THE OUTLINE OF ART

THE OUTLINE
OF ART

EDITED BY

SIR WILLIAM ORPEN

K.B.E., R.A., R.I.

REVISED BY

HORACE SHIPP

LONDON

GEORGE NEWNES LIMITED

TOWER HOUSE, SOUTHAMPTON STREET
STRAND, W.C.2

This new edition, completely revised and enlarged,
has been reset in 12 pt. Bembo type
1950

MADE AND PRINTED IN GREAT BRITAIN BY
MORRISON AND GIBB LIMITED, LONDON AND EDINBURGH

PREFACE

THE word OUTLINE indicates something at once comprehensive and yet free from detail. It came into fame when H. G. Wells, shaken by the disaster of the 1914-18 war, reacted to it by a determination to bring mankind together at least in the understanding of an all-embracing history of the race instead of the ill-balanced national histories which were then available. Wells first, and every creator of an Outline since, believed that its business is to cover the whole ground in one approximately continuous story, and to cover it in comparatively easy fashion so that the uninitiated can follow without being confused. The purpose of an Outline is to enable the reader to see the wood rather than the trees. Afterwards he or she can specialise, differentiate, particularise.

Actually, the specialist vastly learned about some chosen corner of the wide territory, may be rather tantalised by what seems to him sketchy and inadequate treatment of the particular aspect which he knows so thoroughly. We remember how the specialist historians raged at Wells, but that very limitation is the essence of the Outline idea. One moves as in an aeroplane over a continent, flying only low enough to map the outstanding features, whereas the specialist minutely maps one little corner of the ground.

This *Outline of Art* was first published in 1923, the collaboration of one of the greatest painters living at that date, Sir William Orpen, and one of the finest writers upon art, Frank Rutter. A later edition was issued in 1942 after the deaths of both Sir William Orpen and Frank Rutter. This was brought up to date at that time by Bernadette Murphy, a creative writer whose personal friendship with Rutter himself and with many practising artists enabled her to interpret justly many facets of the contemporary movements in painting and sculpture.

After the Second World War it was decided to republish the work in an entirely new edition, resetting the type, changing where necessary the illustrations, and planning a new format, as well as again bringing the text up to date ; and this time the task of revision and extension came into my hands. It was made easier, in one respect, precisely because an absolutely new production was planned, with the illustrations each being given the dignity of a separate page, and the text matter altered in any way I felt necessary.

The most drastic change, the one which I deemed most essential, was to bring the book more truly into line with its title by greatly extending its range. The original OUTLINE had really concerned itself only with European painting and sculpture since the beginning of the Renaissance. It was,

v

therefore, in accord with the wider spirit of this century, with its enormously broader scope, that I extended the range of this OUTLINE in both time and space—in time, to the earliest manifestations of the arts in the prehistoric cave paintings and bone sculpture ; in space, to cover the art of the world. Let the word OUTLINE justify the temerity of this extension since only by such an extension could that title itself be justified.

The specialists, the archæologists with their scientific approach, the modern critics and scholars both of art and anthropology had brought a tremendous amount of new material into the field, and of knowledge of its meaning and significance. We had a much more complete picture of the different periods, and a new idea of the links between them since so many gaps had been filled in. Add to this the new interest in and understanding of the arts of primitive peoples still living—the discovery of Negro sculpture, for instance—and the whole conception of art becomes world-wide and stretches through the ages into the dawn of pre-history.

Into that conception the six hundred years of European painting and sculpture must take its place, even though we grant it a place more important to us than any other contribution because of its nearness to all other aspects of our cultural and social life. But it must not have the sole place. The art of China, for instance, stretching unbroken over five thousand years and achieving in its finest periods something akin to absolute perfection, is *sub specie aeternitatis* as important as European, perhaps even more important. In an ideal Outline of Art it would occupy as much or more space. For our ordinary purposes, however, it can safely be put into a perspective which condenses its size and focus and blurs its details compared to those of our European painters, sculptors, and craftsmen.

The problem of adjusting perfectly these relative values I will not pretend to have solved even to my own absolute satisfaction, and one is prepared for the furious onslaught of some specialist, of say Aztec sculpture or Tibetan silk painting, who feels his life interest slighted in a book which gives inordinate space to Whistler or the French Impressionists. Here, indeed, was another source of doubt which arose out of the very genesis of the book. Sir William Orpen and Frank Rutter had certain enthusiasms—Velazquez, Hogarth, Whistler, and others—and, much as I may myself admire these painters, I would admit that they have undue emphasis even in their story confined to European art. But it was the warm essence of the work and of the writing to include this enthusiasm and personal predilection. The *Outline of Art*, even though its purpose was encyclopædic, was not just an encyclopædia : it was a breathingly human book created by a painter and a writer who *cared* for art, and therefore cared for some more than other. They did justice to all, and a little more than justice to some they loved.

One could have cut and toned down their enthusiasms to some general level ; but at the cost of inspiration, losing thus more than we gained in perfection of balance and proportion. I decided to alter as little as possible the original work and certainly not in the direction of curtailing that enthusiasm which is the first wisdom in art appreciation. I decided to add, rather than take away ; and only here and there, where recent scholarship has thrown new light and changed the aspect of once accepted facts and so would have been likely to have altered the opinions of the original writers, have I made any drastic changes.

One further word : although I have added many new chapters to cover such phases as prehistoric, Egyptian, Cretan, Greek and Roman, Byzantine, Islamic, Chinese, Indian, primitive, and other forms of art on the one hand, and have extended the modern sections as nearly as possible to our own day, I am aware that there are still parts of the vast story inadequately dealt with. Nor have I attempted to touch upon architecture, which is so closely allied to both painting and sculpture that it may be said to be the condition of their changing existence. Only where the coming of some new style in architecture has absolutely dictated a new movement of painting or sculpture have I introduced it as a generality. For these sins of omission we would again take refuge behind the idea implicit in the word OUTLINE. If this volume serves as a broad general introduction, giving so far as it can in comparatively brief space the continuing story of this fascinating creative activity, it will fulfil its purpose. Thousands of specialised books on art can take up that story where this one lays it down. The outstanding ones are indicated in the bibliography. Movements, periods, individual artists, æsthetic theories, technical methods : in ever widening circles of interest this subject radiates to the bounds of space and time, of nature and the spirit of man. Accept this OUTLINE as a pebble dropped in these wide waters to set in motion the expanding wave of enthusiasm.

HORACE SHIPP

CONTENTS

CONTENTS

CONTENTS

LIST OF COLOUR PLATES

LIST OF COLOUR PLATES

The Outline of Art

I

THE MAGIC ROOTS

THE ARTS OF PREHISTORIC MAN

§ I

BEAUTY, Truth, Wonder, Love, Religion. The strange, difficult words lie at the roots of this most curious of all the activities of mankind : Art. The creation of things for use we can understand. The fashioning of the material provided by Nature into clothing and shelter, tools and weapons and utensils : this gave rise to necessary practical operations as the developing mind of man began the tremendous task of adapting his environment to the purpose of his living. The simplest of them—that of providing shelter—even the animals, and still more the birds, also did. But Man was not content with mere utility. Amazingly early in his story we find decoration, pattern, being added to pots and weapons and clothes, and later to his shelters. Even his own body became altered with coloured patterns or with pieces of bone-work through ears, nose, or other parts of the living flesh. The important thing to notice about this is that it is materially useless, it serves no biological purpose, neither hunger nor sex. It does not make the shelter more secure or keep the body warmer or safe from harm. Its actual creation means effort, patience, sometimes even pain and discomfort. Its end is a postponed mental pleasure, and that pleasure has to be anticipated while the work is in progress. We may well wonder what inward urge set the feet of this one among all the species of created things along so strange and apparently meaningless a path. A moment's contemplation of this activity of Art and of its beginnings takes us into deep waters, and it teaches us a great deal about the nature of Man.

A few decades ago, when we knew much less about the science of Man (Anthropology), and of the scientific study of the past (Archæology), we tended to think of Art in little water-tight compartments. Egyptian Art ; Greek Art ; Roman Art ; Modern Art, starting in Italy after the Dark Ages : each was a fresh beginning. Nor was any of it related very definitely with the study of mankind as a whole. Now we have placed

A

this activity of mankind into a definite place in his development ; we have established the continuity of it, and we have thrown its beginnings much farther back in time. Archæologists digging in the earliest known haunts of men have unearthed from beneath the accumulated dust of centuries the evidence of his quest for beauty or his gratification of his sense of wonder and awe, and his interest in the things about him. Anthropologists have watched these same urges at work in the primitive peoples still alive in the world and least touched by civilisation. By these means we have deduced how the mind of early Man worked. We have established links between this activity of Art and that other closely related one, Religion.

Meantime the archæologists, finding the sites of ancient cities, of tombs and temples, and even of settlements before city or temple existed, deciphering hieroglyphics and interpreting symbols, have opened up for us the way Man lived and worshipped. They have established another kind of link also : that between people and people, period and period. So the bounds of history have been pushed farther back into the mists of the prehistoric ; so the known but once disconnected passages of Man's long story have become fused into an epic. There are still obscure periods to which we have not yet found the clue. But beyond all else there is a feeling of continuous movement, and not the least important means of knowing the history of Man lies in the arts. For art reveals in the most permanent forms the mind and spirit of those whose physical bodies have disappeared with the centuries.

§ 2

The earliest chapter which we possess so far was added to that story in the late nineteenth century by a little Spanish girl. Her father was an anthropologist named Santavola, and he shared the wide, and at that date novel, enthusiasm for searching in the floor accretions of likely caves for fresh evidence of the life of the cave-men. At Altamira, in his own district of Santander in Northern Spain, a huntsman had stumbled on a possible cave, or perhaps it would be more correct to say that the fox he was chasing had done so by taking refuge there, and that the huntsman's dog had followed the fox, and the huntsman had followed the dog. Santavola, with an archæologist's zeal, went to the cave to find whether the floor had any of those fragments of weapons, pieces of broken pottery, or other intimations of the occupation by Man in prehistoric times. Suddenly his daughter, going deeper into the cave, pointed to the flattish ceiling of the great cavern and cried :

" Look, father ; bulls ! "

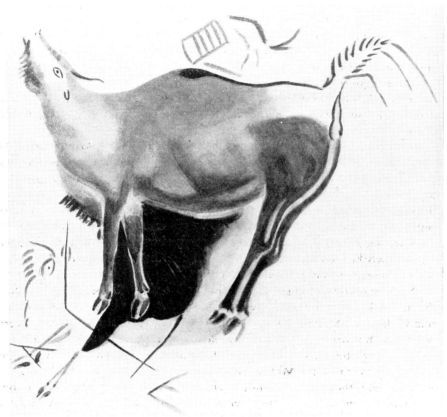

DEER

Altamira Caves, Spain

One of the marvellous animal studies from the walls of the prehistoric cave-dwellings at Altamira, in Northern Spain, painted by artists more than ten thousand years ago. The swiftness of observation and power of expressing the movements of animals have never been better demonstrated in the history of art. They were only proved to be exact when the camera showed the positions of the animals in flight.

There, surely enough, in pigment of red, black, and grey, filling in an incised outline, were some amazing studies of bison, in a cavern which presumably no man had entered for more than twelve thousand years. As his light flashed from side to side of the vast roof Santavola saw more animals by these primitive artists. Reindeer were there—the reindeer which had gone North with the Polar ice at the end of Europe's last ice age. Wolves were there, wild boars, primitive horses, animal after animal wonderfully drawn on an impressive scale.

Santavola wrote a paper on the discovery, but the Academy of Anthropologists, led by Prof. Harlet, called scorn on the idea, even accused him of having the paintings done by a modern artist. The chief argument against him was that the paintings were so magnificent in themselves. The animals were wonderfully observed and drawn in most sensitive outline. They must have been done, it was pointed out, in such a cave by men working by artificial light, and painting above their heads as Michael Angelo worked on the barrel vaulting of the Sistine Chapel. It seemed quite impossible, but it proved to be true.

Soon the archæologists were exploring Northern Spain and the Midi district of France for further evidence, and it appeared in rich profusion in many places of Southern Europe right down to the heel of Italy. Everywhere in this wide region was revealed the artistic presence of these men of the early stone age, who lived by hunting and dwelt in fire-heated caves. In caverns of the Midi were found drawings of the woolly rhinoceros, the cave bear, the hairy mammoth, whilst in the clay of the floor were footprints and hand-prints of the cave-men themselves. As the investigators pressed their search they found sculpture in clay, and, loveliest of all maybe, delicate carvings on bone. The finds varied in artistic value as works of art inevitably will, but they showed a definite evolution, for—happily for the scientific aspect of the search—these men of 12,000 B.C. airily drew their designs right over previous work.

One of the most remarkable of these early carvings is an engraved stag-horn which was found in a grotto in the Pyrenees. At the front of the fragment we have the hind legs of a galloping stag. This is followed by another stag in full gallop, and this by a doe who turns her head and bellows for her young to follow. The intersticial spaces are filled with the forms of fish. The miraculous thing about this incised drawing is that the position of the legs and feet of the running animals is one which was only revealed as exactly true when the instantaneous camera and the cinema came to our aid ! These cave-men had eyes and memories and hands which saw, retained, and subsequently represented the swiftest movements of animals in flight.

In the cave at Altamira another masterpiece is a bison sketched with

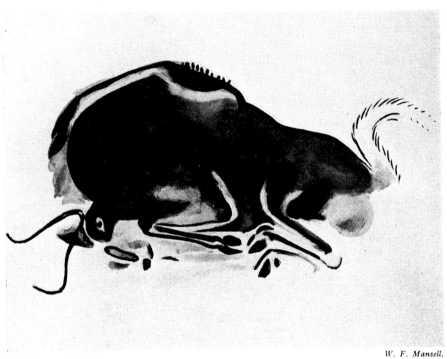

CHARGING BISON
Altamira Caves, Spain
Another study from the walls of the prehistoric cave-dwellings at Altamira.

W. F. Mansell.

DEER

A further picture from the walls of the Altamira Caves, painted by artists o. over a hundred centuries ago.   As with all this animal art of the period, the modelling wonderfully conveys the solidity and relationship of the forms as the sensitive line conveys life and movement.   The purpose of the painting was probably magic : the result was splendid art.

6

amazing lifelikeness, a theme which is echoed often among these cave-drawings. At Dordogne in Périgord another cave has a mammoth in outline which is truly masterly. All told, we have discovered nearly a hundred different kinds of animal in the caves. In one at Périgord a lamp of sandstone was found with a picture of an ibex incised upon it. The find helps to remind us that these men had to do their work by the light of such lamps containing a wick fed with melted animal fat. Indeed, the artist's whole equipment came from the immediate earth and the animals which the hunters killed. His palette was either a flat stone or the flat bone of shoulder blade or pelvis, his paint-tube the hollow bones with the marrow extracted, his brush the hair of the animals. Animal fat again was the medium in which he mixed the ochres and oxides of the earth, the chalk and the charcoal of his simple colours. Often the outline alone had been carved in the sandstone or limestone of the walls and ceilings of the caves with the burins which were subsequently found among the debris. Colour seems to have come later in the evolution of this cave-man art.

At one place there is a piece of fascinating and indisputable evidence of the vast antiquity of the art, for a representation of a bison and a fish have been drawn in the sand of the cave with the finger-tip, and have been preserved for us by a thin coating of stalactitic ice. The fish, here as elsewhere, is exquisitely drawn, and shows the same exactness of observation and the same power of expression which these artists brought to their animal subjects.

Another amazing discovery was made at a cave at Lascaux in this same Dordogne region as recently as the end of 1940. Two schoolboys were roaming the country with their dog, and again as at Altamira the dog played its part, this time by falling into a deep hole. The lads followed to rescue the dog, and found the entrance of a cave—a wonder cave, for the walls were covered with paintings. They took the news to their classics master at the local school, Monsieur Laval, who had talked to his pupils about the prehistoric paintings in the locality, and he went back with them to the cave with a lamp. He found the cave—two passages meeting in an oval high-roofed chamber which is almost symmetrical. And he found along the walls of both galleries and of the chamber the paintings, as the boys had said : scores of drawings wonderfully preserved, some of them larger in scale than any existing prehistoric pictures (one bull is seventeen feet long), deer with exquisitely drawn antlers, cows and bulls, goats, ponies, bison, a woolly rhinoceros, lions, and certain strangely composite beasts, as well as one man. The colours were black, yellow, brown, and purple, and some of the paintings have engraved outline.

Brilliantly clear, this work looked as though it might have been painted a few years ago, but since it is covered in crystals formed through thousands upon thousands of years, there can be no doubt of its antiquity. Indeed, the experts who came to examine the Lascaux Cave pronounced that the paintings belonged to a period thousands of years earlier than the Magdalenian work in the Altamira Cave, and so should be assigned to the Aurignacians, the first men known to have painted.

Even so, this work of animal painting stands at the end of a long line of artistic evolution which began with the merest patterning in lines. There is no evidence of men having lived in the Lascaux Cave. It appears to have been used purely for the evocative magic of that remote time, and the symbols are meaningless to us, although archæologists can make fairly trustworthy guesses at their significance.

Analysis of this art of South-Western France and Northern Spain has revealed that there are two distinct " schools." That of the Midi is especially concerned with large-scale representations of single animals, and there are no human beings depicted ; but over in Spain the subjects are smaller, are concerned with numbers of animals and men in scenes of action. They are full of movement and humanity. It was probably another period, when the first elements which had inspired this art had given place to something nearer art for art's sake, and when the activities of man had extended.

As we look back on all this wonderful heritage of beauty left to the world by the artists of the stone age, we find in it the clue to their lives. These men were, before all else, huntsmen. Upon their success in the chase depended everything—food, clothing, fuel, light in the darkness of their cavern homes, probably their individual standing in the tribe and before their women. Animals ! The whole of their minds must have been centred there ; the whole of their senses at the most alert moments were concerned with the beasts. And it is the very essence of art in every age that the main preoccupation of the humanity of that period and place will inevitably be reflected in it. The arts are verily a picture-book of human life, and a clue to the deepest human interests. Little wonder then that this world of eagle-eyed huntsmen and fishers has given us an art of brilliant animal drawing.

The other factor which we must remember is that one of actual magic. We know from the practice of people living to-day that primitive man tries to influence Nature by evocative magic. The miming of death and resurrection brings back the sun after the winter solstice ; the rattle of the rain-drum brings the healing rain in time of drought ; the enacted fertility rites ensure the growth of the corn. In the days before Man had even settled to agriculture, while he yet was a hunter, it is equally certain that he would use his magic to evoke the things he desperately needed from Nature. The drawn animal on the cave-wall would ensure the coming of the real animal to the waiting huntsman.

8

It is noteworthy that the drawings of the animals were not in the parts of the caves nearest the daylight, but, on the contrary, were usually in the darkest inward recesses. At the Cave of La Mouth, for example, the front part had obviously been used as the living-place, for here were all the remains of the cave-men's normal life, a happy hunting-ground for the searching archæologist. Beyond this a passage-way was discovered leading to a series of pitch-black chambers, and it was in these that a wealth of prehistoric pictures were found. The conclusion cannot but be that these inner chambers were something in the nature of temples, and the activity one of magic and religion.

At one place we have interesting evidence of this practical aspect of prehistoric art : an elephant is painted, and at the place where the heart would be there is a design of a heart—the conventionalised form which we have to-day. It is the oldest piece of conventionalised symbolic shape known in the world. There can be little doubt that its unwonted presence on that painting is part of the killing magic. Possibly, even probably, this art began dim ages before as pure magic, and gradually attained its power and beauty as pure art.

Farther south in Spain it evolves into something more definitely pictorial, concerned with new aspects of human life, and turning to humanity for its themes as the element of magic weakens before the fascination of pure expression. In one cave at Cogul there is a picture probably of an Initiation Ceremony, where women in wonderful flared skirts dance round a naked boy. One other painting in the tiny village of Morella la Vella yields evidence of another grimmer side of humanity, depicting a battle between archers—first record in the world of tribal warfare, and incidentally an indication that bows and arrows date back to more than 10,000 B.C. It is a sprightly and exciting " canvas," full of running, fighting, and most active figures. In the same genre at Baranco de Valltorta we have a realistic " Deer Hunt " ; and elsewhere, more humorously, a representation of a " Man gathering Honey " surrounded by the angry bees as he clings to the tree.

So on the walls and ceilings of cave and rock-shelter we have recorded the lives and interests of these remote ancestors ; depicted there first, no doubt, for reasons of magic, but slowly winning their way as the expression of sheer interest in things for their own sake. The two motives merge imperceptibly as they did in early Italian art, which began as mystical religion and ended as expression of the joy of the senses in the lovely things of this world. History repeated itself at a new level. In this earliest known art we can relive the lives and interests of the men of the stone age.

Then, as the earth swung over towards the sun and the ice-cap moved from Europe towards the Pole, the great plains of shrub and tundra full of

A*

splendid animals gave place to vast forests of giant trees and the moist heat of jungle. In that atmosphere the hunters must have degenerated, migrated, died out. Anthropologists tell us that those who were left moved to the side of the sea and the great lakes, and on narrow strips of land lived the enervated lives of men who had been conquered by the jungle, depending largely on shell-fish for their food. For more than five thousand years nothing exciting seems to have happened to this human race ; or rather we have not yet discovered in which part of the world the thrill of the adventure of human evolution lay. When we contact our kind again it is at the other end of that vast sea-lake which the ancients thought to be situated in the middle of the earth—the Mediterranean. So we move to the great river basins of the Near East, into the Euphrates, the Tigris, the Nile ; and as we do so we pass out of the prehistoric into the beginnings of history.

II

THE ARTS OF DEATH

ART IN EGYPT AND MESOPOTAMIA

§ 1

WHEN next we contact the arts of mankind, after a lapse of five or seven thousand years—almost as long as the whole period of subsequent history—his interest has moved from hunting to agriculture. He still hunts and fishes, but these are supplementary aids to livelihood. Sometime in that misty interim, Man had discovered that seed sown in the right place at the right season brought forth a hundredfold. He had settled in those places, surrounded himself with the domesticated animals which gave him yet more food and clothing without the hazards of the hunt. His settlements had taken on more and more permanency : the tents of the nomads had become houses ; the leaders of the tribes, kings ; the witch doctors and wizards, priests ; and those dim chambers behind the prehistoric caves which had been decorated with symbols of magic, had become temples. Most thrilling of all, Man had become intensely conscious of Nature. The cycle of the seasons meant everything to him ; the sun became his god, the great giver of life. There were many other gods, too, almost inevitably linked with Nature and the phenomena of Nature.

It was the great fertile river valleys which provided conditions most propitious to the new way of life. Water, flat land, the marvellous soil renewed by the spring floods : these things spelled life. In the story of that section of mankind to which we belong, two of those centres play the chief part. One is the vast basin of the river Nile ; the other is the twin valleys of the Tigris and the Euphrates, Mesopotamia—a word that means between the two rivers. Of the former we now possess a rich and wonderful knowledge ; and recent excavations and discoveries in Mesopotamia are opening up for us the story of the civilisations which flourished there five or six thousand years ago.

As with the primitive life of pre-history, so with this of Egypt and Sumeria, much of our understanding comes from precious finds which we are justified in calling works of art. It is well to realise, however, that to these early peoples the statues, the paintings, the low reliefs, the vases and statuettes were not pure art made for the pleasure of their beauty alone, but essentials of magic and religious practices intimately connected with the business of everyday life. Or should we say death ? For it was with death, or rather with the defeat of death, that these people were concerned. It was as if they linked their own survival and return with that of the life-giving sun and the life-given wheat. Perhaps, indeed, the idea of resurrection was born of their preoccupation with Nature's own immortal cycles ; but whether this were so or not, Man from the beginning of his history is obsessed by the urge for continuance after death, and his arts—the most precious expression of his mind—are consecrated to that passion.

§ 2

The art of Egypt is before all else funerary art. The tomb is its centre. For three thousand years before Christ it yields us a practically unbroken record of the life and history of the Pharaohs, for it was one aspect of the Egyptian passion for endurance that the records of these king-gods should be kept, and so on the walls of their tombs we find their stories depicted in paintings and in low reliefs, while they themselves are immortalised in giant sculptures carved in enduring granite, diorite, or other hard stone. Thousands of statues have come down to us, in stone, in bronze, in terracotta, in wood. Around them the hieroglyphics which we are happily able now to decipher, and a language we are able to understand, tell us the history of the dead men, along with the vast religious texts of the so-called " Book of the Dead."

The story of our penetration of the mystery of ancient Egyptian writing is an interesting one. For many years after archæologists had begun to unearth the treasures of Egypt the myriad hieroglyphics remained tantalisingly beyond our knowledge. Then, in 1799, when Napoleon was attacking Syria by way of Egypt, one of his engineers, Boussard, found a great basalt slab near the Nile town of Rashid or Rosetta. The stone was engraved with writing in three kinds of character ; and Napoleon, who had taken with him to Egypt a body of scholars as well as an army, ordered it to be placed in the Institute Nationale which he had just founded in Cairo. More, he caused two lithographers, Citizens Marcel and Gallard, to come from Paris to take impressions of the stone for distribution among the scholars of Europe.

The inscription was in the old picture writing, repeated in the later conventionalised form of this, and again repeated in Greek. Scholars discovered, moreover, that wherever a royal name was mentioned it was placed inside a cartouche, a long oval with flattened top and bottom. From these clues the meaning of the signs, the phonetics even of all the Egyptian early records, were opened up, and the confines of our knowledge were pushed back thousands of years. The Rosetta stone is now in the British Museum, for its possession was made a subject of the British Treaty after the success of British arms in Egypt in 1802. Actually it proved to be a decree made by the Council of Priests at Memphis in 196 B.C. to commemorate the coronation of Ptolemy V. Our concern, however, is not with this comparatively late event but with the thousands of years of history recorded elsewhere which the stone revealed to us for the first time.

This history divides itself into fairly definite periods, and each yields a magnificent contribution to Egyptian art. There is firstly the long predynastic period when these people in the Nile valley were consolidating, a period lasting approximately from 5000 B.C. to 3000 B.C. As early as 4241 B.C. the Egyptian astronomers had established a calendar of 365 days ; and they had an exact knowledge of measurement, encouraged probably by the necessity of re-establishing the boundaries of land inundated by the Nile floods. The worship and dominance of Horus the god who is also accepted as king and served by a great priesthood belongs to this first period, but at approximately 3000 B.C. the office of kingship passes to the Pharaohs. They, too, are divine, but divinity is an attribute of kingship rather than the reverse. The art of Egypt is largely concerned with ensuring the grandeur and the durability of the Pharaohs. In life and in death and in the life to come their state had to be made manifest, and to this end hundreds of thousands of slaves toiled and thousands of scribes and artists worked.

From 3000 B.C. until A.D. 30 there is a continual history divided into four main eras, each grouped around a city where the Pharaoh reigned.

> From 3000 to 2000 B.C. the 1st to the 11th Dynasties reigned at Memphis.
> From 2000 to 950 B.C. the 12th to the 21st Dynasties reigned at Thebes. (This period was interrupted by the coming of the Canaanite shepherd kings in 1580 B.C., so that we usually divide it into a First and Second Theban period.)
> From 950 to 332 B.C. the 22nd to the 31st Dynasties reigned at Sais.
> From 305 B.C. to A.D. 30 the Ptolemies reigned at Alexandria.

This fourth period is not important in the story of Egyptian art ; but the Memphite, the two Theban, and the Saite periods yielded an unbroken heritage of works of art : the oldest known architecture, exquisite statuary sculpture and low-reliefs, wall paintings and illuminated papyrus. The arts of Egypt were concerned with durability, and they have endured.

13

§ 3

In the Memphite era the pyramids were built. They remain among the marvels of the world, these tremendous homes and temples of the dead Pharaohs, with their long corridors leading to inner shrines, their secret chambers where the royal mummy might be hidden from thieves and enemies, their elaborately planned slopes mathematically exact so as to admit the rays of the sun at certain times, their painted and carved walls, and all the pomp and circumstance of death and precautions for resurrection. Cheops of the 4th Dynasty built for his tomb the great pyramid at Gizeh. One hundred thousand men laboured for twenty years at the task, hewing six million tons of stone from quarries fifty miles beyond the Nile, transporting it to the site, erecting it in fifty-ton blocks into the stepped miracle with its elaborate inner structure, and then facing it with slabs of polished granite. The square of its base is almost perfect. How these things were done more than 2800 years B.C., we still do not know.

These vast royal tombs and the lesser but still magnificent ones of the functionaries of court and state, are the rich sources of Egyptian art. Events of the life of the dead man are incised on the walls of the death chamber and the adjoining antechambers, or are sculptured in low relief or painted ; a statue of the great one in granite, diorite, or other durable stone, but sometimes in limestone or wood, is an important feature ; the coffin case itself has a kind of conventionalised portrait painted on it ; and everywhere around are the words of magic power and pictures of the " Book of the Dead," to ensure a safe journey for the soul through the underworld on its way to the Kingdom of Osiris. Every possible means was used to ensure the preservation of the actual body. It was embalmed, anointed with preservative oils and fluids, hidden from robbers, and then surrounded by these magic formulae which would save it from the powers of evil, and evoke the aid of Thoth, the god-advocate, in the Judgment Halls of Souls.

The " Book of the Dead " is really a collection of funerary texts and magic words. It often exists in the form of a long papyrus roll. One of these, the longest papyrus in the world, is in the British Museum and measures one hundred and thirty-three feet long by sixteen and a half inches wide. Along with the hieroglyphic texts are usually fascinating pictures of the magic ceremonials, " The Opening of the Mouth," " The Weighing of the Heart," " The Journey of the Sun God." Amid this elaborate ritual script, the hymns, prayers, and magic litanies, we find scenes from the daily life and work of the deceased set against queer map-like landscapes characteristic of Egyptian painting, which, of course, had not encompassed perspective. The faces of the figures are always in profile and the feet seen

RAMESES II

Turin Museum

A noble example of Egyptian sculpture. Rameses II, who reigned from 1300 B.C. to 1230 B.C., was one of the greatest of the Pharaohs of the 19th Dynasty. Sculpture, as this work proves, was already at the height of its power, combining recognisable portraiture with rhythmic and formal conventions revealed in the beautiful treatment of the drapery and the frontal view, traditional in Egyptian sculpture.

15

from the side, but the bodies until quite late in Egyptian art are shown from the front. All is presented in flat decoration without tones or light and shade.

The climax of this drama of the after-life was " The Weighing of the Heart " which was regarded as the seat of the emotions, desires, and will, and which had to counterbalance the symbolic feather of truth and righteousness. This scene usually calls up the finest art of the illustrator, for here the whole hierarchy of the gods assemble, Thoth uses the words of power and advocacy, and the dead man waits in fear and adoration beside the great scales.

Thus the successful presentation of these funerary texts would make a man victorious on earth and in the other world, ensure him a safe passage through the underworld, allow him to go in and out of his mummified body, *Sahu,* and the statue in the tomb specially made to receive his abstract self, *Ka.* Thus he could eventually scale to the Elysian Fields of Osiris and be prevented from dying the death. Little wonder that an elaborate art of sculpture and picture grew around these adventures of the soul.

§ 4

To the First Theban period belongs the Great Sphinx. It is carved out of a ridge of limestone and is more than sixty feet high and two hundred feet long. This impressiveness by sheer size is itself a feature of Egyptian art. It symbolised power and durability, and naturally used the colossal to achieve its purpose. Not the least important function of this early art— indeed of art of all time—is the impression on the common people of the importance and power of their rulers. Records of great deeds began to be set up in the form of obelisks, four-sided monoliths twenty or thirty feet high expounding the virtues and the powers of the kings.

When in the Second Theban period the great temples were built, it was again an art which impressed by sheer size. Strength, almost crude strength, goes with this. Vast blocks of stone are deposited horizontally, vertically. Floors, pillars, architraves, and roofs are massive. The walls slope outward at the bottom to withstand the immense pressure of the roofs, but—shape of grace—they have a concave outward-sloping moulding at the top which takes away from the mere crude strength.

The temples at Luxor and Karnak are supreme works, that at Karnak, with its great hall of one hundred and thirty-four pillars, some of them seventy feet high (that is as high as the Trajan column in Rome), remaining one of the greatest pieces of ancient art in the world. These temples consisted of : (*a*) an avenue of sphinxes ; (*b*) a pylon entrance gate ; (*c*) a vast court with colonnaded portico ; (*d*) a double pylon ; (*e*) two obelisks

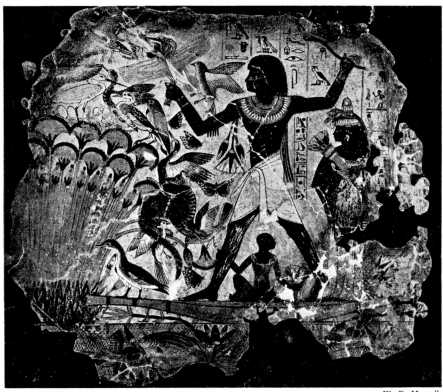

FOWLING SCENE

An Egyptian Mural Painting from a Tomb at Thebes

British Museum

This lively painting from the time of the 18th Dynasty (1600–1450 B.C.) shows how far the art had advanced. The scene from the life of the dead man shows him standing in a canoe, accompanied by his wife and daughter. Papyrus lines the banks, fish swim in the water, the air is full of the birds which he hunts. The figures show the mixture of profile and frontal view typical of Egyptian painting.

THE HEAD OF QUEEN NEFERTITI

Berlin Museum

This piece of coloured sculpture of the famous Queen of Egypt, who preceded Tutankhamen, in the fourteenth century B.C., is one of the most life-like of extant Egyptian sculptures. Her beauty seems surprisingly modern under the charm of the modelling and colour of this head. A copy is in the British Museum.

and two colossal statues ; (*f*) the hypostyle hall with the roof supported by columns and the light coming from an opening near the top of the lateral walls, leaving enormous space for decoration by painting or low relief ; (*g*) the sanctuary of the god ; and beyond this, priests' chambers and sacred groves. All this cried out for the work of the artist, for walls and ceilings and pylons were covered with paintings, conventional decoration, and carvings, whilst statues and carvings of the Pharaohs who were the patrons of the building had their appointed place.

Not the least important part of this Egyptian painting is the decoration by conventionalised natural shapes and ornament, particularly the sacred lotus, and by geometrical forms. These were used to enrich the whole interior space which happened not to be devoted to the pictured myths of the gods and the records of the Pharaohs. Most of the Egyptian motives in decoration have survived down to our own day.

The famous treasure tomb of Tutankhamen belongs to this Second Theban period, for he reigned in Egypt from 1358 B.C. to 1353 B.C., following the lovely Queen Nefertiti, whose painted sculptured head in the Berlin Museum is so modern in its beauty.

The Saite period was in one way an era of decadent art, for the primitive strength had gone, but the artists looked back and tried to revive the glories of the past. There is more elegance but less power ; more complexity, less simple statement. The real decadence sets in with the conquest of Egypt by Alexander the Great in 332 B.C. We find such evidence of attempted novelty as that of making the pillars taper downwards.

Out of this long and wonderful story of a people's life we have a vast treasury of art work. Because of their philosophy and the specific ideas behind it this art tends to be somewhat hide-bound and traditional, but since its tradition was in itself so sound, this is an advantage. The use of tremendously hard stone, such as granite, for the sculpture made for a simplicity and an emphasis of essentials highly acceptable to our modern taste. It also made for wonderful preservation, a factor which was helped by the dry climate of the country. Even the wooden grave figures and the children's toys have not perished despite the enormous lapse of time.

The sculpture of the earliest period is compact, sturdy. Short figures, invariably seated, are a recurring theme. "The Scribe" in the Louvre is one of the very best of these. All statues of the great periods are governed by the Egyptian rule which has been called "the law of frontality," that is, the figure exactly confronts the spectator, the middle of the forehead, neck, and body being in a vertical line, with the weight placed evenly on the soles of the feet. The males may be shown walking, but the females are in repose.

In the painting, as we have seen, the frontal law was retained for the body, but both head and legs were shown from the sides—a queer effect dictated probably by lack of technical prowess, and making for an unrealistic effect. The flat, non-naturalistic painting increased this, but the whole synthesis is a delightful convention which to-day we are able to appreciate and to accept.

The decoration, next to the sculpture and architecture, was the greatest gift of the Egyptians to art—the use of motives from the vegetation of the Nile, particularly of the lotus and the papyrus, being truly wonderful ; and that of the repeated abstract geometrical figures unsurpassed in the story of decoration.

Throughout it all stands that potent idea of duration. Tombs, temples, statues, low-reliefs, paintings, writings : all is done to last the eternal souls for all time, for in Egypt the arts of death were indeed the arts of life eternal.

§ 5

Until comparatively recently it was accepted that the Egyptian civilisation was practically the sole source of Western culture, but the recent discoveries under the guidance of Sir Leonard Woolley in Mesopotamia have revealed a civilisation as old as that of the Nile. Nothing comparable in quantity to compare with the treasures of Egypt has been found in this rival field, but nevertheless much that is very sensitive and beautiful and illuminating in its revelation of these historic beginnings has come to light. Not the least important aspect of the excavations lies in the fact that they bear upon the Bible story and underline the historical fact of the Flood, for at one level a great band of alluvial clay, eight to ten feet in depth, breaks the story of Man's history written in the deposits of pottery, etc. The most interesting site is that of Abraham's city of Ur ; and we have discovered that it was, by Abraham's time, " no mean city," but a highly sophisticated one. By this approximate date of 2000 B.C., Ur had already a history of more than 1500 years. Little wonder then that these brick-built houses of Abraham's time and city were two-storey affairs with good brick stairs and wooden galleries.

The most interesting art finds at Ur, however, were the oldest ; and again it is an art of death. The royal graves go back at least to 3200 B.C., probably to 3500 B.C., and there are even earlier tombs and the evidence of great temples built to the Moon Goddess who was worshipped by this people. The funeral customs of these divine kings and queens demanded or induced what seems to our modern minds appalling human sacrifice, for down the long ramps to the actual tombs the excavators found serried ranks of dead men and women, exquisitely clothed and jewelled, and

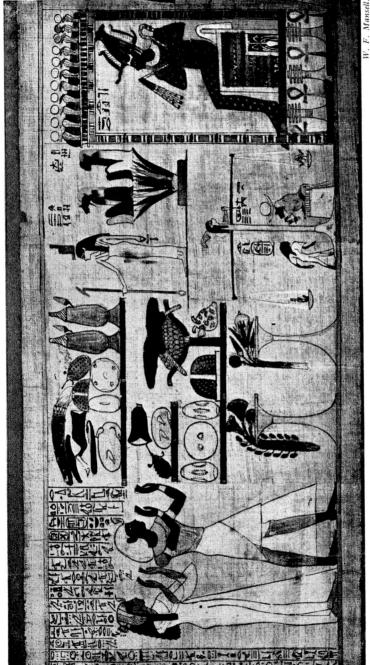

PAPYRUS PAINTING

British Museum

The climax of the drama of judgment depicted in The Book of the Dead : the Weighing of the Heart. This picture shows Queen Netchemet, accompanied by Her-Hern, the first Priest-King, standing in the Hall of Osiris, praying to the god whilst her heart is being weighed in the balance. The mixture of illustration, writing and symbols decoratively arranged to fill the space on the papyrus is typical of the Book of the Dead.

21

bearing weapons, harps, cups, gaming-boards, and other symbols of service to the dead royalty. Beautiful head-dresses of filigree gold, necklaces of lapis lazuli beads, adorned the women ; wonderful golden helmets designed to imitate human hair are found on the men. Gold and the remains of silver, precious stones, and lapis lazuli abound everywhere in these veritable treasure chambers. Much, inevitably, has been taken by tomb-robbers of the ancient days, and so lost to modern science and art.

The number of followers found in each tomb varies. Sixty-eight persons were buried with one king ; twenty-five with the queen. Six men and sixty-eight women are in another grave. The figures lie on their sides, rank upon rank. After more than five thousand years their lovely ornaments still tell of the taste and the craftsmanship of the Sumerians. The fact that the dainty head-dresses are undisturbed indicates that the actors in this macabre performance were not forced : they probably took their arranged places in the great ceremonial of death, prepared to continue to serve the divinity of their old master in the glory of his future state. Under the merciful unconsciousness of some powerful drug they went to death with him. There is no sign of violence ; the skeletons of animals are still beside the chariots ; bones of dainty hands still lie by the golden cups.

There have been some exquisite finds of head ornaments, some most beautiful harps and lyres, silver models of boats, gold cups and vessels of most fragile design, inlaid gaming-boards and weapons. One of the most important finds was a statuette of a ram caught in a thicket, which is now one of the treasures of the British Museum. Another is the " Standard of Ur " a piece of mosaic depicting Sumerian life in Peace and War. These people were masters of mosaic and inlay. The harps with heads of ram or bull in gold plate over a core of wood, the whole body a conventionalised form of the animal, were beautifully inlaid.

We may still be only at the approximate beginning of our discoveries in these river valleys of Mesopotamia. Vast buildings are being unearthed —mountain temples built platform upon platform of sun-baked dried brick with vast ramps running from one to another, and the shrine itself on the smallest and highest of these. The people of these regions probably migrated from mountain country, and on these plains by the rivers they created anew artificially the hill sanctuaries of the ancient gods. The Tower of Babel of Biblical legend was undoubtedly such a structure.

Great cities and palaces grew around these temples, inhabited by a people fierce and predatory. This Chaldean and later Assyrian civilisation shifted its centre around the twin river valleys again and again as the king warriors from one city vanquished another. At Ur and Erech, at Lagash, Tello, Babylon, Nineveh, the great walls and terraces arose, fell, and the

GUDEA, THE BENEFACTOR

Louvre, Paris

One of nine statues n dark-green diorite of this Priest-King of Chaldea, who reigned about 2500 B.C.
The hands are in a religious ceremonial position, the inscription on his knees in cuneiform writing.
In one of the statues he is shown with an architectural plan, to symbolise the builder.

23

STELE OF NARAM-SIN
Louvre, Paris

This low-relief commemorates a victory of the great king of Agadé, who ruled in Mesopotamia, 2678–2641 B.C. A wonderful organisation of plastic forms showing the army triumphantly scaling the mountains beyond the Tigris. The king leads his troops, whilst the Sun, Venus and the protecting stars shine in the sky.

24

ASSYRIAN ANIMAL SCULPTURE

British Museum

The great buildings of Assyria were decorated with massive animal reliefs : bulls and lions depicted with great understanding of the forms. One curious convention was that of showing five legs, so that the animal looked correct from both side and front.

KING ASHURBANIPAL HUNTING

British Museum

During the reign of Ashurbanipal, Assyrian art rose to its highest. He established the library at Kouyunjik so invaluable to our knowledge of the Assyrians, and enriched the building with magnificent bas-reliefs of his exploits as warrior and hunter. They are all triumphant presentations of tremendous energy, and the animals especially are excellently portrayed.

sands drifted over them. At one period statues carved in diorite and other works show definite Egyptian influence. At another there are rich and highly ornamented low reliefs, bronzes, and vases. But our knowledge still has gaps, for the deserts of Mesopotamia are but slowly yielding their secrets to the patient archæologists excavating the sites.

§ 6

After a break of centuries civilisation in this region rises again with the triumph of the Assyrians. From the beginning of the ninth century B.C. to the end of the seventh, the Assyrians were all-powerful. Their buildings are the same as those of the earlier Chaldeans, brick-built in diminishing stages, and by a brilliant use of the brick carrying on the architectural forms of the arch and the cupola. On the earth-filled spaces of the rising platforms palm trees were planted, an ancient Chaldean device which made them mountains of greenery and building and found its climax in the famous hanging gardens of Babylon.

The art of Assyria centred round the vast royal palaces, such as that of King Sargon at Khorsabad. They are fortresses, too, with their high surrounding walls, towers, and few gates stoutly built and guarded. The ornament is often stucco, but the gates were bronze, and on either side were flanked by human-headed winged bulls carved in high relief. Inside such palaces in the grandiose reception halls will be low-reliefs, pictures in tempera or enamelled terra-cotta tiles, vast friezes lauding the exploits of the king, or whole walls covered in cuneiform writing celebrating his greatness.

The reliefs are the most important aspect of this Assyrian art, as the great guardian human-headed bulls are the strangest of its creations. As we see these in the specimens in the Louvre and the British Museum they are tremendously impressive. The bulls are given five legs so that whether they be viewed from the side or from the front they have the appearance of walking. The reliefs, usually in coloured alabaster, were invariably the same so far as subject is concerned right through this Assyrian period. Firstly, strange winged genii protect the king's life ; the king himself and his attendants follow ; then his expeditions, victories, his prisoners being killed or tortured ; his thanksgiving to the gods ; and finally, his life in peace, hunting, or in the gardens with his queen. The king is always fierce and irresistible. Even in the scenes in the pleasure gardens the heads of his enemies hang from the trees. Over men and animals he is shown in triumph.

At the beginning this art of Assyria was highly conventionalised, and even after the practice of centuries the treatment of the human body, of muscles, hair, beard, costume, is mannered to an extreme degree although it has become much more pictorial. Towards the end an element of landscape is introduced. The animals are finely observed and rendered, and for all its brutality (the perennial mark of the art of this conquering people) it takes on a certain refinement. From it we learn much of the life at least of the king-warriors and of those immediately surrounding and supporting them. For centuries this people dominated the regions at the Eastern end of the Mediterranean, and when they gave place at last to the early Persian conquerors in the middle of the sixth century, this art of palace building, modified by the particular mentality of the Iranian people, was continued at Persepolis, Susa, and elsewhere. That story belongs, however, rightly to Persian art. The art of Assyria and the fierce life of these fighters of the river valleys of Mesopotamia had already been broken by the coming of the Medes in 625 B.C.

III

INTERLUDE IN CRETE

ONE of the greatest gaps in human art and story was bridged most fascinatingly towards the end of last century when Heinrich Schliemann, the son of a poor German pastor, followed a life-long dream and re-discovered Troy, pursued it farther and found Homer's Mycenæ " abounding in gold " as Homer had sung of it, and so gave the clue to the Homeric legends which sent us yet farther afield eventually to excavate " hundred-citied Crete." Step by step history was driven back into the legendary past until in Crete we have a culture which has links with that of Egypt and Sumeria, but which has a perfect character of its own. When we contact it, between 2000 and 1400 B.C., the civilisation is at a truly wonderful height, luxurious and perhaps febrile.

Schliemann's romantic story belongs more properly to the record of Greek Art. It concerns us at this point chiefly because it is based on his belief that Homer's cities and characters were historic truth and not mere story-telling. His father told him the story of the Iliad, and in childish picture-books he saw illustrations of burning Troy, of Æneas and Agamemnon. Scholarship in those days had turned all this into fable and folklore, but to young Schliemann it was true. When later he was an assistant in a small grocer's shop, a broken-down, tipsy schoolmaster customer came in, and recited hundreds of lines of Homer. The boy determined to learn Greek, and the dream was born in his mind of visiting the scenes of this magic verse. He tramped to Hamburg, decided to go to sea, and was shipwrecked off Holland. So at nineteen we find him penniless in a foreign land, where he stayed for seventeen more years, becoming an efficient merchant—a " self-made man." Then the Crimean War gave him an opportunity to make a fortune, and determinedly he turned back to his dream and devoted himself to archæology. It was in 1868, after an intensive study of the science in Paris and elsewhere, that he first went to Hissarlik near the Dardanelles in Asia Minor, where he was convinced that Troy was to be found. He was working on clues provided by the second-century traveller, Pausanias. The scholarship of his day, if it did not absolutely deny that Troy had ever existed, mocked at his idea of the site. In face of ridicule and a lack of results for three years,

Schliemann persevered, and in 1873 he proved his dream. City below city he unearthed ancient Troy.

Following his clues the enthusiast turned to Mycenæ, and here, indeed, he found in the tombs of those who were " great before Agamemnon," the piled gold treasures of which Homer spoke.

Not the least part of Schliemann's triumph lay in the fact that he made the world realise that this ancient poetry was concerned with human life, and not merely with grammar and literary expression. The works of art, too, as the excavators and archæologists brought them to light, were revelations of how mankind lived in these legendary times. Schliemann set men asking where the limit was to be set. If Troy were true, what of the earlier legends : Heracles, Theseus, Minos, the Minotaur ? The discoveries went on until a vast Ægean civilisation was discovered, with its centre in Crete and its ramifications back into ancient Egypt and over into Mesopotamia.

Sir Arthur Evans and Dr. Halbhen's discoveries in Crete added a new period of art and civilisation to human knowledge. It arose chiefly from the search for writings, for although Homer had mentioned " dire signs " there was not any trace even at Mycenæ of writing. Some stones were found there with a vague suggestion of picture-writing, slightly suggestive of the Egyptian hieroglyphics, and Evans commenced a search for their source. Following a clue in Crete he found that the village women were wearing these very stones as " milking charms." At Knossos a clay tablet came to light with what looked like an earlier form of the writing, and Knossos was the legendary home of King Minos, the place where Daidalos, the great craftsman-builder, had built the labyrinth for the Minotaur, the " dancing floor " for Ariadne, the king's daughter. To Knossos, so legend said, Theseus had come and won the love of Ariadne, slain the bull-headed Minotaur, and delivered Athens from the yearly tribute of young men and maidens who were sacrificed to the monster.

In 1900 Evans began to excavate, and he unearthed the greatest palace of antiquity. It was three stories high, an enormous complex of buildings—a veritable labyrinth decorated with the double-headed axe, the labrus, from which the name derives. And everywhere was the evidence of the cult of the Bull—wonderful frescoes, low-reliefs, coins, plaques, pottery. The palace was a town in itself. Vast jars held stores of wine, oil, grain ; offices were filled with record tablets ; treasure coffers lined with lead were buried under the flag-stones. Away to the south were the luxurious living quarters approached by a corridor known now as the " Corridor of the Procession," for along its walls is an enormous fresco of a procession of youths and maidens led by the king in glorious robes with a crown of peacock's feathers. Fragments of such frescoes were found

W. F. Mansell.

THE PALACE OF KING MINOS

Knossos, Crete

This vast three-storied building, with its modernity and wonders of engineering and the splendour of its wall-decorations, was revealed to us by the labour and architectural research of Sir Arthur Evans. Its discovery gave the clue to the historical truth of much of the Homeric legend, and showed arts which reached back to Egypt and forward to Greece.

everywhere in the palace. Dainty slim-waisted youths—one depicted carrying a silver and gold vase was so beautiful that the workmen who revealed it treated it as an object of veneration ; women in low-necked dresses with narrow waists and flowing fluted skirts ; acrobats ; a boy painted with blue flesh picking crocuses and putting them into a vase ; a crowd of men and women watching some spectacle. " *Mais ce sont des Parisiennes,*" cried one French scholar at the sight of that 4000-year-old picture ; whilst an Italian, as they unearthed the elaborate sanitary arrangements of the palace, called it " absolutely English."

Bull-sport seems to have been the centre of this luxurious life. On the frescoes, carved on the walls, on seals and rings, engraved on gems and as bronze statuettes, these people of Knossos show us bulls and acrobats. The human figures throw somersaults between the horns. Young men and women alike take part in it. Was it religion or sport, or some amazing marriage of the two ? Was it the origin of the legend of the youths and maidens taken from ancient Athens as tribute and sacrificed to the bull-monster ? Until we are able to decipher the writings of these Ægeans we do not know ; perhaps we shall never know. Meantime we will be content with the revelation of the joy in beauty which this Cretan art affords. The " Hall of the Double Axes," its walls painted with colonnades and the head of every column decorated with the labrus ; the " Dancing Floor of Ariadne " ; the luxury of the women's apartments where were found remains of an enormous number of dainty articles ; a sculptor's studio with one great vase in limestone two feet high and more than six feet round, carved to wonderful thinness, and another in the initial stages ; the frescoes, the statuettes, the fragments of exquisite pottery—all this told the tale of Knossos.

As the digging continued around the site, period after period took this civilisation back to Neolithic man more than 10,000 B.C. Pottery with kinship to Egyptian is found at levels likely to coincide with the earliest Dynasties of Egypt. As the millenniums pass we find this Cretan civilisation echoed at Melos which became an army centre for the Ægean peoples supplying arrows tipped with volcanic glass (the armoury in the Knossos palace contained bundles of them, duly recorded on tablets lying nearby). Then seals appear marked with the picture-writing and signs which are echoes of Egypt of the Fifth Dynasty, about 3000 B.C. This was probably the period of Cretan imperialism and conquest among the islands of the Eastern Mediterranean and the nearby coast. But Knossos remained unfortified, secure probably in its insularity and safe in its naval supremacy. Now the art begins to be increasingly elaborate and to depict costumes of surprising modernity. Some statuettes found at Palaikastro are in costumes which might almost be English Elizabethan ! The pottery

BRONZE MINOAN ACROBAT

This is the most celebrated of all Cretan Bronzes. It shows the acrobat somersaulting over a galloping bull in the bull-sports which probably gave rise to the myth of the Minotaur. The date is about 1600 B.C. in the period we call Minoan I.

becomes increasingly complex and wonderful. In the last phase we have the palace at Knossos with its faintly decadent " Blue Boy " paintings, its luxury sports, and all the signs of fastidiousness and over-refinement. The pottery sometimes has " trickle-glaze " decoration, dependent upon the accidental trickle of the glaze over the clay and a sign always of advanced and even jaded taste. An ivory carving found in fragments in the palace shows a vaulting man so daintily carved that the veins and nails are shown on the hands and the hair is inset gold wire spirals. Luxury, sport, decadence, gaiety : suddenly, at a date which scholars think we can place about 1400 B.C., it all ceases. The great palace at Knossos went down in sudden terrible catastrophe. Fire and destruction overcame this vast home of thousands of highly civilised people. The Ægean civilisation came to an end with catastrophic suddenness. How ? There is little doubt that down from the coasts of Greece the virile Hellenes sped to the conquest and sack of this tempting prize set in the wine-dark sea. The unfortified palace-city ; the weakened and luxurious people ; the wonderful life went down before the swift invaders. Gold and precious things were carried away, everything breakable was broken, the fires licked the towers and columns, and Knossos after thousands of years of civilisation ceased to be.

But the galleys laden with her treasures sped back to the mainland, and at Mycenæ and Tyreus the story of culture continued, and Greek art had its foundations in the shattered ends of Ægean culture.

IV

THE GOLDEN AGE IN GREECE

§ 1

IN an OUTLINE OF ART it is not our business to deal in any detail with
the movements of the peoples in this ancient Mediterranean world.
Suffice it to say that they came southward from the Danubian valleys,
and westward from Asia into these Grecian lands.   The centre of the
invaders from the North was at Mycenæ, but they spread far on to cities
around the sea, and established colonies on the islands, on to the coast of
Asia Minor itself.   They had already established themselves firmly for
hundreds of years when they challenged and overthrew their Cretan rivals
and took back to Mycenæ and nearby Tiryns the treasures of Knossos, and
probably many of the craftsmen themselves as spoils of that terrible victory.

When, therefore, Schliemann turned from Troy, again following the
records of the second-century traveller, Pausanias, who had declared that
at Mycenæ he had seen the great circle where the Homeric heroes were
buried, he found at Mycenæ not only the " abundant gold " of the poet's
description, but cups and hunting knives and gold plaques, engraved gems
and carved ivories which clearly linked up with Cretan art.   Near to the
" Lion Gate "—the oldest existing sculpture in Greece, a pediment showing
a slender column flanked by two lions carved into the massive stone above
the architrave—he found the burial circle and five grave-shafts filled with
treasure.   In one of them alone fifty-six flat golden ox-heads with double
axes between the horns were obviously Cretan.   There were wall paintings
like those subsequently discovered at Knossos ; and down at Tiryns where
a great palace was unearthed was found the remains of a fresco of the
bull-sport.   Elsewhere, at a place near Sparta, some of the most magnificent
golden cups were elaborately decorated with bulls and slim-waisted, belted
Cretans.

Thus the heroic age came to light as historic fact, and the treasures in
the grave-shafts of the heroes revealed its past connections with the prehistoric, legendary world of Theseus and the Minotaur.   But by the time
of the Homeric age this Mycenæan civilisation was itself in decline ; only the
love of beauty worked through the centuries to burgeon anew when the

Ægeans, the Dorians, in a fresh invasion from the North, established themselves at Sparta, and the Ionians, an Aryan people, made Athens their city.

The history of classical Greece almost begins anew with the establishment of the Olympiad, traditionally dated 776 B.C. Every four years this great gathering for athletic contests on the plain of Olympia brought together all the tribes of Greece, and for the period of the games all hostilities among them ceased. The importance of this recurring foregathering, the worship of the same gods, the cohesion of culture which it fostered, the unity emphasised in spite of the continual inter-tribal and inter-civic warfare, and, most important of all, the interest in the perfect human body, gave a direction to Greek art which carried straight forward to the golden age of Pericles at Athens and the vast beauty of Hellenistic art.

One other element which counted was the type of Greek building. That remained uninfluenced by the Cretan modes. It was more Northern. In its primitive form it was a single room centred on the fire, and in its essence it remained precisely that, even though the building became a temple and the fire became the altar and shrine of god or goddess. The necessity for the smoke to escape through the roof forbade the two- or three-storied structure of the Cretans. The essential simplicity of a single gabled roof, the pedimented front, the surrounding colonnade, was an extension of the primitive architecture, and it gave wonderful opportunity for sculpture as well as an ideally lovely architectural arrangement. The wealth of local stone and marble encouraged both these things.

The course of Greek history inevitably played its part, as social and political history always does in the story of a nation's culture. This is no place to trace the tortuous ramifications of the rather ugly record of treachery and violence which for century after century kept these peoples at war with each other and gave them some sort of unity only when they were dubious allies against the might of Persia. Out of the welter of separate states two were of paramount importance : Athens and Sparta. Sparta was what we now call Totalitarian, demanding the utmost consecration of body and mind to the State and particularly to the military necessity of the State ; Athens, although it too was governed by tyrants, had a constitution of democracy (a very limited democracy, of course, which gave no recognition to the helots who were practically slaves). During the sixth century B.C., the great Athenian lawgiver, Solon, had established at Athens a system which gave a great measure of freedom to the Athenians and kept the power of the successive dictatorial tyrants within bounds.

Three events of the fifth century B.C. stand out. Greatest of all is the Persian war ; out of its triumphant waging and conclusion arose the Athenian empire ; and in the reaction caused by the imperialism of Athens

APHRODITE

Lyons Museum and Acropolis Museum.   (Sixth century B.C.)

An archaic Greek statue known as the " Aphrodite of Marseilles " in the Lyons Museum. Fragments were found which are in the Museum at Athens. Greek sculpture started from simple carved wooden cult figures. By the sixth century B.C. they had evolved into slightly more human figures such as this, with the archaic smile, the formal lines of drapery, and even with arms in natural movement which took them away from the figure.

37

" THE CHARIOTEER OF DELPHI "

Delphi Museum

This magnificent bronze statue from a chariot group is typical of the transition to the human work of the great period. The slight turn of the head, the firmly planted feet, the braced shoulders, give life to the work. It is well to remember that all Greek sculpture was coloured and decorated with jewelled craftwork. The eyes of the charioteer, for instance, had bronze pupils set in ivory.

38

came the Peloponnesian war when the Spartans overthrew the Athenian power. The successful resistance to Persia is the truly heroic story of Greek record. Twice the Persians were held, in 492 B.C. and in 490 B.C. That phase of the struggle ended with the thrilling victory of Marathon when a handful of Greeks held the narrow strip of seashore against the hosts of the Medes, when the runner raced back the twenty-five miles to Athens with his almost miraculous tidings, " Rejoice, we conquer," and died as he gave the cry. In the uneasy peace of the next ten years the Greeks watched Xerxes of Persia gather his great army for the war of revenge, and in 480 B.C. again Persia was on the warpath. In the interim, Athens, under the leadership of Themistocles, had made herself a sea-power.

" Whoso can hold the sea has command of the situation," he preached, and Athens had reason to be grateful to the gods that she listened. Xerxes crossed the Hellespont on a bridge of boats, and the battle was brought to a head in the Pass of Thermopylæ where the Spartans died to the last man to hold them back. The sacrifice gained Athens six precious days, and when at last the Persians broke through, the Athenians scorched the earth of their beloved city and took to the waiting ships. Houses and temples and shrines were burned, and the Persians wreaked their vengeance on anything left from the holocaust. But the tide of battle turned. Out at the mouth of the Bay of Salamis the Athenian navy routed the armada of Xerxes and broke the might of Persia.

When they returned to Athens the conditions were ideal for just such an age of great art as in fact occurred. They were in triumphant mood. The gods and heroes had to be thanked and commemorated. The city itself had to be rebuilt. And politically Athens knew that a magnificent Athens would keep for her the lead of the allies which she had obtained by the chances of battle and the forewisdom of her sea policy. Themistocles rebuilt her walls, and when Pericles became tyrant of Athens he turned to the rebuilding of the great shrines on the Acropolis. Greek sculpture came to its climax with the master work of Phidias ; Greek literature at the Dionysian Festivals with Æschylus, Sophocles, Euripides, and Aristophanes ; whilst wall painting, vases, and the crafts flourished as never before. Religion, patriotism, belief in the power of the human mind and body, a sense of freedom and a wonderful site combined to give to fifth-century Athens the perfect conditions for artistic expression.

§ 2

Greek sculpture had already found its direction through the combination of the cult images which the earliest invaders brought from the dark forests of the North with the love of the nude human figure which was a by-product of the athletic games at Olympia and elsewhere. It found its opportunities in the decoration of the pediments and the metope panels of the temples, and in the creation of the figures of the gods and goddesses to whom the buildings were dedicated.

The cult image was at first crude, often little more than a plank of wood vaguely shaped in the form of the human body. The arms were pressed close to the sides, the shoulders barely existed, a slight indication of drapery in rigid folds concealed the rest of the body. By the seventh century B.C. this earliest type began to give place to figures more human but still rigid. The arms, however, show movement, the right hand often holding the drapery ; the face has the frozen " archaic " smile ; the legs are together under the perpendicular folds of the robe. Greek athleticism freed her sculpture. At the great four-yearly festivals of the Olympiad the magnificently proportioned nude athletes ran, wrestled, threw the discus, the javelin. It became a cult to erect commemorative statues to the winners. These sculptures were not portrait statues ; indeed, they were as much Apollo, god of ideal beauty and order, as they were the individual athlete ; as much tributes to the ideal perfection of the human form as to some favourite runner or wrestler. But the artists, with these fine models before them, realised that the human form rose to its thrilling perfection when rigidity gave way to co-ordinated movement and symmetry to the miracle of balance.

All human movement demands a continual change of balance, a swift organisation of counterpoise. The ever-changing centre of gravity in athletics and in the dance must always be met by weight or stress skilfully applied. The fascination of the earliest Greek sculpture is the gradual acceptance of this principle of life into art. The early " Apollo " figures enable us to trace this evolution. For instance, that from the temple at Tenæ, which is in the Munich Museum, just breaks free from the column form, but is a figure " standing at attention " ; that from Piombino, now in the Louvre, walks forward with both arms bent and hands outstretched, and with the stress on one leg. To Dædalus, the legendary craftsman of ancient Greece, the Hellenes themselves paid the tribute that " he made his statues to walk." It has to be remembered that practically all the Greek sculpture which has come down to us, save the low-reliefs from the buildings, consists of Græco-Roman marble copies of the originals, most of which were bronze castings from clay modellings. They are nevertheless true to the Greek designs.

One of the most precious of the statues from this transitional period is the famous " Charioteer " which was found at Delphi and is in the Museum there. Belonging to the early part of the fifth century B.C., it has a static quality of archaic work, yet in the slight twist of the head, the mastery of

" ATHLETE TYING A FILLET," BY POLYCLEITUS

British Museum

A copy of a fifth-century statue found at Vaison. It is one of the most celebrated of the athletic statues. These were idealised studies of the perfect male type, the muscles organised in formal beauty, the poise of the body a marvel of balance and rhythm.

Anderson.

THE " DISCOBOLUS " BY MYRON

Vatican Museum

Myron's contribution to Greek sculpture was largely that of movement. His famous Discus-Thrower, caught at the moment when he is about to hurl the disc, is a wonderful study in balance and the co-ordination of the muscles of the whole body which brings an inevitable rhythm to the work.

the hand gripping the reins, and the balance of the stress on the forward foot, it is essentially a human sculpture, and shows clearly the way the whole art was moving.

§ 3

So the way was prepared for the Golden Age. Two great schools of art arose—the Peloponnesian with its sanctuary of Zeus at Olympia ; the Attic with its sanctuary of Athena on the Acropolis. The celebration by sculptures of athletic victories merged into the commemoration of the national victory over the invading Persians ; the cult statues found their final glory in grandiose statues to the protecting divinities.

Two outstanding names lead the way to that of Phidias : Polycleitus and Myron, both mid-fifth-century artists from the Peloponnese.

Polycleitus carries to its climax the evolution of the athletic statue. His squarely built nude male figures, with the magnificent muscles generalised into something of a formula, are the perfection of the healthy body in repose. Best known, perhaps, is the " Athlete tying a Fillet " or the beautiful " Spear-bearer " at Naples. The thick-set bodies have the grace of noble proportions, the poise is exquisitely balanced. If the art is still a little academic and too studied, it nevertheless has the compensation of ideal repose. His famous " Amazon " statue at Berlin is the female counterpart to these magnificent masculine types.

Myron carries this art one step further forward. His famous " Discobolus," his equally famous " Marsyas," portray a fleeting moment of swift movement when the whole body in action reveals its athletic rhythm. The time was to come when this quality of action would betray Greek art into a violence which destroyed its beauty, but in the hands of Myron it approaches its peak. The discus thrower in the moment when he draws back to the release of the disc ; Marsyas as he reels back from the pipes thrown down by the angry goddess : these are living sculptures. Myron has also left us the noble bust of Pericles which we find in the British Museum.

One other Peloponnesian artist should be mentioned before we turn to Phidias : Pæonius, who is remarkable for the lovely " Victory " of which fragments were discovered at Olympia. This subject of the " Nike," the Victory, brought swift movement to the draped female statues as the celebration of athletic success did to the male. This great winged marble figure of Victory by Pæonius was built on a high pyramidal base which, coloured the blue of the sky, was planned to give the statue the appearance of rushing through the air itself. We must remember that all Greek sculpture was, in fact, painted, or else it was created of differing materials, gold, ivory, and bronze, which gave it colour and some verisimilitude or naturalism.

Phidias himself stood to the noble forerunners as Michael Angelo did to such men as Donatello and Ghiberti. Living from 498 B.C. to 432 B.C. he brought the whole art of Greek sculpture to a splendid climax. He had the opportunity, for when he reached the maturity of his powers Athens under Pericles was enjoying her golden age, the temples and shrines of the sanctuary on the Acropolis were being built, and over at Olympia the rival shrine to Zeus came into being. His two most famous works were the Athena which crowned the temple on the Acropolis, and the Zeus at Olympia. Both were giant works in gold and ivory and bronze over an inner core of wood : the Zeus thirty-five feet high, the Athena more than forty. Far out at sea sailors could see the gleaming gold spearhead of the goddess, memorial to the victory at Marathon and symbol of the power and wisdom of Athens. We only know these great statues from records, from their reproduction on coins and gems, and from reduced antique copies. All the flesh was in ivory, the weapons and armour in gold, the sandals and shield of Athena were ornamented in relief. Indeed, the reliefs on the shield were destined to bring the sculptor to grief and ultimate ruin, for when, in the changing politics of the time, the power of Pericles had waned, Phidias as his friend was arrested on a charge of blasphemy for having introduced portraits of himself and of his patron into the shield reliefs, and he died in prison. The statue of Zeus was equally grandiloquent with that of the goddess at Athens. We know it only from coins and from its description in contemporary writings.

Of one other statue by Phidias we do possess a copy in marble. This is the Lemnian Athena, a beautiful idealised human figure which in the grace of the drapery and the sublimity of the face conveys better than by any external attributes the divinity of the maiden goddess.

In the marvellous architectural sculptures of the Parthenon we may have work from the actual chisel of the greatest of Greek masters ; at least we know they were executed from his designs under his supervision. This most perfect of all Greek temples, built from 447 to 438 B.C. by the architects Iktinos and Kallikrates, crowned the Athenian hill sanctuary and lasted for 2000 years almost unspoiled, until in the Turkish-Venetian war of 1687 the building was used as a powder magazine and was blown up— another outrage by war upon the human spirit ! Its decorative sculptures consisted of three vast series : the ninety-two metopes of which we possess magnificent fragments in the " Elgin Marbles " and of which forty-one are still *in situ* ; the series on the two pediments ; and the processional frieze. All are carved in high relief in Pentelic marble, and were, of course, originally coloured. The metopes tell the stories of the contests between

THE BELVEDERE OF THE PARTHENON

Most perfect of all Greek buildings, the Parthenon on the Acropolis at Athens is the most lovely ruin in the world. This perfection is echoed in the smaller structures which surround it, of which the Belvedere overlooking the bay is one of the most exquisite.

THE PARTHENON FRIEZE (438 B.C.)

W. F. Mansell

British Museum

Part of the so-called " Elgin Marbles " which Lord Elgin brought from the Parthenon ruins for the British Museum, this panel of horsemen is part of the great procession which decorated the frieze. Phidias may himself have worked on these spirited horsemen, and they come down to us as the greatest relief sculpture of all time.

the Greeks and the Amazons, and between Centaurs and Lapiths. Lovely forms of nude youthful warriors, of horses, of the mythological centaurs, of gracefully draped Amazons in attitudes of heroic action carry Greek sculpture to its height. On the pediments were shown the Birth of Athena and the Contest between Athena and Poseidon. The composition of the storied sculpture in these vast triangular spaces is one of the triumphs of Phidias ; the treatment touched the whole gamut of the possibilities of decorative architectural sculpture. Fragments like the statues of Demeter and Core, and the group of the Three Moiræ which are in the British Museum confess the exquisite beauty of pose and drapery which enriched this greatest of all pediment reliefs. The frieze depicted the festival procession of the Athenians to bring the veil to Athena which took place every four years. This work gives us a wonderful picture of Greek life and people, the magistrates, the girls who had spun the wool, men and women of the city, artisans, musicians, warriors in chariots, and young knights. Again we have sections of the frieze in the British Museum, that of the cavalcade of knights being among the finest.

With the Parthenon on the Acropolis stood a number of other buildings and temples, and everywhere we find amazing sculpture from the school of Phidias. The Temple of the Wingless Victory ; the Erectheum, with its—alas !—now ruined frieze but its splendid Caryatides supporting the architrave of the porch, yields yet another phase of this art at the height of its power, when charm, elegance, and that unending inventiveness which shows complete mastery of the craft had been added to the perfect knowledge of the human form in action and repose upon which it is based.

The great sanctuary at Olympia must have been as splendid as that upon the Acropolis, but it has suffered far more, although many magnificent fragments have been found there. It was erected approximately at the same time as the Athenian sanctuary, and here again it was the gold and ivory and bronze statue of Zeus from the hand of Phidias which was the crowning achievement. When excavations were undertaken on the site, enormous numbers of treasures were found, revealing how magnificent the sanctuary must have been. The foundations of more than sixty buildings were laid bare, the remains of 130 statues discovered, and as many as 13,000 objects in bronze, and more than 1,000 in terra-cotta. Most of this work, however, is so broken as to add little to the knowledge that we gain from the better preserved specimens from Athens.

§ 4

Across this golden age came the shadow of internecine war. Athens, swollen with pride, took the dire path of imperialism which turned her allies into vassal states and made her a tyrant rather than a leader. Sparta led the inevitable rebellion against her, and from 431 to 404 B.C. there followed the devastating conflict of the Peloponnesian war, when all Greece was drawn into conflict. The Athenian empire was destroyed, but Sparta's triumph was short-lived. The Greek world lost its semblance of unity, but came together somewhat in 357 B.C. to combat a common foe when Philip II of Macedon marched on the states to the South. Philip won the war and proceeded to reorganise the Greek world, but was assassinated in 336 B.C., and Alexander his son took over the task. Men learned to call him " the Great " for he conquered not only all Greece but Asia Minor, Syria, Egypt, Persia, and the East as far as the North of India, before he died at Babylon in 323 B.C. Then his generals divided his empire among themselves, but already Greek culture and civilisation had been carried far beyond her borders.

All this, indeed, is chiefly important in that it spelled the spread of Greek art and learning. Alexandria, his city at the delta of the Nile, became the centre of learning in the ancient world, the greatest library of manuscripts being established there. In the new cities which sprang up as centres of the new kingdoms, temples and other great buildings en- shrined the localised Greek divinities, and sculptures of these were created for the shrines. These gods of the fourth century B.C. are more human, emotional, passionate, than those of the earlier age. There is often a nervous grace and refinement, but it is paid for by the loss of that sublimity and detachment which marked the former work. The sculptors tended to turn to marble as their medium, and here again there was an influence in that it offered greater subtlety of expression.

Three names stand out from the many of the fourth century B.C. : Scopas of the Peloponnesian school ; Praxiteles of Athens ; and Lysippus, heir of both under the patronage of Alexander himself.

Scopas belongs to the first half of the century. He was born on the island of Paros, stayed for a time in Athens, but formed his style on the Doric example of Polycleitus. His work is remarkable for the expression of tragic grief which he depicts. His noble statue of " Demeter," found at Cnidus and now in the British Museum, is one of the most restrained of the works attributed to him. Other Scopas treasures in the British Museum are the frieze fragments and the statue of " Mausolus " from the great Mausoleum, the memorial sepulchre erected by the widow of King Mausolus of Caria in Asia Minor in 353 B.C. The portrait statue shows the marked movement towards realism and individual likeness which was an increasing tendency of the time. This whole movement was a thrilling by-product of the tomb sculpture and memorial low reliefs which form such a wealth of sculptural Greek art from this time forward.

THE THRONE OF VENUS

National Museum, Rome

One of the musician side panels of the Throne of Venus, the front of which shows the goddess rising from the sea attended by her maidens. The art of sculpture is becoming sentimentalised by this period, but still remains simple and dignified.

49

Of Praxiteles (380–330 B.C.) we are fortunate in possessing some actual work, instead of the Græco-Roman copies which are our usual heritage from the Greeks. The " Hermes with the Infant Dionysus " which Pausanias noted at Olympia was dug up on the spot where he saw it, and there is also a " Head of Venus " in Lord Leconfield's collection. In the work of Praxiteles there is an Attic grace and tenderness which is truly Athenian : slim Apollo figures, dainty Aphrodites, and such works as the " Eros " in the Vatican are conceived in this spirit.

A body of sculpture which we cannot assign to any known masters shows the influence of the two schools as the century proceeds. Two pieces have world fame as the canons of male and female beauty. One is the " Apollo Belvedere " in the Vatican ; the other the " Venus of Melos " in the Louvre. Both reveal how far Greek sculpture had moved earthwards from Olympus in its depiction of gods and goddesses as exquisite, elegant human beings. These lovely pieces compare with the earlier cult figures as the Madonnas of Raphael in their earthly sensuous loveliness compare with these of Duccio or Cimabue in Italian art.

The third outstanding artist of the fourth century B.C. was Lysippus who lived in the latter end of it under Alexander the Great. It is said that Alexander would sit to no other sculptor than this creator of the virile male form. Lysippus concentrated on heroic masculine conceptions —slim young athletes, such as the famous " Athlete using a Strigil " at the Vatican, or mature muscular forms like the " Farnese Hercules " at Naples. In the Louvre, and again at Munich, are portrait heads of " Alexander " by Lysippus.

The mention of these few outstanding names and famous works must suffice to represent the wealth of sculpture of this great fourth century. Even though it had passed its ideal peak, there is such quantity of such high standard that most of the best known and best loved statues belong to this period or to the one following the death of Alexander, when Greek culture ruled the world, even though the empire of Greece and the unity of Greece had passed into that decline which ultimately, in 146 B.C., brought the whole country under the control of the virile, world-conquering Romans.

This Hellenistic Age saw the rise of many great cities : Antioch in Syria, Pergamum in Mysia, Alexandria in Egypt, Rhodes. Each state turned its eyes inward and built grandiose structures and splendid monuments out of their inheritance of the cultural glory of Greece. Inevitably it was all somewhat decadent : more vulgar, noisier, less restrained, restless, and with that touch of flamboyance which contact with the Orient had encouraged. Nevertheless great works emerge.

The " Victory of Samothrace," celebrating a naval victory off Cyprus in

THE VENUS OF MELOS

Louvre, Paris

The best known statue in the world, the Venus of Melos probably dates from about the middle of the third century B.C. This sculpture has long been held up as the ideal of womanly beauty, as the almost contemporary Apollo Belvedere is that of the male. Beauty, calmness, strength, purity and power radiate from this divinity in marble.

51

THE WINGED VICTORY OF SAMOTHRACE

Louvre, Paris

A commemorative sculpture set up about 306 B.C. on a promontory of the island of Samothrace, overlooking the scene of the naval victory which it celebrated. The figure stands on the prow of a ship,
the drapery pressed against the body by the onward rush. This is the splendid realism of Greek sculpture
which has travelled far from the primitive cult statues.

THE LAOCOON

Vatican Museum, Rome

The famous work upon which Lessing wrote his study of poetry and sculpture, shows us the final decline of the grandeur of the art of sculpture in Greece into realism and sensationalism. The choice of subject and its representation by contorted forms and agonised expression is typical of the sculpture of Rhodes and the mainland of Asia Minor towards the end of the history of Greece.

53

306 B.C., is typical of the best in the era. It carries on the tradition of the Victory figures which had long been a feature of Greek sculpture ; but its magnificent movement, the sense of the wind among the draperies as this splendid figure rushes forward through the air at the prow of the ship, has given the " Victory of Samothrace " undying fame.

It was at Pergamum in Asia Minor that this Hellenistic art found its most spectacular expression. A victory over the Gauls by Attilus was celebrated by a number of votive sculptures on the temple of Athena at Pergamum itself and on the Acropolis at Athens. The well-known statues of the " Dying Gaul " belong to theses eries. The other outstanding work at Pergamum was the enormous altar to Zeus. Excavated by a German expedition, portions of this vast structure have been re-erected in Berlin. The great frieze gives all the gods, demi-gods, and heroes of Greek myth-ology under the subject of the contest of the Titans against the Gods of Olympus.

The famous "Laocoon" is another work in this mood of struggle and the utmost effort of the human body and mind. Under the limelight of Lessing's great study this sculpture attracted attention greater, perhaps, than it truly merited. Belonging to the first century B.C., it is yet another step in the direction of naturalism and violence, and to-day we would not give to this tortured depiction of physical and mental agony the high praise which Pliny gave and Lessing echoed.

If from this final flowering of Greek sculpture we have no master-works to compare with those of the preceding ages, we nevertheless have a wealth of minor sculpture. In the private memorial sculpture which com-memorated the dead, usually in the form of delightful low reliefs depicting simple acts of ordinary life, we have a type of genre work which has an intimate grace entirely its own. It links, too, with the realism of portraiture which when this art moved over to Rome was to become so important.

For the next step in the story of classical art was the coming of Rome, the sack of Corinth in 146 B.C., and the subsequent history of the Greek artists as the servants of the Romans creating for their luxurious masters innumerable copies of the most famous of the antique sculptures, from which happily we know the exact form of the lost or fragmentary originals.

V

ROMAN HOLIDAY

§ 1

IT must never be forgotten that art is intimately bound up with human history, and in that history there has probably never been a more important happening than the conquest of the entire Mediterranean and European world by the Romans during the second and first century B.C. and their domination of that vast territory in the centuries which followed. It was, as H. G. Wells has pointed out, a vast administrative experiment, an experiment which is still in a state of evolution in the democracies and imperialisms of the modern world. It established our system of laws and of authority based upon law ; it built up a framework into which the Christian Church was ultimately welded. It needs but little thought to realise how tremendously important the establishment of a world order, law, ethics, and ultimate faith have been in the human story and not least in the history of the arts.

One of the most fascinating aspects of that record is the way that the whole fashion of life and culture was set in the city of Rome itself, centre of that tiny twenty-square-mile state from which the tides of conquest rolled to the Euphrates in the East and to Spain and Britain in the West, inundating all Northern Africa and Southern and Central Europe on their path. City after city throughout this vast region conformed to the original pattern, built its own forum, its theatres and amphitheatres, baths, temples, basilicas, and arenas on the model of the mother city. Private citizens and exiled governors erected on the hillsides of Gloucestershire or the oasis of the Sahara villas which exactly copied the type we unearth from buried Pompeii. Everywhere everything was an extension of Rome and the Roman way of living ; every freeman of the whole empire was a citizen of Rome with the right to vote at the town meetings of the capital—if he could get there ! Thus at Aquæ Salis (which we call Bath) in Britain, at Arles in Provence in Southern France, at Baleek in Northern Africa, at Pergamum in Asia Minor, at Alexandria in Egypt, there was the same life going on as nearly as possible to that of Rome : the same arrangement of the costly villas of the governing Romans and the natives who were helping them carry out their rule or living amiably under it ; the great baths which were clubs, social centres, and museums ; the theatres and circuses where popular entertainment kept the masses from the more dangerous diversion of possible revolt ; the basilicas which were both market places and courts of justice ; the temples where the old Roman gods shared their shrines with indigenous deities in an amazingly cosmopolitan tolerance, so that only the deified statue of the Emperor received its pinch of incense ; the triumphal arches and columns to commemorate the victories of those same emperors. Under the Roman Empire living was recognised as something of an art in itself, and to its adornment the arts ministered. Statues filled the innumerable arches and niches of the baths, theatres, arenas, basilicas ; low reliefs told the story of the triumphs of the Emperors on arch and column ; mural paintings adorned the walls of the private houses as well as some of the public buildings ; portrait busts commemorated the illustrious dead of the noble and governing families in public places, and in private looked down on the splendid tessellated pavements of the fine villas.

This Roman art, although it must be recognised as a definite thing in itself, derives from two distinct sources. One is the Hellenistic sculpture and painting which had already, as we have seen, found its place widely across the civilised world under Greek conquest. The other was a curious funerary and personal art of the Etruscans, the people of Central Italy who were the first to be conquered by the people of Rome in the third century B.C.

§ 2

Etruscan art had risen to a height of pronounced individuality long before the Romans came. Archæologists are still divided as to the origins of this strange people who settled in Italy, coming from Asia Minor somewhere about the fourteenth or thirteenth century B.C., and in a second wave from ancient Greece about the eleventh. They brought from the East a marvellous art of building, solid, massive masonry, of enormous importance in its use of the vault and the arch. Their cities were surrounded by powerful walls, pierced by great arched gates, such as we can still see at Perugia and at Volterra where the titanic sculptured heads at the corbels and on the keystone are typical Etruscan products. The arch was used at these gates, and also to build bridges, drains, and in the tombs which were so outstanding a feature of this Etruscan culture. From these sources they were taken over by the Romans, whose own gigantic structures were rendered possible by this inheritance from Etruria.

It was again, however, an art of death which had inspired the finest and most characteristic Etruscan work. They created magnificent tombs, adorned the walls with paintings of scenes of daily life, and gave the dead

ETRUSCAN SARCOPHAGUS

British Museum

Modern research has thrown doubts upon the absolute authenticity of this work but undoubtedly it is the type of Etruscan funerary art which had so great an influence on Roman sculpture. The sarcophagus itself has low reliefs on its side panels, and is surmounted by male and female reclining figures, probably portraits of the dead shown in lifelike attitudes.

vast sarcophagi often patterned in high relief and with portrait sculptures of their inmates reclining or kneeling on the lids. These Etruscan people seem to have believed that the dead inhabited their tombs for some time, and although they used both burial and cremation they prepared the tombs in the semblance of the houses of the living, which argues a belief in some kind of spiritual body. On the walls and pillars painted low reliefs of household goods were depicted as if the actual objects were in fact hanging there—bags, baskets, pots, utensils, and arms were shown as in the owner's house and lifetime. The walls, like those of the houses, were gay with painted scenes of banquets and dances and with subjects from mythology. On stone benches round the walls, or in the middle of the tomb, sarcophagi contained the bodies or caskets the ashes of the departed, for whom all this was to give a comforting semblance of normal life. Sometimes the bodies were not in coffins at all, but were dressed in their ordinary clothes or armour and seated on the benches or on curious terra-cotta sofas arranged around the tomb. Well may we wonder what strange beliefs inspired all this elaborate organisation of existence in the tomb.

The sculpture of these Etruscan people is remarkable for its amazing realism, especially in the sarcophagal statues. There is an excellent example in the British Museum : the husband and wife in vastly lifelike similitude are lying side by side on the lid in apparently smiling conversation, while the sides of the great coffin are decorated with low reliefs of many figures amid fine patterning. In common with much Etruscan sculpture the very realism gives it a queer sinister feeling. Death masks were often taken and hung around the walls, a custom pursued—perhaps copied from them—by the Romans. Later Etruscan sculpture is sometimes an echo of that of archaic Greek with the frozen smile of the early statues. But by far the most important contribution which the Etruscans made to sculpture is that of their funerary art, with its definitely individual portraiture, for it was this phase which the Romans took over and brought to a high pitch of perfection.

Their wall painting, too, was copied by the Romans. The wall spaces were broken up by painted formal patterns, and often by architectural representation, and in the spaces thus created were delightful designs of dances and banquets, musicians and mummers, and scenes from mythology. Around these were touches of charming pattern. The life of this mysterious people survives for us on these walls and in their tombs, which were themselves fine buildings on occasions although sometimes they were simply carved out of the rocks.

§ 3

The other source of Roman art was, of course, that of the Greeks who had preceded them as masters of the Mediterranean world. At the break

CÆSAR AUGUSTUS

Vatican Museum

This giant marble statue of Cæsar Augustus, clad in armour decorated with low reliefs and bearing the symbol of office, was part of the propaganda of the Roman Empire and its rulers. Probably the finest of all Roman products in the fine arts, it is an idealised portrait owing much to the Greeks, yet having a peculiarly Roman quality.

up of the Empire of Alexander and its ultimate subjection to Rome with the fall of Corinth in 146 B.C. the conquerors were still far too busy with their task of imperialism to deal much in that culture which had become the real contribution of the Hellenes to world progress. So the tutors, the artists, the whole cultural and domestic life of the new Empire in Italy itself at least, and by fashionable reflection in the distant cities as they were added to the Empire, became the business of the Greeks. They taught the sons of the conquerors, they supplied the innumerable copies of their own great sculpture to decorate the gardens and halls of the villas and the great bath palaces, the arches and niches of the theatres and arenas. Something approaching factories of Greek artists arose to cope with the demand of the wealthy Romans for this Greek sculpture. The old bronzes were faithfully copied in the indigenous marble of Italy, and it is not too much to say that almost all we know of Greek sculpture comes from these Græco-Roman copies made by the conquered Greeks for their Roman masters. In the great days of the first century B.C. when Sulla rebuilt Rome, the craze for opulence in which rulers and private citizens vied with each other and with all who had gone before gave the most wonderful chance to these Greek artist-copyists. One theatre alone was decorated with no less than 3,000 statues.

Rome believed in bigness. As rulers of the Western world they knew that size impressed the populace, and consequently they did everything on a massive scale. A great deal of Roman art has to be seen as State publicity. Having to hand the architectural form of the arch, which, as we have seen, they took from the Etruscans, and having discovered the use of concrete as a building material, they were able to erect enormous edifices which impressed by their sheer size. The Circus Maximus held no less than 300,000 spectators on its galleried seats ; the Baths of Caracalla or those of Diocletian could accommodate 3,000 bathers at once in their spacious rooms and galleries ; a whole town was ultimately built inside the walls of the palace of Diocletian across the Adriatic at Split. When Trajan erected his Victory column in the Forum at Rome it was covered with nearly seven hundred feet of pictorial information concerning his campaign in Dacia ; and the whole story of that campaign adorned it, presented with all possible realism, with 2,500 sculptured low-relief figures. Nowadays Government Departments and the printing press have this task of publicity in hand, but the motive is the same. Roman art, therefore, must be seen in the first instance as the publicity of a totalitarian state and its rulers.

This psychological factor, as much as any actual utilitarian purpose which they possessed, accounts for the truly marvellous buildings, roads, aqueducts, bridges, triumphal arches, columns, and palaces. It yielded many of the sculptures and low reliefs with which the monuments were

A ROMAN BUTCHER'S SHOP

British Museum

It is a far step from the idealism of Greece to this intimate and pictorial low relief of a butcher's shop, with the Roman matron as customer, the butcher, and his realistic wares, the block, scales and cleaver. Such plaques were sometimes used as commemorative tablets to the dead.

adorned. Of great importance, too, it gave us the excellently designed Roman lettering, telling in words what the sculptures depicted in form. Clear, beautifully proportioned, this lettering has held its foremost position for two thousand years as most perfectly suited to the purpose. As we have it in its perfection on the Trajan column it is indeed a thing of beauty.

The second phase of Roman art which demanded attention was that of portraiture. This again owes its enormous debt to the Etruscans. In every Roman villa portrait busts of the illustrious dead members of the family decorated the central open hall. Masks in wax taken from the dead gave the basis for these, and the sculptors worked ultimately in bronze and marble or terra-cotta. It was a highly individualised art, and has left for us a magnificent number of Roman portraits. One phase of it was that of the statues of the Emperors for temples or public places. Something of the idealism of the old Greek athletic statues and those of the divinities of Greece was linked with the grandiose feeling of the Roman rulers, and in such a piece as that of the Emperor Augustus at the Vatican—probably the finest extant Roman statue—we have a work of real grandeur. A further aspect of this official portrait sculpture, and a distinctive Roman contribution, was that of the equestrian statue, such as the one of Marcus Aurelius in the piazza of the Capitol. It was a rare thing, but later was to exercise its influence on the great Italians when they came to execute equestrian statuary.

Of all this sculpture, however, the most remarkable was the portrait busts with their definite realism and search for lifelikeness. Those of some of the Emperors, such as the Nero of the Louvre, the Vitellius at Vienna, or the Caracalla at Naples, reveal personality, and are far removed from the remote idealism of Greek work. They link with the private memorial art, and make of this vast Roman Period a breathing and intimate reality, for it was not only emperors and patricians who were thus immortalised. Works such as the high relief of a shoemaker, with his last in low relief as decoration on the frame, remind us that this idea of memorial sculpture was very widespread in the Roman world.

§ 4

With the Romans the art of mural painting, which they had inherited from the Hellenist period of the Greeks and also from the Etruscans, reached a perfection of its own. We have to remember again that the governing-class Roman had made life into an affair of comfort and luxury, and that his villa was a thing of convenience and beauty such as had never been known in the private world before his time. Built around two courtyards, a semi-public and a private one, the Atrium and the Peristyle, these mansions had whole series of apartments for every purpose of civilised living, and

Anderson.

WALL FRESCO FROM POMPEII

An art which the Romans inherited from the tomb painting of the Etruscans and from the luxurious house decoration of the Hellenistic Greeks came to perfection in the villas of the patricians. At first only architectural detail was imitated : panels, pilasters, cornices and the like. Then these became the surroundings for highly realistic scenes as though they opened to views of the distant country ; and finally the panels were decorated with figures.

were decorated in magnificent style. Inlaid mosaic pavements of coloured marbles, noble Corinthian pillars at the doorways, and fine columns around the intimate Peristyle were a basis for this splendour. Mingled with this actual architecture was the painted imitation columns, pillars, and panelling of the walls. These were painted with remarkable realism. It was all an art of illusion, often brilliantly ingenious, an art which had its echo in Italy at the height of the Renaissance when artists painted the walls out of existence and substituted pictured architecture and vistas into the country beyond or into the sky above.

At the beginning, during the second century B.C. there were no actual pictures in the Roman murals, the painting being confined to the imitation of columns, pillars, and cornices and the ingraining of panels to imitate rich marbles. The second period—the first century B.C.—continued this system with yet greater realism, and the panels between the painted pilasters are decorated with " open-air " landscapes with small distant figures, as though one were looking through an aperture into the open countryside. The third style finds the figures given principle importance, while scrolls, patterns, wreathes, floral decoration with birds and other small creatures intermingled justifies the title of Ornate usually given to this period. It was during this time that Nero built his Golden House in the heart of Rome, and made of it a treasure palace of Greek art. Here the " Laocoon " was found, as well as other important Greek sculptures. The Colosseum was later built on the site of a lake in the gardens ; for Vespasian, the emperor who followed Nero, believed in appeasing the gods and the populace rather than in private luxury, and refused to live in the Golden House.

With or without encouragement by the emperors, however, this love of luxury was now ingrained in Roman life, and the art of this Ornate Period degenerated into mere fancifulness in the Intricate Period which followed.

We are fortunate in having had the actual houses of the patrician Romans preserved under the lava of Pompeii and Herculaneum. These cities, with their wonderful position by the seashore, were favourite resorts of the wealthy Romans, and the houses were indeed luxurious and tell us much of the manner of that decadent life of the first century A.D. Some of the wall paintings show a great sense of decoration and pattern for its own sake ; and, if some are frankly lascivious, many are charming and breathe the joy of the Romans in the open-air, and in the flowers and creatures. It reveals that in this Roman civilisation there existed that element we may note in our own day, the love of the rural as a luxury superimposed on an intensely urban civilisation. All this Roman painting has a certain joy in technique ; and if the art of perspective was not yet reduced to the science to which the Renaissance men brought it, there was an extraordinary rightness

WALL FRESCO FROM POMPEII

The sudden overwhelming with the ashes and lava from Vesuvius in A.D. 79 of the luxury towns of Pompeii and Herculaneum preserved for us the consummate, if decadent, art of the period. Realistic and naturalistic, it shows a feeling for mass and perspective which was only equalled when the artists of the Renaissance rediscovered these qualities and made them scientific.

in this painted representation of architecture, landscape, and figures, and a vital sense of decoration in the embellishing ornament.

Despite all its magnificence and its public and private luxury this vast Roman experiment in living was destined to pass away. Its splendid buildings, bridges, and aqueducts are still to be found in all those parts of Europe, Africa, and Asia where once the Imperial eagles of Rome ruled. Its statues, and more importantly, the copies of the greater Greek statues made during those Roman centuries, are the treasures of the museums of the world. The remains of the villas, with their pavements and the fragments of their murals, are places of pilgrimage, whether at unearthed Pompeii or in the remote countryside of England where once fine Roman towns flourished. But the Empire disrupted, the flood-tide of civilisation ebbed, and it was the Christian Church which kept the channels open. It is to Christianity, therefore, that we look for the continuation of the story of art.

VI

THE IMPACT OF CHRISTIANITY

THE ART OF BYZANTIUM AND ITS CUL-DE-SAC IN RUSSIAN CHURCH PAINTING

THE story of art is inevitably blended with the wider history of mankind. It shares its changes and is dependent upon its conflicting political groupings and upon its economic structure as well as upon that deeper and more subtle spiritual urge which persists through all vicissitudes of this material life. So when this heritage of classic art from Greece and beyond was all but squandered by the Romans, the miraculous rise of Christianity in the midst of the tolerant polytheism of the cosmopolitan Empire proved to be even more miraculously the salvation of art and even of civilisation. One writes " more miraculously " because the new religion at first was in every way opposed to art. It was a Semite faith, though Paul early enough widened its boundaries to include the Gentiles ; but its Semitic origin carried with it the distrust of the graven and pictorial image " or likeness of any thing in the heavens above or the earth beneath." It added to this a hatred of the lasciviousness and sensuous luxury which marked much of the later Roman painting and decoration such as that at Pompeii. As a forbidden religion, or at least one intermittently forbidden, it had no places of worship, meetings being held in the houses of the faithful or in some secret place. Actually it was this very aspect of being forbidden which turned the Christians towards art— art not for its own sake or as gratification of the senses, but as a binding factor, a series of secret signs among themselves. Christianity became literally an underground movement. Its intrinsic doctrine of the resurrection, upon which so much depended, caused the Christians to bury their dead rather than to cremate them after the Roman fashion. For this purpose the many underground passages in Rome from which the stones of the city had been quarried, the Catacombs, were chosen. On shelves cut into the walls the dead, sometimes martyred, Christians were encoffined. It was an obvious next step that in times of violent persecution the Christians should use these vast galleries as hiding-places, and anyway as places where they could meet for their forbidden worship. The

Catacombs of Rome became not only cemeteries for the Christian dead but a series of chapels for the living.

As the faith spread to all classes there would equally inevitably be among the converts journeymen whose normal business in the world was precisely that gay decoration, mixture of painted architecture and naturalistic pictures, which was current in the fashionable Roman world. There would be also wealthy adherents used to such decoration of their surroundings. So the catacomb chapels and altars began to be decorated with something akin to the house-paintings of the Roman world, the same painted pilasters and festoons between panels devoted to pictures. It was much cruder, as one would expect under such conditions, but the elements were there.

There was, however, that important difference of purpose. This earliest Christian art was there to convey a message, and often to convey it in a language which had a double meaning. The message was the hope of the new faith, the language had perforce often to be that of pagan Roman symbols. Thus Orpheus or Apollo might be depicted, but the figure stood for Christ. Moses striking the Rock for water symbolised the Baptism ; a figure with two lions was Daniel in the lion's den with its double significance of the resurrection and of deliverance during time of persecution ; so, too, was Jonah. The Christian painting was essentially symbolic ; was, moreover, not an end in itself but a means. If, therefore, it apparently used the light and shade impressionist technique which marked the highly cultivated art of painting under the Romans, a technique which gave form by the use of thrown shadows, if it used the decorative qualities of floral and architectural forms usual in the decoration of the noble houses of Rome, it was not for these things that the spectator looked. And these things, lacking importance, tended to be less technically well done. It was the meaning that mattered, not the method. Art under Christianity became a secret shorthand.

Under the impact of the virile peoples from the North upon an Empire which had lost its early virility, Rome began to fail ; but this once despised and often persecuted religion moved from strength to strength. One happening destined to have great importance for art was that the unwieldiness of the vast Empire necessitated the establishment of a new capital more in contact with the Eastern section than Rome could possibly be. It was founded at the beginning of the fourth century by the Emperor Constantine at Byzantium, and from the beginning rivalled Rome itself. Its vast amphitheatre could seat a hundred thousand spectators ; its palaces and temples were built in the spectacular Eastern fashion and, most important of all, Constantine established the final legal right of Christianity and immediately began an era of church building greater than anything the

Anderson

THE CATACOMBS, ROME

The Crypt of St. Cecilia

In these miles of galleries excavated in the soft stone of the hills around Rome, and used by the early Christians as burial-places, hiding-places, and chapels for worship, art was reborn. It echoed the mural painting of Rome, but was inevitably cruder. Its importance lay in the use of symbols and conventional attitudes, which had significance to the persecuted Christians, but no necessary realism of appearance.

MOSAIC : " THE GOOD SHEPHERD "

Mausoleum of Galla Placidia, Ravenna

In this fifth-century work there is an attempt in the difficult medium of mosaic to imitate the light and shade and perspective of the wall-paintings of pagan Rome. The Sacred Figure and the animals are shown in movement, and the cast shadows are carefully followed.

world had ever known before. Constantinople, as the new capital was called, was a monument to the glory of the Christian Cæsar of the East. Soon Theodosius was to make Christianity the official religion of the Empire ; and the Church, rapidly growing rich under the bequests and gifts of the now wealthy adherents to the faith, took full advantage of its new position and prestige.

The type of building which came into being at Constantinople was itself something new, borrowing on the one hand from the magnificent engineering genius of Rome, and on the other from its Eastern neighbours with their complicated system of dome structure. S. Sophia, the greatest church of the city, was a miracle of strange device. The first building disastrously collapsed in an earthquake, but the second remains to-day one of the most impressive pieces of architecture in the world, a soaring creation of dome above dome supported by arches springing from the piers.

For the interior decoration these people also turned to the East to improve upon a Roman technique. The Romans had for centuries decorated their pavements and to a lesser extent their walls with small pieces of coloured marbles set together as we set a jig-saw puzzle to create a formal pattern and less often a picture. This art of mosaic enlisted from the East the brilliant effect of little cubes of coloured glass and also of gilded glass. In the vast spaces of the new basilicas, amid light coming from thousands of candles to pinpoint the eternal twilight with flecks of living gold, the pictures thus built up of myriad pieces of brilliant material are among the most impressive art creations of the world. The backgrounds of lapis lazuli blue or of sombre gold form a perfect foil to the monumental and majestic figures. These mosaics took over the symbolic simplicity of the catacomb painting, but they were soon fulfilling a new purpose : to tell of the power and grandeur of the Church and of the Emperors. Christianity, which had sent thousands of its sons and daughters to death in the arena or on the crosses of Roman penal law rather than offer worship to the Emperor, found itself the greatest exponent of this grandiloquent art which scarcely stopped short of the ancient ascription of divinity to Cæsar. The religion which began by praising poverty and humility triumphed as one which flaunted riches and power. Byzantine art was entirely removed from the spiritual sources of Christianity and from those mystical sacred figures which had kept faith alive in the Catacombs.

Whatever loss of spiritual or moral value there was, however, it had raised itself to a supreme height as pure art. It had built around itself its own monumental convention. The impressive figures were always depicted standing straight in front of the spectator. There was no action nor gesture ; no drama. The drapery was arranged in formal folds which gave an added simplicity and grandeur. The eyes stared straight forward,

71

large and piercing under heavy brows. All this arose partly from the fact that the method of mosaic permitted no subtlety, but equally because this art, as we have seen, was intended to impress the people, and these factors were impressive ones.

One other form of Christian art had arisen : the illustrations to the manuscripts which were being made by the scribes in the first monasteries, in the great book production centre at Alexandria, and elsewhere. This was different from the Byzantine in that its motive was to tell or illustrate the sacred stories either from scriptures or from the growing Christian legend, and for this purpose it had to have a certain dramatic element, to depict action, and to show some humanity. These book illustrations were usually enclosed in small rectangles and inserted among the text. They were, of course, miniature and tended to depend upon comparatively simple outlines to achieve their aim. Thus they were entirely different from the old Roman painting, and were, in their way, as much an innovation as the mosaics in the basilicas. Sometimes there was a slight inter-mingling of the elements—a mosaic would be built up in the style of the Roman wall-paintings or the best of the catacomb paintings, as, for instance, the magnificent one showing Jesus the Good Shepherd in the Mausoleum of Galla Placidia at Ravenna. Here the effect is gained by representing shadows and reflected lights ; even the lambs are each given their respective shadow. On the whole, however, the lines of the art of mosaic tended more and more to follow the Byzantine method. The central figure would be depicted on a much larger scale than any subsidiary one. Size has always been a psychological factor in propagandist art such as this became, as we have seen in our own time with the giant photographs, paintings, sculptures, and photo-montant glorifying Hitler, Mussolini, Lenin, and Stalin.

The earliest mosaics we have are those in certain fourth-century churches in Rome itself, but in these it is still an art linked with the catacomb paint-ings. We see this in the vault in S. Constanza, a mausoleum built for the daughters of Constantine, where the decoration is in almost purely catacomb style ; the nave of S. Maria Maggiore, which attempts to apply the narrative technique of the books to the depiction of incidents from the lives of Abraham, Moses, Joshua, and Jesus ; and the apse of S. Pudenziana, where an enthroned Christ figure is flanked by groups of half- and quarter-length sacred personages while a vast jewelled cross gleams from the heaven above. All this early Roman work looks backward, save in its use of the mosaic technique. It was at Byzantium itself and at Ravenna that the new art came into its own.

Ravenna to-day yields the greatest thrills of Byzantine mosaic art. Save for the few splendid churches, this now almost abandoned city on the

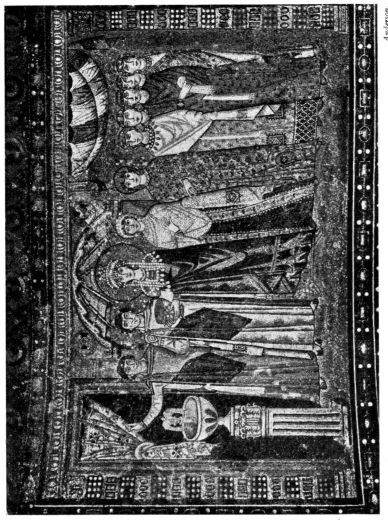

CHURCH OF ST. VITALE, RAVENNA

One of the most perfect examples of Byzantine Mosaic in the world, in the church, built in 526, by the Emperor Justinian. On the walls are shown the Emperor and his Empress Theodora, bringing gifts to the church. She is richly jewelled, haloed to indicate her sanctity, and attended by the ladies of her court. Naturalism has been sacrificed to the frontal attitude, the staring eyes, the stiff folds of drapery which came to be typical of Byzantine art.

Adriatic has nothing of the glory which for two hundred years during the fifth and sixth centuries made it magnificent. It came into primary importance when the Emperor Honorius made it the imperial headquarters in 403, and from that time onward retained its importance as the link between Rome and Constantinople. As such it inherited the art methods of both East and West.

Four of its splendid churches deserve especial mention in this matter of Byzantine art. One is the Mausoleum of Galla Placidia, the sister of the Emperor Honorius. Here among others we have the early mosaic of Jesus the Good Shepherd, previously mentioned, executed in the Roman tradition of light and shade. It belongs to the middle of the fifth century. At the church of S. Giovanni in Fonte we have further frescoes showing the transition to the Byzantine. A Baptism (in which the Jordan is personified in Roman fashion by a presentation of the River God) is still in the Roman tradition, but around this are a series of saints in gold and white on a dark ground with the purely static and decorative quality of the Byzantine. They, too, are fifth-century work. A more definite demonstration of the transition can be seen at the great church of S. Apollinare Nuovo, where in separate rows executed at different periods one can see work in the narrative style of the manuscripts, others in the decorative Roman style, and, dating from fifty years later, a series of martyrs and of virgins of definitely Byzantine type.

A fourth church in Ravenna yields some of the most perfect pure Byzantine mosaics in the world. This is S. Vitale, built in 526, an octagonal church which served as a model to Charlemagne when he erected the cathedral at Aix-la-Chapelle. The erection of this church was part of the vast building schemes under the Emperor Justinian, that strange Roman genius who ruined the Empire by his grandiloquent schemes of building but must be accredited with his splendid work in codifying that Roman law which remains the basis of so much that is good law in the world to-day. If Justinian served Roman law, there was one matter in which he made it serve him, and that was in changing it to support his marriage to Theodora, the courtesan and dancing girl whom he made his Empress. Here on the walls of S. Vitale we see them still in two of the greatest of all Byzantine mosaics. Attended by the ladies of her court, the Empress, weighted down with jewels and haloed to show her somewhat belated saintliness, brings a gift to the church, as her husband does in the companion work. The whole church, indeed the whole city of Ravenna, is rich in this strange Eastern art, but nowhere can we find anything more remarkable than these two pieces.

This static art fought a losing battle with the more lively narrative pictures of the manuscripts. It had its own triumphs. It established certain

74

ILLUMINATED PAGE FROM THE BENEDICTIONAL OF ST. ÆTHELDRED

One other line of development of art was through the illustrations in the great devotional manuscripts. This splendid specimen belonging to about 960 shows a page from one of the great English Manuscripts, where the subject of the Three Maries at the Tomb is shown—a spirited narrative treatment with a noble decorative setting.

conventions—the stiff folds of the drapery, the large eyes which became the symbol of holiness, the long tapering fingers, the plain backgrounds of gold which was the symbolic colour of heaven. When, five hundred years or more later, Italian painting slowly emerged, it was at first to this art of Byzantium that it turned, and all the early painters accepted the conventions of the mosaics as a basis for their art. Whether we look at such a piece as the great Cimabue altar-piece in the National Gallery, or the earlier Margaritone, or to the wall-paintings such as the noble St. Paul on the walls of Canterbury, that influence is there, modified in the case of the Canterbury St. Paul by the more lively narrative pictures from the manuscripts. In the minor arts of the Church : enamels, embroidery, the first carvings, its influence remains. There is a famous Limoges enamel at Cluny which shows us the figure of Christ in perfect Byzantine manner, symbolic, remote, inhuman, with the carefully arranged folds of the drapery, the long slender fingers raised in the symbol of blessing, the large eyes staring straight out of the picture. Only when Giotto and his contemporaries began to decorate the basilicas of that most human saint, Francis, did this, by then archaic, method lose ground.

There remained, however, one curious cul-de-sac wherein Byzantianism persisted : the Greek Orthodox Church. The story of the gradual break between the Eastern Church centred at Constantinople and the Western one at Rome is a long and complicated one. Not the least cause of the quarrel was this very subject of images in the Church. Paradoxically it was the Eastern Emperors, initiators of this great art, who attempted in the eighth century to suppress it as idolatrous, and the Popes at Rome who defended it. Emperor Leo III ordered the removal of all images ; Popes Gregory II and III refused. An armada set out from Constantinople, but the Italians fought for their images, and won ; the Pope, endowed with new power, excommunicated the Emperor, and although there were vicissitudes in the struggle, the images in the West, at least, were saved. In the East the precious creations of three hundred years were in most instances destroyed as a result of this quarrel ; and then, because of their human popularity, the edict was unheeded and the images crept back again. But the break between the two Churches widened, the struggle for power between the Pope of Rome and the Patriarchs and Emperors of the East, intensified. There were doctrinal questions, but chiefly it was a matter of power politics, and eventually the Greek Orthodox Church and the Roman Catholic Church were two diverse arms of Christendom. The Greek Church ultimately came to a compromise on the subject of the church images, forbidding statues, but permitting sacred pictures, " icons," as a concession to the popular demand.

Away to the North of Constantinople stretched the vast lands of what

ENAMEL : CHRIST IN MAJESTY

Cluny Museum

The Byzantine style dominated the early art of the Church and is shown perfectly in the enamel made at Limoges and now in the Cluny Museum, Paris. The stiff attitude, the exaggerated folds of the draperies, the long figures raised in symbolic gesture of blessing : these details were repeated in all the arts and crafts of the church.

we now know as Russia, and it was in 955 that Olga, the widow of its warlike ruler who had himself fought against Byzantium, came to the city and accepted Christianity for herself and her people. It was one of those mass conversions which was assumed to have added to the numbers of the Church without necessarily adding to the godliness or morality of the world. From that remote time until the Bolshevik revolution in 1918 the Greek Orthodox Church was the official Church of this vast territory. First S. Sophia Olga at Kiev was built in the Byzantine manner, and then throughout the whole domain churches were built in this style, with clusters of onion-shaped domes and soaring roof lines. They grew more and more fantastic in shape ; and within, their walls and altars were decorated with barbaric splendour, often with sheets of pure gold. Russia for centuries kept herself apart from the stream of European life. Not until Peter the Great broke the spell did she have any real contact with her neighbours. Within her borders life centred round its Church. The priests wielded material and spiritual power ; the monasteries pursued their strange ingrowing culture. In no country did life remain static for so long a period.

Art also ossified. The curious type which we have seen come into being in Byzantium went on and on in the Russian Church and the Russian home. Enamelled, inlaid, or painted, on metal or on wood, large and small, the art of the icon persisted. If we see an icon of, say, the eighteenth century it is almost exactly the same as one from the fifteenth. Schools of icon makers arose at Moscow, at Kiev, at Novgorod, and elsewhere. They created an unvaried style which charms by its truth to itself and its rigid conventions. The best icons were probably made in the fifteenth and early sixteenth centuries, but the family likeness of these simply told story pictures or pictures of saints makes it difficult for any but the expert to tell at first glance to what period they belong. To us they look like Italian paintings of the very earliest period before the men of the Renaissance conquered anatomy, perspective, and the other factors of representational painting. The colours run to vivid reds, golds, blues, and greens ; the draperies have the naïve folds of Byzantine work, any architecture defies all the rules of perspective, and the scale of the various figures is large or small in the one picture depending upon their importance. So until Russia moved into the orbit of Western culture she retained for us this art which elsewhere yielded to the growing spirit of man. That spirit caused men to discover anew the joys of the senses, to believe in the mind and body, to turn their eyes to the earth ; and as they did so the golden heaven of Byzantium faded into the light of common but marvellous day.

VII

ISLAM CHALLENGES THE CROSS

MEDIÆVAL MOHAMMEDAN ART

§ I

EARLY in the seventh century an event happened which was destined to have far-reaching results on European life and culture. Again it originated in the Near East and again it was the rise of a new religion. A certain young Arab, Mohammed, moved by that genius for monotheistic religion which always seems to have been a characteristic of the Semite peoples, began an intensive campaign against the idolatry of his race. His native city of Mecca was a famous place of pilgrimage where every year thousands came to kiss the black stone in the wall of the Ka'bah temple, and little notice was taken when first this youthful camel driver, who had become the husband of the rich widow whose camels he tended, preached his new faith of the worship of Allah, the One God. But it was an insistent cult, derived partly from the ideas of the Jewish colonies in Arabia, partly from the Christians of the Eastern world who were under the influence of Eastern heresies. In an atmosphere just ready for this advance in the conception of God, the new religion rapidly gained adherents. Mohammed declared that he had received his inspiration from the angel Gabriel, and was given to some sort of trance condition during which his doctrines and ethics were revealed to him. The people demanded miracles, and the prophet declared that the faith itself and its revelation were sufficient miracle. Persecuted in Arabia, the disciples of the faith found refuge in Abyssinia for a time, then scattered again.

In the year 622, under the threat of more violent persecution, Mohammed fled from Mecca to Medina where a fairly large Jewish population gave him the hope of toleration ; but this hope proved ill-founded, for the Jews tended rather to exploit the Mohammedans. Faced by the threat of poverty the prophet began a series of raids on the caravan route to Mecca as it passed near Medina. He preached a holy war against unbelievers, justified the breaking of age-old tribal customs, such as that of tribal peace during certain seasons of the year, by claiming direct command and inspiration from heaven, and attracted an increasing number of followers by the loot which his raids brought. When trained soldiery were sent against the Mohammedans they found themselves defeated by a fanaticism which promised paradise to all who fell in battle fighting for Allah. As with Christianity here was a faith which scorned death itself, which indeed welcomed death. At a great battle at Badr the armies of Mohammed triumphed against an enormously superior number, and from that time onward success begat success. Flushed with these triumphs the prophet began to send letters to the most powerful kings of the Middle East demanding mass acceptance of Islam (the word meant " surrender "). To Persia and to Byzantium and to Coptic Egypt the epistles went. If the demand were refused, the armies of the faithful followed, and wherever they went their fanaticism triumphed. In 630 Mohammed returned to Mecca and made it his holy city, and there he died two years afterwards.

But Islam went on. There were internal dissensions about the succession, but they did not interfere with the policy of conquest. Eastward into Persia and Northern India, southward into Africa, northward into Turkey, westward along the African coast, across the straits of Gibraltar into Spain, the Mohammedans went, carrying their faith by the sword right to the Pyrenees. The holy places of the Christian religion in Jerusalem and at Bethlehem fell into their hands. Alexandria, the greatest centre of culture and book-learning in the mediæval world, was overrun, and record has it that for six months they fed the fires of the baths there with the priceless treasures of the great library. They destroyed much, but they created something as well.

For hundreds of years they held sway alongside Christianity, and the cultural as well as the political and religious life of Europe was enormously affected by them. Science gained immeasurably, for they were deeply interested in learning, and at such vast centres as Baghdad and at Cordova in Spain they established magnificent colleges where mathematics, geometry, medicine, alchemy, astronomy, and other branches of learning flourished. They brought the East into touch with the West, established tolerant relationships as the centuries passed with Christian scholars, so that we read of Hroswitha, the ninth-century nun-dramatist from Gandersheim in Saxony, going down to Cordova to contact the scholars there.

§ 2

The art of Islam inevitably had its own characteristics. One important aspect of it was that Mohammed, in his fear of idolatry which was really the germ from which the faith sprung, adopted the Jewish ban upon the depiction of human and animal forms. Mohammedan art was thus driven back upon pure ornament, and its greatest contribution to the art of the world has been the arabesque, the interlacing, unending line which covered

INTERIOR OF THE MOSQUE, CORDOVA

The spread of Islam established splendid buildings in the Islamic style as far westward as Cordova, Seville and other cities of Spain. Chief of these were the mosques, those vast holy places with forests of pillars linked by horseshoe arches. Cordova in the ninth century became the greatest centre of learning in all Europe, and the beauty of the Mosque remains a monument, though Islam has receded.

the whole surface with intricate abstract design. The Arab mind was not itself creative æsthetically. They were essentially a nomad people, tent-dwellers living far from cities. If they had arts they were rather crafts of weaving and of basket-work, and both of these had their effect on design. The art of the book was cultivated too, for Islam was, even more than Christianity, a book religion, the teaching of Mohammed being gathered into the Koran, most sacred of all sacred literature. Rugs and hangings and books, therefore, embodied their ideals of beauty, and a type of decoration for the surfaces of buildings arose which had much in common with these crafts.

When, after the years of conquest, the Mohammedans settled in the territories they had overrun, they superimposed on the cities their mosques and palaces with vast shadowed forecourts and fascinating fountains and water gardens dear to the heart of a desert people. In almost every instance, however, they accepted something of the spirit of the local culture, adapting it to their immediate needs. The mosques were often simply Byzantine or Coptic churches. The Mohammedans were not perturbed by the earlier associations. Where there were mosaics or frescoes they covered them with a coat of paint or limewash in accordance with their abhorrence of the idolatrous figure worship of which they accused the Christians. Then they hollowed out the *Mihrab*, a niche in the wall of the building, so that the faithful could look towards Mecca at the hour of prayer. Often it became necessary to erect a tower from which the muezzin could call them to prayer. The faith needed no more than this.

With the passing of the centuries all this became elaborated, but the essence remained. Spacious courts and vast halls, broken by forests of columns and low arches, where the adherents could gather with their prayer rugs ; towering minarets ; forecourts with fountains and shadowed arcades. The architecture of the East dominated : the horseshoe arch and the pointed arch with a double curve, fretted walls which allowed the free passage of air yet gave shadow, outer walls of comparatively poor material faced with stucco or with elaborately decorated tiles. The ceilings and the interiors of domes and arches were sometimes broken by a curious honey-comb of stalactites in plaster. Decoration crept over every surface.

From the East, from Persia, and the whole Mesopotamian area came the lovely tiles with which the surfaces were covered. Texts from the Koran, written in the conventionalised forms of the beautiful Arab script, were interwoven with the arabesques. Woodwork was inlaid with similar devices, and thin strips of metal were nailed on to the wood in the same style. It was an art of brilliant if specious surfaces. As one sees it to-day the wonder is that so much has lasted through the centuries. The marvellous beauty of such buildings as the Alhambra at Granada, the Alcazar or

THE ALHAMBRA, GRANADA

Perhaps the most typically Islamic building bequeathed by the modern invasion of Europe is the Alhambra at Granada, in Spain, with its tiled walls, decorated with ceramics in the true style, the honeycomb roofing, the fountains in the lovely courts.

Palace there, the great Mosque at Cordova, remain breath-taking in their fragile loveliness.

The linear ornament building up into the most intricate abstract geometrical design, the perforated stone-work and plaster-work, the brilliant use of polygonal forms, the unending arabesques based maybe on floral or leaf forms but so conventionalised that their representational aspect is entirely lost, the stylised inscriptions : these things are the essence of this Islamic art.

It penetrated Europe, as we have seen, by way of Spain, but was stopped at the Pyrenees. It was all too exotic to have any lasting influence on European art generally. During the years when it was at its most potent, moreover, Christendom regarded the Moslems as deadly enemies, and would not have been likely to admit that any good thing could come from the hated paynims against whom unending war was waged. It was science, therefore, and not art which owes the debt to Islam. Perhaps there was some slight influence of the arabesque, and of abstract geometrical ornament, but on the whole this art receded again to the Near East whence it sprang, yielding lovely fruit in the carpets and book art of Persia particularly, but leaving the European tradition practically unaffected in the hands of the Christian Church.

VIII

THE BIRTH OF MODERN PAINTING

THE ART OF THE FLORENTINE MASTERS, FROM GIOTTO AND
ANGELICO TO LIPPI AND BOTTICELLI

§ I

SOMETIMES a legend, even a doubtful legend, conveys truth as great as that of authentic history. Right at the start of the record of European painting, in the late thirteenth century, there is a story of Giotto, the Italian shepherd boy whose work was destined to revolutionise art. It is that he was drawing pictures of his father's sheep on a slate, when Cimabue, the great artist of the time, happened to be passing by. Struck by the boy's talent, he obtained permission from his father and took the lad with him to Florence as his apprentice. When Cimabue among others was commissioned to decorate the church at Assisi, he entrusted his apprentice with painting the scenes from the life of St. Francis which were to adorn the walls of the upper church. In these frescoes the young Giotto proved himself, in the words of Ruskin, " a daring naturalist in defiance of tradition, idealism, and formalism." Besides his work at Assisi, Giotto also worked at Rome, and important frescoes by him, notably " The Bewailing of St. Francis " and " Herod's Birthday Feast," are in S. Croce at Florence, but the greatest and most famous of all his undertakings is the series of frescoes which he painted in the Chapel of the Arena at Padua. The date of this enterprise can be fixed with some certainty because it is known that in 1306 Dante was Giotto's guest at Padua, and the poet is said to have assisted the painter in his choice of subjects. Petrarch was also the friend of Giotto.

It is interesting to compare Cimabue's " Madonna and Child " and his pupil's " The Bewailing of St. Francis," both reproduced here. To be fair to the elder artist, we must remember what came before. We have only to look at the altar-piece by Margaritone (1216–93) in the National Gallery to see the oppressive type of Byzantine art, destitute of any feeling for beauty or truth to Nature. From whom Cimabue received his training we know not—there was no famous painter before him—but we do know that he was held in high esteem by his contemporaries. The " Madonna "

"MADONNA AND CHILD ENTHRONED," BY CIMABUE (1240–1302)
National Gallery, London

In Cimabue is seen the first sign of the softening of the Byzantine stiffness, shown in the expression on the face of the Virgin in this picture, and also in the more lifelike treatment of the Child. The gilt background, however, is still artificial, and we do not feel that the Virgin is really sitting on the formal throne. Note also the want of proportion between the Virgin and the angels who are supposed to surround her.

he painted for S. Maria Novella aroused such enthusiasm that it was carried to the church preceded by trumpeters and followed by a procession of Florentines. But whatever the advance made by Cimabue, Giotto advanced still further.

§ 2

If we study Cimabue's " Madonna " at the National Gallery we find that his figures, though not entirely lifeless as the heavily gilded Byzantine figures, are wooden, formal, and conventional, while Giotto's figures have individuality and human feeling, and his groups have a new realism and dramatic vigour. Giotto had a more extended range of colour than Cimabue ; he showed a preference for gayer and lighter schemes, and he gave a more careful imitation of Nature than existed in the works of his predecessors. When we hail Giotto as a daring naturalist, we must think of him in relation to the artists who preceded him, and not to those later painters who gradually learnt to give accurate and complete expression to the truths of Nature. Yet his Paduan frescoes show, as it has been well said, " the highest powers of the Italian mind and hand at the beginning of the fourteenth century." Although a shepherd in his youth, it is strange that his drawings of sheep do not appear correct to modern eyes.

As will be seen from his " The Bewailing of St. Francis," his backgrounds, though in a sense true to Nature, are not realistic. His buildings and his trees are far too small, being drawn neither in true perspective nor in correct proportion to the human figures. His hills are bare and jagged cliffs, his trees have only a dozen leaves for foliage ; but it was an innovation for fields, trees, and animals to appear at all, and no imperfections in their rendering can rob the painter of the glory of having extended the subject-matter of his art. Giotto was the first Gothic painter to depict action, to substitute the dramatic human life for the eternal repose of the divine. To his contemporaries his realism must have seemed amazing, and we can understand Boccaccio, after looking at earlier Byzantine paintings, writing enthusiastically in the *Decamerone* :

Giotto was such a genius that there was nothing in Nature which he could not have represented in such a manner that it not only resembled, but seemed to be, the thing itself.

Giotto was not only a painter : he was also an architect. When he returned to Florence in 1334 the city honoured him and itself by appointing him Master of the Works of the Cathedral. Two great architectural works were planned and begun by him at Florence, the West Front of the Cathedral and its detached Campanile or bell-tower. The latter exists to this day as a monument of his genius, although its author did not live to see its completion. But its lower courses were completed from Giotto's design, and

"THE BEWAILING OF ST. FRANCIS," BY GIOTTO (*c.* 1266–1337)

Santa Croce, Florence

St. Francis, the great apostle of humanity, influenced the Italian artists who brought back humanity to painting after the long period of Byzantine artificiality that followed the fall of the Roman Empire.

88

he was able with his own hand to carve the first course of its sculptured ornaments, illustrating arts and industries, before he died on January 8, 1337.

Giotto was the first of the great Florentine painters. Among his immediate successors was Andrea Orcagna, whose famous " The Coronation of the Virgin " is in the National Gallery. Orcagna was painter, sculptor, architect, and poet. More of a dreamer than his shrewd practical predecessor, Orcagna did not so much develop the realistic side of Giotto as refine and intensify his psychology. He carried on the Giottesque tradition of truth and simplicity, but drama and action appealed to him less powerfully than the expression of emotion and deep religious feeling. In his masterpieces we are arrested not by any movement, but by the variety and intensity of the feelings expressed in the figures.

" In the work of Orcagna," Ruskin writes, " an intense solemnity and energy in the sublimest groups of his figures, fading away as he touches inferior subjects, indicates that his home was among the archangels, and his rank among the first of the sons of men."

This religious intensity led to a greater formality than is found in Giotto and to a curious suggestion of a return to Byzantine lack of humanity.

§ 3

While Giotto was laying the foundations of the art of Florence, another school of painting arose in the quiet hill city of Siena. Its founder, Duccio di Buoninsegna (1260–c. 1320), is said to have been so much influenced by the Byzantine style that he has been called " the last of the great artists of antiquity," as opposed to Giotto, the " father of modern painting." It is not easy to understand this comment if one looks at Duccio's pictures, one of which—" Christ Healing the Blind "—we reproduce. In spite of their colour and their gilding the figures are human and life-like, and the picture reflects human emotion entirely in accord with the spirit of St. Francis. There is so much sweetness and grace in the paintings of Duccio and his fellows that they have been called the first lyric painters of modern art.

Among his younger contemporaries the most gifted was Simone Martini (c. 1283–1344), whose work has the pensive devoutness that marks Sienese painting and a gay decorative charm. There is a picture by him at Oxford, and another in the Fitzwilliam Museum, Cambridge, but perhaps his greatest achievement is the series of frescoes at Avignon. These were once attributed to Giotto, but are now recognised to have been the work of Simone Martini and his school.

Among other early Sienese artists the brothers Pietro and Ambrogio Lorenzetti are noted for the dramatic vigour and liveliness of their work Ambrogio Lorenzetti, on one occasion at least, did a new thing in art. His

"CHRIST HEALING THE BLIND," BY DUCCIO (1260-*c*. 1320)

National Gallery, London

Duccio is often called " the last of the Byzantine artists," and if we look at his " Transfiguration " in the National Gallery we may agree. On the other hand this " Christ Healing the Blind " reveals him as dramatic and human in the new style of Giotto.

" HEADS OF FOUR NUNS," BY AMBROGIO LORENZETTI

National Gallery, London

"To paint what one saw," that was a new ideal in art in the fourteenth century. Ambrogio Lorenzetti, who dared to show the view of Siena from the window of the Civic Palace which he was decorating, here makes a study of four nuns in the same vein of tender humanism.

"ST. FRANCIS RECEIVING THE STIGMATA," BY SASSETTA (1392–1450)

National Gallery, London

One of the recent acquisitions of the National Gallery is a series of six panels by Sassetta depicting incidents in the life of St. Francis. The drama of each situation as well as the reverent study of nature gives this artist an important place in the forward movement.

city of Siena had commissioned him to paint an allegory, " The Result of Good Government," for the great room of the Civic Palace, and he graciously went to the window and depicted an idealised version of the lively city from that view. To paint what one saw : it might have started a movement of modernism, but Siena was a deeply mystical city and her painting remained strangely conservative. The sky was still being painted the symbolic gold of heaven, the attitudes of the figures were still ritualistic rather than dramatic, long after the progressive Florentines had found their way into something like naturalism.

One Sienese artist of the fifteenth century, however, shows a mind of particular originality and charm. Sassetta (1392–1450) has a humanity and a clear-cut sense of pattern all his own. He made an altar-piece for the Franciscans at Bolgo San Sepolcro, with a series of panels on the life of the saint, which illustrate his highly individual genius. Some of these have now been bought by the National Gallery, and are among the treasures there.

§ 4

In the Florentine painting of the fifteenth century, the impulse towards naturalism, first given by Giotto, branched out in two opposite directions. One was psychic, the other physical. The expression of intense and strong emotion, together with action and movement, was the aim of one school ; another strove after realistic probability and correctness of representation. This second school, pushed on by its love of truth, attacked and vanquished one by one various problems of technique. The approach to a closer representation of the appearance of realities involved three main inquiries : (1) the study of perspective, linear and aerial ; (2) the study of anatomy, of nude bodies in repose and action ; and (3) the detailed truth of facts in objects animate and inanimate.

The most considerable figure in Florence after Orcagna was the Dominican monk Fra Giovanni da Fiesole, known as Fra Angelico (1387–1455), who belonged essentially to the psychic or spiritual school, and only approached the physical in his loving observation of Nature. Here he was an innovator, for his eye dwells on gentle aspects, and in his landscape backgrounds he introduces pleasing forms of mountains and verd nt meadows multi-coloured with the budding flowers of spring. Indeed, all his painting is flower-like, but this delicate naturalism does not determine its character. It is the soulful quality of his work which gives it supreme distinction. The unworldliness of his art is explained partly by his cloistered existence and the fact that he lived until his fiftieth year in the little hill towns of Cortona and Fiesole. He led a holy and retired life, and, like St. Francis, was a little brother to the poor.

"THE ANNUNCIATION," BY FRA ANGELICO (1387–1455)

St. Mark's, Florence

The note of sweetness and simplicity introduced into art by Giotto is developed with appealing charm by Fra Angelico. Note the perfect realism of the columns and the flowered background : also the religious devotion expressed in the thoughtful countenances of the Virgin and the angel.

"THE ANNUNCIATION," BY FRA FILIPPO LIPPI (1406–69)

National Gallery, London

An example of Lippi's decorative power, enlivened by accurate Nature study. It will be noticed, however, on comparing this work with Angelico's rendering of the same subject, that Lippi, notwithstanding his increased technical dexterity, is less spiritual in his treatment and fails to express the devotional piety found in the work of his master.

If Fra Angelico had his excellencies, he also had his limitations. His angels are so beautiful that, as Vasari wrote, " they appear to be truly beings of Paradise." But his devils inspire us with no terror ; they are too harmless and self-evidently ashamed of their profession to be anything but ludicrous.

" His pictures of martyrdom," says Muther, " create the impression of boys disguised as martyrs and executioners ; and his bearded men, weeping like women, are equally incredible. But when he does not leave his proper sphere, and the problem is to portray tender feelings, a great and silent joy of the heart, a holy ecstasy or tender sadness, his pictures have the effect of the silent prayer of a child."

His frescoes in San Marco at Florence remain the most enchanting visions of the heavenly world, a world he decked with bright joyful colours culled from the flower gardens of earth. Alongside these we should consider those in the St. Nicolas Chapel of the Vatican, Rome, where he shows himself a master of the new realism. Some idea of Fra Angelico's careful and tender art may be gathered from his " Annunciation," which we reproduce.

§ 5

In the expression of feeling, the most famous follower of Fra Angelico was Fra Filippo Lippi (1406–69), but if unable to attain the ethereal spirituality of Angelico his art was full of humanity and delicacy. His Madonnas belong to Florence rather than to heaven and reveal the painter's fine feeling for feminine beauty more obviously than his piety. He was a genial painter, and in his comfortable satisfaction with the things of this life he shared with Angelico a love of flowers. " No one draws such lilies or such daisies as Lippi," wrote Ruskin. " Botticelli beat him afterwards in roses, but never in lilies."

Lippi's geniality is very evident in his " Annunciation," which we reproduce. The figures are human, the scene is homely, characteristics generally suggestive of the Dutch painters of a much later generation.

Fra Angelico and Fra Lippi stand for the imaginative development that followed the death of Giotto. In the other direction, the first great advance in the rendering of physical nature is found in the painting of Paolo Uccello (1397–1475). This artist was far more interested in the technical problems of fore-shortening and perspective than in anything else. Uccello represents the scientific spirit in the art of the Florence of Cosmo de' Medici, where not only artists, but mathematicians, anatomists, and great scholars were congregated. Among his achievements must be reckoned the recommencement of profane painting by his invention of the battle picture, a subject in which he had no predecessor and no successor till a century later.

"PORTRAIT OF JOHN HAWKWOOD," BY PAOLO UCCELLO (1397–1475)

Cathedral, Florence

This equestrian portrait, in addition to its artistic merit, shown in the lifelike painting of the horse, is interesting as representing a famous English mercenary soldier, the son of an Essex tanner, who first went to the Continent with the English army that fought at Crécy.

His early battle piece, the " Sant' Egidio," [1] amuses us by the rocking-horse appearance of the horses. In his absorption with technique, Uccello was indifferent then to realistic accuracy. Truths of colour did not interest him—he painted horses red. The third dimension in space, which Giotto could only suggest experimentally and symbolically, was conquered by Uccello, who clearly separated the planes in which his figures move and have their being. Roses, oranges, and hedges were drawn with botanical precision, and no pains were spared to draw branches and even leaves in correct perspective. The splendid realism to which Uccello ultimately attained is best represented by the intensely alive animal and its rider in the picture we reproduce. Uccello's equestrian portrait of the English mercenary John Hawkwood is a milestone in the history of art.

In that golden age of the Medici this business of art flourished. It is well to remember that it was a business, even in the narrow sense—a matter of workshops, of craftsmanship, of masters and apprentices, of intrigues for Church and aristocratic commissions and of legal agreements. One by one the technical problems of convincing representation, which were now the main preoccupation, were overcome. Two artists in particular made noteworthy contributions : Masaccio and Piero della Francesca.

Masaccio (1401–28), though he died when he was but twenty-seven, became the model for the men of his time. He added to Uccello's discoveries in perspective the important one that objects in the distance not only look smaller, but are less distinct because of the veil of air between. In a famous series of painting which he did in the Brancacci Chapel in Florence he almost abolished the use of line, working in masses and getting his forms by a marvellous use of light and shade. So great were his innovations that practically all the artists of his time studied these works and learned from this young genius.

Piero della Francesca (1416-92) was another power in the art of the time. He was hailed as " monarch of the science of painting," and as we look at such a masterpiece as his noble " Nativity " in the National Gallery we realise how right the title is. He seems to have taken all that went before and to have added to it his own sense of the open air which surrounds his sculpturesque figures.

§ 6

Romantic mysticism, which budded with Fra Angelico, passed by Lippi to flower with all sweetness and beauty in the art of his pupil, Alessandro Filipepi, famed as Botticelli. Sandro Botticelli was born in

---

[1] Though commonly known by this title, Uccello's masterpiece at the National Gallery is now held to represent the Rout of San Romano, 1432.

"THE NATIVITY," BY PIERO DELLA FRANCESCA (1416–92)

National Gallery, London

Piero della Francesca was one of the artists who learned from the youthful genius of Masaccio to give his figures the solidity of three dimensional form and that feeling of being surrounded by air which carried Florentine art yet further forward. His lovely "Nativity" is a magnificent example of his almost sculpturesque art.

99

"THE MAGNIFICAT," BY BOTTICELLI (1444–1510)

In the Uffizi Gallery, Florence

Of all the fifteenth-century Italian painters whose names are famous in history, none surpassed Alessandro Botticelli in the creation of works of sheer beauty. The Madonna of "The Magnificat" is generally regarded as the supreme masterpiece among his many paintings of the Madonna, both for its decorative charm and intense spirituality of expression.

Florence about 1447, and was first apprenticed to a goldsmith. To the end of his life he was a jeweller in colours, but owes little beside the name of Botticelli, by which we know him, to his goldsmith master, whom he soon left, to devote himself thenceforth entirely to painting. The thing that differentiates the art of Botticelli from that of all his predecessors is the intensely personal, even egotistical note that he strikes in all his work. The exquisite, delicate melancholy which pervades the expression, both of Christian saints and Pagan gods, in all his pictures, is his own, not theirs, as though he were sorry for them for being saints and gods, and so, by their very nature, deprived of all those ecstasies alike of faith and of doubt, of conviction and speculation, which are the compensating privileges of human imperfection.

It is this personal quality which makes Botticelli so essentially " modern," and beloved of our time. It is interesting to remember that he remained almost in obscurity and was regarded as a minor painter until about sixty years ago.

The Italy of Botticelli was not the Italy of Fra Angelico. Beauty was no longer the handmaid of religion. The Church was no longer the only patron of art, nor were church walls the only outlet for artists. Cosimo de' Medici and Lorenzo the Magnificent did not worry their painters with theological restrictions ; it was beauty that they wanted. It was not till his master Lippi left Florence in 1467 to undertake a commission at Spoleto, that Botticelli began to develop his own individuality. Pictures before that date, as " The Adoration of the Magi " in the National Gallery, reflect the art of Lippi. But as soon as the young painter was left alone in Florence he mixed with other artists like the brothers Pollaiuoli, who had greater knowledge of anatomy than Lippi, and his art made rapid progress. On another page is shown one of the most beautiful of these early works, " Judith with the Head of Holophernes." Muscular action is finely expressed in the swinging stride of the maid who follows bearing the head of the slain tyrant, while the heroine herself is depicted with all the fresh girlish charm of one of the young Florentine maids who frequented the artist's studio. In the distance the great army of invasion is seen retreating in confusion through a spacious landscape.

Botticelli's chief patron in Florence was not Lorenzo the Magnificent, but a distant kinsman of the Duke with the same name. For the villa at Castello, belonging to this younger Lorenzo de' Medici, Botticelli painted a number of pictures, among them, about 1477, the famous " Primavera." No more beautiful allegory of the coming of Spring has ever been painted than this picture, of which we give a reproduction. In the centre Venus, the Goddess of Love, awaits Spring's coming, with Cupid hovering over her. On her right are the Three Graces, with Mercury, the Messenger of

"THE MOURNING FOR CHRIST," BY BOTTICELLI

In this picture we have an extreme example of the tragic element introduced into Botticelli's last works due to his meditation on the gloomy preaching of Savonarola. There is a strained affectation in the poses of the Apostles which suggests that this picture was finished by pupils after Botticelli's death, but the tense feeling expressed in the central group is entirely in the master's last manner, though only the sweet face of the Magdalene, who is tenderly lifting the feet of Christ, remains to remind us of the earlier Botticelli, whose sole aim was the expression of beauty.

"SPRING," BY BOTTICELLI

In this exquisite allegory of the coming of Spring the vernal season is personified by a brightly garbed maiden, who is being gently pushed forward by Flora, the goddess of flowers, and Zephyr, the west wind; preceding her as a herald (on the extreme left) is Mercury, the messenger of the gods. In the centre Venus, goddess of Love, welcomes Spring's coming, while hovering over her head, Cupid aims his arrow at the Three Graces.

"THE CALUMNY OF APELLES" (DETAIL), BY BOTTICELLI

This striking presentment of Calumny, typified by a black-cowled hag, retreating defeated from the pure presence of the naked Truth, is at once a brilliant re-creation of a lost picture by the famous Greek artist Apelles, who flourished in the fifth century B.C., and is also an expression of Botticelli's indignation against those who calumniated the great preacher Savonarola, even after his martyrdom. It represents the culmination of the painter's devotion to Greek art and the beginning of his submission to the teaching of this fanatical friar.

104

"JUDITH WITH THE HEAD OF HOLOPHERNES," BY BOTTICELLI

Judith, the saviour of her country, is seen here after leaving the tent of Holophernes. The sword is still in her hand, and behind her strides the maidservant bearing the head of the tyrant whom Judith has slain. In the landscape background the discomfited army of Holophernes is shown retreating in confusion across a spacious landscape. This comparatively early work shows the graciousness of Botticelli's conception of womanhood and his power of rendering human beings and landscape with convincing truth.

the Gods; on her left gaily-decked Spring advances, gently pushed forward by Flora, the goddess of flowers, and by Zephyr, who personifies the mild west wind. Where'er she treads the flowers spring to life. Beautiful as an interpretation of old Greek legends, which make a human story out of all the phenomena of Nature, this picture is also an expression of the revived pagan delight in physical form which was typical of fifteenth-century Florence.

The fame of this and other pictures by Botticelli spread to Rome, whither in 1481 he was summoned by the Pope to assist in the decoration of the Sistine Chapel, where three great frescoes, the "History of Moses," "Destruction of Korah, Dathan, and Abiram," and "Temptation of Christ," remain to this day as a monument of his skill, his energy, and his sense of drama and beauty. After two years in Rome, Botticelli returned to Florence, where, in 1483, he painted the most exquisite of all his Madonnas, "The Magnificat." But the happy days of the painter were drawing to an end. After the death of Lorenzo in 1492 and the accession of his worthless son Piero, Florence was agitated by political troubles; and to that city, tired of pleasure and weary of knowledge, came Girolamo Savonarola, the great reformer priest.

When the Medici were expelled from Florence, the young Lorenzo went with them, and Botticelli lost his best patron. During these tumultuous years Botticelli devoted much of his time to executing a wonder-series of illustrations to Dante, the originals of which are still preserved in the Vatican Library and the Berlin Museum. These drawings reveal not only an intimate knowledge of the great poet, but also a profound sympathy with the feelings of the poet. Savonarola preached and Botticelli listened, though happily he did not follow the example of some of his contemporaries, and burn his earlier pictures of pagan subjects. His brother Simone, who lived with him in these later years, was a fanatical disciple of Savonarola, but Sandro himself does not appear to have been wholly converted till the great preacher in turn became the victim of the fury of a fickle populace.

In the same year (1498) in which Savonarola was burned at the stake in the Piazza della Signoria, Botticelli painted his great picture, "The Calumny of Apelles." This work, which we reproduce, had a double purpose. Nominally it was an attempt to reproduce a famous lost picture, "Calumny," by the ancient Greek painter Apelles, from the description of it given by the Greek writer Lucian. But we can have little doubt that the inward and spiritual meaning of this picture, which shows black-robed Calumny (or according to another interpretation, Remorse) slinking from the radiant presence of the naked Truth, was directed against the culminators of the martyred friar. Among all Botticelli's pictures this painting is distinguished by its exquisite finish and richness of detail, and we may

"THE MYSTIC NATIVITY," BY BOTTICELLI

National Gallery, London

One of the last pictures painted by the artist, this typical work reveals the mystical effect of the teaching of Savonarola on the mind of the artist. It is essentially other-worldly, and bears a superscription which indicates that it was painted in 1500 when the painter expected the end of the world. The rhythmic grouping of the figures is one of his individual contributions to art.

regard it as the last great expression of his powers both as a classic and a humanist. Distressed both by the disturbed state of his native city and by the tragic end of Savonarola, Botticelli fretted himself into melancholia during his last years. The few religious pictures of this period which remain—many of them probably finished by pupils after the master's death—contain a strange exaggeration of gesture and facial expression, and an almost theatrical vehemence of action, which are entirely foreign to the poetical fantasies of his earlier manner. As an example of the high-strung emotions of his last years, " The Mourning of Christ " may be compared in these pages with the serene tranquillity of Botticelli's early- and middle-period work. The happiest painting of his last period is the little " Nativity " in the National Gallery.

IX

THE GLORY OF GOTHIC

CHURCH ART AND CRAFT IN NORTHERN EUROPE

§ 1

WHILE Italy blossomed into the wonders of her early art, and before the Flemish made their invention of oil painting, the spirit of man emerging from the Dark Ages was finding its own expression else-where. In Northern France, Flanders, and England, particularly during the thirteenth century, arose the wonder of Gothic art. It was primarily an art of building. Architecture, however, is not only an art in itself, but the occasion of art. Down in Italy the building of the great churches had been followed by the decoration of the wall spaces with the frescoes of the early masters. These, painted directly into the wet plaster, became part of the actual walls, and proved the most indestructible of all known paintings.

In Northern Europe things worked differently. The darker skies caused men to build not to exclude the light, but to take advantage of all possible window space. The new method of building—the Gothic—was altogether less heavy than the earlier Romanesque, when the church or abbey had to be almost as much fortress as place of worship. It was a tremendous advance in the technique of building. The weight was taken by transverse arches and slim piers, the thrust of the roof countered by light supporting buttresses. It enabled men to build higher, vaster, more daringly, and to have enormous window spaces. This new type of building was a thrill and an excitement ; and, in a world dominated by the Church resurgent, it had wonderful results.

Along the valley of the Seine and throughout England a wave of cathedral building gave mankind a heritage of beauty as great as anything that had been known on earth. Under King Louis the Ninth (Saint Louis) in the cities of France it became a passion that spread from town to town. Everybody—priest and citizen, lordly bishop and humble workman—played a part in that ecstatic obsession. Entire townships gave themselves over to it, mobilising all their wealth and labour to build better than their neighbours. We hear of whole populations thronging to drag the trolleys of stone to the sites, singing as they worked, and pouring out their treasures to support the communal effort. Chartres, Amiens, Notre-Dame, Reims, Bourges, Bayeux : simultaneously the vast edifices arose. And in England, under the patronage of Henry the Third, surely if not quite so excitedly, Canterbury, Winchester, Lincoln, St. Albans, Wells, and our other lovely cathedrals came into being. It must be remembered that in those early centuries the cultural link between the two countries through both Church and Court was very strong.

Magnificent art though this architecture proved to be, we are here concerned with its by-product in craftsmanship and painting. For the decoration of these churches, linking up with the work in the monasteries, yielded at least three important contributions to art : sculpture, stained glass, and illuminated manuscripts. There were other crafts : precious metal-work for the altar ornaments ; embroidery for altar-cloths and curtains and vestments ; tapestries ; fine woodwork, ivory carving. All were the servants of the Church, and touched the arts of sculpture and painting at a score of points.

There was, for instance, at Narbonne in France an exquisitely painted silk altar-cloth. It was presented by Charles the Fifth, whom they called Charles the Wise for his love of art and literature which made him put into his rare and lovely books the words : " This book belongs to me, Charles." The Narbonne altar-cloth happens to have been preserved for us, and in its dramatic story-telling pictured in the formally created spaces, as well as in the profile portraits of Charles and his Queen, it links the resplendent craftsmanship of the time with painting proper.

The stained-glass windows are, perhaps, nearer to the art of mosaic than that of painting, but they were among the greatest treasures of this age of beauty. The craft of mixing various metallic oxides into the glass goes back to beginnings in about the tenth century and we probably owe it to those men on Murano near Venice where glass-making has been an art for a thousand years. Who first thought of putting shapes of this coloured glass together between binding strips of lead to make a picture, we do not know. We trace it to a church at Mans near Chartres, but others may have preceded that. What we do know is that the Gothic builders, giving more and more space to the windows, created dreams of loveliness through which the sun streamed till the whole interior was full of jewelled light. Louis built Sainte Chapelle in Paris, and the walls almost disappeared into the many-coloured glass ; Chartres Cathedral told whole ranges of Bible story in its windows ; Canterbury and York led the cathedral churches of England. In the thirteenth century this art of stained glass reached its height ; and the windows from that period, such as the famous Seven Sisters at York, remain as monuments of its triumph.

It is well to remember, too, that in the thirteenth and fourteenth

"OCTOBER," BY POL DE LIMBOURG

Musée Condé, Chantilly

One of the illuminated pages from "Les Très Riches Heures," created for the Duc de Berry by Pol Limbourg and his brothers. This is one of the loveliest manuscript books in the world. From such works the art of landscape painter was really born. The various chateaux of the patron formed the backgrounds.

III

centuries not only the stained-glass windows but the walls of English churches, large and small, were covered with pictures of Biblical and saintly story as a means of conveying these to a people entirely illiterate. The pictures were, alas, not incorporated into the wet plaster at the time of building as those in Italy were, but painted in tempera on it, and so were the more easily destroyed. Nevertheless, of recent years, owing largely to the zeal and patience of Professor Tristram and his predecessor, C. E. Keyser, we have rescued hundreds of these paintings from beneath the whitewash which obliterated them at the time of the Reformation, when thousands of altar paintings on wooden panels perished in the mistaken zeal of the iconoclasts.

At Winchester we have some particularly lovely stories of the Passion dating from the early thirteenth century, whilst at Chichester an exquisite Madonna and Child, rose-pink, yellow, red and green and silver against a background of lapis lazuli, is even earlier, for it was painted when Italy still awaited the coming of Giotto. Both Winchester and St. Albans were leading art centres of Western Europe in the middle of that century, for Henry the Third of England rivalled King Louis in æsthetic and religious enthusiasm. When Henry saw Sainte Chapelle he wished he might bring it away in a cart.

§ 2

It was the work of the illuminators, however, which was destined to yield the most important contribution to art. Every great church had its Scriptorium, where the patient monks worked at service books for the choirs, at scriptures, at lives of saints, and ultimately at those lovely Books of Hours for their patrons. On the vellum of these books the blues and crimsons and greens of the window-glass glowed anew against backgrounds of pure gold. Lovely studies of plants twined in and out of the initials and down the margins ; strange beasts curved among the lettering ; here and there a portrait filled a space ; elsewhere an incident was depicted by way of illustration and decoration.

England had already a long tradition of illumination. The " Lindisfarne Gospels " date from the eighth century, and the marvellous " Benedictional of St. Æthelwold " from the tenth. If the Norman conquest interfered at all with this art it was not for long, for the ultimate cultural result of the invasion was to bind the two countries already strongly linked in the internationalism of the Catholic Church. So under Henry the Third we get the important school at St. Albans under Matthew Paris (1200–59), whose fame alike as artist and historian reverberated across Europe. An interesting fact about much of this early English illumination is that it was in pen and water-colour—a delicate precursor of the triumph of English

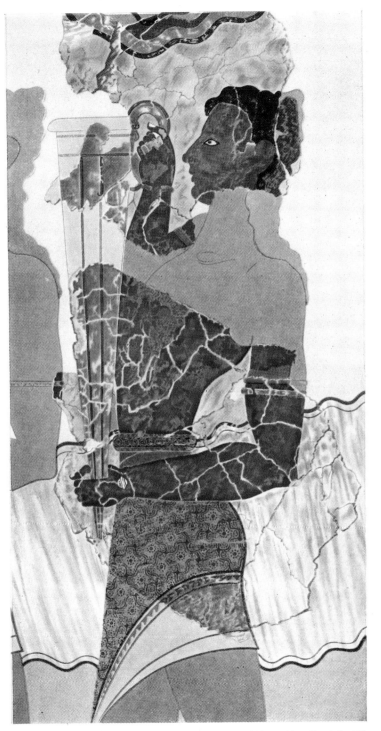

THE CUP-BEARER

Fresco from the mural paintings at the Palace of Minos, Knossos.

The discovery of the lost civilization of Crete by Sir Arthur Evans, so thrillingly described in his book, *The Palace of Minos*, is one of the romances of archaeology. Beside architecture and magnificent ceramics, the walls of the vast palace were decorated with processions, records of the bull sports, and other aspects of the highly civilized life of the Cretans of Homeric days.

STAINED GLASS
Chartres Cathedral

In the thirteenth century when pictorial art was being reborn in Europe, the sculpture, stained glass and embroideries of the ecclesiastical crafts shared its task of telling the illiterate people the sacred story. The supremely lovely glass of Chartres, belonging to this early period, has never been surpassed. This hunting scene has not only marvellous beauty of colour (especially the blues of the background) but is a triumph of design and the filling of the space. Such colouring and designing played a great part in the renaissance of art in Europe.

THE CHICHESTER ROUNDEL

Bishop's Palace, Chichester

A mural painting of the thirteenth century which reveals the charm and grace of the English Gothic painters in those days. Henry III of England rivalled Louis IX of France in his encouragement of the arts in the churches, and the great days of Gothic rewarded his royal patronage.

water-colour nearly a thousand years later. Also it tended to a surprising freedom of form, the subjects straying over the margin rather than staying within rigid rectangular bounds as most of the continental work did.

In the beautiful " Queen Mary's Psalter " and in the " Gorleston Psalter " we find sacred art intermingled delightfully with secular, and often humorous subjects—a sermon of a cat to some ducks and a rabbit's funeral in the East Anglian book, for example. Elsewhere the scriptoria began to produce " Bestiaries " with strange animal forms illustrating the dubious natural history of the texts. Everywhere there were signs that laymen were among the illuminators, and this art of manuscript gradually emerges from the monasteries and the church and overflows under the patronage of the courts and the aristocracy.

Then, in the middle of the century, the peak honours passed over to the French side of the Channel. There had long been a fine school of illuminators at Paris. But it is well, before we consider this definitely French contribution, to note the exquisite " Wilton Diptych " which is one of the treasures of early painting in the National Gallery. Whether it was French work or English does not greatly concern us : the two schools were inextricably interwoven. Sufficient that it is a piece of unrivalled grace and lovely detail. It brings the fourteenth century to a close on a note of beauty unequalled anywhere.

In France this art of the manuscript rose to its height under the patronage of the Dukes of Burgundy and of Berry. The intrigues, the struggles for mastery between these men, was one side—an ugly side—of affairs. The other was their marvellous appreciation of the artists they gathered about them : Jean Malouel and Henri Bellechose at the Burgundian court ; André Beauneveu, the Limbourgs, and later, Jean Fouquet at that of the Dukes of Berry.

Two supreme masterpieces of the illuminator's art came out of that patronage. One was the precious " Très Riches Heures " at Chantilly, painted between 1412 and 1416 by Pol de Limbourg and his two brothers ; the other is the " Hours of Etienne Chevalier " by Jean Fouquet. The story of the first is that the Duke of Berry was shown the " Book of Hours of Turin " by its owner, the Duke of Bavaria. It was the work of the Van Eycks, and forthwith he asked Pol de Limbourg to emulate the work. The fashion and style of these Books of Hours had been started nearly a hundred years before when French artists had made the " Breviary de Belleville." It opened with a pictured calendar of the months, and the illustrations of these and their respective activities sent the artists to Nature and gave us a wonderful series of pictures of contemporary life and conditions. Landscape art owes an enormous debt to those beautiful books.

114

National Gallery.

THE WILTON DIPTYCH

National Gallery, London

This altar-piece, made towards the end of the fourteenth century for King Richard II, shows Richard being presented to the Virgin by St. John Baptist and Saints Edmond and Edward, the patron saints of England. The Virgin is surrounded by angels wearing the king's badge, a white hart, on their shoulders. It is one of the most delicate of all paintings of the period.

Ruskin said of Pol de Limbourg that he was the first artist to set the sun in the sky, and anyway his scenes of springtime and harvest, of summer sunshine and winter snow, of birds and beasts, of men at their work and their play, carried art brilliantly forward. The " Très Riches Heures " is not only a milestone in this French-Flemish borderland painting, but in the whole story of art.

With the fifteenth century comes another masterpiece of this miniature art, the " Livre d'Etienne Chevalier," created for the great secretary of state at the Burgundian court by Jean Fouquet (1415–85). Fouquet is the first truly great name in French painting, and in this book (slightly more archaic in feeling than the work of Pol de Limbourg, although it belongs to a later date) we have sacred history in " modern dress "—the dress of early-fifteenth-century Burgundy. Fouquet has also left us some fine portraits which were not miniatures : the " Man with a Glass of Wine " in the Louvre is almost certainly his ; the portraits of Etienne Chevalier and of Charles the Seventh and his lovely favourite, Agnes Sorel, certainly are.

Thus gradually this art of the miniature and of the illuminated book moved out of the church into the courts as patronage came from the powerful Dukes and their ministers. In the churches, meantime, painting was not confined to the manuscripts but found golden opportunities in the altar-pieces painted on wooden panels. How many of these we have lost we cannot tell, for wood burns, breaks, or can be broken, and in the ages of war and destruction which have intervened almost everything has been lost to us. But a few of these altar-pieces which adorned the great churches and eased the overcharged consciences of their lordly donors have revealed to us the high quality of that lost beauty. Great names of artists mingle with provoking anonymity. The Master of Moulins whose " Virgin in Glory " glowed like a rainbow in the cathedral of that city, and whose " Nativity " at Autun is a dream of grace ; the unknown painter of that " Pieta " from Villeneuve near Avignon in Provence ; Charonton from the same district ; Nicholas Froment, who, under the patronage of King René painted a charming triptych of " The Burning Bush " with the Virgin and Child among the flaming leaves—these and many others circling round the churches and courts of France and England stand at the beginnings of art in Western Europe. It was fundamentally church art, symbolic, mystical, and yet ever reaching out towards the ordinary life of the senses and of Nature, preparing the way for much which was to follow, and withal yielding in its own way treasures which must inevitably be taken note of in this story of the art of Europe. Across its beauty swept the Hundred Years' War and the Black Death, that terrible plague which killed off one-fourth of the population of Europe and came near to throwing civilisation

" THE MAN WITH A GLASS OF WINE," BY JEAN FOUQUET (1415–85)

Louvre, Paris

Portraiture begins when the patrons of the artists have their pictures set in the corner of altar-pieces as the kneeling donors, or in their service books. Fouquet, who made the exquisite " Livre d'Etienne Chevalier " as an illuminated book, also left us this fine portrait of an unknown man.

back into new dark ages. When the world struggled back, the light of the Renaissance was beating too strongly from the South, the Reformation was flooding Central and Western Europe, the discovery of printing was leading art along new channels, and this glory of Gothic was already a part of history.

X

THE INVENTION OF OIL-PAINTING

THE ART OF THE VAN EYCKS, MEMLINC, AND THE EARLY FLEMISH MASTERS

§ I

IN the whole history of painting there are no more remarkable figures than the two brothers Hubert and Jan van Eyck. Never before or since has Art made so mighty a stride in the space of one generation. We get some idea of what they achieved if we compare any King or Queen in a pack of playing cards with a modern photograph of a living monarch.

Just as Molière's " Bourgeois Gentilhomme " was astounded to find he had been talking prose all his life without knowing it, so some readers may be surprised to learn that they are perfectly familiar with mediæval Gothic art, for examples of it may be found in every pack of playing cards, in which the court cards are survivals of mediæval Gothic portraiture.

To obtain the best possible insight into the birth of Gothic art one ought to visit the Cathedral of Brunswick. Here we may see what are probably the best-preserved examples of mediæval wall-paintings. In the choir is a series of pictures, painted about the beginning of the thirteenth century, and one of the best of these represents " Herod's Birthday Feast." It is perfectly childish, of course, but it is childish in a totally different way from that in which the pictures of Giotto and Angelico are childish. Neither the Italian nor the Brunswick pictures show any sense of perspective or give any real effect of space and distance ; but the treatment of the figures greatly differs. In the Italian paintings there is still a faint trace of Greek draughtsmanship distorted by Byzantine dogma, but the Brunswick paintings show quite a new conception of the human body which has nothing to do with Greece or Rome ; it is *pure Gothic*. In these Brunswick paintings the people pictured look like nothing so much as a row of court cards. Herod himself looks as much like a real human being as the King of Hearts looks like H.M. King George VI.

Now we are in a position to appreciate the art of the brothers Van Eyck. To realise the advance they made we must not compare their figures with the portraits of to-day or modern photographs, but with the Queen of Spades and the Jack of Diamonds. And we must remember that little over a hundred years separates the style of court-card portraiture from the realistic forms of Hubert's mighty figures surmounting " The Adoration of the Lamb " and Jan van Eyck's " The Man with the Pinks." Think of the court cards when you look at the illustrations of these paintings.

It is a great misfortune that we know so little about the lives of these amazing men. Many interesting details about the early Italian artists have been preserved to us because Giorgio Vasari, himself an early sixteenth-century Florentine painter, wrote the lives of the preceding and contemporary Italian artists with a fullness and vivacity which make his accounts still fascinating and readable. But there was no biographer of the early Flemish artists, and the few meagre facts we know about them have slowly been unearthed by patient scholarship toiling amid the archives of the cities in which these artists lived.

Therefore it is by the pictures which remain, rather than by any written record, that we must endeavour to reconstruct the flowering of art in Flanders and Northern Europe. But if we do study those works, then it is positively electrifying to behold the mysterious and rapid quickening of the artistic spirit in Flanders.

Of what came between the paintings of Brunswick Cathedral and the art of the Van Eycks, little is known and nothing certain. The very names of the painters of some undoubtedly early pictures are unknown, and all we can say with certainty is that from about the end of the fourteenth century to the middle of the fifteenth century a group of painters flourished on the lower Rhine and became known as the School of Cologne. Several of its members are merely legendary, but the " Bimburg Chronicle " of 1380 contains an authoritative entry : " In this time there was a painter in Cologne of the name of Wilhelm ; he was considered the best master in all German Land ; he paints every man, of whatever form, as if he were alive." This master has been identified as William of Herle (or Cologne), who died about 1378, and though he evidently impressed his contemporaries by his pioneer realism, the work of his school is esteemed in our own time for its spiritual calm and peaceful purity. " St. Veronica " in the National Gallery is probably painted by William of Cologne or by one of his pupils.

Now Hubert van Eyck was born about 1365 near Maestricht, which is no great distance from Cologne. Most probably he studied in the Rhineland capital before he migrated to Flanders and, with his brother Jan, settled in Ghent. The increasing commercial prosperity of Bruges and Ghent attracted artists from the banks of the Rhine, and the School of Cologne declined as the Early Flemish School arose.

Since the time of Vasari, the brothers Hubert and Jan van Eyck have generally received credit for having discovered oil as a medium for painting. Before their time artists had mixed their colours either with water (frescoes) or with yolk of egg (tempera paintings), and though modern scholarship is inclined to doubt whether the Van Eycks were actually the first to make use of oil, they were beyond question the pioneers of the new medium.

Tradition says that Jan, having one day " devoted the utmost pains " in finishing a picture with great care, varnished it and as usual put it in the sun to dry. But the heat was excessive and split the wooden panel which he had painted. Grieving at the destruction of his handiwork, Jan " determined to find a means whereby he should be spared such an annoyance in the future." After various experiments he discovered that linseed oil and oil of nuts dried more quickly than any which he had tried, and that colours mixed with these oils were more brilliant, proof against water, and blended far better than the tempera. Thus was oil-painting invented.

" The Adoration of the Lamb " at Ghent, executed by the two brothers, is not only the earliest monument of the art of oil-painting but it is the most splendid masterpiece produced by any Northern artist before the seventeenth century. Not till Rubens was born, some 200 years later, did Flanders produce the equal of the Van Eycks, and from this fact alone we may deduce the extraordinary mastery of their art.

" The Adoration of the Lamb," an elaborate polyptych, is not one picture but a whole collection of pictures. Originally it consisted of the long central panel showing " The Adoration of the Lamb " and above this three panels of " The Virgin," " God the Father," and " St. John " (all shown in our illustration) ; on the left of the " Lamb " panel—which measures $7\frac{1}{4}$ feet long by $4\frac{1}{2}$ feet high—were two panels of " The Just Judges " and " Christ's Warriors," and these were balanced by panels showing " The Holy Hermits " and " The Holy Pilgrims " on the right. On the upper tier the three central figures were flanked by two double-panelled shutters, the painted subjects on one side being " Angels Singing," " Angels Making Music," and, at the extreme ends, " Adam " and " Eve " ; on the reverse of the shutters are " St. John the Baptist," " St. John the Evangelist," " Jodoc Vydt "—the donor of the altar-piece—and " Wife of Jodoc Vydt."

The complete altar-piece therefore consisted of twelve panels, four painted on both sides, making sixteen pictures in all. The whole painted surface of this composite picture, or polyptych, amounts to over a thousand feet.

The whole altar-piece was undoubtedly planned and begun by Hubert, who certainly painted the three tremendous central figures and the panel of " Angels Making Music." After Hubert's death in 1426 Jan van Eyck completed the altar-piece, and probably did not adhere altogether strictly to his brother's original designs. The difference between the work of the two brothers is one not so much of skill as of temperament. Hubert

"THE ADORATION OF THE LAMB," BY HUBERT AND JAN VAN EYCK

This gigantic altar-piece—the painted surface of which extends to over 1,000 square feet—has in many respects never been surpassed. Originally it consisted of the centre panel, from which the whole takes its name, surmounted by three panels : the Virgin Mary, God the Father, and St. John. These three figures are certainly the work of Hubert. This portion, now at Ghent, is shown above ; but originally the polyptych was completed on either side by two tiers of two panels each.

possessed a solemn spirituality and serious thoughtfulness which was not shared by his more worldly younger brother.

Jan van Eyck, born about 1385, is a more popular and no less eminent figure than his elder brother. He lived on in Ghent and Bruges till 1441 and his works are comparatively numerous, whereas few paintings by Hubert are extant. Shortly before completing the Ghent altar-piece, Jan entered the service of Philip of Burgundy, for whom he undertook several diplomatic missions. In this way he saw Portugal and other foreign countries, and his later paintings betray his affectionate remembrance of the country he had seen in southern climes. Jan was essentially a realist, with his keen gaze ever fixed on the beautiful earth and on human beings rather than on religious doctrines. His real bent is shown in many of his panels for " The Adoration of the Lamb." In the panel of " The Annunciation " his delight in the still-life, in the wash-basin and other furniture of the room, in the street view seen through the window, reveals him to be the true father of genre painting. His portraits of Jodoc Vydt and his wife, shown without flattery as a dull but prosperous Flemish burgher and his wife, prove him to be the father of modern portraiture. Both these qualities, his capacity for realistic portraiture and his infinite exactitude in rendering the detail of an interior, are magnificently displayed in our illustration, " Jan Arnolfini and his Wife," one of the most precious things in the National Gallery.

While Hubert belongs to the austere company of monumental or architectural painters, Jan is a pioneer of domestic painting and one of the first producers of what we now know as a " picture." In this development Jan van Eyck was, doubtless unconsciously, meeting the demand of his time and place.

In Northern churches and cathedrals, which need more light than the Southern, the place occupied by wall-paintings was gradually given over to stained-glass windows, which are marked features in the Gothic architecture of Northern Europe. Wall-paintings, which still led the way in Italy, became secondary in Flanders to the decorative panels introduced into wooden screen-work. This much accomplished, it was a short step to meet the demands of a prosperous commercial community by (metaphorically) detaching a panel from its ecclesiastical frame and adapting its subject and style to a private dwelling-house.

Thus, while Italy remains the home of the religious picture, Flanders and the Netherlands become more and more the home of secular art. Though he painted other religious subjects beside " The Adoration of the Lamb " and the miniature " Altar-piece " which the Emperor Charles V. took with him on his travels, the most famous of the other paintings by Jan van Eyck are portraits. In his portraiture he is uncompromising in his

"JAN ARNOLFINI AND HIS WIFE," BY JAN VAN EYCK (c. 1385–1441)

National Gallery, London

This well-known picture, a favourite with all visitors to the National Gallery, is a splendid example both of Jan van Eyck's truthful and unflattering portraiture and also of his delight in rendering with scrupulous fidelity all the details of an interior. The reflection in the round mirror is itself a miniature within a picture.

"CHRIST'S WARRIORS," BY HUBERT
AND JAN VAN EYCK

Ghent Cathedral

"THE JUST JUDGES," BY HUBERT
AND JAN VAN EYCK

Ghent Cathedral

"THE MAN WITH THE PINKS," BY JAN VAN EYCK

Berlin Museum

Painted about 500 years ago by one of the first artists to use oil-paint, this picture astounds us to-day by its lifelike realism, by its unswerving fidelity to every little detail that can help to give the character of a man and set his living presence before us. Note how the brocade collar of the tunic, showing above the fur collar of the coat, seems to be ornamented with the alternating letters Y and C. It is hoped these may one day afford a clue to the identity of the sitter, who is at present unknown. The bell which, with a cross, hangs by a twisted chain from his neck, suggests that St. Anthony was the patron saint of the person represented.

126

endeavour to state the whole truth ; such details as warts and wrinkles, furrows and stubbly beards, he renders with passionate delight and exactitude. A splendid example of Jan's rugged realism may be seen in our illustration from the portrait, in the Berlin Museum, known as " The Man with the Pinks." Precisely drawn, true to every wart and wrinkle, the face is so full of life and character that we almost listen for speech to come from the slightly parted lips. Who this man was has never been discovered, but from his costume and the handsome ring on his finger we may deduce that he was a person of position.

§ 2

If little is known about the Van Eycks, still less is known concerning their successors. Patient research among municipal records in Flanders, however, has greatly increased our knowledge during recent years. Twenty years ago the very name of the painter of a fine altar-piece in the Abbey of Flemalle, near Liége, was uncertain ; he was alluded to vaguely as " The Master of Flemalle." To-day it has been established that he was a painter of Tournai, called Robert Campin, who was born about 1375 and lived till 1444. There are two good examples of his art in the National Gallery, and he is important, not only for his own work, but as being the master of Roger van der Weyden.

Among religious painters Roger van der Weyden (*c.* 1400–64), who was born at Tournai and settled in Brussels, had a considerable influence. Beside the calm solemnity of Hubert van Eyck, his pictures appear exaggerated in their dramatic intensity and fervour. He was essentially a tragic artist, dwelling on the sufferings of the Saviour and peopling his pictures with wailing figures, whose emaciated faces stream with tears, whose hands are convulsively clutched in agony or outstretched to heaven. In 1450 he visited Rome and is thought to have had some influence on painting in Ferrara and Padua, and there he in turn may have imbibed something of a new spirit, for towards the end of his life his sentiment became more gentle and refined. Van der Weyden is seen at his best in " The Bewailing of the Body of Christ " in the Berlin Gallery, and in this picture his affinity with the school of Van Eyck is shown in the delicate and gently detailed landscape background.

Roger's fellow-pupil Jacques Daret, who died in 1466, is softer and more conciliatory in his religious themes, and his paintings are peculiarly sweet both in colour and temper.

The tragic painting of Van der Weyden was continued by Hugo van der Goes (*c.* 1435–82) of Ghent and Bruges, who is reputed to have begun life as a wild pleasure-lover. Suddenly he withdrew to a monastery near

127

Brussels, and conscious-stricken at his own dissipation he henceforward devoted his talent to sacred subjects, usually accentuating the sorrows of Christ, but always avoiding the wailing and excessive gesticulation which marked the pictures of Van der Weyden. His art is deeper and more quiet, but is certainly not less expressive. The altar-piece with " The Adoration of Jesus " which, under the orders of Portinari, agent for the Medici in Bruges, he painted for Santa Maria Nuova in Florence, is generally accepted as the supreme masterpiece of Hugo van der Goes. We see the continuation of the Van Eyck tradition in the glimpse of landscape, in which light-green branches are boldly contrasted with the deep-blue sky, in the naturalism of the fire-red lily in the foreground, and in the realism of the rough, weather-beaten shepherds who on one side balance the sturdy figure of St. Joseph, who stands praying, on the other. When this picture arrived in Florence, it created a great sensation, and it has been thought that many famous Italian artists, among them Piero di Cosimo, Ghirlandaio, Piero Pollaiuolo, were influenced to the extent of changing their style after they had seen this masterpiece by Hugo van der Goes.

§ 3

The first great figure in Flemish painting who appears to owe little to either of the Van Eycks is Hans Memlinc (c. 1430–94), who probably studied at Cologne before he settled in Bruges about 1467. His paintings in the Hospital of St. John at Bruges are world-famous, and round them has been woven a pretty legend.

Young Memlinc, the story goes, while fighting as a soldier of Charles the Bold, was desperately wounded and dragged himself to the Hospital of St. John at Bruges, where he was kindly received and his wounds tended. When cured, out of gratitude and for no fee, he painted the pictures still to be seen in the Hospital.

Unfortunately, historical research has demolished the legend and reveals Memlinc as no soldier of fortune but as a prosperous citizen and house-owner in Bruges. Yet the legend well accords with the character of Memlinc's paintings, which have been likened to " the visions of a sick man in convalescence."

Just as the name of Michael Angelo is indissolubly linked to the Sistine Chapel in Rome, so is that of Memlinc to the Hospital of St. John at Bruges. But while we are awed by the heroic figures and magnitude of the Italian's paintings at Rome, in Bruges we are fascinated and bewitched by the. bijou qualities of the Fleming's art. Memlinc's large triptych in the Hospital, " The Virgin and Child Enthroned," with panels on either side of " St. John the Baptist " and of " St. John the Evangelist at Patmos,"

"THE VIRGIN OF THE ROCKS," BY LEONARDO DA VINCI

National Gallery, London

It was Leonardo's destiny that so few of his great projects were ever finished, but in "The Virgin of the Rocks" we have his work at its most sublime. There is a quality of eternity rather than of time in this conception of Mary bringing the infant St. John to be blessed by the Christ Child. Leonardo, as usual, foregoes the sensuous appeal of colour for the intellectual force of pure design and noble draughtsmanship.

"BACCHUS AND ARIADNE," BY TITIAN

National Gallery, London

Brilliant colour, dramatic action, an involved rhythm of line which winds through the whole design, Titian's technical qualities are already mature in this picture painted as early as 1514. It is a *tour de force* of figure painting as well as a splendid landscape. The constellation in the sky is the golden crown which Bacchus presented to his bride.

"THE MARTYRDOM OF ST. URSULA," BY MEMLINC (*c.* 1430–84)

Hospital of St. John, Bruges

This illustration, about half the size of the original painting, illustrates the final episode in the story of St. Ursula. Accompanied by a maiden and one of the Pope's Suite, the Saint stands undismayed before the General of the Huns and, refusing to deny her faith, calmly awaits death by the arrow which an archer is ready to let fly. It is characteristic of Memlinc's gentleness and delicacy of feeling that he has preferred suggesting the Saint's martyrdom to painting the Saint's death with the grim realism which we find in the works of other Flemish masters.

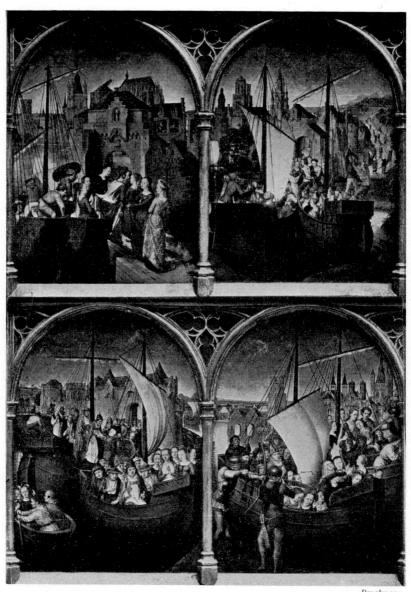

(1) ST. URSULA ARRIVING AT COLOGNE   (2) THE PILGRIMS ARRIVING AT BASLE
(3) THE POPE AND PILGRIMS EMBARK AT BASLE   (4) THE MARTYRDOM OF THE PILGRIMS

"THE MARTYRDOM OF ST. URSULA," BY MEMLINC

Hospital of St. John, Bruges

Memlinc's " Shrine of St. Ursula," is one of the art wonders of the world. It is an oblong gabled casket, the sides of which are adorned with six miniatures illustrating the legend of St. Ursula.

is not the work that takes our breath away : rather is it the " Shrine of St. Ursula," a wonderfully painted casket—made to hold relics of the saint. Though only 3 feet long and less than 3 feet high, this casket is covered with eight panel paintings, and six medallions on the roof slopes. Five of the scenes illustrating the story of St. Ursula are reproduced, and the beauty of their workmanship is manifest.

Looking at these poetical pictures of a romantic story, it seems un-gracious to recall that the legend of St. Ursula, according to modern science, rests on no surer foundation than the discovery in mediæval times of an old Roman burial-ground. From these unknown remains, it is now said, the tale of Ursula and her 11,000 virgins was constructed. Many versions of the legend are in existence ; but none nearer than five or six centuries to the date when the events were supposed to have happened. This is the version followed by Memlinc.

Ursula, daughter of a King of Brittany or Cornwall, either to delay marriage with a pagan prince, or alternately to escape the persecution of the Emperor Maximian, was enjoined to go on a pilgrimage and make 11,000 virgins her companions. The company sailed up the Rhine via Cologne to Basle, and thence went by foot to Rome, where they were received by the Pope with every honour and attention. Returning, they sailed up the Rhine from Basle, with papal benedictions, but on arriving at Cologne they were slaughtered by the Huns. After the martyrdom, their relics were piously collected and buried.

That is the story, and it will be noted that Memlinc, to show how absolutely the Pope was in sympathy with St. Ursula, actually makes him embark with her at the start of the return journey. Incidentally these miniature paintings show that Memlinc knew Cologne well, for in all the scenes which take place in the city he has effectively introduced the cathedral and other of its principal buildings.

The spirituality of Memlinc's portraiture, his power to paint the soul as well as the surface, is beautifully exemplified in " The Duke of Cleves," reproduced from the picture at the National Gallery. His romanticism, a new note which Memlinc definitely contributed to painting, is bewitchingly exhaled from his " Betrothal of St. Catherine " and the " Legend of St. Ursula," both of which are touching in their simplicity, their girlish fresh-ness, and miniature daintiness.

Already the city, so wealthy in the days of the Van Eycks, had become in the time of Memlinc *Bruges-la-Morte*. Something of its sad poetic solitude pervades his pictures. The great house of the Medici had collapsed, the rich merchants had gone elsewhere, and the next great Flemish painter, Quinten Massys (1466–1530), was domiciled in Antwerp.

"THE DUKE OF CLEVES," BY MEMLINC

National Gallery, London

The grace and spirituality of this picture admirably illustrate the portraiture of
Memlinc who, it has been said, "saw not only with his eyes but with his soul."

§ 4

Tradition relates that Quinten Massys, the " smith of Antwerp," became a painter only because his sweetheart would not marry a smith. The swinging brushwork and broad handling which he substituted for the small detailed touches of the earlier painters well accord with the vigour demanded by the work of a smithy. His handling of colour is also new, for instead of placing unbroken blues, reds, yellows, etc., in immediate juxtaposition, he marshals his hues into a uniform colour-scheme. Disliking smallness in all things, he painted figures almost life-size ; and when the size of his picture forbade the full-length, he contented himself with half figures rather than reduce his scale to miniature proportions. " The Banker and his Wife " at the Louvre is a fine example of this innovation.

With the death of Quinten Massys in 1530 the first period of Flemish painting comes to an end. The next generation of Flemings either practised their art in Italy or, like Jan Gossart, called Mabuse (*c.* 1472–1535), imported Italian fashions in painting.

Mabuse, who took his name from the town of Maubeuge, where he was born about 1472, was a Fleming before he naturalised his art. This we may see by studying the magnificent example of his first manner at the National Gallery. " The Adoration of the Magi " was painted by Mabuse before he visited Italy. In the architectural background we get a hint of the influence of Roger van der Weyden ; the thirty figures in their rather pompous costumes are stolid and almost stony in comparison with the grace of his later works.

Some ten years later Mabuse visited Italy in the train of the Duke of Burgundy, and in Florence came under the influence of Leonardo da Vinci. That his first contact with the new naturalism did not have altogether happy results we know by the commonplace realism of his " Adam and Eve " at Hampton Court. Soon, however, the warm air of Italy won him to gentleness, and in his Italianised works it is as a portrait-painter that Mabuse excels. Of his many portraits in Great Britain, the most beautiful is the portrait of " Margaret Tudor," the elder sister of Henry VIII, which now hangs in the Scottish National Gallery at Edinburgh.

After the death of Mabuse in 1533, until the time of Rubens more than one hundred and fifty years later, the art of Flanders was carried on by lesser men, with the exception of Peter Brueghel. Hieronymus Bosch, that painter of nightmare subjects, tortured martyrdoms, and grotesque types, was already dead. Lucas de Heere (1534–84), a capable portrait painter, though born in Ghent had worked chiefly in France and England. A more successful portrait painter, Antonio Moro (1519–78), better known as Sir Anthony More, also began his career in Ghent but found more

"THE BANKER AND HIS WIFE," BY QUINTEN MASSYS (1466–1530)

The Louvre, Paris

This delightfully intimate portrait of a fifteenth-century banker and his wife is deservedly the most popular of Massys' paintings. It is full of charming human touches, and there is no hint of the miser in the expression of the man who is counting and weighing his money. He is just getting on with a necessary piece of business, and both he and his wife, who has turned from her illuminated book—to see if he will be much longer—seem to tell us they will be glad when the day's work is over and nothing is to be done except enjoy their own domestic happiness.

Note how the reflection in the little mirror on the table shows us that these people are facing a window, through which comes the light which illumines them and all the details of the office.

"MARGARET TUDOR," BY MABUSE (*c.* 1472–1535)

Scottish National Gallery, Edinburgh

" A rogue in porcelain "—George Meredith's famous phrase—might fittingly be applied to the subject of this portrait, an English Royal Beauty, the elder daughter of Henry VII. Though she looks so demure the painter has allowed the eyes to betray the real character of this self-willed princess.

If we compare the polished softness of this portrait with Mabuse's earlier work, " The Adoration of the Kings," we learn the extent to which this Flemish painter altered his style after he had visited Italy and had become acquainted with the work of Leonardo da Vinci and his contemporaries.

135

" THE ADORATION OF THE KINGS," BY MABUSE

National Gallery, London

In this remarkable picture we see one of the last masterpieces of pure Flemish art before it became influenced and changed by Italian painting. The words " Roi Jaspar," inscribed on the lid of the chalice offered to the Virgin, reveal the identity of the kneeling king. Behind him stands Melchior with his gift, a monstrance in his right hand, while on our left is the swarthy figure of Balthasar holding before him a gold reliquary. In the original at the National Gallery the signature of the artist " IENNINE GOS . . ." may be deciphered on the torque of the turbaned attendant and also on Balthasar's turban.

"THE ADORATION OF THE KINGS," BY BRUEGHEL (*c.* 1525-6))

National Gallery, London

Brueghel conceives his subject in terms of Flemish realism. The costumes and environment are those of his own time and place, the faces are peasant types of his own district. There is none of the idealism of Italian art, nor the mysticism of earlier periods.

appreciation of his art in Spain and England. His portraiture shows remarkable power of conveying character and personality.

The most important of the immediate predecessors of Rubens were two families of artists, the Pourbus and the Brueghels.

Peter Pourbus (1510–84), a Bruges painter of portraits and religious subjects, had a son, Frans Pourbus (1545–81), who settled in Antwerp. He in turn had a still more famous son, Frans Pourbus the Younger (1570–1622), who painted portraits not only in Antwerp but also at the court of Henri IV at Paris. Young Pourbus, seven years older than Rubens, was one of his few contemporaries in Antwerp who not only never worked for Rubens but may have had some influence on his early style.

The founder of the Brueghel family was Peter Brueghel (c. 1525–69), and it is his work rather than that of either of his sons—" Hell " Brueghel (1564–1628), or " Velvet " Brueghel (the nicknames reveal their typical subjects)—which can claim greatness. A characteristic example of " Hell " Brueghel's work, " An Incantation Scene," may be seen in the Dyce Collection at South Kensington. Jan, the other son, became an assistant to Rubens. The father's work gives us a new note in its time. Studies of peasant life seen with the liveliest imagination and humanity, and set in landscapes of amazing breadth and beauty which reveal the artist's love of Nature. The famous " Four Seasons " at Vienna ; the " Fall of Icarus " where a ploughman gets on with his daily task not heeding the catastrophe to the flyer at the sun ; the " Numbering at Bethlehem," but really charmingly at a typical Flemish village : such works brought landscape into a prominence which presaged the future of art.

It is well to recall that an even earlier Flemish artist, Joachim Patinir (1485–1524), had anticipated this note by painting pictures which made the landscape more important than the small-scale figures which moved in it. He has been called " The Father of Landscape Painting," and although his paternity might be disputed he gave it a new importance, and obviously loved it for its own sake, preparing the way for Peter Brueghel and for the whole grand procession of landscape artists who were destined to follow.

The " Four Seasons " are truly magnificent landscapes, full of light and air, reaching back in spirit to the art of the manuscript books from which landscape, in Northern Europe especially, so certainly derived, and forward to the pure art of painting Nature for its own sake. In them we look down through the trees from the hills to the plains below, see whole villages with all their people at their normal tasks, watch many aspects of the contemporary scene. Indeed it is always with Brueghel this love of the life of his day which charms us. Whether he is painting a classical subject such as " Icarus," a sacred one such as the " Adoration of the Kings," or a landscape, what we really have is the common life of his generation. There is invariably

"THE BIRD-TRAP," BY PETER BRUEGHEL

A typical work by the great Flemish master. The incidents of ordinary daily life are shown, set in wide landscape, whereof every detail is shown with loving fidelity. "The Bird-Trap" landscape, originally painted by Peter Brueghel the elder was brilliantly copied several times by his son.

humour of a satirical kind. He never shirks the brutality of life, or that of the faces of his contemporaries. When he depicts the Holy Family it is surrounded by a group of compelling individualities : they are almost every one ugly, yet we know that they are real people.

His son Jan, " Velvet " Brueghel, became one of the exuberant still-life painters of the period, and when he became an assistant to Rubens he embellished that great man's canvases with literally thousands of studies of fruit and flowers. It is quantitative painting, and flies in the face of our modern asceticism in taste. Its charm is the love which these artists had for the appearance of things in themselves (for Brueghel was part of a whole movement of Netherlandish painting which worked in the same way). Not only fruit and flowers, but butterflies, snails, bees, flies, caterpillars, adorned their canvases. Even a portrait would be surrounded by garlands of minutely depicted flowers and fruits. There was little selectivity, only profusion, and a love of painting things for their own sake.

Meantime a certain Antonello, a native of Messina in Sicily, had seen these works by the Northern masters, and journeyed to Flanders to learn their technique of painting with an oil medium. Full of his secret he went to Venice, where the strong sea air was fatal to the old fresco method. And so the glory of Venetian art was the offspring of this power from the North.

XI

THE WONDER OF THE RENAISSANCE

THE ART OF LEONARDO DA VINCI, MICHAEL ANGELO, AND RAPHAEL

§ 1

"OCCASIONALLY," says the Italian historian Vasari, "Heaven bestows upon a single individual beauty, grace, and ability, so that, whatever he does, every action is so divine that he distances all other men, and clearly displays how his genius is the gift of God and not an acquirement of human art. Men saw this in Leonardo da Vinci, whose personal beauty and grace cannot be exaggerated, whose abilities were so extraordinary that he could readily solve every difficulty that presented itself."

His charming conversation won all hearts, we are told ; with his right hand he could twist a horse-shoe as if it were made of lead, yet to the strength of a giant and the courage of a lion he added the gentleness of a dove. He was a lover of all animals, " whom he tamed with kindness and patience " ; and like other great spirits whose souls are filled with poetry, he could not endure to see a caged bird. Often as he passed the place where birds were sold in Florence, Leonardo would stop, buy the birds, and restore them to liberty.

A painter and sculptor, the perfection of whose work outstripped that of all his predecessors, a scientist and inventor whose theories and discoveries were centuries ahead of his time, a practical engineer who could construct with equal ease and success an instrument of war or a monument of peace, an accomplished musician and composer, a deviser of masques and ballets, an experimental chemist, a skilful dissector, and author of the earliest standard book on Anatomy—is it surprising that this man should have been the wonder of his own and of all succeeding ages ?

Genius is wayward, and as a boy Leonardo—who was born in 1452—was a source of anxiety to his father, Ser Piero da Vinci, a man of good family who, like his father and grandfather, was a notary of Florence. At school, his masters said, he was capricious and fickle : " he began to learn many things and then gave them up " ; but it was observed that however many other things took his fancy from time to time, the boy never neglected drawing and modelling. His father took these drawings to his friend the

W. F. Mansell.

"THE LAST SUPPER," BY LEONARDO DA VINCI (1452–1519)

Sta. Maria delle Grazie, Milan

"Verily I say unto you that one of you shall betray Me." This is the moment the artist has dramatically re-created. Judas (third on the Saviour's right) is guiltily withdrawing the hand extended to the dish, while behind his isolated figure Peter passionately consults the beloved disciple John. On the other side, beyond beckoning Thomas and the amazed James the Great, is the beautiful figure of Philip, whose gesture eloquently speaks to us, "Lord, Thou knowest I am not he !"

Leonardo's masterpiece has so stamped itself on the imagination of the world that we can no longer visualise the scene in any other fashion.

142

artist, Andrea del Verrocchio, who, amazed at the talent they displayed, gladly consented to have Leonardo as his pupil.

One day his master received a commission from the friars of Vallombroso to paint a picture of " St. John Baptizing Christ," and having much work on hand Verrocchio asked Leonardo to help him finish the picture by painting one of the angels. When Leonardo had done this his angel surpassed all the other figures in beauty, so that his master was filled with admiration, yet also with despair that a mere boy should know more and paint better than he could himself. Chagrined, the older artist admitted his defeat ; he is said never to have touched a brush again, but to have devoted the rest of his life to sculpture.

From that moment the reputation of Leonardo was made, and the nobles and princes of Italy sought his services. In 1493 he was invited to Milan by the Duke Ludovico Sforza, who was captivated alike by the genius of the artist and the charm of his personality. While at Milan Leonardo painted his famous " Last Supper " for the Dominicans of Sta. Maria delle Grazie, choosing the moment when the Apostles are anxious to discover who would betray their Master.

Despite his marvellous facility, Leonardo was not a quick worker, and his procrastination in finishing this picture alarmed the Prior, who besought the Duke to reprimand the artist for " mooning about " instead of getting on with the work. When the Duke spoke to Leonardo the latter gently explained how necessary it was for artists to think things out before they began to paint. " Two heads remain to be done," he said. " I feel unable to conceive the beauty of the celestial grace that must have been incarnate in Our Lord. The other head which causes me thought is that of Judas. I do not think I can express the face of a man who could resolve to betray his Master, after having received so many benefits.

" But to save time," added Leonardo, " I will in this case seek no further, but for want of a better idea I will put in the head of the Prior."

The Duke laughed heartily and told the Prior to let Leonardo finish the work in peace.

More famous even than his " Last Supper," and happily in a far better state of preservation to-day, is Leonardo's portrait of " Mona Lisa," third wife of Francesco del Giocondo, a Florentine official. For centuries this portrait with the lustrous eyes and mysterious smile has been regarded as the supreme expression in art of the eternal enigma of womanhood. By a freak of fate the man who commissioned this portrait never had it, for it was still in the possession of the artist—by whom it was considered unfinished—when Leonardo left Italy for France on the invitation of King Francis. The King of France had met Leonardo at Milan, and had long wished to tempt him to his own Court. After innumerable disappointments

"MONA LISA" (OR "LA JOCONDE"), BY LEONARDO DA VINCI

The Louvre, Paris

The most famous painting in the world, this portrait has for centuries been considered the supreme embodiment of the eternal enigma of womanhood. Mona Lisa was the third wife of Francesco del Giocondo, a Florentine official, and Vasari relates that Leonardo hired musicians to sing and play while he painted her in order to preserve the intent expression of her face.

144

in Italy, Leonardo in his old age sought refuge from Italian envy and ingratitude with the French King. Francis received him with every kindness and honour, and when the old man fell sick he frequently visited him.

One day the aged artist was seized with a paroxysm, and the kindly monarch, endeavouring to alleviate the pain, took his head into his arms. "Leonardo's divine spirit, then recognising that he could not enjoy a greater honour, expired in the king's arms." So Leonardo died, as Vasari relates, in 1519.

§ 2

There is no one person in whom the spirit of the Renaissance—that is to say, the rebirth of ancient art and learning—is so completely summed up and expressed as in Leonardo da Vinci. Yet " The Martyrdom of St. Sebastian," by the brothers Antonio and Piero del Pollaiuolo again shows something quite modern in its feeling and expression. These two Florentines were contemporaries of Leonardo. Antonio (1432–98) was of humble origin. His father, who, as his surname shows, was a poulterer, apprenticed the boy to a goldsmith, with whom he soon made a reputation as the most skilful workman in the shop. In time he was able to open a shop of his own, and his reliefs and wax models were much admired by sculptors as well as by his patrons. Meanwhile his younger brother Piero, eleven years his junior, had been apprenticed to a painter, and in early middle age Antonio thought he would like to become a painter also. He had educated himself, learning all he could of anatomy and perspective, and found no difficulty in the drawing, but the colouring was so different from anything he had done before that at first he despaired of success ; but firm in his resolve he put himself under his younger brother, and in a few months became an excellent painter.

Of all works painted by the two brothers the most famous is " The Martyrdom of St. Sebastian," now in the National Gallery.

The many-sidedness, so characteristic of the artists of the Renaissance, which we have already found in Leonardo and Antonio Pollaiuolo, also distinguishes one of the most interesting of their contemporaries. Domenico Ghirlandaio (1449–94), who also was originally a goldsmith, owes his very name to a freak of fashion. He was the first to invent and make fashionable the head ornament worn by Florentine girls. Hence he became known as Ghirlandaio (the maker of garlands), not only because he was the original inventor but also, we hear, because his were of such exceeding beauty that every girl wanted a garland from his shop.

Discontented with his trade, which gave comparatively small scope to his genius for design, Domenico began painting portraits of the people who

"THE MARTYRDOM OF ST. SEBASTIAN," BY ANTONIO AND PIERO POLLAIUOLO
(1432–1498 and 1443–1496)

National Gallery, London

Antonio Pollaiuolo was a pioneer of Naturalism. For four centuries the figures of the stooping cross-bowmen in the foreground of this picture have aroused admiration by their extraordinary realism and sense of tension.

The grouping of the figures forms a pyramid, of which the Saint is the apex, and the lines of the arrows contribute to the symmetry of the composition. The landscape background is the work of Piero.

came to his shop. These were so lifelike and so beautifully painted, that the fame of the artist soon spread, and he was inundated with orders for portraits, altar-pieces, and decorations for the palaces of noblemen. Pope Sixtus IV heard about him and sent to Florence, inviting him to come to Rome and join the band of famous artists who were already at work on what is now known as the Sistine Chapel.

His great work, " The Call of SS. Peter and Andrew," in the Sistine Chapel is a splendid example of the boldness of composition which he contributed to art ; but his small painting at the Louvre, " Portrait of an Old Man and his Grandchild," has a far wider celebrity. We present it not only as a specimen of Ghirlandaio's decorative arrangement and intimate feeling, but as an outstanding masterpiece of Christian art, Christian because the painter has here sought and found that beauty of *character* which was utterly beyond the range of the pagan artists who found beauty in *proportions*.

When we remember that Ghirlandaio began painting late, and was carried off by a fever at the comparatively early age of forty-four, we are astounded at the quantity and quality of the work he left behind. He was a man of immense energy and hated to be interrupted in his work. Once when his brother David bothered him on some domestic matter, he replied : " Leave me to work while you make provision, because now that I have begun to master my art I feel sorry that I am not employed to paint the entire circuit of the walls of Florence."

§ 3

Nine people out of ten if asked to name the greatest artist who ever lived, would reply, Michael Angelo Buonarotti, who was born in 1475 at Castel Caprese, a small town near Florence, of which his father was chief magistrate. The babe was put out to nurse with the wife of a marble-worker, and in later days the great sculptor jokingly attributed his vocation to his foster-mother's milk. His father had other ideas for him, and used a stick freely to impress on the lad the advantages of a commercial career, but Michael Angelo was obstinate and intractable. At last the father gave way, and when the son was thirteen he apprenticed him to Ghirlandaio for three years. Long before his apprenticeship was out, the boy had shown a preference for sculpture. His talent in modelling was brought to the notice of Lorenzo de' Medici, who nominated him for the famous " Garden School " of sculpture which he had founded under the direction of Donatello's chief assistant, Bartoldo. The ruler of Florence, pleased with the progress of his protégé, took him into his household, and made him an allowance of 500 ducats a month. This lasted till 1492, when Lorenzo

"AN OLD MAN AND HIS GRANDCHILD," BY D. GHIRLANDAIO (1449–1494)

The Louvre, Paris

One of the world's great masterpieces, this picture teaches us that true beauty resides in expression more than in regularity of features. The homely countenance of this good old man, despite his deformed nose, is transfigured by his expression of benevolence and affection. Note the perfect balance in the placing of the heads and the way in which the child's hand provides the patch of light needed in one corner to set off properly the view through a window which occupies the other.

148

died, and the youth had to make his own way in the world. Meanwhile a new influence came into his life.

In 1490, when Michael Angelo was a boy of fifteen, Savonarola had begun to preach his impassioned sermons in Florence. The whole city trembled at the terrible voice, which hurled thunderbolts at the Pope himself. All Florence was like a revival meeting ; people rushed about the street weeping and shouting, wealthy citizens became monks, high officials abdicated their positions.

Michael Angelo for the first time in his life was afraid, afraid of the unknown horrors predicted for Florence. He was miserable under the degenerate Piero de' Medici, a stupid tyrant who wasted his time and his talent by commanding him to model a statue in snow ! One night a poet friend of the sculptor dreamt that the dead Lorenzo appeared to him and bade him warn Piero that soon he would be driven from his house, never to return. He told the Prince, who laughed and had him well cudgelled ; he told Michael Angelo, who believed and fled to Venice.

That was in October 1494. A month later Piero fled in his turn, and Florence, with the support of Savonarola, was declared a republic, owning no king but Jesus Christ.

Michael Angelo soon got over his superstitious terrors. That winter he spent at Bologna in learned circles, and forgetting Savonarola, he read Dante and Petrarch ; he was absorbed by the beauty of Nature and the dignity of the antique world. At the very time when his contemporaries at Florence were fanatically indulging in a religious revival, Michael Angelo seemed to assert his paganism by carving a " Sleeping Cupid " so full of Greek feeling that it was sold in Rome to the Cardinal San Giorgio as an antique by a Greek sculptor. When he discovered he had been cheated, the deceived collector was so delighted to think a living Italian could rival the dead Greeks that he sent for the young sculptor and took him under his protection. In 1496, while the Florentines were heaping pagan pictures, ornaments, and books on Savonarola's " Bonfire of Vanities," when his own brother, the monk Leonardo, was being prosecuted for his faith in the Friar, Michael Angelo in Rome seemed anxious to prove himself a pagan of pagans, producing a " Bacchus," an " Adonis," and the lovely " Cupid " which is now at South Kensington.

On May 23, 1498, the fickle populace of Florence turned against its idol. Savonarola was burnt to death at the stake. Still Michael Angelo appeared to take no notice. No mention of Savonarola or his martyrdom can be found in any of the sculptor's letters.

But in his own art he made his own comment. From 1498 to 1501 he worked feverishly, perhaps remorsefully, on a marble group the like of which had never before been seen : a Virgin whose haunting face is

"CUPID," BY MICHAEL ANGELO (1475–1564)

This exquisite marble statue, now in the Victoria and Albert Museum, South Kensington, is an early work of the artist. It was executed in Rome when Michael Angelo was a young man of twenty-two, and reveals a perfection of form which hitherto his contemporaries had thought could only be realised in an antique.

impressed with a " sorrow more beautiful than beauty's self," across whose knees is lying a Christ of such serene physical beauty and perfection that we say, " He is not dead but sleepeth."

This was Michael Angelo's confession to his Maker, the supreme " Pieta " at St. Peter's, Rome : a work of which the exquisite beauty is only equalled by its ineffable sadness. Botticelli, too, was more moved by the end of Savonarola than ever he had been by his preaching. But Botticelli was then an old man : Michael Angelo had but just turned twenty-three and was only on the threshold of his career. Already his pagan days were over. Melancholy claimed him for her own, and never after let him go. In five years he had established his reputation as the greatest sculptor in the world, but then, as now, glory is not necessarily remunerative. His family believed he was making a fortune ; and too proud to acknowledge his true poverty-stricken condition, he starved himself to give alms to his kindred. His own father pestered and abused him worst of all ; his whole family bled him white, and then denounced him as being mean.

In 1501 he returned to Florence to make the famous statue of " David," which was to commemorate the deliverance of the city from her enemies. But no happiness awaited him in his native town. He was foolishly pitted against Leonardo da Vinci, and his envy and jealousy excited by tittle-tattlers. The two great men of the time, who ought to have been understanding friends and comrades, were forced into enmity. Michael Angelo grew morose and suspicious. One day as he was walking through the streets of Florence he saw Leonardo discussing a passage in Dante with a group of citizens. Meaning nothing but kindness, Leonardo hailed his rival and said to his friends, " Michael Angelo here will explain the verses of which you speak."

But the embittered sculptor scented an insult in the innocent remark and passionately retorted : " Explain them yourself, you who made the model of a bronze horse and who, incapable of casting it, left it unfinished— to your shame, be it said ! "

This allusion to his equestrian statue of Francesco Sforza, never finished, wounded Leonardo to the quick. Conscious of his fatal tendency to procrastinate, he reddened as Michael Angelo turned his back on him and strode away.

Unhappy in Florence, Michael Angelo was not sorry when in 1505 Pope Julius II called him back to Rome. Later he was to regret still more bitterly that he ever went. Julius desired a colossal mausoleum to be built for his remains, and the sculptor entered into the project with enthusiasm. He spent eight months in the Carrara quarries selecting his marbles, and in December returned to Rome, where the blocks began to arrive. But a rival artist, Bramante, hinted to the Pope that it was unlucky to build your tomb in your own lifetime. The Pope hastily dropped the idea of the mausoleum, closed his door to Michael Angelo, who was left not only unpaid for his work and time, but in debt for the marbles he had obtained. The sculptor was driven out of the Vatican by a groom, and quivering with indignation the humiliated genius at once left Rome for Florence.

But no sooner was he in Florence than the Pope wanted him back at Rome. Eventually he got him back, and perhaps the eccentric, inconstant Pope meant kindly ; but he reduced Michael Angelo to despair by demanding that the greatest sculptor in the world should spend his time painting the ceiling of the Sistine Chapel. Again the architect Bramante was the evil genius ; he had prompted the command, believing the sculptor would fail ignominiously. What was meant for his dishonour became his greatest glory.

Michael Angelo never wanted to do the work. Already his young rival Raphael had commenced painting the " Stanze " of the Vatican with unparalleled success. The sculptor pleaded that this ceiling should be given to Raphael, but the Pope insisted and his will was law. On March 10, 1508, the distracted artist wrote : " To-day I, Michael Angelo, sculptor, began the painting of the chapel." The next year, on January 27, 1509, he wrote again : " This is not my profession. . . . I am uselessly wasting my time." To-day the whole world thinks otherwise.

Of all the palaces of art which Europe contains, there is not one more wonderful within, or with a meaner exterior, than the Sistine Chapel. The long barn-like structure, lit by twelve round-headed windows, was built over what was once the Library by Sixtus IV. His aim was to ornament the chapel with scenes from the world's history pointing to the coming of Christ. All the greatest artists of the preceding generation, Botticelli, Ghirlandaio, Piero di Cosimo, and Perugino had been called upon to assist in the work, and after the death of Sixtus the completion of the Chapel occupied his nephew Count Giuliano Rovere, who succeeded him as Julius II.

Most artists who had received a papal commission of this magnitude began their work with an army of assistants. Bramante, with a show of giving his enemy every assistance, brought some experienced fresco-painters from Florence and erected a scaffolding whereby they might get at the ceiling. Furious and suspicious of everything and everybody, Michael Angelo began by declaring Bramante's scaffolding to be useless and by raising another. Next he got rid of his assistants. One morning he got there early, destroyed everything they had done, locked himself in, and refused to admit the Florentines.

During the next four years, working feverishly and in secret, the sculptor

" DELPHIC SYBIL," BY MICHAEL ANGELO

Sistine Chapel, Vatican

The description of Michael Angelo as " a sculptor who painted " is aptly illustrated by this noble picture. The introduction of a pagan priestess into a Christian church may seem surprising, but at the time of the Renaissance ecclesiastics revered these Sibyls because one of them had prophesied : " A Child shall be born whose advent will bring peace to the world."

This was believed to be an inspired foretelling of the coming of Christ. Accordingly the Delphic Sybil and her sisters could properly be included among these paintings, all of which point to the preparation of the world, from its earliest moments, for the revelation of Christianity.

153

"HEAD OF ADAM," BY MICHAEL ANGELO

Sistine Chapel, Vatican

This detail from the panel devoted to "The Creation of Man" on the great ceiling reveals Michael Angelo at his most sublime. All the knowledge and genius of a sculptor goes into the painting, and also the tenderly tragic feeling, the foreboding, which in this artist's mind inevitably went with the creation of mankind.

accomplished the mightiest series of paintings in the world. He had endless troubles and difficulties. The work was new to him, and he had to learn its technique as he went along. Hardly had he finished painting one panel, " The Deluge," when the surface became mouldy and he had to do it all over again. All this time his relatives badgered him for money ; the Pope, irritated at his secrecy and seeming slowness, threatened to have him thrown from the top of his scaffolding, and at last, worn out, but still not content with his creations, Michael Angelo, after lying for four years on his back to paint this ceiling, once more stood erect and allowed the scaffolding to be taken down on All Saints' Day 1512.

His worst enemies were amazed at the greatness and magnitude of his achievement. Raphael, great enough himself to fear no rival, was the first to praise it, thanking God aloud that he had been born in the same century. No photographs can do justice to what Raphael and his contemporaries then saw. In default of the original, we can but show a single figure and one detail, and let the imagination do the rest.

Michael Angelo divided the great oblong space of the ceiling into nine principal sections, or rather three groups of three scenes each. The first group, illustrating " The Creation of the World," consisted of (1) " God Dividing Light from Darkness," (2) " God Creating the Luminaries," and (3) " God Blessing the Earth." The second group, illustrating " The Fall of Man," showed (4) " The Creation of Adam," (5) " The Creation of Eve," and (6) " The Temptation and Fall." The last three, illustrating the uselessness of sacrifice under the old dispensation, represented (7) " The Sacrifice of Noah," (8) " The Deluge," and (9) " The Drunkenness of Noah." These nine panels were knit together by a connecting framework in which were placed single figures of Prophets, Sibyls, and other decorative figures, lunettes and triangles, so that the whole appeared as an elaborate architectural roof ornamented with reliefs and sculptured figures among which nine great pictures had been inserted.

The work was completed, but Michael Angelo at thirty seven was an old man. His health was shattered. Working for months on end with his head thrown back had strained his neck and brought on painful swellings of the glands ; his sight was injured to such an extent that for long afterwards he could not read a book or letter unless he held it above his head. Then, when the old Pope, satisfied at last, might have rewarded the heroic artist, Julius died and was succeeded by Leo X, who had work for Raphael, but none for Michael Angelo.

The harassed sculptor went back to Florence, where he set to work on another masterpiece of sculpture, the " Tomb of Lorenzo de' Medici," with its beautiful recumbent figures of " Night " and " Morning," " Dawn " and " Twilight." Worse troubles were in store for him. Disgusted with all things, including himself, he threw himself into the revolution which convulsed Florence in 1527. Though no engineer like Leonardo, the republican revolutionaries put him in charge of the fortifications of the city. Distrustful of everybody, Michael Angelo feared that Malatesta Baglione, the general of the Florentine troops, might betray the city to the troops of the new Pope (Clement VII) ; his warning unheeded by the authorities, he feared the hostility of the powerful commander, and giving way to an attack of nerves he fled to Venice for his life. There he was safe and might have gone to France, but an appeal to his honour brought him back to Florence. Once more he took his place in the fighting line, and six months later Malatesta Baglione, as he foresaw, betrayed the city to the Emperor.

Irony of fate ! The life of the wretched sculptor was spared in order that he might work again for the glory of those tyrants, the Medici, against whom he had fought. In 1534, another Pope, Paul III, called him to Rome to enter on a new project. Again the sculptor was asked to paint, to cover the immense wall at the entrance to the Sistine Chapel with a fresco representing " The Last Judgment." He began the work when he was sixty-one, and again shutting himself up, accomplished the task in a little over five years. It was no work for an old man of nearly seventy, and the following year the sculptor had to turn from painting to architecture ; by command of the Pope he designed the mighty Dome which to all the world to-day is the sign and symbol of the Eternal City.

Vasari, who visited the old man when he was eighty-eight, gives a wonderful picture of Michael Angelo's last years. He lived like a poor man, ate hardly anything but a little bread and drank but a little wine. Unable to sleep, he would get up at night to work with his chisel, and made himself a paper helmet in which a candle was fixed, so that he might have light to work without embarrassing his hands.

On February 12, 1564, he spent the whole day on his feet working at a " Pieta." Two days afterwards he was seized with fever, but with his usual obstinacy refused to see a doctor or to go to bed. On the 17th he consented to be put to bed, and, fully conscious, dictated his will, bequeathing " his soul to God and his body to the earth." About five o'clock on the following afternoon, surrounded by his faithful servant and a few friends, the worn-out genius breathed his last and found that rest which had never been granted him in life.

§ 4

Happy the painter who has no history ! Life, so cruel to Michael Angelo, had nothing but kindness for his young contemporary, Raphael Sanzio. Born at Urbino in 1483, his way was smoothed for him from the

"THE MADONNA OF SAN SISTO," BY RAPHAEL (1483–1520)
Dresden

The Sistine Madonna is justly the most famous and most favoured of all Raphael's Madonnas ; for, though others may rival it in formal beauty, in no other does he reach the same height of spiritual expression. The Christ-child, so solemnly yet naturally gazing at the infinite, the slender, majestic, yet entirely human mother, are figures which, once we have seen them, haunt our memory for ever.

157

W. F. Mansell.

"THE ANSIDEI MADONNA," BY RAPHAEL
National Gallery, London

This famous altar-piece, originally painted for the Ansidei family of Perugia, shows the Virgin and Child in the centre, with St. John the Baptist on one side and St. Nicolas of Bari on the other. In the eighteenth century the picture was purchased from the Church of S. Fiorenzo—where it had hung since 1506—by Lord Robert Spencer, who presented it to the third Duke of Marlborough. It was **bought** from the Marlborough collection at Blenheim for the National Gallery in 1885, at a cost of £70,000.

"THE TRANSFIGURATION," BY RAPHAEL

This picture at the Vatican, Raphael's last masterpiece, shows the transfiguration of Christ, floating over the Mount in clear air, between Moses and Elijah. Prostrate on the earth are Peter, James, and John, in varied attitudes. In the foreground an excited group gathers round the boy possessed of devils.

At the lying-in-state of Raphael, which followed the great artist's death, this picture—which he had painted for the Cardinal Giulio de' Medici—was placed at the head of the corpse in the Hall wherein Raphael had last worked.

"POPE JULIUS II," BY RAPHAEL

Uffizi Gallery, Florence

Giuliano da Rovere, afterwards Pope Julius II, was a nephew of Cardinal Francesco di Savona, who became Sixtus IV and began the erection of the world-famed chapel in the Vatican which bears his name. By his enlightened patronage of contemporary art, Julius II has secured an undying fame, which eclipses any reputation he once enjoyed for theological wisdom or political sagacity.

"VIRGIN ADORING THE INFANT CHRIST" (ALBANI ALTAR-PIECE),
BY PERUGINO (1446–1523)

This central panel of the famous altar-piece in the Villa Albani, Rome, is the most exquisite of all
Perugino's numerous paintings. It exhibits in equal perfection the sweet gracefulness of his feminine types
and the aerial perspective which gives a sense of infinite distance to his tender landscape backgrounds.

moment (1504) that he left the workshop of his master Perugino to begin an independent career. Perugino himself (1446–1523) was a typical painter of that lovely Umbrian countryside, where the Tiber winds down from the Apennines. Art in this region, away from the brilliance of Florence and Rome, was more quietly religious in its feeling, and had the especial quality that the artists loved Nature and invariably introduced exquisite local scenery as their background.

Raphael began as one of the Umbrian painters, but his genius carried him far beyond them. Beautiful as an angel in person, sweet in disposition, charming in manner and conversation, Raphael was a favourite everywhere. After perfecting his art by study in Florence, he was invited to Rome in 1508 to undertake the decoration of the Stanze in the Vatican. These paintings at once established his reputation, and in 1511 he was appointed Chief Architect of St. Peter's, Surveyor and Guardian of the Ancient Monuments of Rome, and overwhelmed with commissions for mighty projects of painting which his gentle courtesy had not the determination to refuse.

He walked through Rome, in those years of his glory, amid a throng of assistants and admirers. Thus meeting him once, grim old Michael Angelo growled out, " You look like a General at the head of an army."

Laughing and quite unspoilt, Raphael wittily retorted : " And you, sir, like an executioner on the way to the scaffold."

As a portrait-painter his " Balthasar Castiglione " at the Louvre, as a painter of altar-pieces his " Sistine Madonna " at Dresden and the " Ansidei Madonna " in the National Gallery, have made Raphael familiar to all and loved by all. In 1520 he was working on his great " Transfiguration " in the Vatican, when a fever struck him down. On March 27 he laid down the brush that he was never to hold again, and on Good Friday, April 6, his birthday, he died as the sun went down, amid the tears of those who mourned not only the artist but the man. He had lived only thirty-seven years, but from that day to this not for one moment has the lustre of his name been dimmed.

XII

SCULPTURE OF THE RENAISSANCE

THE ART OF THE GOTHIC CATHEDRALS AND OF THE RENAISSANCE

§ 1

THROUGHOUT the whole story of the art of the early world—in Egypt and Assyria, in Greece and Rome—the art of sculpture had stood pre-eminent. It may well be that there was a corresponding practice of painting and that we have lost these more perishable treasures ; but the sculpture which has come down to us, especially that from Greece, is among the few perfect creations of the human mind. With the Romans, as we have seen, this art degenerated. During the centuries which followed the fall of Rome it entirely ceased. All the knowledge, all the secrets, all understanding of this sublime art were lost. For six, seven, eight hundred years they remained unknown. If we happen to have any attempt at stone-carving in those centuries, even late in them, it is as crude as the work of any savage people. The marvel is that so much knowledge of beauty could so utterly pass from the earth and " leave not a wrack behind."

When European mankind began again to think in terms of carved stone, it was with the most simple axe-cut patterning and then with such primitive attempts at the representation of human figures as we find on the church of St. Benoit on the Loire. There and elsewhere, round about the year 1000 or earlier, heavy disproportionate figures, scarcely recognisable as humans, were hewn clumsily as part of the pillar itself. We were beginning again at the absolute beginning of sculpture.

It was with the coming of Gothic architecture and that amazing resurgence of spiritual and mental life along the valley of the Seine, that the first wave of the new beauty broke. One of the causes of that Gothic revival was the vogue for relics. Alas ! we must recognise that these multitudinous pieces of the true cross, these finger bones of saints and miracle-working remains of martyrs, were a profitable business alike to the church and to the community gathered around its walls. The Crusades stimulated it. The Holy Land yielded a vast harvest of relics, before which the faithful worshipped. At St. Denis near Paris, for example, there were the remains of no less than three martyrs, and so dense was the crowd of pilgrims to the shrine during the twelfth century that the great Abbot

163

Suger records having seen worshippers crushed to death there. Our own day which shows equal mob-madness for glimpses of film-stars cannot lightly condemn such strange enthusiasms. Out of this relic worship at least came the vast churches and the beauty of Gothic. Under those soaring vaults whole populations could gather for prayer and praise.

It was around these churches with their vast façades, their deeply recessed porches, their innumerable niches, that the art of sculpture was reborn. On the West Front of Chartres Cathedral alone were carved more than seven hundred figures. In the North and South Porches hundreds more. This effect was repeated at practically every cathedral, and created an army of statues quite apart from the decoration of piers, the carving of corbels, pulpits, fonts, screens, and so forth.

As in ancient Greece they evolved from the pillars themselves. At first the human form is planned as a decoration of the stone pillar : there are no shoulders, the arms are solid with the bodies, the long perpendicular folds of the drapery fall to the feet, the braided hair of the women echoes the perpendicular theme. All the skill of the artists was expended on an exquisite decorative effect and on the delicate heads and faces. But gradually the stone became endowed with life as craftsmanship improved. The figures became more and more human. They were no longer carved pillars, but definite statues in the niches between the pillars. The Gothic artists began a search for realism and individuality which was essentially different from the Greek idealisation. The Apostles on the South Porch at Chartres, for instance, and the corresponding Prophets on the North Porch were realised characters. Every figure became no longer symmetrical but a balanced whole, often with one leg taking the weight and the other relaxed, so that we have the whole fascinating rhythm of the stresses and counterpoise of the human body.

Bible story begins to be enacted dramatically between these individualised creations. Such is the charming representation of " The Visitation " at Reims. This was part of the wave of Mariolatry which swept through Christendom during these years. It would be difficult to say exactly what gave rise to that sudden love of the Virgin and worship of woman. It is closely linked with the rise of chivalry and the poetry of the Troubadours, and its effect upon this art of Gothic sculpture was enormous. The lovely " Gilded Virgin " at Amiens, her body leaning slightly backwards and sideways to take the weight of the Child she holds so lovingly on her arm, may be cited as typical of thousands of statues of the Virgin which filled the shrines of the great churches, or was repeated in delicate ivory carvings where the pose beautifully fitted the curve of the tusk. Along with these, but rarer, was the figure of Christ. Again at Amiens there is a supreme example. So the art flourished until there was scarcely a cathedral · in

SCULPTURE, CHARTRES CATHEDRAL

" The Bible of Chartres " Ruskin called it, for the whole scriptural story found its place in the magnificent portals and niches of the Cathedral, and in its stained glass. These statues, slightly elongated and with the drapery arranged in rhythmic folds, became a perfect part of the building.

"MUSICIANS," BY LUCA DELLA ROBBIA (1399–1482)

Cathedral Museum, Florence

Donatello and Luca della Robbia created for the choir gallery of the Cathedral at Florence a series of delightful panels of singing boys and children playing instruments and dancing. Their rhythm gives the very soul of the music which they illustrate. The flow of drapery and the movement of youthful forms make wonderful compositions in these masterly low reliefs.

Northern France or in England or across into the Rhineland but had its own particular treasure of sculpture as well as hundreds of lesser figures, each one a noble work of art.

Not the least fascinating phase of this Gothic art is that which arose when the anonymous craftsmen had slighter tasks to perform—a head on a corbel, a support under a miserere seat, a newel post, a gargoyle—and allowed their humour and fecund imagination play. The satirical, the grotesque, the highly personal, animals strayed from the bestiaries, flowers and plants and every kind of ornament : everything was made for the sheer joy of creating and the expression of minds which were finding the world full of a number of things.

So between sublimity and simple workman's fun this great art of Gothic sculpture flourished for a century or two. Its exponents were anonymous as they laboured for the love of God and of their work. Probably they held themselves of no more account than any other of the craftsmen who were making these great buildings, but they left us a heritage of beauty in stone, and brought back to the minds of men this sublime art of sculpture.

§ 2

Nevertheless the impulse of the Gothic spent itself, and with it this art might have slackened and failed had it not been that down in Italy it came into contact with the spirit of the Renaissance and became magnificently renewed. There in the South, events conspired to turn men's minds back towards the achievements of Greece and Rome. In 1204 the sack of Constantinople in the Crusade released a number of ancient manuscripts. This proved one element in the revival. The discovery in the very soil of Italy of the Roman copies of the original Greek statues was another. The growing abstract passion for knowledge was both cause and effect. Italian political organisation was, in some ways, akin to that of ancient Greece, for it became largely one of independent city states under more or less benevolent tyrants. These cities were tremendously self-conscious ; and the passion for fine building which in the North gave us French and English Gothic, was echoed here in a style of building more suited to the climate and light, and increasingly given over to the reviving classical influence.

It was at Pisa that sculpture awakened. The nearness of the Carrara marble mines may have stimulated it there, but early in the thirteenth century we have Niccolo of Pisa (1205–78), architect and scientist and ardent enthusiast for the Graeco-Roman discoveries. Pisa was a town of political importance and prosperity. Its wealth attracted the vendors of Greek and Roman antiques. Niccolo studied these classical marbles, and eventually abandoned his architectural practice to devote himself wholly to sculpture. He broke away from Byzantinism, founded a new school, and proved to his fellow-craftsmen the advantage of a study from Nature and the antique. The pulpit at Pisa, half-Gothic, half-classical, and wonderful in its storied panels, reveals alike the fertility of Niccolo's mind and its conflict. He was followed by his son, Giovanni, and his pupil, Andrea Pisano ; and Orcagno felt his influence.

Andrea (1270–1348) carried the idea to Florence, that rising city whose enlightenment encouraged any new thing in those teeming years. He made the first doors for the Baptistery, illustrating the life of John the Baptist there. Then, seventy years after, the Merchant Guild of Florence, as a thank-offering for the deliverance of the city from the plague, invited the artists of Italy to compete for the other two doors.

A young painter, Lorenzo Ghiberti (1378–1455), himself a Florentine, returned from Rimini where he was working, to compete. Brunelleschi, the architect of the cathedral dome, and Jacobo della Quercia from Sienna were among the competitors. The judges decided that the exhibits of Ghiberti and Brunelleschi were equally good. The original bronze panels by both artists, illustrating " The Sacrifice of Isaac," are in the National Museum, Florence. Brunelleschi withdrew, and in 1403 Ghiberti received the commission. Those gates became his life-work. He began them when he was twenty-five and he was seventy-four when he finished. The first gate represented scenes from the Old Testament and was set up in 1424 ; the second, still more wonderful, took longer. While Ghiberti was working at the first, Brunelleschi reduced the laws of perspective to a science ; and into the Old Testament subjects for the second gate Ghiberti introduced this newly acquired knowledge. Some panels contain as many as a hundred figures, which, said the artist, " I modelled upon different planes, so that those nearest the eye might appear larger, and those more remote smaller in proportion." The second gate was set up in 1452, and three years later Ghiberti died. After his death, Michael Angelo—never easy to please— viewed his work, and pronounced them " fit to be the gates of Paradise."

Among Ghiberti's other famous works was that which came when the Florentine Guilds turned to the competitive fashion of erecting statues to their respective patron saints in the niches of the Or San Michele. The Silk Workers first put their statue, and soon the other guilds were vieing for the work of sculptors. Ghiberti made three of these—the St. Matthew, St. John Baptist, and St. Stephen. It meant new opportunities in the art ; for whereas the panels of the gates, or that other fine work of his, the bas-reliefs for the shrine of San Zenobia, were pictorial and comparatively small in scale, these life-size figures in the round were in the grand manner which was to lead straight on to the marvels of Michael Angelo.

One other of the men who created the statues for Or San Michele was

" DAVID," BY MICHAEL ANGELO

Florence

The life and art of Michael Angelo has already been considered in an earlier chapter. His sculpture was the climax of that art at the time of the Renaissance ; and the vast " David," carved from a block of marble which had long been lying idle, is one of his masterpieces. All the perfection of proportion and idealism of Greek work is linked in it with the sense of human effort which was characteristic of the Renaissance.

that friend of Brunelleschi, Donatello (1386–1466). He had studied the antique with Brunelleschi at Rome and then returned to Florence. His is one of the greatest names in the history of sculpture. He brought to great perfection the art of carving in low relief, and his many busts and statues have a vigour, humanity, and dramatic power which he was the first to introduce into sculpture. His relief " The Charge to St. Peter," in the Victoria and Albert Museum, South Kensington, is almost an anticipation of the impressionism of Rodin in its suggestion of atmosphere and distance. Of his early period the bronze " David " at the Bargello, Florence, is considered the finest example. The first nude statue thought out independently of its architectural surroundings, since Roman times, it is beautiful both in its proportions and in its simple realism. Human and in a sense gay, it struck a new note. The supreme masterpiece of his later years is the famous equestrian statue at Padua of the Condottiere Gattamelata. Majestic in its repose, yet pulsating with life, this work is one of the two great equestrian statues of the world, the other being the Colleoni Monument at Venice, begun about forty years later by Donatello's pupil Verrocchio, and completed by the Venetian sculptor Alessandro Leopardi. One charming work of Donatello's is the famous " Singing Boys " panels. Both he and Luca della Robbia (1399–1482) made these lovely Cantoria for the choir gallery of the cathedral at Florence, and succeeded in snaring the very soul of music in the stone. Luca della Robbia is otherwise chiefly noteworthy for the delightful enamelled terra-cotta work which bears his name.

All this fifteenth-century sculpture, moving towards a perfection which was able to challenge the work of the Greeks, was, however, but the prelude to the sublimity of Michael Angelo. Apart from him it had already turned from strength to sweetness in the work of della Robbia ; and after him there is practically nothing to record save the able playfulness of Cellini, and the comparatively empty technicality of Giovanni da Bologna. These sixteenth-century men were the decline from the height ; but that height was the sublimest achieved in human art.

XIII

THE ROAD TO VENICE

THE ART OF MANTEGNA, FRANCIA, CORREGGIO, BELLINI,
AND GIORGIONE

§ I

IT takes nine tailors to make a man. So runs the familiar saying, but one tailor of Padua in the fifteenth century sufficed to found a school of painting which has won immortal fame. In all the history of art no stranger figure exists than that of Francesco Squarcione, tailor and embroiderer of Padua. He had little to do with painting or painters till he was past forty, and yet this man was the master of 137 pupils and the " Father " of the glorious schools of Venice, Parma, Bologna, Lombardy, and Ferrara.

Here let us pause to explain that while the succession of painters known as the Florentine School were perfecting their art, as related in the last chapter, groups of artists had already begun to collect in other Italian cities. So far back as 1375, twelve years before the birth of Fra Angelico, a Florentine painter named Justus had settled in Padua ; and when Leonardo da Vinci was born in 1452, Padua was already famous as an art centre.

But to return to our tailor. To the University of Padua came, at one time or another, all the learned men of Italy. Nothing was heard in the streets but talk of ancient lore and the beauty of ancient art. The astute tailor soon found that a fragment of sculpture or a stone with a Greek inscription brought him more and better customers than the display of the latest fashions. Gradually the tailoring and embroidering became a side-line in his complicated business, and the shop of Squarcione gained much fame as a storehouse of antique treasures of art. Artists came to him asking to be allowed to draw his fine old statues.

Squarcione had a keen eye to the main chance, and the power to discover and use the talents of others. Whether he himself ever painted is doubtful, but in 1441, when he was a man of forty-seven, he managed to qualify himself for admission to the Guild of Painters at Padua. His business instinct would not allow him to let slip a ready made opportunity. When students sought to study his unrivalled collection of antique models, they found themselves bound as apprentices to Squarcione ; and henceforward—on the strength of *their* work—Squarcione blossomed into the proprietor of a flourishing art business.

171

In 1443 he was given the contract to decorate with paintings the Chapel of the Eremitani at Padua, and this contract he fulfilled for the most part by the hand of a boy of twelve, whom two years earlier Squarcione had adopted as his son and pupil. This boy was a nameless orphan, who acquired undying fame as Andrea Mantegna. He was only ten years old when, as the " son of Squarcione," he was admitted a member of the Padua Guild of Painters, and from this fact alone we can guess his extraordinary precocity. At the age of twelve Mantegna was employed on important paintings for the Chapel of the Eremitani, and it was the reputation of the pupil, rather than that of the master, which brought students in shoals to Padua.

Another great piece of good luck which befell Squarcione was the arrival in Padua of the Venetian painter, Jacopo Bellini (c. 1400–71), whom the wily contractor inveigled into his business, and there is little room for doubt that Bellini was for many years the actual teacher of painting in the school of the Paduan contractor. Mantegna got his drawing from observing the Greek statues among Squarcione's antiques, but he learnt colouring from Bellini, who was his true master. But so precocious was the genius of Mantegna that at seventeen he had already formed his style and brought his natural talents to mature perfection. At this age he painted an altar-piece for St. Sophia at Padua, a picture which, as the sixteenth-century critic Vasari wrote, " might well be the production of a skilled veteran and not of a mere boy."

Success begets success, and at an early age Mantegna was able to set up for himself. Squarcione became still more furious when Mantegna married the daughter of Jacopo Bellini, who had now broken away from the firm and become a rival. Henceforward the old contractor blamed Mantegna's works as much as he had previously praised them, " saying they were bad, because he had imitated marble, a thing impossible in paint-ing, since stones always possess a certain harshness and never have that softness peculiar to flesh and natural objects."

It is true that Mantegna's sense of form was severe and his figures often remind us of marble statues, but the envious carping of his old master in no wise injured his reputation. His fame spread throughout Italy, and Pope Innocent VIII invited him to Rome, where he was employed on painting the walls of the Belvedere. The payments for this work were not so regular as the painter thought they should have been, and one day he ventured to drop a hint to the Pope, who had come to look at Mantegna's paintings of the Virtues.

" What is that figure ? " asked the Pontiff.

" One much honoured here, your Holiness," said the artist pointedly ; " it is Prudence."

"PARNASSUS," BY MANTEGNA (1431–1506)

The Louvre, Paris

The paganism of this picture illustrates the change that came over Italian art in the fifteenth century owing to that revival of interest in the achievements of Ancient Greece and Rome which is known as the Renaissance.

Andrea Mantegna, who was devoted to Greek ideals, here pictures an imaginary scene on Mount Parnassus, the legendary home of the Nine Muses, personifications of the Fine Arts. On the mountain top stand Venus and Apollo, with Cupid trumpeting their praise, while around them the Muses dance. In the corner stands Mercury, the Messenger of the Gods, with Pegasus, the winged horse, waiting to bear inspiration from these divinities to the poets and artists of the earth. Note how the pyramidical design, helped by the horse's wing, gives dignity to the scene.

173

" You should associate Patience with her," replied the Pope, who understood the allusion, and later when the work was completed we are told Mantegna was " richly rewarded."

After painting in various Italian cities, Mantegna returned to Mantua, where he built himself a handsome house, and there, in 1506, he died at the age of seventy-five. The peculiar qualities of his art, his austere draughtsmanship and compact design may be seen in many works in England, notably in " The Triumph of Julius Cæsar " at Hampton Court, and in his " Madonna and Child " and " Triumph of Scipio " in the National Gallery ; but the most perfect example of Mantegna's art is his great picture " Parnassus," in the Louvre at Paris. Here, as the illustration shows, Mantegna is able to express all his love of Greek art in picturing the home of the Nine Muses, who dance in homage round Venus and Apollo, while Mercury, the Messenger of the Gods, awaits with Pegasus, the winged horse, to bear inspiration from this mythological heaven to the artists and poets of the earth.

§ 2

To enumerate all the artists who were influenced by Mantegna and the School of Squarcione would be to give a list of a hundred names, and to attempt a task beyond the scope of this OUTLINE ; but brief mention must be made of one whose life, and particularly whose death, is of unusual and romantic interest. Francesco Francia (1450–1517) was a goldsmith of Bologna who achieved great fame as an engraver of medallion portraits long before the example of Mantegna inspired him to become a painter also. Francia was one of the first artists to make prints from an engraved plate, and served literature by designing the famous italic type for the press of Aldus Manutius. As a painter, Francia began with portraits and proceeded to altar-pieces, in which he displayed a remarkable psychological insight. Both in ancient times and in modern his lunette of the Dead Christ in the lap of the Virgin has been regarded as a most beautiful work, poignant in the intensity of its expression. This half-moon-shaped picture is the upper part of a famous altar-piece originally painted for the Church of St. Frediano at Lucca, and is now in the National Gallery, London. The main picture below shows the Madonna and Child, with the following saints (from left to right) : St. Sebastian, St. Paul, St. Anne, St. Lawrence, and St. Benedict, while in front of the throne is the figure of the young St. John the Baptist ; and the wan, expressive face of the young Virgin seems to suggest that she is already forewarned of the tragedy commemorated by the picture above.

Francia was at the height of his reputation in Bologna when the young Raphael was working in Rome. The two artists never met, for Raphael

"THE FREDIANO ALTAR-PIECE," BY FRANCIA (c. 1450–1517)

National Gallery, London

This altar-piece was commissioned by the Buonvisi Family for its chapel of St. Anne, in the Church of St. Frediano, Lucca. Francia managed to put his own wonderful feeling into the work, and the upper portion, a *Pieta* showing the Virgin and two angels weeping over the dead body of Christ, is of such tragic intensity that the most hardened sceptic can hardly gaze upon it unmoved.

was too busy to leave the Vatican and Francia was too old to travel. But they heard much of one another, and Francia, as the elder, offered to help his junior in any way he could. He had never seen a picture by Raphael, and longed to view some work by the young man of whom everybody was talking. At last the opportunity came. Raphael was commissioned to paint a panel of " St. Cecilia " for a Bolognese chapel, St. Giovanni in Monte ; and when he had finished the painting he sent it to Francia at Bologna with a courteous letter begging the older artist to " correct any errors found in it," and then set it up on the altar for which it was intended.

When Francia drew the masterpiece from its case and viewed it in a good light, he was filled with amazement and with chagrin, so Vasari says, at his presumption in offering to help so great a genius :

" Francia, half dead at the overwhelming power and beauty of the picture, which he had to compare with his own works lying around, though thoroughly discouraged, took it to St. Giovanni in Monte, to the chapel where it was to be. Returning home he took to his bed in an agony, feeling that art could offer him no more, and died, some suppose of grief and melancholy, due to his contemplation of the living picture of Raphael."

That is the story told by Vasari, and though it may seem incredible to us that any artist should be so fatally affected by seeing the work of another, the fact that so strange a cause of death was related in good faith reveals to us how seriously art was taken in Italy in 1518.

§ 3

To appreciate all that Squarcione's school at Padua did for Italian art, we must trace its influence into the second and third generation. In addition to the sons of Bellini—to whom we shall return—who were the real founders of Venetian painting, the old contractor had among his pupils Cosimo Tura (1420–95), who founded the School of Ferrara. Tura had a pupil named Bianci, who founded a school in Modena, and there had a pupil greater than any of his predecessors, Antonio Allegri, known as Correggio, from the place of his birth. Of the life of this great man singularly little is known, and apart from his art it does not seem to have been in any way eventful. Vasari tells us that Correggio " was of a very timid disposition and, at a great personal inconvenience, worked continually for the family which depended on him. In art he was very melancholy, enduring its labours, but he never allowed difficulties to deter him, as we see in the great tribune of the Duomo of Parma."

It is with Parma that the name of Correggio is always associated, for his greatest works were executed there between 1518 and 1530, and the Cathedral of Parma is the monument of his genius. In its marvellous

"THE EDUCATION OF CUPID," BY CORREGGIO (1494 1534)

National Gallery, London

"The soft beauty of his flesh tints and the grace of his finish," which won the admiration of this artist's contemporaries, still charm us to-day.

In this lovely allegory Correggio shows us Mercury—the patron deity in Greek mythology of schools and colleges—teaching Cupid to spell out love, while Venus, the incarnation of feminine charm, looks on approvingly.

177

complexity and rich invention, his " Assumption of the Virgin " there has no rival in the world. If his fluent and sure drawing was derived from Mantegna, his mastery of light and shade from Leonardo da Vinci, and his tremendous forms and designs borrowed from the storehouse of Michael Angelo, yet his marvellous colouring is entirely his own, and it is as a colourist, above all, that Correggio is supreme.

" It is considered certain," wrote Vasari, " that there never was a better colourist, nor any artist who imparted more loveliness or relief to his things, so great was the soft beauty of his flesh tints and the grace of his finish." Nearly 400 years have passed since these lines were written, but no connoisseur of to-day would change a word in this appreciation. The work of Correggio appeals to every human being who is susceptible to the indefinable quality of charm. Whether his subject be frankly pagan, as in " The Education of Cupid " at the National Gallery, or avowedly religious, as in his " St. Catherine " at Hampton Court, it is on the satisfaction of the eye, and through the eye of all the senses, that Correggio relies.

In Mr. Samuel Courtauld's collection there is a sensitive self-portrait of this great colourist. " He was content with little," says Vasari, " and lived as a good Christian should." A modern critic, Mr. Berenson, has pronounced Correggio's paintings to be " hymns to the charm of femininity the like of which have never been known before or since in Christian Europe," yet from all accounts this artist's private life was singularly free from amours. Correggio was a model husband and father, and the only thing said against him by his Italian biographer is that he " was anxious to save, like everyone who is burdened with a family, and he thus became excessively miserly." This closeness is said to have brought about his premature death. " Payment of 60 crowns being made to him at Parma in farthings, which he wished to take to Correggio for his affairs, he set out with this burden on foot. Becoming overheated by the warmth of the sun, he took some water to refresh himself, and caught a severe fever, which terminated his life in the fortieth year of his age."

§ 4

Soon after the death in 1470 of Jacopo Bellini, there arrived in Venice a young Sicilian painter who, without being himself a great master, nevertheless changed the whole course of Italian painting. This was Antonello da Messina (1430–79), who, having seen at Naples in his youth a Flemish picture painted in oils, was so fascinated by the advantages of the new medium, that he went to Flanders and stayed there for some six years till he had thoroughly mastered the new process of painting. Then he returned to Italy, where he generously communicated his secrets to other artists,

W. F. Mansell.

" ST. CATHERINE," BY CORREGGIO

Hampton Court

All the saints have their symbols, and St. Catherine of Siena is often represented with a book to denote her devotional nature. Correggio, whose art is always sweetly human rather than deeply spiritual, shows us the humanity rather than the saintliness of his subject. She might be a modern beauty immersed in a novel. As an exponent of feminine beauty Correggio ranks among the supreme artists of the world.

179

W. F. Mansell.

"THE CRUCIFIXION," BY ANTONELLO DA MESSINA (1430–79)

National Gallery, London

This Sicilian artist, who went to Flanders for his training, was the first to introduce into Italy the Flemish method of painting in *oils*. We can see the influence of Flemish painting in his rather homely types, but the beautiful landscape with a city in the mid-distance is entirely Italian.

and so popularised in Italy the Flemish method of oil-painting. Antonello was a skilful painter, both of figures and landscape, as his " Crucifixion," from the picture in the National Gallery, proves ; but unfortunately he died at the age of forty-nine, just when he had received commissions for a number of important paintings, and so we can only judge of his talent by the few small pictures and portraits which have survived.

Others reaped where Antonello had sown. Already Venetian painters had shown a certain independence in their art. In this maritime port, where sails were more plentiful than trees, pictures had long been painted on canvas, for wood that warps and plaster that scales and falls were ill-suited to resist the damp that came from the canals. Van Eyck's method of oil-painting, introduced by Antonello, was soon found to be more damp-proof than the old method (tempera) of mixing pigments with yolk-of-egg, besides being lighter in weight and richer in colour.

Among the first to take advantage of the new method were the two sons of Bellini, who had soon followed their father to Venice, after his separation from Squarcione. Gentile, the elder, named after Gentile da Fabriano (Jacopo's first master), was born about 1429 ; his brother Giovanni was a year or two younger. Both these sons far surpassed their father, and the younger outstripped the elder, but throughout their lives there was no jealousy between them.

" Although the brothers lived apart," says Vasari, " they bore such a respect for each other and for their father, that each one declared himself to be inferior to the other, thus seeking modestly to surpass the other no less in goodness and courtesy than in the excellence of art."

We are told that " the first works of Giovanni were some portraits which gave great satisfaction, especially that of the Doge Loredano." This last is the sumptuous painting, reproduced here, now hanging in the National Gallery ; and from this noble portrait of the Head of the Venetian Republic may be obtained a just idea of Giovanni's power of characterisation and of the splendour of his colour when he was still at the outset of his great career. Impressed by the beauty of his portraits and of numerous altar-pieces which he painted for churches in Venetian territory, the nobles of the city desired this great painter, together with his brother Gentile, " to decorate the hall of the great council with paintings descriptive of the magnificence and greatness of their marvellous city." So, beginning with the brothers Bellini, and afterwards continued by painters of equal eminence, there came into being that unrivalled series of mural paintings in public buildings which makes Venice to-day the most wonderful art-city in the world.

Of all the altar-pieces painted by Giovanni Bellini, the most exquisite is the illustration " The Doge Barberigo kneeling before the Infant Christ," a painting formerly in the Church of San Pietro at Murano, but now in the

"THE DOGE LEONARDO LOREDANO," BY GIOVANNI BELLINI (1428–1516)

National Gallery, London

All the pomp, prosperity, and splendour of the maritime State of Venice is summed up in this sumptuous portrait of her Chief Magistrate.

"Bellini," said Ruskin, "is the only artist who appears to me to have united, in equal and magnificent measures, justness of drawing, nobleness of colouring, and perfect manliness of treatment."

182

Accademia, Venice. This Madonna is one of the loveliest in all Italian art, serene, majestic, pensive, but altogether human and lovable.

Softness and gentleness always distinguish the work of Giovanni Bellini from that of his brother Gentile, who inclined more to the severity of his brother-in-law Mantegna. Good examples of Gentile Bellini may be seen in the National Gallery, among them being an " Adoration of the Magi " and his portrait of " The Sultan Mohammed II." The last has an interesting history. Although paintings are prohibited by Mohammedan laws, this Sultan saw some portraits by Giovanni Bellini in the possession of the Venetian Ambassador, and, filled with amazement and admiration, he earnestly desired to see the man who could create such marvels. The Venetian Senate, however, was disinclined to let Giovanni leave the city, but allowed his brother Gentile to go in his stead. Gentile arrived at Constantinople, where he " was received graciously and highly favoured," and after painting a number of portraits, including one of the Sultan and one (by request) of himself, the Grand Turk was " convinced that the artist had been assisted by some divine spirit." He wished to reward the artist richly, and " asked him to name any favour which he desired, and it would immediately be granted."

Tactful and courteous, yet conscious that if he unduly prolonged his stay in Turkey he might excite envy and dangerous religious animosity, Gentile replied that he " asked for nothing but a letter of recommendation to the senate and government of his native Venice." Though loath to let him go, the Sultan was as good as his word. The letter was written " in the warmest possible terms, after which he was dismissed with noble gifts and the honour of knighthood."

So Gentile Bellini returned in honour to Venice, where he lived till he was nearly eighty, when " he passed to the other life," says Vasari, " and was honourably buried by his brother in Santi Giovanni e Paolo in the year 1507." His brother Giovanni survived him by some ten years and continued, fine old patriarch that he was, painting portraits till almost the end of his days. " At length," says our historian, " when Giovanni had attained to the age of ninety years, he passed from the troubles of this life, leaving an everlasting name by the works which he produced in his native Venice and elsewhere. He was buried in the same church where he had previously laid his brother Gentile."

§ 5

Justly famous by right of his own paintings, Giovanni is also renowned as the master of some of the greatest painters Venice ever saw, chief among his pupils being Giorgione and Titian. The first was born at Castelfranco in 1470, and was christened Giorgio, but " from his stature and the greatness

183

" SULTAN MOHAMMED II," BY GENTILE BELLINI

National Gallery, London

The famous portrait of the Sultan of Turkey painted by the artist when he went to Constantinople in the place of his brother Giovanni. The Renaissance compromise with the Mohammedan style is a triumph of adaptation. Such portraits earned for Gentile the favour of the Sultan, and enabled the artist to ask the favour of permission to return to Venice.

184

" THE MADONNA ENTHRONED, WITH SS. LIBERALE AND FRANCIS,"
BY GIORGIONE (1477–1510)

Castelfranco, Italy

This, according to Ruskin, is " one of the two most perfect pictures in existence ; alone in the world as an imaginative representation of Christianity, with a monk and a soldier on either side."

Giorgione was only twenty-seven years of age when he painted this picture, which proves how early his astounding genius developed.

of his mind he was afterwards known as Giorgione," that is to say, " Great George." Though of peasant origin, contemporaries say he was " well bred and polished all his life." He was of a loving disposition and exceedingly fond of the lute, " playing and singing divinely," and this love of music became the new note which Giorgione definitely contributed to art, for not only did he frequently introduce music as a subject in his pictures (e.g. " The Concert " at Dresden, and the man playing a mandolin in " The Golden Age " at the National Gallery, and the " Fête Champêtre " or Musical Party in the Louvre), but all his pictures, as Walter Pater wrote, " constantly aspire to the condition of music." By this it is meant that everything in a Giorgione is subordinated to beauty, and that his first concern is to create *melody* of line and *harmony* of colour.

The gentle nature of the artist, who found grace and loveliness in all men and all things, can be traced in every work of his that has survived the storms of time. In his great altar-piece, " Madonna Enthroned, with St. Liberale and St. Francis," for his native hill-town of Castelfranco, painted before he was thirty, Giorgione charms us alike by the rhythm and balance of the whole composition and by the lovableness of his types. The sweet simplicity of young womanhood in the Virgin, the naturalness of the Child, the knightliness of the soldier-saint Liberale, the welcoming gesture of the nature-loving Saint who could preach to birds and fishes and call them his brethren—all these things are manifest in the illustration of this beautiful picture.

It is a great misfortune that so many of Giorgione's paintings have been lost or destroyed in the course of centuries. Barely a score are known for certain to exist to-day, but among them are some of the most splendid portraits in the world. One of the finest examples of his power in portraiture is the " Unknown Man " in the Querini-Stampalia Collection at Venice. Another, his " Young Man " in the Berlin Gallery, is presented here.

Vasari tells us that Giorgione " did a picture of Christ bearing the Cross and a Jew dragging him along, which after a time was placed in the Church of St. Rocco, and now works miracles, as we see, through the devotion of the multitudes who visit it." We can form some idea of what the exceeding beauty of this painting must have been from the unforgettable head of " Christ Bearing the Cross," which still exists in the private collection of Mrs. Gardner, of Boston, U.S.A.

But, alas ! not a fragment has survived of the famous picture which Giorgione painted to prove the superiority of painting to sculpture. While Verrocchio was in Venice engaged upon the bronze horse of his splendid Colleone Monument, his admirers argued that sculpture, which presented so many aspects of a figure, was superior to painting. Giorgione maintained that a painting could show at a single glance all the aspects that a

"PORTRAIT OF A YOUNG MAN," BY GIORGIONE
Berlin Gallery

Here, according to the great Italian art critic Morelli, " we have one of those rare portraits such as only Giorgione, and occasionally Titian, were capable of producing, highly suggestive, and exercising over the spectator an irresistible fascination."

Note the mysterious " VV " on the parapet. These letters are found in other portraits by Giorgione, and Dr. G. C. Williamson has suggested that they probably indicate the artist's signature, since Giorgione's name was spelt as " Zorzon " or " Zorzi " da Castelfranco by contemporary writers, and in old MSS. the capital Z is frequently made like a V.

" CHRIST BEARING THE CROSS," BY GIORGIONE

Gardner Collection, Boston

The most beautiful conception of Christ in art, this painting (now in an American collection) is either a study for, or a fragment of, a lost picture by Giorgione. Formerly the picture hung in a church in Venice, where, according to the sixteenth-century historian Vasari, its haunting loveliness worked miracles of faith among the multitudes who came to see it.

188

"ADRASTUS AND HYPSIPYLE," BY GIORGIONE

Giovannelli Palace, Venice

Nominally an illustration of the Greek legend how King Adrastus found Queen Hypsipyle disguised as a nurse (after she had been driven out of Lemnos by a conspiracy), this picture is famous as the first expression in art of a stormy landscape. It is a supreme example of Giorgione's skill in pattern building : note how beautifully the broken columns, almost in the centre of the foreground, balance not only the figure of the Queen, but also the tall buildings beyond the bridge.

189

man can present, while sculpture can only do so if one walks about it, and thus he proved his contention :

"He painted a nude figure turning its shoulders ; at its feet was a limpid fount of water, the reflection from which showed the front. On one side was a burnished corselet, which had been taken off and gave a side view, because the shining metal reflected everything. On the other side was a mirror showing the other side of the figure."

The scarcity of Giorgione's work is partly explained by the fact that he died young. In 1510 he was deeply in love with a Venetian lady, who caught the plague, but "Giorgione, being ignorant of this, associated with her as usual, took the infection, and died soon after at the age of thirty-four, to the infinite grief of his friends, who loved him for his talents, and to the damage of the world which lost him."

XIV

THE SPLENDOUR OF VENICE

THE ART OF TITIAN, TINTORETTO, LOTTO, MORONI, AND PAUL VERONESE

§ I

WE never think of Titian as a young man; to all of us he is the Grand Old Man of Italian art, and there is something patriarchal in his figure. He was, indeed, very old when he died. Some would make out that he lived to be ninety-nine, but there is considerable doubt whether he was really as old as he pretended to be. The National Gallery catalogue queries 1477 as the year of Titian's birth, but few modern historians consider this to be accurate. The date 1477 is only given by the artist in a begging letter to King Philip of Spain, when it was to Titian's advantage to make himself out to be older than he was, because he was trying to squeeze money out of a rather tight-fisted monarch on the score of his great age.

Vasari and other contemporary writers give 1489 as the date of birth, but probably the nearest approach to the truth is given in a letter (dated December 8, 1567) from the Spanish Consul in Venice (Thomas de Cornoca), which fixes the year of Titian's birth as 1482. This would make Titian to have been ninety-four when he died.

Whether Titian lived to be ninety-four or, as Sir Herbert Cook thinks, only eighty-nine, is a small matter compared to the greater fact that he was born in the hill-town of Cadore on a spur of the Alps, and spent his boy-hood amid solemn pine-woods and Alpine solitudes. Breathing the keen mountain air, he grew up a young Hercules, deep-chested, his features " sun-browned as if cast in bronze," his eyes clear, with an eagle glance bred of Alpine distances.

So the young Titian (Tiziano Vecellio) came to Venice, a hardy mountaineer among the children of the plain, and all his art bears the impress of his origin. What we call the idealism of Titian is not the result of æsthetic reflection, but, as Muther has pointed out, " the natural point of view of a man who wandered upon the heights of life, never knew trivial care, nor even experienced sickness ; and therefore saw the world healthy and beautiful, in gleaming and majestic splendour."

191

By the early death of Giorgione in 1510, Titian was left without a rival in his own generation, and six years later (1516), when Bellini died, Titian was elected to succeed him as the official painter of Venice. Thenceforward his career was a royal progress. " All princes, learned men, and distinguished persons who came to Venice visited Titian," says Vasari, for " not only in his art was he great, but he was a nobleman in person." He lived in a splendid palace, where he received Royalty, and was able to give his beautiful daughter and his two sons every conceivable luxury, for Titian, says Vasari, " gained a fair amount of wealth, his labours having always been well paid."

Of the dramatic quality in Titian's art we have a splendid instance at the National Gallery in the " Bacchus and Ariadne," which, painted about 1520, is also a famous example of Venetian colour. Nobody before had ever given so dramatic and impassioned a rendering of Bacchus, the God of Wine, leaping from his chariot to console and cherish Ariadne, the beautiful maiden forsaken by her false lover Theseus. There is not only action in the drawing, in the spirited rendering of movement, but there is life also in the colour ; the amber, ruby, and sapphire of the flowing draperies sparkle, quiver, and radiate.

Whence came these qualities so new to Venetian painting ? They came from the great painter's memories of his birth-place, his boyhood's home beside the River Piave roaring down from storm-capped heights, from memories of the wind that swept through the tree-tops and rattled the rafters of the house. Familiar from childhood with the awe-inspiring, dramatic elements of Nature, Titian expressed her majesty and drama in his art.

Amid the wealth of pictorial beauty left by Titian it is difficult indeed to say which is his supreme masterpiece. According to Vasari, Titian's " Assumption of the Virgin " was held by his fellow-citizens to be " the best modern painting," and though it is no longer modern but an " old master," we cannot conceive a more impressive rendering of the subject than this picture, in which we almost hear the wind caused by the soaring ascent of the Virgin, her garments grandly swelling in the breeze by which the encircling cherubs waft her upwards.

Yet to this great painting of his mature years (1541) at least one of his earlier pictures is equal in beauty. To the transitional period in Titian's life, while the direct influence of Giorgione yet lingered, belongs the picture in the Borghese Gallery, Rome, known as " Sacred and Profane Love." But the title is only a makeshift. Nobody knows the true meaning of this picture of two lovely women, one lightly draped, the other in the full splendour of Venetian dress, seated on either side of a well in the midst of a smiling landscape. There is a tradition that the one represents " Heavenly

"JOHANN FRIEDRICH, ELECTOR OF SAXONY," BY TITIAN (*c.* 1482–1576)

Vienna Museum

Out of the most simple elements and with a subject which has little immediate attraction Titian builds this portrait, depending on the monumentality of his design to convey the personality of his sitter. Its absolute simplicity forces us to look at the perfect drawing of the face and hands.

" SACRED AND PROFANE LOVE " (DETAIL), BY TITIAN

Borghese Gallery, Rome

According to tradition, this figure is supposed to typify " Earthly Love," and the one opposite " Heavenly Love " ; but since in the picture these two women are seated on either side of a well, others have interpreted them as Grace and Truth.

Anderson.

"SACRED AND PROFANE LOVE" (DETAIL), BY TITIAN

Borghese Gallery, Rome

Various conjectures have been made as to the meaning of these figures, but the world is content to accept them as supreme examples of Titian's conception of feminine beauty.

"THE MAGDALEN," BY TITIAN

Pitti Gallery, Florence

" This picture most beautiful, moves all who behold it to compassion," writes Vasari, a contemporary of Titian. " The eyes are fixed on Heaven, their redness and the tears still within them giving evidence of her sorrow for the sins of her past life."

196

Love," the other " Earthly Love," but on the other hand a passage in Vasari about another painting by Titian, now lost, gives countenance to the theory that these figures are personifications of Grace and Beauty, or more probably Grace and Truth. A third theory is that the picture illustrates a passage in some lost poem.

Titian's ideal of womanhood is seen not only in this picture but in a number of exquisite portraits and figure paintings. According to Vasari, he painted mostly from his own imagination, and only used female models in case of necessity. Titian's types have little in common with the small, brown, black-eyed maidens we usually associate with Venice. They are nearer akin to the fair-haired Lombard women or the Dianas and Junos of his Alpine home. Further, it is the proud majesty of the mature woman that Titian paints. His beautiful " Flora," in the Uffizi Gallery, Florence, does not suggest springtime but, as Muther has well said, " high summer in its rich, mature splendour." Never old, but never very young, Titian's " mighty women " seem to " beam in an eternal, powerful beauty."

The same mature majesty characterises " The Magdalen," to which Titian's contemporary Vasari pays the following eloquent tribute : " Her hair falls about her neck and shoulders, her head is raised, and the eyes are fixed on Heaven, their redness and the tears still within them giving evidence of her sorrow for the sins of her past life. This picture, which is most beautiful, moves all who behold it to compassion."

" He touched nothing that he did not adorn." So it might be written of Titian, who ennobled all his sitters with something of his own majesty. The supreme example of his powers in this direction is the magnificent " Equestrian Portrait of Charles V," now in the Prado at Madrid. In 1530, when the Emperor Charles V was in Bologna, Titian, by the intervention of his friend the poet Pierto Aretino, was invited to that city and commissioned to paint His Catholic Majesty in full armour. Vasari tells us the Emperor was so delighted with this portrait that he gave the artist a thousand gold crowns, declaring that he would never have his portrait done by any other painter ; and he kept his imperial word, frequently employing Titian thereafter and always paying him a thousand crowns for each portrait.

Never was money better spent. This Emperor of the Holy Roman Empire and King of Spain still fires our imagination, thanks to Titian. The historical truth about Charles V is that he was a pale, scrofulous, emaciated man, a prey to melancholy, full of hesitations and superstitious fears ; so world-weary that in the end he abdicated from his imperial position, and shut himself up in a monastery where, with morbid satisfaction, surrounded by coffins and ticking clocks, he constantly rehearsed his own funeral. Titian shows us nothing of this. His wonderful imagination

" CHARLES V," BY TITIAN
Prado, Madrid

" The personification of the coldness of a great general in battle, and of Destiny itself approaching, silent and unavoidable " : this is what the genius of Titian has made of this portrait. Charles V was both King of Spain and Emperor of the Holy Roman Empire.

Titian has seized on one great moment in this monarch's life and pictured him riding at daybreak over the plain of Augsburg just before the battle in which his troops were victorious.

198

THE ASSUMPTION OF THE VIRGIN," BY TITIAN

Church of the Frari, Venice

Titian's dramatic imagination, rich and powerful both in portraiture and in allegorical decorations for palaces, is here seen applied with equal genius and deep feeling to the rendering of a religious subject.

This picture, formerly in the Academy, Venice, but now restored to its original position in the Church of the Frari at Venice, was thought by Titian's contemporaries to be " the best modern painting."

fastens on one great moment in the Emperor's life, the day when he was the victor at Augsburg. A Black Knight in steel armour, riding over the battlefield at daybreak, the Emperor in this painting becomes " the personification of the coldness of a great general in battle, and of Destiny itself approaching, silent and unavoidable." Charles is here Napoleonic—but Napoleon had no Titian to immortalise his grandeur. Who would not pay a thousand crowns to be so transfigured for posterity ?

Still painting in his ninetieth year with unabated vigour, still able as a nonagenarian to play the host with undiminished magnificence to King Henry III of France, this grand old patriarch finally went down in 1576, like some battered but indomitable man-of-war, with his colours still proudly flying. Even then it was not of old age that he died ; he was a victim to the same pestilence which, sixty-six years earlier, had carried off his young fellow-pupil Giorgione. All Venice went into mourning when the greatest of her sons passed away, and the Senate set aside the decree that excluded victims of the plague from burial within church walls, so that Titian might be laid to rest in the Church of the Frari, within sight of his own picture of " The Assumption."

§ 2

The glowing mantle of Titian fell on the shoulders of Jacopo Robusti, nicknamed Tintoretto (the " Little Dyer ") from the calling of his father, Battista Robusti, who was a dyer, in Italian *tintore*. Tintoretto was born at Venice in 1518 and, having shown his precocious genius by covering the walls of his father's house with drawings and sketches, he was apprenticed as a pupil to Titian. Despite his prodigious capacity, for already the skill and speed of his workmanship were astonishing, he was not a satisfactory pupil. After some time Titian dismissed him, according to one account because he was jealous of his pupil, according to another because Tintoretto " would in no wise give obedience to commands." From all we know of Tintoretto's proud, wilful character the latter reason seems probable.

Left to himself, Tintoretto set up his own workshop, in which he nailed up the legend " The Design of Michael Angelo and the Colouring of Titian." Not only did he live up to his motto as regards his drawing and colour, but to these he added his own supreme understanding of light and shade ; and thus he was able to surpass Titian in the keenness of his literal yet romantic observation, and to outdo even Michael Angelo himself in the furious speed and energy of his execution. Amazing stories are told of Tintoretto's activity. " This artist," remarks his contemporary, Vasari, " always contrives by the most singular proceedings in the world to be constantly employed, seeing that when the good offices of his friends and other methods have failed to procure him any work of which there is question, he will nevertheless manage to obtain it, either by accepting it at a very low price, by doing it as a gift, or even by seizing on it by force."

An instance of this kind occurred when the Brotherhood of San Rocco decided to have the ceiling of their refectory painted with decorations. The four leading painters of Venice—Zucchero, Salviati, Veronese, and Tintoretto—were summoned to San Rocco and invited to submit designs for the project. It was announced that the commission would be given to the artist who produced the best design. "But while the other artists were giving themselves with all diligence to the preparation of their designs, Tintoretto made an exact measurement of the space for which the picture was required, and taking a large canvas, he painted it without saying a word to anyone and, with his usual celerity, put it up in the place destined to receive it.

"One morning, therefore, when the Brotherhood had assembled to see the designs and to determine the matter, they found that Tintoretto had entirely completed the work, nay, that he had fixed it in its place."

Naturally the three other artists were furious, and the head of the Brotherhood angrily inquired why Tintoretto had taken it on himself to complete the work when he had only been asked to submit a design in an open competition.

"This is my method of preparing designs," answered Tintoretto ; "I do not know how to make them in any other manner. All designs and models for a work should be executed in this fashion, to the end that the persons interested may see what it is intended to offer them, and may not be deceived.

"If you do not think it proper to pay for the work and remunerate me for my pains, then," the artist proudly added, "I will make you a present of it."

Thus, as Vasari relates, Tintoretto, "though not without opposition, contrived so to manage matters that the picture still retains its place."

Though he painted numerous portraits and altar-pieces, Tintoretto was essentially a decorative painter, and his mightiest achievements are on the walls and ceilings of the palaces and public buildings of Venice. His "Paradiso" in the Ducal Palace is the largest painting in the world, eighty-four feet wide by thirty-four feet high, and of this stupendous achievement and of most of his other great works no photograph can give any adequate idea. For this reason no attempt to reproduce them is made here. But fortunately the picture which is universally acknowledged to be Tintoretto's masterpiece is not on the same colossal scale. "The Miracle of St. Mark" is one of four large pictures painted by Tintoretto for the School of San Marco in Venice. It represents the Evangelist—who was the Patron Saint

"THE MIRACLE OF ST. MARK," BY TINTORETTO (1518–94)

Academy, Venice

Tintoretto, the most famous pupil of Titian, illustrates in his dramatic picture the legend of how St. Mark, the patron saint of Venice, rescued a Christian slave from Pagan torturers.

of Venice—appearing in the air and " delivering a man who was his votary from grievous torments, which an executioner is seen to be preparing for him : the irons which the tormentors are endeavouring to apply break short in their hands, and cannot be turned against that devout man."

The dramatic element in Titian's work is seen heightened and intensified in many of Tintoretto's paintings, but nowhere is it more splendidly manifest than in this impressive imagining of a supernatural event. Again we seem to hear the rush of air caused by the downward sweep of the Saint, from whom a celestial light irradiates. This great picture is not only an illustration of a saintly legend ; it had a symbolical meaning of great importance to Tintoretto's contemporaries. At this time political relations between Venice and Rome were strained. The Patriarch and Senate of Venice flattered themselves they were better Christians than the Romans, and were delighted to see in Tintoretto's masterpiece a picture in which they saw the Popes as the executioners of the Church, which is to be saved only by the fortunate interference of the Republic of St. Mark.

When Tintoretto died in 1594 there were no more great religious painters in Italy. Unlike Titian, who " had never received from Heaven aught but favour and felicity," and so throughout a long life looked out with ever joyous eyes, Tintoretto, notwithstanding his professional prosperity, was overshadowed by a spiritual gloom which finds expression in his mighty pictures. The works of his manhood and maturity show little of that serene joy in existence which glows from the canvases of Titian ; but in the fitful lighting of their sombre depths, in a constantly recurring hint of tragedy, they reveal a consciousness of stormy days to come, of perils for Church and State, which entitle us to see in Tintoretto a harbinger of the Reformation and the wars of religion.

§ 3

Working side by side first with Titian, afterwards with Tintoretto, was Paolo Cagliari, who, from Verona, the city of his birth, was known as Paul Veronese (1528–88). The whole splendour of Venice is revealed in his paintings, and his decorations in the Ducal Palace give immortality to the pageantry which characterised the Italy of his time.

When the Venetian Senate gave a festival in honour of King Henry III of France, the monarch was received (so history tells us) by two hundred of the fairest damsels in the city, dressed in white and covered with pearls and diamonds, " so that the King thought he had suddenly entered a realm of goddesses and fairies."

This is the realm we enter through a canvas by Veronese, whether his subject be professedly historical, as in " The Family of Darius before

"THE MARRIAGE AT CANA," BY PAUL VERONESE (1528–88)

Dresden Gallery

The luxurious pomp of a Venetian banquet is shown in this sixteenth-century painting, which is far removed from the simple piety of the earlier Italian masters. Veronese, whose opulent sense of colour and splendid design made him one of the great decorative painters of his day, was rebuked by the Inquisition for his worldly rendering of sacred subjects.

Alexander " in the National Gallery, or professedly religious, as in " The Marriage at Cana " at Dresden. We have only to look at this painting with all its worldly pomp and ostentatious luxury to see how far art has travelled from the simple piety of the earlier Primitive Masters.

The monasteries were the chief employers of Veronese, as the eminent critic Berenson has pointed out : " His cheerfulness, and his frank and joyous worldliness—the qualities, in short, which we find in his huge pictures of feasts—seem to have been particularly welcome to those who were expected to make their meat and drink of the very opposite qualities. This is no small comment on the times, and shows how thorough had been the permeation of the spirit of the Renaissance when even the religious orders gave up their pretence to asceticism and piety."

A time came, however, when Veronese went too far even for the depraved ecclesiastics of his day. When he painted " The Last Supper "— now in the Louvre—in the style of " The Marriage at Cana," with the same glitter of crystal, silver, and jewels, the same sheen of silks and satins, the same multitude of serving men and attendants, the stricter clerics were scandalised. Information was laid against the painter, and on July 18, 1573, Paul Veronese was summoned before the tribunal of the Inquisition.

Exactly what happened then is not clearly known : while escaping banishment or severer punishment, the artist was sternly rebuked for his worldly treatment of religious subjects ; and though the reprimand appears to have had little permanent effect on his paintings, it is significant to note that his " Adoration of the Magi " in the National Gallery, which is dated 1573, is both in conception and in execution far more simple and respectful than are the majority of Veronese's pictures of sacred subjects.

The most beautiful picture by Veronese in the National Gallery, and one of the most haunting of all his works, is " St. Helena's Vision of the Cross," which is as reposeful as a piece of antique Greek sculpture and a superbly decorative example of the artist's skill as a maker of patterns. The curious will note in this work how cunningly the painter has arranged the figure to secure decorative balance and rhythm, how the right leg continuing the line of the forearm repeats the diagonal of the cross, while the sharp horizontal of the cherub's wing repeats the line of the window sill. In these devices we recognise the hand of a master-craftsman.

§ 4

A greater than Veronese remains to be mentioned, a painter who was not only a consummate craftsman but also a profound thinker. This was Lorenzo Lotto (1480–1556) who, unlike his great contemporaries, was Venetian born. All the others—save Tintoretto, greatly his junior—came

" ST. HELENA'S VISION OF THE CROSS," BY PAUL VERONESE

National Gallery, London

Reposeful as a piece of antique Greek sculpture, this beautiful painting is also an illuminating example of the artist's skill in pattern-making. Note how the very angle of the Cross, seen by the Saint in her vision, is so arranged as to repeat the lines of her forearm and skirt, thus securing a symmetry which completes the rhythm and decorative aspect of the whole picture.

from the mainland : Giorgione from Castelfranco, Titian from Cadore and Cagliari from Verona.

Few painters have lived so intense a life in the spirit as Lotto ; none has written so plainly as he his soul-history in his works. A true son of Venice, his youthful mind turned to Byzantium rather than to Rome for instruction and inspiration. To him Giorgione and Titian appeared as foreign intruders ; their worldliness shocked him, a follower of Savonarola. Lotto began by putting the Madonna back on a Byzantine throne in the apse of the church from which the painters of the Renaissance had taken her. Ploughing his lonely furrow at Venice he had his doubts, and in 1508 he journeyed south to see what Rome and Raphael had to teach him. What he saw there roused his reforming zeal, as it had that of Savonarola. Four years later (1512) he fled from metropolitan sinfulness and took refuge in the provincial tranquillity of Bergamo.

Here he possessed his soul in peace, and as though touched by the spirit of St. Francis he became reconciled to Nature. No longer is the Madonna enthroned in church, but placed in the open country, where all existing things seem to praise the Creator in their beauty. Lotto became a pantheist and his message is the gospel of love. With his Venetian predecessors and contemporaries the Virgin is either soulful and humble, or aristocratic and proud ; Lotto paints her richly adorned, but imbues her countenance with a beneficent and tenderly maternal expression.

In portraiture Lotto is supreme even in a great epoch. When we look at his portrait in the National Gallery of " The Protonotary Apostolic Juliano," noting through the window the wide and boundless landscape traversed by a river which winds its way to the distant sea, noting also the exquisite Flemish-like painting of the still-life accessories, as well as the grave penetrating characterisation of the man, we cannot agree with Muther that Lotto regards his sitters " unconcerned with their decorative appearance " ; but we do heartily agree that Lotto shows us people " in their hours of introspection."

Why is it that Lotto, as a portrait-painter, strikes chords which, as Muther says, " are echoed in no other Italian work " ? The explanation is this : " Only those whom he loved and honoured were invited into his studio, and this circumstance alone differentiates his portraits from those of Raphael or Titian."

Though never such a great figure in his day as Giorgione, Titian, or Tintoretto, Lotto was not without influence on his contemporaries. One who felt it and gained by it greatly was a painter who came from Brescia to Venice, Giambattista Moroni (c. 1520–78). His " Portrait of a Tailor " is full of human sympathy and almost perfect in craftsmanship. It is deservedly one of the most popular portraits in the National Gallery, and

"THE PROTONOTARY APOSTOLIC JULIANO," BY LORENZO LOTTO (1480–1556)

National Gallery, London

" He looks out from his canvas as if begging for sympathy." So a modern American critic has written of this noble and dignified portrait by the most spiritual of all the great Venetian masters of the sixteenth century. Lotto was remarkable for his pious conservatism, and would undertake the portraiture of no person unless he respected his character.

many of us feel almost equally drawn to Moroni's other great portrait at the National Gallery, " An Italian Nobleman." Together they prove that, like Lotto, Moroni could extend his sympathies to sitters irrespective of their rank or position in life.

It is not easy to over-estimate the abundant excellence of portraiture in sixteenth-century Venice. Just as the wealth and power of her merchant-citizens were the source of the success of the republican State of Venice, so the luxury they were able to afford drew to the island-city of the Adriatic all the artistic talent born on the neighbouring mainland. Of the multitude of artists who during this century were adorning the public buildings and private palaces of Venice, only a few of the most celebrated can here be enumerated. Cima came from Conegliano to Venice in 1492, and worked there till 1516 or later, carrying on in his Madonna the tradition of Giovanni Bellini. Vincenzo di Biagio, known as Catena, was born at Treviso about 1470 and died at Venice in 1531. He was greatly influenced by Giorgione, to whom was once ascribed the beautiful painting " A Warrior adoring the Infant Christ," which the National Gallery catalogue now gives definitely to Catena. Sebastiano del Piombo (c. 1485–1547), who about 1510 left Venice for Rome, where he was influenced by Raphael and Michael Angelo, has a special interest for us because his picture " The Raising of Lazarus " was the beginning of the National Gallery collection. It is still " Number 1." Palma Vecchio (1480–1528) was born near Bergamo, but came to Venice while still a student. Influenced first by Bellini and Giorgione, afterwards by Titian and Lotto, he very nearly reached the first rank, as his " Venus and Cupid," now in the Fitzwilliam Museum at Cambridge, amply proves. He is called Vecchio (= Old) to distinguish him from a later painter Palma Giovine (1544–1628) or Young Palma.

Jacopo da Ponte (1510–92), called Bassano from his birthplace, is also splendidly represented in the National Gallery by " The Good Samaritan," a painting which used to belong to Sir Joshua Reynolds. It is a magnificent example of vigour and muscular action.

In the art, as in the State of Venice, the spark of life lingered long.

This eighteenth-century Venetian Art certainly has its own charm. Canaletto (1697–1768) is one of the finest of painters of city scenes, depicted for the sake of showing the whole layout of the buildings in their setting. He worked in Venice, Rome, and for a good period in England, where he painted some of the very finest views of eighteenth-century London, such as that of the City from Richmond House. His sweeping views painstakingly present every building, the gracious life of the time, and withal the beauty of the sunlit ambient air.

Longhi (1702–85) and Guardi (1712–93) both painted the colourful life and the Venetian scene of their day. Their genre subjects are often

"THE TAILOR," BY GIAMBATTISTA MORONI (c. 1520–1578)

National Gallery, London

"A man's a man for a' that." Heralding the birth of democracy in art and the coming of a time when artists, no longer employed by nobles, could find nobility in the features of working-men, this picture is one of the world's great portraits and a splendid example of Venetian colour before its decadence.

"ITALIAN NOBLEMAN," BY GIAMBATTISTA MORONI

National Gallery, London

All things to all men, Moroni, the most accomplished disciple of Lorenzo Lotto, could depict an Italian nobleman with the same sympathetic skill and dignity that have made his "Portrait of a Tailor" one of the world-masterpieces of portraiture.

211

very charming, and tell us much of the costume and life of the period and its love of carnival.

Giambattista Tiepolo (1696–1770), painting in the tradition of Veronese, earned for himself the proud title " the last of the Old Masters." He was, indeed, the last of the great decorators, with an excellent sense of light and shade set in dramatic contrast and a courageous use of colour—delighting in pale blues and yellows which may have been derived from the newly fashionable love of chinese fabrics of his time. Fine examples of his work are on the ceilings of the Royal Palace at Madrid and in the Bishop's palace at Wurzburg, but the delightful little " Deposition " in our National Gallery will indicate the sensitive quality of his work on a smaller scale.

All this, however, was really a brilliant afterglow. With Tintoretto the last word of Italy had really been spoken, and when he died in 1594 it was left for the artists of other lands to take up the tale of European painting.

XV

THE DAWN OF THE REFORMATION

THE ART OF ALBERT DURER AND OF HOLBEIN THE YOUNGER

§ 1

SO far we have been following mainly the development of art in Italy, but that country had no monopoly of painting and sculpture during the Middle Ages. It was shown in the Tenth Chapter of this OUTLINE how a band of painters flourished on the banks of the Rhine during the fourteenth century.

Ever since the time of the Van Eycks paintings had been produced by natives of most of the great countries of Europe—even in England, where Odo the Goldsmith was employed by King Henry III to execute wall-paintings for the Palace of Westminster—but either because their work was not powerful enough to capture the imagination of Europe or, quite as probably, because they had no historians and biographers to trumpet their praises, the early artists of England, France, and Germany never acquired the fame won by their brethren of Italy and Flanders. With few exceptions their names, and in many cases their works, have been entirely lost.

> Full many a flower is born to blush unseen,
> And waste its sweetness on the desert air.

When all has been said, however, the fact remains that Italy was the centre of the world for mediæval Europe, and to it came all who were desirous of learning, culture, and advancement. In those times the painter born elsewhere made his way to Italy as naturally and inevitably as the artist of to-day makes his pilgrimage to Paris ; and in Italy the stranger artist was treated, not as a foreigner, but as a provincial. Looking at the political divisions of Europe to-day, we are apt to forget that in the Middle Ages the Christian nations of Europe were considered to be one family. Just as the Pope of Rome was the religious Head of all Christendom, so in theory, if not in practice, its secular Head was the Emperor of the Holy Roman Empire. The capital of the Empire, again in theory, was Rome, though in practice the Emperor was usually not very safe outside his own kingdom in Germany.

When the Italian historian Vasari describes the great German artist Albert Durer as a " Fleming," he is making the same sort of mistake that a Londoner might make when he was uncertain whether a west-countryman came from Devon or Cornwall ; and just as some Londoners are so narrow-minded that they cannot imagine any pre-eminent greatness outside the Metropolis, so Vasari in a patronising way wrote of Durer :

> Had this man, so nobly endowed by Nature, so assiduous and possessed of so many talents, been a native of Tuscany instead of Flanders, had he been able to study the treasures of Rome and Florence as we have done, he would have excelled us all, as he is now the best and most esteemed among his own countrymen.

If Vasari thought this talented man had much to learn from Italy, there were Italian artists who thought they had something to learn from Durer. Giovanni Bellini, whose art has been described in Chapter XIII, greatly admired Durer's painting, and found his rendering of hair so marvellous that he thought the artist must have a special brush for the purpose. So when Durer visited Venice and in his polite way offered to do anything in his power for Venetian artists, Bellini begged to be given the brush with which he painted hairs. Durer picked up a handful of his brushes and told Bellini to choose any one he wished. "I mean the brush with which you draw several hairs with one stroke," the Venetian explained. Durer smiled and replied, "I use no other than these, and to prove it you may watch me." Then, taking up one of the same brushes, he drew " some very long wavy tresses, such as women generally wear." Bellini looked on wonderingly, and afterwards confessed that had he not seen it nothing would have convinced him that such painting was possible.

Who was this Durer ? Strangely enough, the artist who most fully revealed the spirit of awakening Germany was of Hungarian descent. His father, Albert Durer the Elder—whose portrait by his son hangs in the National Gallery, London—was born in Hungary. After travelling in the Netherlands for some time, he finally settled in Nuremberg, where his son was born on May 21, 1471. Albert the Younger had everything to foster the development of his gifts, his father was a goldsmith, and his grandfather also ; hence their removal to Nuremberg, a city which was in constant communication with Venice and had already begun to rival it in the arts and crafts of jewellery and metalwork. It is worth noticing that young Albert's godfather was the bookseller and expert printer, Anton Koberger, and through him his godson probably became familiar with fine prints and engravings from his earliest years.

The father intended the son to succeed him in his craft, but as the latter tells us in his memoirs, " I was more inclined to painting, and this I confessed to my father. My father was not pleased," he adds with characteristic

" PORTRAIT OF THE PAINTER WHEN YOUNG," BY ALBERT DURER (1471–1528)
Prado, Madrid

Painted when the artist was only twenty-seven, this beautiful portrait of himself shows the mature precision of a master in every detail.   Note the wonderful painting of the long wavy tresses, a feat which caused the Venetian artist Bellini to believe Durer had a special brush for painting hair.

215

LANDSCAPE DETAIL (FROM "THE RAPE OF AMYONE"), BY ALBERT DURER

Durer's love of Nature which found expression in his delicate yet vigorous drawing of trees, shrubs and clouds, is seen in this landscape.

216

simplicity. Nevertheless young Durer got his way, and in 1486 was apprenticed to Michael Wohlgemut, a local artist then at the zenith of his fame. Wohlgemut had a large art school, which was the most important in Nuremberg, and here young Durer learnt to paint and also, possibly, to practise wood-engraving. But such a master had little to teach so brilliant a pupil, and after three years Durer the Elder wisely took his son away and sent him abroad for four years. Young Albert travelled in the south of Germany and probably paid his first visit to Venice during this period.

Returning to Nuremberg in 1494, Albert Durer—as we shall henceforth call him—married almost immediately Agnes Frei, daughter of a respected citizen. The young artist already had some reputation : in 1497 he painted the portrait of his father, and in the following year the splendid portrait of himself which we reproduce. This comparatively early work, now at Madrid, shows all the characteristics of his later portraits ; it has a simple dignity almost amounting to austerity, remarkable penetration into character, and in execution it shows perfect mastery of drawing and colouring.

In 1498 Albert Durer published a series of wood-engravings illustrating the Apocalypse, which greatly increased his reputation, for in these he was able to show not only the perfection of his drawing and design, but also the extraordinary power of his imagination. No design in this series is more famous than " The Four Horsemen of the Apocalypse."

And I saw, and behold a white horse : and he that sat thereon had a bow : and there was given unto him a crown : and he came forth conquering and to conquer. . . . And another horse came forth, a red horse : and to him that sat thereon it was given to take peace from the earth, and that they should slay one another : and there was given to him a great sword. . . . And I saw, and behold a black horse ; and he that sat thereon had a balance in his hand. And I heard as it were a voice saying, A measure of wheat for a penny . . . and behold a pale horse ; and he that sat upon him, his name was Death.

These are the verses from Revelation (vi. 2–8) which Durer set himself to illustrate ; and since it was executed in a period just previous to the Reformation, some critics have argued that its inner meaning is an attack on the Papacy. It is improbable, however, that Durer was at this time in any way actuated by religious bias ; the series as a whole certainly attacks corruption, both lay and ecclesiastical, but in this woodcut it is more likely that Durer confined himself strictly to his text. The Holy Roman Empire was in a chronic state of war, and Durer must have seen enough of fighting in his youth and early manhood to know who and what were the grim companions of conquest. The meaning of this magnificent rushing design is clear ; it reveals Durer's view of War, war which sweeps mercilessly

"THE FOUR HORSEMEN OF THE APOCALYPSE"

From a Wood-Engraving by Albert Durer

The four riders are Conquest, aiming afar with his arrow : War, with a drawn sword : Famine : and Death. Note the original conception of the third rider, whose rich costume and well-nourished body betray Durer's opinion of the War-Profiteer who fattens himself on the famine of others.

The most wonderful work of art ever inspired by the Book of Revelation (vi. 2–8), this magnificent design displays Durer's inventiveness as a decorative craftsman and the power and originality of his imagination. In our own day it has a peculiar fascination as revealing an Old Master's view of war.

on, sparing neither man nor woman, priest nor layman, and inevitably accompanied by Famine, Pestilence, and Death. The most subtle touch of satire is the third rider with the balances. In portraying Famine as this sleek, well-nourished, handsomely clothed man, Durer seems to hint that he is not ignorant of the existence of the War-Profiteer. The emaciated horse and its rider by his side tell their own tale.

It was by his engravings still more than by his paintings that Durer became famous, for the prints spread throughout Europe and created a great sensation. But though invited to become a citizen of Venice or Antwerp by these municipalities, Durer remained loyal to his native city. He continued to reside in Nuremberg. After his father's death in 1502 his responsibilities increased, for now in addition to his own family Albert had to look after his mother and his younger brother Hans.

When commissions for portraits and altar-pieces were not forthcoming, Durer's wife used to hawk at fairs and gatherings her husband's prints illustrating episodes in the life of the Holy Family, and these wood and copper engravings not only brought in ready money by satisfying a popular demand, but they were the foundation of the artist's reputation as an engraver. The success of these separate prints was immediate, and soon after the publication of the Apocalypse prints, Durer set to work on other sets of engravings, one of which was to illustrate the Passion of Our Lord and another the Life of the Virgin.

At the instigation and by the kindness of his friend, Wilibald Pirkheimer, who lent him the money for the journey, Durer in 1506 paid a visit to Venice, where he was commissioned by the German merchants to paint a panel for their chapel. At first the painters of Venice were inclined to regard Albert Durer as a mere engraver who did not understand how to use colour, but the completion of this panel soon silenced hostile criticism and the work proved to be a veritable triumph for the painter.

In a letter to his friend Pirkheimer, Durer relates how the Doge and the Patriarch of Venice came to see his picture, and still more interesting is his account of how the veteran Venetian painter Giovanni Bellini praised the picture in public and further proved his admiration for the work of the Northern painter. Bellini, Durer wrote, " wanted to have something of mine, and himself came and asked me to paint him something and he would pay well for it. All men tell me what an upright man he is, so that I am really friendly with him. He is very old, but is still the best painter of them all." It was at this time that the incident about the paint-brush already narrated occurred.

Altogether this visit to Venice was a success. It definitely established Durer's reputation as a painter, his small panels sold well, and later he went to Bologna, where he received a great ovation ; but even the flattery of a

"THE GREAT FORTUNE," BY ALBERT DURER

No work has roused more controversy than this famous design, in which Durer imaginatively shows "Fortune" or "Nemesis" with bridles in her left hand to curb the "mad designs" of the proud.

If we are unable to admire the "goddess," we can all see the beauty of the landscape beneath, and viewed from a distance or reversed the rhythmical disposition of the black and white in this engraving makes it stand out as a fascinating pattern.

Bolognese who declared he could " die happy " now he had seen Durer did not turn the artist's head, and he returned to Nuremberg the same modest, conscientious artist he had always been.

The succeeding years were very fertile in paintings, his principal productions being the " Crucifixion," now at Dresden, the " Adam " and " Eve," in which he tried to give his ideal of beauty of form, and the important altar-piece which he painted for the Frankfort merchant Jacob Heiler.

But the artist still found that painting did not bring him in so much profit as engraving, and after he had completed his great " Adoration of the Trinity " in 1511 he gave most of his time to engraving, continuing the first " Passion " series and the " Life of the Virgin." It was after the death of his mother in 1514 that he produced his famous print " Melancholia," a composition full of curious symbolism in which a seated female figure is shown brooding on the tragedies of existence.

Equally famous and still more difficult wholly to understand is the copper engraving known as " The Great Fortune " or " Nemesis." It is supposed that this engraving was suggested by a passage in Poliziano's Latin poem, which may be thus translated :

There is a goddess who, aloft in the empty air, advances girdled about with a cloud. . . . She it is who crushes extravagant hopes, who threatens the proud, to whom is given to beat down the haughty spirit and the haughty step, and to confound over-great possessions. Her the men of old called Nemesis. . . . In her hand she bears bridles and a chalice, and smiles for ever with an awful smile, and stands resisting mad designs.

No work has aroused more controversy than this design ; some have regarded it as a splendid rendering of the physical attributes of mature womanhood, but others have pronounced the ugliness of the figure to be " perfectly repulsive," while others again have found it hard to reconcile the extreme realism of the woman's form with the fanciful imagination shown in her environment.

But however many opinions there may be as to the success of this engraving as an *illustration*, there is only one view about its merit as a *decoration*. T. Sturge Moore, himself an expert and gifted engraver, has well emphasised this point by reminding the readers of his book on Durer " that it is an engraving and not a woman that we are discussing : and that this engraving is extremely beautiful in arabesque and black and white pattern, rich, rhythmical, and harmonious." If the experiment be made of turning the print upside down, so that attention is no longer concentrated on its meaning as an illustration, its extraordinary ingenuity and interest *as a pattern* will at once become apparent.

In 1518 Durer again resumed his activity as a painter : in that year he was summoned by the Emperor Maximilian to Augsburg, where he was employed in painting portraits of the emperor and of many of his nobles. In 1521 he visited the Netherlands and received much attention in Brussels and Antwerp ; though he drew and painted several portraits during his travels, he took up engraving again when he returned to Nuremberg. The series he then began is known as the " Second Passion " ; this set he did not live to complete. He died in 1528. Two years earlier he painted his celebrated " Four Apostles," which have a peculiar interest not only as Durer's last effort in picture-making, but also as an indication of the artist's attitude towards the Reformation.

It was in 1517 that Martin Luther sounded the tocsin for the Reformation by nailing his ninety-five theses on the nature of papal indulgences to the great door of the Church of Wittemberg. It was in the following year that Durer received kindness and attention from his imperial patron, the Catholic prince Maximilian I. The artist was in a difficult position, but though he took no definite side in the great controversy which ensued, his sympathy with the Reformers is shown in this picture by the fact that each of the four Apostles is holding and studying a Bible. It is significant to note that this painting was not a commission, but was painted by Durer to please himself and for presentation to the city of his birth. Here is the letter which accompanied the gift to the Council of Nuremberg :

Prudent, honourable, wise, dear Masters, I have been intending, for a long time past, to show my respect for your Wisdoms by the presentation of some humble picture of mine as a remembrance, but I have been prevented from so doing by the imperfection and insignificance of my works, for I felt that with such I could not stand well before your Wisdoms. Now, however, that I have just painted a panel upon which I have bestowed more trouble than on any other painting, I considered none more worthy to keep it as a remembrance than your Wisdoms.

Therefore, I present it to your Wisdoms with the humble and urgent prayer that you will favourably and graciously receive it, and will be and continue, as I have ever found you, my kind and dear Masters.

Thus shall I be diligent to serve your Wisdoms in all humility.

Possibly it was a remembrance of this picture in particular which prompted Luther, in his consolatory letter to the artist's friend Pirkheimer, to pen this memorable epitaph on Albert Durer :

It is well for a pious man to mourn the best of men, but you should call him happy, for Christ illuminated him and called him away in a good hour from the tempests and, possibly, yet more stormy times : so that he, who was worthy only to see the best, might not be compelled to see the worst.

§ 2

After Durer's death many carried on the tradition he had bequeathed to his country as an engraver—the prints of Aldegraver, Beham, and other followers are still treasured by collectors—but none of them won great fame in painting. Matthias Grünewald (c. 1483–1530), Durer's contemporary, is by far the most important of the lesser men, his fame resting on a few authentic pictures which show the imaginative mind and fine craftsmanship. Chief of these is the famous St. Anthony altar-piece at Colmar in Alsace. Grünewald had a pupil Lucas Cranach (1472–1553), who was much esteemed by his fellow-citizens of Wittemberg and was appointed Court Painter to the Protestant prince Frederick of Saxony ; but we have only to look at the doll-faced " Portrait of a Young Lady " by him in the National Gallery to see how far Cranach's art fell below that of Durer.

Only one other painter of German origin beside Durer has so far succeeded in capturing the world's attention, namely, Hans Holbein the Younger, who when Durer died in 1528 was a young man of thirty-one, painting in England. No more than twenty-six years separate the birth of Holbein from that of Durer, yet within the space of that one generation so great had been the revolution in men's minds that the two artists seem to belong to different ages. Holbein grew up during the greatest Wonder-Time in the world's history. We who have benefited by and taken for granted the astounding discoveries made during what is known as the Epoch of Maximilian (1493–1519), which approximates to the opening of the reign of our Henry VIII, find it difficult to realise the crash of old ideas and the bombardment of new ones which filled the world during this epoch :

That time [as Lord Bryce has told us]— a time of change and movement in every part of human life, a time when printing had become common, and books were no longer confined to the clergy, when drilled troops were replacing the feudal militia, when the use of gunpowder was changing the face of war—was especially marked by one event to which the history of the world offers no parallel before or since, the discovery of America. . . . The feeling of mysterious awe with which men had regarded the firm plain of the earth and her encircling ocean ever since the days of Homer vanished when astronomers and geographers taught them that she was an insignificant globe which, so far from being the centre of the universe, was itself swept round in the motion of one of the least of its countless system.

Nothing but an appreciation of these historical facts can teach us rightly to comprehend the essential difference between the art of the two great German masters : for as the " feeling of mysterious awe " with which all

"JACOB MEYER," BY HOLBEIN (1497–1543)

Basle

Holbein's superlative merit as a draughtsman is seen in this early portrait study of one of his first patrons, the Burgomaster of Basle. Note the union of delicacy and strength in the drawing of this head. As a master of line Holbein in his own style has never been surpassed.

224

"PORTRAIT OF A YOUNG WOMAN," BY HOLBEIN

Windsor Castle

The Holbein drawings at Windsor are famous both in art and history, and it is largely through them that we are able to visualise so clearly the appearance and character of Henry VIII and his circle. This young woman was possibly one of Jane Seymour's maids-of-honour.

his work, whether painted or engraved, is impregnated, makes Albert Durer the last and supreme expression of mediævalism, so an inner consciousness of man's insignificance and a frank recognition of material facts makes Holbein the first exponent in art of Modern Science.

The great Hans Holbein was the son of an artist of the same name, Hans Holbein the Elder, a poor and struggling painter of religious pictures in the flourishing city of Augsburg. Here Hans Holbein the Younger was born in 1497. There was never any doubt as to his calling, for he belonged to a family of painters. Not only his father, but his uncle and his brother were painters also. His father, who was chiefly influenced by the Flemish painter Roger van der Weyden (see Chapter X), had little to teach the son, and when he was seventeen or eighteen young Hans left his father's house in company with his elder brother Ambrosius, and began a foreign tour which eventually ended at Basle. Owing to the lack of any exact records and the constant confusion of the two Holbeins, father and son, the details of Holbein's early life are still a matter of conjecture and controversy. Some hold that the elder Holbein with his family moved from Augsburg to Lucerne about 1514, but the one thing certain is that young Holbein was at Basle in 1515, where he at once found work as a designer with the printer and publisher Frobenius. Through Frobenius he came to know Erasmus, who had recently left France and now graced Basle with his universal fame as a scholar ; and soon the young artist found plenty of employment both as a book-illustrator and portraitist. One of the earliest and most loyal of his patrons was the Basle merchant Jacob Meyer, whose portrait and especially the splendid sketch for the same foreshadowed the future greatness of the artist as a portrait-painter. About 1516 or 1517 Holbein the Younger was in Lucerne, where he decorated a house, and it is conjectured that about this time he also travelled in Italy ; but there is no sure proof, and we can only guess at his movements till he reappears at Basle in 1519. Though but twenty-two, he is now a man and a master. In 1520 he became a citizen of Basle—a necessity if he wished to practise painting in that city—and about the same time he married a widow with two children.

He was a master, but a master of another order to Durer. Holbein was a purely professional painter, anxious to do a day's work and do it as well as he possibly could ; but he did not attempt to show how life should be lived or to penetrate its mysteries : he was content to paint what he saw, paint it truly and splendidly, but like the wise child of a sophisticated age he refrained from a futile endeavour to dig beneath the surface. Holbein can show you the character of a man, as in his portrait of Jacob Meyer ; but Durer would have tried to read his soul.

In 1521 he painted his masterly, though to many unattractive picture,

226

"PORTRAIT OF GEORGE GISZE," BY HOLBEIN

Berlin

There is no more popular element in any picture than the minute rendering of details which betokens a painter's industry and capacity.

This splendidly ornate portrait, in which the accessories are rendered with scrupulous care and brilliance, was a deliberate " show-piece " painted by the artist when he desired to obtain the patronage of " The Merchants of the Steelyard," the title of a Corporation of wealthy German merchants who settled and traded in London during the reign of Henry VIII.

" The Dead Man," horribly realistic some would say, yet in truth it is not morbid. For this outstretched corpse is painted with the calm detachment of a student of anatomy ; it is a manifestation of the sceptical, inquiring, but unmoved gaze of Science confronted with a Fact. In 1522 he painted " Two Saints " and a " Madonna," in the following year a " Portrait of Erasmus," in 1526 a " Venus " and a gay lady styled " Lais Corinthiaca," and in 1529 he painted a great " Madonna " for his friend Jacob Meyer.

The careful reader will have observed that no paintings are given above for the years 1523 to 1525, and indeed these were bad years for all painters. When Giulio de' Medici was elected Pope as Clement VII in 1523, he found, as a historian has said, " the world in confusion, a great movement going on in Germany, a great war just begun between the three most powerful Christian monarchs—a war to which he himself was pledged." Thinking the French would win, he sided with them. Two months after he had signed the treaty of alliance, Francis I of France was defeated and taken prisoner at Pavia, and the Emperor's troops—thousands of Protestants among them—headed for Rome. All the diplomatic wiles of the Pontiff were unavailing, and in May 1527 a horrified world beheld Christian troops, Germans, Spaniards, and Italians, engaged in the sack of Rome.

Basle, then a city of the Empire, though not exposed to the full force of the currents of war, was not untouched by these events, and Holbein, like a shrewd man of the world, began to look out for a shelter from the storm that was convulsing Europe. His native Germany was out of the question, for there paintings already in existence were being destroyed by zealots desirous of " purifying " Protestant churches. During this time of waiting, when commissions for pictures were scarce, Holbein began that series of wood-engravings which have done as much as any of his paintings to make his name illustrious.

No works of Holbein have held a more lasting place in the popular imagination than his little woodcuts illustrating " The Dance of Death." As remote in its origin as the " morality " play, this picturing of the fact that all living beings must die was probably in its beginning a monkish device to compel those who could not read to realise their inevitable fate. This lesson was driven home by the universality with which the theme was expounded. In the older prints of this subject the highest and lowest in the land were shown each dancing with a dead partner of the same rank and calling, a king dancing with a dead king, a bishop dancing with a dead bishop, a merchant with a dead merchant, a labourer with a dead labourer. Whoever you were you could not escape death, that was always dancing at your heels. This was the age-old theme to which Holbein gave new life, and if his version of the Dance of Death has eclipsed all other versions it is because Holbein was the first to present Death as an abstraction, common

Moritur Sacerdos magnus, JOSVE IX.
Et qui reputatus in eius interitum alter, PSAL. 108

THE POPE

Stulte, hac nocte repetent animam tuam, &
qui parasti, cuius erunt. LVCAE. XII

THE MISER

In sudore vultus tui vesceris pane tuo.
GEN. III.

THE HUSBANDMAND

FROM HOLBEIN'S "DANCE OF DEATH"

Like the old morality play *Everyman*, this ancient picture-sequence was intended to drive home the inescapable truth that " in the midst of life we are in death." With a pictorial pageantry unapproached in any previous or later rendering of the subject, Holbein here shows us Death dogging the footsteps of the Pope (and Cardinal), the Miser, and the Husbandman.

"ROBERT CHESEMAN, THE KING'S FALCONER," BY HOLBEIN

The Hague

By this simple and dignified portrait, both lifelike and decorative, of the King's Falconer, Holbein paved the way for his restoration to Court favour, after the execution of his first English patron, Sir Thomas More.

to all prints in the series, and because no other treatment of the theme has excelled his in the pictorial elements of design. Each of these prints is itself a perfect little picture—see how beautiful is the landscape with the setting sun in " The Husbandman." As for its value as preaching, Holbein's series serves a double purpose, emphasising by the skeleton that accompanies all alike, Pope, Cardinal, Miser, Husbandman, and what not, the equality as well as the universality of death. Holbein's message is not only that " all flesh is grass " ; but also that under their skin " the colonel's lady and Judith O'Grady " are very much alike.

In 1526 Holbein found the haven for which he had been looking in England, an isle remote from the European storm-centre. It is probable that he had become known through Erasmus to Sir Thomas More, and so was invited to come ; his painting of " The Household of Sir Thomas More " was one of the earliest and most important paintings executed by Holbein during his first stay in England. In 1528 he returned to Basle for three years, and having dispatched thence his gorgeous portrait of " George Gisze, Merchant of the Steelyard " to show what he *could* do in portraiture, he returned to England in 1531.

This handsome and exceedingly ornate portrait of a young merchant in his counting-house was a deliberate show-piece which had exactly the effect the painter intended. In troublous and uncertain times princes and great nobles were unreliable patrons ; at any moment they might be dethroned, killed, or executed. Like a prudent man Holbein wished to establish a connection with a steadier, yet equally rich stratum of society, namely, the great merchants. Therefore he cleverly set his cap at the wealthy German merchants settled in London, and showed them in this portrait that he could make a merchant look as splendid and imposing as any king or nobleman. He delivered his sample, and human vanity did the rest. The German " Merchants of the Steelyard," as this Corporation was styled, flocked to his studio in London. Three years later his first English patron, Sir Thomas More, was sent to the scaffold by Henry VIII because he declined to declare the nullity of that royal reprobate's first marriage with Catherine of Aragon.

To have been the friend of More was at this time no commendation to the favour of the Court ; nevertheless, Holbein was not the man to miss any opportunity of " getting on " for want of a little tact and diplomacy. Firmly based on the support of the German merchants, he tried another method of approach. Very soon we find him painting his splendid portrait of " Robert Cheseman, the King's Falconer," painting first the minor and then the greater courtiers, till at last, in 1536, he achieved what no doubt had been his aim from the first, and was appointed Court Painter to King Henry VIII.

Never did that sovereign do a wiser or a better thing for himself than when he made Holbein his painter. Not only did the artist present that king to posterity in a manner that mitigates our judgment of his cruelties, but he has made the whole history of that period live for us, as no previous period in English history lives, by his series of portraits and portrait drawings of the English Court. Ford Madox Hueffer has pointedly observed :

How comparatively cold we are left by the name, say, of Edward III, a great king surrounded by great men in a stirring period. No visual image comes to the mind's eye : at most we see, imaginatively, coins and the seals that depend from charters.

Hueffer truly argues that Henry VIII and his men would be just as lifeless without Holbein, and the way he has made them live in our imagination is a tribute not only to Holbein but also to the preserving power of art.

While preparing the way for his advancement in England, Holbein did not neglect the connection he already had on the Continent, and three years before his appointment as Court Painter he sought to widen and enhance his foreign custom by painting another show-piece. " The Ambassadors " was painted as deliberately to force an entry into diplomatic circles as the " George Gisze " had been to secure him the custom of the men of commerce. This remarkable group of Jean de Dinteville, Lord of Polisy, on the left, wearing the French Order of S. Michel, and of Georges de Selve, Bishop of Lavaur, in doctor's cap and gown, on the right, fascinates all beholders by the brilliance with which the accessories are painted—the globe, the turkey rug, the tiling, the mandoline, the astronomical instruments, and in the foreground the anamorphosis (or distorted representation) of a human skull. Many keen imaginations have set their wits to work to find an inner meaning to this curiously elongated death's-head, but the most plausible explanation is found in the fact that Holbein's own name means " skull " in his native language, and this device may consequently be regarded as a fanciful way of putting his seal or cipher on his work. Another interpretation is that here, as in other portraits by Holbein, the skull is introduced to reinforce the lesson of the " Dance of Death," that to this all must come. Whatever the painter's original idea may have been, his work is a complete success ; he painted it to create a sensation, and it has created a sensation for centuries. It may be added that this elongated skull completes the design, by paralleling the line from the one ambassador's hand (holding the dagger) to the head of the other ambassador.

After the death of Jane Seymour, when Europe was searched for marriageable princesses to console the royal widower, Holbein in February 1538 was sent to Brussels to paint his matchless portrait of King Christian's

"THE AMBASSADORS," BY HOLBEIN

National Gallery, London

This famous picture of the Ambassadors Jean de Dinteville and the Bishop of Lavaur is another of Holbein's show-pieces, designed to maintain his Continental reputation and to attract the custom of foreign diplomats. The curiously distorted representation of a human skull in the foreground is an important element in the quadrilateral design and also a rebus on the name of the artist, " Holbein " meaning " skull."

H*

THE " DUCHESS OF MILAN," BY HOLBEIN

National Gallery, London

The grace and sweetness of meditative maidenhood is revealed with matchless beauty in this painting, which is a portrait of a Princess of Denmark (afterwards Duchess of Lorraine).

"HENRY VIII," BY HOLBEIN
Corsini Palace, Rome

As the Court Painter to Henry VIII, Holbein painted many portraits of his royal patron, as well as of the famous people of his court. Many of them, by using the decorative opportunity of the highly ornamented costume of the period, made beautiful a subject which almost defied treatment. Holbein's genius in showing the subtlety of character expressed itself even with his royal and irascible sitter, for we see at once the intelligence and the sensuality in this face.

235

daughter " Christina of Denmark," who, fortunately for herself, escaped Henry VIII. One of Holbein's last works, this is by many accounted his greatest. Here he has painted no show-piece, but set forth with divine simplicity the grace and dignity of meditative girlhood.

From Brussels Holbein went to Burgundy, where he painted other portraits ; and in December of the same year he returned to London. Almost exactly five years later he caught the plague. In November 1543 Holbein died in London, a victim to the same disease that had already killed Giorgione in his youth and was destined, thirty-three years later, to carry off Titian in his old age.

Just as Durer and Holbein had no great forerunners, so they had no great successors, and Europe had to wait thirty-four years before another great master of art was born, outside Italy, in the person of Peter Paul Rubens.

XVI

THE PRIDE OF FLANDERS

THE ART OF RUBENS, VAN DYCK, AND THE FLEMISH PORTRAIT-PAINTERS

§ I

PAINTER, courtier, scholar, and diplomatist, Peter Paul Rubens is one of the most picturesque figures in European history. In origin he belonged to the upper middle class, for though his grandfather had been only a tanner of Antwerp, his father John Rubens had taken his degree at an Italian university and subsequently attained considerable civic importance in Antwerp. At that time Flanders was under Spanish rule, and trouble with the authorities over political and religious matters drove the Protestant John Rubens and his family into exile at Cologne. There he became the intimate counsellor of William the Silent, and unfortunately, too intimate with his patron's wife, the Princess of Orange. Their love affair was discovered and John Rubens was thrown into prison, from which he was only released after the Prince had divorced his wife. He did not long survive his imprisonment, and died at Cologne in 1587.

All this had its influence on young Peter Paul, who was born at Siegen, Westphalia, in 1577, one year after the death of Titian. Political complications had already driven his father from Antwerp, and so the boy spent his early childhood in exile. He was only ten years old when his father died, and then his mother returned to Antwerp, taking her three children with her, Blandina the eldest, a young woman of twenty-three ; Philippe, a boy of thirteen ; and Peter Paul, the youngest. By a curious coincidence, just as only one year separated the birth of Peter Paul Rubens from the death of Titian, so again one year divided the death of John Rubens from that of Paul Veronese (1588), whose art his son was destined to develop and glorify.

After her daughter's marriage in 1590, the widow Rubens was able to say in a letter that both her sons were earning their living—so we know that their schooldays in Antwerp were short : Philippe obtained a place in the office of a town councillor of Brussels, while Peter Paul was Page of Honour to the Princess Margaret de Ligne-Aremberg. This gave the future diplomatist his first experience of court life ; but it was a short one, for already he felt art to be his true vocation, and in 1591 the lad of fourteen

237

was allowed to begin his training as a painter in the studio of his cousin Tobias Verhaeght.

Rubens remained little more than six months with his cousin, who was a landscape artist. His next teacher, Adam van Noort, was a figure-painter, but it is unlikely he learnt much from this morose and often drunken boor. In 1596 he found a more congenial master in Otto Vaenius (1558–1629), who was a gentleman, a scholar, and a man of the world, though as a painter he was even duller and stiffer than his own master, the Venetian Zucchero (c. 1543–1616), well known in England by his numerous portraits of Queen Elizabeth. One thing that Vaenius did was to fire his pupil with enthusiasm for Italian art, and two years after he had come of age and had been admitted a member of the Guild of St. Luke, Peter Paul Rubens arrived in Venice. Here the admirable copies he made of paintings by Titian and Veronese attracted the attention of Vincenzo I, Duke of Mantua, into whose service Rubens almost immediately entered. With the Duke he was at Florence for the marriage of Marie de' Medici to Henri IV (by proxy), and in 1603—after he had visited Rome, Padua, and other Italian cities—Rubens was sent by Vincenzo I on a mission with presents of horses and pictures to Philip III of Spain.

Though not then entrusted with any work for the Spanish monarch, Rubens painted several pictures for his prime minister the Duke of Lerma before he returned to Italy. After working for his patron at Mantua, Rome, and Genoa, Rubens in 1608 was recalled to Antwerp by news of his mother's serious illness. Too late to see her alive when he reached his native city, the grief-stricken painter remained for several months in strict seclusion, whence he was drawn by the rulers of Flanders, the Stadt-holders Albert and Isabella, who, conscious of his growing reputation, persuaded Rubens to leave the Mantuan service and become their Court Painter. In accepting this position Rubens was permitted to live at Antwerp instead of with the Court at Brussels.

His brother Philippe had already married the daughter of his chief, the Secretary of Antwerp, and it was probably at their house that Rubens saw his sister-in-law's niece Isabella, daughter of John Brant, whom he married in 1609. The following year the artist designed a palatial residence in the Italian style, and had it built on the thoroughfare now known as the *Rue de Rubens* : there he took his young and beautiful wife, and there he settled down to found the School of Antwerp. The ensuing ten or twelve years were the most tranquil and probably the happiest in the life of Rubens. An example of Rubens' first manner is the portrait of " Rubens and his First Wife," painted when he was about thirty-two and his newly married wife Isabella Brant little over eighteen. During this period he executed the works on which his fame most securely rests, notably his supreme

"RUBENS AND HIS FIRST WIFE," BY RUBENS (1577–1640)

Pinakothek, Munich

This portrait group of Rubens with his first wife Isabella Brant is a fine example of his early style of portraiture. Note the precision of drawing and wealth of detail which formed the foundation for the artist's later and more dashing style.

239

masterpiece, "The Descent from the Cross," in Antwerp Cathedral. This work, executed in 1612, marks the beginning of Rubens' second manner, just as his "Elevation of the Cross," also in Antwerp and painted in 1609–10, concludes his first or Italian manner.

The late R. A. M. Stevenson, a most penetrating critic, has pointed out how much more original and softer is the later picture :

> It started the Antwerp School, and beyond its ideal scarce any contemporary advanced. The forms are less muscular, the gestures less exaggerated, the transitions suaver, the light and shade less contrasted than in the first period, but the pigment is still solid, and the colours are treated as large, unfused blocks of decorative effect.

The growth of Rubens was gradual, but the extraordinary number of his collaborators makes the tracing of that growth a task of infinite difficulty. Apart from other contemporary evidence, the letters of Rubens himself show the number of artists he employed to work from his designs. The truth is he established a picture-factory at Antwerp, and not only engaged assistants to help him carry out gigantic decorations for churches and palaces, but also farmed out commissions for easel-pictures, landscapes, and portraits. In addition to "Velvet" Brueghel, his collaborators and pupils at one time or another included Snyders (1579–1657), Jordaens (1593–1678), Cornelius de Vos (1585–1651), Antony Van Dyck (1599–1641), David Teniers (1610–90), Jan Fyt (1609–61), and a score of others. A good example of the "team-work" accomplished in the Rubens studio is "Christ in the House of Martha and Mary." In this picture, now in the Irish National Gallery at Dublin, the figures are by Rubens, the landscape by "Velvet" Brueghel, the architecture by Van Delen, and the accessories by Jan van Kessel. Yet all is so controlled by the master-hand that to any but an expert the whole appears to be the work of one man.

A story is told that the Dean of Malines Cathedral was furious when, having ordered a "Last Supper" from Rubens, a young man named Justus van Egmont came down to begin the work. Later on

the great man appeared with his fine calm presence and the urbane manner that was a bulwark against offence or misappreciation. As Rubens corrected the work, enlivened the colour or the action of the figures, and swept the whole composition with his unerring brushwork towards a beautiful unity of effect, the churchman acknowledged the wisdom of the master, and admitted that the money of the chapter had been safely invested.

Even the beautiful portrait of "Susanne Fourment," known as the "Chapeau de Poil," a canvas of 1620, which shows Rubens' second manner merging into his third—in which the pigment is less solid and the fusion of colour more subtle—even this work has been thought by some critics

"THE DESCENT FROM THE CROSS," BY RUBENS

Antwerp Cathedral

Though temperamentally unfitted to be a religious painter, Rubens, by his splendid colour, flowing design, and naturalness of presentation, gives so fine a rendering of this awesome subject that it is counted to be his supreme masterpiece.

241

"CHRIST IN THE HOUSE OF MARTHA AND MARY," BY RUBENS

Irish National Gallery, Dublin

This picture is an example of the co-operative painting carried on by Rubens when he established his " picture-factory " at Antwerp. The landscape is by Brueghel, the architecture by Van Delen, the accessories by Jan van Kessel, and the figures by Rubens, who put the finishing touches which give unity to the whole.

"LE CHAPEAU DE POIL," BY RUBENS

National Gallery, London

This smiling lady in the beaver hat (chapeau de poil) is Susanne Fourment, whose sister Helen became the second wife of the artist. Of the many portraits of women painted by Rubens this is the most famous, and it is a splendid example of his powers at their prime.

243

to be not altogether the work of Rubens. The late R. A. M. Stevenson considered that " the comparatively rude folds of the dress and the trivial details of the feather " betrayed another hand at work.

The fame of the Flemish master had spread all over Europe, and in January 1622 Rubens was summoned to Paris by the Queen-Mother, Marie de' Medici, who wished him to decorate her favourite Luxembourg Palace. The great series of wall-paintings, which were the result of this commission, are now one of the glories of the Louvre. These pictures were designed to emphasise the greatness of the Medicis and the splendour resulting from the marriage of Marie de' Medici to King Henri IV of France. How cleverly Rubens fulfilled his double rôle of courtier and decorator may be seen by our illustration of one of the most notable pictures in this series, " Henri IV Receiving the Portrait of Marie de' Medici." Here, in a wonderful blending of fable with reality, the artist idealises the King as monarch and lover, and turns a marriage dictated by reasons of state into a romantic love-match in which Cupid and all the deities of Olympus are deeply concerned.

Endowed by nature with a splendid presence, tactful in disposition and charming in manners, Rubens was a man to win the confidence of any Court. After the death of the Archduke Albert in 1621, his widow the Regent Isabella took Rubens into her inner counsels and employed him in semi-official visits to foreign courts. The great object of the rulers of Flanders was to keep England and Holland friendly with Spain and apart from France. One of the first missions which Rubens received was to secure a renewal of the treaty between Holland and Flanders, a task which took him to The Hague in 1623. It was at this time that he was ennobled by the King of Spain.

When visiting Paris the painter had made the acquaintance of the Duke of Buckingham, the virtual ruler of England under Charles I, and this nobleman had been greatly taken by the talents of the Fleming both as artist and diplomatist. It was Buckingham himself who suggested that Rubens should be sent to Spain in the summer of 1628 to ascertain the real feelings of Philip IV in the war which Buckingham planned against France through hatred of Richelieu, who had separated him from Anne of Austria. Rubens arrived at Madrid in the course of the summer, bringing with him eight pictures as a present to Philip ; but the assassination of Buckingham on September 2, 1628, changed the political aspect of affairs and enabled Rubens to give his whole attention to art. An important event in the history of painting was the meeting in Spain of Rubens, now fifty-two, with Velazquez, then a man of thirty ; the two became great friends, and we shall see, in the chapter on Spanish painting, that the younger man was considerably influenced by his elder.

" HENRI IV RECEIVING PORTRAIT OF MARIE DE' MEDICI," BY RUBENS

The Louvre, Paris

In this splendid decoration Rubens idealises a marriage made for reasons of state, and presents it as a romantic love-match in which Cupid and all the deities of Olympus are deeply concerned.

245

"THE BLESSINGS OF PEACE," BY RUBENS

National Gallery, London

When visiting England as Ambassador for Philip IV, Rubens presented this picture to Charles I, as a hint of the advantages to be derived if England made peace with Spain. It shows the Goddess of Wisdom pushing back War while Peace receives Wealth and Happiness and their smiling offspring.

246

Politically the great result of the Fleming's stay in Spain was that Philip IV consented to Rubens going as his official representative to King Charles I of England. The artist-diplomat arrived in London on May 25, 1629, and not only arranged the terms of peace between England and Spain but gave a new direction to English painting. Charles commissioned him to paint the ceiling which may still be seen in the Banqueting Saloon in Whitehall, now the United Services Museum, and many of his pictures were bought by the Royal Family and nobility of England.

The tact of the courtier, as well as the splendid powers of the painter, may be seen in our illustration of a famous Rubens at the National Gallery, " The Blessings of Peace," which shows Minerva, Goddess of Wisdom, pushing back War, while Peace receives Wealth and Happiness and their smiling children. This picture was presented to the English king by Rubens soon after his arrival in London as a delicate hint of the advantages to be derived from concluding peace with Spain.

It is said that while he was painting this picture in London an English courtier asked Rubens, " Does the Ambassador of his Catholic Majesty amuse himself with painting ? " " No," replied Rubens, " I amuse myself sometimes with being an ambassador."

On February 21, 1630, Charles I knighted the painter, and soon afterwards Sir Peter Paul Rubens returned to the Continent and again settled in Antwerp. Isabella Brant had been dead about four years, and in December Rubens married Helen Fourment, whom he must have known from childhood. She was one of the seven daughters of Daniel Fourment, a widower, who had married the sister of Rubens's first wife. Helen was only sixteen when she married.

The last seven years of his life were devoted by Rubens to domestic happiness and his art rather than to politics, which he practically abandoned after 1633. He had a fine country estate near Malines, the Château de Steen, of which we may see a picture in the National Gallery, and there for the most part he lived quietly, happy with his girl-wife and only troubled by attacks of gout. During these last years Rubens produced a quantity of fine pictures ; in one year (1638), for example, he despatched a cargo of 112 pictures by himself and his pupils to the King of Spain. The rapidity of the master's execution is well illustrated by a story that, having received a repeat order from Philip (*after* he had received the 112 pictures !), and being pressed by the monarch's brother Ferdinand to deliver the new pictures as quickly as possible, Rubens said he would do them all with his own hand " to gain time ! "

Among these new pictures, sent off in February 1639, were " The Judgement of Paris " and " The Three Graces," both now at the Prado, and generally held to be the finest as well as the latest of the painter's many

"THE RAINBOW LANDSCAPE," BY RUBENS

Wallace Collection, London

This picture shows Rubens' attitude towards Nature, which he approached without awe and with the friendly arrogance of a strong man who respects strength.

pictures of these subjects. But still the King of Spain wanted more pictures by Rubens. Further commissions arrived, and in May 1640 the great master died in harness, working almost to the last on four large canvases.

Excelling in every branch of painting, and prolific in production, Rubens is a master of whose art only a brief summary can be given. A final word, however, must be said on the landscapes which form a conspicuous feature among his later works, and of which we possess so splendid an example in " The Rainbow Landscape " in the Wallace Collection. The healthy and contented sense of physical well-being, which radiates from every landscape by Rubens, has been well expressed in a criticism of this picture by Muther : " The struggle of the elements is past, everything glitters with moisture, and the trees rejoice like fat children who have just had their breakfast."

It has been said that there are landscapes which soothe and calm our spirits, and landscapes which exhilarate. Those by Rubens come under the latter category. He was no mystic in his attitude towards Nature ; he approached her without awe, with the friendly arrogance of a strong man who respects strength. Most of his landscapes were painted in the neighbourhood of his country seat, and in them we may trace not only the painter's love of the beauty in Nature, but something also of the landowner's pride in a handsome and well-ordered estate.

The heir of the great Venetians in his painted decorations, Rubens was a pioneer in all other directions. His portraits were the inspiration of Van Dyck and the English painters of the eighteenth century, his landscapes were the prelude to Hobbema and the " natural painters " of England and Holland ; while in pictures like " Le Jardin d'Amour " and " The Dance of Villagers " he invented a new style of pastoral with small figures which Watteau and other later artists delightfully exploited.

§ 2

Of all the many followers of Rubens, the two most famous were Van Dyck and Jacob Jordaens (1593–1678), another exuberant Fleming, who though greatly influenced by Rubens was never actually his pupil. The " Riches of Autumn " in the Wallace Collection is a fine example of the bacchanalian opulence of Jordaens. The fruit, vegetables, and most of the foliage in this picture are painted by Frans Snyders (1579–1657), a noted painter of " still-life " who frequently collaborated with Rubens and other painters. The skill of Jordaens as a portrait-painter may be seen in his " Baron Waha de Linter of Namur " in the National Gallery, but though a capable and skilful painter of whatever was before him, Jordaens had no imagination and added little of his own to the art of Rubens.

" THE RICHES OF AUTUMN," BY JORDAENS (1593–1678)

Wallace Collection, London

This bacchanalian scene is a typical specimen of the exuberant art of Jordaens. The fruit and vegetables are painted by Snyders.

" CORNELIUS VAN DER GEEST," BY VAN DYCK (1599–1641)

National Gallery, London

How Van Dyck penetrated below externals to the mind and spirit of his sitter may be seen in this wonderful rendering of a man's thought and character.

Antony Van Dyck, who was born at Antwerp in 1599, was supposed to have entered the studio of Rubens as a boy of thirteen, but recent research has shown he was originally a pupil of Hendrick van Balen and did not enter the studio of Rubens till about 1618. He was the favourite as well as the most famous of his master's pupils, and yet temperamentally he was miles apart from Rubens. Where Rubens made all his sitters robust and lusty, Van Dyck made his refined and spiritual. From Rubens he learnt how to use his tools, but as soon as he had mastered them he obtained widely different results. The English Ambassador at The Hague persuaded Van Dyck to visit England in 1620 when he was only just of age, but at that time he made only a short stay, and after his return to Antwerp Rubens urged him to visit Italy. It was good advice. The dreamy, poetic-looking youth, whose charming painting of himself at this time we may see in the National Portrait Gallery, London, was spiritually nearer akin to the Italian than to the Flemish painters. What he learnt from them, especially from Titian, may be seen in "The Artist as a Shepherd" in the Wallace Collection, painted about 1625-26, and from the still more splendid portraits in the National Gallery of the Marchese and Marchesa Cattaneo, both painted during the artist's second stay in Genoa.

Strengthened and polished by his knowledge of Italian art, Van Dyck returned to Antwerp, there to paint among many other fine things two of his outstanding achievements in portraiture, the paintings of Philippe Le Roy and his wife which now hang in the Wallace Collection. These portraits of the Governor of the Netherlands and his wife were painted in 1630 and 1631, when the artist was little over thirty years of age, and in the following year the young painter was invited by Charles I to visit England, where he became Sir Antony Van Dyck, Principal Painter in Ordinary to His Majesty.

His great equestrian portrait "Charles I on Horseback," which we reproduce, passed through several hands before it found a permanent home in the National Gallery. When King Charles's art collection was sold by the Puritans in 1649, this picture passed into the collection of the Elector of Bavaria. Afterwards it was purchased at Munich by the great Duke of Marlborough, from whose descendant it was bought in 1885 for the National Gallery, the price given for this and Raphael's "Ansidei Madonna" being £87,500.

After he had established himself in England, Van Dyck slightly altered his manner, creating a style of portraiture which was slavishly followed by his successors, Sir Peter Lely and Sir Godfrey Kneller.

To speak of the elegance of Van Dyck's portraits is to repeat a common-place, but what the casual observer is apt to overlook is that this elegance penetrates below externals to the mind and spirit of the sitter. Of his

"CHARLES I," BY VAN DYCK

National Gallery, London

Nobody can withhold sympathy from this knightly figure, in which the artist portrays all the virtues of the royal martyr and none of his faults. After the execution of Charles I this picture was sold by the Puritans and passed into the possession of the Elector of Bavaria, from whom it was purchased and brought back to England by the great Duke of Marlborough.

"MARCHESA CATTANEO," BY VAN DYCK

National Gallery, London

The influence of Titian can be seen in this portrait of a Genoese noblewoman painted during
Van Dyck's second visit to Genoa after he had been studying the Venetian painters.

" LORDS JOHN AND BERNARD STUART," BY VAN DYCK

The most beautiful portrait group Van Dyck painted in England : shows the refinement of the artist's portraiture and his capacity as a psychologist.

"PHILIPPE LE ROY," BY VAN DYCK

Wallace Collection, London

This portrait of the Governor of the Netherlands was executed in Antwerp
when the painter was a little over thirty years of age.

"NELL GWYNN," BY LELY (?)

National Portrait Gallery, London

Doubts have been thrown upon the actual subject of this popular picture, and upon Lely's painting of it, but even were it a studio work, it is typical of his style of depicting court ladies of his day. Lely was Van Dyck's successor and tried to follow his delicate and graceful style, but without his master's innate sensitiveness he produced only an echo. Nevertheless, his series of "Beauties" at Hampton Court, or the "Admirals" at Greenwich, show his power and a robustness of his own.

I

powers in both directions an exquisite example is the portrait group of " Lords John and Bernard Stuart," one of the most beautiful pictures he ever painted in England, and a work which proves Van Dyck to have been not only a supremely fluent master of the brush, but also a profound and penetrating psychologist.

Had he lived longer no one can say what other masterpieces he might have achieved : but unfortunately, with all his other great qualities as a painter, Van Dyck lacked the health and strength of his master Rubens. How good-looking he was in his youth, we can see by the National Portrait Gallery picture, but this refined, almost girlish face suggests delicacy and weakness. Weak in a way, he was ; though not spoiled by success, he could not stand the social whirl and dissipation on which a Rubens could thrive. Very superstitious, he was a victim to quacks and spent much time and money in endeavouring to discover the philosopher's stone. It is said that his failure to find this precious fable of the alchemists preyed on his mind and contributed to his collapse in 1641, when, though no more than forty-two, his frail body was worn out with gout and excesses. On the death of Rubens in 1640, Van Dyck went over to Antwerp. It was his last journey, and soon after his return to London he joined his great compatriot among the ranks of the illustrious dead.

Van Dyck established a style in portraiture which succeeding generations of painters have endeavoured to imitate ; but none has surpassed, few have approached him, and when we look among his predecessors we have to go back to Botticelli before we find another poet-painter who with equal, though different, exquisiteness mirrored not merely the bodies but the very souls of humanity.

After Van Dyck's death, numerous imitators, both British and Flemish, endeavoured to copy his style of portraiture, but the next great impetus art was to receive after Rubens came, not from England nor from Flanders, but from Spain. It is to the country of Velazquez and Murillo, therefore, that we must next turn our attention. Meantime the divine inflatus of art swept across Spain and Holland and was gathering new strength in England and France.

XVII

SUNSHINE AND SHADOW IN SPAIN

THE ART OF EL GRECO, VELAZQUEZ, AND MURILLO

§ 1

WHEN one thinks of Spain and art, the name of Velazquez jumps into the mind at once. Indeed, to many people, his is the only name in Spanish painting of outstanding importance. Looking back over the whole history of art in Spain, Velazquez's figure overshadows that of everyone who went before him and of all who have come after him. In a sense, he is the only great painter that country has produced. He interpreted the life of his time in terms that appeal universally, and no art has had more influence than his on modern painters.

How art came to Spain must now briefly be related. Until the fifteenth century there was little painting in Spain, and then, owing to her political connection with the Netherlands, the influence was markedly Flemish. It will be remembered that Jan van Eyck (see Chapter X) visited Spain in 1428, and the brilliant reception he received there induced other Flemish artists to visit the peninsula. Later, when Naples and the Sicilies came under the dominion of the Spanish crown, Italian art set the fashion to Spanish painters and particularly, as we might expect, the art of Naples. The Neapolitan School owed its origin to Michael Angelo Amerigi, called Caravaggio (1569–1609) from his birthplace near Milan. Undaunted by the great achievements of the Italian painters who immediately preceded him, Caravaggio sought to form an independent style of his own based on a bold imitation of Nature. While he was working in Venice and Rome, this astute student of Nature saw his contemporaries falling into decadence because they were artists imitating art. The seventeenth-century painters of Rome, Florence, and Venice degenerated into mere copyists of Titian, Tintoretto, Raphael, and Michael Angelo. Caravaggio saw their error, and perceiving that art based on art leads to decadence, he gave his whole attention to Nature and so became a pioneer of realism. By choice he elected to paint scenes taken from the ordinary life of his day, and " The Card Cheaters " is an admirable example of the novelty both of his subject and of his treatment. The novelty in his treatment chiefly consisted of the use Caravaggio made of light and shade (technically

259

known as *chiaroscuro*) to enforce the dramatic intensity of his pictures. He exaggerated his shadows, which were far too black to be scrupulously faithful to Nature, but by the emphasis he thus gave to his lights he produced original and arresting effects which undoubtedly had a powerful influence on the two greatest painters of the next generation. How widespread was his authority is proved by the extent to which he prepared the way for both Velazquez and Rembrandt.

After working in Milan, Venice, and Rome, Caravaggio settled in Naples, where among those influenced by his realism was the Spanish painter Josef Ribera (1588–1656). " The Dead Christ " in the National Gallery, London, is an example of Ribera's stern naturalism.

Through Ribera the influence of Caravaggio penetrated to Spain, but already that country had had its art sense profoundly stirred by a foreign artist who not merely visited Spain, as other artists had done, but made it his home. This was Domenico Theotocopuli, who from having been born at Candia, Crete, was universally called El Greco, that is to say " The Greek." El Greco (1545–1614), as we shall call him, went to Venice as a young man of twenty-five and worked there for a time under Titian, or Tintoretto. About 1575 he migrated to Spain and settled at Toledo, where he became affected by the great religious fervour which was then agitating the peninsula.

Art is the mirror of life, and a great part of the fascination of old pictures is that in them are reflected the great upheavals of history. We have seen how Florentine art was affected by the preaching first of St. Francis of Assisi and afterwards of Savonarola ; in Chapter XV it was shown how the Reformation influenced the last painting of Albert Durer and the whole outlook of Holbein. Now the most formidable antagonists that the Lutheran Reformers had to face, alike in action and in thought, were the Spaniards. The movement of the counter-Reformation originated and flourished in Spain. As the Spaniards in the Middle Ages had battled against the Moors till they won their land for Christianity, so they fought against the paganism of the Roman Church during the sixteenth century and strove with equal determination later against the Reformers, whom they regarded as heretics. The herald of this last battle was Ignatius Loyola, and he and his creation, the Order of the Jesuits, proved to be the most dangerous and powerful adversary of Protestantism.

El Greco's picture " Christ driving the Traders from the Temple," in the National Gallery, may be regarded as symbolising the purification of the Church by Loyola, but it is by his treatment infinitely more than by his choice of subject that El Greco expresses that vein of " convulsed mysticism " which was the peculiar attribute of Spanish Catholicism. El Greco as he grew older seemed to take delight in distorting natural

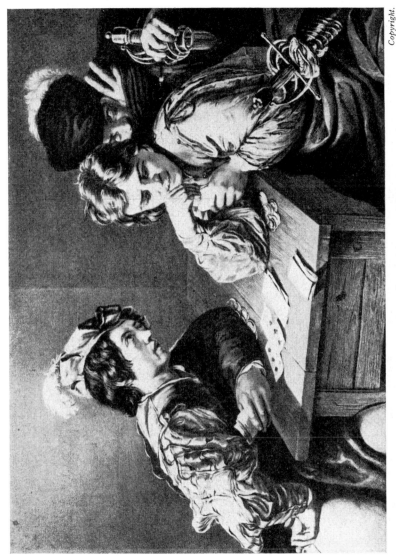

"THE CARD CHEATERS," BY CARAVAGGIO (1569–1609)

Dresden

Life shrewdly seen and truly rendered furnishes the artist with themes as fascinating as any provided by history or legend. This Neapolitan painter, by giving dramatic intensity to scenes taken from the ordinary life of his day, became the founder of Naturalism in art, and his pictures are human documents of never-failing interest.

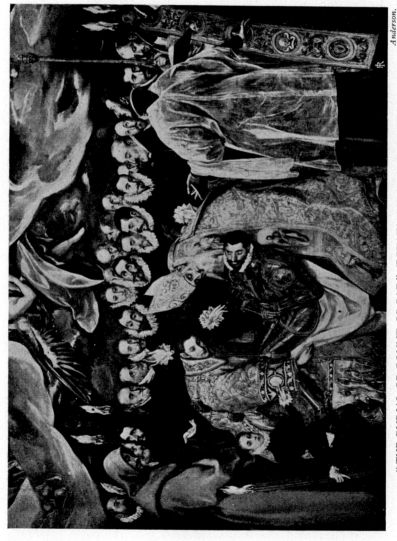

Anderson.

"THE BURIAL OF COUNT ORGAZ" (DETAIL), BY EL GRECO (1545–1614)

San Tomé, Toledo

Reality and unreality intermingled in this picture (which shows a Spanish Count about to be buried in the presence of the members of a knightly order) reveal the heightened imagination of a painter whose art reflects the terrors of the Inquisition.

forms. There is something savage, brutal even, in his art, and his deep earnestness gives grandeur to terrible things. The generally acknowledged masterpiece and most characteristic work by El Greco is his picture in the church of San Tomé in Toledo, in which the members of a knightly order solemnly attend the funeral of Count Orgaz. The corpse is lowered into the ground by two saints, while Christ, Mary, martyrs, and angels hover in the air, and this " abrupt union of actual with transcendental "—as Muther puts it—together with the uncanny, slightly exaggerated forms found in parts of the picture, confess a touch of hysteria.

By a curious coincidence the tercentenary of El Greco was celebrated in 1914, at a moment when the whole of Europe was again in a turmoil and minds were full of hatred and thoughts of violence. To a generation excited by war and rumours of war the suppressed violence in El Greco's pictures was irresistibly attractive. Some very advanced critics and ultra-progressive painters found in his neurotic temperament their ideal Old Master. El Greco was reputed to have held that colour was of far more importance than form or drawing, and if this belief was once regarded as " a curious anticipation of modern ideas," these " modern ideas " are themselves now out of date, drawing and design being now generally accepted as the foundation of all good art. El Greco's pictures are far from being formless. Historically and psychologically the paintings of El Greco are of the highest interest ; but they are a dangerous model for the art student.

Another foreign artist who, if he did not succeed in expressing the spirit of the time, nevertheless influenced Spanish painting considerably was Sir Anthony More, who, as mentioned in Chapter X, visited Spain, and during his stay there, about 1551–52, set a style of portraiture which served as a model for Coello (1515–90) and other Spanish court-painters.

§ 2

These, then, were the principal influences alive in Spanish art when Diego de Silva y Velazquez was born at Seville in 1599. His family was not of Sevillian or even of Spanish origin, for his grandfather Diego Rodriguez de Silva came from Oporto, the home of the Silva family. The name which he made world-famous he took from his mother, Gernima Velazquez, who belonged to an old Seville family. His father Juan de Silva raised no objections when his son desired to study art, and when he was thirteen or fourteen Velazquez was placed in the studio of Francisco de Herrera (1576–1654), who showed something of the fanaticism of El Greco in the flashing eyes and majestic gestures of the saints in his religious pictures. Herrera is said to have been bad-tempered, and after enduring his roughness for about a year Velazquez changed masters and entered the studio of Francisco Pacheco (1571–1654). There he remained five years, and though his master had no great originality or power, he was probably a good teacher, for he was himself a careful draughtsman, a scholar, and the author of a book on painting. Presumably there was also another attraction, for on April 23, 1618, Velazquez married Pacheco's daughter, Juana de Miranda. Henceforward Pacheco did everything he could to advance the interests of his son-in-law.

Within three years occurred the opportunity of a lifetime. Philip III died on March 31, 1621, and the young king, Philip IV, dismissed the Duke of Lerma and made Count Olivarez his prime minister. Now Olivarez, a son of the Governor of Seville, had lived in that city till 1615 and had made himself popular there as a patron of painters and poets. Several of his old protégés at Seville united to praise to the new minister the extraordinary talent of their young fellow-townsman. Velazquez went to Madrid and, after some vexatious delays, in 1623 Olivarez persuaded the young king to give Velazquez a sitting. He conquered at his first brushstroke. The equestrian portrait he painted is now lost, but it pleased Philip so much that forthwith the painter of twenty-four was appointed Court Painter to a king of eighteen.

From the beginning Philip treated Velazquez in the most friendly manner. The king is said by a contemporary to have come to his studio " almost every day," by " those secret passages, hung with pictures, which led from the king's rooms to every part of the old Alcazar." The monotony of the stiff routine of the Court was broken in the autumn of 1628 by the arrival of Rubens, who, as stated in the last chapter, came to Madrid on a diplomatic mission, and for nine months was constantly with the king and Velazquez. According to Pacheco and others, Rubens thought highly of Velazquez, and delighted in his society, while his views of the king appears in a letter Rubens wrote to a friend :

He evidently takes quite a special pleasure in painting, and, in my opinion, this prince is endowed with the finest qualities. I already know him from personal intercourse, as I have a room in the palace, so that he almost daily visits me.

Philip IV appears to have been genuinely interested in painting, a result probably of his intimacy with Velazquez, and after Rubens' visit, and undoubtedly on his advice, the King permitted Velazquez to go to Italy with the great soldier and statesman Spinola, who was to be the Spanish governor of Milan and commander-in-chief in Italy. Velazquez arrived at Milan in the early autumn of 1629 and soon went to Venice, where he made a special study of the work of Tintoretto, who died, it will be remembered, five years before Velazquez was born. From Venice he went

" VIEW IN THE GARDEN OF THE VILLA MEDICI, ROME," BY VELAZQUEZ
(1599–1660)

Prado, Madrid

Painted during his first visit to Rome in 1630, this sketch from Nature shows how Velazquez anticipated the open-air landscape painting of the nineteenth century.

"PHILIP IV AS A SPORTSMAN," BY VELAZQUEZ

Prado, Madrid

With unalterable patience and ever-fresh inspiration, Velazquez painted his King from youth to age. This portrait is an example of the artist's middle period and should be compared with his later "Æsop" to show the painter's progress.

266

to Rome—missing Florence—and after some months there passed on to Naples, where he met Ribera, and returned to Madrid early in 1631. At Naples he painted Philip's sister, Mary of Hungary, and this portrait he brought back with him together with his painting "The Forge of Vulcan."

It is customary to divide the art of Velazquez into three periods, of which the first ends with this visit to Italy. Most critics agree that the finest and most typical painting of his first period is the bacchanalian scene known as "The Topers." In the strongly laid shadows of this painting we see the influence of Caravaggio, and while we admire the virile rendering of form and the well-balanced grouping of the figures, yet we feel that the scene, as R. A. M. Stevenson, the cousin of "R. L. S.," wrote in his classic book on Velazquez, "was never beheld as a whole vision in the mind's eye." The painter's complete mastery of his art was yet to come.

The time between his return to Madrid and his departure in 1649 for a second visit to Italy was the happiest period in the life both of Velazquez and of Philip. Daily the artist advanced in the mastery of his art and in the esteem of his sovereign. R. A. M. Stevenson has pointed out that :

Like Rembrandt, who never ceased to paint his own portrait, Velazquez studied one model, from youth to age, with unalterable patience and an ever-fresh inspiration. He could look at the king's well-known head with a renewed interest, as he went deeper into the mystery of eyesight, and became better informed as to the effects of real light.

Owing to fires and other accidents many of these portraits of Philip have been lost, but twenty-six exist to this day : and they are all different. If we follow the development of the painter's art in these portraits of Philip IV—and nearly a dozen are in England—we shall see the slow transformation of a face, through a hard realism of feature and detail, to the soft, atmospheric impressionism of the final portraits. The bust portrait of " Philip IV : Old " in the National Gallery, London, is a superb example of the painter's last manner and of the way in which he could steep a whole canvas equally in a soft envelope of light.

What this continual painting of the same model did for Velazquez we can see from the portraits : it helped him to realise what every painter in the end must realise if he intends to excel, that it is not the subject but the treatment that makes the masterpiece. Velazquez found his fundamental inspiration, not in the novelty of a new subject, but in the ceaseless pursuit of seeing better and painting better something he had already seen. It is by the ultimate perfection of his rendering of the normal vision of man that Velazquez holds his supreme place among the very greatest masters of art. Other painters have expressed character, ideas, and beauty more poignantly, but nobody before or since has expressed *vision* so splendidly.

What this constant intercourse with a great artist did for Philip IV we can only imagine, but R. A. M. Stevenson again comes to our rescue by picturing in words how lonely is the lot of a king, and particularly in this period of a king of Spain :

To be a king of Spain, to preside at religious executions, to have a wife whom no man, even to save her life, might touch on pain of death, was to be a creature sorely in need of private liberty, and the solace of confidential intercourse. Philip IV seems to have been naturally kind, genial, and affable, and to have divided his leisure between the hunting-field and Velazquez's studio. The two, artist and king, grew old together, with like interests in horses, dogs, and paintings ; thawing when alone into that easy familiarity between master and old servant, freezing instantly in public into the stiff positions that their parts in life required. Painter to the king, when he was scarce twenty-five years old, Velazquez escaped most of the dangers and humiliations of professional portrait-painting, without losing its useful discipline of the eye, its rigorous test of the ever-present and exacting model.

It was when Velazquez was about forty that he was called upon to execute what proved to be one of the two supreme achievements of his art. Olivarez had presented the King with a new palace, Buen Retiro, on the heights above the Prado, and the Court Painters, with Velazquez at their head, were commanded to set about its decoration. For the decoration of this palace Velazquez produced his great historical picture " The Surrender of Breda " which is not only superb as a decoration but as moving in its sentiment as any picture artist ever painted.

The surrender of Breda, a fortified town twenty miles south-east of Dordrecht, was an incident in the memorable, and at first apparently hopeless, struggle which, beginning in 1568, lasted for eighty years and ended in the haughty Spaniards being compelled to recognise the independence of the Dutch Republic. The capture of Breda was one of the last triumphs of Spanish arms before the tide turned against them. This was the subject Velazquez chose for his contribution towards the decoration of Buen Retiro. Notwithstanding the armed crowd and multitude of uniforms, the noble bearing of the principal figures is the first thing that arrests attention. The gestures of Spinola, the Spanish Commander, and of Justin, chief representative of the defeated Dutchmen and bearer of the key to the city, are poignant in expression, and what moves us most of all is the incomparable humanity of the scene. There is no arrogance in the Spanish conqueror, who lays his hand consolingly, almost affectionately, on the shoulder of Justin ; in the Dutchman there is all the tragedy of defeat, but he is still dignified and does not cringe to the victor. It is an ennobling presentment of a historic scene.

While admitting that " The Surrender of Breda " challenges the greatest

" THE SURRENDER OF BREDA," BY VELAZQUEZ

Prado, Madrid

Incomparable in its humanity is this decorative commemoration of one of the last triumphs of Spanish arms in the Dutch war of independence. Spinola, the Spanish conqueror, lays his hand almost affectionately on the shoulders of Justin the Dutchman, who sadly, but with respectful dignity, delivers up the key of the surrendered city.

masters on their own ground, rivalling the highest achievements of Titian, Tintoretto, and Veronese both in its dignity as illustration and in its beauty as decoration, yet R. A. M. Stevenson has affirmed that " it is not the complete expression of the Velazquez eyesight." In a sense it is not ; it has not the amazing actuality of some of the painter's later works, but it may be questioned whether it is desirable that it should have this quality. This painting, we must remember, was first and foremost a decoration painted to adorn a certain wall in a given apartment, and the experience of centuries has shown that ultra-realism does not produce the most effective forms of decoration, which need a certain deliberate convention to emphasise their beauty as patterns. In " The Surrender of Breda " Velazquez gives us the greatest amount of realism compatible with the success of the picture as a decoration : it fulfils its purpose to perfection, and no higher praise than this can be given.

Just about the time of this painting, Velazquez was introduced to a new sitter, the king's little son Balthasar Carlos. Of the many portraits he made of this prince none is more delightful than the one which shows him on horseback. This quaint and rather pathetic little figure on his prancing steed, with the whole of Spain seemingly summed up and expressed in the landscape behind him, is the most adorable picture ever painted of a small boy. For all his pomp and importance (emphasised by the marshal's baton in his hand), the stern, set face—so like his father's—makes us feel sorry for him. He is very human ; we feel that he is a lonely child, and somehow the painter with prophetic insight seems to suggest that he has not long to live. Poor little Balthasar Carlos, born in 1629, did not live to be twenty. In 1646 he caught a cold at Saragossa and died. Thereafter Velazquez had no royal prince to paint, and Philip IV had to lavish all his domestic affection on a little princess, the Infanta Maria Teresa, who had been born in 1638. Soon after her arrival troubles came thick upon Spain. Olivarez mismanaged matters badly and was disgraced in 1643 ; and the same year those lances of Spain, hitherto invincible, which we see in " The Surrender of Breda," themselves suffered the agony of defeat and were utterly crumpled up and crushed at Rocroi by the great French commander Condé. Domestic griefs accompanied these public mis-fortunes, for two years before he lost his son, Philip lost his wife, the Queen Isabella.

In 1649 Velazquez again visited Italy, no longer the follower of an all-conquering army but the agent of a monarch whose power was waning. He landed at Genoa on January 2, and passing through Milan made for Venice, where he purchased several pictures for the King. This, indeed, was the principal object of his journey. From Venice he went to Rome, where he painted the splendid portrait of Innocent X which now hangs

"EQUESTRIAN PORTRAIT OF DON BALTHASAR CARLOS," BY VELAZQUEZ

Prado, Madrid

This quaint and rather pathetic little figure of King Philip's only son is one of the most adorable child portraits ever painted. Note how, with all its apparent naturalness, the artist has fitted horse and rider into a triangular pattern repeated in the landscape in the distance.

271

in the Doria Palace, Rome, and met several artists of note—among them being Salvator Rosa (1615–73), the Neapolitan painter of brigands and wild scenery, and Nicolas Poussin (1594–1665), the polished Frenchman, who in his classical subjects carried on the tradition of the great Renaissance and in his landscapes was a real pioneer.

In the summer of 1651 Velazquez returned to Madrid, where still further honours awaited him. He was made Marshal of the Palace, and as Philip IV had married again during his absence—married his own niece Mariana of Austria, a girl of fourteen—the new Marshal was kept busy organising festivities and tournaments for the amusement of the young Queen. By this second wife Philip had the Princess Margaret, born 1651, who is the central figure in the world-famous " Las Meninas." This picture—in English " The Maids of Honour "—marks the culmination of the third period of Velazquez and is the supreme achievement of his life.

Here, indeed, we have " the complete expression of the Velazquez eyesight," and great and glorious as " The Surrender of Breda " is, we are bound to confess that R. A. M. Stevenson was right in maintaining that this historical picture is not—like " The Maids of Honour "—" an absolutely unique thing in the history of art." Like so many of the greatest pictures in the world, " The Maids of Honour " originated in a spontaneous and unpremeditated flash of intense vision. The story generally accepted is that Velazquez was painting the king, who sat in the spot from which the spectator is supposed to see the picture of " Las Meninas." During a moment's rest the " Infanta " came in with her attendants, and the king was struck with the group which fell together before his eyes. Near him he saw the princess, her maids of honour Maria Sarmiento and Isabel de Velasco (who is offering her water), her dog, and her dwarfs Mari Barbola and Nicolasito Pertusato ; a little farther on the left, Velazquez, who had stepped back to look at his picture ; farther back on the right, a duenna and courtier talking ; while at the distant end of the gallery the king saw his queen and himself reflected in a mirror, and through the open door, Don Joseph Nieto drawing back a curtain. The canvas shown in the picture would naturally be, as Stevenson maintains, the one on which Velazquez was painting the king's portrait. Some, however, will have it to be the very canvas of " Las Meninas," which Velazquez was painting from a reflection in a mirror placed near to where the king had been sitting. R. A. M. Stevenson has justly pointed out that the perspective in the picture hardly seems to agree with this view, but rather makes Velazquez to have been working on the king's right hand. It is not a matter of importance, and the story of the conception of the picture may easily have got mixed in the telling. It is just possible that Velazquez was painting, or was about to paint, a portrait of the Infanta only, when the idea of the large picture

"THE MAIDS OF HONOUR," BY VELAZQUEZ

Prado, Madrid

" An absolutely unique thing in the history of art." This intimate picture of the Spanish royal family is unparalleled for its brilliant actuality and its sense of light, space, and air. In no other painting in the world is the third dimension so perfectly expressed.

273

" ÆSOP," BY VELAZQUEZ

Prado, Madrid

This incomparably real portrayal of a ragged philosopher is a superb example of the last manner of Velazquez, when a soft atmospheric impressionism has replaced the harder realism of his earlier paintings.

suddenly occurred to him or to the king. The canvas of " Las Meninas " is made of separate pieces sewn together, and one of these just contains the Infanta, with room for accessories or a subordinate figure. However it originated, the picture was immediately recognised as a brilliant triumph, and tradition says the Red Cross of Santiago on the painter's breast was painted there by the king's own hand, as a promise of the honour that was to be conferred on him afterwards.

It is hard to conceive of a more beautiful piece of painting than this— so free and yet firm and so revealing. When one stands before this canvas one is not concerned with any consideration of who it was painted by ; it fills the mind and suffices. Like all of the great artists, Velazquez takes something out of life and sets it free. The men and women in his finest pictures are released from what someone has called " mankind's little daily cage " ; and we are startled at the representation. In this portrait group we have life stated so intensely that the ordinary life around us seems almost unreal.

The same intense and startling impression of life is given us by the paintings of single figures executed by Velazquez during his last years. If we compare the shabby but dignified philosopher " Æsop "—a fine example of his late style—with " Philip IV as a Sportsman," which is admittedly one of the best full-lengths of his middle period, we shall begin to realise how far Velazquez travelled during the intervening years, not merely in the rendering of form but in the painting of light and air.

In 1659 Cardinal Mazarin sealed the reconciliation between France and Spain by arranging a marriage between the young Louis XIV and Maria Teresa of Spain. The meeting of the two Courts on the frontier and the organising of the imposing ceremonies required, burdened the Marshal of the Palace with a multiplicity of work and anxiety. The wedding took place on June 7, but it was the last function Velazquez was able to perform. At sixty years of age the strain was too much for him, and a few weeks after he had returned to Madrid he collapsed and died on August 6, 1660.

In a sense it may be said that the most surprising adventures of Velazquez occurred after his death. By birth a hidalgo (i.e. a member of the lesser nobility), Velazquez was buried like a grandee. The entire Court attended his funeral, and knights of all orders took part in the ceremonies. But after the generation that knew the man had passed away, the glory of the painter was strangely and unaccountably forgotten. For two hundred years, during which picture-lovers flocked to Italy and Italian artists became daily more famous, the name of Velazquez was seldom mentioned. Then, about fifty years ago, the sympathy of two or three great artists, notably Whistler in England and Manet in France, broke the spell of silence, and supported by a galaxy of writers, among whom was R. A. M. Stevenson

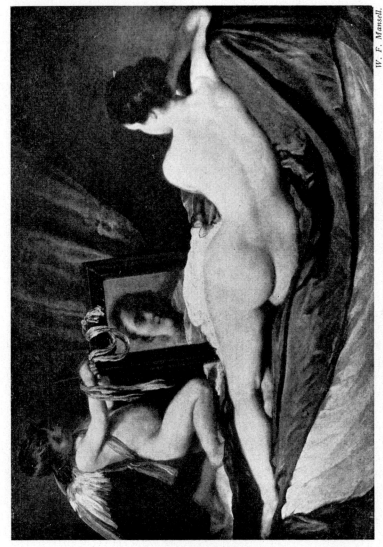

W. F. Mansell.

"VENUS AND CUPID," BY VELAZQUEZ

This superb example of the last manner of Velazquez, unique among all his great works for its refined and natural rendering of a classical subject, was for many years in an English private collection. In 1906 it was exhibited at Messrs. Agnew's gallery and was on the eve of being sold to America, when the National Art Collections Fund by indefatigable exertions raised the sum of £45,000, and in the New Year of 1907 secured the picture for the National Gallery, London.

276

—from whose great book *The Art of Velazquez* we have freely quoted—these enthusiasts made the light of Velazquez to shine before all men, so that to-day he is and evermore will be a star of the first magnitude in the firmament of Art.

§ 3

Contemporary with Velazquez, but influenced in his style of painting not so much by him as by Caravaggio, was the monastic painter Francisco Zurbaran (1598–1662), who, though born in the province of Estremadura, came to Seville when he was only sixteen and is generally regarded as a member of the School of Seville. He is chiefly famous for his religious pictures, and particularly for his monastic visions, among which " The Apotheosis of St. Thomas " in the Museum of Seville ranks as his masterpiece. His monks in white sheets often appear to be carved owing to the effect of high relief obtained by strong contrasts of light and shade, and the feeling of austerity and grandeur they display makes the paintings of Zurbaran illuminating documents of monastic life in Spain during the seventeenth century.

Among the immediate pupils of Velazquez were Juan Battista del Mazo (1600–67), who, in 1634, became his son-in-law and imitated his portraiture so cleverly that some of his paintings were at one time confounded with those by his master ; and one who became still more famous, Bartolome Esteban Murillo (1617–82). Also born at Seville, Murillo passed through a whole gamut of influences before he developed a distinct style of his own. When he was twenty-four he came to Madrid for a couple of years, and when he returned he did not forget the lessons of Velazquez. From this period date those popular pictures of beggar-boys and low-life subjects which were the first to bring him fame. " The Melon-Eaters " is a fine example of this side of Murillo's art. It charms the layman by its warm and graceful sympathy with life ; it delights the artist by the skill and taste shown in the painting of the accessories. The rind of the melon, the bloom of the grapes, the wicker of the woven baskets, all are depicted not only with great beauty of colour but with rare fidelity to the *textures* of the different objects.

Later in life Murillo altered his methods and employed a softer and more suave style, in which outlines are lost in the delicate fusion of graduated colours. The mysterious vaporous effect thus obtained was a variant of Correggio's famous " smoky " style (see Chapter XIII), but has been distinguished from his by being technically described as *vaporoso*. Among the multitude of Murillo's religious paintings in this style the most famous is " The Immaculate Conception," which the French Government acquired in 1852 for the sum of £23,440. The change in the type of religious

" THE MELON-EATERS," BY MURILLO (1617–82)

Munich

Taken from life, this picture is an example of the painter's early style, and gives pleasure both by its warm humanity and by the realistic painting of the still-life accessories.

"ST. JOHN AND THE LAMB," BY MURILLO

National Gallery, London

Murillo was inspired by John the Baptist's words, quoted by the Apostle John :
" Behold the Lamb of God, which taketh away the sin of the world."

279

"THE IMMACULATE CONCEPTION," BY MURILLO

The Louvre, Paris

Innocence and sweetness characterise this ideal of the Virgin, whose upward gaze seems to indicate not longing, so much as naïve astonishment. Compared with El Greco's burial scene (page 262) this painting indicates a great change in the type of religious presentation.

presentation is marked if we compare this painting with the frenzy of El Greco or the dramatic action displayed in a Titian or a Tintoretto. The storm and strife of the Reformation and counter-Reformation is passing away, and the enervation of the once combative Spain finds expression in a soft serenity that dreams of an ideal world. Not tragedy nor power, but innocence and sweetness characterise this vision of Mary, whose eyes, as a modern critic has pointed out, are not filled with inspiration and longing, but " astonished as those of a child gazing upon the splendour of the candles of a Christmas-tree."

Murillo was very famous in his lifetime, and the sweet sentimentality of his paintings appealed so strongly to the eighteenth and nineteenth century that for nearly two hundred years after his death he was considered the foremost of Spanish painters. To-day at least three Spanish painters, Velazquez, Goya, and El Greco, are rated more highly. Señor A. de Beruete y Moret, the learned director of the Prado Museum at Madrid, has stated that

The art of Murillo is of less interest than formerly, owing to present-day preferences, which seek spirituality in art, a force, and even a restlessness which we do not find in the work of this artist. . . . His conceptions are beautiful, but superficial. There is in them no more skilful groundwork, dramatic impulse, nor exaltation than appears at first sight. To comprehend and enjoy them it is not necessary to think ; their contemplation leaves the beholder tranquil, they do not possess the power to distract, they have no warmth, nor that distinction which makes a work unique.

Historically the art of Murillo must be regarded as a sign of the decadence of Spain, and it was not till a century later that the country gave birth to another great artist ; then the agony of the Wars of Succession found expression through the grim, satirical powers of Goya, whose work will be considered when we come to the art of the Napoleonic period.

It is interesting that in our day this work of Goya, and in particular his bitter realistic series of paintings showing the horrors of war as it came to his country, and the work of El Greco with its intense religious feeling and its deliberate distortions have become more popular than any other Spanish painting. The experiences of our time have given us a greater understanding of the things Goya had to say ; and the non-naturalistic method of working of the great Cretan master, who became Spanish only because of his long residence in the country, is now easily understood and entirely acceptable to us.

Strangely in all Spanish art there is a sense of the tortured and the hysterical. It may be something in the nature of the people which makes the sufferings of the saints and of common humanity so close to their feelings. Save with Murillo it is unhappy painting. Even Velazquez, man of the world, favourite of fortune and great courtier though he was, seems to have about him an atmosphere slightly unhealthy.

The political power and prosperity of Spain rose to its zenith between the reigns of Philip II and Philip IV, and flowered in the paintings of El Greco and Velazquez. But as the power of Spain weakened and her prosperity dwindled, so also did the glory of her art begin to wane. It is not without significance that all the great painters of Spain, Murillo included, were born before 1648, the year in which the humbled Spanish empire was compelled to recognise the independence of the Netherlands by the Peace of Münster. Immediately after Velazquez we must look for the great masters of the seventeenth century, not in decaying Spain, but in Holland, victorious and independent, the country of Hals and Rembrandt.

XVIII

HOW ART ROSE WITH THE DUTCH REPUBLIC

THE WORK OF FRANS HALS AND REMBRANDT

§ I

SHORTLY before the Spanish army began its seven months' siege of Haarlem in the winter of 1572–3, a burgher of that city named Pieter Hals made his escape with his wife and family, and found shelter in Antwerp. Well for the world that he did so, for had he taken part in the heroic defence of his native city he might have been killed in the general butchery that followed when the Spaniards at last took the town ; and then one of the world's greatest painters would never have been born.

Of the life of his son comparatively little is known, but it is tolerably certain that Frans Hals was born at Antwerp in 1580, that is to say, about five years after El Greco's arrival in Spain. Exactly when the Hals family returned to Haarlem is not known, but since the younger son, Dirk Hals (1591–1656), is reputed to have been born in Haarlem, it may be conjectured that the Hals family returned some time between 1590 and 1600. By the latter date Frans Hals was certainly working in Haarlem, and there he remained all his life.

The police records of Haarlem show that on February 20, 1616, Frans Hals was summoned for maltreating his wife (Anneke Hermans), was severely reprimanded, and dismissed on the undertaking that he would eschew drunken company and reform. On this one fact, which is indisputable, gossip has built up a legend that Hals was a man of imperfect morals and a continuous and habitual drunkard. But, as Gerald S. Davies has pointed out, drunkenness is not only a moral but a physical matter, and it is physically impossible that a confirmed inebriate should have had a hand steady enough to paint the pictures Hals painted when he was sixty and older.

We must admit an ugly passage in the painter's life—though, as a Scottish critic once observed, we do not know what provocation Hals' wife gave him !—and we must conclude that his first marriage was miserable. The poor woman died soon after the police-court case—though not, it would seem, as the result of her husband's misconduct—and a year later Hals married again. His second wife became the mother of many children,

283

surviving her husband after fifty years of married life, and since she never had occasion to take him to the police court, we may reasonably conclude that Hals was *not* an habitual wife-beater.

He appears to have been a jovial and very human being, fond of a glass in good company, and now and then, perhaps, taking one too many ; a real Bohemian, as his paintings of gipsies and strolling players attest ; but he was not a social outcast, or he would not have been constantly employed by respectable citizens and important corporations, nor would he at the age of sixty-four have been appointed a director of the Guild of St. Lucas, which protected the interests of the artists and craftsmen of Haarlem.

Yet towards the end of his life, when his honourable position cannot be assailed, he was in sad financial difficulties. At one time he supplemented his income by teaching, and Adriaen Brouwer (1605–38) and A. J. van Ostade (1610–85) were among his pupils ; but this connection did not last, and in 1652 he was distrained upon for debt by his baker, Jan Ykess. Ten years later his distress was such that he had to apply to the Municipal Council for aid, and was given the sum of 150 florins ; two years later he had to apply again, and this time (1664) the Council voted the old man a yearly pension of 200 gulden. That year Hals, now eighty-four years of age, painted his last two pictures, portraits of the " Managers of the Almshouses at Haarlem," and in 1666 he died, and was buried on September 7 in the choir of the Church of St. Bavon.

Properly to appreciate the art of Frans Hals, there is one thing we must never forget, namely, that all the work of his maturity was done during the excitement of war. It was a war which must have thrilled every Dutchman through and through, for it was waged to defend hearth and home and to deliver the fatherland from a foreign yoke ; it was a war in which one of the smallest nations in Europe had the hardihood to challenge the mightiest empire of the time. It began in 1568, about twelve years before Hals was born, and as he grew up the apparent hopelessness of the conflict disappeared, and the gaiety and elation of victory in sight began to sparkle in his paintings. When Hals first painted the officers of the St. Joris' Shooting Guild in 1616 the issue was still doubtful ; when he painted the last of his great series of military groups in 1639, again of the " Officers of St. Joris' Shooting Guild," the ultimate triumph of Holland was a foregone conclusion. In the earliest group many of the faces appear anxious and worried, but see how happy they all are even in the " Reunion of the Officers of the Guild of Archers of St. Adriaen " a picture painted in 1633. These stout fellows bear their fortune with varying demeanours ; some are smiling and jovial, some are grave and stern, one or two are evidently elated, one or two are thoughtful, but *all are confident*. In no countenance can a trace of doubt be

"THE LAUGHING CAVALIER," BY FRANS HALS (1580–1666)

Wallace Collection, London

"One of the most irresistible things ever painted" is the smile of this unknown young officer. "He looks out at you with an air of supreme contempt at one moment, of supreme good-nature at another," says the Rev. G. S. Davies, Master of Charterhouse ; "but the expression is full of changefulness, full of that electric current which plays over the human face and tells you while you look at it at one moment what to expect from the next."

"NURSE AND CHILD," BY FRANS HALS

Berlin

Look well at the face of this babe and you will see it " just beginning to ripple all over with the laughter that will come in a minute." The picture shows the artist's power to seize a fleeting expression, and the keen eye and steady hand needed to paint the elaborate details of lace and embroidery.

286

felt, and their freedom from anxiety finds its parallel in the flowing brush of the painter, equally confident and unerring.

If in the intoxication of victory, coming and assured, some of the soldier-patriots of Holland became boisterous in their exuberance, who will blame them ? And who will blame Hals if in this great and exhilarating period his art also becomes boisterous and exuberant ?

It was nearly a quarter of a century before the final victory and the Spanish acknowledgment of Holland's independence, when Frans Hals about 1624 painted that portrait of an officer known all over the world as " The Laughing Cavalier." The treatment and the subject are in complete unity, for the swagger of the brushwork is in harmony with the swaggering pose of the officer. G. S. Davies, the Master of Charterhouse, has commented on the extraordinary mobility of feature in the expression of this portrait—how at one moment the face of the cavalier seems provocatively disdainful, at another full of amused good-humour. Another brilliant example of the unrivalled power of Hals to catch a fleeting expression will be found in his later painting, " Nurse and Child," a work which with its wonderfully elaborate and intricate detail no alcoholic hand could possibly have painted. Look well at this babe with its odd little old face, and you will see it " just beginning to ripple all over with the laughter that will come in a minute." G. S. Davies thinks Hals must have learnt the knack of this from watching his own children in his own home, and surely we may say with conviction that the man who could paint babies with so penetrating an eye was a good father.

Splendid as these two paintings are, good as the portraits by Hals in the National Gallery, London, yet to know Hals to the uttermost it is necessary to visit his home-town of Haarlem and to see there the series of great portrait-groups he painted of the Guilds, the " Archers of St. George " (Joris) and the " Archers of Saint Adriaen." These shooting guilds may be roughly described as equivalent to our own Honourable Artillery Company when it was first instituted.

It is in these paintings of the citizen-soldiers of his own city that Hals displays his highest gifts both as a decorator and as a painter of actuality. The figures are so real that we who look at them seem to be one of the company ; but though the arrangement appears so natural our eyes are always gladdened by a beauty of pattern, a flow of line, and a balancing of masses which testify to the painter's science of design. There is nothing with which we can compare them save " The Surrender of Breda," and in making this comparison we must not forget that if Velazquez was his contemporary he was also by nearly twenty years the junior of Hals. It is easy to count up the qualities lacking in the art of Frans Hals, who had neither the grave dignity and mastery of light that Velazquez possessed nor the

"REUNION OF THE OFFICERS OF THE GUILD OF ARCHERS OF ST. ADRIAEN,"
BY FRANS HALS

Haarlem

Very similar to our own Honourable Artillery Company when it was first instituted, these Guilds of
Dutch citizen-soldiers played a gallant part in the eighty years' struggle with Spain which ended in
the independence of the Dutch Republic.

scenic splendour of Rubens, nor the thought of his contemporary Rembrandt ; but a painter, like a man, must be judged by what he is—not by what he is not—and Hals keeps his place among the great masters by his own peculiar gifts as an exuberant, and indeed an inspired, portrayer of the bravery of Holland in her greatest hour.

§ 2

There is this initial difference between Hals and Rembrandt, that whereas Hals passed the greater part of his working life during a time of war, Rembrandt attained his maturity and executed most of his greatest work after the conclusion of peace. Hals lived in and depicted a life of action, when men must be up and doing and there was no time to think ; Rembrandt's middle years and old age were spent in an age of comparative peace and quiet, when Holland had the leisure to think and to meditate not only on the greatness of her political achievements but on the problems of life. Hals expressed the gallantry of Holland in action ; Rembrandt, the profundity of her thought.

One ought not to lay too much stress on a mere coincidence, yet when we remember the philosophical temper of his art it seems peculiarly appropriate that Rembrandt should have been born in the university town of Leyden, the headquarters of Dutch philosophy and learning. He came into the world on July 15, 1607, being the fifth and youngest son of Hermon Gerritzoon van Rijn, a prosperous miller who possessed a mill, several fields, and other property. The parents were ambitious for their youngest son and sent him to school " to learn the Latin tongue to prepare himself for the Academy of Leyden, so that in the fulness of time he might serve the city and the Republic with his knowledge."

The boy, however, did not take kindly to book-learning, but was for ever drawing and designing. At school Rembrandt is said to have been one of the idle pupils who " during their writing lessons, when they ought to be writing, scrawl figures of vessels and animals all over the margins of their books." He was at the University in 1620, but it soon became clear to his father that it was unprofitable for Rembrandt to continue his studies there. His aptitude for art was unmistakable, and accordingly he was apprenticed first to Jacob van Swanenburch, and afterwards to Pieter Lastman, of Amsterdam, a fashionable portrait-painter of the day.

Six months were enough to satiate this earnest young student with the smooth and flattering trivialities of a fashionable merchant of likenesses, and in 1624 he returned to Leyden to study and practise painting by himself. One of the earliest of his known and dated pictures is " St. Paul in Prison," painted in 1627, now at Stuttgart. This picture shows the precise rendering

K
289

of detail characteristic of his early style, but also anticipates the light effect of his later work by the way in which the light is concentrated on the head of the apostle. That the painter had already attracted some attention is clear from the fact that in the following year Gerard Dou, a promising boy of fifteen, was placed with him as a pupil.

About 1631 Rembrandt removed from Leyden to Amsterdam, an important step taken no doubt owing to the increasing number of portrait commissions he received from the rich merchants of this flourishing city. He had also made some reputation for himself as an etcher, and in 1632 Hendrik van Uylenburg, who had previously published some of his etchings, commissioned Rembrandt to paint a portrait of Saskia van Ulyenburg, a young cousin of the print-seller. The acquaintance thus begun soon ripened into love, and the form and face of this dainty little patrician, an orphan who had lost both her parents, suddenly becomes the prevailing theme both in the painted and etched work of Rembrandt. The attraction was mutual, and though her relatives disapproved of the attachment, considering the painter not good enough for a well-dowered young lady of quality, yet love won the day, and Rembrandt and Saskia were married in 1634. The veiled hostility shown by his bride's relations led the painter to relieve his feelings by painting a series of pictures illustrating the life of Samson, in which Saskia is the Delilah, the artist Samson, and the Philistines, of course, are his wife's relatives. These paintings not only express the artist's defiance of family pride, but also his attitude towards the world at large, and his recurring amazement at his having won for himself so sweet a maid. The joyous picture of himself with Saskia on his knee, shows Rembrandt at the zenith of his happiness. Still popular as a painter, his portraits were sought after, he had a crowd of pupils, and a charming wife who brought him a moderate fortune. The young couple felt that the world was their own, and behaved like children in their utter disregard of the value of money. Rembrandt kept on buying new jewels and fine stuffs with which to deck his beloved and paint her in a new guise : he bought the works of other artists and beautiful objects of all kinds, wishing to create a fairy world around a fairy wife. But soon all this luxurious beauty was overshadowed by sorrow. Two children died one after the other, and in 1642 Saskia herself died after giving birth to the boy Titus.

Rembrandt had had his fun, and now came the time to pay. Already money was beginning to be scarce, and his popularity as a portrait-painter was beginning to wane. In the year Saskia died, Rembrandt had completed his great picture, the " Sortie " or " Night Watch," which though to-day the most popular of all his works and universally ranked among his greatest achievements, almost destroyed the contemporary reputation of the painter and began that decline of his fortunes which ended in his bankruptcy.

"THE ARTIST AND HIS FIRST WIFE," BY REMBRANDT (1607–69)

Dresden

In this early picture Rembrandt shows himself feast-making with his bride. It is almost the only riotously joyful self-portrait painted by an artist whose life was full of sorrow.

"THE NIGHT WATCH," OR "THE SORTIE," BY REMBRANDT

Amsterdam

" Turn out the guard ! " This dramatic rendering of a company of militia about to march displeased the officers who had commissioned the painting, because Rembrandt had painted a scene mysterious in its light and shadow. The officers wanted a collection of recognisable likenesses. Now acknowledged as a great masterpiece, the picture ruined Rembrandt's practice as a portrait-painter.

The subject is explicitly stated on the back of a copy of it in water-colour : " The young Laird of Purmerlandt (Frans Banning Cocq) in his capacity as Captain gives to his Lieutenant, the Laird of Vlaerdingen, the command to march out his burgher-company." This amply justifies the more correct title of " The Sortie," but the purpose and hour of this " going out " of a company of civic militia are not easy to define. In the eighteenth century it was assumed to be a nocturnal watch turning out on its rounds by artificial light, hence the French name for the picture " Ronde de Nuit," which has been anglicised as " The Night Watch." But as Prof. Baldwin Brown of Edinburgh University justly pointed out, the time is " certainly the day and not the night. The shadow of the captain's outstretched hand and arm is thrown by the sun upon the yellow dress of the second in com-mand, and it is easy to see by the relative positions of object and shadow that the sun is still pretty high in the heavens."

Before we too hastily condemn those who condemned this splendid picture, we must put ourselves in their position. To see what Captain Banning Cocq and his friends expected we should turn back and look at Hals' portrait group of the Guild of Archers. They expected to be painted like that, and Rembrandt painted them like this ! In point of fact, Rem-brandt did not paint *them*, he painted the *scene*. Hals shows a collection of individual officers, each of whom is clearly seen and recognisable. Rem-brandt shows a patrol, many of whose members are lost in shadow and unable to be identified. As a picture Rembrandt's work has splendid qualities of drama, lighting, and movement which we cannot find in the Hals ; but Captain Banning Cocq and his friends did not want to see these qualities, they wanted to see themselves. Rembrandt had painted a great picture, but he had dealt a heavy blow to human vanity, and his contem-poraries could not forgive him.

It must be admitted that Rembrandt was wilful and wayward. He would go his own way, and he was only justified by the greatness of his genius. He was, as Muther has said, " the first artist who, in the modern sense, did not execute commissions, but expressed his own thoughts. The emotions which moved his inmost being were the only things which he expressed on canvas. He does not seem to think that anyone is listening to him, but only speaks with himself ; he is anxious, not to be understood by others, but only to express his moods and feelings."

An interesting example of the liberties Rembrandt took with his nominal subject will be found in the Wallace Collection. The picture now known as " The Centurion Cornelius " used to be called " The Unmerciful Servant," and commentators explained that the figure in the turban and red robe was Christ, and enlarged on the displeasure shown in his face and the guilt and fear of the Unrighteous Servant, whom they took to be the central of the three figures to the right. Then a mezzotint by James Ward, published in 1800, was discovered, and in this reproduction the correct title was given. The red-robed figure proved to be Cornelius, in no way " displeased," while the remaining three figures are " two of his household servants, and a devout soldier of them that waited on him continually " (Acts x. 7). This widely-spread error shows how easy it is to misread pictures if they are approached with preconceived ideas. The misunderstanding, of course, has been brought about by Rembrandt's fondness for oriental splendour, which led him to put a Roman centurion in Asiatic costume ! It is not " correct " in the way that Alma-Tadema's classical scenes are ; but real greatness in art does not depend on accuracy of antiquarian details—however praiseworthy this may be—but on largeness of conception, noble design, and splendid colour.

Overwhelmed by his domestic sorrows—he lost his old mother two years before Saskia died—neglected by his former patrons, Rembrandt turned to Nature for consolation. He wandered about the country-side recording all he saw. Practically all his landscapes were painted between 1640 and 1652. Many of his most beautiful landscape etchings were also executed during this period. The most famous of them all, " The Three Trees " was done in 1643. It shows a view of Amsterdam from a slight eminence outside the town, and a storm-cloud and its shadow are used to intensify the brilliance of the light and the dramatic aspect of this mood of Nature. This is landscape in the grand style ; but its homelier, more intimate note appealed equally to the artist. A lovely example of the picturesque corner portrayed for its own intrinsic beauty is the etching executed in 1645 known as " Six's Bridge." Tradition relates that this plate was etched against time for a wager at the country house of Rembrandt's most loyal friend, Jan Six, while the servant was fetching the mustard, that had been forgotten for a meal, from a neighbouring village. There is nothing impossible in the story, for Rembrandt is known to have been an impetuous and rapid worker on occasion ; but if this little masterpiece was done in haste, we must not forget that it was also done with " the knowledge of a lifetime."

Even while Saskia was alive Rembrandt was in want of ready money, and when on his mother's death in 1640 he inherited a half-share of a mill, he hastened to have it transferred to his brother Wilhelm and his nephew. Though he lost money by the transaction, he probably gained his end in keeping all the mill in the family instead of a share going to his creditors. Then in 1647 he became involved in lawsuits with Saskia's family, who objected to Rembrandt's connection with his servant Hendrickje Stoffels, and wished to prevent him from being trustee for his and Saskia's son Titus. These lawsuits, which lasted till after 1653, and ended in Saskia's relatives

"THE BLINDNESS OF TOBIT," ETCHING BY REMBRANDT

Never has the pathos of a blind man's groping been more movingly expressed than in this etching.

W. F. Mansell.

"THE THREE TREES," ETCHING BY REMBRANDT

Though we see to the left a distant view of Amsterdam, this masterly etching is not merely a transcription of something seen, but a dramatic rendering of a mood of Nature. Its grandeur is unequalled in etching and has rarely been approached in painting.

"SIX'S BRIDGE," BY REMBRANDT

Etched for a wager while a servant was fetching mustard, forgotten for lunch, from a neighbouring village, this delightful little landscape shows the delicacy of Rembrandt's handling and the swift sureness of his drawing.

W. F. Mansell.

"CHRIST WITH THE SICK AROUND HIM, RECEIVING LITTLE CHILDREN,"
ETCHING BY REMBRANDT

The most famous of Rembrandt's etchings, this is popularly known as the "Hundred Guilder Print" from the price it once realised at auction early in the eighteenth century. No work shows more splendidly Rembrandt's command of the etcher's art and his deep insight into manifold phases of human character and emotion.

298

obtaining the trusteeship but not the custody of Titus, greatly contributed to Rembrandt's difficulties.

His marriage with Hendrickje Stoffels, a woman of humble birth, was another cause of offence to aristocratic patrons ; all the same, it was a wise action. This devoted woman mothered Titus with loving and unremitting care ; she made great efforts to stem the tide of ill-fortune, and when the crash came and Rembrandt was made bankrupt in 1656, she loyally shared her husband's troubles and used her wits to rebuild their fortunes. As soon as Titus was old enough she combined with him in keeping an old curiosity shop, starting, one imagines, with some relics of the treasures Rembrandt had amassed for Saskia. Money, or the want of it, however, was not a thing which could profoundly trouble a philosophic dreamer like Rembrandt. If he had it, he spent it royally ; if he had it not, he went without. Only a year after his bankruptcy he achieved one of the world's masterpieces of portraiture, " The Artist's Son Titus," in the Wallace Collection. If you look at the Pellicorne portraits, also in the Wallace Collection, you will obtain a fair idea of Rembrandt's ordinary professional style in 1632–34, when his painting was still popular. But how thin and shallow these early portraits seem beside this haunting and passionate portrait of the son he loved so dearly. Turning to the " Titus " after these early works, we see how far Rembrandt has travelled. Three or four years later he painted the wonderful " Portrait of Françoise van Wasserhoven," in the National Gallery, one of the most reverent, sympathetic, and intimate studies of old age ever painted.

Throughout his life Rembrandt was a keen student of human nature, and no painter has ever penetrated further than he did into the inner lives of the men and women he painted. His wonderful insight into character made him the greatest psychologist in portraiture the world has yet seen, and since he searched faces above all for the marks of life's experience which they bore, old people—who had had the longest experience—were inevitably subjects peculiarly dear to him and subjects which he interpreted with con-summate mastery. His own face he painted over and over again, and if we study the sequence of his self-portraiture from early manhood to ripe old age, we see not only the gradual development of his technical powers but also the steady advance made by Rembrandt in expressing with poignant intensity the thoughts and emotions of humanity.

Of Rembrandt's technique Sir John Everett Millais wrote : " In his first period Rembrandt was very careful and minute in detail, and there is evidence of stippling in his flesh paintings ; but in the fullness of his power all appearance of such manipulation and minuteness vanished in the breadth and facility of his brush, though the advantage of his early manner remained. . . . I have closely examined his pictures in the National Gallery, and have

"THE 'LANSDOWNE' MILL," BY REMBRANDT

In his appreciation of the veil of beauty which atmosphere casts over a scene, as well as in his capacity to find strangeness in the familiar and beauty in the commonplace, Rembrandt anticipated the romantic landscapes of the nineteenth century. A few years ago this picture was sold for £100,000 by Lord Lansdowne to an American collector, Mr. J. E. Widener.

FRANÇOISE VAN WASSERHOVEN, BY REMBRANDT

National Gallery, London

This noble rendering of the dignity of age teaches us that while physical beauty may be only
" skindeep " and quickly fade, beauty of character endures while life lasts.

"HENDRICKJE STOFFELS," BY REMBRANDT

First his maidservant, and then his second wife, Hendrickje was a loyal helpmate to Rembrandt.
By her own efforts she practically supported him during his worst financial crisis, and she was a devoted
mother to Titus, his son by his first wife.

"THE ARTIST'S SON, TITUS," BY REMBRANDT

Wallace Collection, London

In this portrait of his only son we see a superb example of Rembrandt's later style which should be compared with his earlier portrait group on page 291. The features here are built up boldly by patches of light and shade, and the portrait has a consequent softness and richness as compared with the earlier work.

actually seen beneath the grand veil of breadth, the early work that his art conceals from untrained eyes—the whole science of painting." Among his contemporaries the minute detail in the work of his earlier period was far more admired than the " veil of breadth " which he cast over his later paintings, and it was long before people who admired his early portraits could be persuaded that his later paintings were not only equally good, but vastly superior both in workmanship and expression.

Gradually among the discerning few the outstanding excellence of Rembrandt's portraiture was again acknowledged, and in 1661 he received a commission for another official picture. He was asked to paint a portrait group of five officials of the Clothmakers' Company, and staging them on the dais on which they presided over a meeting, Rembrandt produced the wonder-work known as " The Syndics." Avoiding the dangers of " The Sortie," Rembrandt places all five figures in a clear light and yet gives them the unity of a scene taken from life.

Alas ! this fresh artistic triumph was dearly paid for by more domestic misfortunes. Soon after this work was completed, Hendrickje, the loyal helpmate, died. Titus, now grown up, married his cousin, and after less than a year of married life he also died. Now, indeed, Rembrandt was alone in the world, and though a posthumous daughter to Titus was born in 1669, the artist, now in his sixty-third year, was too worn out to struggle much longer against " the slings and arrows of outrageous fortune." He lived long enough to see his little grand-daughter Titia christened after her father, and then, crushed by the accumulated sorrows of a lifetime, passed to his long rest on October 4, 1669. To all appearance the illness and death of the greatest man Holland ever produced passed unnoticed, and only the bare fact of his burial in the Westerkerk, Amsterdam, is attested by an official entry.

XIX

DUTCH PAINTING IN THE SEVENTEENTH CENTURY

THE ART OF CUYP, DOU, HOBBEMA, DE HOOCH, POTTER, MAES,
RUISDAEL, VAN DE VELDE, AND VERMEER OF DELFT

§ I

WE saw in the previous chapter how, after a long struggle, the yoke of the Spaniards was broken, and the independence of the Dutch Republic was established in 1648 by the Peace of Münster. This event is commemorated by Terborch's picture in the National Gallery of the signing of the Treaty; in this it will be noticed that the Protestant Dutch delegates raise their hands to affirm, while the Roman Catholic plenipotentiaries of Spain lay their hands on the Gospels to take the oath. Careful and exact both in the portraiture of those present and in the painting of every little detail, this moderate-sized picture expresses the sober spirit in which Holland celebrated her victory.

While of considerable historic interest, this picture is not a supreme masterpiece of art; it is not so effective as the same painter's " Portrait of a Gentleman," a small full-length figure which also hangs in the National Gallery. Historical subjects did not call forth the highest powers of the painters of the Netherlands. The art of Holland was neither an ecclesiastical nor a state art: it was a domestic art which produced pictures, not for churches or public buildings, but for the private homes of citizens. So wonderful was the artistic activity inspired by the wave of patriotism which swept through Holland, that the name of these so-called " Little Masters " is truly legion, and no attempt can be made in this OUTLINE to mention each by name. Only a few representative artists can be selected for individual notice.

Chronologically, the first place among the Little Masters is claimed by Adrian Brouwer (1605–38), whose " Boor Asleep " is one of the most precious Dutch pictures in the Wallace Collection. It is still a matter of dispute whether Brouwer was born in Holland or Flanders, but he certainly spent his youth in Haarlem, where he studied under Frans Hals. Afterwards he worked both in Amsterdam and Antwerp. How highly Brouwer was esteemed by other painters of his time is shown by the fact that Rubens

Wallace Collection, London

The absolute realism of later Dutch Painting sent its masters to the ordinary life of the people for
their subjects. They showed us men and women often at their least dignified, but sometimes, as
in this masterpiece, invested them with dignity nevertheless.

possessed seventeen of his pictures, while even Rembrandt, in spite of his financial difficulties, managed to collect and retain eight Brouwers. A humorous vividness of vision, concise and vigorous drawing, and an enamel-like beauty of colour are the distinctive qualities of his art.

Apart from the landscape-painters—whom we must consider subsequently—most of the Dutch painters of the home descended artistically either from Hals or from Rembrandt. Gerard Dou (1613–75), one of Rembrandt's many pupils, was the most successful painter financially of his day. He made his fortune by never progressing beyond the first manner of his master and by painting with a careful literalness which demanded no exercise of the beholder's imagination. " The Poulterer's Shop " is a typical example of Dou's minutely finished style. It has always been popular because it is much easier to recognise industry than to understand inspiration, and in rendering this everyday incident in a shopping expedition Dou has spared no pains to render each detail with laborious fidelity.

How even in the rendering of detail there is all the difference in the world between the Letter of Exactitude and the Spirit of Truth may be seen when we compare the pictures of Dou with those of similar scenes by Terborch, De Hoogh, or Vermeer. Each one of these three exquisite painters has an eye for detail as keen as that possessed by Dou, but they all have far more ability than Dou possessed to subordinate details to the unity of the whole. The eldest of these three masters, Gerard Terborch or Terburg (1617–81), has already been mentioned. As a young man he studied at Haarlem, where he was probably influenced by Hals and Brouwer, but Terborch did not found his style only on what he found within the borders of Holland. He was more a man-of-the-world than most of his artist contemporaries. He visited England, Germany, France, Italy, and Spain, and in the last country he certainly studied the paintings of Velazquez, who was only eighteen years his senior. Like Velazquez, but unlike most of his fellows in Holland, Terborch was aristocratic in the temper of his art, so that his pictures as a rule show us a higher strata of Dutch society than that depicted by the majority of Dutch artists.

Here it may be well to pause in order to emphasise the fact that these Dutch painters were preoccupied with rendering the *manners* of their time. This characteristic, which gives their work a lasting historical value, has caused their little pictures of courtyards, interiors, tavern scenes, conversations, toilet-scenes, and the like to be known as " genre " painting, from the French word *genre* (*i.e.* manner or style). A few, like Terborch, show us the manner of dress and living of the upper classes ; others show us the middle classes, and still more concern themselves with the manners of the peasants and lower classes. Among these last the best known is Jan Steen (1626–79), who is often amusingly satirical in his outlook ; other painters

"THE POULTERER'S SHOP," BY GERARD DOU (1613–75)

National Gallery, London

A typical example of the precise, minutely finished style of this artist, a pupil of Rembrandt, who made his fortune by imitating the first manner of his master. Though Dou lacked imagination and dramatic grandeur, his faithful rendering of everyday incidents makes him a valuable chronicler of the manners of his time.

of a similar style were Adrian van Ostade (1610–85) and the Fleming David Teniers (1610–90).

These painters may amuse us for the moment, but they do not hold us spellbound as some of the others do. The greatest rival of Terborch was Peter de Hooch or de Hoogh (1629–77), who was only twelve years his junior. De Hooch's figures may not be so aristocratic as those of Terborch, but they are seen as finely and have their being in the same clear light which both these masters observed and rendered so lovingly. This passion for the rendering of light began to show itself in the paintings of Brouwer ; it becomes still more marked in the work of Terborch, and it approaches perfection in the pictures of De Hooch. His chief interest, as the late Sir Walter Armstrong remarked, " is always absorbed by the one problem, that of capturing and bottling the sunlight." How supremely well he succeeded in his object is shown by our illustration of " A Girl Reading," a masterpiece of interior illumination, in which every object is not only perfectly rendered but keeps its proper distance within the room owing to the painter's delicately exact notation of the relative degrees of lighting.

In his youth, as Armstrong has pointed out, De Hooch liked the broadest daylight, but with advancing years he preferred " merely to suggest the outside sun, as it creeps down tiled passages, through red curtains and half-open shutters." An interesting example of De Hooch's earlier period when he chose the broadest daylight for his scene is the " Interior of a Dutch House." Nothing could be more brilliant or more faithful to Nature than the bright sunlight which streams down on the group near the window. It is instructive to observe here that the standing figure by the fireplace was an afterthought, put in by the artist to improve his design. This woman forms the apex of a triangle of which the wall with the windows forms the base. We know that she was an afterthought because the artist had already painted the black-and-white tiled floor right up to the fireplace before he began the figure, and that is why we can still see the tiling through the woman's skirt. This correction would not have been visible to De Hooch's contemporaries, but it is a peculiar property of oil paint that an underpainting, invisible when the paint is fresh, will in time work its way up to the surface. Since De Hooch was a consummate craftsman whose handling of pigment approached perfection, the fact that even he has been unable to disguise a correction is a useful lesson to a living painter that he must get his picture right from the start, or otherwise, however clever he may be, his errors will be found out after his death. In De Hooch's interior, this emergence of what it was endeavoured to hide is too trivial and unimportant to affect seriously the beauty and merit of the painting.

W. F. Mansell

"INTERIOR OF A DUTCH HOUSE," BY DE HOOCH (1629–77)

National Gallery, London

The artist's joy in painting sunlight is delightfully expressed in his brilliantly lit interior. The figure standing before the fireplace is an afterthought added to improve the design of the grouping after the picture had been finished, and that is why the black and white tiling of the floor can be seen through the woman's skirt.

Bruckmann.

"A GIRL READING," BY DE HOOCH

Munich

Whatever his subject, de Hooch was absorbed by one problem, that of " capturing and bottling the sunlight." Compare this masterpiece of illumination with Dou's picture and it will be seen how Dou's details appear hard and unsympathetic, while every object in de Hooch's interior is soft and atmospheric owing to the greater subtlety of his lighting.

§ 2

Jan van der Meer, commonly known as Vermeer of Delft (1632–75), is one of the Old Masters whom modern research has rescued from unmerited neglect. Houbraken, a historian who wrote only forty years after his death, does not even mention him, and for two centuries his name was almost forgotten and his paintings were sold as works by De Hooch, Terborch, Metsu, or even Rembrandt. Then in the middle of the nineteenth century a French exile named Thoré spent three years (1858–60) studying records and archives in Holland and patiently searching out Vermeer's paintings. Since Thoré published his account of his studies, the fame of Vermeer has rapidly spread and increased. To-day he is one of the most costly and one of the most popular of the old masters.

Of his private life very little is known. Vermeer was three years younger than De Hooch, and fifteen years younger than Terborch. We know that as soon as he came of age in 1653 he married Catherine Bolenes and by her had eight children. He was evidently esteemed in his native city, for in 1662 and again in 1670 he was elected one of the principal officers of the Guild of St. Luke of Delft. But fame is one thing and fortune is another. When Vermeer died in 1675 he had nothing to leave his wife and family but twenty-six unsold pictures. If these were put into the market to-day they might fetch anything *over* a quarter of a million pounds, but there were no American millionaires in the seventeenth century ; so poor Vermeer was judged to have died insolvent and his widow's affairs had to be put in the hands of a liquidator, who happened to be the naturalist Leeuwenhoek.

To explain in words the incomparable charm of Vermeer's painting is as simple and as difficult as to explain the beauty of light. The illumination in his pictures is as perfect as it is in the best works of De Hooch ; and if the pictures of Vermeer are still more beautiful than those of De Hooch it is because Vermeer was a still finer and more subtle colourist. He was, indeed, one of the greatest colourists the world has ever known. He excelled in all subjects. His " Head of a Young Girl " is one of the loveliest portraits in the world. This young girl is not strikingly beautiful in herself. She has a sweet face, and Vermeer has brought out the sweetness of her disposition and the charm of her youth ; but he has done more than this : by the loveliness of his colour—particularly by the contrast of the blue and lemon-yellow of which he was so fond—Vermeer has made her a joy for ever. Colour of this lyrical beauty sings its own sweet song.

Vermeer's " View of Delft," also at The Hague, is the loveliest street scene or town view in art. It has the crystal purity of colour and limpid atmosphere of Delft itself, which a living writer has described as " the

"HEAD OF A YOUNG GIRL," BY JAN VERMEER OF DELFT (1632–75)

The Hague

" The Perfect Painter " is the name E. V. Lucas gave to this artist, who, long numbered among the " Little Masters " of seventeenth-century Holland, is now recognised to have been probably the greatest colourist who ever lived. This head is his masterpiece in portraiture.

"VIEW OF DELFT," BY VERMEER

The Hague

The loveliest view of a town in art, this picture is exquisite in its quality of light and sense of airiness. Nothing could be more natural, more true to the thing seen.

"THE PEARL NECKLACE," BY VERMEER

Berlin

In this picture of a lady looking in a mirror to see how her necklace suits her, we are fascinated by
the artist's rendering of light, which softly illumines every object in the scene.

cleanest city in Europe, looking as if all the houses were thoroughly scrubbed down and polished each day before sunrise." Nothing could be more natural, more true to the thing seen, than this painting, yet nothing could be more perfect in every quality that goes to the making of a work of art.

These two pictures are exceptional even among the paintings of Vermeer, and when we come to consider his more numerous paintings of small figures in interiors, the richness he offers us makes selection embarrassing. It would be perilous to say " The Pearl Necklace " is better than " The Milkmaid " or other pictures one could mention ; but it is certainly one of the best and shows how Vermeer could compete with De Hooch in " bottling sunlight " and beat that master even at his own favourite game.

Vermeer's art undoubtedly affected his contemporaries, those of his own age as well as those who were his juniors. Gabriel Metsu (1630–67) sometimes comes near to Vermeer, and the colour of " The Letter Writer Surprised " in the Wallace Collection has a tenderness which is apt to make even a Terborch look a little hard. Metsu knows how to set his stage decoratively ; his pictures are always sprightly ; but his observation is less subtle, and his research into light and shade is not carried to the point of perfection reached by De Hooch and Vermeer.

Nicolas Maes (1632–93), another pupil of Rembrandt, though less gifted than Metsu, used to be thought of chiefly as a portrait-painter, but is now much esteemed for the anecdotal pictures he painted in his youth. " The Idle Servant " is an amusing example of his work in this style, and shows both his own powers of observation and what he learnt from Rembrandt in the way of using lighting to enhance a dramatic effect. But if we look critically at the picture, say at the cat stealing the plucked bird, or at the whole area of the tiled floor, we shall have to admit that in drawing Maes was inferior to Dou, and in illumination far inferior to De Hooch or Vermeer. All these subject pictures were painted between 1655 and 1665, after which date circumstances drove Maes into " pot-boiling " portraiture.

§ 3

We have seen now with what variety and perfection the Dutch artists painted their national hearthside : and next we must consider how they painted their homeland. Midway between the genre painters and the landscape-painters stands Aart van der Neer (1603–77), who forms a bridge, as it were, between the two groups. Born three years before Rembrandt, he, like Jan van Goyen (1596–1656), is one of the early pioneers of landscape painting, yet by the little figures in his landscape he tells us a great deal of the life of Holland. Thus his " Skating Scene " in the Wallace Collection has been ranked by the famous Dr. Bode as " among the most perfect landscape

"THE IDLE SERVANT," BY NICOLAS MAES (1632–93)

National Gallery, London

An amusing example of this artist's powers of humorous observation.   Maes was a pupil of Rembrandt and enjoyed a considerable vogue as a portrait-painter, though his drawing was not equal to Dou's, and his illumination is far less perfect than that of de Hooch or Vermeer.

" A SKATING SCENE," BY VAN DER NEER (1603–77)

Wallace Collection, London

One of the " most perfect landscape delineations of winter," this picture also illustrates the life of Holland in times of frost when the canals and rivers become highways for the traffic of the country.

delineations of winter," but it is also a charming picture of manners, giving us a glimpse of the life in seventeenth-century Holland.

Towards the end of his life Aart van der Neer deteriorated as other "Little Masters" did also ; in addition to painting, he kept a tavern, and possibly business losses in the wine-trade drove him to do inferior but more immediately saleable work during his last years. Nearly all his best work was done before 1665, when he was not dependent on painting for a livelihood, but a happy amateur who could paint what he liked. He was one of the first artists to attempt painting night scenes, but though the novelty of his moonlight views attracted attention, his winter landscapes in daylight are usually considered to be his best work.

Agriculture has always been an important industry in Holland, and the local artists who catered so well for the needs of the citizen did not forget to make an appeal also to the farmers. Of many who made a speciality of painting cattle, Paul Potter (1625–54) is the most celebrated, though he died in his twenty-ninth year. His big picture " The Bull " is a favourite showpiece at The Hague, where guides—most conservative critics—wax enthusiastic about its accuracy. Courageous people, however, have been known to confess that they find its precise statement of fact a little dull, though few dare to be so severe as Muther, who once described Potter's cattle as " essentially Dutch, for they know neither passions, nor struggles, nor movement, but chew the cud phlegmatically or lie down in comfortable repose."

Cattle also figure largely in the paintings of Albert Cuyp (1620–91), who is splendidly represented in English collections. Cuyp was no mere animal-painter : his principal interest lay neither in the beast nor in the earth, but above in the mighty vault of the heavens. He does not so much set out to paint cattle as to *use* cattle, and we may see in his " River Scene " how effectively cows can be used as dark spots which bring out by contrast the luminosity of the sky, and as prominent objects in the foreground which emphasise the great stretch of flat landscape which reaches out to the horizon. The glowing light and golden colour of Cuyp have placed him among the great sky-painters of the world, and his work has for centuries been an example and an incentive to British landscape painting.

Apart from all other Dutch painters of landscape—seeming, indeed, to belong to another race—stands the austere and majestic figure of Jacob van Ruisdael (1628–82). Though he took all Nature for his province, and in his youth painted her more peaceful aspects, we instinctively associate his sublime spirit with holy spots " both savage and enchanted." It is difficult to think of him as eight years younger than Cuyp, for so serious and austere is his vision that we can hardly believe Ruisdael was ever young. Even when he paints a simple seaside scene like " The Shore at Scheveningen " he gives dramatic intensity to the scene by the rolling clouds in the sky

"THE BULL," BY PAUL POTTER (1625–54)

The Hague

One of the earliest and most celebrated cattle-pictures in the world, Potter's "Bull" is a show-piece which delights farmers to-day as it did in the seventeenth century.

Rischgitz.

"RIVER SCENE," BY ALBERT CUYP (1620–91)

National Gallery, London

The glowing light and golden colour of Cuyp's skies have placed him in the front rank of those painters who "set the sun in the heavens." In this picture we see how effectively he uses cows as dark spots which bring out the luminosity of the sky and lend enchantment to the distant horizon.

"THE MILL," BY JACOB VAN RUISDAEL (1628–82)

Amsterdam

" His grave and solemn mind gives to the simplest and most commonplace of landscapes a look of sad importance, which is almost like a reproach of lightmindedness to any other man's work which happens to hang alongside."

" THE SHORE AT SCHEVENINGEN," BY JACOB VAN RUISDAEL

National Gallery, London

Scheveningen to-day is a fashionable watering-place, but this beautiful picture shows it as it was nearly three hundred years ago, when the majesty of Nature was undisturbed by the villadom of Man.

which seem to repeat the restlessness of the agitated waves. Again, in his famous painting of " The Mill," for all the stillness of the scene, we feel that this is the calm before the storm—as, indeed, the sky betokens. Grandly designed as this painting is, it is one of the quietest works of the artist, who, though infinitely varied in his choice of subject, delighted especially in painting waterfalls, cascades, and rocky cliffs. Ruisdael, says a gifted American painter, John La Farge,

is as different from Cuyp as shadow is from sunshine ; and his grave and solemn mind gives to the simplest and most commonplace of landscapes a look of sad importance, which is almost like a reproach of lightmindedness to any other man's work which happens to hang alongside.

Meindert Hobbema (1638–1709) was Ruisdael's pupil and friend, but as different in temperament from his master as a man could well be. Ruisdael approaches Nature with the devoutness of a worshipper approaching a shrine ; Hobbema, with the unconscious ease of a man entering his own home. He painted the same subjects over and over again, but he painted them so naturally, so freshly and convincingly, that they take us straight back to Nature, not to the pictures of another artist. In the humbleness and sincerity of his naturalism he expresses everybody's feeling of delight and thankfulness in sunny weather and fresh country air. " The Avenue " is probably the best beloved landscape in the National Gallery, London, and this and other works by Hobbema have had a profound and far-reaching effect on British landscape. Out of his smiling and friendly art grew our Norwich school of landscape. Gainsborough acknowledged his worth by word and deed, and the last sentence ever uttered by John Crome was, " Oh, Hobbema, my dear Hobbema, how I have loved you ! " It is sad to think that this simple, honest, and most easily understood painter, a man of genius who has given happiness to millions for six generations, fared so poorly in his profession of painting that when he was thirty he sought another means of livelihood. He sought and obtained a small position in the wine-customs, and thus made himself independent of picture-buyers and dealers. He saw his master, the great painter Ruisdael, battling with poverty and becoming no more prosperous as the years rolled on, so Hobbema wisely determined to look elsewhere for his bread-and-butter and make landscape painting his hobby and pastime. It is significant to note that his supreme masterpiece, " The Avenue," was painted some years after he had become a civil servant, and when, without having to think of what the buyer might or might not like, he could indulge to the full his feeling for the pattern in landscape and his sense of beauty in the elements of Nature.

It must be admitted that if Holland had a galaxy of artistic talent during the seventeenth century she did little to encourage genius. As so often

"THE AVENUE," BY HOBBEMA (1638-1709)

National Gallery, London

The most popular landscape in the National Gallery, this masterpiece expresses the joy and thankfulness we all feel for bright weather and fresh country air. For all his genius Hobbema could not earn his living by painting, and at thirty he had to take a small position in the Civil Service.

happens in modern times, the mediocre painters made the best income, while the men of genius starved. This state of affairs is not satisfactory, but it is not inexplicable. The men who prospered and made money were, as a rule, painters like Gerard Dou, who painted every feather on a bird, every scale of a fish, the shine of a copper pan, and the lustre of an earthenware pot. These were things within the range of everybody's observation and interest, and demanded no imagination, no culture. Therefore the painters of pots and pans, of insects, fruit and flowers, all prospered, while great artists like Rembrandt, Hals, Vermeer, and Ruisdael, who concentrated their attention on higher things, were neglected. Anybody could understand a picture of a cat stealing a fish, but to appreciate the beauty of pearly light stealing through high windows to lighten an apartment, presupposes some sense of poetry in the mind of the beholder.

§ 4

All classifications of so individual a thing as art are bound to be artificial and imperfect ; but just as we may say that the genre-painters of Holland depicted the life of the city, and the landscape-painters the life of the country, so a third group of artists mirrored another phase of national activity in constituting themselves painters of shipping and the sea. Holland, as England once knew to her cost, was, and still is, a great maritime nation, and her sea-captains and shipowners inevitably set up a demand for pictures of the element on which they triumphed and prospered. Moreover, this low-lying land was at the mercy of the sea, which was only kept back by the dykes, so that every Dutchman may be said to have had a personal interest in the ocean. One of the earliest painters of sea-pieces with shipping was Hendrik Dubbels (1620–76), who was the master of a more famous sea-painter, Ludolf Bakhuizen (1631–1708). Bakhuizen is as much a painter of shipping as of the sea, and in addition to being a picture-painter he was a naval architect who made constructive drawings of ships for the Russian Tsar Peter the Great. There is a great deal of spirit in his sea-pieces, particularly in his tempestuous subjects, but his storms, as John Ruskin pointed out, were storms that belonged to melodrama rather than to Nature.

We do not feel, however, that there is anything theatrical in the marines of his far greater contemporary, Willem van de Velde the Younger (1633–1707), who belonged to a famous family of artists settled in Amsterdam. Some critics hold that the younger Van de Velde is at his best when depicting shipping in a calm, and assuredly he has painted the stillness of the sea with a beauty and true dignity which go straight to the heart of every sailor. But there are pictures also in which Van de Velde has portrayed crashing waters under a charged sky, and if he rarely essayed to express the terrors of

"A GALE," BY WILLEM VAN DE VELDE (1633–1707)

National Gallery, London

" It was in Holland that marine painting first began to play an important part, for the sea was both the glory and the menace of this low-lying naval power." By a strange freak of fortune Van de Velde, born in the country of De Ruyter, came to England in later life as marine painter to Charles II. He died at Greenwich after his own countryman, William of Orange, had ascended the throne of England.

a great storm, yet he succeeds perfectly in conveying the excitement and somewhat perilous exhilaration of a stiff breeze. An example of his powers in this direction is " A Gale," in which we see the waves washing over a fishing-smack in the foreground, while farther on a frigate proudly approaches with bellying sails, and still farther in the distance a second frigate rides out the gale at anchor beneath the dark clouded sky. This gale is not awe-inspiring, as it might have been had Ruisdael painted it, but it is a picture that instinctively makes us square our chests and brace ourselves to meet the wind. Both the Willem van de Veldes, the father and the son who soon surpassed him in accomplishment, came over to London in 1677 and entered the service of Charles II. Willem van de Velde the Younger died at Greenwich, and owing to his long sojourn in England his pictures are plentiful in our public galleries, where they have served as models for Turner and other British sea-painters.

Painting, so flourishing in Holland at the beginning of the seventeenth century, was dead or dying when the next century dawned. The rapid rise of art to the eminence attained by Rembrandt was followed by an equally rapid decadence, so that in the early years of the eighteenth century Dutch painting, while maintaining a creditable level of craftsmanship, had sunk to the meticulous and uninspired painting of fruit, flowers, and the odd collections of inanimate objects known as " still-life." In the Netherlands the vein of Rubens was now exhausted, and his true heir appeared in France in the person of that strangely attractive painter, Antoine Watteau.

XX

THE RISE OF FRENCH PAINTING

THE ART OF WATTEAU, CHARDIN, BOUCHER, FRAGONARD, AND GREUZE

§ I

COMING events in the world of politics cast their shadows before them on the field of art, and as soon as we begin to study closely the national painting of France during the seventeenth and succeeding century, we become conscious of two streams of tradition, one democratic and derived from the Low Countries, the other aristocratic and inspired by Italy.

These two French schools of painting, which mirror respectively the life of the nobles and the life of the peasants, give us warning of that sharp division of the classes which were afterwards to meet and mingle in the clash and conflict of the French Revolution.

The seventeenth century, which in its beginning and middle period had seen art flourishing in Holland with the rise of the Dutch Republic, witnessed towards its close the shifting of political interest from Holland to France, and the rapid growth and development of a group of artists who added to the glory of the Court of Louis XIV. Although France had given birth to artists of considerable distinction long before the end of the seventeenth century, it was not till the reign of the " Grand Monarch " that she evolved a distinct national style of her own.

When, after the Hundred Years' War, French art slowly crept back into existence, it was no longer the church art of the earlier centuries. The French painters were still almost wholly under the influence first of Flanders and then of Italy. Thus Jean Clouet, who in 1516 was appointed Court Painter to King François I, was the son of a Brussels artist, and both he and his son François Clouet (c. 1510–72), who succeeded him, carried on a Flemish tradition. Though the feminine grace of the drawing of the Clouets has been held to be characteristic of France, yet the style of both artists was so close to that of their great contemporary Holbein that it can hardly be accepted as distinctly national.

Flemish again in character was the work of the three brothers Le Nain— Antoine and Louis, who both died in 1648, and Matthieu, died 1667—who came from Laon and settled in Paris. The gentle seriousness of their paintings of rustics foreshadows the peasant masterpieces of Jean François Millet. They are the ancestors of the democratic painters of France. Another painter closely associated with the age of Louis XIV, Philippe de Champaigne (1602–74), who painted numerous portraits of Cardinal Richelieu, was actually born in Brussels, though he established himself in Paris at the early age of nineteen. His portraiture, with its clear outline and suave colouring, is also northern rather than southern in character.

Nicolas Poussin (1594–1665) and Claude le Lorrain (1600–82) were great masters whose innovations left an indelible impress on landscape painting— the development of which will be traced in a subsequent chapter—but though born in France, both of them spent the greater part of their lives in Rome. Their art belongs to Europe generally rather than to France. The portrait-painter Pierre Mignard (1610–95) and his great rival Charles le Brun (1619–90), who as architect and sculptor as well as painter dominated the Louis Quatorze period, were both trained in Rome and were entirely Italian in style.

None of these men was strong enough to found a distinct and national French style ; and the kind of painting which we look upon to-day as being essentially and characteristically French was not born till Antoine Watteau left his home in Valenciennes for Paris. It was this weakling, whose frail form was prematurely ravaged by consumption, who founded the greatest and strongest of all the modern schools of painting.

Antoine Watteau was born in 1683 at Valenciennes, near the Franco-Flemish frontier. His father, a tiler and carpenter, was in poor circumstances, and the boy is said to have had an unhappy childhood. Watteau senior bore the reputation of being a hard man, and wanted his son to become a tiler like himself ; and when young Antoine at last obtained permission to work in the studio of a local artist, one Guerin, who was painter to the munici-pality of Valenciennes, the father refused to pay the expenses of his son's education.

After the death of Guerin in 1702, Antoine Watteau, then aged nineteen, ran away to Paris with a scene-painter called Metayer. But when they had arrived in Paris, this man soon abandoned his young companion when he had no more work to give him, and henceforward Watteau, already in delicate health and disowned by his father, was alone in Paris, without money, clothes, or resources of any kind. In desperate poverty he at last found employment in a wretched workshop where cheap religious pictures were produced by the dozen, to be retailed by country shopkeepers. Nowa-days chromolithographs have saved artists from this kind of drudgery, but in the early eighteenth century even the lowest-priced coloured card had to be done by hand. What was required of Watteau and his fellow-labourers was rapidity of execution in making copies of popular subjects, and for this

" BEGGARS," BY LE NAIN

Victoria and Albert Museum, London

With the work of Le Nain we have a beginning in French Art of that tradition of democracy which was destined to be so definitely its spirit. His groups of simple people, posed rather rigidly, have a delightful dignity because they are treated so seriously as subjects for art.

work the pay was the equivalent of half-a-crown a week and one daily meal of soup !

Yet even in this miserable trade Watteau managed to distinguish himself, and was entrusted with the reproduction of a " St. Nicholas " that was in great demand. One day the mistress of the workshop forgot to give Watteau the " St. Nicholas " to copy, and remembering her oversight later in the day, she climbed up to Watteau's attic to scold him for idling. After she had worked herself up into a passion, Watteau amazed her by showing her his day's work, a perfect St. Nicholas, which he had completely finished from memory.

Through all this period of drudgery and semi-starvation, Watteau never despaired, and snatched every opportunity to improve his art, drawing from Nature at night and during his rare holidays and leisure moments. Then by a happy chance he made the acquaintance of the decorative artist Claude Gillot, who, after seeing Watteau's drawings, invited the young man to live with him.

Rescued from his miserable factory, Watteau worked with enthusiasm at the ornamental painting of his new friend, who was then chiefly engaged in representing scenes from Italian comedy. Watteau, who in his poverty and ill-health worshipped elegance and all the graces of life, soon rivalled and surpassed his tutor in painting slim Harlequins, simple Pierrots, dainty Columbines, and other well-defined characters of Italian comedy ; and it may be that Gillot grew jealous of his *protégé*. After a period of warm friendship, the two artists parted on bad terms, and though Watteau in after-life never ceased to praise Gillot's pictures, he kept silent about the man, and would never answer when questioned about the breach between them. Gillot, on the other hand, tacitly acknowledged his pupil's superiority, for some time after the quarrel he abandoned painting and devoted himself to etching.

When Watteau left Gillot, his fellow-assistant, Nicolas Lancret (1690–1743), who afterwards became his pupil, left with him, and both young men found employment with Claude Audran, a painter of ornaments, who was also a guardian of the Luxembourg Palace. This stay with Audran had a profound influence on the art of Watteau. There were no gardens of the Luxembourg in those days, and the park attached to the royal palace was full of wild and natural beauty which appealed to the young artist, and drew forth his powers as a landscape-painter. It was here that he discovered and learnt to paint those noble clumps of trees which form the background to the figures of his idylls and pastorals.

Inspired thus by the externals of the palace, Watteau was also profoundly moved by what was within, the picture-gallery containing the series of great paintings by Rubens which illustrated the life of Marie de' Medici.

332

"LADY AT HER TOILET," BY ANTOINE WATTEAU (1683–1721)

Wallace Collection, London

Unique as the "Venus" of Velazquez, this picture is held by many to be the most beautiful Watteau ever painted. Though almost directly inspired by the figure paintings of Rubens, which Watteau studied at the Luxembourg, this charming little painting is exquisite in its grace and refinement.

333

Watteau viewed these spirited paintings again and again ; he copied them with zest, and became so saturated with Rubens that eventually he was able to deflect his fellow-countrymen from Italian ideals and revivify French painting with the vigorous realism of Rubens. His worship of the great Fleming, to whom he felt himself related by ties of race as well as artistic sympathy, never degenerated into servile imitation : " by means of a gradually widening realism," says the distinguished French critic Camille Mauclair, Watteau " arrived at the point of preserving in his small canvases all Rubens' admirable breadth, while achieving a masterly originality of grouping." A superb example of Watteau's powers in this respect is his exquisite " Lady at her Toilet " in the Wallace Collection. Here a theme, in which Rubens could hardly have avoided a certain coarseness, becomes a model of grace and refinement.

Once again the jealousy of a senior threatened Watteau's progress. Watteau showed his master a realistic painting of soldiers on the march, and Audran, who naturally did not want to lose so talented an assistant, advised him not to paint realistic pictures lest he should lose his skill as a decorator. But Watteau, determined to devote himself to original work, was now diplomat enough to avoid a quarrel, and desirous of leaving Audran courteously, he informed him that he must return to Valenciennes to visit his family. At Valenciennes the young artist continued his studies of nature and contemporary life, and he painted a series of military pictures illustrating camp-life, marches, and outpost duty. But after staying there long enough to justify his visit, he returned to Paris, where he was now not altogether unknown.

At this time his great desire was to win the Prix de Rome and to visit Italy, and with this object he competed in 1709, the subject set by the Academy being " David granting Abigail Nabal's Pardon." The prize, however, was won by a student named Grison, Watteau being placed second and thus losing his opportunity of visiting Rome.

Still desirous of studying in Italy, and still hopeful that the Academy might help him to accomplish his desire, Watteau three years later contrived to get two of his military pictures hung in a room through which Academicians were in the habit of passing. Several admired the " vigorous colouring, and a certain harmony which made them appear the work of an old master," and one Academician, de la Fosse by name, made inquiries as to the painter. It was then discovered that this young painter, already twenty-nine, was so modest that all he wanted from the Academy was its influence with the King that he might receive a small grant to enable him to study in Italy.

Attracted by his talent and modesty, de la Fosse sought an interview with Watteau which had the most surprising results. With a rare generosity the Academician told the young man that he had no need to seek instruction in Italy, that he undervalued his own ability, and the Academicians believed he was already capable of doing them honour ; in short, he had only to take the proper steps to be accepted a member of their society. The young artist did as he was told, and was immediately received as a member of the French Academy.

In all the long and memorable history of the Academy of France no incident similar to this has ever been recorded. That a young artist, without friends or fortune, who had failed to win the Prix de Rome and humbly begged for help in his studies, should spontaneously and unanimously be elected an Academician, is a miracle without precedent or sequel in the history of all Academies. This unique event was the turning-point in Watteau's career, and henceforward his fame was assured and he was able to earn his living in comfort.

It was on August 28, 1717, that Watteau was definitely admitted to the Academy. All successful candidates are required to deposit a diploma work after their election, and it was for this purpose that Watteau eventually painted his famous masterpiece, " L'Embarquement pour Cythère," which is now in the Louvre. In this poetically conceived picture, which shows a crowd of gallant youths and fair maidens about to embark for the legendary isle of perfect love, Watteau revealed a science of colour harmony which was one hundred and fifty years ahead of his day. He had already excited the admiration of his contemporaries by a method of painting which was as successful as it was original. He would cover his canvas copiously and, to all appearance, vaguely with a thick layer of pigment, and on this he would proceed, so to speak, to *chisel* out his detail. Figures, sky, and landscape background were then built up by a series of minute touches, which gave his pictures a peculiarly vibrating and scintillating effect. His division of tones and his wonderful orchestration of complementary colours make Watteau a forerunner of the prismatic colouring of the more scientific painters of the nineteenth century.

Unfortunately he was not destined to enjoy long the fame and fortune which now awaited him. The privation and hardship of his early manhood had undermined his always frail constitution and left him a prey to phthisis.

As if he knew the end was approaching, he worked feverishly during his last years. For a time he lived with a wealthy collector named Crozat, for whose dining-room he painted a set of " The Four Seasons." Though very comfortable at Crozat's house, which was filled with precious things and with paintings and drawings by old masters he admired, a desire for more complete independence led Watteau to leave it and live with his friend Vleughels, who afterwards became Principal of the Academy at Rome. In 1718 he left Vleughels, and shut himself up in a small apartment alone with his dreams and his illness, displaying then that craving for

"THE CONVERSATION," BY ANTOINE WATTEAU

Fitzwilliam Museum, Cambridge

Conceived in a poetical spirit, in spite of the artificial atmosphere of the mock pastoral style of his day, this typical example of Watteau's art enchants us by the exquisite precision of his observation, the light brilliancy of his colour, and the gentle melancholy which pervades even the fairyland of his creation.

336

"A LADY WITH A FAN," BY VELAZQUEZ

Wallace Collection, London

This treasure of the Wallace Collection reveals Velazquez at the height of his powers creating a wonderful harmony of subtle colour and a monumental design. The ivory white of the gloves set against the blue-white cuffs ; the brown of the dress between the warmer tones of the fan and the black of the mantilla : such things as these have caused Velazquez to be called " the Painter's Painter."

"PALLAS ATHENE," BY REMBRANDT

Gulbenkian Collection, National Gallery, London

Rembrandt's passion for rich materials and the opportunities they gave for effects of chiaroscuro and of lighting led him often to this use of precious armour and of cloaks. This picture and the " Mars " in Glasgow were probably companion pieces. In both, the crimson and gold flood the shadows with warmth.

solitude which is said to be one of the symptoms of phthisis. Later, some-body having spoken well of England, he suddenly had an almost morbid longing to cross the Channel.

In 1719 he came to London, where he painted and had some success, till the climate made him ill and unable to work. He returned to France more exhausted and weaker in health than he had ever been before, but slightly recovered during a six months' stay with his friend, the art-dealer Gersaint, for whom he painted a sign, an exquisitely finished interior with figures, in the short space of eight mornings—he was still so weak that he could only paint half the day. Then, hoping that he might recover his strength in the country, he moved to a house at Nogent which had been lent to him, but there his health rapidly declined and he gave himself up to religion, his last picture being a Crucifixion for the curate of the parish. Still pathetically hopeful that change of air might do him good, he begged his friend Gersaint to make arrangements for him to journey to Valenciennes. But while waiting for strength to move to his native town the end came, and on July 18, 1721, he died suddenly in Gersaint's arms. He was only thirty-seven years old.

The real sweetness and generosity of Watteau's nature is well illustrated by a touching incident during the last months of his life. His pupil, Jean Pater (1696–1736), had offended him, as Lancret had also done, by imitating his own style and subjects too closely, and in a fit of ill-temper he dismissed him from his studio. But during his last illness Watteau remembered how he had suffered in his youth from the jealousy of his seniors, and he re-reproached himself with having been unjust as well as unkind to Pater. He besought his friend Gersaint to persuade Pater to return to him, and when the latter arrived the dying man spent a month giving Pater all the help and guidance that he could in order to atone for his former injustice.

Pater, though possessed of less individuality than Lancret, was in many respects the best of Watteau's followers, and, like his master, he also died young. He was haunted by a fear that he would become old and helpless before he had saved enough to live upon, and he worked so incessantly and feverishly to gain his independence that eventually his health broke down and he died in harness at forty.

Lancret, who lived on till 1743, continued Watteau's Italian comedy manner, and had considerable success with his theatrical portraits, two of which are in the Wallace Collection. He is seen at his best in the portrait of an actress known as " La Belle Grecque," which has a vivacious charm of its own and is full of life. The pose of the figure is particularly happy and conveys admirably a sense of movement. But while they could imitate more or less cleverly the superficial appearance of Watteau's pictures, neither

337

PORTRAIT OF AN ACTRESS (" LA BELLE GRECQUE "), BY LANCRET (1690–1743)

Wallace Collection, London

This superb portrait of an actress shows that in quality, that of dramatic force, Lancret surpassed his master Watteau. We can almost hear this graceful creature recite her lines, and her gesture is eloquent of the point she has turned to make.

Lancret nor Pater were able to give their paintings that undercurrent of pathos which lifts Watteau's work high above the trivial.

Only a very superficial observer of Watteau's pictures would accuse him of being a painter of frivolities, a chronicler of picnics. Watteau lived in an artificial age, and being a true artist he could not help reflecting something of its artificiality. The French Court life of his day had the splendour of autumn leaves about to fall. Watteau, himself a dainty rose with canker in the bud, shows us the hectic charm of a civilisation already being consumed by mortal malady; but his honesty and intellectual insight prevented him from pretending that the happiness of his puppets was anything more than a passing moment of self-deception. His pictures haunt us, not because of their gaiety, but by reason of their gentle, uncomplaining melancholy; and the late Sir Frederick Wedmore penetrated to the secret of Watteau when he laid stress on " the reflective pathos, the poignant melancholy, which are among the most appealing gifts of him who was accounted the master of the frivolous, of the monotonously gay."

Watteau is unique in his qualities of drawing and colour. There have been many painters who were great draughtsmen, and a number of painters who have been great colourists; but those who were supreme both in drawing and colour we can count on the fingers of one hand. Watteau is among them. If we look at the little figures in a typical Watteau like " The Conversation," we perceive that the drawing rivals that of Raphael in its perfection of form and that of Rembrandt in its expressiveness. Watteau's draughtsmanship may be studied still further in his chalk drawings in the British Museum Print Room.

As for his paint, hardly among his predecessors will you find anything so exquisite in colour and so jewel-like in quality. The brightness of his palette, and the little touches with which he laid on his colour, make his pictures vibrate and sing as those of no other artist had done before. Watteau was not only a great master; he was one of those pioneer artists whose original research and brilliant achievements have given a new impetus to the art of painting.

§ 2

While Watteau was laying the foundation for the romantic and impressionist painting of modern France, another group of French figure-painters were evolving a national " grand style " for French portraiture. This new style first made its appearance when Largillière began painting Louis XIV and his family, and a typical example of it may be found in the Wallace Collection.

Nicolas Largillière (1656–1746), who was nearly thirty years older than Watteau, was born in Paris, but worked for many years in London, where he was an assistant to Sir Peter Lely and a great favourite with King Charles II. But unlike his master Lely—who rivalled the Vicar of Bray in keeping in with both sides—Largillière was a Royalist through and through, and like the fallen Stuarts he returned to France and made Paris his home during the latter part of his life. His drawing is accurate but rather hard, his colour harmonious and lighter in hue than that of his predecessors Mignard and Le Brun, and his great canvas at the Wallace Collection of Louis XIV with the Dauphin, the Duc de Bourgogne, the infant Duc d'Anjou (afterwards Louis XV), and Madame de Maintenon, shows how magnificently he could stage and present a royal group.

Among his contemporaries were Hyacinth Rigaud (1659–1743), and his pupil Jean Baptiste Oudry (1686–1755), who won much fame as super-intendent of the royal tapestry manufactories of the Gobelins and Beauvais ; but his most famous successor was Jean Marc Nattier (1685–1766), a Parisian-born, who became one of the favourite portrait-painters at the Court of Louis XV. Nattier commenced his career as a historical painter, and only took up portraiture in 1720 after he had lost all his savings through the speculations of John Law, the Scottish financier and adventurer. His paintings are also a little hard, but they are light and gay in colour and remarkably stately in their grouping and arrangement.

Another Paris-born artist acquired still wider fame. This was François Boucher (1703–70), who gained the first prize at the Academy when he was only twenty years old and afterwards studied in Rome. " No one," wrote the late Lady Dilke of this artist, " ever attacked a greater variety of styles ; his drawings—often extremely good—are to be met with in every important collection. Innumerable were his easel pictures, his mural decorations, his designs for tapestries at Beauvais or the Gobelins, his scene paintings for Versailles and the Opera."

No artist more completely illustrates and represents French taste in the eighteenth century than François Boucher, who was indeed the leader of fashion in this direction, and by his creative genius brought a new note into European painting. He introduced a lighter and gayer scheme of colour into tapestries and decorative paintings, pale blues and pinks being pre-dominant in his colour-schemes. He designed many paintings and decora-tions for the famous Madame de Pompadour, and the sweet colour now generally known as rose du Barry was invented by Boucher and was originally called rose Pompadour.

To do justice to the French portraiture of the late seventeenth and early eighteenth centuries, we must remember the ornate gilt furniture of the period with which they were surrounded. Portraits like Nattier's " Made-moiselle de Clermont " and Boucher's " Marquise de Pompadour "—both of which are in the Wallace Collection—must not be judged as easel paintings,

" LOUIS XIV AND HIS HEIRS," BY LARGILLIÈRE (1656–1746)

Wallace Collection, London

The desire of Louis XIV to be a great patron of the arts failed to attract to the Court of France the greatest artists. Largillière and Rigaud attempted to create something of lasting value, but the artificial life and costume defeated them. This group-portrait is one of the best of the period.

MARQUISE DE POMPADOUR, BY BOUCHER (1703–1770)

Wallace Collection, London

This notorious favourite of the King of France possessed an unerring instinct for beauty, and during the twenty years of her reign she exerted a great and, on the whole, a beneficial influence on the arts. " Her death in 1764," says Lady Dilke, " deprived the great group of artists employed by the Crown of a court of appeal whose decisions were ruled by a taste finished to the point of genius."

342

but as items in an elaborate scheme of interior decoration. There is nothing like them in the history of portraiture, just as there never was a Court exactly like that of the "Grand Monarch" or of his immediate successors. These portraits reconvey to us all the splendours of Versailles, its luxury and its heartlessness. They are the quintessence of aristocratic feeling, so full of culture that there is little room for humanity. The pride they express ends by alienating our sympathy, for they are the most pompous pictures the world has ever seen.

§ 3

Side by side with these aristocratic painters whose art reflected the temper of the French Court, we find now and then an artist of genius who expresses the life and feelings of the people. The greatest of these was Jean Baptiste Simeon Chardin (1699-1779), who was also born in Paris. Though he worked for a time under the Court painter Van Loo at Fontaine-bleau, and was elected a member of the Academy in 1728, Chardin was never a favourite with the nobles of France, nor did he make any effort to pander to their taste. His pictures, like those of his predecessors the brothers Le Nain, were "tainted with democracy," and the intense humanity of Chardin links him to his great contemporary on the English side of the Channel, William Hogarth.

Though Chardin, as Lady Dilke once said, " treated subjects of the humblest and most unpretentious class, he brought to their rendering, not only deep feeling and a penetration which divines the innermost truths of the simplest forms of life, but a perfection of workmanship by which every-thing he handled was clothed with beauty."

Like the Persian poet, Chardin could compose a song about a loaf of bread and a glass of red wine—as his beautiful still-life in the National Gallery, London, proved—while "The Pancake-Maker" shows what beauty and tenderness he could find in the kitchen.

Amid all the artificiality of the gaudy Court of Versailles, Chardin stands out as the supreme interpreter of the sweetness and sane beauty of domes-ticity. He was a poet with the unspoilt heart of a child who could reveal to us the loveliness in the common things of life.

How strong a character Chardin must have been to resist the current of the time and adhere unswervingly to his simple democratic ideals we realise when we contemplate the talent and career of Jean Honoré Fragonard (1732–1806), who was for a time his pupil. We have only to look at Fragonard's charming domestic scene, " The Happy Mother," in the National Gallery, London, to see that this artist also might have been a painter of the people. He shows us here the home of a blacksmith, whose forge is seen in the

"LADY MAKING TEA," BY CHARDIN (1699-1779)
Hunterian Museum, Glasgow

Revealing a power of observation and justness of lighting which rivals the exquisite work of the best Dutch Masters, this painted fragment of everyday life also shows a grace and subtle refinement which is characteristic of France.   Its beauty is as indisputable as its truth.

"THE PANCAKE-MAKER," BY CHARDIN

Hunterian Museum, Glasgow

Unmoved by the affections of his age and the artificialities of the French Court, this great artist painted humble scenes of domesticity with a penetration that divined their innermost truths and with a perfection of workmanship that invested them with beauty.

"THE SWING," BY FRAGONARD (1732–1806)

Wallace Collection, London

In this picture we have an example of that affectation of rustic simplicity which thinly veiled the real sensual character of Court life at Versailles. After squandering his great artistic gifts on pandering to the taste of a depraved nobility, the greatest decorator of his age lived to see his patrons sent to the guillotine and though the painter himself escaped the worst terrors of the French Revolution he died in poverty.

background, while in the centre the young mother with her three children sits at a table, and beyond another woman rocks a cradle.

For good or ill Fragonard chose another path, and after he had gained from Chardin a knowledge of sound craftsmanship which he never afterwards lost, he chose a more fashionable master and became the pupil of Boucher. In 1752, at the age of twenty, he won the Prix de Rome, and in 1756 he went for four years to Italy, where he made a particular study of the decorative paintings of " The Last of the Venetians," namely, Giovanni Battista Tiepolo (1696–1769). He returned to Paris in 1761 and almost immediately became a favourite with the French nobility.

" In Fragonard," wrote Lady Dilke, " Boucher found his true heir. The style of Court fashions and customs, highly artificial even in the affectation of nature and simplicity, the temper of society, purely sensual in spite of pretensions to sentiment, gave birth to innumerable fictions which took their place in the commerce of ordinary life. Eternal youth, perpetual pleasure, and all the wanton graces, their insincere airs masked by a voluptuous charm, came into seeming—a bright deceitful vision which cheated and allured all eyes. . . . The hours float by in waves of laughter, and the scent of flowers which breathe of endless summer fills the air. Existence in the gardens of Fragonard is pleasure ; it penalties and pains are ignored just as sickness and sorrow were then ignored in actual life."

Highly typical of the period and of the manner in which Fragonard catered for the taste of his patrons is his picture " The Swing," painted to order and exhibiting all the characteristics which Lady Dilke has so brilliantly analysed in the passage quoted. The workmanship is beautiful, the drawing and colour are alike charming, but these displays of so-called " gallantry " are detestable to many people, and through it all we are conscious of the insincerity of a clever and highly gifted painter.

Pictures which Fragonard painted purely to please himself, like " The Happy Mother " and the " Lady Carving her Name," are less typical of Fragonard, but often pleasanter to gaze upon than his commissions and elaborate decorations. But even in these subjects Fragonard is always frolicsome and playful where Chardin was serious and earnest, and it is impossible to escape the conclusion that Fragonard's was essentially a shallow nature. For all his cleverness he paid the penalty of his insincerity ; he outlived his popularity and ultimately died in dire poverty. In 1806 the times had changed : Napoleon and the French Revolution had swept away the frivolities of Versailles.

"GIRL WITH DOVES," BY GREUZE (1725–1805)

Wallace Collection, London

Though she appears the incarnation of sweet innocence and simplicity, the original of this portrait broke Greuze's heart by her infidelities and eventually robbed him of his savings. She was the daughter of a Paris bookseller. The artist married her in haste, and by his paintings made her a reigning beauty of her day.

§ 4

Contemporary with Fragonard was a painter who, though never the equal of Chardin as a craftsman, nevertheless approached him in the democratic temper of his art. Jean Baptiste Greuze (1725–1805), who was born near Macon and came to Paris in 1746, suddenly acquired fame and popularity when he was thirty by exhibiting at the Salon of 1755 his picture " A Father Explaining the Bible to his Family." This familiar scene, with its everyday details and its personages taken from humble life, made an immediate appeal to the bourgeois, who found in it those new ideas of simplicity and morality which Jean Jacques Rousseau had spread among the middle classes. Lady Dilke, who evidently suspected the moral sincerity of Greuze, pronounced his pictures to be " stained by artificiality." His pictures were rendered attractive, she argued, by " a vein of wanton suggestion which found an echo in the dainty disorder in which his heroines are dressed."

There are some strange parallels between the life of Greuze and that of Watteau, who died four years before his birth. Greuze's father was also a carpenter, and he also opposed his son's determination to become an artist. Greuze also began his career in extreme poverty, but fortunately he had a more robust constitution and withstood hardship better than Watteau. Greuze's father whipped him when he caught him drawing, and Greuze also ran away to Paris with another painter, and he, too, when he got there, found that nobody wanted to give him any employment. Both men were close on thirty before the turning-point came, Watteau by his election to the Academy, and Greuze by the exhibition of his picture at the Salon. But there the parallel ends, and the close of Greuze's life is more like that of Fragonard. For he also outlived his popularity and died in poverty.

It seems extraordinary that Greuze, the most popular of painters at all times, should have fared so badly at the end of his life. We cannot account for it by saying that Greuze could not accommodate himself to the change of taste brought about by the French Revolution, for throughout his career he was distinctly a bourgeois rather than an aristocratic painter.

The miserable truth is that the seemingly sweet and innocent little person, who looks out at us continually from those pictures of girls' heads which have brought the painter his greatest posthumous fame, was the cause of her immortaliser's wretched end. To look at all the portraits of her which hang in the Wallace Collection, or at the one entitled " Girl Looking Up," which is in the National Gallery, is to find it difficult to believe that the original was an arrant little baggage. Yet some people, who profess to be judges of character, say that the Greuze girl is not so innocent as she pretends to be.

349

"HEAD OF A GIRL LOOKING UP," BY GREUZE

National Gallery, London

A beautiful example of one of the many fanciful portraits of his lovely but erring wife by which this artist has attained world-wide fame and popularity.

MLLE. SOPHIE ARNOULD, BY GREUZE

Wallace Collection, London

No artist owes so much of his fame to the beauty of his models as Greuze did, but it must be admitted that he knew how to present them to advantage and to paint them with a rare tenderness and atmospheric softness. He also, like Fragonard, outlived his popularity and died in poverty.

351

In fact she was the daughter of a bookseller on the Quai des Augustins, Paris, and Greuze, attracted by her beauty, is said to have married her to save her reputation. He married Anne Gabriel in haste, and he repented at his leisure. Owing to her husband's constant exposition of her charms, Madame Greuze became one of the noted beauties of the day, and though her husband was devoted to her and gave her crazily everything he could that she wanted, the ungrateful little hussy repaid him by robbing him not only of his peace of mind but of large sums of money that he had saved.

It is easy to be wise after the event, and John Rivers in his book on *Greuze and his Models* maintains that every feature of Anne Gabriel "announced a hasty, passionate, and rather voluptuous nature"; nevertheless we are inclined, as human beings ourselves liable to error, to give our sympathy to Greuze and praise him for a generous and chivalrous action rather than to condemn him for having made an imprudent marriage. Though he painted other beautiful women, it is by his various fanciful portraits of his erring wife that Greuze has obtained his world-wide popularity, and there is hardly another instance in art of a painter who has achieved so great a fame by his exposition of the physical charms of a single model.

So, as the rumbling of the Revolution sounded just around the corner of time, this art of Chardin and Greuze heralded it. Lightness, gaiety, frivolity gave place to earnestness, moral purpose, and concern for the ordinary affairs of the average man which was the growing philosophy of those years.

" A LADY STANDING AT THE VIRGINALS," BY VERMEER

National Gallery, London

The utmost serenity of Dutch seventeenth-century art is enshrined in the still, sunlit interiors of this most perfect of Dutch painters. The wealth of exquisite possessions, the rich stuffs of the costumes, the security of that golden age, is expressed in compositions statically built in rectangular patterns and brilliant with cool, clean colour.

"VISCOUNT KILMOREY," BY GAINSBOROUGH

National Gallery, London

A typical Gainsborough Portrait with the landscape setting which he loved. It is fascinating to notice how differently he has modelled the face as compared to the tree trunk. Despite the charm of the background the focus is on the portrait, with its profound indication of individuality and character.

XXI

ENGLISH MASTERS OF THE EIGHTEENTH CENTURY

THE ART OF HOGARTH, RICHARD WILSON, AND REYNOLDS

§ I

IN this eighteenth century which was witnessing the rise of painting in France, art in England rose to a peak. Throughout the preceding centuries it had been overshadowed by one after another of the foreign artists who received patronage from the court and the aristocracy. Since those very early days of the cathedral builders and the church crafts which accompanied it, no outstanding names, no great achievements mark English art. Mors, Holbein, Van Dyck, Rubens, had been doing the work which English artists might have done. English painting had either been imitation of this foreign art, or had tended to turn towards miniature of which we had had an incomparably brilliant school. Nicholas Hilliard (1547–1619) in the reign of Elizabeth and James was truly a splendid artist as his miniatures at South Kensington reveal. We have not paid sufficient attention to, nor sufficiently valued, Hilliard, who had in him the qualities of a great artist, and was genuinely and essentially English. A goldsmith, a sculptor, a painter, a miniaturist, he was Court Illuminator to Elizabeth and afterwards to James the First. An author also, he wrote a delightful treatise on painting, full of common sense.

One of the most delightful of his miniatures is that " Portrait of a Young Man " at South Kensington, an open-air study of a gallant which has all the poetry of Spenser in it. Interestingly, too, it is taken out of doors (another prophecy of the English tradition) with a gay pattern of roses. An exquisite portrait of his wife in the Buccleuch collection is another work which shows Hilliard's quality. Yet few have heard of him, for his native genius was overshadowed by the brilliance of Holbein, and, less justly by the third-rate art of the Gheeraedts, father and son.

This art of miniatures remained the English glory through late Tudor and Stuart times. The Olivers, Isaac (1564–1617) and his son Peter (1594–1648) did lovely and important work on the small scale which seems always to have appealed to the British temperament. A score of other artists worked in the same genre. Of larger-scale work the foreign tide still swept everything away : Van Dyck succeeded Holbein worthily ;

M

Martha Wife of
Joshua Horton Esq.
of Sowerby.

"MARTHA HORTON OF SOWERBY," BY JOHN RILEY(?)

National Gallery, London

We cannot certainly say that this picture of an English Puritan lady is by Riley, but we can claim that it is one of the finest portraits of its period. The homely features are given a beauty by the magnificent handling of the paint and the fine draughtsmanship of an artist who suffered neglect while British patronage went to lesser men from abroad.

354

but there were the Gheeraedts, Lely, and Kneller. Meantime our own portraitists, Cornelius Johnson (1593–1664), Robert Walker (1600–58), the painter of Cromwell, William Dobson (1610–46), and John Riley (1646–91), found it more profitable to imitate the foreigners than to pursue their own vision. Yet as one looks at the masterly portrait of "Martha Horton of Sowerby" in the National Gallery we realise what greatness was lost. This is one of the great portraits of the world, depending for its value upon no tricks of pose or embellishment or fine costume. The sitter is far from beautiful, but the portrait is so full of character and so honestly painted that she is immortalised as truly as the "Mona Lisa" or Holbein's "Duchess of Milan." This fine work is attributed to Riley before he succumbed to imitation of Lely, who was himself an echo of the true quality of Van Dyck.

And Riley's pupil was a certain Jonathan Richardson to whom Joshua Reynolds acknowledged his debt. So the English tradition persisted : a thin stream through the marsh of foreign influence to flood at last into the widespread glories of the eighteenth and nineteenth centuries. Reynolds, Gainsborough, Romney, Raeburn and their fellow portrait painters ; then the marvellous line of landscape artists from Wilson to Turner and Constable, Girtin, Crome, Cotman, Cox ; such men made it impossible for even the British to neglect their artists. Certain strongly marked characteristics marked the British art. One was our love of water-colour in which our artists had always led the world, and still do. Another was our interest in small-scale work, and a certain distrust of the flamboyant. A third was our love of nature which was destined to bring recognition at last to the British painters, at the beginning of the nineteenth century. But the great days of our painting began a hundred years earlier when genius strangely asserted itself in the person of Hogarth.

§ 2

In all the annals of British Art there is no more illustrious name than that of William Hogarth. Not only was he, as E. V. Lucas has pointed out, " the first great national British painter, the first man to look at the English life around him like an Englishman and paint it without affectation or foreign influence, but he was the first to make pictures popular. Hogarth's engravings from his own works produced a love of art that has steadily increased ever since. During Hogarth's day thousands of houses that had had no pictures before acquired that picture habit which many years later Alderman Boydell and his team of engravers were to do so much to foster and establish."

That is where Hogarth differs from the French democratic painters, from

Chardin and Greuze, mentioned in the previous chapter ; he was an engraver as well as a painter, and so was one of the first artists in Europe to devote talent of the highest order to providing art for the masses as well as the classes. People who could not afford to buy oil-paintings could buy engravings, and it was by his engravings that Hogarth first acquired fame.

William Hogarth was born in Bartholomew Close, Smithfield, on November 10, 1697. He was the son of a schoolmaster and printer's reader, who was apparently a man of some education and had the intelligence to recognise his son's talent for drawing, and to place no obstacle in his path. At an early age young Hogarth was apprenticed to a silversmith near Leicester Fields (now Leicester Square), for whom he chased tankards and salvers, and two years after his father's death in 1718 he felt sufficiently confident in his powers to set up as an engraver on his own account. Meanwhile he had taken every opportunity of improving his drawing, and had attended classes at the art academy of Sir James Thornhill (1676-1734), a portrait-painter and decorative artist much in favour with Queen Anne. Thornhill was especially renowned for his ceilings, and the Painted Hall at Greenwich is a famous example of his art.

Hogarth did not get on very well with Thornhill and his method of tuition, which consisted principally of giving his pupils pictures to copy. This did not suit a youth so enamoured of life as Hogarth, who had a habit of making notes on his thumb-nail of faces and expressions and enlarging them afterwards on paper. In this way he trained his memory to carry the exact proportions and characteristics of what he had seen, so that his drawings, even done from memory, were extraordinarily vivacious and full of life. " Copying," Hogarth once said, " is like pouring water out of one vessel into another." He preferred to draw his own water, and this sturdy determination to see life for himself set him on the road to greatness. Previous English artists had not done this ; they had looked at life through another man's spectacles, and their pictures were more or less good imitations of the manner of Van Dyck, Lely, and Kneller.

Nevertheless he continued for a long time to frequent Thornhill's academy, the real attraction being not the master's tuition but his pretty daughter Jane. In the end Hogarth eloped with Miss Thornhill, whom he married without her father's consent and very much against his will. At the time the match was considered a *mésalliance*, for Thornhill was a Member of Parliament and a knight, whereas Hogarth had as yet acquired little fame and had rather scandalised society by bringing out in 1724 a set of engravings, " The Talk of the Town," in which he satirised the tendency of fashionable London to lionise foreign singers.

Four years later, however, the tide was turned in Hogarth's favour when Mr. Gay lashed the same fashionable folly in *The Beggar's Opera*, which,

"THE SHRIMP GIRL," BY HOGARTH (1697–1764)

National Gallery, London

" Life more abundant in her face you see."

Though hardly more than a sketch in its lightness of handling and reticence of colour, this is the most
famous of all Hogarth's portraits for its amazing vitality and actuality.

produced at the Lincoln's Inn Fields Theatre in January, 1728, proved to be as great a popular success then as it has been in our own day. Hogarth was naturally attracted to a piece that revealed a spirit so akin to his own, and he painted several pictures of its scenes, one of which is now in the Tate Gallery. His genial, bohemian temperament delighted in the society of actors and writers, and Hogarth's association with the company of *The Beggar's Opera* indirectly led him to take up portrait-painting. One of his earliest portraits is " Lavinia Fenton as *Polly Peachum*," the gay young actress who created the part and became Duchess of Bolton.

This portrait is a wonderful achievement, as indeed are all of Hogarth's. It has nothing of the manner of Lely or Kneller or any of his predecessors ; it is fresh, original, unmannered, and sets life itself before us. To some extent, perhaps, he was influenced by Dutch painting, which has the same quality of honesty, but in the main he was " without a school, and without a precedent." Unlike the portrait-painters who preceded and those who immediately succeeded him, Hogarth does not show us people of rank and fashion. His portraits are usually of people in his own class or lower, his relatives, actors and actresses, his servants. Hogarth was too truthful in his painting and not obsequious enough in his manner to be a favourite with society, and it was only occasionally that a member of the aristocracy had the courage to sit to him. Simon Fraser, Lord Lovat, did, and the magnificent little full-length in the National Portrait Gallery shows how vividly Hogarth grasped and expressed his character.

Still more amazing as an example of Hogarth's vivid characterisation and vivacity of expression is " The Shrimp Girl." It is only a sketch, mostly in greys with a few touches of other colours, but there is no work in the National Gallery more abounding with life. These portraits, painted with joy for the painter's satisfaction, never produced an income. He made his living by other pictures, and especially by his engravings, which had a wide sale and made his name a household word. The series of pictorial dramas which he invented brought him both fame and fortune ; and after " The Rake's Progress " and other sets had firmly established Hogarth in popular favour, Sir James Thornhill became reconciled to his son-in-law, whom he now saw to be capable of earning a good living.

Narrative pictures were not a new thing in the history of art ; the reliefs of Trajan's Column at Rome tell the story of the Emperor's Dacian campaigns, and we saw in Chapter VIII how Giotto and other early Italian painters recounted Bible stories and the lives of the saints in a series of pictures. But no painter before Hogarth had invented the story as well as illustrating it. Without any text familiar to the public, Hogarth by paint and engraving told new and original stories of his own time, and told them so clearly that they were universally understood. Sometimes these stories

"MARRIAGE À LA MODE," BY HOGARTH

Scene I.   The Marriage Contract

National Gallery, London

The first scene in Hogarth's celebrated picture-drama.   Note how the young lawyer (" Silvertongue ") is already beginning to court the bride, while her prospective husband admires himself in the mirror.

In a splendid apartment the father of the bridegroom points to his pedigree, while the rich alderman, father of the bride, studies the marriage settlement.   " The three figures of the young nobleman, his intended bride, and her inamorato, the Lawyer, show how much Hogarth excelled in the power of giving soft and effeminate expression. . . . Nothing can be more finely managed than the differences of character in these delicate personages."   HAZLITT

359

"MARRIAGE À LA MODE," BY HOGARTH

Scene II. Shortly after Marriage

National Gallery, London

The mutual boredom resulting from a "marriage of convenience" is the moral Hogarth points in this morning scene, adorned with a wealth of exquisitely painted details.

Note the delicious touch of satire in the four pictures of saints which adorn the walls of a worldly interior. An old steward, shocked at the way things are going, is leaving with a bundle of bills and one receipt. The wife sits yawning at breakfast, while the card-tables and the candles, still burning, in the room seen beyond, show how the husband, lazing in his chair, has spent the night. "The figure, face, and attitude of the husband are inimitable. Hogarth has with great skill contrasted the pale countenance of the husband with the yellow-whitish colour of the marble mantelpiece behind him, in such a manner as to preserve the fleshy tone of the former. The airy splendour of the view of the room in this picture is probably not exceeded in any of the productions of the Flemish school." HAZLITT

"MARRIAGE À LA MODE," BY HOGARTH

SCENE III. THE VISIT TO THE QUACK DOCTOR

National Gallery, London

The harsh faces of the quack and his companion and the gay unconcern of the Earl are contrasted with the rigid figure of the little girl, the victim of his profligacy, in this third scene, which shows how the married couple are drifting apart.

The peer, with a cane in one hand and a box of pills in the other, rallies the sardonically smiling quack for having deceived him. " The young girl, who is represented as the victim of fashionable profligacy, is unquestionably one of the artist's chefs-d'œuvre. The exquisite delicacy of the painting is only surpassed by the felicity and subtlety of the conception. Nothing can be more striking than the contrast between the extreme softness of her person and the hardened indifference of her character."

HAZLITT

W. F. Mansell.

"MARRIAGE À LA MODE," BY HOGARTH
SCENE IV. THE COUNTESS'S DRESSING-ROOM
National Gallery, London

Hogarth's powers as a satirist find their fullest expression in this mocking picture of a polite company enduring an exhibition of " culture."

" *The gradations of ridiculous affectation in the Music Scene are finely imagined and preserved. The preposterous, overstrained admiration of the Lady of Quality, the sentimental, insipid, impatient delight of the Man, with his hair in paper and sipping his tea, the pert, smirking, conceited, half-distorted approbation of the figure next to him, the transition to the total insensibility of the round face in profile, and then to the wonder of the negro boy at the rapture of his mistress, form a perfect whole. The sanguine complexion and flame-coloured hair of the female virtuoso throw an additional light on the character. . . . The gross, bloated appearance of the Italian Singer is well relieved by the hard features of the instrumental performer behind him, which might be carved of wood. The negro boy holding the chocolate, both in expression, colour, and execution, is a masterpiece. The gay, lively derision of the other negro boy, playing with the Actæon, is an ingenious contrast to the profound amazement of the first.*"

HAZLITT

"MARRIAGE À LA MODE," BY HOGARTH

SCENE V.   THE DUEL AND DEATH OF THE EARL

National Gallery, London

"*Silvertongue, the young lawyer whom in the last scene we saw passing a masquerade ticket to the Countess, has now been found out.   The Earl, who surprised him with his wife, has fought a duel and is dying as the result, while the young lawyer escapes through a window as the Watch enters.*"

HAZLITT

" MARRIAGE À LA MODE," BY HOGARTH

SCENE VI. THE DEATH OF THE COUNTESS

National Gallery, London

The last act showing the suicide of the Countess, while her father seems more intent on securing her rings than on consoling the orphan daughter, whom a nurse holds up to the dying mother.

" *A bottle of poison on the floor shows that the Countess's death is self-sought, while the paper near it, with the words* ' *Counsellor Silvertongue's Last Dying Speech,*' *reveals the end of another leading character in the drama. While the father absent-mindedly draws the rings from the fingers of his dying daughter, the half-starved dog ravenously snatching the meat from the table suggests with subtlety the straitened resources of the household as a result of previous prodigal expenditure.*"

HAZLITT

364

were almost wholly humorous, as in " The Election " series, but more often they had a serious intention and amusing incidents were introduced only by way of light relief.

To regard Hogarth as a satirist first is wrong : he was more than that : he was a great moralist. For though no man more severely scourged the folly of his time, Hogarth taught his lessons not only by exposing the ridiculous, but also by revealing the tragedy of wrong and the beauty of goodness. Among his many inventions none more beautifully display his method than the " Marriage à la Mode " series which we reproduce from the original paintings at the National Gallery ; and though each one of these pictures tells its own story clearly, it may be helpful to summarise the action of each scene, and add the illuminating comments made by the great critic Hazlitt.

While the merited success of his prints and subject-pictures made Hogarth a very prosperous man, he preserved his simple character to the last, and on one occasion he walked home in the rain, completely forgetting that now he had his own coach, which was waiting for him. He had a town house at 30 Leicester Square (now rebuilt) and a country house at Chiswick, now a Hogarth Museum, and when he died in 1764 he was buried in Chiswick Churchyard.

§ 3

The greatest of Hogarth's contemporaries, the link indeed between him and Sir Joshua Reynolds, was the artist known as " The Father of British Landscape," Richard Wilson. His is one of the saddest stories in British Art, for, though acknowledged to be one of the most eminent men of his day, and attaining a modest measure of success in middle life, Fortune, through no fault of his own, turned her back on him, and his later years were spent in the direst poverty.

Richard Wilson was born at Penegoes in Montgomeryshire on August 1, 1714, the day Queen Anne died and George I ascended the throne. His father was a clergyman of limited means, but his mother was well connected, and one of her well-off relatives took sufficient interest in young Richard's talent for drawing to have him sent to London to learn painting. Though it is by his landscapes that Wilson acquired lasting fame, he began life as a portrait-painter ; one of his earlier portraits of himself is in the National Portrait Gallery, while a very much later portrait, in the Diploma Gallery of the Royal Academy, we reproduce. This magnificent work, which speaks for itself, is enough to prove that even in portrait-painting Wilson had, among his immediate predecessors, no equal saving Hogarth.

Like Hogarth, Wilson was of a sturdy, independent disposition, little inclined to truckle to the conceit of fashionable sitters or to flatter their

"PORTRAIT OF THE ARTIST," BY RICHARD WILSON (1714–1782)

Diploma Gallery, Royal Academy

A noble and dignified portrait of himself by the artist, who won lasting fame as " The Father of British Landscape." Owing to an ill-timed jest, Wilson lost Court favour, and his later years were spent in pitiful poverty and privation.

vanity, and consequently he was not the man to make it the staff of his professional practice, though in 1748 he had acquired a considerable eminence in this branch of art. In this year he was commissioned to paint a group of the Prince of Wales and Duke of York with their tutor—a portion of which now hangs in the National Portrait Gallery—and with the money earned by this and other commissions he decided in the following year to carry out a long-cherished wish to visit Italy.

Hitherto there has been a general belief that Wilson did not attempt landscape-painting till he found himself in Italy, but it has recently been ascertained [1] that he unquestionably painted landscapes before he left England.

In Italy Wilson devoted more and more of his time to landscape till he finally established himself in Rome as a landscape-painter, only doing an occasional portrait. His beautiful pictures of Italian landscapes, in which dignity of design was combined with atmospheric truth and loveliness of colour, soon gained him a great reputation in that city, and his landscapes were bought by the Earl of Pembroke, the Earl of Thanet, the Earl of Essex, Lord Bolingbroke, Lord Dartmouth, and other Englishmen of high rank who were visiting Italy. Consequently, when he returned to England in 1756, his reputation preceded him and he enjoyed a considerable measure of success when he first established himself in London at Covent Garden. But unfortunately for Wilson, the taste of the eighteenth century was severely classical, and after the first novelty of his Italian landscapes wore off, only one or two enlightened patrons, like Sir Richard Ford, were capable of appreciating the originality and beauty of the landscapes he painted in England. Thanks to the discrimination of Sir Richard and Lady Ford, the best collection in the world of landscapes by Richard Wilson is still in the possession of the family, and by the courtesy of Captain Richard Ford we are permitted to reproduce two fine examples in these pages. It is only in the Ford Collection that the full measure of Wilson's greatness can be seen, for while the splendour of the flaming sunset sky in " The Tiber, with Rome in the Distance " reveals how Wilson showed the way to Turner, the sweet simplicity and *natural* beauty of " The Thames near Twickenham " proves him also to have been the artistic ancestor of Constable.

Wilson's English landscapes went begging in his own day. His memorandum-book, preserved in the Victoria and Albert Museum, South Kensington, shows how he sent them out on approval and often had them returned. As his fortunes dwindled, Wilson despairingly set about painting replicas of the Italian landscapes which he had found more saleable, and these repetitions of his Italian scenes have done much harm to his reputation in succeeding years, for the later Italian pictures do not always attain the

[1] Cf. *Richard Wilson and Farington*, by Frank Rutter, 1923.

By courtesy of Capt. Richard Ford

"ITALIAN LANDSCAPE," BY RICHARD WILSON

A beautiful example of Wilson's poetic rendering of Italian scenery, and of his power to render the glow in the sky and
the limpid atmosphere in a spacious landscape. Note also the dignity and harmony of the carefully balanced composition.

quality of the first version when the painter was freshly inspired by the original scenery.

Nevertheless, with the help of one or two unaffected lovers of art and Nature, who bought his English landscapes, and more who bought repetitions of his Italian scenes, and with the fees of his pupils—among whom was the diarist, Joseph Farington, R.A.—Wilson managed for some years to make a tolerable living, and when the Royal Academy was established in 1768, George III—who in his boyhood had had his portrait done by this landscape-painter—nominated Richard Wilson as one of the founder-members of the Academy. At the Academy exhibitions Wilson exhibited with credit, if without much commercial success, and nothing serious happened till 1776, when he sent a picture of " Sion House from Kew Gardens," which the King thought of buying.

Unfortunately he sent Lord Bute to bargain with the artist, and this canny nobleman thought the price asked, sixty guineas, was " too dear." " Tell His Majesty," said Wilson roguishly, " that he may pay for it by instalments." Had an Irish peer been the intermediary he might have seen the joke and have made Wilson's fortune, but Lord Bute belonged to a race that is reputed to take money very seriously, and to be not too quick at grasping the English sense of humour. He was shocked and scandalised, deeming the answer insulting to royalty.

The harmless gibe cost Wilson what little Court favour he had, and proved to be his ruin. Fortunately, before this disastrous retort had been made, he had secured the Librarianship of the Royal Academy, and the salary of this post, fifty pounds a year, was all Wilson had to live on during his later years. His few patrons fell away from him, his brother Academicians —most of whom had been rather jealous—now shunned him, and he lived in a miserable garret in Tottenham Street, Tottenham Court Road, existing chiefly on bread and porter. He had always been fond of the last—" though not to excess," said Beechey, R.A., who knew him intimately.

Just before the end he had a year or two of quiet and comfort, for he left London and made his home with his relatives in Wales, where he died, at Llanberis, in 1782. Wilson did not altogether abandon portrait-painting when he returned from Italy, and in addition to the noble portrait of himself, there is in the Academy's Diploma Gallery a very beautiful full-length of the young artist Mortimer, whom he painted about the same time. A splendid portrait of Peg Woffington, very rich in colour, which hangs in the Garrick Club, is another example of Wilson's portraiture after his return from Italy.

Richard Wilson was the first English artist to show his countrymen not only the beauty of Nature but the beauty of their own country. He should not be judged by such large pictures as " Niobe " and " The Villa of

"THE THAMES NEAR TWICKENHAM," BY RICHARD WILSON

Capt. Ford's Collection

Perfect in its rendering of the light in the sky and on the water, this wonderful landscape anticipates Constable in the absolute fidelity
with which it mirrors the sweet natural beauty of English scenery.

370

Mæcenas," which he painted " to order," but rather—so far as the National Gallery is concerned—by his exquisite " Italian Coast Scene " (No. 2646) and " On the Wye," which together show how beautifully and truly Wilson rendered the characteristic scenery of the two countries he so deeply loved.

§ 4

When Richard Wilson was already learning the business of portrait-painting in London, Joshua Reynolds was a little boy of six. He also was the son of a clergyman, the Rev. Samuel Reynolds of Plympton Earl, near Plymouth, where Joshua, the seventh son, was born on July 16, 1723. Sir Godfrey Kneller died the same year.

Nature and Fortune were both kind to Reynolds : the first endowed him with courtly manners as well as talent, the second gave him opportunities to use these to the best advantage. Doubtless Reynolds would have made his way to the front, by one path if not by another, but it was a piece of good luck for him when Commodore Keppel of the *Centurion* put in at Plymouth for repairs, and met the young painter at the house of Lord Mount-Edgcumbe. Keppel took a liking to the painter and offered him a free passage on his ship to the Mediterranean. Reynolds gladly accepted, and after a long stay with Keppel at Minorca, went on to Rome, where he gave himself up to that worship of Michael Angelo that he retained all his life. His well-known deafness dates from this early period, and was the result of a cold which he caught while copying at the Vatican.

From Rome, Reynolds went to Florence, Venice, and other Italian cities, returning to England in 1753, and then he settled in London, never to leave it again except for a holiday. His youngest sister Frances kept house for him, and he never married ; like Michael Angelo, the object of his worship, Reynolds said he was " wedded to his art." After living for a time at 104 St. Martin's Lane, and then at 5 Great Newport Street, he made his permanent home at 47 Leicester Square.

Reynolds did not capture the town at the first assault ; the deep richness of the colouring he had adopted from the Venetian masters, and the atmospheric contours of his forms, did not appeal to connoisseurs accustomed to the lighter colour and harder outlines of Kneller ; but supported by the influence of Lord Mount-Edgcumbe and Admiral Keppel, he gradually became acknowledged as the head of his profession. When the Royal Academy was founded, his appointment as President met with universal approbation, for it was felt that no painter could fill the office so well. Reynolds, as E. V. Lucas points out, " was sought not only for his brush, but also for his company ; and though he did not court high society, he was sensible of the advantages it gave him. Other and finer intellects also

"THE AGE OF INNOCENCE," BY REYNOLDS (1723–92)

National Gallery, London

This delightful portrait of his little grand-niece, Theophila Gwatkin, aged six, while showing in its harmonious arrangement all Reynolds's mastery of the " grand style," also reveals the tenderness of his emotions and his reverent affection for the innocence of childhood.

"THE INFANT SAMUEL," BY REYNOLDS

National Gallery, London

Reynolds once told Hannah More that he was mortified to be asked by even his more enlightened sitters for information "who" Samuel was!

373

welcomed him—such as Dr. Johnson, Burke, and Goldsmith—and his house became a centre of good talk."

Reynolds was not only a great painter, but a great gentleman, for long before the King knighted him in 1769, five days before the opening of the first Academy exhibition, he had shown Court and Society " that a painter could be a wise man and a considerable man as well."

The story of Sir Joshua's life is not dramatic ; it is the placid, smoothly running story of his art, of well-chosen friendships, of kindly actions, occasional displays of professional jealousy—for he was human and not an angel—and of a happy domestic life. When his brother-in-law Mr. Palmer died in 1770, Sir Joshua adopted his daughter Theophila, then thirteen, and later her sister Mary Palmer also came to live with him, so that though a bachelor Reynolds was not without young people in his house. Both his nieces remained with him till they married, and it was Theophila's daughter, little Theophila Gwatkin, who was the original of one of Reynolds's most charming and popular paintings, " The Age of Innocence."

His grand-niece was six years old when Reynolds, in 1788, painted her portrait, a work which in conception and in every touch proclaims that it was " a labour of love." Indeed, nowhere do the simplicity, the benevolence, and the affectionate nature of the man shine out more beautifully than in his paintings of children. Splendid and decorative in its colour-scheme and open-air setting, his " Mrs. Richard Hoare with her Infant Son " in the Wallace Collection has the same winning simplicity of intention ; for it is much more than a portrait, it is a tender expression of a mother's love.

The other side of Sir Joshua's art, " the grand manner," is seen in the famous " Mrs. Siddons as the Tragic Muse " and in other of his pictures. This was the side most admired by his contemporaries, and we must admit that Reynolds had a rare power of dramatic presentation, which found its happiest outlet when he was dealing with contemporary subjects. " The Tragic Muse " is something of a wreck to-day, because in his desire to emulate the deep, rich colouring of the Venetians, Reynolds made use of bitumen, a pigment which gives brilliant immediate results but never dries, and in time trickles down a canvas in channels, ruining its surface. This pigment, which liquefies like asphalt when the sun is hot, is chiefly responsible for the poor condition to-day of many paintings by Reynolds.

When Sir Joshua was sixty-six he lost the sight of his left eye, and from this calamity and the dread of losing the other, which was threatened, he never recovered. For three years he lingered on, seeing his friends and bearing his infirmity with fortitude, but the will to live was gone when he could no longer practise his art with assurance. He died on February 23, 1792, and was buried in state at St. Paul's Cathedral.

" I know of no man who has passed through life with more observation

W. F. Mansell.

"MRS. SIDDONS AS THE TRAGIC MUSE," BY REYNOLDS

Dulwich Gallery

The most famous example of the " grand style " introduced by Reynolds into English portraiture :
the great actress is shown as a queen of tragedy seated on her throne. As he put his signature at the
bottom of the painted skirt, Reynolds, in his courtly manner, told the sitter he would go down to
posterity on the hem of her garment.

375

"MRS. HOARE AND HER INFANT SON," BY REYNOLDS

Wallace Collection, London

Unsurpassed as a decorative example of the typically British "open-air portrait," this picture is also a supremely beautiful expression of the tenderness of a mother's affection.

"MISS EMILY POTT AS THAIS," BY REYNOLDS

Reynolds's dramatic power is finely displayed in the arresting pose of the figure in this theatrical portrait. "Thais" was an Athenian beauty who accompanied Alexander the Great on his expedition to Asia. After his death she was claimed by Ptolemy, to whom she bore three children.

377

than Reynolds," said Dr. Johnson ; " when Reynolds tells me anything, I consider myself as possessed of an idea the more." Sir Joshua himself was distinguished by his literary abilities, and his " Discourses on Painting," which formed his yearly addresses to the students of the Royal Academy, are treasured and read to-day both for their literary merit and their instructive art teaching.

XXII

EIGHTEENTH-CENTURY BRITISH PORTRAITURE

THE ART OF GAINSBOROUGH, ROMNEY, RAEBURN, HOPPNER, AND LAWRENCE

§ I

SHORTLY before little Joshua Reynolds celebrated his fourth birthday in the West of England, there was born in the Eastern Counties a babe destined to become his greatest rival in life and death. Thomas Gainsborough was born in 1727 at Sudbury, in Suffolk. He was one of a large family, his father being a wool manufacturer and clothier of moderate means, while his mother was a woman of education, the sister of a schoolmaster and herself a skilful painter of flowers. Thomas inherited his mother's love of Nature and her talent for art, and spent his boyhood rambling about the countryside and sketching the scenery round Sudbury. His gift for catching a likeness revealed itself early. One day, having seen a man robbing an orchard, he made a quick sketch of him, with the result that the robber was recognised from Gainsborough's drawing and arrested. The boy's faculty for copying, however, was not always exercised in the interests of law and order ; and on another occasion, when he desired to play truant, he forged his father's handwriting in a letter to the schoolmaster, asking for a day's holiday. The ruse succeeded, but was subsequently found out, and seeing clearly that the boy would work at nothing but his drawing and his sketching, the father wisely sent his son at the age of fifteen to London to study art under the French engraver Henri Gravelot. Young Gainsborough also studied at the St. Martin's Lane Academy, and later became the pupil of the portrait-painter Francis Hayman (1708–76), with whom he continued nearly four years. In 1745 he returned to his native town of Sudbury, where he began practice as a portrait-painter and occasionally painted a small landscape for his own pleasure.

Unlike Reynolds, who was " wedded to his art," Gainsborough married when he was only nineteen. He fell in love with Margaret Burr, a beautiful girl of eighteen, who fortunately possessed an income of £200 a year of her own, and as no obstacles were raised to their wedding, the boy-and-girl couple settled down at Ipswich, where Gainsborough soon acquired a considerable local reputation as a portrait-painter. Here his two daughters were born, and the painter led a happy domestic life, sketching in the country between the intervals of his professional portraiture and spending his evenings playing the violin—for he was devoted to music—either in his own home or in the houses of some of his friends.

In 1760 he was tempted to leave this simple life at Ipswich and moved to Bath, a fashionable centre to which everyone who was anyone in London society came sooner or later. From a professional point of view this move was the beginning of Gainsborough's fortune, for the fashionable world soon flocked to the studio of this " new man " who made his sitters look so august and distinguished ; and the modest provincial, who had begun painting three-quarter lengths at five guineas apiece, now asked eight guineas, and was soon able to increase his figure to something nearer London prices. But while his fortune waxed, his happiness waned, and having now secured the entry into the fashionable world, Gainsborough began to pay attention to other ladies and so excite his wife's jealousy. His home life was no longer simple or happy, and as time went on his private troubles increased, for both Mrs. Gainsborough and his two daughters became subject to mental derangement. To the world, however, he continued to show a cheerful face, and his sprightly conversation and humour made Gainsborough a welcome favourite in all society.

In time the fame of the Bath painter spread to London, where Gainsborough occasionally exhibited at the Society of Artists, but though in 1768 he was chosen as one of the foundation members of the Royal Academy, he did not immediately leave Bath. He came there when he was thirty-three ; and it was not till he was forty-seven that he was persuaded to move to London. In 1774 he took a part of Schomberg House in Pall Mall, and his success was immediate. " The King sent for him and Duchesses besieged his studio." Society was rent in twain, divided into a Reynolds faction and a Gainsborough faction, and under these circumstances it is not altogether surprising that Sir Joshua's jealousy did not allow him to be quite fair to his rival, whose power of securing a likeness he once formally denied.

Many stories are told of the rivalry between the two painters, and they have mostly increased with the telling in the course of years. As an example of the growth of legends, we may cite the widely circulated story that Reynolds at an Academy banquet once proposed the health of " Mr. Gainsborough, the greatest landscape-painter of the day," whereupon Richard Wilson is said to have retorted, " Ay, and the greatest portrait-painter, too."

The original version of this incident is told by Thomas Wright in his *Life of Richard Wilson*, published in 1824, and here we learn that the dialogue took place, not at an Academy banquet, but at the Turk's Head in Gerrard Street, shortly after Gainsborough had arrived in London from Bath.

"THE MARKET CART," BY GAINSBOROUGH (1727–88)

National Gallery, London

This artist confessed once that he painted " portraits for money, landscapes for love." His delight in the simple happiness of country life is eloquently expressed in this masterly rendering of a typical scene in rural England.

Meeting Richard Wilson there, Reynolds in a bantering spirit said, " Have you heard, sir, that our greatest landscape-painter has come to Town ? "

" Nay, Sir Joshua," retorted Wilson, " you mean our greatest portrait-painter." Thus what was originally a piece of good-humoured chaff between two great artists has been twisted by inaccurate repetition into a display of maliciousness on both sides.

Nevertheless it must be admitted that there was a decided coolness between Reynolds and Gainsborough, and this was natural enough, for not only were the two men competitors for the patronage of Society, they were also temperamentally too far apart to understand one another completely. " With Reynolds," Sir Walter Armstrong has said, " deliberation counted for much ; Gainsborough's good things are impromptus." The seriousness and slight pomposity of Reynolds could not mix easily with the free-and-easy gaiety of Gainsborough. To Gainsborough, Reynolds seemed something of a pedant ; to Reynolds, Gainsborough appeared rather a frivolous person.

In his discourse to the Academy students in 1778, Reynolds observed that blue should not be massed together in a picture, whereupon Gainsborough proceeded subsequently to paint his famous " Blue Boy " and, by his brilliant success with the boy's blue dress, put Reynolds in the wrong. It is highly probable that the blues which figures so prominently in his beautiful portrait of " Mrs. Siddons " are another expression of Gainsborough's disapproval of Sir Joshua's dogmatic teaching. We have only to compare this Gainsborough portrait with Reynolds's painting of the same actress as " The Tragic Muse " to realise the difference between the two artists. Reynolds painted his picture in 1783, Gainsborough his in 1784, when Mrs. Siddons was twenty-eight ; but, though actually a year younger, everyone will agree that the actress looks years older in Sir Joshua's picture. Reynolds emphasised the intellectual qualities of the great tragedienne, his endeavour was to show the sublimity of her mind ; Gainsborough was content to show the charm and vivacity of her person, and that is why Mrs. Siddons looks younger in his portrait. Another temperamental difference between the two artists is shown in their hobbies ; while Sir Joshua was interested in Literature and delighted in conversing with the learned, Gainsborough's ruling passion was Music. He was not only a good musician himself but was completely carried away by the playing of others. Once when a talented amateur, a Colonel Hamilton, was playing the violin at his house, Gainsborough called out, " Go on, go on, and I will give you the picture of ' The Boy at the Stile ' which you have so often wished to buy of me." The Colonel " went on " and eventually returned home with the coveted picture as his reward. This love of music makes itself felt in Gainsborough's pictures, which are lyrical, the paintings of an artist who sings, while those

"PORTRAIT OF MRS. SIDDONS," BY GAINSBOROUGH

National Gallery, London

The most popular of all Gainsborough's portraits of women, this picture represents the celebrated actress, Sarah Kemble, afterwards Mrs. Siddons, in her prime. She was the daughter of an actor and the sister of John Philip Kemble. The painting was in the possession of the great actress till the day of her death, and Mrs. Jameson relates that once she found Mrs. Siddons, when she was seventy, seated beside this portrait, and " the likeness was still remarkable."

383

W. F. Mansell.

"MISS HAVERFIELD," BY GAINSBOROUGH

Wallace Collection, London

The most charming of all Gainsborough's portraits of children, this picture admirably illustrates the lightness of his touch. This little lady is as exquisite and fragile as the flower growing at her feet.

of Reynolds are more philosophical, the pictures of a man who thinks in paint.

Of all the English eighteenth-century portraitists Gainsborough is the lightest and airiest, and in freshness of colour and in gracefulness without affectation his portraits more than rival those of Reynolds. His " Miss Haverfield " is more of a little lady than any of Sir Joshua's children, and though her gentility may not be accounted a virtue, and while we must admit that Reynolds's " Age of Innocence " has more psychological profundity, yet we cannot find another portrait in the world which excels this Gainsborough in rendering the flower-like charm of childhood.

Though by his portraits Gainsborough acquired so considerable a fortune that he could afford to have country houses at Richmond and in Hampshire as well as his town house, his landscapes rarely found buyers, and remained " admired and unsold till they stood ranged in long lines from his hall to his painting-room." At his death his house was filled with his own landscapes. The end came with some suddenness. A pain in the neck, to which he had paid little attention, turned out to be due to a cancer, and when the physicians pronounced his case hopeless, he settled his affairs with composure and prepared to meet death. He was particularly anxious to be reconciled with Sir Joshua and begged him to visit him on his death-bed. When Reynolds came an affecting reconciliation took place : " We are all going to Heaven," said Gainsborough, " and Van Dyck is of the party." Thomas Gainsborough died on August 2, 1788, and by his own desire was buried as privately as possible in Kew Churchyard. Sir Joshua Reynolds was one of the pall-bearers, and in his presidential address to the Academy in the following year he paid an eloquent tribute to the memory of his former rival.

§ 2

The third great English portrait-painter of the eighteenth century was George Romney, who never exhibited at the Royal Academy, and all his life was hostile to that institution and to its president, Sir Joshua Reynolds. Romney was born at Dalton-in-Furness, Lancashire, in 1734, when Reynolds was a boy of eleven and Gainsborough a child of seven. He was one of eleven children, and his father was a man of many occupations—farmer, builder, cabinet-maker, and dealer—and little prosperous in anything he undertook. George Romney consequently had his education neglected : at eleven years old he was helping his father in the workshop, and there he displayed precocious ability in drawing portraits of the workmen and other people. When he was twenty he made the acquaintance of a vagabond artist named Christopher Steele, who journeyed from place to place making portraits, and in 1755 this man secured Romney as his pupil and took him with him on his travels. In the following year Romney fell ill with a fever and was tenderly nursed by his landlady's daughter, a domestic servant named Mary Abbott, and being a highly-strung romantic youth Romney married this girl in the first burst of his gratitude, and later found her utterly unsuited to be his mate. Steele meanwhile had settled at York, and summoned Romney to join him there as soon as he was well enough, and since he was not earning enough to keep a wife, Mrs. Romney had to go back to service when her husband rejoined the man to whom he was apprenticed.

There was little good that Steele, a mediocre artist and a loose liver, could teach Romney, and their association was more profitable to the older than the younger man. After a year or two in bondage at York, Romney managed to purchase his freedom, and he then made a home for his wife at Kendal. With this town as his headquarters, he rambled about the Lake Country painting heads at two guineas each and small full-lengths at six guineas, till in 1762 he had at last managed to save a hundred pounds.

Romney was now twenty-eight, and he felt that if ever he was to make his fortune by his art he must seek it in London. So giving £70 to his wife, with the remaining £30 he came to the capital, where he at once competed for a prize offered by the Society of Arts for an historical picture on " The Death of Wolfe." Romney was at first awarded a prize of fifty guineas for his version of this theme, but later the judges reversed their verdict and awarded the fifty guineas to John Hamilton Mortimer (1741–79), a young friend of Richard Wilson and Reynolds, and gave Romney only a consolation prize of twenty-five guineas. Romney, not unnaturally, believed this reversal of the first judgment to be the result of favouritism, and to the end of his life he thought that it had been brought about by Reynolds, who had been actuated by fear of a rival. In 1766 Romney again gained a premium for his " Death of King Edward " from the Society of Arts, to which he was now admitted a member, and henceforward he exhibited regularly at the Society's exhibitions, but always held aloof from the Academy. In 1767 he paid a visit to his wife and two daughters at Kendal, and returning alone to London soon established himself in public favour, and in the early 'seventies he was making over a thousand a year by his profession. He thought the time had now come when he should visit Italy, and in March 1773 he set off for that country in the company of a brother artist, Ozias Humphrey (1742–1810), who afterwards became a famous miniature-painter. At Rome, Romney separated himself from his fellow traveller and led a hermit's life, shunning the society of his compatriots, and giving his whole time to work and study. In 1775 he made his way back to England via Venice and Parma, studying with advantage the work of Correggio in the latter city, and reaching London in the month of July. Greatly improved now in his colouring and confident in his increased

"THE PARSON'S DAUGHTER," BY ROMNEY (1734–1802)

National Gallery, London

Known throughout the world by the title under which the picture was first exhibited, this pensive beauty, whose powdered auburn hair is bound up with green ribbon, is still an enigma whose identity has never been discovered. The charm of her person and the delicacy of the painting have combined to make this Romney's masterpiece.

knowledge and power, Romney boldly took the house and studio of Francis Cotes, R.A. (1725-70), who had been one of the chief of the older portrait-painters, at 32 Cavendish Square, and there seriously entered into competition with Reynolds. Gainsborough, it will be remembered, did not come to London till 1779, so that Romney, though the younger man, was the first formidable rival that Reynolds had to endure. Charging fifteen guineas for a head life-size, Romney soon found himself surrounded by sitters, and Reynolds was alarmed at the way in which his practice for a time was diminished by the painter to whom he contemptuously referred as "the man in Cavendish Square." Later Romney had so many commissions that he was able to put up his prices, but even so he received only about eighty guineas for the full-length portraits which now fetch many thousands of pounds when they are sold by auction at Christie's. When Reynolds died he left a fortune of £80,000 earned by his brush, and though Romney was not successful to this extent he made a good living, his income in the year 1785 being £3635.

But Romney was never a mere money-grubber, and when at the age of forty-eight he first met his most famous sitter, the dazzlingly beautiful Emma Lyon, known to history as Lady Hamilton, he was so fascinated by her extraordinary personality, that time after time he refused all kinds of wealthy sitters in order that he might continue uninterruptedly to paint the lovely Emma. In 1782 the future Lady Hamilton was a mere girl of twenty or twenty-one, living under the protection of Charles Greville, who four years later—when he was in money difficulties—heartlessly handed her over to his uncle, Sir William Hamilton, who treated her more kindly and honourably. For five years Romney painted this fascinating creature continually in a variety of characters, and though gossip soon busied itself making scandal out of their relations, there is no evidence that the painter's affection for her was anything but platonic. Of his many paintings of her we reproduce one of the most charming, the "Lady Hamilton" in the National Portrait Gallery.

In the art of George Romney there is a peculiar feminine quality which gives an extraordinary winsomeness, almost a pathos, to his paintings of frail women. There is a paternal tenderness rather than the passion of a lover in his paintings of Emma Hamilton and of another famous beauty, Mrs. Robinson, known as "Perdita." Romney's beautiful portrait of the last in the Wallace Collection was done while this gifted actress was under the protection of the Prince of Wales, afterwards George IV. But that royal rascal soon tired of her, and at the age of twenty-four she had already been abandoned by "the first gentleman in Europe." When he sent her away the Prince gave her a bond for £20,000 ; but he never paid it, and "Perdita" Robinson died in 1800, poor and paralysed.

"LADY HAMILTON," BY ROMNEY

National Gallery, London

For nearly five years Romney neglected wealthy sitters in order that he might devote himself without interruption to portraying, in various guises, the inexhaustible fascination of the wonderful woman known to history as " Nelson's enchantress."

Nobody has yet discovered who was the original of Romney's most famous masterpiece, " The Parson's Daughter," but we may imagine that this beautiful creature, with a gentle melancholy behind her smile, was also one of the frail sisterhood to which both Lady Hamilton and Mrs. Robinson belonged. The extraordinary sweetness and simplicity of Romney's portraiture of women has the same tender reverence for the sex that we find in *The Vicar of Wakefield*, and the peculiar winningness of Romney is perhaps best described by placing him as the Goldsmith of English painting.

Though he never brought his wife and family to London—where it is probable that they would have felt ill at ease in a sphere to which they were not accustomed—Romney supported them in comfort, and when after years of hard work in London his health broke down, he went back to his wife at Kendal. She received him without reproaches, and under her affectionate care the tired, worn-out genius " sank gently into second childhood and the grave." He died at Kendal on November 15, 1802.

§ 3

The greatest portrait-painter that Scotland has ever produced, Sir Henry Raeburn, R.A., belonged to a younger generation than any of the artists whose lives we have so far recounted. Raeburn was born at Stockbridge, a suburb of Edinburgh, on March 4, 1756, and so was thirty-three years younger than Reynolds, twenty-nine years younger than Gainsborough, and twenty-two years younger than Romney. His father, a well-to-do manufacturer, died when young Henry was six, and his elder brother then looked after him, had him educated at Heriot's School—where he showed his leaning by making caricatures of his masters and school-fellows—and apprenticed him at the age of fifteen to an Edinburgh goldsmith. There he also began to paint miniatures, and these gradually attracted attention till Raeburn broadened out into oil portraits and landscapes.

Like Gainsborough, he loved to ramble about the countryside sketching, and in one of his open-air sketches he introduced the figure of a charming young lady whom he had seen crossing the meadow. Some time later this young lady presented herself at Raeburn's studio to have her portrait painted. She was the widow of a wealthy Frenchman, Count Leslie, but herself a Scottish girl, her maiden name having been Ann Edgar. During their sittings the artist and his model fell deeply in love with each other ; there was no one to hinder their union, so they were quickly married, and at the age of twenty-two young Raeburn found himself the possessor of a charming wife, a fine house at Edinburgh, and a comfortable income which made " pot-boiling " unnecessary.

"MRS. MARY ROBINSON," BY ROMNEY

Wallace Collection, London

Famous as " Perdita," this beautiful actress was at one time loved by the Prince of Wales, afterwards George IV, but though a reigning beauty in her day her vogue did not last, and she died in 1800 poor and paralysed.

Under these happy circumstances he rapidly came to the front as a portrait-painter. About 1785 he visited London and called on Sir Joshua Reynolds, who, himself now almost an Old Master, showed the young artist every possible kindness and gave him much good advice. Reynolds urged him to visit Rome and " saturate " himself in Michael Angelo, generously offering to lend him money for the journey. This, however, Raeburn did not need, but he followed the advice of the veteran, and went to Rome, where he remained for nearly two years and greatly strengthened his art. In 1787 he returned to Edinburgh, and soon after, inheriting some property from his brother, he built himself the splendid studio and picture gallery in York Place, which still stands and is known as " Raeburn House."

From this time on till the day of his death in 1823, the career of Raeburn, was an unbroken sequence of happiness and success. Acting, it is said, on the advice of Lawrence, he wisely preferred to be the best painter in Edinburgh rather than one of several good painters in London. But though he never resided in England, he exhibited regularly at the Academy from 1792 to the year of his death ; he was elected an Associate in 1812 and made a full Academician three years later. He was knighted when George IV visited Edinburgh in 1822 and soon afterwards appointed His Majesty's Limner for Scotland.

Raeburn was probably wise to remain in Scotland, for it is by no means certain that the rugged truthfulness which was the chief characteristic of his portraiture would have pleased London society. He was the most vigorous of all the eighteenth-century British portrait-painters, and none of them succeeded so well as he did in setting on canvas the splendid figure of a man. Though he has left us many noble and dignified paintings of women, Raeburn is held to have excelled himself in male portraiture, and his masterpiece, " Sir John Sinclair," can hold its own for vitality, solidity, and dignity with any painted man in existence.

Raeburn was one of the most methodical and industrious of all the world's great portrait-painters. He rose at seven, breakfasted at eight, entered his studio at nine, and worked there till five in the afternoon. It is said that he spent more time looking at his sitters than in painting them, for he would search the countenance before him till he had penetrated to the character of the person, and then beginning with forehead, chin, nose, and mouth, he would paint away rapidly, never making any preliminary drawing, and never using a mahl-stick to support his brush. His method was free and vigorous, and the results he obtained by it preserved the freedom and vigour of his process.

"SIR JOHN SINCLAIR," BY RAEBURN (1756–1823)

This Highland Chieftain in the tartan of his clan is one of the most superb male portraits ever painted. In truth, distinction, and dignity without haughtiness, Raeburn's masterpiece surpasses the elegance of Van Dyck and rivals the supreme achievements of Velazquez.

§ 4

Within the space of this OUTLINE it is not possible to enumerate all the talented painters who made England during the eighteenth century the most prolific country in Europe for the production of notable works of art. The wealth of the country and the patronage extended to art by the Court and Society brought painters from all over the world to London, and in addition to the native-born artists many foreign painters settled in London, among them being the two American historical painters, John Singleton Copley (1737–1815) and Benjamin West (1738–1820), who succeeded Reynolds as President of the Royal Academy.

In portraiture, however, the true heir of Reynolds was John Hoppner (1758–1810), who, though born at Whitechapel, was from childhood brought in touch with the high personages he was afterwards to paint. His mother was employed at Court, and his father—though there is some mystery about his birth—is said to have been a surgeon. George III was certainly interested in the boy when he was a chorister at the Chapel Royal, and perceiving his aptitude for art he made the lad a small allowance, and in 1765 got him admitted as a student to the Academy schools. There Hoppner gained the gold medal in 1782, and later when he settled at 18 Charles Street, St. James's Square—close to Carlton House—he at once had the favour of the Court. He painted Mrs. Jordan for the Prince of Wales, and the three princesses for the King, and soon became the fashion. Though too much influenced by Reynolds to be considered a very original artist, and too hard as a rule in his colour and not strong enough in his drawing to be considered that great man's equal, Hoppner has nevertheless left us many charming portraits, among which " The Countess of Oxford " is usually considered to be his master-work. In this thoughtful head we see that Hoppner, like Reynolds, was also a scholar and a thinker, and he not only had great intelligence but the capacity to express his thoughts clearly and well. He was associated with Gifford of the *Quarterly Review*, to the first numbers of which he contributed some brilliant articles, which do credit to his powers of literary expression, to his artistic judgment, and to his goodness of heart, but, owing to his intimate relationship with this famous Whig periodical and its editor, he gradually lost the favour of the Court, which was given to the Tory party and its protégé, Thomas Lawrence.

Sir Thomas Lawrence (1769–1830), who succeeded West as President of the Royal Academy in 1820, had the romantic career of a child prodigy. His father was an innkeeper who, when young Thomas was three, kept the " Black Bear " at Devizes, where people of fashion used to stay on their

"COUNTESS OF OXFORD," BY HOPPNER (1758–1810)

National Gallery, London

Jane Elizabeth Scott, wife of the 5th Earl of Oxford, was a celebrated beauty who counted Lord Byron among her lovers.   She was twenty-five when Hoppner painted this portrait.

way to and from Bath. Though the child got little education, he was wonderfully gifted and a lovely child in appearance. He was petted by his father's guests and entertained them by quaint recitations and by drawing their likenesses with a precocious skill which soon made the child at the " Black Bear " the talk of the Bath Road. He was allowed to copy pictures in the great houses in the neighbourhood before he was ten years old, and once he was taken to London to be exhibited as a phenomenon, for his father, a complete adventurer, lost no opportunity of making money out of his son. Finding his son likely to be more profitable than his innkeeping, the father settled at Bath, where the pretty boy opened a studio and drew heads in charcoal for a guinea apiece.

In 1785, when he was only sixteen, Lawrence began to paint in oils, and two years later his father thought it worth while to remove to London, and this youth of eighteen was given a studio at 4 Leicester Square, near the great Reynolds, upon whom he called, and who was exceedingly kind and encouraging. While continuing to keep his family by the pictures he painted for money, Lawrence was now able to study at the Academy schools. Prosperity increased as his talent matured, and soon after he had turned twenty he took a larger studio at 24 Old Bond Street ; he was already the talk of the town and the darling of Society. As gracious and charming in his manners as he was in his art, royalty delighted to honour him, and in 1791 George III compelled the Academy to admit him as an Associate, though according to its rules twenty-five was the minimum age at which an Associate could be elected, and Lawrence had only just turned twenty-two. The King's will broke through the Academy's law, and when Reynolds died in the following year, Lawrence, at the age of twenty-three, was appointed the King's principal portrait-painter-in-ordinary.

The way was now open for his unbroken triumph. John Opie (1761–1807), the Cornish painter, whose art was much stronger and more robust, might have been a formidable rival had he not been too abrupt and caustic in his speech to please a public that liked to be flattered. It was Opie who, when asked once how he mixed his colours, made the famous reply, " With brains, sir."

Hoppner also had lost his chance by attaching himself to the wrong political party, so young Lawrence had it all his own way, and after being made a full R.A. when he was only twenty-five, on the death of Benjamin West in 1820 he was unanimously elected the new President. Five years before this he had been knighted, and during the interval between his knighthood and his Presidency he had visited the chief Courts of Europe and painted more crowned heads than any other English artist before or since. His prices were higher than those of any artist before him : for a head he received 200 guineas, for a full-length his usual terms were 600 to

"LADY BLESSINGTON," BY LAWRENCE, (1769–1830)

Wallace Collection, London

At the beginning of the last century the Countess of Blessington was famous for her beauty, her wit, and her Salon. The last was frequented by all the men of talent and all the men of fashion, including Count d'Orsay, celebrated as " the last of the dandies."

397

700 guineas, but for some portraits—like that of "Lady Gower and Child"—he received as much as 1500 guineas.

Like Reynolds, Lawrence never married, but he was engaged for a time to the daughter of Mrs. Siddons, and treated the poor girl so badly that a tragedy ensued. He was so notorious a flirt that when he was painting the portrait of Caroline of Brunswick he was required to draw up an affidavit as to the propriety of his conduct. Though popular and tremendously successful, the private life of Lawrence was not particularly happy; and though he made great sums he was often in financial difficulties owing to foolish purchases. He was constantly tempted to pay extravagant prices for paintings by Old Masters, and his numerous acquaintances—for he had few real friends—often took advantage of his kindness and generosity. His fame is lower to-day than it was in his lifetime, for there was an inherent weakness both in his art and in his character. The refinement of his drawing is still to be admired, but he had not the love of truth which distinguished his great predecessors, and beside their work the portraits of Lawrence are apt to appear artificial and insipid. He is seen at his best in his portrait of "Lady Blessington" in the Wallace Collection, and looking at this elegant portrait of an elegant woman we perceive the subtlety of what Campbell said about the artist. "Lawrence," the poet remarked, "makes one seem to have got into a drawing-room in the mansions of the blest and to be looking at oneself in the mirrors."

Another precocious child artist of the eighteenth century was the famous woman-painter, Angelica Kauffmann (1741–1807). She was the daughter of a mediocre Swiss portrait-painter who settled in England, and when she was ten years old Angelica was executing portraits in crayons with the assurance of a professional. Owing to the sex prejudice which existed in her day, she was taken by her father to the Academy *in boy's clothes*, so that she might improve her drawing. When she was in her middle teens she accompanied her father to Milan, Florence, Rome, and Venice, and it was at the latter city in 1764 that she made the acquaintance of the wife of the English Ambassador, who took a great fancy to the clever young artist and brought her back with her to England. Thus introduced to England in 1765, she soon became a general favourite, the young Queen being particularly attracted by her scholarly mind and amiable personality. In 1769 she was nominated one of the foundation members of the Royal Academy. The same year she was unhappily deceived into a secret marriage with the valet of Count de Horn, who had passed himself off for his master. This scoundrel treated her badly, and she only managed to buy back her liberty by giving him £300 on condition that he took himself off to Germany and did not return to England. With the exception of this painful episode, the private life of Angelica Kauffmann was as happy and serene as her own

"PORTRAIT OF THE ARTIST," (SELF) BY ANGELICA KAUFFMANN (1741–1807)

This artist, with the flower-painter Mary Moser, R.A. (1744–1827), was one of the two first women members of the Royal Academy. Speaking four languages fluently, skilled both in vocal and instrumental music, and amiable in disposition, she was as accomplished in her person as in her art.

pictures, and after the false count had died she married again in 1780. Her second husband was a Venetian painter, Antonio Zucchi, with whom, and with her father, she returned to Italy two years after her marriage, and finally settled in Rome, where, happy, popular, and universally esteemed, she lived twenty-five years till her death in 1807. " The Portrait of the Artist," which we reproduce, gives a good idea of the personal charm of Angelica Kauffmann as a young woman, and of the soft graciousness which distinguishes her painting.

XXIII

THE FRENCH REVOLUTION AND ITS INFLUENCE ON ART

THE WORK OF DAVID, VIGÉE LEBRUN, GROS, INGRES, AND GOYA

§ 1

TO look at the calm and serene British portraits illustrated in the two previous chapters, it is difficult to realise that England was engaged in warfare almost continuously during the century in which they were painted. While Reynolds, Gainsborough, and their successors were building up the reputation of English art, statesmen, soldiers, and sailors were laying the foundations of the present British Empire, Wolfe in Canada, Clive in India, and Nelson on the high seas. We have seen how profusely art flowered in England while her empire abroad was expanding, and we must now turn our attention to the progress of art in that country which throughout the century was England's constant foe.

To appreciate the effect of the French Revolution on the painters of France, it is advisable to consider briefly the condition of artists in the eighteenth century. The French Academy, founded in 1648 for the advancement of art, had become a close body, exercising a pernicious tyranny. Artists who were neither members nor associates were not allowed to exhibit their works in public, and even Academicians were not supposed to show elsewhere : one of them, Serres by name, was actually expelled from the Academy because he had independently exhibited his picture " The Pest of Marseilles " for money. The only concession the Academy made to outsiders was to allow them once a year, on the day of the Fête Dieu, to hold an " Exhibition of Youth " in the Place Dauphine, which was open for only *two hours*.

At the last Salon held under the old monarchy in 1789 only 350 pictures were exhibited : in 1791 the National Assembly decreed that an exhibition open to all artists, French and foreign, should be held in the Louvre, and the number of pictures shown was 794. In the year of the Terror (1793) the number of exhibits exceeded 1000 : in 1795 the number of pictures shown increased to 3048. These figures tell their own story, and show that the first thing the French Revolution did for art was to give painters a fuller liberty to display their work to the public. Further, notwithstanding the exhausted

401

state of the finances, the Revolutionary Government encouraged artists by distributing annual prizes to a total value of 442,000 francs, and began the systematic organisation of public museums. On July 27, 1793, the Convention decreed that a museum should be opened in the Louvre, and that art treasures collected from the royal palaces, from monasteries, and from the houses of aristocrats who had fled the country should be placed there. At the same time a sum of 100,000 francs was voted for the further purchase of works of art.

While in some parts of the country an ignorant and savage mob ruthlessly destroyed many precious monuments, libraries, and art treasures, the leaders of the Revolution throughout showed a special solicitude not only for contemporary art but also for the monuments of the past. Yet while the Revolution did everything it could to foster contemporary art, and to preserve and popularise the best art of the past, it could not produce one really great master of painting or sculpture. Now, if ever, we might expect to find a realism and a rude, savage strength in art ; yet the typical painting of the French revolutionary period is cold and correct, and its chief defect is its bloodlessness. While in England the taste, as we have seen, was all for a happy Romanticism in art, the taste of revolutionary France was for a stern Classicism. A nation aspiring to recover the lost virtues of antiquity was naturally disposed to find its ideal art in the antique, and just as politically its eye was on republican Rome rather than on Athens, so its Classicism in art was Roman rather than Greek. The man who gave a new direction to French painting was Jacques Louis David (1748–1825), a distant relative of Boucher. For a time he worked under that master, whose art in later years he cordially detested. Later he became the pupil of Vien (1716–1809), whom he accompanied to Rome when Vien was appointed director of the French Academy in that city. In Rome David became absorbed in the study of the antique, and began painting pictures of classical subjects, which were well received when exhibited in Paris. During the Revolution David became an enthusiastic supporter of Robespierre, and though he was in danger for a time after the fall of Robespierre, he escaped the perils at the end of the Terror by wisely devoting himself to art and eschewing politics. When the Directory created the Institute of France on the ruins of the old monarchical academies, David was appointed one of the two original members of the Fine Arts section and charged with the delicate mission of selecting the other members.

Henceforward David was omnipotent in French art. Like so many other revolutionaries, he was completely carried away by the genius of the First Consul, who seemed to him the right Cæsar for the new Romans. One morning, after Bonaparte had given him a sitting for a head, David spoke enthusiastically of the General to his pupils. " He is a man to whom

" M. SÉRIZIAT," BY DAVID (1748–1825)

Louvre, Paris

We think of David as the painter of those semi-classical pictures in praise of the Empire under Napoleon, but his highly organised and technical art was capable of creating fine portraits as this striking picture proves.

"MME. RÉCAMIER," BY DAVID

The Louvre, Paris

Reputed to be the most brilliant conversationalist of her age, Mme. Récamier was famous for her "salons," which were attended by all the most eminent men of the Directory and First Empire. This refined and sympathetic portrait shows the most gracious and human side of a painter who was fanatical in his adoration of Greek and Roman art. Even the furniture in this picture is said to have been made from classical models designed by David.

404

altars would have been erected in ancient times ; yes, my friends, Bonaparte is my hero." But the portrait of his hero was never completed, and only the head remains to-day, for Napoleon disliked long sittings and did not care for exact likenesses. What he demanded from an artist was a picture to rouse the admiration of the people, and to satisfy this demand David painted " Bonaparte crossing the Alps," " Napoleon distributing the Eagles to his Army," and similar pictures which, though correct and precise in drawing, seem cold, strained, and dull to-day.

The best works of David are not his official pictures, but some of his portraits, which have more force and life. The most celebrated of these portraits is his " Madame Récamier," now in the Louvre, though the painter himself did not regard it as more than an unfinished sketch which he once threatened to destroy. The sitter greatly displeased David by leaving him when the portrait was half finished and going to his pupil Gerard (1770–1837), who had suddenly become the fashion, to have another portrait of herself painted by him. A few years later Madame Récamier, tired of Gerard's flattering portraiture, came back to David and begged him to go on with his picture. " Madame," he replied, " artists are as capricious as women. Suffer me to keep your picture in the state where *we* left it."

After Waterloo and the restoration of the Bourbons, David, who had taken so prominent a part in the Revolution, was exiled from France in 1816, and not being allowed to go to Rome as he wished, he settled in Brussels, where he continued painting classical pictures, now chiefly of Greek subjects, till he died in 1825. Even in exile David was still regarded as the head of his school, and few painters of so moderate a talent have so profoundly influenced the art of Europe. He completely crushed for the time being the ideals of Watteau and his school and of Boucher—" cursed Boucher," " that Boucher of ridiculous memory "—as he called him ; and as a good republican he delighted other republicans by maintaining that the art of the last three Louis represented " the most complete decadence of taste and an epoch of corruption." To David and his pupils Europe owes that revival of classical subjects which was a feature of nineteenth-century painting in all north-western Europe, and France owes him in addition that tradition of fine drawing which has characterised her art for the last century.

§ 2

Most attractive of all the portraitists of this period is the woman artist Madame Elizabeth Louise Vigée Lebrun (1755–1842). Her father, a portrait-painter himself, died when she was only twelve years old, and his daughter carried on his practice almost at once, for when she was only fifteen she was already painting portraits with success and talent. While still young she married Lebrun, a prosperous and enterprising picture-dealer, who managed her affairs well, and whose stock of Old Masters afforded the young artist many models which she studied with good results. In 1783 Vigée Lebrun was admitted to the French Academy, and during the last years of the French monarchy she was a favourite at Court and painted several portraits of Marie Antoinette and her children. In 1789, alarmed at the way things were going in France, she went to Italy, where she was received with enthusiasm and made a member of the Academies of Rome, Parma, and Bologna. Thence she went to Vienna, where she stayed three years, and subsequently visiting Prague, Dresden, Berlin, and St. Petersburg, she only returned to France in 1801. Thus she escaped the Revolution altogether and saw little of the Empire, for about the time of the Peace of Amiens she came to England, where she stayed three years, and then visited Holland and Switzerland, finally returning to France in 1809.

Entirely untouched by the Revolution and by the wave of Classicism which followed it, Mme. Vigée Lebrun was a cosmopolitan artist whose art belonged to no particular country, and whose style had more in common with English Romanticism than with the asceticism then in vogue in France. Among all her portraits none is more charming than the many she painted of herself, and of these the best known and most popular is the winning " Portrait of the Artist and her Daughter " at the Louvre. Though in time she belongs to the revolutionary era, Mme Lebrun is, as regards her art, a survival of the old aristocratic portrait-painters of monarchical France.

§ 3

How great was the influence of David on the painters of his generation is revealed by the tragic story of Antoine Jean Gros (1771–1835), who killed himself because he thought he was bringing disgrace on the tradition of his master. Gros entered David's studio in 1785, and though he was unsuccessful when he tried for the Prix de Rome in 1792, in the following year his master helped him to get a passport for Italy, and so Gros got as far as Genoa, where in 1796 he made the acquaintance of Josephine, afterwards Empress. Josephine carried him off to Milan and presented him to Bonaparte, who took a liking to the young man, attached him to his staff, and allowed him to paint that wonderful portrait, now in the Louvre, of " Napoleon at Arcole," which is the most haunting and poetic of all the many portraits of the Emperor.

Thenceforward the career of Gros was outwardly a series of triumphs. Owing to his experiences in Italy—where, in 1799, he was besieged with the French army at Genoa—he had a closer acquaintance with the realities of war than any of his artist contemporaries.

" THE ARTIST AND HER DAUGHTER," BY E. L. VIGÉE LEBRUN (1755–1842)

The Louvre, Paris

One of the first woman-painters to reach high distinction in her art, Mme. Elizabeth Louise Vigée Lebrun painted Queen Marie Antoinette in her youth and lived late into the nineteenth century. She married very young, and this charming portrait of herself and her daughter was painted shortly before the outbreak of the French Revolution.

" BONAPARTE AT ARCOLE," BY BARON GROS (1771–1835)

The Louvre, Paris

A poetic portrait of the young Napoleon as he was at the beginning of his Italian campaign by an artist who finally committed suicide because he was unable to paint in accordance with his ideals.

In Genoa and elsewhere Gros had made a particular study of the work of Rubens and Van Dyck, and in his canvases he now endeavoured to emulate the opulent colour of the Flemish School. Consequently his battle-pictures were so informed with knowledge and inspired by feeling and fine colour that they aroused high enthusiasm in Paris. When his picture " Les Pestiférés de Jaffa " was shown in the Salon of 1804, all the young artists of the day combined to hang a wreath on the frame in honour of the life, truth, and colour in the work of Gros.

Already there was a beginning of a reaction in Paris against the ascetic Classicism of David, and while Gros, as an old pupil of that master, still commanded the respect of the classicists, his spirited renderings of contemporary events pleased the younger generation who were later to give birth to the Romanticists. Thus, for a time, Gros pleased both camps in painting, and his position was unimpaired when Napoleon fell and the Bourbons were restored. In 1816 he was made a member of the Institute, he was commissioned to decorate the cupola of the Panthéon, and in 1824, on the completion of this work, he was created a Baron.

Meanwhile David, exiled in Brussels, was uneasy about the style of his former pupil, whom, on leaving Paris, he had left in charge of the Classical Movement. From Brussels he wrote constantly to Gros, begging him to cease painting " these futile subjects and circumstantial pictures " and to devote his talent to " fine historical pictures." By this David meant, not those paintings of the battles of Aboukir, Eylau, the Pyramids, etc., which *were* fine historical pictures, but paintings depicting some incident in the history of Greece or Rome. These alone, according to David, were the fit themes for a noble art, and he could not accept the rendering of events of his own times as true historical pictures. Unfortunately Gros, in his unbounded veneration for his old master, took David very seriously. He saw with alarm that the younger generation of painters were departing from the classical tradition and heading for Romanticism, and he blamed himself for leading them astray.

In the very year when he was made a Baron, his fellow-pupil, Girodet (1767–1824), died, and at the funeral of this follower of David, Gros lamented the loss of a great classic artist, saying : " For myself, not only have I not enough authority to direct the school, but I must accuse myself of being one of the first who set the bad example others have followed."

Conscience-stricken at falling away from his master's ideals, and particularly so when David died in the following year, Baron Gros now did violence to his own talent by forcing himself to paint subjects of which David would have approved. While the truth of his war pictures had shocked the Classic School, the artificiality of his new classical pictures roused the mocking laughter of the young and increasingly powerful Romantic School.

His " Hercules and Diomed " in the Salon of 1835 was openly sneered at ; the younger critics treated him as a " dead man," till, wearied out and depressed by the disgrace and shame which he thought he had brought on the school of David, poor Baron Gros, on June 25, 1835, lay down on his face in three feet of water at Meudon, where on the following day two boatmen discovered his body.

That leadership of the Classic School, for which Baron Gros both by his art and his temperament was utterly unfitted, was eventually assumed with honour and credit by his junior, Jean Dominique Auguste Ingres (1780–1867). A pupil of David and the winner of the Prix de Rome in 1801, Ingres was not at first regarded as a " safe " classic by the purists of that school. To these pedants, who worshipped hardly any art between the antique and Raphael, Ingres was suspicious because of his loudly proclaimed admiration of the Italian Primitives. On his way to Rome, Ingres had stopped at Pisa to study the frescoes by Benozzo Gozzoli and his contemporaries in the Campo Santo. " We ought to copy these men on our knees," said the young enthusiast, and his words were repeated to David, who regarded them as ominous.

Though he gained the prize in 1801, Ingres was not sent to Rome till 1806, and then he remained in Italy for nearly eighteen years. These were years of quiet, fruitful labour, during which the artist, in his own words, was " drawing to learn and painting to live," and by living abroad he escaped all that contemporary drama of victories and disasters, of changes of dynasties and changes of opinion, that was going on during this period in his own country. Nevertheless, from Italy he sent pictures now and again to Paris, where they attracted attention in the Salons, though they were criticised by the followers of David. When he exhibited in 1819 his " Paolo and Francesca da Rimini," the work was pronounced to be " Gothic " in tendency, and in this small historical painting we can recognise the influence of the Primitives whom Ingres admired for the purity and precision of their drawing.

When Ingres returned to Paris in 1824 the battle between the Classicists and the Romanticists was in full swing, and with Girodet dead, David in exile and dying, and Gros incompetent, the former were glad to welcome the support of Ingres, and soon made him the chief of their party. Ingres was amazed and enchanted at his sudden popularity and the honours now thrust upon him. He was speedily elected to the Institute, and later was made a Grand Officer of the Legion of Honour and a Senator. The full story of the war between the Classicists and Romanticists must be reserved for a later chapter, but it may be said at once that Ingres threw himself heart and soul into the championship of the classics by precept and example.

But where Ingres differed from his predecessor David was that with him it was the treatment rather than the subject which was all-important. A

"JOAN OF ARC AT REIMS," BY INGRES (1780–1867)

The Louvre, Paris

The faultless drawing in this picture admirably illustrates the point of view of the artist, who said
" A thing well drawn is always well enough painted."

" PAOLO AND FRANCESCA DA RIMINI," BY INGRES

Chantilly

An early example of the painting of this master, showing the delicacy and precision of his line and the extent to which he was first influenced by the work of the Italian primitives.   While Paolo is embracing Francesca, her husband, Malatesta, is seen in the background drawing his sword to slay his brother Paolo.

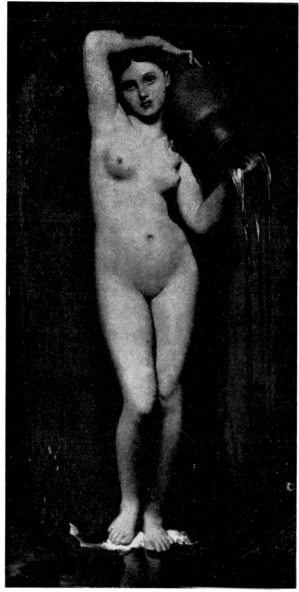

W. F. Mansell.

"LA SOURCE," BY INGRES

The Louvre, Paris

Begun as a study in 1824, this exquisite work, the painter's masterpiece, was taken up again in 1856 and completed when Ingres was seventy-six. It is unrivalled as a happy blending of truth to Nature with ideal beauty.

fanatic for drawing from the first, he held strong and peculiar views on colour. " A thing well drawn is always well enough painted," he said ; and his own use of colour was merely to emphasise the drawing in his pictures. " Rubens and Van Dyck," he argued, " may please the eye, but they deceive it—they belong to a bad school of Colour, the School of False-hood." From his early Roman days Ingres had shown himself to be a faultless draughtsman of the human figure, and his drawings and paintings of nudes are the works on which his fame most surely rests to-day. The most celebrated and perhaps the most beautiful of his works, " La Source," has an interesting history, for, though begun as a study in 1824, it was not till 1856, when the artist was seventy-six, that he turned it into a picture. One of the most precious gems of painting in the Louvre, this picture pre-serves the freshness of a young man's fancy, while it is executed with the knowledge of a lifetime. " It is a fragment of Nature, and it is a vision," is the comment of a great French critic on this picture.

If Ingres was the greatest artist the classical movement produced in France, yet he belongs too much to the nineteenth century to be considered a true product of the revolutionary and Napoleonic period. Indeed, the greatest Continental artist of that period was not a Frenchman, and it is to Spain that we must turn to find a man of outstanding genius whose protean art fully expresses the surging thoughts and feelings of this time of changes.

§ 4

The life-story of Goya is as full of storm and stress as that of his unhappy country, which between 1788 and 1815 saw more misery and more changes of government than any other country in battle-scarred Europe. Under the rule of Charles IV and his depraved consort, Queen Maria Louisa, Spain was in a miserable condition ; its Court was a frivolous, shallow imitation of Versailles, and its monarchy and government were even more rotten and more corrupt than those of France under Louis XVI. A young lieutenant of the Guards, Manuel Godoy, was made Prime Minister because he was the Queen's favourite lover, and the King was a puppet in the hands of this Spanish Messalina. Public offices were openly sold to the highest bidder, and eighteen thousand priests drained the purse of the people and stifled their intellects. Art seemed dead and past the hope of revival till Goya came to Madrid.

Francisco José de Goya y Lucientes was born on March 30, 1746, that is to say, twelve years after Romney, and ten years before Raeburn. He was the son of a peasant in a village in Aragon, and legend relates that, like Giotto, he was found drawing sheep by an amateur who recognised the boy's talent and sent him in his fourteenth year as pupil to a painter in

"DOÑA ISABEL CORBO DE PORCEL," BY GOYA (1746–1828)

National Gallery, London

Unrivalled as a satirist when painting people he disliked, Goya could also render marvellously, as we see here, the ethereal charm of a Spanish beauty of aristocratic lineage. At a time when all artistic Europe was in raptures over the "antique," Goya anchored his art to Nature and became the greatest painter of his age.

415

Saragossa. There the boy grew up strong, handsome, wild, and passionate, continually involved in love affairs and quarrels. In one of the last three men were left wounded and bleeding, and as a result of this midnight affray Goya had to leave the city hurriedly.

In 1766 he was in Madrid, and there his adventurous disposition soon got him into trouble. He was wounded in some love quarrel, placed under police supervision, and chafing at this restraint he escaped from the city with a band of bull-fighters and sailed to Italy. At the end of the 'sixties he was in Rome, where he appears to have been much more interested in the teeming life of the people than in the antiquities of the city. Here again his amorousness got him into trouble, for it is said that one night he made his way into a nunnery, was nearly captured, and only escaped the gallows by a headlong flight from the city.

In 1771 he returned to Saragossa and found shelter in a monastery, where he seems to have reformed his manner of living, for four years later this scapegrace adventurer, the hero of a hundred fights, reappeared in Madrid as a respectable citizen, married to the sister of Bayen, a painter of good standing. Through his brother-in-law he got to know people of a better class, and he was finally introduced to the Court and permitted to paint the portrait of Charles III.

Goya's pictures of this period reflect the manners of the Spanish Court, for pictures like " The Swing " and " Blind Man's Bluff " at Madrid are obviously imitations of Watteau and his school, as the Spanish Court imitated the artificiality of Versailles, only Goya, a cynic from his youth, does not give his figures the daintiness of the Frenchmen. With almost brutal realism he depicts the rouge on the women's cheeks and the pencilling of their eyebrows, and seems to take a delight in unmasking their falseness and dissipation. While he was intelligent enough to perceive the rottenness of Spanish society, Goya was no moralist himself and lived the life of his time. Countless stories are told of his relations with women of high society, and Goya is said to have been the terror of all their husbands. In this connection one inevitably thinks of his famous double picture at Madrid, " The Maja Nude " and " The Maja Clothed," the latter being an almost exact reproduction of the former with the garments added, and these are so filmy, so expressive of the limbs underneath, that the second picture has justly been said to reveal a woman " naked in spite of her dress." The story runs that the lady was the Duchess of Alva, and that when the Duke desired to see Goya's work, the painter hurriedly produced the clothed portrait and concealed the other.

When Charles IV came to the throne Goya became still more firmly established in Court favour, though he produced the most impudent portraits of royalty that have ever been painted. Nowhere can we find a more pitiless

Anderson.

"THE MAJA NUDE," BY GOYA

The Prado, Madrid

This unconventional portrait of a Duchess, said to have had a weakness for the artist, is one of the most famous paintings of the nude. A companion picture exists in which the Duchess is shown in the same attitude, only clothed, and the story goes that this second picture was painted for the Duke, and the one illustrated for the artist's own pleasure.

Rischgitz.

"CHARLES IV ON HORSEBACK," BY GOYA

The Prado, Madrid

Uncompromisingly truthful even in the portrayal of Royalty, Goya shows the King of Spain, who was a puppet in the hands of his dissolute wife, as " a monument of serene and complacent stupidity."

exposure of serene stupidity than his " Charles IV on Horseback." " He sits there, asthmatic and fat, upon his fat asthmatic horse . . . like a Moloch," says Muther, " an evil god who has battened upon the life-blood of his people." When he painted the Queen Maria Louisa, Goya portrayed her as the brazen old courtesan she was ; he shows up the Crown Prince as a sly, spiteful, hypocritical meddler, and the favourite minister Godoy as a nincompoop and a panderer. When the French novelist Gautier first saw Goya's large portrait group of the Spanish Royal Family and its favourites, his comment was, " A grocer's family who have won the big lottery prize " ; and that is exactly the impression the picture gives us, a collection of stupid, ill-bred people who owe their fine clothes and position to no talent or merit of their own but to sheer luck. It is amazing that this daring satirist of royalty should have gone unpunished and unreproved, but the King and his family circle were themselves too stupid to realise that the artist was holding them all up to the ridicule of the world.

As, while outwardly a courtier, he insidiously undermined the pretences of the Spanish monarchy, so while appearing to respect the observances of Catholicism, Goya surreptitiously attacked the Church which was blinding the eyes of the people. In 1797 he began to produce a series of engravings which, under the title of " Caprices," pretended to be nothing more than flights of fancy, but which were in reality biting satires on the social, political, and ecclesiastical conditions of his age. He drew devout women with rolling eyes worshipping a scarecrow, priests drawling out the Litany with obvious indifference, and in one fantastic plate—which he had the audacity to dedicate to the King !—he showed a corpse rising from the grave and writing with its dead finger the word Nada, i.e. " Nothingness." It was tantamount to saying that the hope of immortality held out to the people was only a blind to make them endure want and misery without murmuring, while kings and priests grew fat at their expense. If the Court and high ecclesiastics were too stupid to comprehend Goya's message, the people understood, for the revolutionary era was at hand.

A more subtle example of Goya's anti-clerical tendency is the little picture in the National Gallery, " The Bewitched," in which, while professing to do no more than paint a stage scene from a popular comedy of the time, the artist shows us a priest frightened by demons in forms of a goat and jackasses.

Like most of the intellectual men in Spain, Goya had at first welcomed the coming of Napoleon, for anything seemed to promise a hope of better things than the old regime. But, later, the piteous spectacle of his country in the throes of warfare seemed to rouse the patriot in him, and he began to champion its rights in a series of the most moving paintings and engravings. In 1810 he began to execute a series of engravings entitled

"THE BEWITCHED," BY GOYA

National Gallery, London

A priest, frightened by demons in the form of jackasses, hurriedly pours oil into a lamp held by a goat.
In this painting of a scene from a comic play, the artist satirises the Spanish clergy of his time and hints
his opinion of the value of the " light " they profess to throw on the unknown.

"The Disasters of War," which were absolutely a new thing in art. Hitherto artists, with few exceptions, had shown only the imposing side of war, its panoply and splendour, its daring and heroism. Goya was the first artist to make a deliberate and systematic impeachment of Militarism. Not only did he refuse to glorify the old adage that " it is sweet and decorous to die for one's country," but he persistently showed all the blood and misery with which military glory was bought. In his engravings of the war he shows the unchaining of the " human beast," and his prints of the torturing of prisoners and the shooting of deserters are ghastly in their revelation of raging madness and the distortions of death agonies.

In his paintings also Goya told the terrible story of the tragedies which ensued when the Spanish volunteers took up arms against Napoleon's soldiery. There is no more awful war picture in the world than Goya's painting of an incident in 1808, in which we see the gleam of the gun-barrels, and poor wretches who have been condemned by court-martial falling forward prone before the musket-fire of the troops. The despair of the condemned, and the cold-blooded energy of the executioners are appalling.

Yet while he lamented the sufferings of the patriots during the Peninsular War, Goya could not rejoice at the restoration of the Bourbons after the fall of Napoleon. For when King Ferdinand returned to Madrid in 1814, Goya saw that all hope of liberalism and freedom of thought had vanished, and that the powers of darkness, which for the time had been scared away, again settled on the land and obscured truth, progress, and enlightenment. The last " disaster of the war " was the resettlement of the Bourbons, who had " learnt nothing and forgotten nothing," on the throne of Spain, and Goya with his old fearlessness expressed his view of the matter in his engraving " The Death of Truth," in which he showed the naked figure of Truth suffering martyrdom at the hands of the priests.

We might expect that this outspoken work would have proved too much even for the most stupid, priest-ridden Court to swallow, but nothing that Goya could do ever brought home to royalty what the artist really thought of them and their government. King Ferdinand confirmed Goya's appointment as Court Painter, and even persuaded him to paint a portrait of him in the purple mantle of empire, but now the artist himself was too old and too sick at heart to play the hypocrite at Court and paint grandees with his tongue in his cheek. Gradually Goya withdrew from public life and established himself in a simple country house on the outskirts of Madrid. His wife and son were both dead ; since 1791 he had himself been afflicted with deafness ; and in this villa the lonely painter lived out his life in company with his art. His last protest against the tendencies of the time were some small paintings of the interiors of prisons and torture-chambers, in which he

"A MILITARY EXECUTION IN 1808," BY GOYA

The Prado, Madrid

From this tragic picture of the execution of Spanish volunteers by Napoleon's soldiery, Goya reveals his sympathy with the patriots and his horror at the brutality of warfare. Goya was the first artist to attack Militarism.

"THE BULL-FIGHT," BY GOYA

Accad. S. Fernando, Madrid

The artist who painted all conceivable aspects of Spanish life, could not ignore this national institution, and in his paintings of bull-fights Goya displays a professional knowledge of the sport which he gained in his youth, when he ran away once with a band of bull-fighters.

reminds us that the Inquisition had again raised its head under King Ferdinand. Among his last works were scenes of bull-fights, of the details of which Goya, in his youth, had acquired a professional knowledge. Greatly as all humanitarians must detest this horrid sport, its colour and movement appeal to the artistic sense, and the decorative aspect of the scene is the dominant note in Goya's renderings of the subject.

After nine years of this lonely life Goya seems to have felt himself no longer very secure in Spain. Perhaps he feared that the clerics would in the end perceive his purpose and have their revenge on him. At all events, in 1824 he sought and obtained leave of absence for six weeks to visit the sulphur springs of Plombières in Lorraine on account of his gout. But this appears to have been merely an excuse to get out of Spain, for he never went to Plombières, but after visiting Paris, settled at Bordeaux, where, on April 16, 1828, he died as the result of a stroke of apoplexy. In his last years he was not only stone deaf but half blind, and consequently his creative work in France was small, but one engraving remains to show that the old cynic never swerved from his faith and still had hope for the future. " Lux ex tenebris " is the pregnant title of this work of his old age, and in it he shows us a shaft of light falling on a dark spot of earth (Spain ?) and scaring away from it owls, ravens—and priests !

XXIV

THE RISE OF LANDSCAPE PAINTING

THE ART OF CLAUDE, GEORGE MORLAND, J. M. W. TURNER, GIRTIN,
DAVID COX, AND DE WINT

§ I

THE greatest difference between the art of the nineteenth and that
of the preceding centuries is the increasing importance attached to
natural scenery. The Old Masters were not altogether inattentive
to inanimate Nature, but it did not occur to them that scenery alone could be
a sufficient subject for a picture. In the East, as we shall see in a later chapter,
Nature had always preoccupied the minds of the finest artists, and in China
landscape was regarded as the highest branch of art ; but in Europe men
thought otherwise, and it was only slowly that landscape crept forward
from the background and gradually occupied the whole of the picture.

The artist who is usually considered to have been the father of modern
landscape painting was a Frenchman, or rather a Lorrainer, Claude Gellée
(1600–82), born near Mirecourt on the Moselle, who at an early age went
to Rome, where he remained practically for the rest of his life. Claude's
interest was entirely in Nature, and particularly in the illumination of
Nature. He was the first artist who " set the sun in the heavens," and he
devoted his whole attention to portraying the beauty of light ; but though
his aerial effects are unequalled to this day, and though his pictures were
approved and collected in his own day by the King of Spain, Pope Urban
VIII, and by many influential Cardinals, yet the appreciation of pure landscape was so limited then that Claude rarely dared to leave figures out of his
pictures, and was obliged to choose subjects which were not simply landscapes
but ostensibly story pictures which gave him an excuse for painting landscapes.

Nobody to-day pays very much attention to the little figures in Claude's
" Marriage of Isaac and Rebecca " at the National Gallery. We are not
disposed to ask which is Isaac and which Rebecca, or to try to discover
what all these figures are doing, because to us the beauty of the landscape is
an all-sufficient reason for the picture's existence. Our whole attention is
given to the beautiful painting of the trees and the lovely view that lies
between them, to the golden glow of the sky, to the flat surface of the water

W. F. Mansell.

"THE MARRIAGE OF ISAAC AND REBECCA," BY CLAUDE (1600-82)

National Gallery, London

When this picture was painted in 1648, the beauties of natural scenery were so slightly appreciated that it was politic for an artist to put in figures and pretend he was illustrating a story from the Bible even when, as here, his whole interest was in a lovely landscape.

426

with its reflected light, and to the exquisite gradations of the tones by which the master has conveyed to us the atmosphere of the scene and the vastness of the distance he depicts.

Similarly, in his " Embarkation of the Queen of Sheba," we are at once conscious that the glorious rendering of the sun in the sky and of its rays on the rippled surface of the sea constitute the principal interest of the picture ; this was what primarily interested the painter, and his buildings, shipping, and people are only so many accessories with which he frames and presents to us his noble vision of light.   But to Claude's contemporaries these titles and the figures which justified them had far more importance than they have to us, and it was by professing to paint subjects which the taste of his day deemed elevating and ennobling that Claude was able to enjoy prosperity and paint the landscapes which are truly noble.

Another Frenchman, also a contemporary of Claude, Nicolas Poussin (1594–1665), must be regarded as a pioneer of landscape painting, though he was also a figure painter of great ability who upheld the classic style of the antique in his Biblical and pagan figure subjects.

For the first years of his life he struggled on as a painter in Paris, but his eyes were fixed on Italy, and at the age of thirty he went to Rome and established himself on the Pincian Hill where already Claude was living.

His reputation as a painter of classical subjects spread rapidly, and in 1640 he was invited to return to Paris to decorate the great palace of the Louvre for Louis XIII.   But he hated the Court life and intrigue, and although ostensibly he was a figure painter and thought of himself as such it was in reality the lovely Italian landscape which lured him back to Rome.

This second Roman period lasted for more than twenty years, and in it Poussin painted his greatest pictures.   They were over-intellectual, for he was steeped in classical thought, and at first the classical and scriptural figures took the stage, large-scale against a background of golden scenery. Gradually, however, those backgrounds became the important thing, and the classical landscape style evolved as the now small-scale figures took a minor place in surroundings of compelling and placid beauty.   The " Diogenes " of the Louvre with its Tiber landscape, or " The Deluge " with its dramatic harmony between man and nature stand out among these.

In the National Gallery we have his " Nativity " which yields some idea of his powers as a landscape artist.   He himself did not believe in pure landscape for he stated : " Without action drawing and colour fail to influence the mind."   Nevertheless we turn away from his highly organised classical figure subjects finding them cold and unfeeling.   Rather we look at the wonderful construction of the landscapes of the Campagna or of the mountains of Alba behind his dramatically posed figures.   It was the

427

" NATIVITY," BY NICHOLAS POUSSIN (1594–1665)

National Gallery, London

The immediate claim of any picture by Nicholas Poussin lies in its majestic composition. His classic style (which causes him here to lay the scene of the Nativity not in a manger but amid classical architecture) finds expression in the noble scale of the figures and the highly conscious rhythms and balance of the picture.

solidity of their construction which caused Cézanne to say that the modern landscape artist should aim at " Poussin painted from nature " ; for Cézanne, turning away from the insubstantiality of the Impressionists of his own day, found in the old Franco-Roman painter, with his brown trees and his sense of the gravity of the solid earth, a model for his ideals.

Poussin, having no son, adopted his wife's younger brother, Gaspar Dughet (1613–75) who took the name of Gaspar Poussin and continued to explore the avenue which his benefactor and master had opened. He became an excellent landscape painter as his work " Abraham and Isaac " in the National Gallery testifies. He saw nature with a fresher vision than did Nicholas, saw trees as green, and noted the changing clouds. With Claude he brought to something like perfection this balanced designing of landscape, framing far vistas in foreground trees. He, too, believed he was concerned with human incident, but actually landscape was playing an even greater part than it did with the elder Poussin.

This group of artists rightfully find their place at the beginning of this chapter upon the rise of landscape art in Britain because in the eighteenth century when that art emerged their painting was held to be the correct method by connoisseurs and artists alike. Their serene golden Italian skies, the balanced foreground trees, the carefully arranged distance of river and mountains, the ancient classical buildings, the small-scale figures : these things constituted an ideal landscape—and a saleable one.

We have already seen how Richard Wilson endeavoured to popularise landscape-painting in England, and it will have been noted that so long as he also pretended to paint classical subjects, as in his " Niobe," he had a moderate measure of success ; but when he painted pure landscape, as in " The Thames near Twickenham," the taste of his day could not follow him, and his finest work was ignored and went begging.

§ 2

According to a great historian, Dr. S. R. Gardiner, much of the best literature of the early nineteenth century was inspired by the " better side " of the French Revolution, " its preference of the natural to the artificial, and of the humble to the exalted." This same preference is clearly visible in the art of George Morland (1763–1804).

Morland, who was born in London on June 26, 1763, was the son and the grandson of artists. His father, Henry Robert Morland (1730–97), discovered his son's talent at an early age, and proceeded to force it with unparalleled avarice and tyranny, so that his unfortunate son had no life at all outside the garret in which he was kept earning money for the needy household. George Morland began drawing when he was three ; at the age

"THE ALEHOUSE DOOR," BY GEORGE MORLAND (1763–1804)

National Gallery, London

A pioneer of democratic art, Morland painted the every-day life around him ; his boon companions were frequently his models. His rustic scenes, happy in their simple truth and fresh harmonious colour, have the charm and interest of authentic human documents.

430

of ten he was exhibiting in the Royal Academy ; but while his hand and his eyes were trained to accomplish remarkable feats of painting, the rest of his education was absolutely neglected, so that he grew up empty-headed, with a great longing to escape the paternal tyranny and be able to enjoy himself.

Inevitably, when he did at last break away from his father, he plunged into dissipation, and divided his time between drinking and painting. In 1786 he married and pulled himself together for a time, but he was so fond of his liberty that he refused an offer from Romney of £300 a year for three years to be his assistant, and preferred to ramble about the country painting rustic scenes and spending too much time and money in alehouses.

For a little while, before his health was ruined by drink, he was in easy circumstances, for his paintings of domestic scenes and farm life were exceedingly popular, and he was better known to the people than any of his august contemporaries. All his principal works were engraved, and these coloured prints after Morland's pictures found their way into many humble homes. It is probable that his well-known painting at the National Gallery, " The Interior of a Stable," was painted about 1791, which would nearly coincide with the period of Morland's greatest prosperity. The stable is said to be that of the White Lion Inn at Paddington, where Morland once had as many as eight horses, but partly owing to his drinking habits and partly owing to his unbusinesslike methods his prosperity soon dwindled.

Notwithstanding his dissipation—and a day rarely passed in which he was not drunk—he was not idle, for Morland was the author of four thousand pictures and of a still greater number of drawings. But his intemperance and his dependence on dealers gradually impoverished his art, and the man who had a genuine love and understanding of country life, and ought to have been one of the world's greatest rustic painters, sank into " pot-boiling," painting what the dealers wanted instead of what he wanted to do himself. His terms were four guineas a day—and his drink ! Morland had got into the state when he " didn't care," though in his sober moments he must have seen the irony and impropriety of a man of his character painting Hogarthian moralities like " The Fruits of Early Industry," " The Effects of Extravagance and Idleness," and so forth. Indeed, these in his own day were Morland's most popular works, and though some of them show the degeneration of his drawing, and his carelessness in their " woolly " rendering of form, even to the end a little painting more carefully handled and jewel-like in colour will now and again show what a great painter he might have been. His last miserable years, 1800–4, were spent in a debtor's prison, yet even here, with a brandy-bottle always handy, he was still industrious, and for one dealer alone during this period he painted one hundred and

"INTERIOR OF A STABLE," BY GEORGE MORLAND

National Gallery, London

But for drink, which wrecked his career and brought about his death at the age of 41, Morland might have been one of the greatest of English painters. He was the author of 4000 pictures, but owing to his intemperance most of them are mere "pot-boilers," and few approach the excellence of this work, which shows what the artist might have done had he been industrious and sober.

ninety-two pictures. At the early age of forty-one George Morland died, completely wrecked, the victim of his own want of education and of roguish employers.

§ 3

The establishment of landscape in the popular estimation as a branch of art, equal to the highest achievements of portraiture or historical painting, was finally achieved by Turner, the greatest glory of British art. Joseph Mallord William Turner was born, appropriately enough, on Shakespeare's birthday, April 23, 1775 ; appropriately, because he was destined to become the Shakespeare of English painting. He was the son of a London hairdresser in humble circumstances, who lived and had his shop at 26 Maiden Lane, Covent Garden. As a boy he showed ability as a draughtsman and colourist, and his father exhibited some of the lad's drawings in his shop, where now and again they found a purchaser. One or two artists who went to the elder Turner to be shaved noticed his son's drawings, and urged the father to give his son a proper artistic training. So at the age of eleven young Turner was sent to the Soho Academy and had lessons from Thomas Malton, who grounded him well in perspective, and also from Edward Dayes ; and in 1789, when he was fourteen, he was admitted to the school of the Royal Academy.

Meanwhile he was managing to support himself by selling a few sketches now and then, by putting in backgrounds for architects who wanted nice drawings to show their clients, and by colouring prints for engravers. While tinting prints for John Raphael Smith (1752–1812), the mezzotinter, who made a fortune by engraving the work of Morland, Turner met the brilliant water-colourist, Girtin, with whom he made friends, and Girtin introduced him to the friendly house of Dr. Thomas Monro, at 8 Adelphi Terrace. Here the two young men and other students were welcome every evening, for Monro was an enthusiastic connoisseur who had a studio fitted up for his protégés to work in ; he gave them oyster suppers, a few shillings for pocket-money when they had nothing of their own, and free medical attendance if they became ill.

In 1797 Turner exhibited his first oil picture, a study of moonlight, at the Royal Academy, but most of the views he painted at this time were in water-colour. In 1792 he was commissioned to make a series of topographical drawings for a magazine, and this enabled him to make the first of those sketching tours which ever afterwards were a feature of his artistic life and to which we owe his enormous range of subject. In the following year he opened his own studio in Hand Court, Maiden Lane, where he exhibited and sold the drawings he had made on his tours.

Turner never had any difficulty in making a living, and we may account

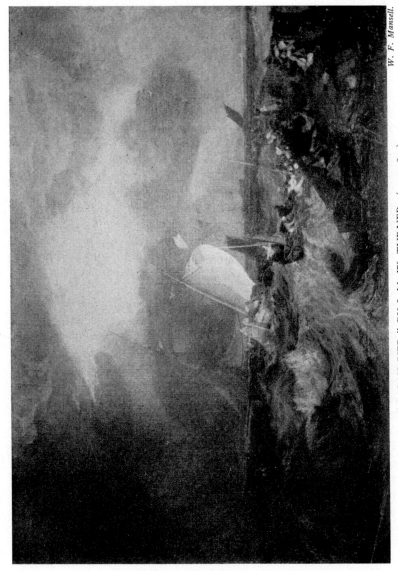

"CALAIS PIER," BY J. M. W. TURNER, (1775–1851)

National Gallery, London

This picture, painted in 1803, shows the English Packet arriving off Calais while French fishermen are preparing for sea. It is considered to be the first masterpiece of Turner's early style, and reveals the artist's power of painting *weather* when he was still in his twenties.

434

for his success where so many other landscape artists had failed by the fact that he established his reputation in water-colour before he proceeded to oils. From the time of Richard Wilson there had always been a demand for topographical drawings in water-colours, and Wilson's contemporary, Paul Sandby, R.A. (1725–1809), the " father of water-colour art," was one of the first to popularise landscape by going about the country and sketching gentlemen's mansions and parks. Landowners were pleased to purchase his and other artists' water-colours of views on their estates, and their pride in their own property was gradually converted by these artists into a real appreciation of the beauties of Nature.

At Dr. Monro's house Turner met John Robert Cozens (1752–99), a most poetic painter in water-colours and the son of a water-colour artist, Alexander Cozens, who died in 1786 ; and while Turner owed most to his diligent study of Nature, he always owned his obligation to Cozens, who was indeed his immediate predecessor in water-colour and the first to produce those atmospheric effects which Turner rivalled and excelled.

In 1799, at the age of twenty-four, Turner was elected an Associate of the Royal Academy, and henceforward, surer of himself and his public, he eschewed the merely topographical imitation of landscape for a nobler art. He looked beyond the mere details to a larger treatment of Nature, seizing all the poetry of sunshine, and the mists of morn and eve, with the grandeur of storm and the glow of sunset. In feeling his way to this period of his first style Turner looked not only to Nature but also to the example of his great predecessors, Claude, Richard Wilson, and the Dutch painters of the seventeenth century. The influence of the Dutch School, and particularly of Van de Velde, is apparent in many of these early works, even in " Calais Pier," which, painted in 1803, was held by Ruskin to be " the first which bears the sign manual and sign mental of Turner's colossal power." Already, however, Turner had improved on Van de Velde, who was never able to interpret weather so truly and vigorously as it is painted in the rolling sea and windy sky of this stimulating sea-piece.

The year before this picture was painted, Turner was elected R.A. (1802), and during the succeeding years he spent much time in travelling, visiting France, Switzerland, Italy, and the Rhine, and producing innumerable water-colours, as well as some of his finest oil-paintings.

That splendour of the sky, which was to be the peculiar glory of Turner, is first indicated in his " Sun rising through Vapour," painted in 1807, and it was possibly because this was the first picture in which he was able to obtain the effect after which he strove most earnestly that he was so attached to this picture. He sold it, but twenty years later, at the De Tabley sale of 1827, he bought it back for £514 10s. in order that he might bequeath this to the nation, together with his " Dido Building Carthage " on condition

"THE EMBARKATION OF THE QUEEN OF SHEBA," BY CLAUDE

National Gallery, London

One of the earliest and one of the grandest endeavours to paint the actual source of light, this picture has for two centuries been an inspiration to landscape painters by the beauty of its sky and the sunlight shining on the water.

W. F. Mansell.

"DIDO BUILDING CARTHAGE," BY J. M. W. TURNER

National Gallery, London

The artist loved this picture (painted in 1815) so much that he once declared his wish to have it wrapped round his dead body and buried with him. He changed his mind, however, and bequeathed it to the nation, directing that it should always be hung beside Claude's masterpiece (see opposite page) as a perpetual challenge.

they should be hung in perpetuity beside Claude's " Marriage of Isaac and Rebecca " and " Embarkation of the Queen of Sheba." Conscious of his own powers and confident in the verdict of posterity, Turner was jealous of other painters' fame, and he was enraged at the way in which English connoisseurs extolled the pictures of Claude while they neglected his own works.

The pictures already mentioned, together with the lovely " Crossing the Brook," a view near Weir Head, Tamar, looking towards Plymouth and Mount Edgcumbe, also painted in 1815, may be regarded as the chief master-pieces in oils of Turner's first period. After 1820 a great change was manifest in his manner of painting. In the early paintings dark predominated, with a very limited portion of light, and he painted solidly throughout with a vigorous and full brush ; but his later works are based on a light ground with a small proportion of dark, and using opaque touches of the purest orange, blue, purple, and other powerful colours, Turner obtained infinitely delicate gradations which produced a splendid and harmonious effect. This new manner is first seen in his " Bay of Baiæ," painted in 1823, and six years later, in 1829, it is revealed in all its glory in one of Turner's most beautiful and poetical works, " Ulysses Deriding Polyphemus," in which, as Redgrave has said, " while in no way gaudy, it seems impossible to surpass the power of colour which he has attained, or the terrible beauty in which he has clothed his poetic conception." In this glorious picture, " a work almost without a parallel in art," the nominal subject has little more power over us to-day than it had in Claude's works. Turner's painting attracts us primarily, not as an illustration to a familiar story from Homer, but as a glowing piece of colour, a magnificently decorative transcription of a flaming sunrise. And with all this the picture is a " magic casement " through which our imagination looks out on a world of romance, for in this colour is all the intoxication of triumph, of final victory after perils escaped ; and though Turner himself probably did not know it, and few who look upon his masterpiece are conscious of the fact, this picture subconsciously expresses the elation, the pride, and even the touch of insolence, that all England felt after her victorious issue from the Napoleonic wars.

As Turner altered his style of oil-painting, so also he revolutionised his practice in water-colour. Originally, in common with the older members of the Early English Water-colour School, Turner began a drawing by laying in the gradations of light and shade with grey or some other neutral tint, and afterwards represented the hue of each object by tinting it with colour ; but this he found resulted in a certain heaviness of aspect. Accordingly, in his later water-colours he proceeded to treat the whole surface of his drawing as colour, using at once the pigments by which the scene might most properly be represented. By delicate hatchings he achieved wonderful qualities of

" CROSSING THE BROOK," BY J. M. W. TURNER

National Gallery, London

Painted in 1815, this beautiful picture illustrates the second manner of Turner, and in its classical arrangement shows how he was influenced by Richard Wilson. The river seen in the middle distance is the
Tamar, which divides Devonshire from Cornwall, and looking towards Plymouth and Mount Edgcumbe
we see Calstock Church beyond Poulston Bridge. Thus, though idealised by the painter's imagination,
the scene is founded on fact.

439

"THE FIGHTING *TÉMÉRAIRE* TOWED TO HER LAST BERTH," BY J. M. W. TURNER

National Gallery, London

The *Téméraire* fought at Trafalgar in 1805, and was broken up in 1838. With poetic imagination Turner visualises her last voyage, the old man-of-war looking almost ghostly in the silvery light of the moon, while the sun is setting on the tug that tows her home.

440

broken hues, air tints, and atmosphere, so that the view when finished glowed and sparkled with the brilliance of Nature's own colours. This method of putting on the colour direct, without any under-painting of the subject in light and shade, has been to a great extent the foundation of modern painting.

Determined to outshine his fellows, Turner had a habit, dreaded by other artists, of coming to the Academy on Varnishing Day armed with his paint-box, and putting a brilliant touch or two on his own canvas when necessary to heighten its effect if its brilliance happened to be in any way challenged by that of a neighbouring picture. The brightness of the yellows and reds in his " Fighting *Téméraire* being Towed to her Last Berth " is said to be due to after-touches put on to " kill " a highly coloured painting by Geddes which hung near it in the Academy of 1839. Towards another landscape painter Turner was merciless, but he had respect and kindly feeling for Sir Thomas Lawrence, and on one occasion he darkened a landscape of his with lamp-black because it injured the effect of pictures by Lawrence on either side.

As he grew older, and particularly after his visit to Venice in 1832, Turner became more and more ambitious of realising to the uttermost the fugitive radiances of dawn and sunset. Light, or rather the colour of light, became the objective of his painting, to the exclusion of almost everything else, and few of his contemporaries could follow him as he devoted his brush more and more to depicting the pageant of the heavens. His work when exhibited was severely criticised and held up to ridicule and mirth by Thackeray and other wits ; he was regarded as a madman and accused, as other artists after him have been, of " flinging a pot of paint in the public's face." Even " The Fighting *Téméraire*," which seems to us so poetic to-day in its contrast of moonlight with sunlight, to match the contrast between the sailing-ship that was passing away and the steamer that heralded the future, even this work was deemed to be exaggerated and extravagant, and to most of the admirers of his earlier pictures paintings like " The Approach to Venice " were utterly incomprehensible.

Fortunately, Turner was now independent of patrons and could paint as he liked. During the earlier part of his career he had amassed a considerable fortune, a great part of which was derived from the engravings of his works, for he was a good business man, able to drive a close bargain with publishers, and clever enough to retain an interest in his works. He had commenced in 1808 the series of etchings known as the " Liber Studiorum," and the excellence of these plates—now of great rarity and value—had led to his employment as an illustrator, and his fame was greatly increased and extended by the beautiful work he did for books like Rogers' *Italy*, and *Poems, The Rivers of France, Southern Coast Scenery*, etc. He had a fine studio at what is now 23 Queen Anne Street, and he also owned a house at Twickenham, where he lived with his father, who had retired from business and made his home with his son from about 1807 till his death in 1829. Here, with his father and an old housekeeper, Turner led a retired life ; but though habitually taciturn and reserved, he could be jovial at a convivial gathering of artists which he now and then attended.

In 1840, when Turner was sixty-five, he met a young man of twenty-one, fresh from Oxford, who, from the time he first saw the illustrations to Rogers' *Italy*, had worshipped the genius of Turner, and was destined to become his persistent and most eloquent champion. This was John Ruskin, who, in 1843—the year in which Turner painted " The Approach to Venice " —published the first volume of his *Modern Painters*, an epoch-making book, the real subject of which was the superiority of Turner to all painters past and present. Henceforward, however others might laugh at and ridicule his magical colour visions, Turner had an enthusiastic defender whose opinion yearly became more authoritative and more widely respected. It is no exaggeration to say that to the constant eulogy of Ruskin is due in no small measure the universal esteem in which Turner is held to-day.

Though he never married, Turner had a natural liking for a quiet domestic existence, and after his father's death he began to lead a double life. Under the assumed name of Booth he formed a connection with a woman who kept a house at 119 Cheyne Walk, where he had been accustomed occasionally to lodge, and " Puggy " or " Admiral " Booth became a well-known character in Chelsea, where he was reputed to be a retired mariner of eccentric disposition, fond of his glass, and never tired of watching the sun. On the roof of the house in Cheyne Walk there was a gallery, and here " Mr. Booth " would sit for hours at dawn and sunset. The secret of his double existence was not discovered till the day before his death, for he had been accustomed to absent himself from Queen Anne Street for long intervals and therefore was not missed. Suddenly those who knew him as Turner learnt that the great artist was lying dead in a little house at Chelsea, where his last illness had seized him, and where he died on December 19, 1851. The body was removed to the house in Queen Anne Street, and afterwards buried in the crypt of St. Paul's Cathedral.

Turner left a fortune of £140,000, and after making a number of small annuities left the bulk of it for the benefit of art and artists ; but his will, drawn by himself, was so vague and unskilfully framed that, after four years' litigation, a compromise was arranged on the advice of the Lord Chancellor. The Royal Academy received £20,000, which it set aside as the Turner Fund for the relief of poor artists not members of their body, and the National Gallery acquired the magnificent gift of 362 oil-paintings, 135 finished water-colours, 1757 studies in colour, and thousands of drawings and sketches. The task of sifting, arranging, and cataloguing the water-colours

"ULYSSES DERIDING POLYPHEMUS," BY J. M. W. TURNER

National Gallery, London

Never in the history of art had the flaming splendour of a sunrise been so gloriously depicted in vivid colours as when Turner painted this picture in 1829.

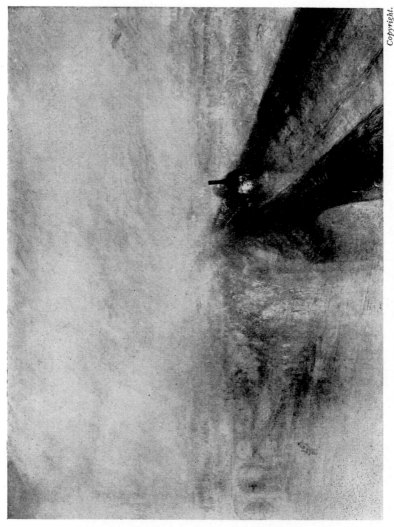

" RAIN, HAIL, AND STEAM," BY J. M. W. TURNER

National Gallery, London

Turner's final period was one in which he was concerned only with colour and light. He found a subject in this early railway train rushing across a bridge in bad weather. The forms were lost in the wild rush of the elements and the steam from the engine. How far is such treatment removed from the topographical art of his first period, but how linked it is with the work of the French Impressionists who were to follow.

444

and sketches which Turner bequeathed to the nation was rightly placed in the sympathetic hands of his great advocate, John Ruskin.

The life of Turner, as we have seen, was full of strangeness and contradictions, and it is possible he may have inherited some of his eccentricities from his mother, a woman of fierce temper, who eventually became insane. There was little correspondence between his art and his life, for, as E. V. Lucas has justly said : " Turner's works are marvels of loveliness and grandeur ; Turner was grubby, miserly, jealous, and squalid in his tastes. He saw visions and glorified even what was already glorious ; and he deliberately chose to live in houses thick with grime, and often to consort with inferior persons." The evidence before us compels us to believe that he was really happier as " Puggy Booth " with a few cronies in a Chelsea bar-parlour than as " the famous Mr. Turner " in the company of his patron, Lord Egremont, or in the hospitable mansion of Mr. Fawkes of Farnley Hall.

§ 4

Jealous as he was of other painters, there was one of his contemporaries for whose art Turner had nothing but admiration. " Had Girtin lived," he once said, " I should have starved," and he roundly admitted that painter's " White House in Chelsea " to be better than anything of his own up to that time. Thomas Girtin was born in 1773 at Southwark, where his father was a rope manufacturer, and, like Turner, he was for a time the pupil of Dayes. But for his short life—for he died in 1802 at the early age of twenty-seven—he would probably have rivalled Turner as a painter in oils, and though his career was cut short he lived long enough to make himself one of the greatest of our painters in water-colours. In this medium his style was bold and vigorous, and by suppressing irrelevant detail he gave a sense of grandeur to the scenes he depicted. His chief sketching-ground was the northern counties, and particularly their cathedral cities, and his favourite subjects were the ruins of our old abbeys and castles, and the hilly scenery of the north. The water-colour at South Kensington of " Kirkstall Abbey " is a fine example of his power to present his subject with truth and majesty.

A younger fellow-student with Turner and Girtin in the hospitable house of Dr. Monro was another artist who achieved fame chiefly as a painter in water-colours. This was Peter De Wint, born at Stone in Staffordshire in 1784. His father was a Dutch physician belonging to an old and respected Amsterdam family who settled in England. Peter, his fourth son, was originally intended for the medical profession, but was allowed to follow art, and placed with the engraver, John Raphael Smith, in 1802. Five years later he was admitted to the Royal Academy School, and the same year (1807) he exhibited at the Academy for the first time, sending three

W. F. Mansell.

"KIRKSTALL ABBEY," BY GIRTIN (1773–1803)

Victoria and Albert Museum, London

A masterly example of the water-colour art of this short-lived painter of whom Turner said, "Had Girtin lived, I should have starved."

446

"THE TRENT, NEAR BURTON," BY DE WINT (1784–1849)

Victoria and Albert Museum, London

Dutch by descent, though born in England, De Wint was at his best in painting flat stretches of river scenery under a placid luminous sky. This water-colour of a hayfield with a hay-barge on the river is a happy example of his rural idylls.

landscapes, and thereafter he exhibited there occasionally till 1828. But his reputation was principally made by the drawings he contributed to the Water-colour Society, of which he was elected as Associate in 1810 and was long one of the chief ornaments.

De Wint loved to paint direct from Nature, and was never so happy as when in the fields. His subjects are principally chosen in the eastern and northern counties, and though often tempted to extend his studies to the Continent, the love of England and English scenery was so strong that, except for one visit to Normandy, he never left these shores. He formed a style of his own, notable for the simplicity and breadth of his light and shade, and the fresh limpidity of his colour. He was a great purist in technique and objected to the use of Chinese white and body colour, which he thought tended to give a heavy effect to a drawing. He excelled in river scenes, and " The Trent near Burton " in the Victoria and Albert Museum, South Kensington, is a beautiful example of his tender and faithful rendering of a typical English scene.

While De Wint excelled in painting the placid aspects of landscapes, his contemporary, David Cox, was at his best on a windy day or in stormy weather. Cox was the son of a blacksmith and was born at Deritend, a suburb of Birmingham, on April 29, 1783. During his school-days he had an accident and broke his leg, and this misfortune proved to be his good fortune, for having been given a box of colours with which to amuse himself while he was laid up, young David made such good use of the paints that his parents perceived the bent of his genius, and when he was well again apprenticed him to a painter. David Cox received his first tuition from an artist who painted miniatures for lockets, but when his master committed suicide young Cox went to the other extreme of painting, and at the age of seventeen he became an assistant scene-painter at the Birmingham Theatre. It is said that he even took a small part now and then at this theatre, which was then managed by the father of Macready.

From Birmingham David Cox went to London to paint scenery—at four shillings a square yard !—in the Surrey Theatre, varying this work with sepia drawings, which he sold to a dealer at two guineas a dozen for school copies. Meanwhile he made every endeavour to improve his art and took lessons from John Varley (1778–1842), an artist of refined accomplishment, who was one of the founders of the Water-colour Society in 1804. Varley, who had had his own struggles before he made a position for himself as one of the best water-colourists of his time, liked Cox so much and thought so highly of his talent that he would not allow the young man to pay him for his lessons.

Under Varley's tuition Cox rapidly improved his art and his circumstances ; he was able to quit the theatre and earn money in his turn by giving

"A WINDY DAY," BY DAVID COX (1783–1859)

National Gallery, London

Among all the remarkable landscape artists of his day, David Cox was notable for the freedom of his handling and his vigorous rendering of weather. In this picture we can almost feel the wind that is blowing across the common in the face of the woman with her dog.

P

lessons, and in 1805 he made his first visit to Wales, where he discovered Bettws-y-Coed, ever after to be his Mecca. On his return he exhibited his Welsh water-colours, which attracted some attention, and in 1808 he married and settled down in a little house on Dulwich Common. Here he gave lessons to pupils and polished his own art by the diligent study of the surrounding scenery, learning to render the varied effects of Nature and the aspects of morning, noon, and twilight. In 1813 he was elected a member of the Water-colour Society and became one of the principal contributors to its exhibitions.

In 1829 he made a tour on the Continent, choosing his subjects on the coasts and in the market-places of Antwerp and Brussels, and the crowded bridges of Paris, but he liked best the scenery of his own country, particularly the mountainous country of Wales and Scotland, whose gloomy passes he painted with great effect and grandeur. He also painted many views of the Thames and of the country round London, but till he was past fifty he worked exclusively in water-colours.

In 1839, however, when he was fifty-six, Cox became acquainted with a young Bristol painter, William James Müller (1812–45), who had just returned from a long journey through Greece and Egypt. Müller was himself a very brilliant colourist and a skilful painter in oils ; the man and his work made a deep impression on Cox, who studied Müller and watched him at work, and henceforward devoted himself more to oils than to water-colours. About 1841 Cox left London and settled at Greenfield House, Harborne, near Birmingham, and there, with an annual excursion of some weeks to his beloved Bettws-y-Coed, he lived till the day of his death on June 7, 1859. During these later years Cox gave himself chiefly to oil-painting ; his best pictures were seldom seen in London during his own lifetime, and when shown were not generally appreciated. It was only after his death that his merit as an oil-painter became widely recognised.

Whether in oil or in water-colour the work of David Cox is distinguished by its light, its vigour, and its spaciousness. His picture " A Windy Day," also known as " Crossing the Common," is a happy example of the scene and weather he excelled in rendering.

XXV

NATURAL LANDSCAPE

THE ART OF CONSTABLE, BONINGTON, CROME, AND COTMAN

§ 1

UNQUESTIONABLY the two greatest English painters of landscape, and probably the two greatest English painters of any kind, were Turner and Constable, who were born within a year of one another. Turner, as we saw in the last chapter, amassed a large fortune ; Constable, on the other hand, could hardly earn a bare living, and not until 1814, when the artist was thirty-eight, did he sell a picture to any but his own personal friends.

How was it that, from a worldly point of view, Constable failed where Turner succeeded ? The explanation is to be found in the totally different character of the landscapes painted by these two artists. Turner, as Claude had done before him, made frequent use of nominal subjects as an excuse for his pictures of Nature ; there was a dramatic element in his art which appealed to the popular imagination, and even when, as in many of his later works, people found difficulty in apprehending the elements of his style, they were insensibly affected by the splendour of his colour and brought to admit that these pictures, if difficult to understand, were paintings in the " grand style."

Constable never made use of fictitious subjects and titles as an excuse for painting landscapes. His works were wholly free from any dramatic or foreign interest, and following the example of the Dutch landscape painters of the seventeenth century, he whole-heartedly devoted himself to painting the simple, homely beauty of the scenery in his native land. He modestly confessed that he thought there was room for a " natural painter," and by this he meant a painter who would devote himself to painting as truly as he could the beauty of Nature without importing into his pictures any extraneous reference to Homeric legend or to events in the past or present.

His landscapes were long unappreciated because they appealed to a pure love of Nature which was not fully awake in the artist's lifetime. " My art," said Constable a little bitterly in his middle years, " flatters nobody by imitation, it courts nobody by smoothness, tickles nobody by petiteness, it

451

is without either fal-de-lal or fiddle-de-dee ; how can I then hope to be popular ? "

John Constable was born on June 11, 1776, nearly fourteen months, to be precise, after the birth of Turner. He was the son of a miller who owned watermills at Flatford and Dedham and two windmills at East Bergholt in Suffolk. It was at the mill house in East Bergholt that John Constable was born, and here he passed the greater part of his youth. His father wished him to enter the Church, but Constable had no inclination in this direction, and after he had finished his education in the local school, at the age of eighteen he assisted his father in the mill at East Bergholt which figures in so many of his landscapes.

Meanwhile his love of Nature and art was encouraged by a great amateur who happened to have his seat in the neighbouring county of Essex and was quick to recognise the talent of young Constable. Sir George Beaumont (1753–1827) was something of a painter himself, he had been a pupil of Richard Wilson ; and he was an enthusiastic patron of art and artists. He had peculiar ideas about colour, and his well-known saying that " a good picture, like a good fiddle, should be brown," was not helpful to a painter like Constable, who saw the lovely greens in Nature and painted them as he saw them ; but at this time Constable was a beginner, and the friendly encouragement and advice of Beaumont decided Constable's career.

One of the best things about Sir George Beaumont, to whose zeal and generosity we owe in large measure the establishment of the National Gallery, was his unremitting efforts to make England appreciate the genius of her own artists. As a young man he had waggishly shown up the ignorance of the public and its ridiculous passion for foreign artists by advertising in the newspapers that a wonderful German had arrived in Bond Street who could take likenesses by a new method of heating the mirror in which the sitter looked, and for ever fixing and preserving the reflection ! On the next day a crowd of fashionable folk flocked to Bond Street, only to be laughed at by the practical joker and his friends.

Sir George Beaumont not only encouraged young Constable to go on with his sketching, but lent him works which might serve as models for his practice. Among these were two water-colours by Thomas Girtin, which Constable always maintained set his feet firmly in the right road, and also Claude's " Landscape with the Angel appearing to Hagar," a work Beaumont so loved that he took it about with him wherever he travelled. In 1826 he gave this with fifteen other pictures to the nation, but finding he could not live without it he asked for it back till his death, which occurred in the following year. This Claude is now in the National Gallery.

The opinion of this artist-baronet naturally carried weight with Constable's father, and as a result of his influence John Constable was permitted

" BOAT-BUILDING NEAR FLATFORD MILL," BY JOHN CONSTABLE (1776–1857)

Victoria and Albert Museum, London

This peaceful scene, painted in 1815, is a perfect example of Constable's early style before he had acquired the vigour and freedom which distinguish his later works.

to go to London in 1795 to study art. Here he was encouraged by Joseph Farington, R.A. (1747–1821), who communicated to him some of the precepts he had himself derived from his master Richard Wilson, and in 1799 Constable, through Farington's influence, was admitted to the Royal Academy Schools. Although the first painting Constable exhibited at the Academy was a landscape, shown in 1802, he began his professional career as a portrait painter, which was then the only profitable branch of art. But after painting some portraits and altar-pieces for Brantham in 1804 and for Nayland in 1809, he came to devote himself more or less exclusively to landscape, which was the true bent of his genius. He felt he could paint his own places best, he delighted in the flats of Dedham, with its trees and slow river " escaping from milldams, over willows, old rotten planks, slimy posts, and brickwork " ; and so he finally settled down as the painter of the rural scenery among which he had been born. In 1803 he had written, " I feel now, more than ever, a decided conviction that I shall some time or other make some good pictures ; pictures that shall be valuable to posterity, if I do not reap the benefit of them."

These words were prophetic, and for some years almost the only patrons the young artist had were a kindly uncle and his friend Archdeacon Fisher, the nephew and chaplain of the Bishop of Salisbury. Had Constable been content to be a merely topographical artist as Farington and most of the older water-colourists were, he would probably have found it easier to sell his works and make a respectable income ; but from the first it was his desire not merely to paint " portraits of places," but to give a true and full impression of Nature, to paint light, dews, breezes, bloom, and freshness. The multitude of his sketches—of which a fine collection may be seen in the Victoria and Albert Museum, South Kensington—show how earnestly and assiduously he studied Nature in all her aspects to attain this end, and though a love of Nature and of truth is discernible even in his earliest works, it was only gradually that Constable acquired the breadth and freedom which distinguish his later works.

If we compare even so beautiful an example of his early style as " Boat-building near Flatford Mill," painted in 1815, with " The Hay Wain," painted in 1821, we at once perceive the tremendous advance made by the artist in the intervening six years. It is not altogether without significance to note that the greatest strides forward in his art were made during the early years of his married life, and it may not unreasonably be surmised that the happiness of his private life and domestic contentment compensated Constable for public neglect and helped to give him increased confidence in his own powers.

It was in 1816 that he married Maria Bicknell, with whom he had been in love since 1811, and the correspondence between the two during these

"THE HAY WAIN," BY JOHN CONSTABLE

National Gallery, London

Almost unnoticed when shown at the Academy in 1821, this picture created a sensation when it was exhibited in the Paris Salon of 1824. Constable was awarded a Gold Medal, and his example led French artists to adopt a new and truer style of landscape painting.

five years—several letters of which still exist—shows the simple nature of the writers and the complete trust each had in the other. The marriage was delayed owing to the long opposition of Constable's father, and eventually it took place against his wishes, but there was no serious breach between father and son, and neither Constable senior nor Mr. Bicknell, who was also very comfortably off, allowed the young couple to be in actual want. Two years before his marriage Constable had for the first time sold two landscapes to total strangers, but as yet he had no real success, and the young couple set up house modestly at 76 Charlotte Street, Fitzroy Square.

In 1819, when Constable was forty-three, he exhibited at the Academy a large landscape, " View on the River Stour," which was keenly appreciated by his brother artists and resulted in his being elected an Associate, and in the following year his love of Nature led him to take a house at Hampstead.

When " The Hay Wain " was exhibited at the Royal Academy in 1821 it attracted comparatively little attention, but three years later it was sold to a French collector, who sent it to the Paris Salon of 1824, where it created a veritable sensation. Constable was awarded a gold medal, and his picture had an immediate and lasting effect on French art. His pure and brilliant colour was a revelation and an inspiration to French painters, and under the glamour of " The Hay Wain " Delacroix, the leader of the French Romanticists, obtained leave to retouch his " Massacre of Scio " in the same exhibition. In a fortnight he repainted it throughout, using the strongest, purest, and most vivid colours he could find, and henceforward not only were Delacroix's ideas of colour and landscape revolutionised by Constable's masterpiece, but a whole school of French landscape painters arose, as we shall see in a later chapter, whose art was to a great extent based on the example and practice of Constable.

It was in France, then, that Constable had his first real success, and Frenchmen were the first in large numbers fully to appreciate his genius. It is a piece of great good luck that " The Hay Wain " ever came back to England, but fortunately it was recovered by a British collector, George Young, and at his sale in 1866 it was purchased by the late Henry Vaughan, who gave it to the National Gallery.

In 1825 Constable, now possessing a European reputation though still neglected in his own country, sent to the Academy his famous picture " The Leaping Horse," which is generally considered to be his central masterwork, though many shrewd judges consider that the essence of his fresh, naturalistic art is still more brilliantly displayed in the big preparatory six-foot sketch of the same subject, now in the Victoria and Albert Museum. It was Constable's habit to make these large preparatory sketches for pictures of special importance, and the great difference between the sketch and the picture is that the former was done in the open, directly from Nature, while

W. F. Mansell.

" STUDY FOR THE LEAPING HORSE," BY JOHN CONSTABLE

Victoria and Albert Museum, London

This magnificent six-foot sketch, painted direct from Nature in 1825, gives the essence of Constable's fresh, naturalistic art. Compare this study with the colour reproduction (Plate X) ; in completing the picture the artist made important alterations.

the latter was worked up in the studio. Consequently the sketch always contains a freshness and vigour, something of which is lost in the picture, though this last may have refinements of design not to be found in the sketch.

For example, in the " Sketch for the Leaping Horse," the bent willow is to the right of the horse and its rider, as it doubtless was in the scene that Constable actually beheld ; but in the picture of " The Leaping Horse " in the Diploma Gallery of the Royal Academy, the tree is shifted to the other side of the horse and rider, more to our left, in order to improve the design and emphasise the rhythm of the diagonal accents from the big tree on our left to the water-weeds in the opposite lower corner. This transposition of the willow-tree is exceedingly instructive, for it proves that Constable did not, as some have maintained, simply paint " snapshots " of Nature ; he understood the science of picture-making as well as any artist, and while desirous above all of presenting the *general* truth of the scene before him, he did not scruple to alter the position of one particular tree or other object if thereby he thought he could improve the composition of his picture.

Constable was now fifty, but still he was only an A.R.A. Neither " The Leaping Horse " nor " The Cornfield " which he exhibited in 1826, moved his brother artists to make him an Academician, and though " The Corn-field " attracted a good deal of attention and was one of the first pictures to make Constable talked about in London, it did not sell, but remained in his possession to the day of his death. There would seem to be no denying that to the end a number of Academicians were unable to appreciate the genius of Constable, and after the death of Joseph Farington in 1821 he had no keen admirer with influence within their ranks. The story is told that one year, after he had at last been elected R.A. in 1829, Constable submitted one of his works labelled with another name to the Academy jury. When the majority had voted for its rejection, Constable admitted his authorship and quietly remarked, " There, gentlemen, I always thought you did not like my style of painting."

When official recognition came it was " too late," as Constable sadly said. Fortunately he was not in want, for in 1828 his wife's father had died and left Constable the sum of £20,000. " This," wrote Constable, " I will settle on my wife and children, and I shall then be able to stand before a six-foot canvas with a mind at ease, thank God ! " From this exclamation it would certainly appear as if the painter himself took more pleasure in his six-foot sketch than in painting a picture from it for the market.

Any pleasure he might have experienced in his election to the Academy as a full member in 1829 was counteracted by his grief at the loss of his wife, who had just previously died. It was the thought of this faithful companion

"THE CORNFIELD," BY JOHN CONSTABLE

National Gallery, London

Though much admired by the discerning when it was first exhibited at the Academy in 1826, this brilliant example of Constable's genius remained unsold till after the artist's death, when a number of his admirers clubbed together to buy the picture from his executors and presented it to the nation. The church in the distance is Stratford St. Mary, Suffolk.

459

"FLATFORD MILL," BY JOHN CONSTABLE

National Gallery, London

At a time when fashionable opinion held that " a good picture, like a good fiddle, should be brown," Constable dared to paint Nature truly in her own colours and became the pioneer of " natural " landscape painting.

Flatford Mill belonged to the artist's father, and it was while assisting his father as a boy that Constable acquired his knowledge and love of Nature.

and helper that prompted Constable to say his election as R.A. was " too late."

Though it would be a gross exaggeration to say that Constable ever obtained anything like popularity in his own lifetime, his landscapes after 1831 began to be known to a wider public by virtue of the mezzotints of some of his best paintings by David Lucas (1802–81). Lucas was an engraver of genius, who brilliantly translated into black-and-white the beauties of Constable's light and shadow, but when he first approached the artist for permission to engrave his work Constable was dismally despondent about the project. " The painter himself is totally unpopular," he said, " and will be so on this side of the grave. The subjects are nothing but art, and the buyers are wholly ignorant of that." Nevertheless Lucas persisted with his mezzotints, which did much to spread the fame of Constable, and these engravings are now eagerly sought for at high prices by collectors.

Though never becoming actually despondent or embittered, Constable naturally craved for the appreciation which he felt he deserved, and in the endeavour to court notice he even went so far as to advertise in the newspapers :

" Mr. Constable's Gallery of Landscapes, by his own hand, is to be seen *gratis* daily, by an application at his residence."

But few except other artists applied, and as he grew older his house became fuller and fuller of unsold pictures. After his sixtieth birthday, in 1836, his health became uncertain, and on March 30, 1837, he died suddenly in his house at 76 Charlotte Street. Almost immediately after his death the world awoke to his genius, and in the same year a number of gentlemen who admired his work clubbed together and bought from the executors his picture " The Cornfield," which they presented to the nation. Strangely enough this artist, who was so little known during his own lifetime, has since his death become a familiar personality, thanks to the pious solicitude of his friend, the genre-painter C. R. Leslie (1794–1859), whose *Memoirs of John Constable, R.A.* is one of the best biographies of a painter ever written. It is a classic which, for the intimate insight it gives us into the character of the man, may be compared with Boswell's *Johnson*. All who met Constable were attracted by his simple, kindly, affectionate nature, and perhaps the most touching tribute to his memory was paid by a London cab-driver who, when he heard that he would never drive Constable again, told Leslie he was " as sorry as if he had been my own father—he was as nice a man as that, sir."

Leslie had always been a firm believer in the genius of Constable, and wrote of his works : " I cannot but think that they will attain for him, when his merits are fully acknowledged, the praise of having been the most genuine painter of English landscape that has yet lived." Subsequent generations

" SALISBURY CATHEDRAL," BY JOHN CONSTABLE

Victoria and Albert Museum, London

One of Constable's earliest patrons and most constant friends was the Rev. John Fisher, nephew and chaplain to the Bishop of Salisbury. Owing to this friendship the artist painted several pictures of the Cathedral, among which this painting is notable for the brilliance and beauty of its lighting.

have corroborated Leslie's opinion, and another genre-painter, Sir J. D. Linton, who was born three years after Constable's death, has testified to the genius of Constable and to the effect of his painting. "His art," wrote Linton, "has had the widest and most lasting influence both at home and abroad. . . . Although Turner is accepted as the greatest master of landscape painting, and his work has not been without very great influence, Constable's robust and massive manner has affected the modern schools more universally."

While we admire Turner we love Constable the more dearly, perhaps because his art is so essentially English. Never did a landscape painter travel less than Constable in search of a subject. While Turner toured all over Europe, Constable opened his door and found beauty waiting to be painted. With exceptions so few that they do not bulk largely in his work, all Constable's landscapes are drawn either from his birthplace, that is to say the borders of Essex and Suffolk about the Stour, now known as "the Constable country," or at Hampstead, where his house yet stands. The hill with a clump of firs on it, close to the Spaniard's, is to this day spoken of as "Constable's Knoll." His only other sketching ground of real importance was Salisbury, whither he was doubtless drawn by his friendship with the Rev. John Fisher. Of his many paintings of Salisbury Cathedral, one of the most beautiful is the painting in the South Kensington Museum, from which we see that had his bent been that way Constable could have painted architectural subjects as truly and beautifully as he did landscapes.

It was the supreme distinction of Constable to destroy Beaumont's fallacy that a "brown" landscape was a "good" landscape, and to paint all the greenness in Nature. He loved to paint the glitter of light on trees after rain, and the little touches of white paint with which he achieved the effect of their sparkle were jocularly alluded to as "Constable's snow." No painter before him had painted with so much truth the actual colour of Nature's lighting, and since Constable the true colour of Nature in light and shadow has increasingly become the preoccupation of the "natural" landscape painter.

§ 2

Constable was not the first nor was he the last English painter whose art was appreciated in France long before his talent was duly recognised in his own country, and it may be argued that his triumph at Paris in 1824 was to some extent anticipated by the warm welcome which the Parisians had already given to his young compatriot Richard Parkes Bonington. The father of Bonington was an extraordinary man who had originally succeeded his father as governor of the Nottingham county gaol, but he lost this appointment through his irregularities and then set up as a portrait painter,

"COAST OF PICARDY," BY R. P. BONINGTON (1802–28)

Wallace Collection, London

Bonington's brilliant open-air work was one of the pronounced influences upon the French art of his time. Although he was so young, and died after only seven years of painting, his assured genius made itself felt. Light and air are everywhere in these delicate shore scenes which he painted in France.

464

while his wife kept a school which was the real mainstay of the family. His son Richard was born at Arnold, a village near Nottingham, on October 25, 1801, and at an early age showed a talent for drawing which made him another infant prodigy, like Lawrence.

Meanwhile his father's love of low company, intemperate habits, and violent political opinions had broken up his wife's school, and about the time of the fall of Napoleon the family fled to France, first to Calais and then to Paris. Henceforward Richard Parkes Bonington, though still a boy, was the chief breadwinner for the family. In 1816 he obtained permission to copy pictures at the Louvre, where he was said to be the youngest student on record, and he also worked in the studio of Baron Gros, where his improvement was so rapid that his master soon told him he had nothing more to learn in that studio, and advised him to go out into the world and paint from Nature on his own account. This advice Bonington took, travelling extensively in France and also visiting Italy in 1822. His oil-paintings and water-colours, which were exceedingly rich in colour and full of vitality, were quickly appreciated and the reputation of Bonington rapidly increased in Paris. In 1824, when Constable received his gold medal, another gold medal was also awarded to Bonington for the two coast scenes which he had sent to the Salon.

Though he had visited England now and again, Bonington was quite unknown here till 1826, when he exhibited at the British Institution two views on the French coast which surprised the English painters and at once gave him a name among his own countrymen. In the following year he exhibited another marine subject at the Academy, and in 1828—though still residing in Paris—he sent to the Academy a view on the Grand Canal, Venice, and a small historical painting of " Henri III of France." Though but twenty-six years of age, Bonington for some time had been greatly esteemed in France, and now commissions flowed upon him from England also. Anxious to fulfil them, the artist worked feverishly during the hot summer, and after a long day sketching under a scorching sun in Paris he was attacked by brain fever, followed by a severe illness. When his health had slightly improved he came over to London for medical advice, but it was too late. He had fallen into galloping consumption, and the brilliant promise of his career was cut short by his death on September 23, 1828. He was buried in the vaults of St. James's Church, Pentonville.

The early deaths of Girtin and Bonington were the two greatest blows British art had received, and had they lived it seems probable that Bonington might have gone even further than Girtin. His range for his years was remarkably wide, and he was as skilful in painting figures as he was in land-scapes and marine subjects. His art was picturesque, romantic, and often dramatic, while he had an opulent sense of colour and was able to imbue his figure paintings with a wonderful sense of life. In the Louvre, Paris, where the artist studied as a boy, the examples of Bonington's art are more numerous and important than those at the National Gallery, London, which possesses two only, a Normandy landscape, bequeathed by Mr. George Salting, and "The Column of St. Mark, Venice." Happily Bonington's work is well represented in the Wallace Collection, where there are ten of his paintings and twenty-four water-colours, among the former being the picture of "Henri IV and the Spanish Ambassador," which so long ago as 1870 fetched the considerable price of £3,320 in a sale at Paris.

§ 3

Another great landscape painter who during his lifetime never took the place in the world that his genius warranted was John Crome, frequently called "Old Crome," to distinguish him from his son, who also became a painter. Crome, who was born at Norwich on December 21, 1768, was the son of a poor weaver and began life as an errand-boy, carrying bottles of medicine for a doctor, but when he was about fourteen or fifteen his love of art led him to apprentice himself to a house and sign painter. While following his trade during his apprenticeship, Crome took every opportunity of sketching the picturesque scenery which surrounds his native city. He was very, very poor, but he persevered and his perseverance gained him friends.

Chief among these friends was Mr. Thomas Harvey, of Catton in Norfolk, who possessed a fine picture gallery and encouraged Crome to study and make copies of the pictures he had collected. Mr. Harvey's collection included landscapes by Richard Wilson—by whom Crome was greatly influenced—Gainsborough's "Cottage Door," and many fine examples of the Dutch painters of the seventeenth century, notably Hobbema, for whose art Crome then conceived a passionate admiration which lasted all his life. Mr. Harvey not only introduced Crome to other Norwich amateurs, but also obtained him some pupils to whom he taught drawing, though at this time the artist was only an awkward, uninformed country lad, whose deficiences of education were to some extent compensated for by his great gifts and his natural shrewdness.

Meanwhile Crome had formed an intimate friendship with a lad of his own class, Robert Ladbrooke (1770–1842), then a printer's apprentice, but also ambitious to become an artist. After living together for some two years, Crome and Ladbrooke married sisters, and abandoning their original trades they established themselves in partnership as artists, Ladbrooke painting portraits at five shillings apiece, and Crome selling his landscapes for what they would fetch—which was not always as much as five shillings ! But for Crome's practice as a drawing-master he could hardly have kept

"THE COLUMN OF ST. MARK'S, VENICE," BY R. P. BONINGTON

National Gallery, London

Though he died when he was only twenty-six, this artist greatly influenced his contemporaries by his rich colour and romantic feeling. Had he lived he would undoubtedly have been one of the greatest artists of his time.

The view shown is of the Piazzetta at Venice, with the column supporting the winged lion of St. Mark and the companion column, on the right, which is crowned by a statue of St. Theodore, the first patron saint of Venice.

467

himself, let alone a family, in these early years, but gradually he acquired a local reputation and his landscapes found occasional purchasers, though at pitifully low prices.

In February, 1803, Crome gathered round him the artists of his native city for their mutual improvement, and from this beginning arose the Norwich Society of Artists, founded in 1805. The Society held annual exhibitions to which Crome was a large contributor, for he rarely sent his pictures to London for exhibition and consequently was little known there. Crome's pupils and associates, among whom the most distinguished were John Sell Cotman, James Stark (1794–1859), George Vincent, and his eldest son, John Bernay Crome, formed what is known as the " Norwich School." The inspiration of this school was derived chiefly from Crome, but also from the Dutch painters by whom he was influenced.

The Norwich School prospered exceedingly, more so than any other body of provincial artists has ever done in England, and their success was due not only to the excellence of their own work but also to the fact that they laboured in a field well prepared to receive art. It will have been observed how many of the great English landscape painters belonged to the Eastern Counties—Gainsborough and Constable were both Suffolk men— and the extent to which the art of all of them was influenced by the art of Holland. The explanation is to be found in the intimate trade relations which had existed for centuries between East Anglia and the Netherlands. Owing to this commercial intercourse numbers of Dutch and Flemish pictures found their way into East Anglian homes, and while London during the eighteeenth century worshipped Italian art almost to the exclusion of all other, well-to-do people in Norfolk and Suffolk took a keener delight in the homelier art of the Dutch and Flemish Schools. Thus at the very time that Constable was being neglected in London, John Crome was enjoying esteem and wide popularity in Norfolk.

It is true that Crome never made a fortune ; to the end his lessons brought him in more money than his paintings, for any of which fifty pounds was a large and rarely attained price ; but Crome did sell his pictures and in time became quite comfortably off. In 1801 he moved into a big house in Gildengate Street, he kept two horses, and managed before his death to acquire many good pictures and to form a library. Norwich was proud of her distinguished painter, and a special seat was always reserved for him in the parlour of the old inn in the market-place, where in his later years he was treated as an oracle, revered by all.

Under these circumstances we can understand why Crome continued to reside in his native Norwich and was never tempted to settle in London. In 1806 he exhibited for the first time at the Royal Academy, but between then and 1818 he sent only thirteen pictures in all to be exhibited there. He

"A WINDMILL ON MOUSEHOLD HEATH," BY JOHN CROME (1768–1821)

National Gallery, London

Founder of the Norwich School, Crome devoted his life to painting the beauties of the country round his birthplace, and never attempted to establish himself in London. His feeling for light, air, and space are splendidly revealed in this noble landscape.

visited London occasionally, twice he went to Cumberland (in 1802 and 1806), once to Weymouth, and in 1814 he made a tour in France and Belgium, but his chief subjects were almost exclusively local. He was perfectly satisfied with the lanes, heaths, and river-banks surrounding Norwich, without wishing to journey further afield. In his great tree picture, " The Poringland Oak," he rivalled his own idol Hobbema ; in " Moon Rise on the Yare," he surpassed the moonlight paintings of Van der Neer, by whom it was inspired ; while his masterpiece, " Mousehold Heath," at the National Gallery, will always rank Crome amongst the grandest of landscape painters. Asked by his son why he had painted this last subject, Crome made the memorable reply : " For air and space."

In addition to his oil-paintings Crome executed a few water-colours and also a number of etchings. In 1834 a series of thirty-one of his etchings was published under the title of " Norfolk Picturesque Scenery."

While out sketching in his fifty-third year he caught a chill, and after a few days' illness died on April 22, 1821. On the day before he died he addressed to his son the words so often quoted : " John, my boy, paint, but paint only for fame ; and if your subject is only a pigsty, dignify it." The art of Old Crome is indeed a perpetual reminder that a masterpiece of painting is due far more to the treatment than to the subject, and nobody knew better than the Norwich master how to give dignity to the humblest subject by its stately presentation in a well-balanced composition.

Though his landscape art is limited in comparison with that of Turner and Constable, within his own self-imposed limits Crome is second to none. He did not set out, like Turner, to mirror the blazing glories of dawn and sunset, nor did he, like Constable, hold himself ready to paint Nature and weather in every aspect : Crome waited for the quieter moods of Nature in his own homeland, and he painted these to perfection.

§ 4

The Norwich School owes its fame to two stars of the first magnitude, Crome and Cotman, and to a host of lesser luminaries. John Sell Cotman was fourteen years younger than Crome, and though also born at Norwich, on June 11, 1782, he did not, like Crome, acquire his art education in his native city. Cotman from the first was in a very different position. He was the son of a well-to-do draper, received a good education at the Norwich Grammar School, and was intended to enter his father's shop ; but when his bent for art clearly declared itself his father was sensible enough to allow his son to make it his vocation and sent him to London.

Cotman remained in London from 1800 to 1806, and probably the most fruitful part of the education he received there was his association with the

"WHERRIES ON THE YARE," BY JOHN SELL COTMAN (1782–1842)

National Gallery, London

So little was the genius of Cotman appreciated in his own day that this beautiful painting was sold
at Norwich in 1834 for eighteen shillings !

471

group of artists who frequented the house of Dr. Thomas Monro, who has already been mentioned in this OUTLINE as the friend of Turner and Girtin. In Dr. Monro's house at 8 Adelphi Terrace, Cotman made the acquaintance of and worked with all the most brilliant young artists of the day, and in addition to the studies he made there under these stimulating circumstances he joined a sketching club which Girtin had founded.

To Girtin, who was not only an inspiring genius but also a most generous and affectionate friend, Cotman probably owed most at this stage of his career, and it must have been a great shock to him when Girtin died at the early age of twenty-seven. After Girtin's death in November, 1802, London was not the same place to Cotman, and though as a young struggling artist he could hardly complain of want of success—for he had exhibited no fewer than thirty paintings at the Royal Academy between 1800 and 1806—he made up his mind to return to his native city.

In London Cotman had applied himself especially to architectural subjects, and it is possible that even in these early days he was influenced in this direction by the gifted West Country artist, Samuel Prout (1783–1852), who excelled in water-colours of these subjects, and was living in London from 1802 to 1804 ; but when he returned to Norwich in 1806 or 1807, Cotman at first set himself up as a portrait painter. Gradually, however, under the influence of Crome—who was thirty-nine when Cotman was twenty-five—he devoted himself more and more to landscape. He became a member of the Norwich Society of Artists and was for a time its secretary.

Cotman was a prolific worker at this time, and to the Society's exhibition in 1808 he contributed no fewer than sixty-seven works. In 1809 he married, and soon afterwards removed to Yarmouth, where he added to his means by teaching drawing as well as painting in oils and water-colours, and also etching. In 1811 he commenced a publication by subscription of his " Architectural Etchings," and having made a number of topographical tours throughout the country, he published in 1816 his " Specimens of Norman and Gothic Architecture, Norfolk Churches," etc. He formed a useful association with Dawson Turner, the Norfolk antiquary, for whose antiquarian publications Cotman drew and etched the illustrations, and during the next three years (1817–19) he made annual expeditions into Normandy with this writer, whose *Architectural Antiquities of Normandy*, illustrated by Cotman, was published in 1822. All the time that he was engaged on drawings for these and other publications Cotman was exhibiting oil-paintings and water-colours both in Norwich and in London, but though several of these found purchasers the prices were so low that, notwithstanding his immense industry, Cotman could not have supported his wife and family if, in addition to all his other activities, he had not continued to give drawing lessons.

"GRETA BRIDGE, BY JOHN SELL COTMAN
British Museum, London

The artist's masterpiece in water-colour, majestic in design, splendidly strong and massive in its drawing, and rich and harmonious in colour.

In 1825, when he was again living in Norwich, Cotman was elected an Associate of the Water-colour Society in London, and from that year was a constant contributor to the Society's exhibitions ; but though his work was known and respected both in London and Norwich, the genius of Cotman was never recognised in his lifetime nor indeed for many years after his death. The struggle to make a living began to tell on his nerves and health, and it was in the hope of giving him some ease by assuring him a regular income that his steadfast friend Dawson Turner, the antiquary, succeeded in getting Cotman appointed in 1834 as drawing-master at King's College School, then in the Strand. Removing to London in view of this appointment, Cotman settled himself at 42 Hunter Street, Brunswick Square, but the change seemed to do him more harm than good. His health gradually declined, and the nervous depression to which he was a victim became more and more severe till in the end his mind became slightly unhinged. His eldest son, Miles Edward Cotman (1811–58), a water-colourist of moderate ability, succeeded him as drawing-master at King's College School, and on July 28, 1842, John Sell Cotman died and was quietly buried in the churchyard of St. John's Wood Chapel. How little Cotman was appreciated then was made painfully evident when·his remaining oil-paintings and water-colours were sold at Christie's in the following year. Works for which collectors would now gladly pay hundreds of pounds hardly realised as many shillings in 1843, and the highest price then obtained for a painting by him was £8 15s. ; the highest price given for a Cotman water-colour was £6.

To discover exactly why an artist, afterwards recognised to be a genius, is not appreciated in his own lifetime, is never an easy task, but it is certain that many of his contemporaries considered Cotman's work to be " unfinished " because it had that vigorous breadth which now wins our admiration. Whether we look at an oil-painting like his " Wherries on the Yare," or a masterly water-colour like the " Greta Bridge " at the British Museum, we cannot fail to be impressed by the grandeur which the artist has given to his rendering of the scene by his subordination of detail and suppression of all that is irrelevant.

Cotman took a big view of Nature, and the breadth and simplicity of his masses materially help to give his pictures, whether in oil or water-colour, a monumental majesty unsurpassed even by his great contemporaries.

XXVI

THE PRE-RAPHAELITES

THE ART OF FORD MADOX BROWN, ROSSETTI, HOLMAN HUNT, MILLAIS,
AND BURNE-JONES

§ I

AMONG the pupils of John Sell Cotman when he was a drawing-master at King's College School was a strange, foreign-looking boy, the son of an Italian poet and patriot living in exile in London. This boy was Dante Gabriel Rossetti, who afterwards combined with Millais and Holman Hunt to found the Pre-Raphaelite Brotherhood. Innumerable books have been written in which it has been sought to show that first one and then another of these three young men was the real motive-power in the founding of a new style of painting ; but the fact remains that it was not till all three came together in 1848 that any revolution was effected, and it was the peculiar and diverse gifts which each brought to the common stock which made their union so formidable and enabled them eventually to triumph over opposition and hostile criticism.

Rossetti, according to Ruskin, was " the chief intellectual force " in the association ; his fire, enthusiasm, and poetic feeling were valuable assets, but technically he was the least accomplished of the three. He had ideas, but at first he was weak in translating them into drawing and painting, and he shirked the drudgery of the discipline necessary to perfect his powers of expression. Millais, on the other hand, was not remarkable for original ideas, but he had brilliant powers of eye and hand ; he was a precocious genius in technique to whom the problems of drawing and painting presented no difficulty. Holman Hunt had neither the facility of Millais nor the impatience of Rossetti, but he had a high seriousness of purpose and a deter-mined perseverance which held the others steadily together and chained their endeavours to lofty ideals.

Before considering what " Pre-Raphaelitism " was, and what it ulti-mately became, it will be helpful to glance briefly at the origin of its three founders. William Holman Hunt, the eldest of the trio, was born in Wood Street, Cheapside, on April 2, 1827. His father, the manager of a city ware-house, opposed his wish to be an artist and placed him at the age of twelve in the office of an estate agent. His employer encouraged young Hunt's artistic leanings, and the father reluctantly allowed the boy to spend his salary on lessons from a portrait painter. In 1843 Hunt was at last allowed to devote himself to art, but entirely at his own risk, and the sixteen-year-old boy bravely struggled along, studying half the week at the British Museum and supporting himself by painting portraits on the other three days. Eventually he was admitted as a probationer to the Academy Schools, where he soon made friends with his junior, Millais, and while studying still managed to earn a bare living.

The youngest of the three was John Everett Millais, who was born at Southampton in 1829. He came from a Norman family settled in Jersey, and his early childhood was spent in that island, at Le Quaihouse, near St. Heliers. His father was a popular, gifted man with some artistic talent, who delighted in and encouraged the precocious ability his son soon showed in drawing. In 1837 his parents came to live in Gower Street, London, and on the advice of the Irish artist Sir Martin Archer Shee (1769-1850), who was then President of the Royal Academy, young Millais was sent to Henry Sass's art school in Bloomsbury. Here his progress was so phenomenal that when he was only nine years old he won the silver medal of the Society of Arts. Two years later he was admitted to the Royal Academy Schools as the youngest student who ever worked there, and " The Child," as he was then called, was already considered to be a marvel of precocity whose achievements rivalled those of the youthful Lawrence.

When he was twelve years old he painted his first picture in oils, and in 1845, when he was sixteen, he was able to earn £100 a year by painting in backgrounds for a dealer and selling him some of his sketches. In the following year he exhibited " Pizarro seizing the Inca of Peru," a large painting of remarkable maturity, now in the Victoria and Albert Museum, South Kensington ; and in the next year, 1847, he was awarded a gold medal for his " Young Men of the Tribe of Benjamin seizing their Brides." In neither of these pictures do we perceive any tendency of the artist to revolutionise the style of painting then in vogue ; both of them are more or less in the manner of William Etty (1787-1849), whose art, like that of Sir Joshua Reynolds, was chiefly based on the Venetian masters and whose colour was rich, but heavy and dark. At the Academy Schools Millais had already made the acquaintance of Holman Hunt, but though the two young students may have been discontented with the pictorial ideals of the time, and may have discussed aims and methods in private, they did not show any signs of a new faith in their works till after they had made the acquaintance of Rossetti.

After leaving King's College School, Rossetti studied art at Cary's Academy in Bloomsbury, and though he was not able to gain admittance

"OPHELIA," BY MILLAIS (1829–96)

Tate Gallery, London

Painted on the Ewell, near Kingston, this picture is famous for the precise study of Nature shown in the foreground and background. The figure was painted in his studio from Miss Siddal, who had to lie in a bath of water ; one day Millais forgot to fill the lamps which kept the water warm, with the result that this beautiful and gifted woman, afterwards Mrs. Rossetti, contracted a serious illness which eventually shortened her life.

W. F. Mansell.

"THE LAST OF ENGLAND," BY FORD MADOX BROWN (1821–1893)
Birmingham Art Gallery

Though an older artist, Madox Brown was influenced by the "Brotherhood," and the picture—
which shows emigrants taking their last look at the "old country"—is "Pre-Raphaelite" in its exact
rendering of details and in its serious thoughtfulness of expression.

into the life-class, he worked in the Antique School of the Royal Academy in 1845 and 1846. Born in London in 1828, Dante Gabriel Rossetti was a year younger than Holman Hunt, and a year older than Millais, but though so near their own age, he was from an art-master's point of view far below them, so that he was kept drawing from casts of antique statues when they were already drawing and painting from living models. This was dull work for Rossetti, who was passionately interested in life, and he looked around to see where he might obtain more congenial tuition. He had been greatly attracted by a picture he had seen in an exhibition, " Our Lady of Saturday Night," and he went to the painter, Ford Madox Brown, and besought him to accept him as a pupil. After some demur Brown consented, but when Rossetti, though allowed brushes and colours, found that his new master's method of tuition consisted in setting him to paint studies of still life, his impatience at discipline soon overcame him, and declaring that he was tired of painting " pots and pans," when his head was full of exciting pictures of romantic women and knightly men, he broke away from Brown after an apprenticeship that only lasted some four months.

Ford Madox Brown (1821–93) was never a member of the Pre-Raphaelite Brotherhood, but he was so much in sympathy with their aims and his art was so nearly related to their own, that some brief account of him must be included in any review of this phase of English painting. Madox Brown was six years the senior of Holman Hunt. He was born in Calais at a time when David and the Classicists had imposed a new artistic ideal on France, and when he began to paint about 1835 this classical ideal was being attacked by a new romantic movement to which Madox Brown was attracted. He was from his childhood, therefore, conversant with Continental art movements—as the majority of English painters were not—and after studying at Bruges, Ghent, and Antwerp, where he was the pupil of the Belgian historical and romantic painter, Baron Wappers, he worked for three years in Paris. His desire then was to become a painter of large historical pictures, and in 1844 he came to England in order to enter a competition for the commission to paint decorations for Westminster Hall. In this he was unsuccessful, and in the following year he went to Rome, where he became acquainted with two curious German painters named Cornelius and Overbeck. These artists were leading semi-monastic lives, and in so far as they deliberately cultivated the devotional frame of mind of the Italian masters who preceded Raphael, they were the first " Pre-Raphaelites." Cornelius and Overbeck, who were both devout Catholics, worked in cells, and like the mediæval monastic painters, they prepared themselves for their work by scourging, vigil, and fasting. In order that their work might be free from all taint of " fleshliness," they avoided the use of human models. It is not likely that their dry and rather affected painting influenced Madox Brown to any great extent, but they doubtlessly opened his eyes to the excellencies of the earlier Italian painters, and showed him that there was more than one way of looking at Nature.

It cannot be too strongly emphasised that for the connoisseurs of the eighteenth and early nineteenth centuries, the " Old Masters " began where in the opinion of to-day they end. We look upon Raphael, Michael Angelo, and Leonardo da Vinci as the *end* of a great school of painters ; but our fore-fathers were inclined to regard them as the *beginning* of a great school. Their successors, men like Annibale Carracci (1560–1609), Domenichino (1581–1641), and Carlo Maratti (1625–1713), were at one time esteemed as Masters, though to-day we recognise that their art was decadent and debased. Cornelius and Overbeck were perfectly right in preferring the painters before Raphael to those who followed him, but they made the deadly error of merely imitating the pictures of the Italian Primitives, instead of going, as they had done, direct to Nature. Thus the German painters made exactly the same mistake as the late Italian painters had done, and their art was sterile also for the same reason, because it was " soup of the soup " art based wholly on preceding art.

The effect of the early Christian painters on Ford Madox Brown was to cause him, not to imitate their work slavishly, but to look at Nature for himself, as they did. When he did look he perceived that Nature was far brighter than it appeared to be in the pictures of his British contemporaries. Since the time of Reynolds, Sir George Beaumont's dictum that a good picture must be a brown picture had been the general opinion, and though certain landscape painters rebelled against this doctrine as we have seen, no English figure painters made any serious stand against it till Ford Madox Brown and the Pre-Raphaelites began to exhibit.

How had this cult in brown pictures arisen ? The explanation is very simple. Painters had observed that the pictures by the recognised great masters, Rembrandt, Titian, Tintoretto, etc., were usually brown in tone, but this brownness was often due, not only to the pigments originally used by the masters, but also to the grime of centuries, to the " tone of time." Seeking to be praised as " Old Masters " in their own lifetime, painters used artificial means to make their pictures look brown, and were in the habit of painting on a brown bituminous ground in order to give to their pictures a fictitious quality of golden-brown light and " Rembrandtesque " shadow. Ford Madox Brown reversed the general practice of his day by painting his pictures on a white ground, and immediately his colour became brighter and truer to Nature.

By the time he was back in England in 1846, Madox Brown had come independently to very much the same conclusions that Hunt and Millais were now whispering to one another, and he had begun to adopt a method of

W. F. Mansell.

"THE ORDER OF RELEASE, 1746," BY MILLAIS

Tate Gallery, London

This brilliant and pathetic painting of a Highlander, wounded in the '45 Rebellion and unexpectedly delivered from prison, his wife having brought an order for his release, won for the artist his A.R.A. in 1853.

The woman is a portrait of Mrs. John Ruskin, who afterwards became Lady Millais.

"GIRLHOOD OF MARY VIRGIN," BY DANTE GABRIEL ROSSETTI (1828–82)

Lady Jekyll's Collection

The first picture ever painted by Rossetti, who under the guidance of Holman Hunt here shows an exactitude in the painting of details which he never surpassed later. The artist's mother sat for St. Anne and his sister Christina for the Virgin.

painting very similar to that subsequently practised by the Brotherhood, to whom we must now return.

§ 2

Unknown to one another, Rossetti and Holman Hunt both had a passion for the poetry of Keats, and it was this that first really brought them together. It was in 1848 that Rossetti persuaded Madox Brown to have him as a pupil, and to the Academy of that year Hunt had sent a painting, inspired by a poem of Keats. In the memoirs which he wrote in his old age, Hunt gave an account of how he met the younger artist in a picture gallery and what ensued :

Rossetti came up to me [he wrote] loudly declaring that my picture of " The Eve of St. Agnes " was the best in the collection. . . . Rossetti frankly proposed to me to come and see him. Before this I had been only on nodding terms with him in the schools, to which he came but rarely and irregularly. He had always attracted there a following of clamorous students who, like Millais's throng, were rewarded with original sketches. Rossetti's subjects were of a different class from Millais, not of newly culled facts, but of knights rescuing ladies. A few days more and Rossetti was in my studio.

The upshot of these meetings was that Rossetti left Madox Brown and shared a studio with Holman Hunt, under whose guidance he began painting his first picture, " The Girlhood of Mary Virgin." Intimacy with Hunt naturally led to intimacy with his friend Millais, and it is said that the immediate occasion of the founding of the Brotherhood was an evening spent by the three friends in the house of Millais's parents looking at engravings of the early Italian wall-paintings in the Campo Santo at Pisa. According to Hunt, it was Rossetti who insisted that their union should be a close one, and that it should be styled a " Brotherhood." The term " Pre-Raphaelite " originated as a nickname, somebody exclaiming when they had expressed a preference for the painters before Raphael to those who succeeded him, " Why, then you must be pre-Raphaelites." The title was adopted as an official label which fitly conveyed their aims. These aims were to paint Nature with minute fidelity and to regain the intense sincerity of the early Italian painters, but undoubtedly Rossetti held that the latter also implied intense poetic expression.

Thus the Pre-Raphaelite Brotherhood was established, and in addition to the three founders, membership was extended to Dante Gabriel's brother, W. M. Rossetti, and to three of their friends, Woolner, a sculptor, James Collinson, and F. G. Stephens. James Collinson was probably elected on the strength of his picture, " The Charity Boy's Debut," in the Academy of 1847, and would doubtless have been a more important figure had he not ceased exhibiting after 1870 and retired to a monastery. His most important

picture, " St. Elizabeth of Hungary," painted in 1851, is now in the Johannesburg Gallery, William Rossetti and Stephens soon abandoned painting ;
both became art critics, and their eloquent and enthusiastic articles did much
to convert the public to an appreciation of the work of the other Brothers.

It is no unusual thing for art students or young artists to form themselves
into clubs and societies, to hold regular meetings, and to discuss their aims,
methods, and ideals ; but so often the talk leads to nothing. In the case of
Millais and Hunt it led to a revolution of their painting ; in the case of
Rossetti it led to something approaching a masterpiece at the first effort.
In 1848 Millais had exhibited " Cymon and Iphigenia," another painting
in the style of Etty ; in 1849 he exhibited " Lorenzo and Isabella," now at
Liverpool, and but for the conclaves of the brethren and the stimulating
encouragement of comradeship he could never in one year have leapt the
gulf which separates the two pictures. Holman Hunt's " Rienzi " was an
equally sensational advance on his " St. Agnes's Eve," but in many respects
the most remarkable achievement of all was Rossetti's " Girlhood of Mary
Virgin." Finely painted as " Lorenzo and Isabella " is, it has not the touching
simplicity of Rossetti's first painting ; it is more imitative, a skilful exercise
in the manner of the early Italian masters. It was immensely clever, but it
was not quite what the Pre-Raphaelite Brotherhood set out to do.

Rossetti's maiden effort may appear childish in places when compared
with the accomplishment of the Millais, but it is a much better example of
true Pre-Raphaelitism in its absolutely honest and unconventional attempt
to render what the painter saw. Hunt has told us that every detail in
this picture was painted directly from life under his supervision, and it says
much for his patient influence that in the first year of the Brotherhood its
most romantic member should have painted the most naturalistic picture.

The trouble with Rossetti, owing to his teeming, poetic imagination, had
been that he had always wanted to paint things " out of his head " at a time
when his hand and eye needed to be educated by an endeavour to paint truly
what was before him. With infinite tact Holman Hunt let him set to work
on a romantic subject, the choice of his heart, but he took care that every
detail in this imaginative scene should be painted truly and carefully from
facts. In Madox Brown's studio Rossetti had rebelled at painting so prosaic
an object as a pot ; Holman Hunt led him to paint the same object with
delight because it held the symbolical lily needed by his subject. For the first
time in his life Rossetti became passionately interested in *things*, because he
had been made to see that they helped him to express his ideas. He borrowed
big books from his father, and window curtains from his parents' house in
Charlotte Street. His sister Christina sat for the Virgin, and his mother for
St. Anne. He borrowed a child's nightgown and painted that on a small
lay-figure, which probably explains why the figure of the little angel is not

"THE BELOVED," BY DANTE GABRIEL ROSSETTI

Tate Gallery, London

"My beloved is mine and I am his." This poetical conception of the Bride in the Song of Solomon
was commissioned by Mr. George Rae in 1863 and painted by Rossetti in 1865.

so convincing as the head ; but when we remember that Rossetti was painting every object in the picture for the very first time we are compelled to stop fault-finding to marvel at the wonder of his achievement.

"Rienzi" and "Lorenzo and Isabella" were exhibited in the Academy of 1849 ; "The Girlhood of Mary Virgin" in the Hyde Park Gallery known as the "Free Exhibition" ; but somewhat to the disappointment of their authors they attracted very little public attention. Even the "P.R.B." after Rossetti's signature on his picture appears to have escaped comment. Undismayed, if a trifle disappointed, the young revolutionaries set about more vigorous propaganda by means of new pictures, and a periodical, *The Germ*, in which they could ventilate their opinions and doctrines.

It was with the idea of writing a journal for this magazine that during the summer Hunt and Rossetti made a tour in France and Belgium, and this journal was duly written, though later it was considered too personal to be published in *The Germ*. In their judgments of the pictures they saw abroad the young artists were terribly severe. Van Eyck and the early Flemings they admired intensely, but the works of the later painters from Rembrandt to Rubens were dismissed in two words as "filthy slosh."

After what they had seen abroad they held more firmly than ever before that it was not enough for a picture to be correctly drawn and well painted, it must also enshrine a worthy idea. In accordance with this doctrine, now added to the rules of the Brotherhood, Hunt, Millais, and Rossetti all chose serious subjects for the pictures they intended to exhibit in 1850. Hunt painted "An Early Christian Missionary escaping from Druids," Millais his famous "Christ in the House of His Parents," and Rossetti "The Annunciation," or "Ecce Ancilla Domini" as it was originally called. Curiously enough Rossetti, who in the previous year had been the most, was now the least Pre-Raphaelite of the three. His strangely beautiful work is not a vision of things seen, but a reverie, the romantic rendering of a mood. Again his sister Christina sat for the Virgin, and Thomas Woolner posed for the head of the Archangel.

Millais, on the other hand, had now thoroughly grasped the principle of Pre-Raphaelitism, and no longer giving a clever imitation of an Italian Primitive, he outdid Hunt himself in the thoroughness with which each detail in his picture was studied from Nature. In order to get absolute truth, Millais took his canvas to a carpenter's shop to paint the details ; he painted the figure of Joseph from the carpenter because that was, he said, "the only way to get the development of the muscles right." He was not able to get sheep, but he purchased two sheep's heads from a butcher and painted the flock from them ; and it will be observed that the sheep in the picture only show their heads, the bodies being tactfully concealed by wickerwork.

By the time the Academy of 1850 opened, the existence and doctrines of

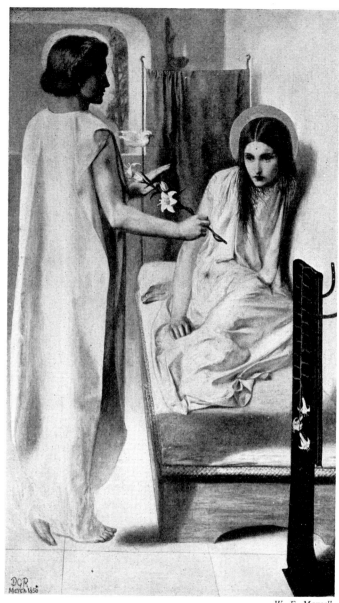

"THE ANNUNCIATION," BY DANTE GABRIEL ROSSETTI

Tate Gallery, London

In this, his second attempt to paint a picture, the poetic nature of the artist finds exquisite expression in his haunting conception of wistful, meditative maidenhood. His sister, Christina Rossetti, the poetess, posed for the figure of the Virgin.

487

the Brotherhood had become more widely known, and this year there was no opportunity to complain of any want of public attention. The three pictures aroused a storm of criticism which fell with particular fury on the head of Millais. The true meaning of " Pre-Raphaelite " was not very well understood, and the popular view was that a group of young painters had set themselves up to be " better than Raphael " and deserved to be trounced for their vanity and impudence. And trounced they were. " Their ambition," wrote one newspaper critic, " is an unhealthy thirst which seeks notoriety by means of mere conceit. Abruptness, singularity, uncouthness, are the counters by which they play the game."

The title " The Carpenter's Shop," by which Millais's picture is now generally known, was contemptuously applied to it by enemies of the Pre-Raphaelite movement. The artist originally exhibited it at the Academy with no other title than an extract from Zachariah (xiii. 6) :

And one shall say unto Him, What are these wounds in Thine hands ? Then He shall answer, Those with which I was wounded in the house of My friends.

The very humanity which endears the picture to us to-day and makes it irresistibly winning was at that time a cause of offence. Millais was accused of dragging down the Saviour to " the lowest of human levels, to the level of craving human pity and assistance." The picture was described as " a pictorial blasphemy " from which right-minded people would " recoil with disgust and loathing." Even Charles Dickens took part in the general attack, and denounced the picture in *Household Words* as follows :

In the foreground of the carpenter's shop is a hideous, wry-necked, blubbering red-haired boy in a nightgown, who appears to have received a poke in the hand from the stick of another boy with whom he had been playing in an adjacent gutter, and to be holding it up for the contemplation of a kneeling woman so horrible in her ugliness that (supposing it were possible for a human creature to exist for a moment with that dislocated throat) she would stand out from the rest of the company as a monster in the vilest cabaret in France, or the lowest gin-shop in England.

Since the famous novelist's abuse was directed far more at the persons than the painting, it is interesting to recall that the " blubbering boy " was little Noel Humphreys, the son of an architect, while the " monster horrible in ugliness " was Mrs. Henry Hodgkinson. Not one of the people in the picture was painted from a professional model, and though the body of St. Joseph is that of the carpenter the head is a portrait of the father of Millais.

This shower of vituperation affected the fortunes of the brethren, and Woolner, who had unsuccessfully competed for a commission to execute a Wordsworth Memorial, abandoned sculpture for a time and set sail for the gold-diggings in Australia. There eventually he returned to sculpture, and

W. F. Mansell.

"CHRIST IN THE HOUSE OF HIS PARENTS," BY MILLAIS

Tate Gallery, London

Dreadfully abused as "mean, odious, revolting, and repulsive" when it was first shown at the Academy in 1850—Charles Dickens joining in the attack—this picture is now generally considered to be the painter's noblest masterpiece. John Ruskin was the first great writer to praise it, and his eulogy turned the tide of public opinion.

in later years he had a modest success in Australia and England with his portrait busts. Holman Hunt, who could not lean on his parents, as Millais and Rossetti could, had a desperate struggle with poverty, and was compelled to take on the job of washing and restoring the wall paintings by Rigaud (1659–1743) at Trinity House. Stephens was employed with Hunt on this work, and William Rossetti got a place in the Inland Revenue Office. Millais, though the most abused, was the best off of the band, for a dealer named Farrer had the courage to pay him £150 for his picture and showed his faith in the artist by pasting all the adverse criticisms on the back of the canvas. Late in the year a purchaser was found also for the picture by Hunt, who then abandoned his restoration, and set to work on his splendid picture " Two Gentlemen of Verona," now in the Birmingham Art Gallery. Millais at the same time began painting his " Woodman's Daughter," and in these pictures the artists obtained a greater brilliancy of colour than they had yet secured by painting upon a *wet* white ground. They prided themselves on having rediscovered one of the secrets of the early Italian masters, and later on Hunt communicated the " secret " to Madox Brown, whose pictures certainly gained much in luminosity and brightness of colour immediately after 1851.

Rossetti had begun an oil-painting of a subject from one of Browning's poems, but he did not get it finished, so that Millais and Hunt alone had to sustain the renewed attack which was made when their pictures were exhibited in the Academy of 1851. In addition to " The Woodman's Daughter," Millais exhibited " Mariana of the Moated Grange " and " The Return of the Dove to the Ark," and again he and Hunt were told that their paintings were " offensive and absurd productions," displaying nothing but " puerility " " uppishness," and " morbid infatuation." This year, however, they were not without defenders. William Rossetti had begun his career as an art critic and upheld Pre-Raphaelite aims and ideals in the columns of the *Spectator*. Still more important were two letters of chivalrous and wholehearted appreciation which appeared in *The Times*, signed by " An Oxford Graduate," and everybody knew that the writer was the great John Ruskin. In the same year appeared a new volume of *Modern Painters*, in which Ruskin wrote of Millais and Holman Hunt :

Their works are, in finish of drawing and splendour of colour, the best work in the Royal Academy, and I have great hope that they may become the foundation of a more earnest and able school of art than we have seen for centuries.

It is difficult to exaggerate the revulsion of feeling produced by Ruskin's pronouncements, for at that time he was almost a dictator of taste in England. Slowly the tide began to turn in favour of the brethren, but it was very nearly too late for Hunt. His picture returned to him unsold from the

W. F. Mansell.

"THE TRIUMPH OF THE INNOCENTS," BY W. HOLMAN HUNT (1827–1910)

Walker Art Gallery, Liverpool

Rigidly faithful all his life to Pre-Raphaelite principles, Holman Hunt visited Palestine twice in order that he might be able to paint sacred subjects with literal truth to Syrian landscape. With poetic imagination the artist depicts the flight into Egypt as a royal progress in which " only the Child's eyes are open to see the children whose wakening souls are His retinue."

Academy, he was absolutely penniless and had nothing to tide him over until better times ; indeed, he was on the point of abandoning painting and seeking his fortune as a sheep-farmer in Australia when Millais and his parents came to the rescue. Millais had made a little money, and with his parents' consent he gave it to his comrade in order that he might make one more attempt. This generous help bound the two " Brothers " still more closely together, and they spent the late summer and early autumn in the country near Surbiton, searching the backwaters of the Thames to find just the right background for the picture of " Ophelia," which Millais had decided to paint, and studying the meadows for the scene of Hunt's crucial picture " The Hireling Shepherd." But Hunt did not have to wait till this, perhaps his most perfect picture, was finished and exhibited before learning that the tide was turning ; for while he and Millais were painting in the fields a letter was brought them announcing that the Liverpool Academy had awarded a prize of £50 to the painter of " Two Gentlemen of Verona."

" The Hireling Shepherd " embodies the essence of Pre-Raphaelitism and indicates its high-water mark. In the heedless shepherd, who dallies with a coquettish beauty while a wolf is worrying his sheep, a worthy moral lesson is inculcated ; while its bright, jewel-like colour reveals the minute fidelity with which Nature has been painted. When it was shown in the Academy of 1852 the battle was nearly over, for though there was still considerable opposition, the Pre-Raphaelite picture had now become an accepted type of painting, and other Academy exhibitors were beginning to change their practice and paint in a similar style.

The battle was won, but the Brotherhood was beginning to break up ; Woolner was in Australia, Collinson thinking about retiring to a monastery, William Rossetti and Stephens had definitely become writers, and worse still, Dante Gabriel Rossetti was beginning to drift away. From 1850 to 1853 Rossetti produced no large picture. He was steeping himself in Dantesque literature and his mind was more occupied with poetry ; now and again he produced some lovely little water-colours—Ruskin, who had become his principal patron, encouraging him in this direction with his purse as well as his praise. In 1853—the year in which he painted " The Order of Release "—Millais was elected A.R.A., and in the following year Holman Hunt, who had just painted and sold for £400 " The Light of the World," set sail for Palestine in order that he might be able to paint incidents from the life of Christ with literal truth to the nature of the country in which He lived. To the end Holman Hunt remained the most consistent of all to the principles of Pre-Raphaelitism.

For a little while after his departure the influence of Holman Hunt lingered in England. " Autumn Leaves " and " The Blind Girl," both painted in 1855, are true Pre-Raphaelite pictures, and they were the last

W. F. Mansell.

"THE HIRELING SHEPHERD," BY W. HOLMAN HUNT

Manchester Art Gallery

One of the three founders of the Pre-Raphaelite Brotherhood, Holman Hunt was throughout his life the most faithful adherent to that accurate observation of Nature which was its early ideal.

paintings by Millais that Ruskin blessed. For gradually, as he went on his way alone, Millais deteriorated, and though his work rapidly won public favour so that his career henceforward was, from a wordly point of view, one of uninterrupted success, his pictures ceased to be inspired by the noble seriousness of Holman Hunt or by the poetry of Rossetti. What had been sentiment degenerated into sentimentality, and as his subject-matter became commoner in quality, so an increasing laxity crept into his style of painting. " Bubbles," the child picture so extensively popularised as an advertisement by a firm of soap-makers, is the best known example of his later style, but the achievements which come nearest to the distinction of his early work are some of his portraits, notably that of John Charles Montague, an ex-sergeant of the 16th Lancers, whom Millais painted in the uniform of " The Yeoman of the Guard." This picture was painted in 1876, and thirteen years earlier Millais had been elected R.A. In 1885 he was created a baronet, and in 1896, after the death of Lord Leighton, he was made President of the Royal Academy ; but already his health was failing, and shortly after his election he died, on August 13 of the same year, and was buried in St. Paul's Cathedral by the side of his mighty predecessor, Sir Joshua Reynolds.

§ 3

Meanwhile Rossetti had been treading another path, forsaking the naturalism of Holman Hunt, but avoiding the anecdotal triviality that tempted Millais ; his pictures became more and more dream-like in their imaginative aloofness from life. The popularity that Millais courted was shunned by Rossetti, who, relying on the patronage of Ruskin and other admirers, ceased to exhibit his pictures except in his own studio.

In 1857 Rossetti went to Oxford with the intention of executing wall-paintings in the Debating Hall of the Union Society, and there he gathered round him a brilliant band of pupils, chief among whom were two under-graduates from Exeter College, William Morris and Edward Burne-Jones (1833–98). Unfortunately the English climate is fatal to true fresco painting, but though the Oxford decorations rapidly perished, and to-day are hardly visible, they remain historic as marking the starting-point of a new phase of Pre-Raphaelitism, in which the naturalist element was lost and its place taken by a more deliberately decorative and romantic mediævalism. Of this new school Rossetti was as definitely the leader and inspirer as Holman Hunt had been of the original Brotherhood, and though for many years the pictures produced by Rossetti and his followers continued to be commonly described as " Pre-Raphaelite," it is now clear that their productions really had little to do with the original Pre-Raphaelitism, but formed part of what became known later as the " Æsthetic Movement."

W. F. Mansell.

"THE BLIND GIRL," BY MILLAIS

Birmingham Art Gallery

One of the last paintings in which Millais strictly adhered to the principles of the Pre-Raphaelite Brotherhood, this picture moves us equally by the pathetic tenderness of its subject and by the beautiful precision of its rendering of Nature.

495

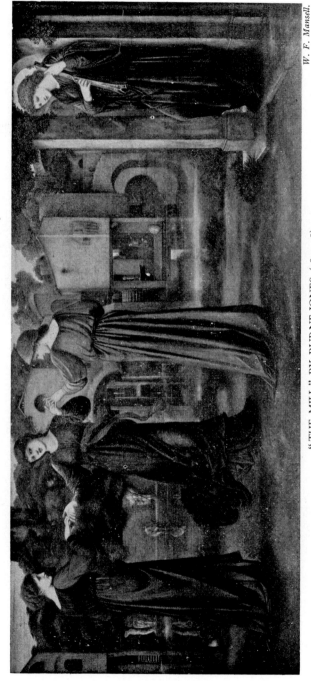

"THE MILL," BY BURNE-JONES (1833–98)

Victoria and Albert Museum, London

This vision of an imaginary world remote from actual life shows how Burne-Jones's idea of womanhood differs from that of Rossetti, and how far removed are his pictorial ideals from the naturalism of Millais and Holman Hunt.

"VENICE," BY J. M. W. TURNER

Victoria and Albert Museum, London

Turner, concerned with the effects of light and the reflection of light, found in Venice his ideal painting ground, and canvas after canvas showed the insubstantial beauty of the city set on the waters, its buildings and shipping poised between the light of the sky and their own image in the lagoons. This painting of his middle period has not yet dissolved the forms in radiance as he later did.

"THE LEAPING HORSE," BY CONSTABLE

Diploma Gallery, Royal Academy, London

In 1824 Constable attained a European reputation with "The Hay Wain," and the next year he painted "The Leaping Horse." Happily we possess both the finished picture and the large sketch for it (see p. 457), and so we are able to see the important alterations which the artist made for the sake

In 1862 Eleanor Siddal, who for ten years had been Rossetti's model and constant inspiration, died, and at first the bereaved husband was so prostrated with grief that he was totally unfitted for work. But two years later he recommenced painting in oils, and reached the highest point in his " Lady Lilith " of 1864, and " The Beloved " painted in 1865–66. Though nominally a subject from the Song of Solomon, this voluptuous presentation of feminine beauty, which for sheer loveliness rivals a Botticelli, is far removed from the simple and comparatively stern Biblical paintings of the artist's youth. The subject is clothed in the garb of mediævalism, enveloped in the romance of a fairy-tale, and heightened by a brilliance of colour unsurpassed in the painter's work.

Rossetti's pictorial work may be divided into three periods, each of which is dominated by an ideal of womanhood derived from a living woman ; in the first period she is his sister Christina, in the second his wife Eleanor Siddal, and the inspiration of the third was Mrs. William Morris. Of the many pictures she inspired one of the most beautiful is " The Daydream " in the Ionides Collection at South Kensington, but though he painted her in many characters, he never painted Mrs. Morris as Dante's Beatrice. That character was sacred to his wife, and it was in memory of her that he began to paint in 1863—though it was not finished till much later—the " Beata Beatrix," now in the Tate Gallery. The picture, according to Rossetti, " is not intended at all to represent death, but to render it under the semblance of a trance, in which Beatrice, seated at a balcony overlooking the city [Florence], is suddenly rapt from earth to heaven."

Rossetti died at Birchington in 1882, but his ideals were faithfully carried on by the most celebrated of his pupils, Edward Burne-Jones, who had been intended for the Church, but after meeting Rossetti at Oxford felt he must be a painter. One great difference between their pictures lay in their different ideals of womanhood, for while the women of Rossetti were fullblooded and passionate, those of Burne-Jones were of so refined a spirituality that to many people they appear anæmic. Otherwise the paintings of Burne-Jones are as remote from naturalism as the later works of Rossetti ; he also gives us dream pictures of an imaginary mediævalism ; and while Rossetti, as became his Italian descent, found his ideal in the Florence of Dante's time, the Welshman Burne-Jones fittingly found his in the legendary court of King Arthur. Both, however, were inspired by the same feeling for chivalry and romance, and the distance that had been travelled from Holman Hunt's naturalism may be traced in the famous confession of Burne-Jones that he longed to paint " the light that never was on sea or land."

In 1884 he exhibited one of his best known and most popular works, " King Cophetua and the Beggar-Maid " at the Grosvenor Gallery, and two years later, at the age of fifty-three, he was tardily elected A.R.A., but

"THE DAY-DREAM," BY DANTE GABRIEL ROSSETTI

Victoria and Albert Museum, London

A beautiful example of Rossetti's third and last phase, during which his model and inspiration was the beautiful wife of his disciple, William Morris.

498

" KING COPHETUA AND THE BEGGAR-MAID," BY BURNE-JONES

In this dreamlike picture of the King about to lay his jewelled crown at the feet of the beggar-maid, we may trace the mediæval romanticism of Rossetti refined by the spirituality of a Celtic mystic.

499

he was never much in sympathy with the Academy, seldom exhibited there, and in 1893, five years before he died, he resigned his Associateship.

In addition to his pictures and water-colours, Burne-Jones designed a number of tapestries and stained-glass windows for his lifelong friend William Morris, whose unbounded artistic energy found more congenial occupation in reviving crafts than in practising painting. In Morris the mediævalism of Rossetti found a furiously eager and thoroughgoing exponent, and though many of his ideas were unpractical, his inauguration of the Arts and Crafts Society was one of the most fruitful art movements of the Victorian era, and to him more than to any other man we owe not only the revival of tapestry and stained glass but a great improvement on fine printing, in furniture, pottery, wall-papers, and interior decoration generally.

Holman Hunt, the eldest of the Pre-Raphaelites, survived them all, and after painting a series of sacred pictures unique in English art for their religious fervour and geographical exactitude, he died in September, 1910, at the great age of eighty-three.

XXVII

THE VICTORIAN AGE

THE ART OF LANDSEER, LEIGHTON, POYNTER, ALFRED STEVENS,
ALBERT MOORE, ORCHARDSON, AND G. F. WATTS

§ I

SEVERAL of the artists already mentioned in this OUTLINE—among
them being Turner, Cotman, and David Cox—were alive and working when Queen Victoria ascended the throne in 1837, but we are not
in the habit of thinking of any of these as typical artists of the Victorian era.
Even the Pre-Raphaelites, whose art, as described in the previous chapter,
shed so much lustre on the Queen's long reign, were a group apart from the
general trend of the times, and none of these painters—with the one exception of Millais in his later years—showed in his art those peculiar characteristics which we are now inclined to label broadly as " Victorian."

Just as in politics the reign of Victoria was distinguished, before all things,
by the growth of Democracy, so painting during this reign approached
more closely than it had ever done before to popular ideals. Under Queen
Victoria English painting became a homely, easily understandable art,
appealing to the people by clear representation of simple themes often
founded on everyday life, and almost always tinged by a sentiment per-
ceptible and congenial to the humblest intelligence. Subject was of
paramount importance, every picture told a story, and the story was
usually of a simple nature that required no erudition for its comprehension,
one that all who ran could read.

Of a host of pictures of this description only a few can be mentioned
here. The quintessence of Victorianism may be found in the paintings of
William Powell Frith (1819–1909), whose " Derby Day," now in the Tate
Gallery, created a sensation in 1858, and whose " Railway Station," painted
four years later, is a still more dramatic assemblage of the " all sorts and
conditions of men " who go to make the world. No knowledge of the Old
Masters or of the technique of painting is needed to enjoy Frith's " Railway
Station " ; everybody can recognise the bridal couple being " seen off" by
their friends, the boy who is going to school, the new recruit taking leave of
his parents, and the criminal who is being arrested at the moment when he
thought to escape. This picture is not only full of the incidents which may

be seen at any railway station ; it is full of the simple human emotions which all have experienced and all can understand.

Very much the same qualities—though the subjects are entirely different —can be found in the works of Sir Edwin Landseer, R.A. (1802–1873), who was reputed to have been Queen Victoria's favourite painter, and was certainly one of the most popular and most successful painters of his day. Edwin Henry Landseer was born in London and was one of a family of artists. He was the third son of John Landseer, A.R.A., a painter and engraver ; his brother Charles Landseer (1799–1879) also became a successful painter of historical and animal pictures ; and his eldest brother, Thomas Landseer, became an expert engraver, whose prints after his brother's pictures materially contributed to the wide-spread fame and popularity which Edwin Landseer enjoyed. Animals specially appealed to the young artist, and some of his earliest studies were made in a menagerie at Exeter Exchange, where the Strand Palace Hotel now stands. The first distinction he received was a premium from the Society of Arts for his drawing of " A Horse for Hunting," and at the age of fourteen he was admitted as a student to the schools of the Royal Academy, where he had already made his debut as an exhibitor with a painting of " The Heads of a Poynter and Puppy."

Up to about 1820 his subjects had chiefly been dogs and horses, but he soon added other animals to his repertory. Among his father's friends was the historical painter Benjamin Robert Haydon (1786–1846), and on the advice of this artist Landseer, while still an Academy student, learnt to dissect and make anatomical studies of animals. Taking advantage of the death of a lion in one of the menageries, he diligently studied its anatomy, and the knowledge thus gained gave him a power in the drawing of that animal notable in his future works. The first fruits of these studies were his pictures " A Prowling Lion " in the Academy of 1821 and " A Lion Disturbed " in the following year. In 1824 he exhibited " The Cat's Paw," a picture of a monkey seizing a cat's paw to take roasting chestnuts from a fire, this being one of the first of his animal paintings in which an obvious moral was happily combined with humour.

In this year, when Landseer was twenty-two, he accompanied his friend and fellow-student C. R. Leslie (1794–1859) on a visit to Scotland, where the two young artists had the honour of staying with Sir Walter Scott at Abbotsford. Landseer drew the dogs of the author of *Waverley*, and was introduced by the novelist to the deer forests of Scotland. Henceforward the " monarch of the glen " became one of Landseer's favourite subjects, and deer-stalking was the sport which he loved beyond all others ; but it is said that the sportsman was often vanquished by the artist, and that when a particularly noble animal came in sight, Landseer was apt to fling down his rifle and pick up instead his sketch-book and pencil.

"DIGNITY AND IMPUDENCE," BY LANDSEER, (1802–73)

Tate Gallery, London

Landseer, who was Queen Victoria's favourite painter, is the most famous interpreter in art of canine intelligence and fidelity. In this, the most popular of his pictures, the artist humorously contrasts the stateliness of the bloodhound with the " cheekiness " of a little Scotch terrier.

In 1826 he was elected A.R.A., and his prosperity being now assured he left his father's house and established himself at 1 St. John's Wood Road, where he lived unmarried till the day of his death. Landseer now widened the field of his art, and painted pictures of various subjects, among them being several portraits. One of the most successful of the last was " Lord Cosmo Russell," a picture of a little boy on a rough pony scampering over the heather ; but while he never lacked patrons even for portraiture, his fame and popularity depended chiefly on his animal pictures, and particularly on his paintings of dogs. A witty canon of St. Paul's, who was advised to have his portrait painted by Landseer, laughingly declined with the remark, " Is thy servant a dog that he should do this thing ? "

In 1834 he exhibited at the Royal Academy " Bolton Abbey in the Olden Time," one of the best known and most popular of all his works, which has been made familiar throughout Great Britain not only by engravings but also by innumerable copies in needlework. In 1837 he increased his already great reputation by his picture of a faithful dog watching beside a coffin, entitled " The Old Shepherd's Chief Mourner," a work of intense pathos, and in the following year he painted a noble Newfoundland dog as " A Distinguished Member of the Humane Society." No painter ever surpassed Landseer in rendering all the varied aspects of canine character, and while in some of his pictures he attained a sublimity of pathos so that some captious critics accused him of making his dogs " too human," in others he showed a subtle humour which is irresistible. Probably no English picture has ever enjoyed a wider popularity than " Dignity and Impudence," in which Landseer amusingly contrasts an old bloodhound of the Duke of Grafton breed with a little Scotch terrier called " Scratch." Landseer loved dogs and kept a troop of them in his home at St. John's Wood.

From 1839 onwards the artist enjoyed a considerable intimacy with the Royal Family. He taught both Queen Victoria and the Prince Consort to etch and painted many pictures for them, one of his largest being " The Drive, Shooting Deer on the Pass." He had been elected R.A. in 1831 and in 1850 he was knighted. He was a sculptor as well as a painter, and in 1859 he was commissioned to execute the lions for the base of Nelson's Column in Trafalgar Square. On this work the artist was engaged, off and on, for some half a dozen years, and his lions were finally uncovered at Trafalgar Square in 1869. Two of the studies which Landseer made at the Zoo for these lions are now in the National Gallery (Nos. 1349 and 1350).

Three years earlier, on the death of Sir Charles Eastlake (1793–1865), Landseer had been offered the Presidency of the Royal Academy, but he declined the honour, for though a general favourite, popular alike at Court, in society, and with the public, he was subject to fits of depression brought about by an almost morbid sensitiveness and a certain constitutional delicacy.

" SYMPATHY," BY BRITON RIVIÈRE (1840–1920)

Tate Gallery, London

This favourite picture of a little girl in disgrace and her canine comforter never fails to appeal to all who love children and dogs and have remarked the unspoken sympathy which exists between them.

Towards the end of his life he suffered continually from nerves, and his general state of health was sadly impaired by a railway accident in November 1868. This accident not only left a scar on his forehead but affected his memory, so that his last years were much clouded. He died in his house in St. John's Wood on October 1, 1873, and was buried in state at St. Paul's Cathedral.

The tradition of painting animals with affectionate insight, founded by Landseer, has been followed with success by many other British artists, prominent among them being Briton Rivière (1840–1920), who, after being influenced at first by the pictures of the Pre-Raphaelites and by Tennyson's poetry, soon turned his attention to the painting of pictures in which animals played an important part. His well-known " Sympathy," in the Tate Gallery, is a characteristic Victorian picture in the Landseer tradition, but in gayer and more agreeable colours. It tells its own story clearly, and can never fail to appeal to all who love children and dogs and have noted the unspoken sympathy which exists between them.

§ 2

Victorian painting was essentially a story-telling art, but the stories were not limited to one country or to one century. The classical revival, the delight in pictures representing the life of ancient Greece and Rome, which marked, as we have seen, the art of France during the Revolutionary Period, did not show itself in England till nearly half a century later. The man who introduced this style of picture into England was Frederick Leighton, who, though born at Scarborough in 1830, spent the greater part of his early life abroad. Leighton was the son of a physician and spent his boyhood in Italy. When he was only ten years old he studied drawing at Rome, and afterwards lived in Florence, where he was taught by several Italian artists. When he was eighteen he visited Brussels, and in the following year he continued his art studies in Paris, where he attended a life-school and copied pictures by Titian and Correggio in the Louvre. In 1850 he went to Germany, visiting Dresden and Berlin, but staying longest at Frankfort, where he worked for two years under a painter named Steinle, and was to some extent influenced by the painters Cornelius and Overbeck, who were mentioned in the last chapter. From Germany he returned to Paris, where he had a studio in the Rue Pigalle. At this time he was much enamoured of the earliest Italian artists, and his first oil-painting, executed at Frankfort, represented " Giotto found by Cimabue among the Sheep." It was from Paris that Leighton sent to the Academy of 1855 his picture of " Cimabue's Madonna carried in Procession through the Streets of Florence." This picture, with its precise drawing, elaborate design, and fresh, clear colour, created a tremendous

"THE BATH OF PSYCHE," BY LORD LEIGHTON, (1830–96)
Tate Gallery, London

sensation in London, and when it was bought by Queen Victoria the reputation of the painter was immediately made. It was not till five years later,
however, that Leighton left Paris and settled in London.

Leighton was now thirty years old, and he was an accomplished, much-
travelled man of the world. He had charming, courtly manners, and his
prestige in the arts was equalled by his social success. He executed a number
of illustrations for the Brothers Dalziel, but he had no lack of other patrons,
and received numerous commissions for decorative paintings and subject
pictures. He gave himself largely to the illustration of Greek history and
legend, two of his most famous pictures in this style being " Daphnephoria "
and " The Return of Persephone," now in the Leeds Art Gallery. He was
generally considered to have recaptured the spirit of Greek art better than
any artist since Raphael, and " The Bath of Psyche " is a famous example
of the almost waxen perfection of his figures, and of his manner of
idealising the nude.

The graceful sense of form noticeable in his paintings was also displayed
in Leighton's works of sculpture, of which the best known are " The
Sluggard " and " Athlete with Python," both in the Tate Gallery. From
the moment he set foot in England, Leighton's career was a series of unbroken
successes. He was elected A.R.A. in 1864, R.A. in 1868, and ten years later,
after the death of Sir Francis Grant in 1878, he was elected President of the
Royal Academy and received a knighthood. He was created a baronet in
1886, and on January 1, 1896, a few months before his death, he was made
Baron Leighton of Stretton, being the first British painter elevated to the
peerage.

Leighton never married. He built himself a handsome house, with an
Arab Hall, from his own design, at No. 2 Holland Park Road, and his home,
now known as Leighton House, is preserved as a memorial of his art.

Looking backward, we may surmise that the wide popularity enjoyed by
Leighton and his followers was not altogether unrelated to the revival of
interest in antiquity and archæology which, beginning in the reign of Queen
Victoria, has continued undiminished to this day. At a time when the mind
of the public was roused by reports in the newspapers of the discoveries made
by excavators in Greece, Egypt, and elsewhere, it is not surprising that
visitors to the Academy should have made favourites of those pictures which
sought to portray life as it was in Greece or Egypt in the olden days.

Among a number of scholarly artists who were influenced by the example
of Leighton, one of the most distinguished was his eventual successor in the
presidency of the Royal Academy, Sir Edward John Poynter (1836–1919).
This artist was born in Paris and was the son of an architect, Ambrose
Poynter, who was himself a skilful painter in water-colours and had been an
intimate friend of R. P. Bonington. E. J. Poynter studied art first in the

"FAITHFUL UNTO DEATH," BY POYNTER (1836–1919)

Walker Art Gallery, Liverpool

This inspiring picture of a Roman sentinel, steadfastly remaining at his post amid the scenes of terror which accompanied the destruction of Pompeii by the eruption of Mount Vesuvius is generally regarded as the masterpiece of one of the most eminent of the Victorian classical painters.

Academy schools and afterwards in Paris, where one of his most intimate friends and fellow-students was the illustrator George du Maurier, author of *Trilby*. Poynter first exhibited at the Academy in 1861, and during the earlier part of his life he designed a number of decorative works, among them being mosaics for the Houses of Parliament and for St. Paul's Cathedral. He also, like Leighton, executed illustrations—some of which appeared in *Once-a-Week*—and painted portraits as well as landscapes ; but though his activities were many and various, he was best known by his paintings of Greek, Roman, and Egyptian subjects. His first great popular success, and probably the most moving picture he ever conceived, was painted in 1865 ; " Faithful unto Death," now in the Walker Art Gallery, Liverpool, shows a Roman soldier standing unmoved at his post while Pompeii is being destroyed by volcanic eruption, and in this picture the artist not only shows exactitude in archæological detail, but also expresses a nobility of purpose which every human being can understand and admire. In 1867 he painted " Israel in Egypt," but in later years he seldom approached the high serious-ness of these early pictures, and though he maintained his popularity with scholarly and agreeable renderings of classical scenes, like " A Visit to Æsculapius " in the Tate Gallery, the subjects of these pictures tended to become lighter and sometimes trivial.

In addition to his work as a painter Sir E. J. Poynter was overwhelmed by official duties. He was elected A.R.A. in 1869 and two years later he was appointed the first Slade Professor at University College, London, a post which he held till 1875, when he became Director of the Royal College of Art at South Kensington, over which he presided for seven years. Mean-while he had in 1876 been elected R.A., and henceforward his influence in the Academy council steadily increased. In 1894 he was appointed Director of the National Gallery, London, and he held this post till 1905, although in 1896 he had been appointed President of the Royal Academy, in succession to Millais. He was knighted in 1896 and made a baronet in 1902.

The wealth of Victorian England not only fostered native art, but naturally drew to these shores a number of foreign artists. Among them was one of the most famous of our modern classical painters, Sir Lawrence Alma-Tadema. This artist was born in Holland in 1836, and after studying art in Antwerp gave his attention to historical painting. He began with early French and Egyptian subjects, but commenced his series of Greek subjects about 1865. In 1869 he sent his painting " The Pyrrhic Dance " to the Academy in London, where it was so well received that the painter decided to settle in England and became naturalised in 1873.

In the hands of Alma-Tadema the classical picture became historical in detail but playful and fanciful in subject. The Victorian anecdote reappeared in a Greek or Roman dress, as in his picture " A Silent Greeting " at the Tate

"LOVE IN IDLENESS," BY ALMA-TADEMA (1836–1912)

Among the classical painters of his time, Alma-Tadema, who was born in Holland, won wide popularity by illustrating the lighter side of life in ancient Greece and Rome. This dream-like picture of wistful maidenhood is a characteristic example of his art, and exhibits the scrupulously painted marble accessories which this artist delighted to introduce into his pictures.

Gallery, in which a Roman warrior places a bunch of roses in the lap of a sleeping lady. " Love in Idleness " is a characteristic example of his art and shows the wonderfully painted marble accessories which he was so fond of introducing into his pictures. Though full himself of antiquarian knowledge, and often called upon by Irving and other theatrical producers to assist in giving verisimilitude to the costumes and scenery for historical plays, Alma-Tadema never wearied the public with his learning, and his pictures were in the nature of agreeable dreams which made no serious demands upon the intellect or high emotions of the spectator. In the course of a long and successful career Alma-Tadema was elected A.R.A. in 1876, R.A. in 1879, knighted in 1899, and received the Order of Merit in 1905. He died while staying at Wiesbaden in 1912.

While all these artists enjoyed fame and fortune in their lifetime, other artists of equal or superior gifts were less appreciated by their contemporaries, though in several cases their fame is higher to-day than that of the popular favourites of their day. If we number Albert Moore (1841–93) among the Victorian classical painters, we must be careful to draw a distinction between his art and that of Leighton, Poynter, and Alma-Tadema. For, whereas these three artists emphasised the illustrative element in painting, Albert Moore laid more stress on its decorative element. Moore was not anecdotal, and for this reason his decorative compositions did not make so easy and obvious an appeal to his contemporaries ; but he was filled with the Greek spirit of beauty, and his painting " Blossoms " is now one of the most admired of the quasi-classical pictures in the Tate Gallery. Moore was born at York and was the son of an artist, but though he was trained in the Academy schools and began to exhibit at the Academy in the 'sixties, he was not well received there, and subsequently exhibited chiefly at the Grosvenor Gallery and the Old Water-colour Society. He was never elected a member of the Academy, but associated with Whistler and other independent artists. An admirable draughtsman and designer, Albert Moore was also gifted with a refined and delicate sense of colour equalled by few of his contemporaries.

His brother Henry Moore (1831–95), an excellent marine painter, received more official recognition ; he was elected A.R.A. in 1886, R.A. in 1893, and in 1885 his " Catspaws off the Land," in the Tate Gallery, was bought for the nation.

§ 3

Apart from all the other artists of his time stands the lonely figure of Alfred Stevens (1817–75), who, though never fully appreciated by his own contemporaries, is now generally recognised to have been probably the greatest and most complete artist that England ever produced. Stevens was

"THE SCAPEGOAT," BY HOLMAN HUNT

The Lady Lever Art Gallery, Port Sunlight

With the money earned from the sale of "The Light of the World" Holman Hunt fulfilled his dream of a journey to Palestine to paint Biblical subjects in the Pre-Raphaelite ideal of absolute truth to natural fact. This picture was one of the first results. The detailed landscape beside the Dead Sea is made the setting for a subject of religious significance and symbolism.

"LA LOGE," BY RENOIR

National Gallery, London

A picture which shows Renoir working as a semi-portraitist outside the Impressionist manner we usually associate with him. He builds up a brilliant composition with the black and white of the woman's dress and the man's evening clothes, set against the crimson and gold of the theatre decoration.

" BLOSSOMS," BY ALBERT MOORE (1841–93)
Tate Gallery, London

cast in a heroic mould and ought to have lived in a heroic age ; painter, sculptor, and architect, he possessed the universality of some giant of the Renaissance ; and no other artist of any country has approached more closely in his work to the temper of Michael Angelo. Yet this great English-man was never recognised or honoured by the Royal Academy ; throughout his life he had a hard struggle to make a living, and while his Wellington Monument and Prophets for St. Paul's Cathedral prove that he was capable of executing works of the mightiest genius both in sculpture and in painting, for want of more appropriate employment Stevens was con-demned to spend a great part of his life in designing stoves, fenders, etc., for commercial firms.

Alfred Stevens was born at Blandford in Dorset in 1817. He was the son of a heraldic painter, whom he assisted from an early age, and while he was still in his teens his rare genius was recognised by some of the better-off residents in the district, who subscribed a purse to enable him to study art in Italy. Thus assisted, Stevens went to Italy in 1833, and stayed there for nearly nine years, studying painting, sculpture, and architecture, chiefly in Florence and Rome. In the latter city he was for two years (1841–42) assistant to the Danish sculptor Thorwaldsen (1770–1844), author of the famous Lion of Lucerne, carved in the solid rock in memory of the Swiss Guards who died in defence of Louis XVI and Marie Antoinette.

When Alfred Stevens returned to England in 1842 he was, according to modern authorities, " the most thoroughly educated artist the country has seen," but his erudition and genius long failed to find suitable employment. In 1844 he competed, unsuccessfully, for a commission to execute decorations in Westminster Hall, and in the following year he accepted an appointment as Master of Architectural Drawing, Perspective, Modelling, and Orna-mental Painting to a new School of Design at Somerset House. To Stevens, however, teaching was never more than a stopgap ; he knew that his real business in life was to create works of art, and consequently as soon as he was given an opportunity to do creative work he resigned his appointment and in 1847 he began to decorate Deysbrook, near Liverpool. For the next few years he managed to make a living by working for other architects ; in 1849 and 1854 he worked for Cockerell on St. George's Hall, Liverpool ; he designed the bronze doors for Pennethorn's Geological Museum in Jermyn Street ; he designed the lions for the British Museum railings in 1852 ; but work of this kind was so uncertain that in 1850 he had been glad to accept a position as designer in the firm of Hoole at Sheffield. Thanks to Alfred Stevens, this firm secured first prize for their stoves and fenders in the Great Exhibition of 1851.

Occasionally he received a commission for a painting, and his noble portrait of Mrs. Mary Ann Collmann, at the National Gallery, was painted

MRS. MARY ANN COLLMANN, BY ALFRED STEVENS (1817–75)

National Gallery, London

Painter, sculptor, and architect, Alfred Stevens recalled the universality which distinguished the giants of the Renaissance. Towards the end of his life he was entrusted with the execution of the Wellington Monument for St. Paul's Cathedral, but for many years his genius was frittered away by his being compelled to earn his living by designing minor objects for architects and commercial firms. This noble portrait of the wife of an architect who employed him at one time, shows the regal dignity and perfection of his painting.

in 1854, the lady being the wife of an architect, Leonard Collmann, who sometimes employed Stevens.

In 1850 Stevens began the chief work of his life with his competition model for the Wellington Monument. Originally he was placed only sixth in the competition and awarded a prize of £100, but fortunately on further consideration the superior merit and appropriateness of his design was perceived and the commission for the monument was definitely given to Stevens. For the remaining seventeen years of his life the artist was at work on this monument. It was all but completed at his death, with the exception of the crowning equestrian statue of the Duke, which, by a strange caprice, was ruled out by the Dean because he did not like the idea of a horse in a church! Eventually this pedantic objection was overruled, and the equestrian statue, carried out from Stevens' model, was placed in position as recently as 1911, so that the whole monument as conceived by Stevens may now be seen in St. Paul's. Other memorials of the genius of Stevens in St. Paul's are the four mosaics of Prophets in the spandrels under the dome, which he designed in 1862. The original cartoon for the mosaic of " Isaiah " is now in the Tate Gallery, and nothing equal to it can be found nearer than the Sistine Chapel at Rome. Concurrently with these great masterpieces, Stevens worked at the decoration of Dorchester House, Park Lane, where he completed for Mr. Holford two chimney-pieces, a buffet, and other features, and designed a painted ceiling, the whole being a scheme of unequalled splendour in English interior decoration. Worn out by the strain of his monument and his severe battle with life, Alfred Stevens died on May 1, 1875, in the house he had designed and built for himself at 9 Eaton Villas, Haverstock Hill. Apart from the works already mentioned, only a few fragments remain of the art of Alfred Stevens, but while we must always deplore that more opportunities were not given to so great and various an artist, enough exists to prove to all time the measure of his genius.

If Stevens was neglected in his lifetime, we have since grown to appreciate greatly the perfection of his art and realise that in him we had an English master comparable to the noble figures of the Renaissance. His drawings are now much sought after, and a particularly fine collection of more than a hundred of them, as well as other work by him, enriches the Walker Art Gallery at Liverpool. There also can be seen some of his early portraits, some of the work from Dorchester House, and other examples of his art and craft. Because of his connection with St. George's Hall at Liverpool and with Deysbrook House in that locality, it is fitting that the city should thus honour him. In the presence of any such collection of his work we realise that his quality was that of the Renaissance masters, and that this great Victorian was the last artist to remain true to the ideals of Greek culture.

W. F. Mansell.

"HOPE," BY G. F. WATTS (1817–1904)

Tate Gallery, London

Blindfolded, with lyre in hand, and sitting on the globe in the dim twilight of the world, Hope " strives to get all the music possible out of the last remaining string."

This beautiful allegory is the masterpiece of an artist who sought in all his works to " appeal to the imagination and the heart, and kindle all that is best and noblest in humanity."

517

§ 4

Born in the same year as Stevens was another great artist, who, though he certainly gained honours and rewards during his lifetime, nevertheless found himself hampered by the circumstances of his time in carrying out the desires of his art. George Frederick Watts was born in London on February 23, 1817, the son of a Welsh father, who encouraged his artistic bent and permitted him to study at the Academy schools and also under the sculptor William Behnes (1795–1864). When he was twenty-five Watts entered the competition for the best designs for decorating in fresco the new House of Lords, and won the first prize of £300 with his " Caractacus led Captive through the Streets of Rome." This was the competition in which both Alfred Stevens and Ford Madox Brown were unsuccessful. On the strength of this prize Watts in 1843 went to Italy, where he remained for four years, mostly in Florence, and was befriended by Lord Holland. Returning to England, Watts entered another competition in 1847 for decorating the House of Lords, this time in oils, and again won the first prize of £500 with his " Alfred inciting the Saxons to resist the Danes." As a result of these successes Watts was employed for the next ten years on mural decorations, painting " St. George overcoming the Dragon " for the House of Lords and his allegory of " Justice " for the great hall of Lincoln's Inn ; but though his desire was to continue painting in this style, further opportunities were denied him. He offered to give his time freely in painting decorations for Euston railway station, but the offer was declined, and balked of his intention to create elevating works of art in public buildings, he began that great series of painted allegories with which his name is most closely associated.

Explaining his own ideals Watts once said : " My intention has not been so much to paint pictures that charm the eye, as to suggest great thoughts that will appeal to the imagination and the heart, and kindle all that is best and noblest in humanity." Successful in his early years and never covetous of great wealth, Watts was able in his middle years to paint exactly as he pleased without thinking of sales and patrons. He painted portraits, but he never portrayed any person he did not respect and admire, and the noble series of pictures of the great men of his time which he gave to the National Portrait Gallery shows how little, even in portraiture, did Watts paint for money. Similarly, the pick of his allegorical paintings, a cycle of the history of humanity, was kept for years in his own gallery at Little Holland House, till in 1897 he generously presented the collection to the Tate Gallery. Watts was essentially a philosophical artist and he has not inaccurately been described as " a preacher in paint," for, in his opinion, it was not enough for an artist to portray noble aspirations, he must also " condemn in the most trenchant manner prevalent vices," and utter

518

W. F. Mansell.

"MAMMON," BY G. F. WATTS

Tate Gallery, London

A powerful indictment of ruthlessness in the pursuit of wealth. The artist shows us the god of riches, with ass's ears, in gold brocade and crown, seated on a blood-red throne surmounted by skulls, with money-bags in his lap. With heavy hand he crushes the head of Woman, whose green garment (symbolic of hope) has fallen from her, while Man is stripped and prostrate beneath his foot.

519

"LOVE AND LIFE," BY G. F. WATTS

Tate Gallery, London

Love, strong in immortal youth, guides Life upwards over a rocky path, sheltering her with his broad wings from stormy winds. Even in this barren soil violets spring up where Love has trod.
An exquisite allegory by the most thoughtful of Victorian painters.

"THE TENDER CHORD," BY ORCHARDSON, (1835–1910)

This engaging picture of a Victorian young lady, arrested by some memory evoked by " the tender chord," is a typical example of the domestic art of this distinguished Scottish painter, who retained the respect of his brother artists by his polished powers of painting and design, and won the affection of the public by his power to suggest a story and convey a sentiment.

" warning in deep tones against lapses from morals and duties." All aspects of Watts's art may be seen to advantage in the room devoted to his works at the Tate Gallery, where his beautiful " Hope " and his " Love and Life " reveal noble aspirations of humanity, while his unforgettable " Mammon " and " The Minotaur " condemn prevalent vices and warn against lapses from morals.

As a sculptor Watts is represented at the Tate Gallery by his bronze bust of " Clytie," but his most important work in this medium is his equestrian group " Physical Energy," originally designed as a monument to Cecil Rhodes and set up as a memorial to the great Empire builder on the slopes of Table Mountain, Cape Town. A replica of this fine statue has been placed in Kensington Gardens.

The life of Watts was long and full of honours. He was elected A.R.A. and R.A. in the same year, 1867 ; twice he was offered and refused a baronetcy, but two years before his death he accepted the Order of Merit. He died in 1904 at the great age of eighty-seven, his last years having been spent chiefly in his country house at Compton, Surrey, where a large permanent collection of his works is still visible to the public.

§ 5

Watts for nobility of thought and conception and Stevens for grandeur of design and execution will, in all probability, be considered by posterity to have been the two most eminent artists of the Victorian era, but though it may be less easy to find, among the painters, the outstanding giants who mark the same period in literature, the very number of names as distinguished as they are familiar show how active and flourishing the arts were during the Queen's long reign. Many artists who enjoyed, and still enjoy, a wide popularity must necessarily be omitted from this OUTLINE, but no survey, however hasty, of Victorian painting can ignore the band of Scottish artists who won fame in the south as well as in the north. Among them we may mention the historical and romantic painter John Pettie (1839–93) ; Peter Graham, the cattle painter ; John MacWhirter, the popular painter of the Highlands ; William M'Taggart, unrivalled in his delicate yet vigorous renderings of foaming seas and windy shores ; and Sir W. Q. Orchardson, the leader of this band of Scottish students, and one of the most polished, typical, and popular of all Victorian artists. William Quiller Orchardson (1835–1910) was born in Edinburgh and came to London about 1862, and thereafter maintained and held his position as one of the most popular of Academy exhibitors. He excelled in a variety of subjects ; his " Sir Walter Gilbey " and " Master Baby "—a group of his wife and child—rank among the great portraits of the nineteenth century ; " Napoleon on Board the

W. F. Mansell.

NAPOLEON ON BOARD THE *BELLEROPHON*, BY ORCHARDSON

Tate Gallery, London

A dramatic, thought-provoking vision of the deposed Emperor on his way to St. Helena. The officers of his staff, from left to right, are Col. Planat, General Montholm, Surgeon Maingaut, Count Las Cases, Generals Savary, Lallemand, and Bertrand. The boy Las Cases leans upon the rail.

Bellerophon " is one of the best known and most admired of modern historical paintings ; but perhaps the best loved of all his works are those paintings of contemporary life, like " The Tender Chord," which, without being positively " anecdotal," yet suggest a story and convey a sentiment. It was the distinction of Orchardson that his story-telling was never crude and obvious, his sentiment was always gentle and refined, his execution was suave and accomplished, so that his pictures, often representing moods of wistful reverie, charmed the eye of the beholder and at the same time conjured up a scene which dwelt in the memory and made its own appeal to the imagination.

XXVIII

THE ROMANTIC MOVEMENT IN FRANCE

THE ART OF DELACROIX, GÉRICAULT, COROT, MILLET, AND THE BARBIZON SCHOOL

§ 1

SOME thirty years before the Pre-Raphaelite Brotherhood began its triumphant fight in England for the free expression of new ideals in art, a similar struggle between old and new schools of artists was waged with extraordinary vehemence in France. We saw in Chapter XXIII how under the Revolution and the Empire a cold Classicism was the dominating tendency in French painting, and how gradually there arose among the younger artists a reaction against this traditional art. The spirit of unrest, which profoundly agitated France after the restoration of the Bourbons and culminated in the revolutionary explosion of 1848, first began to show itself in the art and literature of the younger generation. On one hand were the defenders of tradition, of the " grand style " of Academic painting, defenders of the classic ideal based on the sculpture of ancient Greece and Rome ; on the other were ardent young reformers, intoxicated with the colour and movement of life itself, who found their inspiration, not in the classics, but in romantic literature, in Dante, Shakespeare, Goethe, Byron, and Scott. Passion, movement, the imaginative expression of life were the aims of this group of artists, who became known as the Romantics.

"Who will deliver us from the Greeks and Romans ? " was a catchword among the young enthusiasts who found more beauty in life and Nature than in the masterpieces of ancient sculpture. The deliverer was found in the ranks of the reactionaries, in a young artist who was the pupil of Guérin the classicist. Jean Louis André Théodore Géricault was born at Rouen in 1791 and came to Paris about 1806, studying first with Carle Vernet and afterwards with Guérin. His method of drawing was so different from that approved by the school of David, that it exasperated his " correct " and academic master, who told Géricault he had better give up art because it was evident he would never succeed in it.

One day as Géricault was walking along a road near St. Cloud, a dapple-grey horse in a cart turned restive and plunged about in the sunshine. Géricault whipped out his sketch-book and jotted down notes of the movement of the animal and the play of light and shade on his dappled coat, and these notes gave him the idea of a great picture. He would paint an equestrian portrait, not the stiff image of a man on a wooden horse, but a vivid present-ment of the plunging, sun-illumined animal he had seen. He persuaded his friend Lieutenant Dieudonné to pose for the rider, and he had a cab-horse brought round each morning that he might freshen his eye with the points of the horse. Working with the highest enthusiasm and energy Géricault, in the space of a fortnight, produced his " Officier des Chasseurs à Cheval," now in the Louvre. This picture created a sensation in the Paris Salon of 1812.

Two years afterwards Géricault repeated his success with a companion picture, " The Wounded Cuirassier," and after a short period of military service—when he had further opportunities of studying his favourite equine models—he went in 1817 to Italy, where he " trembled " before the works of Michael Angelo, who henceforward became his inspiration and idol.

When Géricault returned to France in 1818, he found all Paris talking about nothing but a naval disaster of two years earlier, an account of which had just been published by two of the survivors. The drama of the shipwreck of the *Medusa* seized upon the imagination of the artist, who determined to make it the subject of a picture. He spent months in collecting material for this work. He found the carpenter of the *Medusa* and induced him to make a model of the famous raft by which the survivors were saved. He spent days in hospitals studying the effects of illness and suffering. He persuaded two of the surviving officers of the ship to give him sittings, and painted one leaning against the mast and the other holding out his two arms towards the rescuing ship on the horizon. All his models were taken from life, and it is interesting to note that his friend, the famous artist Eugène Delacroix, posed for the man who lies inert on the left with his head against the edge of the raft.

These methods of painting—though afterwards employed by the Pre-Raphaelites—were then a complete innovation in painting, and the painting was so novel in conception, so contrary to the received ideas of the time, that when it was at length completed and shown in the Salon of 1819 it was at first greeted with nothing but abuse. Nevertheless, this picture marks a turning-point in the history of French painting ; it brought strong feeling and pulsating life into the barren and frozen official art, and gave new ideals to the younger generation.

At the time the genius of Géricault was more highly appreciated in England than in France, and after the exhibition of his masterpiece the artist visited London, where his drawings and paintings of horses were intensely admired, and Géricault did signal service to the art of both countries by returning to Paris full of praise for the painting of Bonington and Constable,

"THE RAFT OF THE *MEDUSA*," BY GÉRICAULT (1791–1824)

The Louvre, Paris

Inspired by the heroic endurance of the survivors from a sensational shipwreck in 1816, this picture of a contemporary event, painted with scrupulous fidelity to the facts as obtained from eye-witnesses, marks a turning-point in the history of French painting. It brought back life and feeling into a petrified, official art, and gave new ideals to the younger generation.

527

whose pictures he introduced to and made known in Paris. Unfortunately for the world this great genius was short-lived. Early in 1823 he was stricken down by a mortal illness, and after eleven months of terrible suffering, borne with fortitude and composure, he died in January 1824 at the early age of thirty-three. His place at the head of the Romantic School was taken by Delacroix, who had been his friend and fellow-student in the studio of Guérin.

Ferdinand Victor Eugène Delacroix was born at Charenton in 1798, but spent his early years at Marseilles, where he gained that love of vivid colour and bright sunshine which afterwards distinguished his painting. His father, an ex-foreign minister under the Directory and subsequently prefect of Marseilles and Bordeaux, did not take kindly to the idea of his son becoming a painter, but he died before his son came of age, and Eugène Delacroix then found shelter with a married sister in Paris, where he overcame family opposition and was allowed to study art.

His father, however, had left him penniless, and the young artist was so poor that in 1822, after painting his first great picture, " The Barque of Dante," he could not afford to buy a frame, but sent the canvas to the Salon surrounded by four laths which he had coloured with yellow powder. There it was seen by Baron Gros, who generously recognised the great talent of the poor artist, and not only persuaded the administration to give the picture a handsome new frame, but hung it in a place of honour in the Salon Carré.

" The Barque of Dante " made the painter famous at once, and did not offend the Classicists. Gros said the picture was " Rubens reformed," and paternally advised the artist, " Come to us ; we will teach you how to draw." Delacroix was grateful to Gros for his kindness, but went his own way, and two years later he shocked the Classicists and delighted the Romantics by his picture " The Massacre of Scio."

It will be remembered that Constable's " Hay Wain " was exhibited in the Paris Salon of 1824, and when Delacroix saw it he was so overwhelmed by its colour that he obtained permission to retouch his own " Massacre of Scio." In a fortnight he completely repainted this picture, using the purest and most vivid colours he could find, with the result that it now became as brilliant in colour as it had already been in action and movement. The turbulent energy in this painting was too much for the Classicists, and Gros, playing on the title, said, " This is the massacre of painting." On the other hand, enthusiastic young critics lauded the picture with extravagant praise, one of them asserting that it showed up " all the horror of despotism " in art as in life.

In this picture, which was the real beginning of his lasting fame, Delacroix proved himself to be one of the world's great colourists, and laid the

"THE BARRICADE," OR "LIBERTY GUIDING THE PEOPLE," BY DELACROIX
(1798–1863)

The Louvre, Paris

This remarkable picture by the great leader of the Romantic Movement in France is a true rendering of an incident during the street fighting of the revolution in July 1830—when the Parisians deposed the unpopular Charles X and placed his cousin Louis Philippe, Duke of Orleans, on the throne—and at the same time the heroine of the Barricade may be regarded as an allegorical figure of Liberty guiding the People.

foundations of the new handling of colour which became the greatest pictorial triumph of the nineteenth century. Colour in his hands was no dead thing, it became something alive, scintillating and vibrating ; his results were obtained not only by the happy choice of individual tints, but still more by the science with which he knew how to juxtapose one colour against another so as to accentuate the brilliancy of each and secure a glowing harmony.

The art of Delacroix is distinguished by three things—its colour, its poetry, and its decorative qualities. He turned naturally to Dante, Shakespeare, and Byron for subjects, not so much because they provided him with good themes to illustrate, as because in their poetry he found those passionate ideals and aspirations which animated his own mind. When actual events aroused a similar intensity of emotion, he painted them also. Though usually he eschewed political subjects, the Revolution of July 1830 moved him to paint his famous picture " The Barricade," now known as " Liberty Guiding the People," a picture which is at once a fragment of actuality and the embodiment of an ideal. For this is a true historical picture in so far as it does represent with fidelity a typical incident during the street-fighting of the Revolution ; and at the same time the heroine of the barricade, with her Phrygian cap, streaming tricolour, and musket, is an allegory of Liberty, liberty for the people and liberty for art. Exhibited in the Salon of 1831 this picture perplexed the authorities, who could neither deny its excellence as a work of art nor altogether approve of its firebrand politics. The Director of Fine Arts temporarily solved the problem by purchasing the picture for the nation, and then turning its face to the wall ! To-day the picture is one of the chief treasures of the French School in the Louvre.

In the same year Delacroix made a journey to Morocco which had a considerable effect on his art, for he delighted alike in the brilliant colours and picturesque costumes of this sunny land, and on his return exhibited a number of pictures of Eastern subjects, which were enthusiastically received, and, inspiring other artists to do likewise, he gave birth to a school of artists known as the " Orientalists." Delacroix himself, however, was too big and varied a genius to confine himself to one subject, and having given a lead to the Orientalists he now devoted much of his time to decorative painting.

Though regarded by his great rival Ingres and by the classical painters as a revolutionary, Delacroix was full of respect for tradition, only whereas David and Ingres adhered to the tradition of Raphael and Leonardo da Vinci, Géricault and Delacroix upheld the tradition of Michael Angelo, Titian, Veronese, and Rubens. Though his own researches into colour were perhaps his most valuable legacy to the art of France, the intention of Delacroix was not to break with tradition but to bring back the colour and methods of the old masters into modern painting. The romanticism of Delacroix was a half-way house between the old Classicism and the Realism that was coming, and as he in his youth had challenged the position of Ingres and the Classicists, so in his later years his own romanticism was challenged by Courbet the Realist.

Owing to this long battle between the classics and the romantics, the doors of the Academy were closed against Delacroix for five-and-thirty years, and it was not till he was sixty—and so barred by age from holding a professorship at the École des Beaux-Arts—that he was at last admitted as a member of the Institute. The artist did not long enjoy the distinction, for he died at Paris in 1863.

§ 2

While Géricault, Delacroix, and other " Romantics " were liberating the painting of history, poetry, and real life from the trammels of Classicism, another group of French painters was engaged in rescuing landscape-painting from the deadness and artificiality which had overtaken it since the days of Poussin and Claude Lorrain.

Among the earliest of the French artists to paint Nature as she is, and not as the pedantic " classics " thought she ought to be, was Jean Baptiste Camille Corot (1796–1875). Born in Paris, the son of a small linen-draper having a shop in the Rue de Bac, Corot was for eight years a commercial traveller in the cloth trade. It was not till he was twenty-six that he was reluctantly allowed by his family to abandon trade and devote himself to painting. His father made him an allowance of sixty pounds a year, and till he was nearing fifty this was practically all Corot had to live upon.

In 1822 he entered the studio of Victor Bertin (1775–1825), a painter of classical landscape so successful in his day that the French Government, attracted by his own work and that of his pupils, created a new Prix de Rome for Landscape Painting. This prize was usually carried off by Bertin's pupils, who thus came to regard Rome as the finishing school of their artistic education. The turning-point in Corot's life came in 1826, when he also went to Rome, and there he formed a friendship with another French painter, Aligny (1798–1871), who had some influence on his early efforts. Aligny, though a classical painter, had a much more honest feeling for Nature than most of his kind, and though his pictures are rigid in execution they show unusual carefulness in composition and detail. The early Roman paintings of Corot are distinguished by precise drawing, careful composition, and a deliberate soberness of detail, but they also have a lovely limpidity of colour unequalled in the work of his contemporaries, and a delicate feeling for light and air. Breaking away from the brown convention of his day,

" THE POOL," BY COROT (1796–1875)

The Louvre, Paris

The most poetic of landscape painters, Corot was long neglected by his contemporaries. Beginning life as a commercial traveller, he exhibited his first painting when he was thirty-one, but he never sold a picture till he had turned sixty.

"THE LADY IN BLUE," BY COROT

Universally admired as a landscape painter, Corot is less known as a figure painter because these subjects are rarer and until recently have been hidden away in private collections. This beautiful work, painted when the artist was a veteran of seventy-eight, is one of his last pictures and reveals his exquisite skill and refinement in portraiture.

Corot painted southern landscape and architectural subjects in delicate tints of pale blues and greens, light biscuit-colour and pearly greys.

For some seven or eight years Corot remained in Italy, gradually forming a style which was absolutely his own and in which, while remaining true to the actual facts of Nature, he expressed her most poetical aspects. Occasionally he also painted pictures with small figures, and these, with their precision and delicate colour and subtle lighting, were nearer akin to the Dutch style of Vermeer and other seventeenth-century masters than to the accepted styles of Italian figure-painting.

It is strange to think that the paintings of Corot—for which millionaires now eagerly offer thousands of pounds—were for long years utterly neglected by his contemporaries. He exhibited regularly in the Paris Salon from 1827, but his exhibits aroused neither censure nor admiration—they were simply ignored. *For thirty years he never sold a picture.* The first critic to notice his work was the poet Alfred de Musset, who praised his picture in the Salon of 1836; but with the exception of two favourable notices received in 1837 and 1847, he was generally as neglected by the press as by the public. It was not till he was sixty that Corot began to capture the attention of the critics and collectors.

The one great compensation that Corot possessed during these years was the affection of a number of his brother artists, who both admired the artist and loved the man. Corot possessed a sunny, tender, tranquil nature that endeared him to all who came in contact with him. He was never embittered by his want of success, but lived the life of a peasant, happy in his art. " Le Père Corot " became the beloved patriarch of a colony of artists who had settled in the little village of Barbizon in the forest of Fontainebleau, a spot attractive to artists by the richness and variety of its sylvan scenery and at the same time reasonably near to the exhibition centre, Paris. In this district Corot painted the most famous pictures of his later days, *e.g.* " The Pool " and " Souvenir of Mortefontaine." He particularly delighted in the poetic effects of early morning and approaching eve, " when all Nature sings in tune," and during the glare of the noonday sun he would retire indoors, for effects of brilliant sunshine did not make the same appeal to him. He preferred the minor to the major chords of Nature's colouring, and was the supreme interpreter of her moods of wistfulness, mystery, and reverie.

Though the dreamy poetical beauty of Corot's later landscapes, with their willowy trees and mysterious atmosphere, made an unprecedented appeal to American and British collectors towards the end of the nineteenth century, so that extravagant prices were paid for typical examples—in one year more so-called " Corots " were said to have been imported into the United States than Corot himself could ever have painted—it is only in comparatively

" SPRING," BY COROT

This delightful picture of a young girl gathering flowers shows the power of Corot in interpreting
moods of wistfulness and reverie, whether in Nature or human beings.

535

W. F. Mansell.

"SOUVENIR OF MORTEFONTAINE," BY COROT

The Louvre, Paris

One of Corot's most famous masterpieces, this picture is an example both of his poetic feeling and of his adherence to classic methods of composition. Note how the picture is divided diagonally into two triangles of light and shade, an arrangement which contributes to the feeling of repose which the painting inspires.

recent years that the supreme excellence of Corot's early works and figure-paintings have become recognised.

More immediately successful than Corot was his friend Jules Dupré (1812–89), whom Corot called " The Beethoven of Landscape." Dupré was the son of a porcelain manufacturer at Nantes and, like several other distinguished artists of the time, began his career by painting on china. He was one of the pioneers of " natural " landscape in France, turning away from the medley of the classical painters to render with fresh observation and expressive detail the characteristic beauties of rural France, her pastures, forests, and villages.

One of the most vigorous and famous of the Barbizon School, Théodore Rousseau (1812–67) was born in the same year as Dupré and, like him, was an enthusiastic admirer of Constable. Rousseau was the son of a Paris tailor and, though town-born, he experienced the fascination of the forest in his early boyhood, when he stayed with an uncle who had sawmills near Besançon. This uncle persuaded his parents to allow Théodore to study art, and accordingly the young man was placed in a Paris studio. From his masters, mediocre painters of classic landscape, Rousseau learnt less than from Nature, and a very early picture, painted in the open air at Montmartre —then almost country—showed a remarkable mastery in rendering air, light, and the details of Nature. In 1831 his first landscape was accepted and hung in the Salon ; in 1833 he began his studies in the Forest of Fontaine-bleau, and again exhibited with credit ; and in 1834 his picture of " A Cutting in the Forest of Compiègne " was awarded a medal, and was bought by the young Duke of Orleans. This early success, far from bringing him fortune, proved disastrous, for the older landscape painters, jealous of his growing reputation and his power, cruelly determined henceforward to exclude his work from the Salon. Accordingly in 1836 his magnificent " Descente des Vaches "—a great picture of herds of cattle coming down in autumn from the high pastures of the Jura—was rejected by the Salon. The picture is now one of the chief treasures of the Mesdag Museum in The Hague.

For fourteen years the work of Rousseau was excluded from the Salons ; as a result of this attack Rousseau in 1837 left Paris for Barbizon, where he was joined by other independent painters. After the Revolution of 1848 the work of Rousseau began to be known and appreciated, but though his pictures now began to sell and he was awarded a first medal in 1849 and the Legion of Honour in 1852, he made no change in his life and continued at Barbizon till his death in 1867.

Corot, with characteristic modesty, once said : " Rousseau is an eagle ; as for me, I am only a lark who utters little cries among the grey clouds." There was indeed a great difference between the two men, for Rousseau did not look at Nature with the dreamy gaze of a poet, but with the fiery glance

"THE OAKS," BY THÉODORE ROUSSEAU (1812–67)

The Louvre, Paris

The most vigorous of the Barbizon School, Rousseau, as we may see in this picture, delighted in the infinite variety of Nature and while strongly characterising her details, yet contrived to preserve her breadth and majesty.

Braun.

"ON THE BANKS OF THE OISE," BY DAUBIGNY (1817–78)

A characteristic example of the peaceful river scenes which this artist painted with tender fidelity and poetic feeling.

539

of a scientist who would wrest all her secrets from her. He delighted in the infinite details of Nature, and while preserving her breadth and majesty, he delicately differentiated between plants and weeds, mosses and lichens, brushwood and shrubs. Nothing was too great for his soaring imagination, nothing too small for his earnest attention. His vigorous rendering of form and his searching characterisation of Nature may be seen in " The Oaks."

Friendship and admiration for Rousseau had a great effect on the life of Virgilio Narcisse Diaz de la Pena (1808–76), commonly known as Diaz. This painter was born at Bordeaux, whither his father, a political refugee, had fled from Spain, and after his death, which occurred soon afterwards, Mme. Diaz removed to Sèvres, where she supported her young family by giving lessons in Spanish and Italian. When he was fifteen years old he was apprenticed to learn china painting, but he soon tired of working at the factory, and spent all his spare time in painting romantic Eastern scenes from his imagination. About 1830, while still earning his living by painting on porcelain, Diaz met Rousseau in Paris, and this acquaintance ripened into a lifelong friendship. Taught by Rousseau how to use pure and brilliant colours so that his pictures glowed like jewels, the pictures of Diaz appealed to the public by their subjects and were soon sought after. At first Diaz painted nymphs and bathers, mythological subjects and Oriental scenes, the last so brilliant in colour that it is difficult to believe Diaz never saw the Orient and never travelled farther than a few hundred miles from Paris.

Though he had little to complain about on his own account, Diaz shared the fortunes of his friend Rousseau, and accompanied him to Barbizon in 1837. There he gave his mind almost entirely to landscape, and made a new reputation by his brilliant forest pictures with light glancing on the tree stems.

Like Diaz and Dupré, the famous cattle painter Troyon (1810–65) began as a painter on porcelain. His father, who had been employed at the Sèvres Porcelain Factory, died early, and Troyon and his brother, while quite young boys, earned a living by painting on china at the manufactory, and in their spare time sketched from Nature in the surrounding country. It was not till he was thirty-two that Constant Troyon was able to leave Sèvres and commence his studies in Paris, and for some years his progress was hampered by the somewhat niggling style of painting he had acquired from the habit of decorating porcelain ; but devoting himself especially to the painting of animals he gradually acquired strength and breadth, though he was nearly forty before he gained the power that has since made him famous. When he did find himself, however, the success of Troyon was immediate. He was speedily recognised by his contemporaries as the greatest animal painter since Cuyp and Paul Potter, and the demand for his work was so great that Troyon sometimes employed other painters to put in

"OXEN GOING TO WORK," BY TROYON (1810–65)

The Louvre, Paris

The masterpiece of the most celebrated painter of cattle in the nineteenth century, this picture is remarkable not only for the lifelike rendering of the beasts but also for its brilliant expression of the full glory of a summer morning.

backgrounds and accessories. Troyon excelled in showing living beasts in their natural surroundings, and the landscapes in his cattle pictures are not mere " back-cloths " but genuine studies which interpret with sincerity the weather, the time of day, and the season of the year. His most famous masterpiece is his great painting " Oxen going to Work " in the Louvre, in which the superb rendering of the animals is equalled by the splendour with which the artist has rendered the full glory of the early morning landscape.

Though much influenced by Corot, who regarded him almost as a son, Charles François Daubigny (1817–78) evolved another distinct type of landscape and excelled in his poetic renderings of placid river scenes. His father was a journeyman painter of mediocre ability, and as a boy Daubigny painted decorations on clock-cases, glove-boxes, fans, and other articles of luxury. When he was seventeen he and a friend saved up a little over fifty pounds with which they set out on foot for Italy, and there maintained themselves for nearly a year. Returning to Paris, Daubigny gave himself for a time to figure subjects, but about 1840 he turned definitely to landscape, which he discovered to be his true vocation. His favourite sketching-ground was near Valmondois on the Oise, where he had spent happy days in his childhood. Though his landscapes were exhibited regularly in the Salon from 1841 to 1847, Daubigny had a hard struggle during these years, but in 1848 he received a second medal for his five landscapes in the Salon, and thereafter the State began to buy his pictures for provincial museums and his sales generally improved.

" On the Banks of the Oise " is a beautiful and characteristic example of the art of Daubigny, and reveals that exquisite calm and repose which is a feature of many of his paintings, though occasionally he painted stormy scenes ; for Daubigny was not limited in his subjects, but painted various aspects of Nature. He was one of the pioneers in the truer rendering of Nature's own colouring, and his famous saying, " We never paint light enough," became a watchword to the younger generation of artists.

§ 3

The great struggle for liberty and truth in art, begun by the Romantics and landscape painters already mentioned, was carried a stage further by Jean François Millet (1814–75), who was the first to paint the peasant, not as a sort of " stage property " in a landscape, but as he truly lived and moved. Millet came of peasant stock, and during his boyhood worked hard in the fields with his father, whose home was in the hamlet of Gruchy, near Cherbourg. When he was eighteen, his father, recognising the lad's talent, allowed him to study art in Cherbourg, but as the eldest son he returned to manage the farm on his father's death in 1835. His heart, however, was

"THE SOWER," BY MILLET (1814–75)

This world-famous figure is a noble expression of Millet's feeling for the dignity of labour, and can also be regarded as a universal symbol of the Present sowing the Future.

still in his art, and seeing this his mother and grandmother heroically determined not to allow him to sacrifice himself, but soon persuaded him to return to Cherbourg. There his talent was recognised by the Municipality, who gave him a grant of forty pounds, and with this he went to Paris in 1836 and entered the studio of the historical painter Paul Delaroche (1797–1856). During the next twelve years, spent partly in Paris and partly in Normandy, Millet experienced nothing but trouble, distress, and discouragement. Though always in poverty, he married in 1841, and his wife died in 1844 ; at the end of 1845 he married again, and found a devoted and courageous helpmate in his second wife.

At this period of his life Millet chiefly painted portraits and small pictures of classical or mythological subjects, and already his colour—in which he was considerably influenced by Correggio—began to attract attention and the admiration of other artists. He became friendly with Diaz, and through Diaz got to know Rousseau and others. In 1847 his picture " Œdipus taken from the Tree " was favourably noticed in the Salon by Théophile Gautier, who prophesied that the painter would become famous, and in the following year Millet's picture of a peasant woman was given a place of honour in the best room at the Salon. It looked as if the painter was on the point of achieving a popular success, for he had also been finding a ready sale for small pictures of nude figures, which he painted with great skill. But about this time he accidentally overheard somebody speaking of him as " Millet, who paints nothing but naked women," and this chance remark so upset him that he then and there determined never again to paint the nude. Already town life and town manners were distasteful to him ; he longed for country air to breathe and the peasant people whom he knew and loved to paint.

In 1849 he decided to change his manner of life, and with his wife and babies he removed to Barbizon, where Rousseau and Diaz were already settled. In this peaceful village Millet made his home, and found his true vocation in chronicling in a series of noble paintings the dignity of peasant labour. To the Salon of 1850 he sent his unforgettable picture of " The Sower," a work of epic grandeur which seems to symbolise the Present preparing the Future in the guise of an agricultural labourer fulfilling his common task. During the next ten years Millet painted some of his greatest pictures, " The Gleaners " in 1857, " The Angelus " in 1859, but all this time Millet was harassed by money difficulties, and with a growing and increasing family he had a hard struggle for mere existence. His new pictures were not popular ; not only did they fail to find purchasers, but they were often attacked because many of them were thought to be " socialistic," and " The Gleaners " was particularly abused on its first appearance as a work expressing subversive political principles. Millet and his family might have starved at this time, but for the good deeds stealthily don by his more

"THE GLEANERS," BY MILLET

The Louvre, Paris

This master of democratic art painted the common life of the peasant in the field with a depth of feeling, sympathy, and understanding that had never previously been approached. There is epic grandeur in the figures of these three women, whose sturdy forms are contrasted with the still beauty of the sunlit landscape.

fortunate comrades. In 1855 Rousseau secretly bought one of his pictures for £160, and Troyon also bought several of Millet's works, pretending that he was acting for an American collector who had no real existence. By this tactful generosity Millet was prevented from ever knowing how much he owed to the devotion of his friends.

It was not till the Great Exhibition at Paris in 1867 that Millet came into his own, and his opportunity came then because his friend Théodore Rousseau was President of the Jury. In this exhibition Millet was represented by " The Angelus," " The Gleaners," and seven other important paintings. He was awarded a first-class medal for the collection, and in the following year was made a Chevalier of the Legion of Honour. He was now at the height of his fame, but the honours and fortune which followed came too late to be enjoyed. The artist was deeply smitten by the death of Rousseau in December 1867, and his own health began to fail in 1870. During the disastrous Franco-Prussian war he retired to Cherbourg, where his work was interrupted by frequent illnesses. When he returned to Paris, the new Republican Government gave Millet a commission in 1874 to paint a set of decorative panels of " The Four Seasons " for the Panthéon, but though he at once began charcoal sketches for these subjects he was never able to execute the paintings. Throughout the autumn his health declined, and surrounded by his devoted family he died on January 20, 1875.

Closely associated with Millet, whom he accompanied to Barbizon, was Charles Jacque (1813–94), who, though less powerful than Troyon, was one of the best animal painters of his time. He excelled in painting flocks of sheep in the open or on the edge of a forest. The painting of peasant life, inaugurated by Millet, was continued by Bastien Lepage (1848–84) and the still more popular Jules Breton (1827–1906), who, though weaker in drawing and less rich in colour, reaped where Millet had sown. Associated with Diaz, and still more fantastic than this painter in the exotic pictures of his earlier years, was Adolphe Monticelli (1824–86). Born at Marseilles, Monticelli brought the warmth of southern colouring and imagination to Barbizon : he was the most romantic of the romantic landscape painters, and his canvasses, loaded with rich pigment, from which radiant fairy-like figures emerge and seem to quiver with life, are magical masterpieces of jewel-like colour.

Belonging to a slightly later generation, but encouraged in his youth by Corot, Daubigny, and Millet, the exquisite sea painter Eugène Boudin (1825–1898) is a link between the Barbizon School and the Impressionists. Boudin was born at Honfleur, where his father was a sea-captain, and during his early years he assisted Troyon by painting the skies in some of his pictures. This was a department of painting in which Boudin excelled, and his rendering of the clouds and the blue vault of heaven excited the keen admiration

W. F. Mansell.

"THE HARBOUR OF TROUVILLE," BY BOUDIN (1825–98)

National Gallery, London

A link between the Barbizon School and the Impressionists, Boudin excelled in rendering the pearly tints of clear grey days. His marine paintings are pitched in a higher key of colour than that usually employed by the Barbizon painters.

of Corot, who hailed his young contemporary as " the monarch of the sky."
Boudin spent the greater part of his life in the neighbourhood of his birthplace, and never tired of painting the shipping, shores, and harbour scenes
of this part of the Normandy coast. His paintings are pitched in a slightly
higher key of colour than those of Corot and Daubigny, and the prevalence
of luminous pearly greys in his work have caused his paintings—together
with similar paintings of similar subjects by his slightly older contemporary,
the Dutchman Bartholde Jongkind—to be known as *la peinture gris, i.e.* the
" grey " school of painting. " The Harbour of Trouville " in the National
Gallery is a beautiful example of Boudin's delicate realism and of his sensitive
feeling for the wind in the sky and the light on the water.

XXIX

REALISM AND IMPRESSIONISM IN FRANCE

THE ART OF COURBET, MANET, DEGAS, RENOIR, AND MONET

§ I

THE French Impressionists were the offspring of the Realists, and to trace their artistic pedigree we must return to painting in France in the middle of the nineteenth century. It was shown in Chapter XXVIII how the Romantics had rebelled against a false Classicism, but only the barest hint was given of how the struggle for liberty and truth in art reached a further stage in the 'forties by the development of a new group of artists known as the Realists. The leader of this movement and the man who perhaps did more than any other to change the whole modern outlook on art was Gustave Courbet (1819–77).

Courbet was the son of a wealthy farmer of Ornans in the Doubs. His father intended him for the law, and with this object sent him to Paris. Arrived there, Courbet threw law to the winds and set about learning the one thing that interested him, painting. A rigid republican, both by education and inclination, Courbet was penetrated by a passionate sympathy for the working classes, and he found the subjects for his pictures in the ordinary life of the people. Further, holding tenaciously that painting, " an art of sight," ought to concern itself with things seen, he was as opposed to Romanticism as the Romantics had been, in their day, to Classicism. Intensely earnest and serious by nature, Courbet regarded it as mere frivolity to make pictures out of imaginary incidents in poems and romances when all the pageant and pathos of real life waited to be painted. His point of view is made clear by a reply he once made to a patron who desired that he should execute a painting with angels in it for a church. " Angels ! " said Courbet, " but I have never seen angels. What I have not seen I cannot paint."

After the Revolution of 1848 Courbet's new style of democratic painting had a temporary success. In 1849, before the political reaction had begun, he was awarded a medal at the Salon for his picture, " After Dinner at Ornans." This medal placed him *hors concours*, that is to say it gave him the right of showing pictures in future Salons without his works having to obtain the approval of the Selecting Jury. Courbet took full advantage of this privilege in the following year, and to the Salon of 1850, in addition to two landscapes and four portraits, he sent two large pictures entitled " The Stone-breakers " and " A Funeral at Ornans." The political reaction was in full tide, and the two last pictures raised a storm of fury, because their subjects were supposed to be " dangerously social- istic." It will be remembered that it was in the Salon of the same year that J. F. Millet showed his first great democratic painting, " The Sower."

" A Funeral at Ornans " became one of the milestones in the progress of modern painting, for, notwithstanding the abuse showered on Courbet, the sincerity of his work appealed to a younger generation of artists. Here was a man who saw life steadily as a whole, and painted life just as he saw it. Each figure in it, from the clergy to the mourners, from the grave- digger to the dog, is painted simply but with a truth and power that make it a living thing. Courbet was the first of modern painters to break away from the classic traditions of Italy and turn towards the open-air realism of Velazquez and Frans Hals. He not only had much direct influence on Whistler and on Manet, but pointed out to them the road along which they should travel.

In 1855 Courbet painted a picture which summed up his life of the past seven years. He called it " The Studio of the Painter : a Real Allegory." On the right of this large canvas were the types he had been painting, the beggar, the labourer, the tradesman, the priest, the poacher, the gravedigger ; on the left was a group of his personal friends, among them Baudelaire and Proudhon ; between the groups was Courbet himself painting a landscape of Ornans.

In an introduction to the catalogue of a private exhibition of his works held in the same year, Courbet explained his endeavour to replace the cult of the ideal by a sentiment of the real :

To translate the manners, the ideas, and the aspect of my own times according to my perception, to be not only a painter but still more a man—in a word, to create a living art, that is my aim.

During the reign of Napoleon III Courbet became more and more incensed against all authorities, political or artistic. The former thought him revolutionary because of his subjects, the latter because his style was based on Dutch and Spanish painting instead of on the accepted Italian masters. Nevertheless, his position as leader of the Realist school was such that in 1870 he was nominated Chevalier of the Legion of Honour. Courbet wrote a violent letter to the Ministry refusing to accept this decoration, and when the Commune broke out in 1871 he took a prominent part in the Revolution and became President of the Commission of Fine Arts. Courbet has been much blamed because during his brief presidency

"A FUNERAL AT ORNANS," BY GUSTAVE COURBET (1819–77)

The Louvre, Paris

In this great picture of a country funeral, every figure from the clergy to the mourners, from the kneeling gravedigger to the dog is painted simply and sincerely with a truth and power that gives it life and individuality. Courbet was the founder of modern realistic painting, seeking character rather than formal beauty, and painting real incidents in ordinary life which he had seen with his own eyes.

he allowed to be pulled down the Column commemorating Napoleon I in the Place Vendôme. This was part of a scheme to efface from Paris all traces of the Empire, whether First or Third, and though the Column was a historic monument it had no great artistic interest. On the other hand it was Courbet who, during the fury of the Commune, not only preserved intact the art treasures of the Louvre, but with difficulty secured the safety of the Arc de Triomphe. He was full of concern for this monument because of its great artistic qualities, notably the sculpture by Rude with which it was decorated, and he managed to persuade those who urged its demolition that the Arc de Triomphe ought to be spared because it stood not so much for the glory of Napoleon as for the heroism of the revolutionary armies of France.

Still, when the Commune had been suppressed with an iron hand, the good deeds of Courbet during the insurrection were forgotten : the unfortunate artist was arrested in connection with the demolition of the Vendôme Column, condemned to six months' imprisonment and to defray the whole cost—some 400,000 francs—of the reconstruction of the Column. This utterly ruined him, and though Courbet eventually succeeded in crossing the frontier he was broken in health and spirits. He died in exile in 1877.

§ 2

Manet was the heir of Courbet with this difference, that the temper of his art was more aristocratic. He also built up his pictures by the direct application of planes of colour rather than by working up an underpainting based on linear design and light-and-shade ; he also used the blonde palette of Velazquez and Hals, and he also chose his subjects from the life around him ; but he painted the people and life of the middle-classes, while Courbet had concentrated on the proletariat.

Edouard Manet was born at Paris in 1833. His father was a magistrate and, like Courbet, Manet was originally destined for the bar, but he eventually overcame family opposition, and when he was about eighteen he was permitted to enter the studio of Couture (1815–79). Thomas Couture was an accomplished artist whose rich coloured paintings were a discreet compromise between Romanticism and Classicism, but his orthodox instruction appealed little to Manet, who from the beginning desired to observe Nature closely and reproduce it according to his own feeling. After travelling in Germany, Austria, and Italy to study the Old Masters, Manet finally found in the paintings by Velazquez and Goya at the Louvre the answer to all his questionings and aspirations for light and truth. Influenced by these masters and by the example of Courbet, he gradually evolved a new technique which presented modern aspects by modern methods. Observing how one colour melted into another in Nature, he declared " There are no lines in Nature," and in his pictures he abandoned the convention of the outline and shaped his forms by a modelling obtained by subtle gradations of tints which fused into one another. The problem of just illumination was to Manet a matter of primary importance. Once when he was asked to point out the principal figure in a group he had painted, he made a reply that has become historic. " The principal person in a picture," said Manet, " is the light."

Manet made his first appearance at the Salon in 1861 with a portrait of himself and his young wife, and another painting, " The Spanish Guitar-player." Over both the cry of " Realism " was raised, and Realism was unpopular at the moment; nevertheless the Jury, inspired by Delacroix, gave Manet an Honourable Mention. But during the next two years the partisans of the classical tradition obtained the upper hand again, and Manet was excluded from the Salon of 1863. As we have recorded, so many artists of admitted talent had their works rejected *en bloc* by the Salon jury this year, that the Emperor Napoleon III, inspired by a praiseworthy liberal thought, insisted that these innovators should at least have the right to exhibit together in a special room. Thus there came into being what was known as the *Salon des Refusés* : among the exhibitors there, in addition to Manet and Whistler, were Alphonse Legros, Fantin Latour (1836–1904), celebrated both as a portraitist and as a painter of flowers, Harpignies, Renoir, Claude Monet, and many others who have since become famous. One of the paintings in this exhibition, a sunset by Claude Monet, entitled " Impressions," excited much laughter among the crowd that came to jeer at the " rejected," and henceforward the custom arose of alluding to the new school of painters as " Impressionists." Originating as a term of derision, the word remained in use, and the painters to whom it was applied adopted it as an official label which would serve, as well as any other, to cover their varied aims.

Prior to the *Salon des Refusés* Edouard Manet had little or no knowledge of Claude Monet, who was seven years his junior, but now the similarity between their names and the abuse showered upon both drew the two men together. Through Monet, Manet came to know Renoir and Sisley, who had been fellow-students with Monet in the studio of Gleyre, Whistler's master ; and this group was joined, among others, by two older artists, Camille Pissarro and Degas. As in the case of the Pre-Raphaelites, it was friendship and unjust derision which created the solidarity of the Impressionists, though the individual painters had by no means identical aims. Manet, we now realise, was far more a Realist than an Impressionist, and it is important to remember that he passed as an innovator years before Impressionism existed or was even thought of. It was more than ten years

s*

after the *Salon des Refusés* before Manet became influenced by the new ideas of colour evolved by Pissarro, Monet, and Renoir. In his fine portrait " Le Bon Bock," painted in 1873, Manet still reveals himself as the heir, not only of Courbet, but of Velazquez, Hals, and Goya. Nothing could be further from the once popular notion of an " Impressionist " picture as a daub hastily put together, than this careful, if unconventional, portrait of his friend the engraver Belot enjoying a glass of beer. M. Belot gave Manet no less than eighty sittings before this portrait was finished. It is freer than Courbet, with a greater simplifying of planes and values, but it is no revolution, it is a continuation and development of Courbet's realism.

Quite different in style is " A Bar at the Folies-Bergère," painted in 1882. We may say at once that the chief difference between the two pictures is in the colour, for—to borrow a term from the wine-list—the colour in " Le Bon Bock " is " still," while that in the " Bar " picture is " sparkling," sparkling especially in the wonderful painting of the bottles and glasses as we may see even in a photograph. Both pictures are magnificent, both are marvellously lifelike, but in the second there is a more searching pursuit of colour, in shadow as well as in light, and a more vivacious statement of its actuality. In a word, it is a typical " Impressionist " picture : and here we may well pause to inquire what is meant by " Impressionism."

§ 3

If we look at all the bottles in " A Bar at the Folies-Bergère " we shall notice that the treatment of detail here is totally different from the treatment of detail, say, in Millais's " Ophelia " (cf. page 477). In his picture Millais looked at each leaf, flower, and branch separately, and set them down separately on his canvas like a sum in addition. But all the bottles in Manet's picture are seen simultaneously in relation to each other : it is a synthesis, not an addition. Impressionism, then, in the first place, is the result of *simultaneous vision* that sees a scene as a whole as opposed to *consecutive vision* that sees Nature piece by piece. Let us suppose, for a moment, that we are staying at a house on the banks of the Seine opposite the church at Vernon. Let us suppose that, having arrived there in darkness the previous evening, we jump out of bed in the morning, open the window, and put out our head to see the view. Monet's picture " The Church at Vernon " shows us what we should see *at the first glance* ; the glance, that is to say, when we see the scene as a whole, before any detail in it has riveted our attention and caused us unconsciously to alter the focus of our eye in order to see that detail more sharply. Another way of putting the matter is to say that in an Impressionist picture there is only one focus

"A BAR AT THE FOLIES-BERGÈRE," BY MANET (1832–83)

Painted the year before he died, this picture of a bar in a popular Parisian music-hall shows the final style of an artist who said, "The principal person in a picture is the light." Though crowded with glittering details all sparkling with reflected light, the picture is a true impression of a scene viewed "steadily and as a whole."

"THE CHURCH AT VERNON," BY MONET (1840–1927)

A typical landscape by this famous Impressionist showing his immediate concern with a fugitive effect of light. All details in the landscape are subordinated to the illumination which falls upon them. Even deprived of their magical colour, the reflections in the water show the vibration of light, the sense of movement and life, obtained by Monet's method of painting with broken touches.

throughout, while in a Pre-Raphaelite picture there is a different focus for every detail. These two methods of painting represent different ways of looking at the world, and neither way is wrong, only whereas the Pre-Raphaelite looks *particularly* at a series of objects, the Impressionist looks *generally* at the whole.

This way of viewing a scene broadly, however, is only a part of Impressionism. It was not a new invention, for Velazquez saw and painted figures and groups in a similar way, therefore Impressionists like Whistler and Manet (in his earlier works), who adopted this broad style, were in this respect developing an existing tradition rather than inventing a new one. But a later development of Impressionism, which was a complete innovation, was the new palette they adopted. From the time of Daubigny, who said, " We never paint light enough," the more progressive painters had striven to make the colours in their pictures closer to the actual hues of Nature. Delacroix was one of the pioneers in the analysis of colour. When he was in Morocco he wrote in his Journal about the shadows he had seen on the faces of two peasant boys, remarking that while a sallow, yellow-faced boy had *violet* shadows, a red-faced boy had *green* shadows. Again, in the streets of Paris, Delacroix noticed a black and yellow cab, and observed that, beside the greenish-yellow, the black took on a tinge of the complementary colour, violet. An advertisement issued by a well-known soap firm will have made many readers familiar with the phenomenon of complementary colour. The name of the soap was printed in bright red letters on a white paper, and we were asked, after gazing at this steadfastly for a few moments, to look up at a white ceiling, when we should see the name of the soap in *green* letters. Every colour has its complementary, that is to say, an opposing colour is evoked by the action of the human eye after we have been gazing at the said colour ; consequently all colours act and react on one another. Delacroix discovered that to obtain the full brilliance of any given hue it should be flanked and supported by its complementary colour. He did not attain to full knowledge ; it was left for a later generation to make nicer distinctions and to recognise that if violet is the right complementary for a greenish-yellow, an orange-yellow requires a turquoise blue, and so on.

The nineteenth was a scientific century during which great additions were made to our knowledge of optics. The French scientist Chevreuil wrote a learned book on colour, which was studied with avidity by the younger painters. It became clear to them that colour was not a simple but a very complex matter. For example, we say that grass is green, and green is the *local colour* of grass, that is to say, the colour of grass at close range, when we look down on it at our feet. But grass-covered hills seen at a great distance do not appear green, but *blue*. The green of their local colour is affected by the veil of atmosphere through which we view it in the distance, and the blue we see is an example of *atmospheric colour*. Again, the local colour of snow is white, but everybody who has been to Switzerland is familiar with the " Alpine glow " when the snow-clad peaks of the mountains appear a bright copper colour owing to the rays of the setting sun. This " Alpine glow " is an example of *illumination colour*, and since the colour of sunlight is changing throughout the day, everything in Nature is affected by the colour of the light which falls upon it.

The landscape painter, then, who wishes to reproduce the actual hues of Nature, has to consider not only " local colour," but also " atmospheric colour " and " illumination colour," and further take into consideration " complementary colours." One of the most important discoveries made by the later Impressionist painters was that *in the shadows there always appears the complementary colour of the light*. We should ponder on all these things if we wish to realise the full significance of Manet's saying, " The principal person in a picture is the light."

This new intensive study of colour brought about a new palette and a new technique. For centuries all painting had been based on three primary colours, red, blue, and yellow ; but science now taught the painters that though these might be primary colours in *pigment*, they were not primary colours in *light*. The spectroscope and the new science of spectrum-analysis made them familiar with the fact that white light is composed of all the colours of the rainbow, which is the spectrum of sunlight. They learnt that the primary colours of light were green, orange-red, and blue-violet, and that yellow—though a primary in paint—was a secondary in light, because a yellow light can be produced by blending a green light with an orange-red light. On the other hand green, a secondary in paint because it can be produced by mixing yellow with blue pigment, is a primary in light. These discoveries revolutionised their ideas about colour, and the Impressionist painters concluded they could only hope to paint the true colour of sunlight by employing pigments which matched the colours of which sunlight was composed, that is to say, the tints of the rainbow. They discarded black altogether, for, modified by atmosphere and light, they held that a true black did not exist in Nature : the darkest colour was indigo, dark green, or a deep violet. They would not use a brown, but set their palettes with indigo, blue-green, yellow, orange, red, and violet, the nearest colours they could obtain to the seven of the solar spectrum.

Further, they used these colours with as little mixing as possible. Every amateur in water-colour knows that the more he mixes his paints, the more they lose in brilliancy. The same is true of oil paints. The Impressionists refrained, therefore, as much as possible from mixing colours on

"LE BON BOCK," BY MANET

A splendid example of the realistic portraiture of the artist's middle period. It presents M. Belot, an engraver, who gave his friend eighty sittings before this lifelike picture was completed. Bock is the common term in France for a glass of beer; hence the title may be rendered in English as "A Good Drink."

their palettes, and applied them pure in minute touches to the canvas. If they wanted to render secondary or tertiary colours, instead of mixing two or three pigments on the palette, they would secure the desired effect by juxtaposed touches of pure colours which, at a certain distance, fused in the eye of the beholder and produced the effect of the tint desired. This device is known as *optical mixture*, because the mixing is done in the spectator's eye. Thus, whereas red and green pigment mixed on a palette will give a dull grey, the Impressionists produced a brilliant luminous grey by speckling a sky, say, with little points of yellow and mauve which at a distance gave the effect of a pearly grey. Similarly the effect of a brilliant brown was given by the juxtaposition of a series of minute touches of green, red, and yellow ; and this association of minute touches of three pure colours set up a quivering vibration which had greater luminosity than any streak of brown pigment. It was an endeavour to use paints as if they were coloured lights.

Various names have been given to this technique. It has been called " Divisionism," because by it the secondary and tertiary colours were divided into their constituent elements. It has been called " Pointillism," because the colour was applied to the canvas in points instead of in sweeping brush-strokes. It has been called " Luminism," because the aim of the process is primarily to express the colour of light with all its sparkle and vibration. This last is the best name of all, because it serves to emphasise the new outlook of the new painters. The tendency before the Impressionists was to regard colour from the standpoint of black and white. Thus, in considering a grey, it would have been asked is it a dark grey or a light grey, does it approach black or white ? The Impressionists took quite a different attitude and asked whether it were a bluish grey, or a greenish grey, or a purplish grey, or a reddish grey : in a word, not whether it were light or dark, but to which colour in the solar spectrum it most closely approached.

To the Impressionists shadow was not an absence of light, but light of a different quality and of different value. In their exhaustive research into the true colours of shadows in Nature, they conquered the last unknown territory in the domain of Realist Painting.

To sum up, then, it may be said that Impressionist Painting is based on two great principles :

1. *The substitution of a Simultaneous Vision that sees a scene as a whole in place of a Consecutive Vision that sees Nature piece by piece.*

2. *The Substitution of a Chiaroscuro based on the colours of the solar spectrum for a Chiaroscuro based on Black and White.*

This new technique, with all the research and experiment which it implies, was not the invention of one man, but the outcome of the life

"THE LITTLE SERVANT," BY CAMILLE PISSARRO (1830–1930)

National Gallery, London

A typical work of Camille Pissarro, showing an obvious love of a structural pattern linked with the broken brushwork of the Impressionists. The picture was bequeathed by his son, Lucien Pissarro, to the National Gallery.

studies of a whole group of men. Most prominent among those who brought Impressionist painting to perfection in theory and practice were Camille Pissarro, Claude Monet, and Auguste Renoir.

§ 4

Camille Pissarro (1830–1930) was born at St. Thomas in the Danish West Indies and came to Paris with his parents when he was twenty-five. He became a pupil of Corot, and his earlier works show the influence of Corot as regards style and colour and of Millet in subject and drawing. He was the eldest of the Impressionists, being two years older than Manet ; but throughout his life Pissarro was an ardent student, never ceasing to investigate and experiment, always ready to listen to the theories and to observe the practice of a junior who claimed to have discovered a new truth. Though darker in colour than his later work, a small landscape now in the Musée des Arts Decoratifs at Paris, painted by Pissarro in 1869, shows that even at this time he was experimenting in the division of tones. Unfortunately nearly all the earlier paintings of Camille Pissarro are lost, for his home and studio were in the line of approach of the destroying Prussians in 1870. Owing to the war Pissarro and Monet came to London in 1871, and there they saw the later paintings of Turner, which confirmed their ideas about colour and encouraged them to paint brighter and still brighter.

Claude Monet was ten years younger than Pissarro. Though born in 1840 at Paris, where his father was a merchant, he spent much of his boyhood at Havre, where he learnt a good deal about painting from Boudin. After completing his military service in Algeria, Monet returned to Paris and entered the studio of Gleyre. Here he formed a close friendship with two fellow-students, Renoir and Sisley, and became acquainted later with Manet, as has already been related. Monet's earliest paintings, however, are not lighter than those by Boudin and Corot, and he was first influenced by these and others of the Barbizon School.

Auguste Renoir (1841–1919) was born at Limoges, where his father was a tailor in a small way of business, and at the age of thirteen young Auguste began to earn his living as a painter on porcelain. This early apprenticeship left a certain trace on his art which was always decorative and even elegiac in spite of its later realism. In time Renoir saved up enough money to go to Paris and become a pupil of Gleyre, but while his friends were landscapists Renoir was first and foremost a figure painter.

Alfred Sisley (1839–99) was born in Paris of English parents, and his development was parallel to that of Monet, whose work his own pictures closely resemble. We may say that all these young men, together with

"THE UMBRELLAS," BY RENOIR (1841–1919)

Tate Gallery, London

The strange spectacle presented by an array of umbrellas on a rainy day in a public place has here inspired the artist to give one of his most original and ingeniously designed impressions of Parisian life. Renoir excelled in rendering the actual colour of sunshine on human flesh and figures, and this picture is as true to Nature's own colouring as it is true to life in its intimate observation of human character and behaviour.

Pissarro, were discontented with the state of painting before 1870. They looked at their pictures and they looked at Nature ; but while they realised how far their painting fell short of their intention, they had not yet found the way to secure greater brilliancy and truth. That way was discovered during the 'seventies, after Pissarro and Monet had seen the Turners in London and returned to Paris. It is possible' to exaggerate the influence of Turner on the new movement, for it had really begun earlier with Delacroix, but the sight of the Turners undoubtedly hastened its accomplishment as far as Pissarro and Monet are concerned. Not the beginning of Impressionism, but the first public revelation of Impressionism, was an exhibition held at Nadar's galleries, Boulevard des Capucines, in 1874. Here were gathered together works by many of the " rejected " of 1863— Manet being the best known of them and generally considered the leader of the movement—and also works by new adherents to Impressionist doctrine. The exhibition provoked much controversy, but it was sufficiently talked about to be something of a success, and thereafter for several years a *Salon des Impressionistes* was an annual event. But in 1874 the science of colour was still in its infancy, and if the exhibitors were " Impressionists " they were not all " luminists." Even Renoir's famous picture of people in a theatre-box, painted about this time, is sombre in colour, in comparison with the scintillating canvases he was to paint later.

Another contributor to this exhibition, whose picture, " The Dancing Lesson," attracted much attention, was Degas. Friendship with Manet drew Degas into this circle, though he never entirely accepted all the principles of Impressionism. Edgar Hilaire Germain Degas (1834–1917) was born in Paris, the son of a banker, and, like Courbet and Manet, was originally destined for a legal career. In 1855, however, he entered the École des Beaux Arts, and also studied under Lamothe, a pupil of Ingres. All his life Degas, who was brought up in the classical tradition, had the deepest veneration for Ingres. He was also an admirer of Holbein and Clouet, whose pictures he copied. In 1856 he went to Rome and remained two years in Italy studying the work of the early Italian masters. Returning to Paris, he began as an historical painter, his last picture in this style being " A Scene of War in the Middle Ages," shown in the Salon of 1865. But about this time he came into contact with Manet, and through him with Pissarro, Monet, Renoir, and others who frequented the Café Guerbois in the Batignolles, and there endlessly discussed their artistic aims and ideals. Because of this centre for social intercourse the Impressionist group was at one time nicknamed " The School of Batignolles." Owing to the powerful new influences surrounding him, Degas was led to abandon his historical works and devote himself to painting scenes of modern life. Always intensely interested in the rendering of movement, Degas was

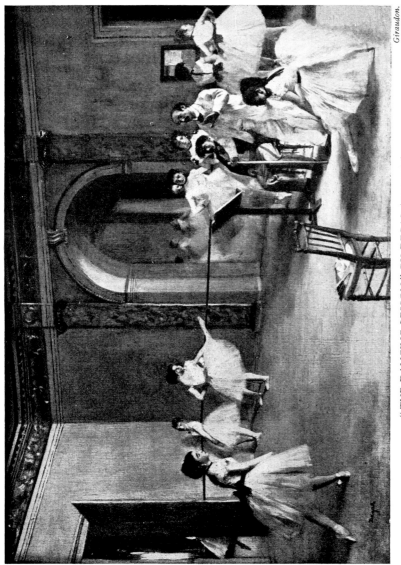

Giraudon.

"THE DANCING LESSON," BY DEGAS (1834–1917)

A passionate interest in movement and life drew Degas to the study of professional dancers, and his pictures of the Ballet are world-famous and unique. In this comparatively early work he shows us the hard realities which lie behind the fairyland of the stage. The varied attitudes of the dancers, in difficult positions, reveal his mastery of drawing, while the aerial spaciousness of the scene as a whole results from his perfect rendering of light and air first attracted to subjects he found on the racecourse, one of the earliest successes in his new manner being " A Carriage at the Races." He also painted washerwomen at their work, scenes in cafés and in theatres, and revealed himself as an artist passionately absorbed in the spectacle of city life, though with rather a cynical outlook. Degas was the greatest draughtsman among the Impressionists, and in his pictures of modern life he relied upon line more than any other of the friends with whom he exhibited. Like Whistler, he was much influenced by Japanese colour prints, which gave him new ideas of pattern and design.

After the Franco-Prussian war, during which he served in the artillery, Degas concentrated on the Ballet, a subject for which he became famous throughout the world, and which occupied his best attention for twenty years. In these works Degas stands revealed as an uncompromising Realist. What he usually shows us is not the glamour and illusion of the Ballet from the spectator's standpoint ; Degas gets behind the scenes and exposes the work and discipline which lie behind this artificial fairyland ; he strips the dancers of their tinsel, compelling us to see that they are not lovely young nymphs, but plain, tired, hard-worked women, often middle-aged. The beauty of his pictures is to be found not in any prettiness of his models, but in the lighting, the arrangement, the drawing, and later, in the colour, in the convincing truth of his vision, and in the decorative charm of his design. In the later 'seventies and thenceforward, Degas worked more frequently in pastel than in oils, and in these later pastels he adopts the prismatic hues of Luminism, based on the rainbow colours of the solar spectrum, so that these works, in addition to their masterly drawing and decorative design, have the additional beauty of shimmering, iridescent colour. A superb example of his later style is the pastel " A Dancer on the Stage " in the Luxembourg, Paris. Here, for once in a way, Degas forgets his cynicism and shows us the magical glamour of a *première danseuse* quivering with movement, bathed with light, and happy apparently in her moment of success. After 1886 Degas retired almost completely from the public eye, living the life of a recluse on a fifth floor in Montmartre ; refusing for the most part to sell his works or even to show them to collectors, though his fame continually increased and the value of his earlier works rose to sensational prices. Before his death his picture " Dancers at the Bar," which he had originally sold for £20, was bought by an American collector for £17,400, this being the record price obtained to-day at public auction for a picture by any living artist. But Degas was equally contemptuous of praise or criticism, and to the end he declined all honours.

Claude Monet, who died in 1927, had also seen pictures he sold for £4 bring thousands of pounds in America and elsewhere. Devoting himself

" A DANCER ON THE STAGE," BY DEGAS

The Luxembourg, Paris

This pastel, which gives a wonderful impression of a ballet-dancer almost floating into the brilliant light of the stage from the obscurity of the " wings," should be compared with the earlier painting by the same artist on page 565. It is miraculous in its suggestion of quivering movement.

to the painting of landscapes in bright sunlight, he carried the pitch of painting into a higher key than any artist before him had done. " Pine-Tree at Antibes " is a beautiful example of his style at its maturity ; radiant colours are laid side by side in small broken touches to suggest the vibration of light, while the decorative arrangement shows that Monet also has taken hints for design from the artists of Japan. Light is always the " principal person " in Monet's landscape, and since he always aimed at seizing a fugitive effect, he insisted on consistency of illumination at particular hours of the day and season. With this object he adopted, since the early 'eighties, a habit of painting the same subject under different conditions of light. He would set out early in the morning with a carriage-load of canvases, and arriving at his destination he would start his day's work, changing his canvas every couple of hours as the light changed. In this way he painted a series of views, all of the same subject, but all different in colour and lighting. Among the most famous of these series are those known as " Haystacks," " The Poplars," " The Thames at Waterloo Bridge," " Rouen Cathedral," and " Water-lilies," the last being a scene in his own riverside garden at Giverny. When he was a young man Monet once said, " I want to paint as a bird sings," and all his pictures have this delicious lyrical quality. While he adopted the rainbow palette and the technique of the small touch—" the procedure by the touch " as it is called in France—Monet was never dogmatic in his use of divisionism.

The elaboration of Divisionism into a rigid scientific theory of painting was the work principally of two younger men, Georges Seurat (1859–91) and the living artist Paul Signac, born at Paris in 1863. But for his early death Seurat, who was a genius in design as well as a great colourist, would have obtained a foremost place in modern art. It was Seurat about 1880 who definitely established the superiority, for the purposes of brilliance and intensity, of " optical blending " to actual blending on the palette. The division of colour, which was never more than a convenience to painters like Monet and Sisley, became a law not to be departed from in the work of Seurat and Signac. This new scientific development of Impressionism became known as " neo-Impressionism." For a time Pissarro also practised this method of Divisionism with scrupulous exactness, but eventually he adopted a broader and freer manner, though still retaining the general principle of divided colour. In addition to Seurat and Signac, the chief exponents of neo-Impressionism have been Henri-Edmond Cross (1856–1910) and the Belgian painter, Théo van Rysselberg. This method of painting and the scientific theories on which it is based are fully described in M. Paul Signac's book *D'Eugène Delacroix au Néo-Impressionisme* (Paris, 1898).

Courtauld.

"PINE-TREE AT ANTIBES," BY MONET

This view from a promontory on the Riviera is a beautiful example of true impressionist or "luminist" painting in which the artist uses the radiant hues of the rainbow to get the actual colours of sunshine and small "broken touches" of paint to suggest the vibration of light. Note how full of colour are the shadows, also the decorative balance of the composition, which betrays a hint of Japanese influence.

Copyright.

"LA BAIGNADE," BY GEORGES SEURAT (1859-91)

Tate Gallery, London

Seurat, feeling that the broken colour of Impressionism lost the form, attempted to regain this while keeping the brilliant effects of light.
In this picture of lads bathing at the river bank he has strong form and vivid flickering colour.

"VENICE, SAN GEORGIO," BY PAUL SIGNAC (b. 1863)

Signac endeavoured to counteract the looseness and loss of form in Impressionism by building up his pictures with carefully placed almost rectangular brushstrokes. By this means he hoped to bring back the outline which had been sacrificed, without losing the new brilliance of colour.

The effect of this art method of Impressionism on the art of our own day is enormous, especially upon art in England where we have taken to the idea of broken paint and bright tones. It is true to say that the vast majority of artists are now painting in the way they are because of this theory of the effect of light upon forms and colour which the French artists first put forward in the latter part of last century. Actual divisionism or *pointillism* is not so evident ; but something akin to it in broken colour, loosely put on to the canvas with more regard for the effects of light than for the basic form permeates contemporary art. As we shall see later, a reaction from this ideal, already noticed in Seurat and Signac, but becoming definite in the theories and practice of Cézanne, is equally important.

XXX

THE REVIVAL OF SCULPTURE

THE ART OF RODIN, MEŠTROVIĆ, MILLES, EPSTEIN, AND OTHERS

§ 1

DURING all these years, centuries even, since Michael Angelo had carried the art of sculpture to a supreme height in Renaissance Italy and Cellini had rounded off the period with his decorative fancy, surprisingly little had happened in this sister art. While painting flourished marvellously in seventeenth-century Spain and Holland, no important sculpture was produced in either country. When the vortex swung to England in the eighteenth century and painting in France climbed steadily to its climax, a few names appear in sculpture, but nothing comparable to the galaxy of painters. If anything were done during those centuries it was a cold imitation of the antique. Flaxman (1755–1826) in England achieved something so completely Græco-Roman that it has a merit of its own. Happily he found a niche in designing for the new Wedgwood Pottery which gave that coldly classical work a real beauty. His sculpture was a perfect expression of the Augustan spirit. Antonio Canova (1757–1822), the Italian, simultaneously worked in this classical spirit, a mood that was tremendously abroad in the world largely as the result of the writings of Winkelmann and the excavations at Herculaneum. Canova's monument to Clement XIV in Rome created a sensation unknown since the days of Michael Angelo and sent sculpture for many years along this path of Neo-classicism. Sometimes he swerves over to a sentiment which has little in common with the Greek spirit, as in his well-known " Cupid and Psyche," and often he is a noble worker, and he turned the eyes of Europe again to the possibilities of his form of art.

Thorwaldsen (1770–1844), the Dane, took up this story, and in turn produced a vast body of work in the tradition. His work can best be studied in Copenhagen where a gallery is devoted to it ; but when inspiration comes from art to art and not from life to art, the influence tends soon to slip down into decadence, and the rest of the sculptors in this vein are of little importance, until we come to Alfred Stevens, that great artist who came near to the perfection of Michael Angelo in the comparatively small amount of work which he did. Stevens worked in Thorwaldsen's

573

studio as a young man, and when he returned to England from this Italian period he applied himself to work which was in the best Renaissance tradition. There was, alas, little call for the kind of big thing he might have done and he turned to the designing of ironwork—a passion in England in the mid-nineteenth century. The Wellington Memorial in St. Paul's cathedral, the delightful lions around the railings of the British Museum, and a magnificent fireplace at Dorchester House are the outstanding works of this man who, in a more propitious time, might have created so much more.

Meantime, throughout the eighteenth and nineteenth centuries such interest as there was in sculpture was in France. From the time of Louis XIV, France had had a thin trickle of talented sculptors, but until the coming of Impressionism none of genius. Then in Auguste Rodin she produced a great world artist, one whose name might truly stand with that of Michael Angelo.

Among the earlier French sculptors Jean Baptiste Pigalle (1714–85) was a pioneer of realism, his vigorous and fertile imagination giving his work a certain amount of life and originality. Jean Antoine Houdon (1741–1828), his pupil, was famous for the power and truth of his portrait busts. The head of his " Voltaire " is probably one of the best known pieces of sculpture in the world. François Rude (1784–1855) was a still greater liberator of French sculpture from cramping classicism. His famous group " La Marseillaise " on the Arc de Triumphe, shows Rude's realism and the fervour of his expression of patriotic feeling. This passion of patriotism, allied to a flamboyance which continually overstepped the bounds of good taste, became the mark of French sculpture of the nineteenth century. It was absurdly pictorial, had little sense of form, and, indeed, none of sculptural form, which depends for its beauty on the relationship of the masses one to another.

§ 2

Into this decadence about the middle of the century came Antoine Louis Barye (1796–1875), painter and sculptor, the contemporary and friend of the Barbizon School men. Like them Barye turned to Nature, and as they looked for their truth in landscape, in field and sky and woodland, he sought the truth and beauty of form in animals. Barye held an appointment as Master of Drawing at the Paris Zoological Gardens, and he made himself a master of animal form. His lifelike work opened a new path in the art.

It was a pupil of Barye, an even greater modeller than himself, who was destined to achieve the greatest fame won by any sculptor since Michael

Angelo. Auguste Rodin (1840–1917) was of humble origin, and in his youth had to earn his living working in a mason's yard, where he became familiar with the material he was destined to master. For years his only studio was his humble bedroom, and it was here that he modelled his early bust," The Man with the Broken Nose." At first, in 1864, it was rejected by the Salon, the judges being shocked by the absence of ideal beauty in the work. When, however, it was accepted it was acknowledged to be a masterpiece of realism modelled with a power and truth unknown for many generations.

In 1877 his beautiful statue, " The Age of Bronze," was exhibited at the Salon, and the authorities were so astonished by its masterly modelling that Rodin was accused of having taken a cast from life. To prove the falsehood of this accusation the sculptor made his next statue, " St. John the Baptist," rather more than life-size, and again the modelling was miraculous in its perfection and lifelikeness. If " The Age of Bronze " with its polished rendering of the graceful form of adolescence reminds us of the best Greek sculpture, this second powerful and lifelike rendering of a mature man is comparable to the figures by the master sculptors of the Renaissance.

It has often been asked why a statue by Rodin is different from any other, and the explanation is simple : instead of copying Greek work as others had done, Rodin did as the Greeks did—he went direct to Nature. He had learned that from his master, Barye. " Everything," said Rodin, " is contained in Nature, and when the artist follows Nature, he gets everything." And again he said : " I am not at the orders of my model, but at those of Nature."

Rodin taught his contemporaries that distinction in sculpture is obtained not by selecting a certain type of figure, but by the gift of modelling the natural truth in any figure. He was essentially a modeller, with a marvellous eye for seeing form, a miraculous hand for expressing it. When, as in his earlier style, he worked realistically, he would with infinite patience recreate every twist and turn of the planes in his subject. Later, he felt that in order to present a true appearance of form it was necessary to fashion the " holes and lumps " as he called them, not exactly as they existed in anatomy, but as they appeared to the human eye when the subject was enveloped in atmosphere and bathed in light. Thus he introduced Impressionism into sculpture.

However he chose to work—realistically as in the " St. John Baptist " ; impressionistically as in the great " Balzac " ; symbolically as in " The Hand of God," a great hand holding a male and a female figure—he always makes his work seem to hover on the borders of actual living itself. It has a curious mobility, a restlessness almost. It is full of emotion, an

575

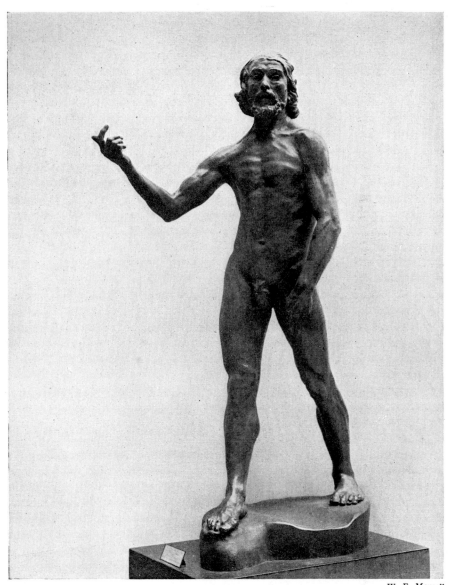

"ST. JOHN THE BAPTIST," BY RODIN (1840–1917)

Victoria and Albert Museum, London

Falsely accused of having taken a cast from life and shown it as an original statue, Rodin modelled this heroic figure larger than life to prove his ability in modelling. It was first intended to portray nothing more than " A Man Walking," but while he was working on it Octave Mirbeau told the sculptor it was an ideal St. John, and Rodin accepted the title.

emotion arising from life itself and from thought about life, and not necessarily from abstract form. This quality, less acceptable to a later generation than it was to Rodin's own, has been brought against him in criticism. It makes him essentially a dramatic sculptor.

His famous monument, "The Citizens of Calais," is remarkable thus not only for the pure beauty of its workmanship as sculpture, nor for the truth and atmosphere of this procession and its sense of movement as it winds its way slowly and sadly along, but for the poignant expression of the different characters of the various figures. These are no graveyard figures, but living men moving and breathing in the air which surrounds them. This fine work, erected at Calais, was repeated in a copy on the Victoria Embankment, London, close to the House of Lords, thanks to the generosity of English admirers of the French sculptor.

The rugged technique by which Rodin obtained his wonderful effects of atmospheric reality was long in establishing itself in public favour, yet there have been few sculptors animated by a more profound respect for the basic material of their art. It was Rodin's love of marble itself which led to a new development of his style, in which he would leave rough the matrix from which his sculpture was hewn, so that the delicate heads and figures seemed to grow like flowers out of the marble of their origin. A memorable example of this is "Thought," in which a feminine head of exquisite refinement and spirituality emerges from a rough-hewn block of marble.

Rodin reached his extreme limit of Impressionism in sculpture with his colossal statue of "Balzac," which, when exhibited in the New Salon of 1898, threw the world of art into a condition bordering on frenzy. A man who twenty years before had been declared too skilful to be genuine was now accused of not knowing the elements of his craft. Yet the sublime simplicity of this figure, loosely wrapped in a dressing-gown, with the upturned face, the lion-maned head of genius, soaring as it were to heaven, revealed Rodin at his highest not only as a master of impressionist model-ling, but also as a pyschologist who could conceive and create an unforget-table expression of the very soul of genius.

§ 3

Rodin brought this art of sculpture back into the front line of æsthetic expression. Or it may have been that the time was ripe for a renaissance of the art, and he was a product of that new spirit. Certain it is that all across Europe there was a revival of interest and almost every country produced men of fine achievement, and some gave us artists who stand in the front rank.

E. Druet.

"BALZAC," BY RODIN

The upper part of Rodin's statue of Balzac which caused a sensation in the Salon of 1898. This powerful rendering of the great novelist, loosely wrapped in his dressing-gown, shows the extreme limit of impressionism in sculpture.

From France itself came two men of exceptional merit. Emile-Antoine Bourdelle (1861–1929), though he did not achieve the profundity of his master (for he confessed the strong influence of Rodin), brought back to sculpture an element of formalism a little nearer the classic spirit. In his great " Heracles " outside the Luxembourg, or in the " The Centaur," the very subjects show where much of his inspiration and enthusiasm lay. One of his very finest works, however, " The Virgin of Alsace," a vast figure made to go on a hillside in Alsace as a war memorial, is quite different in spirit, allying the early French Gothic to certain formal qualities which one associates with such artists as the great Serbian sculptor, Meštrović.

Aristide Maillol (1861–   ) belongs more definitely to the modern movement in sculpture. Starting from discipleship to the later Rodin, he grew to think of his art much more in its creative self-containedness than simply as a means of representing Nature or presenting thought. Forms and masses—Rodin's " holes and lumps "—became the subject-matter of Maillol's art almost for their own sake. The human figure was used as a basis, but as a basis for formal design and not of pictorial representation. Details were simplified away ; actual forms were distorted or changed to yield the effect in design which he desired. Sometimes, as in " The Young Runner," Maillol would get the utter simplicity and beauty which we associate with Greek sculpture. At others—some of his Bathing Women, for example—there is a wilful and therefore a challenging distortion. Always there is a calm and self-poise about his work which corrects the tendency to restlessness in that of Rodin. As Miss Bernadette Murphy says : " Maillol's work most clearly demonstrates the reaction of the generation of sculptors immediately following Rodin to that great master's work. For whereas the emphasis with Rodin was on the intellectual and emotional content of the conception, Maillol's chief concern has been with pure plastic beauty, the noble beauty of form. Yet he has never confined himself to this alone. His many lovely nudes, the draped and undraped female figures, seated, standing, kneeling, are expressive of emotion because the sculptor's aim has been to reveal the beauty of living form."

Rodin himself, in much of his later work, was moved by the same impulse, and in following this line taken by the master, Maillol has continued his tradition and has been an enormous influence on contemporary sculpture.

§ 4

Meantime, some of the smaller European countries had produced sculptors of international importance and highly individual achievement.

Constantin Muenier (1831–1905) of Belgium used realism to express the industrial age and found his models and his subjects among the workers. Their movements as they laboured ; their clothes given significant form by the very nature of their work ; their features and hands, beautiful in their very ugliness and made dignified by toil : these things were his theme and subject. Less a pure artist than either Rodin or his disciples, Muenier said in bronze what Millet was saying in paint.

Another supreme sculptor belongs to Dalmatia. Ivan Meštrović was born in 1883. A child of peasants, he began his life as a shepherd boy, but soon he went to the little town of Spalato and there became a mason's assistant, working in the local marble from which ultimately he was to create his masterpieces. Meštrović was perhaps fortunate in that his environment gave him a theme, the theme of passionate nationalism, with its already created legends and subjects, its instant appeal to an audience, and its deep emotional content. For centuries Serbia had suffered under foreign rule, and when Meštrović was a lad the country, newly possessed of its independence, was keenly alive to its own past. Moreover, its geographical position, placing it between the classical traditions of Italy and Greece and the Byzantine East, gave to the young sculptor a confluence of artistic spirits of which he made full use. Born, too, in a country rich in marbles, Meštrović was as essentially a carver as Rodin was a modeller— that is to say, he cut back into the block of stone to create his forms instead of building them slowly up in clay and then having them cast in bronze. The effect was one of greater simplicity, less naturalism, more formalism and convention.

When in 1915, at a great exhibition at South Kensington, London first became actively aware of Meštrović, it was a new light upon sculpture. These legendary Serbian heroes, these weeping widows and immobile caryatid figures, the highly conventionalised lines of the hair and drapery, the stern classicism of the typically Serbian faces : all were new to us. In stone and in wood, in the round and in low relief, Meštrović's sculpture was a revelation. Often it was built on a series of definite planes, with the indications of form incised into these. Its archaic strength was matched by its intensely modern sense of decoration, and both by its originality— for Meštrović imitated nobody. His country's spectacular and tragic part in the 1914–18 War, gave an added link which endeared this highly nationalistic art to the western world of England, France, and America.

In 1920 he had a great opportunity when he was commissioned to build a mausoleum at Cavtat above Regusa on the Dalmatian coast for the old family of the Racić. The creation became a shrine of his art at its most splendid and typical, the formal angels bearing aloft the souls of the dead being triumphs of design and execution.

One other Dalmatian sculptor of high standing was Toma Rosandić.

" MOTHER AND CHILD (BRONZE)," BY IVAN MEŠTROVIĆ

Using typical Serbian types, and giving his work strong emotional power, Meštrović brought something new to European sculpture.

" ORPHEUS," BY CARL MILLES

Stockholm

Carl Milles's work has created a highly individual new Baroque. The forms are graceful
and fanciful, the whole conception brought into unity by the play of the water.

He was an older man than Meštrović, but worked in much the same mood, often carving in wood.

§ 5

If the renaissance of sculpture produced these men in the Near East it also had its representatives in Northern Europe and in England. Greatest of the splendid band who hail from the Scandinavian countries is Carl Milles of Sweden. Milles's work has a high imaginative quality greater probably than that of any other living sculptor. There is a sense of enormous fertility in this pronouncedly personal style and choice of subject. Baroque ? Perhaps, but with a difference, a grace of its own.

Although Milles now works in America, it is to Sweden one must go to see his work in its exuberance—statues, great fountains, architectural decorations. Stockholm is full of treasures from his hands, and near by at Lidingo is his lovely home—one of the most truly beautiful places in the world, with a terraced garden devoted to his sculpture. This exquisite place is to be given to his country at his death as a home of rest for artists. Meantime, lovers of his art have little difficulty in obtaining permission to visit it.

Some of Milles's finest work has been in connection with fountain schemes. In Sweden they seem to understand fountains, and Milles has created them in a number of towns. There is, for instance, the great fountain at Göthenburg in the centre of the Square flanked by the Concert Hall, the Theatre, and the Art Gallery. It is an amazing arrangement of sculptured groups synthesised, as Milles's fountains so rightly are, by the lines of the water thrown in living parabola from one to another, or quivering in great granite basins.

Early in his career the little town of Linköping, a place of only 25,000 inhabitants, adjudged Milles the winner in an open competition for a great fountain, and gave him the opportunity to carry out a noble scheme. The black granite basins and vast vases he surrounded with reliefs presenting the history and legends of the kings of Sweden, and over the centre he created the fine equestrian group of Folke Filbyter, the king whose son was stolen by the monks. This work is probably the noblest in Milles's early, comparatively simple style. Another work in this early manner is the enormous polychrome carved wooden statue of King Gustav Vasa in the National Museum at Stockholm. It is one of the greatest pieces of wood sculpture in the world, and Milles worked on it for eighteen years, from 1907 to 1925.

We associate him, however, rather with an almost feminine gracefulness and fancifulness in form and conception : The Apollo Fountain outside the Concert Hall in Stockholm ; the Europa Fountain with its wonderfully

" THE VISITATION," BY JACOB EPSTEIN

Tate Gallery, London

Epstein is primarily a modeller and a romantic, and in this life-size bronze he conveys all the mystery and resignation of his great subject. There is invariably in his work something of the elemental.

" PROSPERO AND ARIEL," BY ERIC GILL

Broadcasting House, London

Great simplification of the carved stonework gives to Eric Gill's sculpture an early Gothic note.
He unites the beauty of mediæval sculpture with his own definite Modernity.

curved Tritons. Attenuated figures rise out of his stonelike flower forms ; lines radiate, catch at each other across space ; complicated form leads the eye through almost infinite convolutions. Whatever else may be said of the work of this Swedish sculptor it is highly individual and is already exercising an influence on European sculpture.

In something of a renaissance the Scandinavians have produced many modern sculptors, less individual than Milles, but nevertheless important. Sinding and Kai Neilsen of Denmark ; Väinö Aaltonen of Finland ; Vigeland of Norway ; Einer Jonsson of Iceland ; David Edstrom of Sweden : a few names stand out from the many who work nobly in stone or wood in these Northern countries with their highly cultured and sensitive peoples.

§ 6

Here in England sculpture during recent years has also had something of a real revival, with a high standard of fine talent producing conscientious if unspectacular work, and a few names of world renown and challenge. The Royal Society of British Sculptors has done much to keep the standard of the art high and to obtain recognition for it along orthodox academic lines. Because of the challenge of their work the names of Jacob Epstein and Eric Gill in particular demand attention.

Epstein has, indeed, almost suffered from too much publicity. He has a restless mind which, having freed itself from the strict limitations of naturalism, has sought in a dozen styles to express its ideas. Each new work has been greeted with an outburst of objections, accusations, and defence— almost all overstated in the heat of controversy. The Wilde Memorial in Père Lachaise Cemetery in Paris with its decorative Byzantinism ; the Cubist " Venus " ; the Expressionist " Ecco Homo " ; the almost Egyptian figures of " Day " and " Night " on the Underground Building (where also are some interesting sculptures by other contemporary modern sculptors depicting the Four Winds) ; the Rodinesque modelled portrait busts and statues : in each of these Epstein explores a different vein. Often the result is brilliant, and it is invariably forceful—a fact which gives the lead to his studies of strong male personalities. Sometimes, inevitably, there is a sense of unsuccessful experiment. Fundamentally Epstein is a modeller rather than a carver. His strong personal temperament colours his work to an unusual degree, and may account for the vehemence of controversy which flares up with the exhibition of each new creation. " The Visitation " in the Tate Gallery remains one of the most all-round successes of Epstein's sculpture.

One other British sculptor whose work had evoked a great deal of controversy is Eric Gill (1882–1942). Gill was a Roman Catholic, a

" SUSANNAH," BY FRANK DOBSON

Tate Gallery, London

Bought as long ago as 1926 by the Contemporary Art Society and lent by them to the Tate Gallery for several years, this fine early work by Dobson was presented by the Society to the nation in May 1939. It is typical, in its massiveness and the simplification without distortion, of those sculptural qualities which make Dobson one of the leading British sculptors of the day.

mediævalist, a craftsman. He graduated into sculpture from his carving of lettering, and much of his notable work, such as the beautiful " Stations of the Cross " in Westminster Cathedral, still have a quality derived from this. Apart from his creative work as an artist he has written a great deal of exposition of what art is to him, and therefore what it should be in his view as a social activity. One of his most interesting works is the " Prospero and Ariel " on the B.B.C. building.

Apart from these men with international reputations this art of sculpture is being practised by a surprising number of good artists in this country working in the sound academic tradition and producing modelling and carving of fine craftsmanship. On the other hand, stand the rarer experimentalists, such as the ill-fated Gaudier-Brezska who after a start of great promise was killed in the 1914–18 War. Frank Dobson is another modernist of note, whose manipulation of natural form in the interests of design intrigues the non-naturalists. In England, however, a natural conservatism in art and a long tradition of craftsmanship tends to keep the art of sculpture within a decorative-realistic bound.

Germany contributes to the story of modern sculpture a very interesting figure in the person of the wood-carver, Barlach. His studies of peasants seem to be part of the wood from which they hardly emerge and yet they remain instinct with life. The outstanding sculptor in more normal vein is George Kolbe, a fine if not very daring exponent, whose " Dancer " is justly a favourite.

XXXI

THE MODERN DUTCH SCHOOL

THE ART OF JOSEF ISRAELS, ROELOFS, MAUVE, MESDAG,
BLOMMERS, AND THE BROTHERS MARIS

§ 1

FOR more than a hundred years after the deaths of Hobbema and William van de Velde, Holland produced no painter of European importance. The Dutch School, which during the seventeenth century had risen, as we have seen, to the highest eminence, sank during the eighteenth century into trivial virtuosity. Pictures became conjuring feats rather than true works of art, for they evoked neither tender sentiments nor noble thoughts, but only excited wonder by their manual dexterity. In craftsmanship many of these paintings were remarkable in their meticulous detail, and while some painters—like Willem van Mieris (1662–1747), whose " Fish and Poultry Shop " is in the National Gallery—carried on the traditions left by Jan Steen and Gerard Dou, still more made a reputation among their contemporaries by their minute rendering of fruit and flowers. These they painted with the patient skill of a miniaturist, and they delighted in introducing into their pictures flies and other small insects whose tiny, but marvellously realistic forms, had to be discerned with the aid of a magnifying-glass. Among the artists who excelled in this style of painting may be mentioned the woman-painter of Amsterdam, Rachel Ruysch (1664–1750), and her contemporary, Jan van Huysum (1682–1749), both of whom are represented in the National Gallery. Here we may see how skilfully they both painted flowers, how cunningly the one introduces a butterfly, the other a snail ; but we soon weary of this pettifogging cleverness, which may amuse our eyes for a few moments, but can never touch our hearts.

It was not till towards the middle of the nineteenth century that any great revival of painting showed itself in Holland. One who helped to prepare the ground for the new generation was Johannes Bosboom (1817–91) who painted impressive pictures in oils and water-colours of the interiors of Dutch churches and cathedrals. He was influenced by the seventeenth-century painter Emanuel de Witte (1607–92), who had also painted these subjects not only with great accuracy of linear perspective but with broad effects of light-and-shade ; Bosboom painted these interiors still more

589

broadly and invested them with a dim atmosphere of grave grandeur and solemnity.

Bosboom always gives us a more or less generalised vision, and contrasted with the particularity of the painters who immediately preceded him, he may be said to have given a new direction to Dutch painting.

Another pioneer and forerunner of the modern movement was Willem Roelofs, who was born at Amsterdam in 1822, and went to France, where he made the acquaintance of Corot and other members of the Barbizon School. For some time Roelofs lived with these artists in the now famous village, and painted the forest of Fontainebleau in their company ; then he returned to the Netherlands, taking with him new ideals of landscape painting. Though he lived chiefly in Brussels, Roelofs had a considerable influence on Dutch painting. He was never an imitator of Corot, Daubigny, or Troyon, though he learnt something from all of them, as we may see in his picture " A Summer's Day," and it was through him that a knowledge and appreciation of their paintings first spread through Belgium and Holland. Roelofs helped to found at Brussels in 1868 the *Société Libre des Beaux Arts*, of which Corot, Daubigny, and Millet became honorary members, and to this exhibition both Dutch and Belgian artists contributed. It became the rallying-point of the younger generation and of those painters who were beginning to be affected by the Barbizon pictures which so many of them had seen in Paris. After living in Brussels for forty years Roelofs moved to The Hague, where he died in 1897.

§ 2

The debt of the modern Dutch painters to France cannot be ignored, but we must remember that Holland possessed in Rembrandt one of the greatest of the Old Masters, and though his influence seemed to slumber for two centuries in his own country, it was shortly to prove itself to be alive once more. The greatest figure in this school is Josef Israels, and his art must be regarded as a blending of the influence of Rembrandt with that of Jean François Millet, plus the remarkable personality of the painter himself. Israels was one of the earliest as well as one of the greatest of the modern Dutch painters. He was born on January 27, 1824, at Groningen, of Hebrew parents, his father being a money-changer and broker. As a boy his first ambition was to be a rabbi ; at an early age he studied Hebrew and buried himself in the Talmud, and he was well in his teens before he displayed a marked leaning towards art. Meanwhile his father intended Josef for a business career, but while working under his father as a stockbroker's clerk, Josef Israels surreptitiously obtained lessons in painting from local artists, and though their talent was but mediocre their pupil soon began to display such

"A SUMMER'S DAY," BY WILLEM ROELOFS (1822–97)

One of the pioneers of the Modern Dutch School, Roelofs worked at Fontainebleau with the painters of Barbizon and introduced their ideals of landscape painting into the Netherlands. This picture is a fine example of his tender fidelity to Nature and of the radiant beauty of his lighting.

"A HAPPY FAMILY," BY JOSEF ISRAELS (1824–1911)

In this exquisitely lighted picture of the humble home of a Dutch fisherman, the painter gives us a touching study of domestic contentment and bids us ponder on the lives of people who can be happy with so little.

"FRUGAL MEAL," BY JOSEF ISRAELS

Glasgow Art Gallery

One of the greatest democratic painters of the nineteenth century, Israels interpreted the indoor home-life of the peasant as the Frenchman Millet recorded his labour in the fields. Making a stay in the little fishing village of Zantvoort, near Haarlem, Israels discovered the human drama and pathos of everyday life. In this characteristic picture he shows us " the treasure of the humble " and invests a homely repast with the solemnity and poignancy of a sacrament.

593

unmistakable gifts that parental opposition was overcome and he was allowed to go to Amsterdam to study art. He lodged with an orthodox Jewish family in the Ghetto, and all that he saw in the Jewish Quarter himself, combined with the religious paintings and etchings of Rembrandt based on the life in that quarter—which had altered so little since Rembrandt's time—made a profound impression on him, and had a more lasting influence than anything he learnt from his master, Jan Kruseman, who, though a successful portrait-painter of his time, was a dry and uninteresting artist. In 1845 Israels left Amsterdam to study in Paris, but here again he was not very fortunate in his master. He entered the studio of Picot, who had been a pupil of David, and so far from being in touch with the ideals of the " men of 1830," he was brought up to admire historical paintings in the classical style. When Israels returned to Amsterdam in 1848 he was chiefly influenced by the French historical painter Delaroche, and he began painting historical and dramatic subjects in which, beneath the French polish, the influence of Rembrandt was nevertheless discernible. But Israels had not yet found himself, and it was some years before he did. The critical period in the artistic career of Israels was about 1856. In 1855 he showed in the Paris Salon a historical picture, " The Prince of Orange for the first time opposing the Execution of the Orders of the King of Spain " ; in 1857 his exhibits at the Paris Salon were " Children by the Sea " and " Evening on the Beach," two tender impressions of commonplace, everyday scenes on the coast near Katwijk. These last pictures are by the Israels we know ; the picture of 1855 might have been by almost any historical painter of the period. How did this change come, and what brought it about ?

It was life, not art nor any artist, that changed the whole spirit of Israels's painting. He had a serious illness while he was living at Amsterdam, and when convalescent went to Zantvoort, a little fishing village close to Haarlem, to recruit his health. He lodged there with a ship's carpenter, and living the life of these simple, kindly seafaring folk, Israels was struck by the drama, pathos, and tragedy in the common lot. At Zantvoort he made the same discovery that Millet had made at Barbizon, namely, that to a sympathetic and understanding spectator the common life of the people even in a remote, secluded village is as full of romance, thrills, and tragedy as the pages of any history book. Israels discovered that " the events of the present are capable of being painted and the sorrows of the poor are as deep as the tragical fate of ancient heroes." A new vein of artistic expression was now opened to him, and henceforward he painted the life of the poor and humble, and found in typical, everyday episodes motives for expressing with peculiar intensity his wide human sympathy.

It may be said, therefore, that the art of Josef Israels, though he received his training in Paris, was far more the fruit of his own experience of life than

W. F. Mansell.

"ALONE IN THE WORLD," BY JOSEF ISRAELS

"The sorrows of the poor are as deep as the tragical fate of ancient heroes." In this moving picture of a wife who has just lost her beloved husband, Israels expresses his deep feeling for the daily tragedy of life.

the outcome of French influence. We feel that even if Millet had never existed, Israels would not have painted otherwise than he did, and though the subject-matter of their respective pictures are akin, there are considerable differences between them. Millet painted his peasants out of doors in the light of the sun ; Israels pictured his fisher-folk by preference indoors, in dim interiors. Hence his pictures are usually more subdued in colour than those of Millet. Israels painted low life in low tones and built up his visions of life, whether in oil-paintings, water-colours, or etchings—and he worked in all three mediums—by broad masses of light and shade. Further, his tendency is to be more tragic than Millet, and many of his pictures have not inaccurately been described as " piercing notes of woe." One of his most famous pictures, " Alone in the World," contains the essence of his art. In the treatment, in the rays of light illuminating the gloom which befits the subject, we see the influence of Rembrandt ; while in the bowed figure of the lonely widow, with her open Bible by her side, we have a poignant expression of the artist's deep feeling for the daily tragedy of life.

In 1870 Josef Israels left Amsterdam and moved to The Hague, where he lived till he died on August 12, 1911, respected, honoured, and world-famous. He was a painter who appealed equally to the general public and to connoisseurs, and though so many of his works are tragic, this never interfered with his popularity, because he pictured the tragedies of common life which all have experienced and all can understand. Further, if he reached his highest intensity of expression in rendering sorrow, suffering, endurance, and the pathos of old age, Israels was not wholly tragic in his art. Pictures like " A Frugal Meal " and " A Happy Family " show the reverse of the medal—the compensations of poverty and the happiness of the humble. But even in these scenes of domestic contentment there is something touching, and the philosophy of Israels seems to bid us to ponder on the life of people who can be happy with so little.

When Josef Israels was a young man, working as a clerk under his father, one of his frequent duties was to take a money-bag to the bank of a Mr. Mesdag. This banker had a son Hendrik Willem Mesdag, born at Groningen on February 25, 1831, who also became a famous painter. For many years Mesdag practised art as an amateur, and it was not till he had amassed a considerable fortune in business that he retired from banking and devoted himself entirely to painting. Thus Mesdag was not only in the independent position of being able to paint what he pleased without thinking of the taste of buyers, but he was also wealthy enough to help his brother artists whose works he admired.

In 1866, when he was thirty-five years of age, Mesdag went to Brussels, where his friend and relative, Alma-Tadema, was then residing. Roelofs also was living in Brussels, and it was under his guidance that the banker began

" A SEASCAPE," BY H. W. MESDAG (1831–1915)

Originally a banker by profession, Mesdag retired from business at the age of thirty-five and hence-forward devoting himself to art he became the foremost marine painter in Holland. This picture is a fine example of his vigorous rendering of the life and movement of the waves and of his skill in placing shipping, so that his picture is at once absolutely natural and also decorative.

" ON THE BEACH," BY B. J. BLOMMERS (1845–1914)

A typical example of the happy art of this painter, displaying his love of children and his knowledge of sea and sky. A disciple of Israels, Blommers developed the lighter side of that master's art.

the serious studies which should fit him to make art henceforward his profession. Mesdag stayed three years at Brussels and returned in 1869 to The
Hague, no longer an active man of business but an artist. He was not only
a painter himself but a collector of paintings, and in course of time he formed
a very important collection of modern pictures, chiefly of the Barbizon and
Modern Dutch Schools, which in 1903 he generously presented to the public.
The Mesdag Museum at The Hague is a lasting monument of his own taste
and of the genius of his contemporaries. As a painter Mesdag gave himself
almost exclusively to the painting of the sea, and his marines are remarkable
for their luminosity, truth, and the vigour of their handling. " A Seascape "
is a good example of his power of suggesting the life and movement of the
waves and of his skill in placing shipping, so that his picture is at once
absolutely natural and yet decorative in design.

The numerous painters of the Modern Dutch School—almost as numerous
as the " Little Masters " of the seventeenth century—may broadly be divided
into two classes, the figure or genre-painters for whom Israels was the chief
influence, and the landscape painters who were inspired by Roelofs and the
French painters of Barbizon. Among the genre-painters we may mention
Albert Neuhuys, born at Utrecht in 1844, who approaches closely to Israels
in his grave tender renderings of humble interiors ; David Adolf Constant
Artz (1837–90), who, in addition to interiors, painted the fisher-folk of
Scheveningen out of doors, frequently at moments when they were resting
on the sandhills ; and Bernardus Johannes Blommers, born at The Hague in
1845, who developed in his own way the lighter side of the art of Israels.
There is nothing tragic in the pictures of Blommers, whose favourite
subjects are children playing on the sands at Scheveningen or paddling
in the water. " On the Beach " is a typical example of the happy seaside scenes in which the artist displays alike his love of children and his
knowledge of sea and sky.

§ 3

Of the landscape painters of nineteenth-century Holland, the nearest to
Corot—nearest in the delicacy of his colouring and in the lyrical note that
rings out clearly in all his work—is Anton Mauve (1838–88). The son of a
Baptist minister, Mauve was born at Naandam and brought up in a strict
Protestant home, where art was not encouraged. It was much against the
will of his parents that he eventually took up art, and he made little progress
under his first master, Van Os, a dry academic painter whose stiff style had
little attraction for his sensitive, rather dreamy pupil. The earliest paintings
of Mauve were tightly drawn and highly finished, but later, after he had made
the acquaintance of Israels, Willem Maris, and other artists in Amsterdam,
he completely changed his style, his handling became looser and broader,

and he restricted his palette to delicate greys, greens, light fawns, and pale blues. When he was thirty he exhibited at the Free Society in Brussels, and he was influenced by the French artists who exhibited there, particularly by Corot and by Daubigny, whose works he saw in the house of Mesdag and other places in Holland. Mauve soon began to excel in landscape, rendering the soft hazy atmosphere that lingers over the meadows of Holland with infinite tenderness and poetic truth. The sand-dunes near Scheveningen were for many years his favourite sketching-ground, and it was there that he painted one of the most popular of his pictures, " The Sand Cart." It is a painting that captivates us at once by its winning simplicity, its entire truth, and the atmosphere of repose which it exhales ; and this reposefulness is a general characteristic of the art of Mauve, though his subjects are usually taken from workaday life. We do not think of him primarily as an animal-painter, though his love of animals is made clear by the frequency with which he introduces them into his pictures. But Mauve's animals never seem to have been painted solely for their own sake ; they are part and parcel of the landscape, in which they take a natural place, fulfilling their alloted function as aids to human activity. Each of Mauve's landscapes has the animals appropriate to it. He painted horses—for many years his " Watering Horses," belonging to Mr. J. C. J. Drucker, was lent to the National Gallery—but he also painted donkeys on the seashore, cows in meadows and on the road, sheep at pasture and in their pens. The fine collection of Mauve's work in the Mesdag Museum at The Hague contains examples of all these subjects. Towards the end of his life Mauve painted sheep more frequently than any other animals, the reason being that after living at Amsterdam and The Hague he settled at Laren, which is in the heart of the sheep country to the north-east of Amsterdam. Mauve took all rural and seashore life for his province : he painted fishermen and fish-wives at a fish-auction on the beach, he painted groups of peasants gathered together at a timber sale, drawing the various types of faces with great insight and humour, but in all his pictures life is pleasant and work proceeds placidly in an atmosphere of peace and contentment.

§ 4

Three of the most famous and most interesting of the nineteenth-century Dutch painters were members of one family, all born at The Hague and the sons of a struggling printer. This printer, Maris by name, was of foreign extraction, being the son of a Bohemian soldier of fortune who left his native city of Prague, married a Dutch wife, and settled in the political capital of Holland. The printer also had some experience of fighting, for in 1830 he was called up as a conscript to fight on the side of the Netherlands

W. F. *Mansell.*

"THE SAND CART," BY ANTON MAUVE (1838–88)

This tender rendering of a typical incident in the workaday life of the seashore captivates us by its winning simplicity, its entire truth and its atmosphere of repose.   Mauve was the most lyrical of the Dutch painters, and his pictures have a serene quality of placid contentment.

in the war which resulted in the independence of Belgium. After this war the printer returned to a life of unbroken toil, married, and had three sons. Of these the eldest was Jacob (or James) Maris, born in 1837, next came Matthys (or Matthew), born in 1839, while the youngest, Willem, was born in 1844. In speaking of these brothers we shall here use the English equivalents of their names by which they are usually known in Great Britain and the United States.

All three sons showed at an early age remarkable talents for drawing, and notwithstanding his poverty their father appears to have realised the wisdom of allowing each to follow his artistic bent. In their early years James and Matthew were closely associated. In 1855 the talent of the latter came to the notice of Queen Sophie of Holland, who made him an allowance, and the thrifty father considering that this allowance was enough for two, both James and Matthew were able to spend a year studying and painting at the Antwerp Academy. At Antwerp the two brothers lived in the same house as Alma-Tadema, and through him they got to know his relative Mesdag, the banker-painter, Josef Israels, and other Dutch artists. But in these early days neither brother was much affected by the art of his immediate contemporaries. They laboured strenuously to master the technicalities of their art, and James was guided in his first efforts by a master named Van Hove. This artist, though of mediocre ability, was a very conscientious draughtsman, and under his influence James Maris produced pictures remarkable for the minuteness of the details. One of his early pictures, " Interior of a Dutch House," painted when the artist was twenty-three, is in the Mesdag Museum, and is quite in the style of Pieter de Hooch. In the middle-distance, on the left, is a sunny nook ; in the foreground is the figure of a servant-girl standing in the entrance hall, holding in her right hand a basket and in her left a pewter can. All these details are painted with scrupulous exactness, and the same characteristics may be found in other domestic scenes and interiors which he painted in these early years.

It was not till he was nearing thirty that James Maris changed his manner of painting and acquired the style which eventually brought him fame. In 1865 he went to Paris, where he remained for six years, and there, under the influence of the Barbizon masters, he gradually broadened his style, abandoning his former intimacy of detail and now aiming at a more general effect of grandeur. Henceforward he devoted himself almost exclusively to landscape, and though the change of his style was brought about by French painting, his mature work is akin to that of Ruysdael in the nobility and majesty of its outlook. We can hardly escape thinking of Ruysdael's " Mill " when we see " The Stone Mill " by James Maris in the Mesdag Museum ; a picturesque stone mill, with an open gallery round it, makes a stately figure against a sky with white drifting clouds. In the foreground are sandhills, in

"DORDRECHT," BY JAMES MARIS (1837–99)

A majestic vision at eventide of the "Venice of the North," with its Groote Kerke, its wide canals, and its shipping. It is a fine example of the manner in which this artist, the eldest of the three brothers, subordinated details to the grandeur of the general effect.

the distance the red roofs of a village, but though the accessories taken together make up a scene quite distinct from that shown in Ruysdael's famous picture, both pictures have a touch of sublimity in the dignity of their design. Equally characteristic of the way in which this artist subordinates particular objects to the general effect is his painting of " Dordrecht." All details are merged in these masses of light and shade, yet everyone who has seen this town at eventide will agree that the painter has given us the essential characteristics of the " Venice of the North," its Groote Kerke, its shipping, its wide canals, and the rolling grey sky overhead, and has presented these with incomparable dignity and grandeur.

William Maris is more limited in his range than either James or Matthew, and though in their early days the work of all three showed a certain similarity of style, William's work altered least in style and in subject. He is nearer to Roelofs than either of his brothers, and his favourite subjects were landscapes with cattle, which he painted, as a rule, in full daylight, so that his pictures are rather brighter and gayer in colour than those of his brothers. A meadow extending along the border of the sandhills, in which are seen a few stunted trees and some cows, a pond perhaps in the immediate foreground, and a cloudy sky overhead, this is a typical William Maris subject. Less poetic than Mauve, less grand than his brother James, and less romantic than his brother Matthew, William Maris was a happy realist whose rich-coloured pictures are full of sunshine and mirror the luxuriant greens of Holland's pasture-lands.

Matthew Maris stands apart from his brothers and from all the Dutch artists of his generation. He was different in his temperament, different in his life, and different in his art. Tracing it to his foreign extraction, to his Austrian, or, as we should now say, to his Czecho-Slovak blood, Professor Muther says there broke out in Matthew Maris a " Teutonic mediæval mysticism " from which his brothers were free. Matthew no doubt possessed a romantic mystical temperament, but it is possible that he was influenced by the romantic mediævalism of Rossetti. It was in England that Matthew Maris painted his most characteristic pictures, and in England, where he lived for forty-five years, he drifted apart from his brethren in his art as in his life.

The beginnings of Matthew were almost parallel with those of James. The two brothers studied, as we have seen, at The Hague and Antwerp, and they were together in Paris. One incident must be chronicled which appears to have had far more influence on Matthew than on James. In 1858 the two brothers were back from Antwerp at The Hague, and three years later, having made some money by copying pictures, the two set out together on a tour through the Black Forest to Switzerland, returning through France by Dijon to the Puy-de-Dôme. Matthew was tremendously

"ENFANT COUCHÉE," BY MATTHEW MARIS (1839–1917)

W. F. Mansell.

An example of "the delightful quality of faëry and enchantment which so strangely characterises some of the works of Matthew Maris." It has a quality "for ever young and simple as of the glorified vision of a child."

impressed by the romantic castles and buildings he saw in Central France ; to his poetic imagination they were enchanted palaces. The recollection of this tour never faded from his mind, and in pictures painted years afterwards we catch echoes of the turrets and battlements which remained fixed in his memory. We may see evidence of this in the background of " Feeding Chickens," painted in 1872.

Nevertheless it is important to note that there is not the same note of romanticism in pictures he painted only two years earlier. In 1868 Matthew joined his brother James in Paris, and we may see in the National Gallery a little picture he painted there in 1870. " Montmartre," as it is called, shows us dust-carts tipping rubbish on the side of a hill which has a windmill at the top. It is beautifully painted, perfect in its refined realism, but it is not romantic.

When the Franco-Prussian war broke out, James Maris returned to Holland. Matthew remained, went through the siege of Paris, and, like other residents, was enrolled in the Municipal Guard and called our for duty. His post was on the fortifications, opposite Asniéres and just under Mont Valérien, and he suffered considerably from the bitter cold during night duty. Military life was not congenial to this gentle artist, and the thought of killing anybody was abhorrent to him. He confessed afterwards, " I never put a bullet in my gun, but only pretended to do so ! "

His war experiences certainly did Matthew Maris no good ; they saddened him and tended to make him shrink into himself, so that he became more and more of a recluse. After the siege Matthew Maris came to London in 1872, and there he remained to the end of his days. He had rooms at first in the house of an art decorator named Daniel Cottier in St. James's Terrace, Regent's Park ; and Cottier, a strong active business man, had much influence over him, telling him what sort of pictures he ought to paint. Although Cottier, an admirer of Rossetti, undoubtedly encouraged the romantic element in the Dutch artist, Matthew Maris rebelled at painting under his direction and professed that he was thoroughly unhappy in his house. Yet between 1872 and 1875, when he was under the spell of Cottier, Matthew Maris painted what are generally considered to be his finest pictures. Among them we may mention " The Girl at the Well " and " Feeding Chickens," painted in 1872 ; " The Christening " and " Enfant Couchée," in 1873 ; " He is Coming "—a most Rossetti-like vision of a little princess at her spindle with a prince seen approaching through the open door—in 1874 ; and " The Sisters " in 1875. Yet even these works, full of indescribable poetry and romantic beauty, failed to satisfy the artist, who in after years would speak of them as " pot-boilers " which he had been compelled to paint by a tyrannical taskmaster.

Though discontented and professedly unhappy, Matthew Maris was

"FEEDING CHICKENS," BY MATTHEW MARIS

This picture, painted in 1872, shows how the artist could invest a commonplace incident of farm life with the magic of poetry. The "enchanted towers" in the background are probably a memory of the romantic castles and buildings in Central France which made a lasting impression on the artist when he saw them in 1861 while travelling from Dijon to the Puy-de-Dôme.

slow to leave what he regarded as a house of bondage, and it was not till 1887—and then chiefly because Mrs. Cottier was in ill-health—that he finally left. He went to 47 St. John's Wood Terrace, intending to remain there only a fortnight, while he looked around for a more convenient studio, and he stayed there nineteen years. In 1906 he found a home at 18 Westbourne Square, Paddington, in a half-flat with a small painting-room, and in this modest abode, tended by a faithful housekeeper, he remained till he died on August 17, 1917. He seldom went out and he had few visitors, the most intimate friends of his later years being the Dutch picture-dealer, Mr. E. J. Van Wisselingh and his wife, a Scottish lady, daughter of Mr. Craibe Angus, of Glasgow, who had been one of the earliest British patrons of Matthew Maris. His later paintings became more and more mysterious ; instead of the clear outlines of his earlier pictures, forms were seen dimly as through a mist, and these pictures he would work over and over many times, each re-painting seeming to cast a new veil over faces and figures that became more and more spiritual. Had he wished, Matthew Maris might have had fortune as well as fame, for there were ardent collectors in many countries eager to secure examples of his works, but his means were straitened largely because he could with difficulty bring himself to part with a picture and desired to keep them all in his painting-room. In 1911 a Dutch admirer of his work, Mr. Thornsen, offered to the compatriot of whom he was proud a small pension. This the painter accepted, and the pension was continued till his death.

An abnormal being, Matthew Maris was " alone in the world " because he chose of his own accord to live the life of a hermit shut up with his dreams.

XXXII

OUR EYES TURN EASTWARD

THE ARTS OF CHINA, JAPAN, INDIA, AND THE BUDDHIST EAST

§ I

DURING all the thousands of years that this Western Art had been developing in Europe, another as rich, varied, and in some ways even more wonderful and exquisite had pursued its own course in the Far East. There had been little or no contact between the two. On rare occasions, such as when Alexander's Empire contacted Central Asia, or when the Mongols swept Westward in a tide of conquest, or when rare travellers such as Marco Polo, the enterprising Venetian, carried his ambition for trade to the East in the thirteenth century, there had been links ; and some sort of a legend of a civilisation away there beyond the farthest wanderings of European man had sprung up. Cathay : the word was a spell. China for her part deliberately chose to isolate herself over long periods, and the vast ranges of the mountains of Western Asia, the almost trackless Gobi desert, and the wide encircling seas ensured her isolation. As transport became more competent, and the lure of the riches of India and the spice islands took men Eastward, the legend of the beauty and civilisation of Cathay began to take shape as tangible fact. Slowly it was accepted, and ultimately Europe was stirred by the art and craft which came from this strange land.

It was during the eighteenth century that the decorative and applied arts of the West became fully aware of this exotic beauty, and a new wave of æsthetic idea, of Chinoiserie, brought fresh motives to fabrics and wall papers and ceramics. Great vases whereon dragons and phœnixes were interwoven with arabesques of flowers were brought back from the East by the rich nabobs and their agents who were making fortunes in India and the East Indies. Carpets of exquisitely cool blues and delicate pinks came to the floors of the Salons of France and England. Quaintly carved furniture in rich ebony, or stools and cabinets of fretted lacquer-work, found themselves in strange company in the drawing-rooms of the great. Some of our finest furniture designers were influenced to modify the severity of the prevailing classic, by shaping wood into faint echoes of this Eastern work. A pagoda—most amusingly Chinese of all forms—eventually

U

found itself, an object of surprise and wonder, in the Royal Gardens at Kew. During the nineteenth century, when taste everywhere had degenerated under the influence of the *nouveau riche* of the Industrial Revolution, this initial fascination of connoisseurs became a spate of mere acquisition. Birmingham imitated in brass what China had conceived in jade ; and the Chinese themselves, forced out of their isolation by the enthusiasm of missionaries and the enterprise of trade backed by gunboats, responded to the demand by producing Chinoiserie in shiploads. The vases were larger, more tortured in shape, more set about by ever more fantastic dragons ; the lacquer was fiercer in colour ; the furniture more deliberately contorted ; the ornaments more dreadfully ornamental. So Chinese art came to Europe at its most debased, and so it was accepted when it was least worthy.

Little did we dream in those days that the crest of this wave of beauty had passed a thousand years before. Little did we realise that during the whole of the period wherein our own art had been building up from the ruins of the Dark Ages this of the East had been degenerating. Two periods of three hundred years each—the *Ming* and the *Ch'ing*—stood between our enthusiasm for Chinoiserie and the days when, as Marco Polo records, Kubla Khan ruled over cities which were dreams of loveliness. And, if we would reach the golden age of Chinese art, we must go further back still, past the *Yuan*, that century of Mongol domination, to the period of the *Sung* which stretches backwards in time from 1279 to 960 ; and beyond again to the *Tang* which takes us back to the year 618. Those were the days of poets and painters and sculptors ; of the builders of temples and palaces of exquisite grace and beauty ; of embroiderers of banners like moving flames ; of painters of dainty scroll pictures on silk, revealing a civilisation of the utmost suavity and an understanding of nature Wordsworthian in its mysticism ; of the creators of ornaments of jade, of vases and bowls which have never found an equal in their subtlety and grace.

In those days Chinese culture was already incredibly old, and, in contradistinction to that of the West, it was unbroken. The period of the great civilisations of Egypt and Mesopotamia stretched from 3000 B.C. or beyond it. But whereas Egypt, Ur, Nineveh, Babylon, Crete, Greece, Rome, Italy, passed each in its turn, the dynasties of China formed a practically continuous culture, even through war and civil war and foreign invasion. Twenty-three centuries B.C. China had a Golden Age. The dynasties went by : the *Hsia*, the *Shang-yin*, the *Chou*, the *Ch'in*. During the sixth century B.C. came two great thinkers : Confucius, the sage, the teacher of ordered morality ; and Lao-Tsze, the mystic philosopher of Nature. Confucius (551–478 B.C.) collected and edited the already ancient writings of China and from them evolved an ethical doctrine of honesty, decorum and good manners based on the right relationship and dignity of individuals in the family and the state. His nine books, the five *Shus* and the four *Kings*, are the classics containing his teaching. Lao-Tsze, on the other hand, preached a mystic Pantheism, urging men to tread the *Tao*, the Way of tranquillity and gentleness, and to get back into unity with universal being through the contemplation of Nature and the acceptance of her way. His was a doctrine of inaction, of receptivity. He was the librarian of a Prince of the *Chou* dynasty, but retired to a hermitage and wrote his *Canon of Reason and Virtue*, the sacred book which embodies his teaching. Art in China is so closely allied with the philosophies of these two great teachers and with that of Gautama Buddha that we have to bear in mind their teachings if we would rightly appreciate it.

The great *Han* dynasty followed. It stretched from 206 B.C. to A.D. 219, and it was in the middle of this period that Buddhism spread from India and linked itself with Taoist ideas. China in *Han* times was sending her caravans along the great Silk Road towards the West, and so had communications with India and Persia. The link with her neighbours brought Buddhist Art as a lovely gift to China. Four hundred years of internecine war followed the *Han* dynasty owing to the disintegration of the separate parts of China into individual states ; but there was nevertheless a deep-seated civilisation. Buddhism rose to its height, and despite the unsettled conditions a delicate art flourished. Out of it emerged the *Tang* dynasty (618 to 906), and China enjoyed one of her greatest periods of political quietude and prosperity. Her borders extended to the shores of the Caspian Sea and touched India. Taoism was the official religion, and Buddhism modified it, whilst Confucian ethics and orderliness kept life gracious and sure. Buddhism, so closely akin to Taoism in its ideals of quietude, simplicity, and universal kindness and toleration, gradually swamped the older faith into which it seeped. Exquisite temples and shrines arose, with some of the noblest sculpture the world has ever seen, with frescoed walls and paintings of Buddhistic story and of the saints of the religion on silk and precious manuscripts. This gracious civilisation continued for yet another three hundred years of the *Sung* period (960–1279). The æsthetic emphasis gradually moved from sculpture to painting, an art closely allied to the magnificent literature which marked the time.

In 1212 Ghengis Khan and his Mongol warriors swept over the Great Wall which was to have protected China from the North, and it seemed for a moment that this precious civilisation was to be destroyed. But China, vast and wonderfully established on its deep foundations of ancient culture, absorbed her conquerors. Her own symbol of man, created from the wisdom of the *Tao*, was the bamboo which bent but did not break. The *Yuan* dynasty lasted for a century, and in that short time

611

these fierce Mongol war lords had become more Chinese than the Chinese themselves. There were new motives in the paintings : the horses which the Mongols loved, portraits of the overlords and of the priests. There were palaces and temples set graciously amid the water-gardens.

> " In Xanadu did Kubla Khan
> A stately pleasure dome decree."

Coleridge saw these cities in his dreams, as Marco Polo saw them in the reality of their incredible beauty. Travellers to-day can still imagine the loveliness, though more than six centuries have passed since they were built, though war and fire and revolution have passed over them during the troubled times of China's decline. During the following periods of the *Ming* (1368–1644) and the *Ching* (1644–1911) Confucianism gained ascendancy over Buddhism, and the old Taoist religion declined almost absolutely. Culture, under the influence of the Confucian doctrine with its worship of the traditions and its belief in stabilisation, tended to imitate the past, or if it changed at all moved towards an over-elaboration and an over-ornamentation which compares badly with the perfection and harmony of the earlier periods. Now, after the years of the great revolution which in 1912 overthrew the last dynastic house and established the republic, after seven years of the terrible devastation of modern warfare with a foe as ruthless as Ghengis Khan, but armed with weapons of modern destructive power, after contacts with the vulgarisation of the West and the proletarian culture of Soviet Russia, we may well fear for the continuity of the Chinese spirit which has persisted for five thousand years. But it may be that China will again conquer by the might of her spirit, and that something specifically Chinese will arise out of her ruin and sorrow.

§ 2

No people in the history of mankind more closely associated art with their social life and philosophy than the Chinese. We must, therefore, approach the paintings, the sculpture, even the applied arts, the early bronzes, the ornaments of jade, the ceramics, in an entirely different spirit from that with which we consider Western art and craft. In the first place there is a conscious underlying symbolism in everything, based on the fundamental Chinese view of the universe. In the second we must see the painting as an evolution of that art of calligraphy which is one of the most treasured in this Eastern culture. Unless we are viewing Chinese art with the Chinese eye we are debasing it to an art of surfaces such as we cultivate in our material Western world, and thereby missing its meaning. A landscape of mountain and lake with the mist ascending ; a thicket of bamboo in which a tiger lurks ; a river running between giant rocks : these things have their own hidden language based on Taoistic philosophy and on a conception which has held sway in China since thousands of years before even Lao-Tsze incorporated it in the *Tao*.

That conception was of two balancing principles which by their inter-action held the balance and created the life of things : the *Yang* and the *Yin*. The one was associated with the heavens, the other with earth ; the one with masculine, the other with feminine. That was the basis. All things grouped around these fundamentals. Water, cloud, mist belong to the heaven principle ; rocks, trees, and all such to the earthly. Moreover, the movement of water, descending as rain, flowing as rivers, or ascending as mist, came to symbolise the interpenetration of earth with the life of heaven. Thus, when an artist draws what to our Western eyes is merely a delicate representation of craggy pine-clad mountain peaks rising to the sky, with a waterfall rushing down between the rocks, a soft mist over the lake below, a foreground of swaying bamboos, he is not only depicting the beauty of his beloved landscape with a touch as sensitive as that of a bow on a violin, but he is speaking of the unity and arrangement of the universe with Man in its midst.

Somewhere in all this, very small in scale, you may find Man : a hermit listening to the distant bells of the temple, a little group of pleasure-seekers on a terrace looking at the evening star, a solitary fisherman. Humanity is a tiny integral part of Nature in this Taoist Chinese art ; it does not sprawl across the whole conception of the universe as it does in Western art of practically any period. Each Chinese picture is a mood. It is akin to quiet music in its gentle stirring of the spirit ; it aims at uniting Man and Nature through contemplation. Wordsworth among our poets came near to its spirit, and even he had a tendency to spoil its effects by the interpolation of the insistent human ego.

The other thing we must realise in approaching Chinese painting is the method, the technique arising out of the most ancient art of calligraphy and still being basically concerned with line-drawing in ink on silk. There are no shadows as in Western art. Indeed, when the Jesuits in the seven-teenth century showed to the Chinese European portrait-paintings with shadows on the faces, the naïve Orientals enquired whether it was our custom to wash only one side of the face ! Nor is there the perspective from only one point of view which our painting achieved under the science of the Renaissance. The shapes of the pictures are different also, for the silk is mounted on rollers either at top and bottom or at either side ; and in certain landscapes, such as that magnificent one, " The Thousand Miles of the Yellow River," which was one of the many glories of the Chinese Art Exhibition at Burlington House in 1936, we are meant to unroll it section

LANDSCAPE BY WANG MENG, YUAN DYNASTY

Every Chinese landscape is full of symbolism which adds up to a balance between the heavenly and the earthly principles : cloud and water ; rocks and stones. The celestial water, as lake, ascending mist, cloud and returning waterfall, interpenetrates the material earth. Somewhere the tiny habitations and figures of man take their subordinate place in the design.

by section and read its beauty from end to end as one reads a book. To the Chinese connoisseur every stroke of the brush can be appreciated for its sensitiveness, and not least the brush-work of the writing which may be found somewhere on the design expressing in the words of some tiny poem the mood and meaning of the subject.

The symbols, the characters of the language carry us back into the mists of pre-history. Early bronzes are already decorated with elaborate pattern, often an ornament something like the Greek meander, which to the Chinese was and is the symbol for thunder and cloud, and thereby bespeaks the heaven principle. Strange shapes of jade (itself a symbolic material, for it is regarded as the product of both earth and water and therefore the unity of heaven and earth, of *Yang* and *Yin*) also embodied symbols of the dual principle ; and ceramics—creation of the earth clay and the heaven water and fire—were at once beautiful in themselves, and full of significance in shape and ornamentation. We find these things in the earliest tombs of prehistoric times. They were used in the ceremonial doubtless as emblems of specific powers and offices, in that search for the perfect adjustment between *Yang* and *Yin* which lies behind all Chinese thought and art.

In the twenty-eighth century B.C. the Emperor Fu Hsi is credited with having reduced these all-important principles to a few significant symbols which were the beginning of Chinese writing. The *Yang* became represented by a long stroke ——, the *Yin* by two short ones – –. Out of this came eight further picture symbols :

heaven ——	earth – –
water ——	fire – –
river ——	wind ——
mountain – –	thunder – –

These symbols rapidly extended to a vast vocabulary of picture-writing, and this calligraphy was cultivated as a supreme art. The brush and the medium of ink on silk constituted the method ; and Chinese painting evolved from this and still retains its quality.

In the first century A.D. we have evidence of painting on silk and paper, and the tradition is unbroken. We possess delightful paintings of this type dated as early as the fourth century A.D. In the British Museum is a horizontal scroll painting, " The Admonitions of the Instructress," ascribed to one of the noted artists of the period, Ku K'ai-Chih, whereon the dainty figures depict the canons of good behaviour and conduct. Also in the British Museum is a later copy of another work by this master, a fairy-tale subject of a poet who loved a river nymph but—alas for the frailty of the love of poets !—not sufficiently to share her watery existence, so the lady swept out of his unchivalrous existence on a chariot drawn by six dragons. This type of fantasy is typical of one important side of Chinese painting and literature.

During the period preceding the *Tang* dynasty six canons of good painting were drawn up and accepted, and it is interesting that the first and most important of these is that which is called " rhythmic vitality," a quality which aims at expressing life in the very lines of the composition and the manner of the brush-strokes. There seems little doubt that the *Tang* period itself was really the golden age of Chinese painting. It was, indeed, one of the great periods of Chinese life. The silk routes to the West brought her into close touch with the Buddhists of India, the Zorastrians of Persia, and even with the various doctrinaires of Christianity in the Near East. Buddhism especially had enormous power. As it decayed in India the more earnest of its priests and monks moved into China, bringing with them the Hindu and the Hellenist-Hindu forms of art. Sculpture rose to magnificent heights, and in painting Buddhistic art yielded a magnificent harvest.

Sir Aurel Stein in 1908 opened up a series of rock shrines at Tun-huang on the Turkestan border, and disclosed thousands of manuscripts and paintings as well as carvings of Buddhist sacred figures. " The Cave of the Thousand Buddhas " it was called by the excavators ; and, as the treasures from it in the British Museum confess, it was indeed a revelation of the fineness of this painting even in a remote province of the country. From the monumental picture of Buddha preaching, to the hundreds of smaller works, scenes in paradise, Bodhisattvas (those beings whose compassion for erring humanity cause them to forgo their right to the bliss of Nirvana in order that they may return to help here on earth), priests, learned Lohans : these paintings give us some idea of the riches of this period.

Of the frescoes we have only tradition. One great master, Wu Tao-Tzu, is said to have painted no less than three hundred on the walls of temples. At this time such artists as Wang-Wei started that so-called Southern School of gracious landscape which came to its maturity in *Sung* times. There

女史司箴敢告庶姬

"ADMONITIONS OF THE INSTRUCTRESS" BY KU K'AI-CHIH
British Museum

One of the earliest extant paintings of the world, this drawing in ink with washes of colour on a scroll of brown silk, belongs to the 4th century A.D. Its delicacy and exquisite draughtsmanship are typical of Chinese painting in every great period.

U*

"THE FISHERMAN," BY MA YUAN, SUNG DYNASTY

The mood of complete peace is upon this picture. The bamboo is always symbolic of man. This picture bears the stamps of the succeeding owners, and another characteristic of Chinese painting—a tiny poem.

618

were wonderful animal painters, too ; more especially painters of horses, for the Chinese loved horses. Another vein which was explored was that which we have already noted in the " Admonitions of the Instructress," the gentle depicting of the activities of women. " Preparing Silk," " Listening to Music in a Garden " : how gracious it all is, how civilised ! We have to remind ourselves that these paintings of delicately clad girls engaged in these highly æsthetic occupations were made about two hundred years at least before the Norman Conquest of England, a period when Europe was still immersed in the internecine struggles for the barest existence at the end of the Dark Ages.

If we have lost many of the treasures of the *Tang* period, we have been more fortunate with those of *Sung* times. The landscape art, those " mountain and water " pictures as the Chinese call them, rose to absolute perfection in the hands of two masters especially : Kuo Hsi and Hsia Kuei. The son of the former has left on record how his father prepared himself spiritually for his painting, sitting at a bright window and allowing the calm of Nature to flow in upon him until he felt impelled to create out of the treasure of his well-stocked and sensitive mind. Kuo Hsi himself has written his philosophy, and records that the love of landscape is granted only to him who wishes to free himself from care and routine and to find among the hills and streams that which is refreshing. The landscape must be viewed from a distance so that the mind is free to wander in its noble vistas, and also that one may realise the unity of form amid its vast diversity. So this painter-philosopher sat at his window, burned incense to either side, washed his hands, took the finest brush and ink, and " let the thoughts settle in his soul " before he commenced work.

Hsia Kuei, perhaps the greatest of all the *Sung* masters, gave us the magnificent study of " The Thousand Miles of the Yellow River," tracing the stream from its source, the waterfalls among the rocks, until it merges with the broad flood of the open sea. Only Chinese Art could encompass such a conception, and when we were privileged to see it at Burlington House we realised that here was the absolute grandeur of landscape with which no landscape-painting in the Western world could compare.

Along with the name of this artist stands that of Ma Yuan, the master of pine trees and solitary crags. But he can also convey his mood of unity with Nature by showing a single fisherman sitting in his boat among the reeds. Often he painted tiny album pictures, but their size did not prevent him from expressing in them a vast conception of Nature. Not the least fascination of these Chinese pictures of Nature is the use made of the mist to obliterate detail and create great rest spaces from which the eye returns refreshed to the intricate details of crag and tree and bamboo. All this

Sung art has a quality of pure feeling which no other landscape art in the world has ever achieved.

When it turns to purely Buddhist subject—the portrayal of learned Lohans or of Bodhisattvas—the emotion is the same : a calm which has found the repose at the heart of things. There is a splendid study of three Bodhisattvas in the British Museum which is a supreme example of the religious work of the period. At other times the art concentrates on one tiny aspect of Nature—a bird on a bough, a group of reeds, a single flower, three fish moving through water, a tiger, two geese. Always we feel that there is an understanding of essentials. One of the most famous pieces, a little album picture of a bird on a spray, which is in the Eumorphopoulis collection, is a masterpiece in its miniature way.

With the overthrow of the dynasty by the Mongol invasion it seemed that all this gracious life, quietist philosophy, and poised culture might have been lost. But the Chinese have always conquered their conquerors, and soon these fiery Mongols were accepting absolutely the beauty and culture of the people they had defeated. There were new motives, particularly that of the horses which these Northern warriors loved and which the Chinese could depict so vitally. Portraiture, too, came to the fore, for these Mongol lords were proud builders of empires who did not share the Chinese humility. Even the sacred art turned to the depicting of the priests and dignitaries of the Zen Buddhist and Taoist faiths by such artists as Yen Hui. But still the lovely landscape art persists in the hands of Ni Tsan and other great masters of the time.

Had we not the challenge of these wonderful early periods we might rightly feel that the painting of the period of the *Ming* dynasty, which roughly coincided with the great centuries of Italian painting, was marvellous indeed. There are exquisite things belonging to it, as one must realise in face of such a work as the " Wild Geese by a Mountain Stream," by Lin Liang, which is in the British Museum, or the quite delightful "Fairy with a Phœnix " which is in the same collection. In every important gallery all over the world beautiful works from this time may be found ; and if this art loses some of the inner feeling, it yet retains the command of the medium, the sweep of the brush-stroke, the simplicity, the power of suggesting vast spaces, which had characterised Chinese art of the greater early centuries. But gradually the external conquers. In the *Ming* period, that last three hundred years before the revolution of 1911, Chinese art succumbed to the temptation of marvellous repetition. Most of the old spirit had gone, leaving a surface art of elegant decoration. Silk paintings of this later time, as we have seen, came to be accepted in Europe as representative of the wonderful culture from which the soul had almost departed centuries before. Now we are better able to compare the later with the

"TWO GEESE," BY A CHINESE ARTIST OF THE SUNG PERIOD (950–1250)

British Museum, London

The most simple subjects opened the door of Nature to the sensitive Chinese masters
with a beauty both symbolic and objective.

621

MARBLE—SEATED BUDDHA

Buddhism, introduced into China in the fifteenth century brought her a new beauty and symbolism much in accord with her own spirit of quietude. The highly decorative qualities of Eastern Art found a new purpose.

earlier work, we have adjusted our values, and we look back another thousand years for the crest of that wave in whose shallows we so long disported, thinking them to be the ocean of Chinese art.

§ 3

From China we turn to the arts of Japan, so closely related to, and, indeed, derived from those of the mainland. Painting and sculpture were introduced to the islands some time during the fifth century under the spreading of Buddhism ; and although there have been periods when Japan has closed her doors to all outside influences, the Chinese power has invariably returned bringing fresh inspiration. Against this has to be set the distinctive characteristics of the Japanese people which inevitably have become expressed in their arts. They are, they always have been, more virile than the Chinese, less contemplative, more given to action. In many respects they seem more concerned with the immediacies of life here and now, and even though their art began with the other-worldiness of Buddhism it developed into realism again and again as though drawn by some invisible magnet. From one time of revolution we have a series of battle pictures and scenes of violence unequalled in the world ; at another more recent period arose the democratic Ukioye type of painting and woodcut, the genre " pictures of the passing world " making no claim to religious content or idealism but devoted to depicting the life of the common people. It was this latter school which came to marvellous fruition in the cheap woodcuts and colour-prints, perhaps the most brilliant contribution of Japan to the art of the world ; the woodcuts which, discovered by chance in a shop in Paris by the early Impressionists, had so remarkable an influence on modern French and Western art.

The earliest Japanese painting and sculpture is the Buddhist work centred round the ancient capital of Nara. There in a temple we have the vast bronze figure of the Buddha, fifty-three feet high ; there we have the paintings of the Ajanta type which tell of the roots of this art in distant India. At this early stage the influence, however, is distinctly Chinese and Korean, and it was only when the capital was moved in 794 to Kioto that Japan began to have her own characteristic art. Those were the days of the magnificent court of the Fujiwara clan with its great culture. The Shingon sect of Buddhists, founded by the priest-artist, Kobo Daishi, made the practice of painting a sacred calling, and although under the patronage of the highly sophisticated court art swung over to secular themes, the temple paintings of the period yield some of the finest examples of early mediæval Buddhist art. At the end of the Fujiwara period, however, we have the school of the Tosa painters depicting the decadent life of that court, where even the men used cosmetics and cultivated effeminate elegancies which ultimately led to its downfall.

The most outstanding name of the period is that of Kosé-no-Kanaoka, painter of the lovely study of the " Nachi Waterfall " with its exquisite blending of colour and that genius for stylised form which the Japanese had inherited from China. In these years the distinctive forms of the *makimono* (the long horizontal scroll) and the *kakimono* (the vertical hanging scroll) established themselves firmly as the conventional shapes for Japanese paintings. Under Buddhistic influence, with its acceptance of the sacredness and unity of all life, the artists made perfect studies of the minutiæ of Nature, of frogs and grasshoppers, of single reeds and blossoms, of birds and leaves and sprays, with a reverence for Nature which had yet to wait hundreds of years before it was manifested in Europe.

In the British Museum we have the splendid examples of the " Ascending and Descending Buddha," painted by the Shingon priest, Yeshin Sodzu, whose date was 942 to 1017. One other curious aspect of Fujiwara art came at the extreme end of the period in that of the priest, Toba Sojo, who humorously depicted his fellow priests and worshippers under the guise of monkeys and geese and frogs—a form of satire which we find occasionally in the manuscripts from the monasteries of mediæval Europe, and evidently a world-wide ecclesiastical joke. A famous work of his in more serious vein is the " Shigazan makimono," depicting a series of miracles as its ostensible subject, but valuable for its lively portrayal of the contemporary life. In such work we have the beginning of the " pictures of the passing world " which were later to become Japan's most characteristic contribution to Eastern art.

With the overthrow of the noble Fujiwara clan this gracious art of court and cloister yields to the vivid depiction of the incidents of the civil war which caused their downfall. The painter Mitsunaga and his fellow artists give us terrible pictures which stand among the greatest battle studies of the world : the burning of palaces, the flight of the terrified court, the clash of armed horsemen, the swirl and terror of fleeing crowds. Into these long horizontal scrolls, so eminently suited in shape to the delineation of such subjects, the masters put a liveliness far removed from anything that had ever been attempted in the East. Sumiyoshi Keion has left us three of these twelfth-century masterpieces ; and his successor, Kosé Korehisa, carries even further this war realism. One other master of the period demands mention : Nobuzane (1177–1265) carried on the work of the earlier court painters, and shows us the new court with a wider freedom and less conventionality, and with daring colour harmonies that are dreams of beauty. His masterpiece is the portrait of Kobo Daishi, the founder of the Shingon sect, as a boy saint.

When in the middle of the thirteenth century the Mongols swept down upon China and destroyed the *Sung* dynasty, it seemed for a time that their tide of conquest must extend Eastward to the islands of Japan, but the great armada which was to take them across the narrow gulf was devastated by storm, and Japanese independence continued. At first the effect was one of encouraging Japanese insularity, but later the flood of cultured refugees who had fled before the terrors of Ghenghis Khan caused a revival of Chinese influence. This Ashikaga period of Japanese art, extending from 1335 to 1573, is thus a reflection of *Sung* painting and sculpture.

Its early master was the monk, Cho Densu (1351–1427), greatest of all Japanese Buddhist masters, and imbued with a deeply religious spirit which recalls to us that of his Italian contemporary, Fra Angelico. One outstanding development of the school was that of quiet monochrome painting. Again it was a heritage from China, for its inaugurator was the Chinese priest, Josetsu, and its greatest exponent his pupil, Shiubun, whose landscape study in the British Museum is a splendid example of this monochrome work. The whole Ashikaga period was one of deep and restrained culture in which all the most characteristic arts and crafts of Japan, her poetry, her music, her unique flower arrangement, her formalised gardening, her calligraphy, and the delicate crafts such as those of the carved and jewelled sword-hilts, rose to their climax at the court of Yoshimasa. Here worked that most versatile and fastidious of Japanese æsthetes and artists, Noami, whose painting of a tiger is in the British Museum along with some of his landscapes and other work.

Sesshiu (1420–1506) is, however, the most considerable artist of this period. The Chinese influence in his work is predominant, but in landscape and figure subjects alike he used the swift calligraphic brush-stroke as no other master could. He also is well represented in the British Museum collection, not the least fascinating of his works being the " Hotei and Children," painted in his old age just before his death.

Towards the end of this great period of Japanese art came the famous Kano school of painters who received the official recognition which had hitherto belonged to the old court artists of the Tosa school. Motonobu (1476–1559) was its real founder, although he had been trained by his father, Kano Masanobu. His picture of " Shoriken crossing the Sea on his Sword " which we have in the British Museum, is a powerful example of his figure studies, but he was also a master of landscape, of birds and flowers, and he excelled alike in the old brilliantly coloured style and in the new method of monochrome. For seven or more generations the brilliant work of the Kano school went on from father to son and then it continued practically to our own day in the hands of brilliant disciples.

The seventeenth century brought a great change to Japan with the accession to the all-powerful Shogunate (the headship of government of which the semi-divine Mikado is only the nominal chief) of Iyeyasu, who pursued a policy of isolating his country from foreign influences and cultivating her inner resources. Under this policy the arts and crafts of Japan rose to exquisite loveliness, especially the art of lacquer and that of ceramics. To this Tokugawa period belongs the artist whose work has deservedly found such favour in Western eyes, Korin (1655–1716). Most famous as a painter and designer of screens, his lovely creations on backgrounds of gold and silver are among the treasures of this time. His conventionalising of form is brilliantly daring—witness the formalism of waves and rocks in the noble " Wave Screen " in the British Museum. Everything he touched was marked by this magnificent creative power.

It was, however, another direction taken by seventeenth-century Japanese art which was destined to have the most remarkable results. A school of popular painters arose, the Ukioye school, which deliberately planned to cater for the ordinary people. The word means " pictures of the passing world," and the subjects were to be those of contemporary life rather than the idealisations of religious art or the now highly formalised art of landscape or Nature. Morunobu (1625–94), created the vogue, although an earlier man, Matabei, is credited with founding the school. In the hands of Morunobu, however, the grace and charm of ordinary life shown in an idyllic fashion caught the popular taste. He took the step of having the more popular of his paintings translated into woodcuts. At first these were confined to the main design being cut and printed in black, the colour being added by hand by the artist ; but they laid the foundation for the whole process of colour-printing, since with later artists each colour was made the subject of a single block which could be overprinted upon the basic design. By this means many prints could be taken from each set of blocks, so that the cost of these Japanese colour-prints came within the reach of everybody who wished to possess the work of the fine artists who created them. Theme and price, therefore, were definitely popular ; and the men who took up this new form of pictorial art were themselves largely recruited from the artizan classes and catered for their tastes. One of the liveliest and most popular of themes was that of the theatre—a subject which would never have been permitted in the older conservative art, but which the common people loved. Actors in character and theatre scenes, therefore, became one of the most acceptable and regular subjects of these colour-prints.

Harunobu (1718–70) brought the art to perfection, adding a number of colours, devoting himself to delightful studies from daily life rather than to the theatre prints, and giving us the complete Japanese colour-print

"RIVER SCENE WITH BRIDGE AND FUJIYAMA IN THE DISTANCE," COLOUR PRINT BY HOKUSAI
(1760–1849)

British Museum, London

An impressive example of the naturalistic and decorative powers of the greatest of the democratic artists of Japan. We have only to compare it with "Old Battersea Bridge" to learn how Whistler was influenced by the design of Hokusai.

627

"JEHEI AND MISS KOHARU," BY UTAMARO

This colour-print, in black, pale-blue, Indian red and grey with a touch of yellow on the candle-stick,
is typical of the feminine grace, delicate drawing and fine design of Utamaro's work.

as we know it to-day. Alongside him stands Utamaro (1753–1806), depictor of beautiful women in designs dominated by the most lovely rhythms of curves. Then, towards the end of the eighteenth century, came that great master of the school, Hokusai (1760–1849), " the old man mad with painting " as he termed himself, and one of the most brilliant of all Japanese artists. He and Hiroshige (1797–1858) turned again to the art of landscape, but of landscape seen through the new convention of the colour-block and not through the traditional one of the reed brush. Hokusai is perhaps most famous for his brilliant series, the Thirty-six Views of Fuji. They are now part of the artistic heritage of the world, a revelation of the beauty of the sacred mountain in aspect after aspect of her loveliness expressed in the wonderful simplicity of this subtle art. Most famous of all his prints in another vein is " The Wave," that brilliant study of laden boats between moving walls of water. It emphasises yet another characteristic of these later masters of the colour-print : their genius for getting into the tiny space of their woodcut a sense of vastness which brings to us the immensity of Nature. It was the discovery of some of this series of designs which so greatly intrigued the French Impressionists when one of their number found them in a tiny shop in the Latin Quarter of Paris, or—according to a more romantic legend—discovered the first of them through the happy accident of being served with a piece of cheese wrapped in one of these popular Japanese prints. But for Hokusai's method of doing whole series of studies of one subject, Monet would not have conceived the idea of the famous Rouen Cathedral series, the Waterlilies, or his other manifold versions of individual subjects, under different aspects of light. Hokusai, who was draughtsman, poet, journalist, and *bon viveur*, issued a kind of art journal, *Mangwa*, which contained many of the delightful and tremendously vital sketches wherein the whole life of Japan of his day breathes for us.

If the Impressionists owed a debt to Hokusai, Whistler found much of the inspiration for his work in the beauty of the woodblock prints of the other nineteenth-century master, Hiroshige, who delighted in the simplicity and subtlety of evening scenes.

Their work was a brilliant finale to this school which had lasted for a hundred and fifty years—a brilliant end, indeed, to this whole story of Japanese art before the influences of the West submerged it. There came a day when American gunboats shelled Japan to force her to open her doors to the trade and the culture of the Western world. At first reluctantly, and then with all the virility and acquisitiveness of her people, she obeyed ; and mechanism, materialism, and the curse and temptation of power politics flooded over her age-old traditions. Perhaps the day may return when Japan again finds her own real life in the charm of the Tea Ceremony and the quietism of her native art. Or perhaps she is now for ever lost in the cosmopolitanism of the contemporary world, and her art must remain as museum pieces telling of a fairy-tale past and a beauty that is gone from the earth.

§ 4

India, so rich in literature and individual in architecture, yields fewer treasures of painting and sculpture. Much of the early work may have perished, for her climate, hot and moist as it is, has none of the preservative qualities of Egypt and Mesopotamia. That its civilisation is as old recent excavations in the Indus valley testify. Great cities are being unearthed there, coeval with Ur and the centres of civilisation in ancient Sumeria, cities with wide streets town-planned on a definite rectangular method, with two-storied houses complete with bath-rooms and a drainage system, with well-made brick-built wells and every evidence of a communal life planned by some central authority. But so far these homes of bronze-age culture have yielded no treasures of art, unless we except the seals and amulets engraved with animal forms often, or the terra-cotta figurines which tell of the elaborate jewellery worn by the women. Much has yet to be learned, however, of this civilisation. We have not yet deciphered the script, so there is no external literary evidence ; no temples seem to be among the ruins, no fortifications in all the six or seven city sites so far unearthed. That they lasted for many centuries is revealed by the fact that at the chief of them, Mohenjo-Daro, no less than six city levels have so far been discovered. Strangely the record, such as it is, breaks both at the beginning and the end, for there is no first link with primitive village settlements and this whole civilisation of the Indus valley ultimately disappeared, leaving no trace.

Art in India, therefore, practically begins with Buddhist work, although this echoes the woodcarving of the worship of the gods and goddesses of the Hindu cosmogony. Indeed, it is essential to remember how closely related Buddhism is to the old religion which it came to reform, that religion partly brought into India by the invading Aryans from the North and partly evolved by the native Dravidians whose doctrines of karma and of reincarnations and whose practice of Yoga were all made part of the new faith when Gautama, in the fifth century B.C., preached his doctrine of purification.

It was during the third century B.C., however, in the reign of that enlightened king, Asoka, that Buddhism was firmly established, and in the enormous wave of temple-building and shrine-making of those wonderful days. Something like the passion for religion and its expression which swept over France under Saint Louis and left us the beauty of the Gothic cathedrals belongs to this period of the missionary king of the

Buddhistic East. He stabilised the faith and its doctrines. He caused to be erected great pillars at various holy sites carved with inscriptions of the now orthodox doctrines. More than this he established the rock-hewn cave temples and the great *stupas*—the grave-mound shrines—at places where the relics of Gautama were reputed to be. Each of these had as its centre the traditional dome-shaped edifice, symbol of the lotus of heaven, and around it a four-square processional path approached by great decorated gateways and stone railings. Alongside the processional path as it climbed the mount would be low-relief panels carved to tell the story and legends of the faith.

Thus came the first stone sculpture, for contact during the previous century with Hellenistic tradition and the Western world through the invasion of Asia by Alexander the Great had taught the Hindus the value and durability of stone as a building material in place of their own method of wooden structure. It did not break down the forms which obviously belong to wood and woodcarving, and these decorative-pictorial panels, these great gateways, and the various symbols of the Buddha with which the shrines are enriched were all conceived in a wood tradition even when the medium was stone. The Eastern gateway of the stupa at Sanchi in Bhopal, with its elaborate carvings both in low relief and in the round, may be studied from the cast in South Kensington Museum. Not the least fascinating of these sculptures are the delightful figures of the tree-spirits with which it is adorned. How elaborate these stupas could become may be deduced from the fact that one of them, built at Amaravati, had nearly seventeen thousand square feet of low relief carvings. This magnificent work was unhappily almost destroyed by fire during last century, but precious fragments remain in the British and other Museums.

In those first shrines and in the great temples excavated and carved from the solid rock which were part of the stupendous early Buddhistic architecture there was no representation of Buddha himself, and it was in the districts most in touch with the Hellenistic tradition that during the first century A.D. a school of sculpture arose which began to create images of the Buddha. The traditional attitude of contemplation prescribed for the Yogi became the most widely accepted. This attitude had been poetically described in the *Bhagavad-Gita* :

" Abiding alone in a secret place, without craving and without possession, he shall take his seat upon a firm seat, neither over-high nor over-low, and with the workings of the mind and the senses held in check, with body, head, neck maintained in perfect equipoise, looking not round about him, so let him meditate and thereby reach the peace of the abyss : and the likeness of one such, who knows the boundless joy that lies beyond the senses and is grasped by intuition, and who swerves not from truth, is that of a lamp in a windless place which flickereth not."

631

WALL PAINTING FROM THE CAVES AT AJANTA

One of the greatest series of frescoes in the world, the paintings at Ajanta, Hyderabad, stand in Buddhist Art as those at Assisi do to Christian. The Indian work belongs to the Gupta period (A.D. 320–530).

632

Such an ideal of static repose was an inspiring motif for sculpture, and from it came the marvellous Buddha figures of the Eastern world. One of the noblest and most massive of these early Buddhas is the giant one at Anuradhapura in Ceylon which belongs to the second century.

Once the way had been opened, however, to the representation of the great teacher, the cult of statuary inevitably spread. Many incidents, many traditions of his life offered themselves. During the Gupta period, which extended from A.D. 320 to 530, this Buddhistic sculpture became more experimental and elaborate. Groups of figures, haloed saints, studies of the Buddha as King or as Bodhisattva, individual figures framed with low relief panels : the inspiration never waned, until Buddhism itself lost something of its hold upon India and found its home farther East.

Meantime, India tended to revert to the gods of earlier Hinduism, and it was upon these that the later Hindu artists were able to expend the fecundity of their imagination in form. The vast literature of legend contained in the Vedic hymns composed by priest-poets as early as 1500 B.C. and written between 800 and 500 B.C. contained thrilling conceptions of the gods and their attributes derived from the earliest animism and Nature worship and partly refined in the spiritual imagination of this great people. Siva, Vishna, and Brahma were the three leading deities in whose activities the whole processes of the universe became symbolised, and in all of whom aspects of terror as well as of benevolence were accepted. The Hindu mind, not so literal nor anthropomorphic as that of the West, conceived these deities in forms which to our eyes have a certain monstrosity. Siva has many limbs ; her son Ganesha has an elephant's head to signify world-wisdom ; Sakti as the dark consort of Siva had any form of terror. All the terrible fecundity of a jungle country became expressed in the sculptured forms of these Nature gods and goddesses in a conception of the interwovenness of life which twisted darkly between the animal and the human. It is only by seeing Indian sculpture and painting of the last few hundred years from this native viewpoint that the Westerner can free himself from an obsession with what to us seems monstrous.

With the domination of Western influences, however, there remains little new life in those age-old conceptions or in this Hindu art. Nothing now can compare with the glories of the Gupta period when not only the great sculpture of Buddhism but the wonderful series of paintings in the Caves at Ajanta—a series which stand in Buddhistic art as the Franciscan paintings of Giotto stand in Christian—left us their treasures. Nothing can equal the marvels of the great Stupa out at Borobudur in distant Java which in the eighth century retold the whole legend of Buddha and symbolised the sevenfold path in a miracle of carved stone ; or of that vast temple, the Angkor Wat, away in Cambodia which was built during the

633

eleventh and twelfth centuries. Once in the sixteenth century, under the influence of that noble spirit Akbar, Mughal and Rajput painting, stimulated by the genius of near-by Persia, had a brief period of loveliness, achieving a delightful decorative quality and a charming character of its own. But the school passed away, as that unity of religion which Akbar had inaugurated broke down again after his death. India became the field for vast exploitation and her own people lost grip of their destiny. Only in recent years, at the instigation of such master-spirits as that of Rabindranath Tagore and his artist brother Abanindro Nath Tagore, has there seemed to be a new hope for a revival of Hindu art based on the magnificent traditions of her own great past.

XXXIII

THE INFLUENCE OF THE FAR EAST

JAPANESE COLOUR-PRINTS AND THE ART OF WHISTLER

§ 1

THE beginning of the artistic influence of Japan on Europe is generally dated from the International Exhibition held at London in 1862, when examples of Japanese art shown made a profound impression on all who studied them. Seidlitz, in his *History of Japanese Colour-Prints*, gives the same date, but this authority traces the first discovery of Japanese art in Europe to a Japanese shop in the Rue de Rivoli, Paris. This shop, known as " La Porte Chinoise " and owned by a dealer named Soye, was frequented by a number of artists who delighted in the colour-prints by Hokusai, Hiroshige, and others which they found there. To this shop came Manet, Degas, Monet, and other French artists afterwards to become famous, and to it also came a young American artist, James McNeill Whistler. The Japanese have a perfect instinct of decoration, and consequently these colour-prints made an immediate and powerful appeal to a young artist who already had within him the instinct of decoration. In the work of Hokusai and Hiroshige, Whistler recognised those qualities which above all he desired to have in his own work.

§ 2

Among the artists of the nineteenth century Whistler holds a unique position. He was the first great painter of American birth to win universal renown. His life was a long struggle against hostile criticism and misunderstanding, and he defended his art and his ideals with the pungent brilliancy of a wit and with the undaunted pugnacity of a soldier. By example and precept he eventually revolutionised English ideas about art and interior decoration. He compelled people who stubbornly repeated " Every Picture tells a Story," to realise at long last that *every picture ought to sing a tune*, that is to say, it ought to utter forth a melody of line and a harmony of colour ; in a word, he compelled all England and the United States to recognise the decorative as well as the illustrative element in painting. More than any other English-speaking man Whistler opened our eyes to the true value of Velazquez and Hokusai, and he invented a new style of portraiture in which

Spanish realism was exquisitely wedded to a Japanese sense of decoration. A stranger within our gates, he revealed England to the English and recorded, both in his etchings and in his paintings, poetic aspects of London's riverside, aspects to which hitherto all artists had been blind, aspects the beauty of which all can now see.

Whistler was born on July 10, 1834, at Lowell, in Massachusetts, and was baptized there with the Christian names of James Abbott. This second name he dropped in later life and substituted for it his mother's maiden name, McNeill. His father, Major George Washington Whistler, after leaving the United States army, became a railway engineer, and in 1842 journeyed to Russia with his wife and family : he had been appointed chief adviser of the railway under construction between Moscow and St. Petersburg. The most important consequence to James Whistler of this boyhood stay in Russia was that in St. Petersburg he learnt to speak French fluently. His father died in 1849, when the widow returned with her children to the United States.

Following in his father's footsteps, James Whistler in 1851 entered the military college of West Point, but after three years of desultory study he was dismissed, chiefly owing to his deplorable failure in chemistry. The first question in his oral examination floored him completely, and later in life Whistler humorously said, " If silicon had been a gas I might have become a general in the United States army." Even from his Russian days Whistler had shown a remarkable capacity for drawing, and his delight in sketching prompted his relatives, after his West Point failure, to obtain for him a post as draughtsman in the Government Coast Survey Department at Washington, thinking that this occupation might be more congenial to him. To some extent it was, for here he learnt to engrave and etch, and he executed an excellent plate of a view, taken from the sea, of cliffs along the coast ; but the fancy heads and figure which he irrelevantly added in the margin showed that he could not take his topographical studies seriously as a preliminary to map-making, but only as an excuse for sketching. In February, 1855, he resigned his position, and the end of the year found him an art student in Paris.

Many painters have spent joyous student-days in Paris, but few of them bear the traces of it in their lives as Whistler did. He had barely turned twenty-one when he arrived in Paris, and his high-spirited temperament and sense of fun delighted in all the antics which then distinguished the Bohemians of the Latin Quarter. In those days the art students lived a life apart, making themselves noticed by wearing unorthodox clothes, playing all sorts of practical jokes, affecting to despise the common mortal, and never so happy as when they succeeded in shocking and bewildering what they called the " bourgeois." Whistler plunged hot-foot into this way of life, and, as the distinguished French critic Théodore Duret, who knew him

"AT THE PIANO," BY WHISTLER (1834–1903)

This early work, painted in 1859, was the first picture the artist exhibited in London. It shows us Whistler's favourite niece, Annie, and her mother, Mrs. Seymour Haden, who was the artist's half-sister.

well, has remarked, there was grafted on him " the habit of a separate pose, whimsical attire, a way of despising and setting at defiance the ' vulgar herd ' incapable of seeing and feeling like an artist.   This combination of the distinctive characteristics of a French art student and the manner of an American gentleman, in a man otherwise full of life, spirit, and individuality, made of Whistler a quaint original who could not fail to be remarked everywhere."

But all the time he was amusing himself he worked, not so much in the studio of Gleyre—his official place of training, but irregularly attended—as in the streets and cafés of Paris and in his rooms.   He divided his time between etching and painting, and in the former he appeared almost as a master in the first " French Set " published as early as 1858.   In the following year he produced his first great individual achievement in painting, " At the Piano," which, though rejected by the Paris Salon of 1859, was hung at the Royal Academy in 1860 and subsequently purchased by the Academician John Philip, R.A. ·In this picture, which represents his half-sister, Mrs. Seymour Haden, seated, playing the piano, against which her little daughter Annie, in white, is standing, Whistler already shows the influence of Velazquez.   Philip was well known as an intense admirer of this master, and it was doubtless the Spanish qualities in Whistler's painting which led the older artist to buy it.   Two years later Whistler set out for Madrid with the intention of seeing the pictures by Velazquez in the Prado, but on the way he stopped at a seaside resort, where he nearly got drowned while bathing and had to return to Paris without going to Madrid.

In 1863 he made his second attempt to exhibit in the Paris Salon, and again the jury rejected his picture, the full-length portrait of a young Irish girl, known as " Jo," dressed in white, holding a white flower, and standing against a white curtain.   " The White Girl," as it was first called, was the beginning of a series of pictures in which Whistler deliberately experimented in improvising a colour harmony based on the infinitely delicate gradations of one dominant colour.   It was afterwards entitled " Symphony in White No. I."

So many paintings by artists of great talent were rejected by the Salon this year that the Emperor Napoleon III intervened, and by his order a selection of the rejected works was shown in a special room which became famous as the *Salon des Refusés*.   Of this epoch-making exhibition more will be said in the next chapter, when dealing with French painters who were Whistler's contemporaries, but for the moment it must suffice to say that among the works there exhibited was " The White Girl," which elicited high praise from the more advanced critics.

From 1859 Whistler had divided his time between Paris and London, and though he had many friends and admirers in the former city, he was

W. J. Stacey.

"THE LITTLE WHITE GIRL," BY WHISTLER

National Gallery, London

For sheer beauty this portrait of his once favourite model, afterwards Mrs. Joanna Abbott, was never surpassed by Whistler. This picture inspired Swinburne to write his poem " Before the Mirror." In 1919 it was bequeathed by Mr. Arthur Studd to the National Gallery.

639

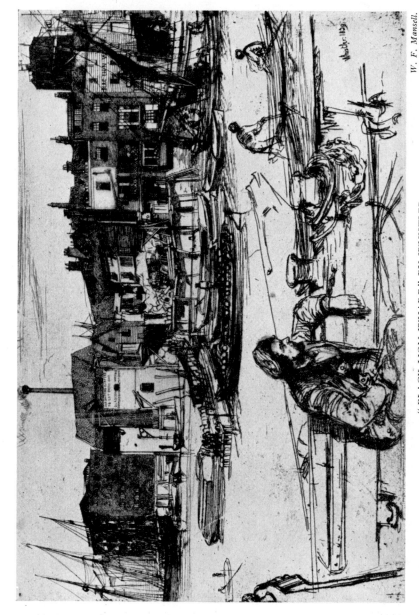

"BLACK LION WHARF," BY WHISTLER

One of the most famous etchings in his early "Thames Set," this work shows the precision and delicacy of Whistler's draughtsmanship in 1859. He was the first artist to perceive and record the picturesqueness of the Thames in mid-London.

hurt at the lack of official recognition. In 1863 he fixed his residence in London, where several of his family were already established. Whistler's father had married twice, and one of the daughters by his first wife had married the English surgeon Seymour Haden, who afterwards made a great reputation as an etcher. Whistler's mother also had now left America and was living in London with her second son William, a doctor. James Whistler himself had not only stayed and exhibited in London, but had worked there, for in 1859 he had already begun the series of etchings known as "The Thames Set," which marks the culminating point of his first etching period. One of these, "Black Lion Wharf," may be taken as an example of the perfection of his technique in 1859, of the lightness and elasticity of his line, and of the vivacity of the whole. Though he afterwards produced etchings, perfect of their kind, in quite another style, Whistler never did anything better in their own way than some of the plates in "The Thames Set."

Whistler settled down in Chelsea, and became friendly with his neighbour Rossetti, who shared his taste for blue-and-white Chinese porcelain and for Japanese colour-prints, and during his first years in London the artistic influence of the Far East became more pronounced in Whistler's art. He surrounded himself with Oriental objects and introduced them constantly into his pictures. In 1864 he painted "The Gold Screen," against which sat a young woman in Japanese costume, surrounded by other variously coloured objects from the Far East. About the same time he painted the beautiful "Princesse du Pays de la Porcelaine," in which brilliant colours are again afforded by a Japanese dress. The original of this portrait was Miss Christina Spartali, daughter of the Greek Consul-General in London. Her sister Marie Spartali, afterwards Mrs. Stillman, had been a pupil of Rossetti and sat to him for "Fiametta" and other paintings. Owing to the family likeness common to the two sisters, it has been said that at this time Whistler was subject to Rossetti's influence, but the resemblance between their works is a superficial one due only to the likeness of their respective models. There is no evidence that Whistler borrowed any of Rossetti's methods, and the chief influences during the years in which Whistler formed his style of painting were Courbet and Manet—as we shall see in the next chapter—Velazquez and the masters of Japan. In etching he was principally influenced by Rembrandt and Méryon.

"The Princess of the Porcelain Country," accepted by the Salon in 1865, was the first work by Whistler to be shown in any official exhibition in Paris. Other pictures of this Japanese period were "The Lange Leizen," in the Academy of 1864, "The Balcony," in the Academy of 1870, and, most beautiful and best known of all, "The Little White Girl," also known

"LA PRINCESSE DU PAYS DE LA PORCELAINE," BY WHISTLER

One of the masterpieces of Whistler's pronounced Japanese period, this picture is a costume portrait of Miss Christina Spartali, daughter of the Greek Consul-General in London. It was formerly in the possession of the shipowner, Mr. F. R. Leyland, and occupied a central position in the famous " Peacock Room " decorated for him by Whistler.

"PORTRAIT OF MISS CICELY HENRIETTA ALEXANDER," BY WHISTLER

This charming portrait of the younger daughter of Mr. W. C. Alexander is one of Whistler's most daring colour-schemes, a bright harmony of grey and green. Note the butterflies in the left-hand top corner, which give a note of summer-time gaiety to the composition and repeat Whistler's own "trade-mark," the butterfly signature on the wall.

643

as " Symphony in White No. II," shown at the Academy in the same year. The Japanese fan in the girl's hand is the only direct confession of Oriental influence in this picture, which otherwise unites the Spanish gravity and realism of " At the Piano " with the gay-coloured decorativeness of a Hokusai or Hiroshige. After having seen this picture in Whistler's studio, Swinburne wrote the poem afterwards included in *Poems and Ballads* :

BEFORE THE MIRROR

Come snow, come wind or thunder,
High up in air,
I watch my face and wonder
At my bright hair.
Nought else exists or grieves
The rose at heart, that heaves
With love of her own leaves, and lips that pair.

I cannot tell what pleasures
Or what pains were,
What pale new loves and treasures
New years will bear ;
What beam will fall, what shower
With grief or joy for dower,
But one thing knows the flower, the flower is fair.

Whistler also painted a " Symphony in White No. III." In this, two girls, one in cream, one in white, recline on a white sofa, while a fan on the floor and the flowers of an azalea in a corner repeat the dominant whites. The motive of the artist in choosing these colour-schemes and calling the pictures " symphonies " was at this time beyond the comprehension of even professional art critics, and one of them wrote of this picture in the *Saturday Review* :

In the " Symphony in White No. III " by Mr. Whistler there are many dainty varieties of tint, but it is not precisely a symphony in white. One lady has a yellowish dress and brown hair and a bit of blue ribbon, the other has a red fan, and there are flowers and green leaves. There is a girl in white on a white sofa, but even this girl has reddish hair ; and of course there is the flesh colour of the complexions.

To this Whistler promptly retorted :

Bon Dieu ! did this wise person expect white hair and chalked faces ? And does he then, in his astounding consequence, believe that a symphony in F contains no other note, but shall be a continued repetition of F, F, F ? . . . Fool !

This was one of the earliest of Whistler's critical encounters, taking

"THE ARTIST'S MOTHER," BY WHISTLER

Luxembourg, Paris

When M. Bourgeois, Minister of Fine Arts, expressed a desire to purchase this work for the French Nation, Whistler replied : " The picture you have chosen is precisely the one I could most earnestly wish to see become the object of so solemn a consecration."

place when the picture was exhibited at the Academy in 1867, and the critics were soon to learn that here was a painter who could hit back with interest.

As the successive exhibition of Whistler's pictures enabled the tendencies and peculiarities of his work to be more clearly seen, the public, the critics, and the Royal Academy itself became more and more hostile to him, and finally took up an attitude of undisguised ill-will. In 1872 his characteristic painting of his mother, now universally recognised to be one of the great portraits of the century, was narrowly rejected by the Academy, and its final acceptance was only due to the staunch championship of the veteran Sir William Boxall, R.A., who threatened to resign from the Council if the picture were not hung. Doubtless Whistler's habit of giving his works titles borrowed from musical terms prejudiced the public against them. An extremist far more in his titles than in his actual manner of painting, Whistler went so far as to call his picture of his mother, " Arrangement in Grey and Black." He defended this title by saying :

That is what it is. To me it is interesting as a picture of my mother ; but what can or ought the public to care about the identity of the portrait ?

In his desire to emphasise the importance of decorative design and colour in painting, Whistler became a little inhuman. As one of his younger critics pertinently observed, we can find an " arrangement of grey and black " in a coal-scuttle ; we find far more in Whistler's " Mother," we find reverence for age, character, tenderness, and affection. It has become one of the great pictures of the world, not only because it is a pleasing pattern of colours, but because it is a true work of deep emotion tenderly expressed.

No longer welcome at the Royal Academy, Whistler was fortunate in soon securing a new exhibition centre. Sir Coutts Lindsay, a rich banker and amateur painter who patronised the arts, had the Grosvenor Gallery built in Bond Street, and at the first exhibition opened there in May 1877 Whistler was represented by seven pictures. These included the portrait of Carlyle, now at Glasgow, a painting similar in style to the artist's " Mother," described as " An Arrangement in Brown " ; a full-length of Irving as Philip II of Spain, described as " Arrangement in Black No. III " ; and four nocturnes, two in blue and silver, one in blue and gold, and one in black and gold. Whistler had not confined his studies of the Thames in mid-London to his etched work ; he had used these subjects for paintings in the 'sixties, among them being " Old Battersea Bridge," and " Chelsea in Ice," but in this new series of evening effects by the riverside he shocked the conventions of the day more than he had yet done by his " symphonies."

NOCTURNE—BLUE AND GOLD—" OLD BATTERSEA BRIDGE," BY WHISTLER
Tate Gallery, London

One of the celebrated nocturnes exhibited at the Grosvenor Gallery in 1877, when Ruskin accused Whistler of " flinging a pot of paint in the public's face." The painter was awarded only a farthing damages in the libel action which ensued ; but two years after Whistler's death, this picture, for which he had asked 200 guineas, was purchased at 2000 guineas for the National Gallery.

These poetic paintings of night represent the extreme point of originality to which Whistler went. Particularities of scene and landscape exist in these nocturnes only as accessories ; the real subject is the limpidity of the atmosphere, water illumined by the pale rays of the moon, mysterious shadows, the great silhouettes of dark nights, the darkness intensified sometimes by a splash of fireworks against the sky. To-day, though Cremorne is no more, we can recognise the truth as well as the beauty in " Cremorne Lights " and similar works, for Whistler has now taught us to use our own experience in looking at these pictures of moonlight and lights reflected in the water. But at the time of their first appearance these nocturnes were incomprehensible to most people, who looked in them for topographical details which the veil of night would naturally conceal. In an eloquent and moving passage in his lecture, known as the " Ten o'Clock," Whistler afterwards explained what he saw and painted by the Thames at eventide :

When the evening mist clothes the riverside with poetry as with a veil, and the poor buildings lose themselves in the dim sky, and the tall chimneys become campanili, and the warehouses are palaces in the night, and the whole city hangs in the heavens, and fairyland is before us—then the wayfarer hastens home ; the working man and the cultured one, the wise man and the one of pleasure, cease to understand as they have ceased to see, and Nature, who, for once, has sung in tune, sings her exquisite song to the artist alone, her son and her master, her son in that he loves her, her master in that he knows her.

But in 1877 Whistler's views on the poetry of night were unknown, and the magic of his brush could not immediately convert the public to appreciation of pictures the like of which had never before been seen in Europe. Something approaching them had been seen in Japan, as we may see by comparing Hokusai's bridge pictures with those of Whistler, but Hokusai and Hiroshige were not known then as they are to-day. Whistler's nocturnes were regarded by the majority as a smear of uniform colour in which no distinct forms could be considered. The painter was looked upon as a charlatan and buffoon, and among those who attacked him, sad to relate, was the stout defender of Turner and the Pre-Raphaelites. John Ruskin, no wiser in this respect than the others, permitted himself to write the following in *Fors Clavigera* on July 2, 1877 :

For Mr. Whistler's own sake, no less than for the protection of the purchaser, Sir Coutts Lindsay ought not to have admitted works into the gallery in which the ill-educated conceit of the artist so nearly approached the aspect of wilful imposture. I have seen, and heard, much of cockney impudence before now ; but never expected to hear a coxcomb ask two hundred guineas for flinging a pot of paint in the public's face.

Strange that Ruskin did not remember that the selfsame phrase about

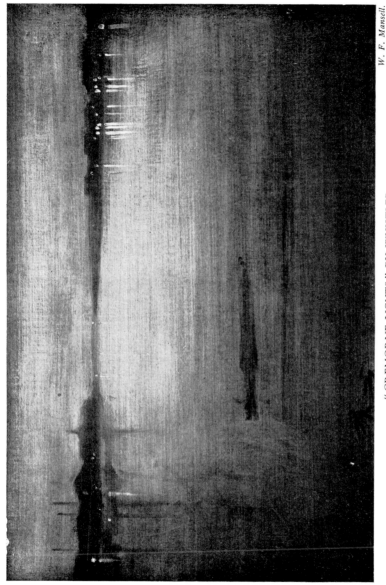

W. F. Mansell.

"CREMORNE LIGHTS," BY WHISTLER

National Gallery, London

"When the evening mist clothes the riverside with poetry, as with a veil, and the poor buildings lose themselves in the dim sky, and the tall chimneys become campanili, and the warehouses are palaces in the night, and the whole city hangs in the heavens and fairyland is before us."—*J. McNeill Whistler.*

X*

649

" flinging a pot of paint " had been used a generation earlier by a critic of one of Turner's sunsets. Then Ruskin had been on the side of the artist, now he did not understand and stood with the Philistines. Time has avenged the insult to genius uncomprehended, and the " Nocturne—Blue and Gold—Old Battersea Bridge " which Ruskin in 1877 thought not worth two hundred guineas, was in 1905 eagerly purchased for two thousand guineas and presented to the nation.

Whistler's exhibits brought him all the publicity any artist could desire —all London was talking of his nocturnes—but the hostility of the critics, and particularly the savage onslaught of Ruskin, scared away purchasers. When he exhibited for the second time at the Grosvenor Gallery in 1878, Whistler found that Ruskin's denunciation was stopping the sale of his pictures and, after some hesitation, he decided to bring a libel action against him.

The case was heard on the 25th and 26th of November 1878, before Mr. Justice Huddlestone and a special jury. It created a great sensation, but Whistler was ill-advised to bring the action, because artistic questions can never be satisfactorily settled in a court of law. Popular sympathy was with the critic, who had so often been right in the past, and Whistler's brilliant repartees in the witness-box did him no good, for they only tended to confirm the opinion that he was an amusing jester who was not to be taken seriously. In cross-examination the opposing counsel elicited the fact that the " Nocturne in Black and Gold " had been painted in two days, and then said, " The labour of two days, then, is that for which you ask two hundred guineas ? " " No," replied Whistler with dignity ; " I ask it for the knowledge of a lifetime."

The point at issue really was whether the nocturnes were or were not works of art, and this was a matter obviously over the heads of the jury. Albert Moore, giving evidence for Whistler, praised his pictures highly and declared that they showed not " eccentricity " but " originality." William Rossetti also pronounced the nocturnes to be true works of art, but on the other side Frith declared they were not, and Burne-Jones agreed with him because, though he admitted that the nocturnes had " fine colour and atmosphere," he considered that they lacked " complete finish." Tom Taylor, the art critic of *The Times*, giving evidence for Ruskin, attempted to explain what Burne-Jones meant by finish, and for this purpose produced a picture by Titian. But when this was handed to the jury, one of them, mistaking it for a picture by Whistler, exclaimed, " Oh, come ! we've had enough of these Whistlers," and they all refused to look at it !

In the end Whistler was awarded the contemptuous sum of one farthing damages. This meant that he had to pay his own law costs, and since nobody would buy his pictures now, he was soon in money difficulties.

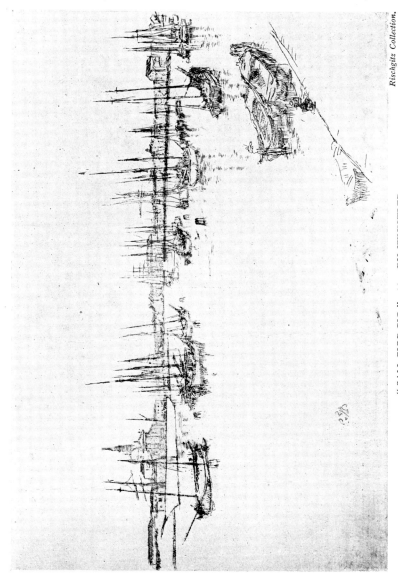

Rischgitz Collection.

"SAN GIORGIO," 1880, BY WHISTLER

A brilliant example of Whistler's second manner in etching which he developed in Venice, where he stayed for some months after his bankruptcy. Again "fairyland is before us," and with the utmost economy of means the artist has suggested a characteristic aspect of Venice and its shipping, flooded with light and air.

He revenged himself by issuing a pamphlet, *Art and Art Critics*, in which his enemies were neatly and wittily put in their places, but this did not help him to live. To put an end to an untenable situation, early in 1879 he had to abandon his residence, " The White House," in Chelsea. He became a bankrupt and all his belongings were sold to satisfy his creditors.

Another man might have been crushed by the misfortunes which now crowded on him, but fortunately Whistler was an etcher as well as a painter, and at this moment, when his pictures were unsaleable, he again turned to etching. He came to an arrangement with a firm, which advanced him a sum of money on etchings he engaged to execute, and with this he went in 1879 to Venice, where he developed a new and beautiful style in etching. In comparison with his earlier work, these Venice etchings were lighter in handling and more simplified in line. " San Giorgio " shows how spacious an effect Whistler was able to secure with a minimum of means.

These new etchings were not at first popular with the public and the critics any more than the nocturnes, but they were appreciated and purchased by many discriminating print-collectors, and when Whistler returned to Chelsea towards the end of 1880 his position gradually improved. In 1883 he held a second and larger exhibition of his Venetian pieces at the Fine Art Society, and prepared an extraordinary catalogue, in which under each numbered exhibit appeared quotations taken from influential journals and well-known writers, *all hostile*, and beginning with this extract from *Truth* : " Another crop of Mr. Whistler's little jokes." The exhibition, which was beautifully arranged and staged, together with this quaint catalogue, caused an immense sensation. Never before had an artist made fun of his critics to this extent. Visitors could not fail to recognise the refinement in works like " San Giorgio," and when they read a sentence like " Whistler is eminently vulgar," the criticism recoiled on the writer, not the artist. The tide began to turn, and a considerable opinion now became definitely favourable to Whistler. He began to paint again, people like Mrs. Meux, the wife of the brewer, and Lady Archibald Campbell came to him for portraits, and his position was immensely strengthened when his " Portrait of the Artist's Mother " obtained a medal and a brilliant success in the Paris Salon of 1883. Later this work was bought by the French Government for the Luxembourg.

For the next few years Whistler made Paris his principal exhibition centre. Exhibited at the Grosvenor Gallery in 1881, his " Portrait of Miss Cicely Alexander " had been dreadfully abused by English critics ; but in the Paris Salon of 1884 it was singled out for general approbation. For a brief season Whistler exhibited at the Royal Society of British Artists, of which he was elected President in June 1886, and under his presidency this Society held the most brilliant exhibitions in its history. But in 1888 there was a cabal against him by members discontented with his rule. Whistler was compelled to resign, and was followed by a number of talented artists whom he had persuaded to join the Society. When asked to explain what had happened, the ex-President replied, " It is quite simple ; the artists have left and the British remain."

The year after Whistler met with this rebuff in London, he was made a Chevalier of the Legion of Honour, which showed the esteem in which he was now held in France, and in 1892 he took a house at Paris in the Rue de Bac. He can hardly be said to have settled there, however, for he returned several times to London. In 1890 he had published a collection of letters and various controversial matter, including a report, with his own marginal comments, of the Ruskin trial, under the title of *The Gentle Art of Making Enemies*, and this publication not only increased his reputation as a wit but showed that he possessed a distinct literary style of his own. This was followed some years later by *The Baronet and the Butterfly*, a pamphlet giving the artist's version of a quarrel and lawsuit with Sir William Eden over a portrait of Lady Eden. Whistler had early adopted the device of a butterfly as his sign-manual and signature, but he was a butterfly with a sting, as he confessed himself to be in the little drawings with which he decorated his publications.

All the quarrels and encounters of his stormy life cannot be recounted here, but in the end he was victorious in London as in Paris. The purchase of his " Mother " by the French Government helped to turn the scale in England. A new generation of artists gave Whistler a banquet in London to celebrate the event, and in the same year (1892) the most important one-man-show of his pictures yet held anywhere was opened in the old Goupil Gallery in Bond Street. This included nearly all his most famous works, among them the disgraced nocturnes, but now only a minority objected to his pictures or his titles, and the success of the exhibition revealed the change which the course of years had brought about in London opinion. The Royal Academy was no longer the power it had been in his earlier days ; its prestige had declined, and there was now a powerful body of outside artists who admired Whistler. In 1898 the most eminent of these formed the " International Society of Sculptors, Painters, and Gravers," and invited Whistler to become its first President, a position he held till his death on July 17, 1903. The exhibitions of this new Society proved that Whistler was not only respected by artists, but had become fashionable with all persons of taste.

To sum up, it may be said that after forty years of incessant battling, Whistler enjoyed a decade of tranquil success, but his last years were saddened by private trouble. In 1888 he had married the widow of E. W. Godwin, an architect, and his wife's death in 1896 was a great blow to the artist. With his loneliness he grew restless, and though his continued devotion to his work saved him from melancholy, he travelled about a good deal. He was visiting Holland in the summer of 1902 when he was seized with a heart attack, and though he gained enough strength to return to London, and even to begin working again in the winter, a relapse in the following June prostrated him, and on Friday, July 17, he was seized with syncope and died. France, Italy, Bavaria, and Dresden had all conferred distinctions on him ; but in America, his birthplace, and in England, where he lived and worked for the greater part of his life, Whistler received no official recognition.

§ 3

In his treatment of buildings, particularly in his earlier etchings, Whistler was undoubtedly influenced by the work of Charles Méryon, one of the earliest and greatest etchers of architectural subjects. The life of this artist is one of the saddest stories in modern art. Charles Méryon was born in 1821 ; he was the son of a French dancer, and his father is said to have been an Englishman of good family, but during his early life he had little assistance from either of his parents, and from his boyhood he had to struggle to make his own way in the Bohemian underworld of Paris.

During Méryon's lifetime, unfortunately, etchings were not so popular as they are to-day. For a century and a half after Rembrandt etching, as a pure and separate art, lay comparatively unnoticed ; but undeterred by want of patrons, poverty, and ill-health, Méryon devoted himself to the revival of this almost forgotten art, and became one of its greatest masters that the world has yet seen. To record on copper the beauty and interest of the architecture of Paris became the passion of Méryon's life, and his etchings are unique for the imagination and emotional force they display, combined with scrupulously exact drawing of the architectural features which form his theme. His famous etching " Le Stryge," showing us a view of Paris from Notre Dame, with one of the quaint gargoyles of the Cathedral occupying a prominent place in the foreground, reveals not only the perfection of his technique, with its fine, nervous line and rich velvety blacks, but also the blend of realism and imagination which characterises this artist's work.

These masterly views of Paris were offered for sale by the artist at the price of one franc (then worth about tenpence in English money), but even at this ridiculous figure they did not find enough purchasers to enable him to keep body and soul together. Privation, hardship, and want of proper nourishment inevitably told on his health, and eventually his nerves gave way and he was put away as insane in the hospital of Charenton. But though of a nervous temperament, his brain was not diseased, and

654

Insatiable vampire L'éternelle Luxure
Sur la Grande Cité convoite sa pâture

Autotype Co. Ltd.

"LE STRYGE," BY MÉRYON (1821–68)

The career of this great French etcher is one of the saddest tragedies in art history. Unable in his lifetime to sell his prints at tenpence in sufficient numbers to save him from starvation, Charles Méryon died in a hospital literally from want of proper nourishment. A few years after his death his genius was so appreciated that his etchings were eagerly bought at £5 a piece, and in recent years collectors have paid over a thousand pounds for an etching which the artist could not sell for a franc.

655

after some months of good feeding in the hospital Méryon became normal, and it was seen that his breakdown was wholly due to starvation. He was allowed to leave Charenton and began to work again, drawing and etching in Paris, but the unhappy genius had no better fortune and seemed unable to secure the minimum amount of food that a human body requires. Again he starved, with the same result, his mind became unhinged, and he was taken back to Charenton, where he died in 1868.

By a cruel irony of fate the etchings began to be appreciated almost immediately after the etcher's death. Never before or since has the art world seen so rapid and sensational an increase in value. The explanation is that the interest excited by the plates of Whistler and Seymour Haden led to a feverish hunt after other etchers, and so the fame of Méryon was established. Within a few years of his death the etchings he had vainly tried to sell for tenpence apiece were changing hands at five pounds ; the prices of them rose rapidly and steadily from tens to hundreds of pounds, and within recent years rich collectors have paid more than a thousand pounds to secure a fine impression of an etching by Méryon.

XXXIV

POST IMPRESSIONISM, CUBISM, AND FUTURISM

THE ART OF CÉZANNE, VAN GOGH, GAUGUIN, MATISSE, AND PICASSO

§ I

WHAT is " Post impressionism " ? This term was invented by the English painter and art critic, Roger Fry, to cover various art movements which came *after* Impressionism, and since some of these movements have been developments of Impressionism, while others have been a reaction from it, confusion can only be avoided by considering separately the principal movements and the artists associated with them.

The reader of this OUTLINE will have observed that, from the days of Giotto down to the close of the nineteenth century, the development of the main stream of European painting was in the direction of a more perfect representation of the appearances of natural forms. In the nine-teenth century two causes contributed to change the direction of painting. One was the invention of Photography, which set painters wondering what part the representative element really played in a picture ; the other was the new Colour-science of the Impressionists, who seemed to have pushed truth of representation to a point where further developments were im-possible. Ambitious painters sighed, like Alexander, for new worlds to conquer : the problems of foreshortening, of perspective, of the true colour of shadows, all had been solved triumphantly by their predecessors. What was there left to be done by a painter who did not wish to imitate the work of any other artist ? It was inevitable that a reaction should set in. Painting, according to the neo-Impressionist formulas described in the previous chapter, had become, as we have seen, a highly complicated and scientific business. A new generation began to argue that, after all, painting was not a science but an art, and that its primary function was not the accurate representation of Nature but the expression of an emotion. A fresh start was made in a new direction. Emphasis was now to be laid on expressing an idea rather than on rendering appearances, and it was held that by reducing the facts of phenomena to a minimum the idea might

657

be able to shine forth more brightly. The vessel of art having become overloaded, it was thought advisable to lighten the ship by throwing some of the cargo overboard.

Already there had been a forerunner in this direction. Honoré Daumier (1808–79), though chiefly known to his contemporaries as a pungent caricaturist and lithographer, also executed oil-paintings which have become highly esteemed since his death. These pictures, sometimes satirising the Law Courts whose "justice" roused him to fury, often based on some illuminating incident in the history of Don Quixote and Sancho Panza, were unlike any other pictures of his time, and always expressed an idea with a maximum of intellectual force and a minimum of colour and pictorial means.

Half a century before his time, he had the courage to eliminate trappings and redundancies from his painting, and to give us plastic conceptions of rugged simplicity. In so doing he anticipated the most interesting and fruitful of modern pictorial movements.

It was from the heart of Impressionism itself that the most powerful reaction began, and the artist usually regarded now as the "Father of Post-Impressionism" is Paul Cézanne (1839–1906), who during his lifetime exhibited with the Impressionists and was long thought to be one of them. But though the friend and companion of Pissarro, Renoir, and Monet, Cézanne differed from them in many ways. To begin with, he was a southerner, born at Aix in Provence, while all the others belonged to Northern France ; secondly, while accepting their colour theories, he never wholly adopted in practice their prismatic palette ; thirdly, while they were primarily occupied with registering fugitive effects of light, he was always most concerned with eternal verities. His aim is best explained in his own words : "I wish to make of Impressionism something solid and durable, like the art of the Old Masters."

If we look at his landscapes, or his "Card Players," or his portrait of himself, we do not think first of the light by which these things are seen, but rather of the weight, density, and solidity of the forms depicted. The art of Cézanne is simpler and less complicated than that of Monet and Pissarro ; his analysis of colour is more summary, his expression ruder and more forcible. His colour is entirely his own, and the prevalence of browns in his pictures itself separates him from the other Impressionists ; but this brown with him is not a convention, it is true to the colour of the sun-scorched landscape of his home, of the South of France, in which he chiefly worked. His paintings may seem clumsy in handling beside the delicate work of Renoir and Sisley, but by reason of his whole-hearted sincerity and honesty of purpose they make a deep and strong impression.

E. *Druet.*

"PORTRAIT OF THE ARTIST," BY PAUL CÉZANNE (1839–1906)

This is the painter who said, "I wish to make of Impressionism something solid and enduring, like the art of the Old Masters." His rugged painting of himself in middle age gives us an impression of substance and weight, which proves that the artist has achieved his object.

"THE CARD PLAYERS," BY PAUL CÉZANNE
The Louvre, Paris

A new phase of Impressionism is seen in this homely picture of two villagers playing cards in a rustic café. Light is no longer the " principal person " in the picture, for though the illumination is just, the sense of space and air admirably preserved, and the figures generalised and broadly treated, our interest is concentrated on the two men whose forms and characters are presented with a monumental simplicity and grandeur. This is not an effect of light, but a fragment of life.

E. Druet.

"LANDSCAPE IN PROVENCE," BY PAUL CÉZANNE

This essentially naturalistic painting of a scene in Southern France contains the germs of Cubism, for in his desire to give an effect of solidity and substance to houses and land, Cézanne here emphasises cubic forms and tends to sharpen curves into angles.

Cézanne was not a conscious revolutionary ; his pronounced style was the result of a strong, incorruptibly honest mind struggling to express what his eye could see without any preconceived ideas as to the manner of expression. His private life was simple and uneventful, devoted to unremitting toil which was never recognised or honoured. After studying in Paris he returned to the South of France, where he lived and married on an allowance of £12 a month made him by his father, a banker. After his father's death he inherited a share of his fortune, but made little change in his manner of living. He did not paint to make money, but to learn more about Nature and life, and to express what he felt vaguely in his soul. It is related of him that after he had finished a study out of doors, he would often leave his painting against the nearest bush. With the last brush-stroke, his interest in the painting ceased : he had done all he could ; and it was his wife who surreptitiously followed in his footsteps and garnered in the canvases so difficult at that time to sell.

Of Cézanne it may truly be said that he did not paint to live, but lived to paint, and owing to his absorption in the art of painting, and his consequent detachment from life, he tended to paint human beings as if they were still-life. So it comes about that some of Cézanne's most impressive paintings are simple pictures of still-life. In his work, as Duret has pointed out, " a few apples and a napkin on a table assume a kind of grandeur, in the same degree as a human head or a landscape with sea." In painting fruit Cézanne seemed able to suggest the tremendous power of Nature, so that pears and apples spread idly on a dinner-table become a revelation of the hidden forces of Nature, which brings fruits to birth. It is only now and again in his figure paintings that we get a glimpse of the passion for humanity which warms the work of a Rembrandt.

This quality, however, is abundantly present in the work of his younger contemporary, Vincent Van Gogh (1853–90), who exclaimed in one of his letters, "I want to paint humanity, humanity, and again humanity." A Dutchman by birth, Van Gogh was slow to find his true vocation, and he was close on thirty before he began painting. His brief life is full of romance and pathos. Always of a fanatical temper, and the son of a Lutheran pastor, Vincent began to earn his living as assistant to an art-dealer, but soon shocked his employers by his habit of quoting the Bible to prospective purchasers and pouring forth passionate sermons if they showed signs of purchasing pictures which he considered to be trivial and unworthy. For a few months he was a schoolmaster in England, but in 1877 he returned to Amsterdam, purposing to become a clergyman. He grew impatient in the dry atmosphere of a theological college, and set out as a missionary to the mining district of Borinage, in Belgium. Here his ardent sympathies with the hardships of the workers soon got

" SELF-PORTRAIT," BY VINCENT VAN GOGH (1853–90)

This haunting portrait of himself was painted by Van Gogh after he had cut off his right ear in a fit of frenzy ; hence the bandage round his head. The face, compared with the earlier portrait, betrays the tragedy of the artist's life, but the extraordinary vitality and power of the painting show that after recovering from his first mental breakdown Van Gogh's eyes were as keen and his hand as sure as ever they had been in the past.

E. *Druet.*

"THE PRISON YARD," BY VINCENT VAN GOGH

A masterpiece by an artist who once exclaimed, "I want to paint humanity, humanity, and again humanity." In this extraordinarily vivid impression of convicts taking their monotonous exercise in a prison yard, Van Gogh compels us to recognise the tragic dreariness of imprisonment and his own compassionate pity for outcasts of society who, whatever they may have done, are still human beings, doomed to feel and suffer.

him into trouble with the authorities ; he gave away all that he had with reckless generosity, and nearly starving himself, he began to relieve his emotions by drawing the people he could not help or comfort. Henceforward art claimed him, and though he had no prospect of being able to support himself in this way, he was encouraged to persevere, and entirely supported by his brother Theo, who had a good position in Paris. At first Van Gogh took Millet for his model, but after he had joined his brother in Paris in 1886 he was influenced by Pissarro and Seurat, and adhered to the neo-Impressionist ideals of painting. But in adopting their palette and technique Van Gogh showed his own individuality by using for the separation of colour, not points or patches, but fine lines of pigment, lines whipped on with extraordinary nervous force and passion. His colour touches are so alive that they have not inaptly been described as " wriggling little snakes." His portrait of himself with a beard shows his style of painting soon after he had learnt the secrets of Impressionism, and also reveals his own peculiar character. Van Gogh was not the inventor of a new technique ; but he rapidly developed a distinctive style of his own, remarkable for its vehemence of attack. " He was the most passionate of painters, and the extraordinary intensity of his vivid impressions may be likened to our vision of things seen momentarily in the duration of a lightning flash."

From Paris Van Gogh went to Arles in the South of France, where he exposed himself to the risks of sunstroke by frequently painting in blazing sunshine without any head-covering. A curious incident made public the fact that he was becoming abnormal. Teasing him for a present, a girl in a café once playfully said to him, " Well, if you can't give me anything else, give me one of your big ears." Shortly before Christmas this little waitress, whom the artist admired, was horrified to receive a parcel which was found to contain a freshly severed human ear. Van Gogh was found in bed with his head bleeding and with raging brain fever. Subsequently he was taken to an asylum, but his portrait of himself with a cap on his head and his head still bound, painted after this breakdown, proves that his hand had not lost its steadiness nor his eye its power to see essentials with brilliant intensity.

In the summer of 1889 he was well enough to leave Arles, and after a short stay in Paris, his brother arranged for him to live in the house of a doctor at Auvers-sur-Oise. Van Gogh appeared to be in the best of health and spirits, and there is no doubt that he fought bravely against the clouds which threatened his keen intellect. But the day came when he felt himself to be a doomed man, with nothing but mental darkness ahead, and on July 28, 1890, in a fit of depression he shot himself fatally. The fact that his mind eventually became unhinged, so that some of the pictures of his last years betray an abnormal vision, does not invalidate the splendid sanity of the bulk of Van Gogh's productions. Technically Van Gogh got his modelling by sweeping contours, instead of by a series of petty planes, and so gave weight to objects, while cleanly preserving their silhouettes as co-ordinated parts of a decorative design. We are impressed by his strength, as we are by that of Cézanne ; but it is not physical strength alone, but also moral force. His colour is of a high order and pitch, showing a fine sensibility for the splendour of pigment, but Van Gogh was too seriously absorbed in life and humanity for his painting ever to degenerate into mere decorations. One of the pictures in which he most completely expressed himself was " The Prison Yard," in which he conjures up with forcible economy the tragic aspect of these prisoners pacing their monotonous round, makes the high walls eloquent of the impossibility of escape, and without a touch of sentimentality contrives to express his compassionate pity for these dregs of humanity who are yet " men and brothers."

§ 2

Paul Gauguin (1848–1903) also learnt painting from Camille Pissarro, whose style he copied closely in his early work, but at heart he was never a Realist. His father was a Breton, but his mother was a Peruvian Creole, and a passion for the Tropics was in his blood. As a boy he ran away and went to sea, but after several voyages in various parts of the world he returned to Paris and entered business life. One day in a shop window he saw some pictures which brought back memories of the light and colour he had seen in the Tropics ; he made inquiries as to the authors, and so became acquainted with Pissarro. Gauguin was thirty at this time, and though he began painting now as an amateur, it was not till two years later, in 1880, that he began to exhibit, and another year passed before he decided to give all his time to art. Gauguin soon broke away from the dogmas of the neo-Impressionists, though his debt to them is confessed in the splendour of his colour—and for a time he was influenced by Cézanne, this influence showing itself in a tendency towards simplification. Gauguin made certain innovations of his own, he deliberately simplified forms and reintroduced the fashion of binding them with heavy dark outlines, and while his style grew more decorative his subjects became more imaginative.

In one of his letters Van Gogh records that while Gauguin was living with him at Arles he (Van Gogh) was for a while " led into working from imagination."

The association of Gauguin and Van Gogh was unfortunate, for their aims and temperaments were too distinct to mingle with ease. Van Gogh

" THE TAHITIANS," BY PAUL GAUGUIN (1848–1903)

Convinced that modern European civilisation was diseased and unhealthy, Gauguin sailed to the Pacific to paint a primitive people in a primitive style.   This picture of two natives of Tahiti is a typical example of the decorative simplicity and imaginative charm which distinguish his later works.

was all humility, Gauguin was proud and haughty, and though the warm-hearted Dutchman venerated his friend, the latter's cold cynicism often got on his nerves and contributed to his depression. Van Gogh wanted to devote his life to suffering humanity ; Gauguin wanted to forget the suffering and dwell in an " enchanted land." After Van Gogh's mental collapse at Arles, Gauguin went to Brittany and established himself at Pont Aven, where he found " big, simple mortals and an unspoilt Nature." But even rural France was too sophisticated for a man whose romantic temperament found its ideal among the unspoilt barbarians of the Pacific. In 1891 Gauguin sailed for Tahiti, where he fulfilled his intention to paint a primitive folk in a primitive style. Admitting the technical interest and decorative merit of Gauguin's Brittany pictures, it remains doubtful whether he would have been so great a figure in modern art had he not, like R. L. Stevenson, been fascinated by the life and manners of the Kanakas. His Tahitian pictures with their exotic subjects made a wide appeal to the popular imagination, though they did not become generally known till after the artist's death in 1903. But if he complained bitterly at the lack of purchasers for his pictures, Gauguin delighted in his new home, and never regretted having left Europe. " I have escaped everything that is artificial, conventional, customary. I am entering into truth, into Nature." Nevertheless he idealised the Nature he found in the Pacific ; he dwelt in a land of dreams and his pictures were charming conventions. When a literary friend in Paris quarrelled with his ideal, Gauguin replied : " Your civilisation is your disease, my barbarism is my restoration to health."

In the closing years of the nineteenth century Gauguin appeared to Paris, not only as the inventor of a new style of picture, but also as the protagonist of a new mental attitude towards life and art. At that period there was a certain lassitude among the highly cultured, expressed by the term *fin de siècle*—and it was not difficult to make out a case for regarding modern civilisation as a disease. There is much in city life that is repugnant to some temperaments, and the yearning for simplicity among artists had its parallel in the " back-to-the-land " movement in politics. The argument put forward by a new generation of artists was this : " If modern life is diseased, modern art must be diseased also. We can only restore art to health by starting it afresh like children or savages." Thus began the reaction against the complexity of neo-Impressionist painting, and this movement, chiefly influenced by the example of Gauguin, gave birth to a group of painters known in Paris as the *fauves* (*i.e.* " the wild beasts "). This Fauviste movement was an extreme emotional reaction against the cold intellectual tendencies of hyperscientific painting. In so far as these " wild-beast " painters sought to make painting simpler and less complicated, it may be argued that they were moving in a right direction.

668

A similar reaction in England, fifty years earlier, had led Holman Hunt and Millais to go back to the painters before Raphael for qualities of line and colour which they thought desirable. But the French painters, in their rage against civilisation, went much further back : one by one all the Old Masters were swept away by revolutionaries who sought inspiration from the rudimentary art of savages and barbarians. Forcible, childlike scrawls began to appear in Paris exhibitions, and these paintings were based not so much on any new view of Nature as on the savage art of Polynesia and Central Africa. The rough-hewn intensity of negro carvings excited jaded minds which were satiated with the plastic perfection of the sculpture of Michael Angelo.

The passion for simplicity and the desire to secure a maximum of expression with a minimum of means—which are the chief virtues of the Fauves—are found in the highest degree in the work of Henri Matisse, who is generally regarded as the leading exponent of this school. Born in the North of France in 1869, Matisse as a young man made a great reputation among connoisseurs by the extraordinary power of his drawing. Beginning as an almost academic draughtsman, influenced at first by Impressionism and then by Gauguin, painting landscapes, figures, and still-life, the art of Matisse has passed through a number of phases, each of which has had offshoots in a band of imitators. If Gauguin has been the most lasting influence, Matisse is in no sense an imitator of this master. Though he retained the high-keyed Impressionist palette of bright, clean colours, Matisse abandoned the mosaic method of painting, using a sweeping brush and large planes of colour to fill in the masses of what are essentially linear designs. Many of his drawings are wonderful in their summary expression of form and movement, but while in his pictures we admire the masterly sureness and simplicity of his drawing, we are often bewildered by his wilful distortion of natural form.

One of his defenders has sought to explain that Matisse exaggerates deformity in a model by a temperamental necessity which pushes him to affirm a truth without discretion to the point of paradox. Most people will find it difficult to accept a passion for realism as a reasonable explanation why an artist should present the calf of a leg as having a greater circumference than a thigh ! On the other hand, decorative intent is patent in all the pictures of Matisse, and we frequently find that distortions of form are used to help and emphasise the rhythm and equilibrium of the linear pattern ; accordingly it seems more reasonable to conclude that these distortions are wilful, not accidental, and that the painter subordinates natural representation to formal design, and desires us to admire his pictures, not because they are " true," but because he has created a pattern of line and colour which should appeal to pure æsthetic sensibilities. Matisse is

E. Druet.

"HEAD OF A WOMAN," BY HENRI MATISSE

Leader of a movement to simplify modern painting, Matisse in this striking picture secures a powerful effect with a rigid economy of means. A few heavy lines are sufficient to express a face which, whether we like it or not, we shall not easily forget.

historically important, therefore, as a pioneer of the doctrine that mere " actuality " is unimportant to pictorial art. He may also be regarded as the introducer of " shock tactics " into art. Even if we dislike his pictures, we find it difficult to forget them, because they make so forcible an impact on our vision. His " Head of a Woman " is an example of the powerful effect he achieves with the utmost simplicity and economy of means.

§ 3

If we look at the southern landscape by Cézanne we shall perceive that in his desire to make the objects look solid and enduring the artist has sharpened some curves into angles and emphasised cubic forms. This method of expressing the volume of objects was seen to be powerful and effective, and was seized upon by certain of the Fauves, who, desirous above all things of being forcible, elaborated their discovery into a dogma. Further, they supported their practice by a specious theory based on a smattering of science. We have seen how at the beginning of the present century there was a craze for the Primitive among a certain section of artists. These young men picked up from mineralogists the idea that the *crystal* was the *primitive form* of all things. A strange new test was applied to pictures : Did they or did they not show evidence of " crystallisation " ? A phrase torn from a scientific handbook was adopted as an æsthetic watchword :

All *secondary* forms arise from the decrement of particles from the *edges* and *angles* of these primitive forms.

Therefore to restore natural objects and human beings to their " primitive " forms, it was necessary to eliminate all curved lines and to reconstruct forms and faces in their " primary " form, octahedron, dodecahedron, six-sided prism, or whatever other geometrical figure might be most suitable. Among the earliest pictures embodying this new doctrine were landscapes in which meadows were crumpled up into crisp, candy-like masses, and marines in which all the waves had a sharp edge. These pictures were the work of a young Frenchman named Georges Bracque ; and it is still a matter for considerable argument whether Bracque or the Spanish artist Pablo Picasso is to be regarded as the true founder of Cubism.

Picasso was born at Malaga in 1881, and appeared in Paris about the end of the nineteenth century as an accomplished and masterly draughtsman. His early work " Mother and Child " shows the normality of his art and his genuine gifts before he attached himself definitely to the

Fauviste movement. Possessed of the quick and fertile brain of an inventive engineer, Picasso poured forth in quick succession a number of paintings of startling novelty in a variety of styles before he reached the mode that is now known as Cubism. On his practice, the outcome of a restless search for novelty of effect and of tireless experiments in pattern-making, others built up a new pseudo-philosophy of art. As a theory Cubism was based on two dogmatic assertions and a fallacious conclusion. It was argued :

(1) Strength is Beauty.
(2) A straight line is stronger than a curved line.

It is hardly necessary to point out how faulty are both these contentions, for in the first place nothing is more beautiful or weaker than a flower, and in the second it is a commonplace of construction that an arch is stronger than a horizontal on two perpendiculars. Nevertheless, blind to the error of their major and minor premise, the Cubists with a parade of logic proceeded to the conclusion that a painting wholly composed of straight lines is stronger and therefore more beautiful than a painting containing curved lines. Picasso's " Head of a Lady in a Mantilla " illustrates the first phase of Cubism, in which the human body is cut up into geometrical forms. It is a " crystallisation " of a human head, which looks less like a painting than a wood-carving executed by a savage with a blunt instrument, yet once our eyes have grown accustomed to the strange barbarism of the technique we have to acknowledge that this head is not altogether wanting in expression.

The first phase of Cubism is simple in comparison with the second, for if the first consisted in cutting up natural objects into geometrical shapes, the second consisted in shuffling the pieces. This curious development, with which the name of Picasso is chiefly associated, professed to show, not merely one aspect of objects, but a number of sectional aspects seen from different standpoints and arbitrarily grouped together in one composition. By this method the painting of a simple object like a teacup is transfigured into an unrecognisable figure—consisting of fragments of the cup as seen from above, from the sides, and, as held up in the air, from below. These ingenious conglomerations, professing to give us " the greater reality " of things seen, leave us as bewildered, confused, and uninformed as a metaphysician's analysis of truth and error. As an example of the second phase of Cubism we give Picasso's " Portrait of M. Kahnweiler," in which all we can recognise are fragmentary frontal aspects of his waistcoat (with watch-chain), left eye, left ear, and one side of his nose drowned in a chaotic sea of various aspects of receipt-files and other unrecognisable objects. Thus a movement which originated in an attempt

672

"HEAD OF A LADY IN A MANTILLA," BY PABLO PICASSO

An example of the first phase of Cubism in which all curved lines are eliminated in order to give greater " strength " to a picture, and human features are consequently cut up into geometrical forms. Executed at a period when primitive and savage art was idolised by advanced artists, this head looks less like a painting than a wood figure carved by a savage with a blunt instrument.

Y

"PORTRAIT OF M. KAHNWEILER," BY PABLO PICASSO

An example of the second phase of Cubism when, owing to the arbitrary shuffling of the geometrical shapes into which natural forms had already been cut up, only infinitesimal fragments of objects can be identified by the uninitiated. In this "puzzle-picture" a glimpse of a waistcoat with watch–chain can be seen in the centre, above it are indications of an eye, nose, and ear, but the rest of M. Kahnweiler appears to be smothered under the papers and files of his office.

to secure a primitive simplicity was led astray by false doctrines, till it finally wandered into a blind alley of complexity, for the complications of neo-Impressionist painting were child's play in comparison with the entanglements of the puzzle-pictures of the later Cubists.

Following upon the distortions of Matisse and the strange pictures of the Cubists, in which the facts of vision were either ignored or so juggled with that they became incomprehensible, it is not surprising that yet another school of painters arose who abandoned representation as an indispensable element in picture-making and argued that painting should be as free as music to give emotional pleasure without any appeal to association of material ideas. This claim that painting should be abstract, and not concern itself with the concrete, was argued by the Polish artist Wassily Kandinsky, working at Munich in 1914, more convincingly in his book *The Art of Spiritual Harmony* than in his kaleidoscopic pictures. In theory it seems plausible enough that if a musician is free to weave melodies without reference to natural sounds, a painter should be free to construct compositions without reference to natural forms. It is also true that the emotional pleasure we derive from the stained-glass windows of an old cathedral does not depend on the subject painted. We are enchanted with the radiant beauty of the pattern of colour. So far so good, but now comes the point that no artist living or dead has yet succeeded in convincing the world that these stained-glass windows would give us any keener or purer emotional pleasure if they had no subject, nor has any artist been able himself to produce an abstract painting more beautiful in colour and pattern than paintings based on concrete forms.

Kandinsky, however, went a step further, and claimed that his abstract paintings were not mere dream-patterns, but had a meaning for the initiated in that they were based on the psychological effect on the observer of various lines and colours. But these effects are by no means definitely established, they are still a subject for speculation, and till they are fixed by the common consent of mankind, experiments in the " art of spiritual harmony " must necessarily be uncertain and inconclusive. Indeed, in Kandinsky's own " Compositions "—as his abstract paintings are entitled— outward and visible signs alone give us a clue to the inward and spiritual meaning, and it is by discerning faint traces of a gun-carriage, a puff of smoke, and falling houses in one of his pre-war pictures, painted in 1913, that we obtain a sense of that " clash and conflict of ideas in the spiritual world " that the painting is said to express.

The sectional representation of divers aspects of different objects was developed, with an added emphasis on the expression of movement, by the group of Italian painters known as the " Futurists." Futurism was a literary as well as an artistic movement, and it was largely a protest against

675

" A LADY AND HER DOG," BY GIACOMO BALLA

An example of a Futurist painting in which an endeavour is made to represent movement by showing in various positions the moving paws and tail of the dog, the swing of his chain, and the step of his owner's feet. Here painting attempts to rival and surpass the achievements of the rapid-motion camera.

the tyranny of the past on the part of ardent nationalists, who resented that the present achievements of their country should be obscured by the glory of its past. The leader of the movement was a writer, Signor Marinetti, and his skilled pen justified the extraordinary practices of his artist friends by sonorous phrases. A pictorial record of the commonplace fact that the seat of a chair is visible after the sitter has got up and walked away, was majestically alluded to as an example of " the plastic interpenetration of matter." As regards colour, the Futurists accepted the divisionism and complementarism of the neo-Impressionists, but in the rendering of form they sought to introduce new principles : " Universal dynamism must be rendered in painting as a dynamic sensation ; movement and light destroy the materiality of bodies." An amusing example of the " dynamic decomposition of matter " is Giacomo Balla's painting " A Lady and her Dog," which may be regarded as a synthesis of rapid-motion photography. A multiplicity of paws and tails indicates that the animal is trotting with wagging tail, four ghostly chains suggest the whirling of his lead, and an army of shoes presents the movement of his owner's feet. In concentrating their endeavours on the expression of movement, the Futurists attempted to convert painting from an art of space to an art of time. Their daring experiments have produced few pictures likely to stand the test of time, but possibly an exception may be made for Signor Balla's " Centrifugal Force." This painting of revolving spheres shooting forth golden sparks into an azure void was not only decorative in design and colour, but also nobly expressive of the Force that shoots meteorolites through the universe. An abstract painting that succeeds in expressing an abstract idea is clearly legitimate art, but pictures of this calibre are unfortunately the exception among abstract paintings.

Nevertheless it would be wrong to assert that the experiments of the modern extremists in painting have been wholly valueless. Technically they have widened the horizon of painting and opened the road to a new Realism in which the firm structure and rigid design of the Cubists can be combined with a truth and beauty of colour derived from the Impressionists. Psychologically their work is of profound interest to every student of history. Coming events cast their shadow before them on the field of art. The patient reader who has followed this history thus far will have observed the increasing endeavour on the part of painters to give an expression of Strength. In examining their works he will have noticed that, however greatly they may vary in their aspects and styles, nearly all of them contain an element of Violence. These Fauviste, Cubist, and Futurist paintings never soothe us to rest ; they aim at galvanising us into action. All of them must be regarded as symptoms, as expressions in art of the unrest, agitation, and suppressed violence seething subterraneously in Europe prior

677

to the outbreak of the first World War. The effect of the war on art will be considered in another chapter, but long before August 1914 premonition of the coming hostilities were given in the tumult of modern painting.

The important thing to remember, however, with all modern experimental art is that it no longer depicts something *seen by the eye* at one moment of time but something *conceived in the mind,* where—as we know from our dreams—neither time nor space are rigid. Cézanne's intellectual concepts about the geometrical solids underlying all natural appearances ; Van Gogh's introduction of emotional values which could be emphasised at the expense of outward form and colour ; Gauguin's movement towards primitive simplification : all these were the beginning, though these three still based their pictures to some extent on the appearance of things in Nature. Each proved an opening to the newer theories of the purposes of art. Form for form's sake ; emotion for emotion's sake ; the primitive as an ultimate simplification. These elements, pure or intermingled, will be found as the basis of practically all contemporary art.

It is fascinating to realise that the whole movement of thought in the twentieth century has been towards a greater subjectivity than prevailed during the materialistic nineteenth ; and art reflects this. Freud has tremendously stimulated our interest in the subconscious and the irrational ; the scientists and physicists have come near to dissolving all matter into energy and motion. Modern art must be seen in the light of such movements of human thought. Thus it was not only an underlying violence and revolt, but a growing anti-materialism which was the ferment in the new art.

XXXV

ART DURING THE FIRST WORLD WAR

A SURVEY OF THE WORK OF OFFICIAL WAR ARTISTS AND OTHERS

§ I

IT was shown in the previous chapter how at the beginning of the present century the art world was deluged with theories and " isms," while several of the pictures illustrated afforded evidence that a sinister violence and subterranean unrest became manifest in European painting before it exploded in European politics and precipitated a great war. On the Continent—and to a slighter extent in England also—the " wild-men " of painting had betrayed in form and colour that spirit of merciless aggression which eventually provoked Armageddon. The principal British contribution to the extreme left of modern painting was a development of Cubism known as " Vorticism," and it is not altogether without significance that the leader of this movement, P. Wyndham Lewis, should have begun in the early spring of 1914 a series of abstract paintings with titles taken from military text-books. His " Plan of Campaign," exhibited at London in June 1914, was based not on any vision of landscape and figures, but on such a diagram of a battle disposition as we may find in any history book. The parallel lines and blocks stand for the divisions of contending forces, and the heavy blocks in the upper right-hand corner are supposed to represent the extended left wing of one army outflanking and falling with superior strength on the right wing of the other army. This is the " plan of campaign." Here again we have a curious premonition of the war expressed in paint. The case of Wyndham Lewis typifies the general effect the 1914–18 war had on art. When a student at the Slade School Lewis was already remarkable for the uncommon power of his drawing. Caught up in the vortex which swept so many ambitious young artists into the whirlpool of " abstract painting," because of their desire to attain novelty at all costs, Lewis was led in the years immediately preceding the 1914–18 war to paint " abstract " pictures, incomprehensible to the multitude and difficult for even the initiated to understand. Then in 1918, after two years' experience with the heavy artillery in France, he returned to London and returned to realism. " The Gun

679

Pit," which he painted for the Canadian War Memorials, was no abstract picture, but a perfectly comprehensible painting based on vision, on his remembered experience with the big guns and of the big-built men who worked them.

The chief effect of the 1914–18 war on painting, therefore, was to bring about a return to realism, but it was a new realism modified, as we shall see, by certain principles derived from movements which, in themselves, appeared to be extravagant. Not only did the war restore to sanity many of the most promising of the younger artists, it also prepared the public to accept and understand their works. Youthful artists, who in peace-time might have waited till middle age before their talent was recognised, became famous in a year or two. The wall of prejudice was broken down by the unparalleled upheaval of our normal world, so that even conservative minds were ready to consider impartially a new vision of new events. Further, though there was no slackness on the part of the younger artists in joining the colours, the artistic activity of Great Britain may be said to have reached its zenith during the years of the 1914–18 war. Never before had so much official and State patronage been given to British artists ; never before did the British public so clearly recognise that picture-making was not a mere pastime but an activity which had its own function and purpose of usefulness to humanity.

As early as 1914–15 the first public recognition of the artist's value to the State in war-time came in connection with the recruiting campaign. " Art for art's sake " was dead and done with, but in its place was substituted a new gospel of " Art for the Idea's sake." Art was recognised as an element of education and social progress, because nothing else in the world could impress an idea so vividly and lastingly on the human memory. During the first winter and spring of the first World War nearly a hundred posters were commissioned from various artists by the Parliamentary Recruiting Committee, and 2,500,000 copies of these posters were distributed throughout the United Kingdom. In addition to these official posters, generous contributions were made to the campaign by several private firms. The recruiting posters issued by the London Electric Railways will be long remembered for their efficiency and artistic qualities, notably Frank Brangwyn's " Remember Belgium " and G. Spencer Pryse's " The Only Road for an Englishman." Later, the use as a poster during the War Savings Campaign of a reproduction of Whistler's portrait of his Mother (see page 645)—as a gentle reminder that " Old Age Must Come "—was significant of a growing belief on the part of Authority that the most artistic picture can make the widest public appeal.

Simultaneously with the appearance of the recruiting posters on the hoardings, came the war cartoons in the newspapers. It is impracticable

"PLAN OF CAMPAIGN," BY P. WYNDHAM LEWIS

A curious premonition of the first World War, this painting—exhibited at London in June 1914—is based on the diagram of a battle disposition which we may see in any history book. The parallel lines and blocks stand for divisions of contending forces, and the heavy blocks in the upper right-hand corner are supposed to represent the superior forces of one army turning and crushing the right wing of the other.

to give a list of the British artists who did excellent work in this direction —every reader will remember notable drawings.

Meanwhile, what of painting ? It was said rather bitterly in 1916 that " no visitor to the Royal Academy would know that there was a war on." It may be admitted frankly that the exhibitions in these years looked much the same as those in years of peace. Pictures of the war were infrequent, and when present they were rarely successful. The failure of the older artists to grapple with the situation was neither surprising nor shameful. They did not possess the requisite experience. Some endeavoured to be topical, and envisaged the war after their memory of Crimean pictures, changing the uniforms into khaki but repeating the old arrangements. But sword-waving officers, swaggering cavalrymen, and neatly brushed infantry were no longer convincing even to civilians. Standing before an Academy picture of a charge, a wounded New Zealander was overheard to remark : " That's absurd ! one man with a machine-gun would wipe out the lot." New methods of warfare demanded new methods of painting for their efficient expression. The battle in art, as at the Front, was for the young, and the first man to capture the imagination of London by his war pictures was a young artist hitherto practically unknown.

§ 2

Before 1914 Christopher R. W. Nevinson was only known to the few as a young artist of promise. After studying at the Slade School of Art, he had formed ties of friendship in Paris with the Italian artist Gino Severini, and so had become influenced by Futurism. He was also interested in Cubism, and though he never definitely adhered to " Vorticism," he exhibited on one occasion with Wyndham Lewis, Edward Wadsworth, William Roberts, and other Vorticists. During the early stage of the war Nevinson was driving a motor-ambulance behind the Belgian Front, and being invalided with rheumatic fever early in 1915 he was able to resume painting during his convalescence. Thus he was practically the first artist who had the opportunity to exhibit in London pictures of the war based on personal experience of the realities of modern fighting. It was in the spring of 1915 that Nevinson showed his first three war pictures in the exhibition of the London Group at the Goupil Gallery, and though these betrayed Futurist and Cubist influence, they were perfectly intelligible as illustrations of actual incidents.

Dr. Johnson maintained that there was some good to be got out of every book, and similarly it may be argued that there is some good to be got out of every artistic theory. It was the peculiar distinction of

Reproduced by permission of the London Passenger Transport Board.

'THE ONLY ROAD FOR AN ENGLISHMAN," BY G. SPENCER PRYSE

Still remembered for its effectiveness during the Recruiting Campaign of 1914–15, this poster with its dignified design and noble appeal, shows how vividly art can be used to implant an idea in our minds.

"LA PATRIE," BY C. R. W. NEVINSON,

An intensely tragic vision of " the broken debris of the war-machine." The treatment of the figures shows a modified use of the Cubist method, which is helpful here as an indication that " war is a process in which man is not treated as a human being but as an item in a great instrument of destruction."

"REMEMBER BELGIUM," BY FRANK BRANGWYN,

This striking poster was specially drawn by Frank Brangwyn for the famous series of artistic recruiting appeals issued by the London Electric Railways.

685

Nevinson to leave aside all the extravagances of Futurism and Cubism, and snatch from them the two things which helped him to render realistically a new world in a new way. The particular good thing in the work of the Italian Futurists was their successful suggestion of movement. By a generous use of slanting lines in the composition, Nevinson gave a vivid sense of movement and life to his early painting " Returning to the Trenches." His French soldiers, with packs on their backs, their bodies and rifles sloping in the direction in which they were marching, were not portrayed as they would be shown in a photograph : the aim here was not to portray a group of individual soldiers, but to express the onward rush of an advancing army, and this impression was vividly and irresistibly conveyed. Further, the use of straight lines and avoidance of curves— characteristics derived from Cubism—suggested that the movement was that of a vast machine rather than of a collection of human beings.

The distinguished art critic, A. Clutton Brock, has pointed out in one of his essays that for fifty years or more a belief has been growing on us that man is a machine and " should be conscious of the fact that he is one." The popular play " R.U.R. " was an expression of this conscious-ness in dramatic form ; in painting it was confessed by the Cubist method which, as Clutton Brock has said,

does express, in the most direct way, the sense that in war man behaves like a machine or part of a machine, that war is a process in which man is not treated as a human being but as an item in a great instrument of destruction, in which he ceases to be a person and is lost in a process. The cubist method, with its repetition and sharp distinction of planes, expresses this sense of a mechanical process better than any other way of representation.

Familiarity with the working of the " war -machine " prepared the mind of the public to accept that vision of the world as a complicated piece of mechanism which is the essence both of Cubism and Futurism. The first World War offered to the Cubists one of the few subjects which their technique was fitted to express, and the marvel is that this opportunity, missed by the French and Italian inventors of the new method, was seized upon with conspicuous success by a handful of almost unknown British artists.

From the first Nevinson stood out from all previous painters of war by reason of his power in suggesting movement, and the implication in his pictures that modern war was not the affair of human individuals but the creaking progress of a complicated machine. His remarkable painting of the interior of a hospital, " La Patrie," which was purchased by Mr. Arnold Bennett, is tragical in its intensity, but it is the tragedy of automata crushed and mangled in the revolutions of a pitiless machine.

686

"THE ROAD FROM ARRAS TO BAPAUME," BY C. R. W. NEVINSON,

From the Painting in the Imperial War Museum

The son of a famous war-correspondent, Nevinson was the first artist to make a reputation by his original and intense interpretation of scenes on the battlefields. This painting of a road familiar to thousands of British soldiers is a typical example of his later pictures of the Great War, in which mannerisms and inessential details have alike been suppressed, and the main characteristics of the remembered scene are stated with emphatic simplicity and clearness.

687

Other artists have painted the interiors of base-hospitals, pictures of men bandaged but smiling, and attended by a bevy of comely nurses, so that the spectator might imagine it was rather pleasant than otherwise to be wounded ; but Nevinson permits no falsifying of the facts ; he shows us the reality of the thing, the broken debris of the war-machine, the pain and the suffering and, above all, the relative insignificance of the individual pawn in this mighty war-game.

The versatility of Nevinson and the way in which he alters his style to suit his subject is seen in " A Group of Soldiers." The great truth about the English " Tommy " after 1915 was that he was the British working-man in disguise, and here with unerring accuracy Nevinson has penetrated to the man behind the uniform, and unveiled the man of toil, the unit of the machine. Some have demurred that in the foremost figures the hands are exaggerated, but while the point is open to debate, a slight exaggeration is permissible as emphasising the fact that these men belong to the horny-handed class. In this group, where there is no movement to be registered, Futurist devices would be out of place and they are avoided, but there is still a faint trace of Cubism in the definite angles of the simple modelling, and this helps to give a monumental sense of strength and doggedness to the sturdy figures.

In landscape, as well as in his figure paintings, Nevinson contrived to get at the reality behind the thing seen. " The Road from Arras to Bapaume " is neither impressionistic not photographic, but it gives the essential truth of a scene acutely remembered. All the inessential details have been suppressed, with the result that the main recollections of the truth—the white, switchback track of Roman straightness, the lopped-down tree-trunks, the stream of moving traffic, and the limitless expanse —are recorded with increased strength and intensity. This is one of Nevinson's later pictures of the war, and while he no doubt enjoyed greater facilities and privileges when he returned to France in 1917 as an " official artist " than he had done in 1914–15 as a motor-mechanic, the essential qualities in his pictures remained the same. His reputation was made with the earlier pictures, in which the mannerisms were most marked ; in the later works these mannerisms were pruned to a vanishing point, and realities were stated without any serious loss in strength and with increased clarity.

It is no wonder that the war-pictures of Nevinson took London by storm in the early days of the war. He was the first to show the grim inner realities of modern fighting, and others who dealt only with appearances seemed in comparison remote from the heart of the subject. When other young artists were released from the fighting line, a new series of visions of men as automata expressed the new outlook of a new generation,

" A GROUP OF SOLDIERS," BY C. R. W. NEVINSON,
From the Painting in the Imperial War Museum

After 1915 the British soldier was the British workman in disguise. In the above picture the artist has unveiled the man behind the uniform and expressed this truth with convincing simplicity and force. Faint traces of Cubism, revealed in the definite angles of the modelled forms, help to give strength and doggedness in the sturdy figures.

689

but their work did not begin to appear in exhibitions till nearing the time of the Armistice in 1918.

The first serious rival to Nevinson appeared in April 1916, when a large painting, " The Kensingtons at Laventie," by Eric H. Kennington, was exhibited in Regent Street. Kennington, a young painter of promise in whom William Nicholson had taken an interest, was an artist of quite another type. He was untouched by the most modern movements, except that he had a leaning towards simplicity of drawing and emphasis of design : this, together with a knowledge of the war from within, was all he had in common with Nevinson. After only three months' training in England as a Territorial, Private Kennington went to France at the beginning of November 1914 with the 13th Battalion of the London Regiment (" The Kensingtons "). He returned to England in 1915, when he was discharged unfit for further service, and then began to paint this great picture of a typical moment in the life at the Front during the terrible winter of 1914–15. The moment chosen for representation in this picture was when his platoon, after serving for four days and nights in the fire trenches, enduring the piercing cold of twenty degrees of frost and almost continuous snow, had at last been relieved. The men have emerged from the communication trench terminating in a ruined farmyard, and are forming up along the ruined village street. Each figure in the picture is an actual portrait, and the artist has given the following description of his work :

Corporal J. Kealey is about to give the order, " Fall in, No. 7 Platoon." . . . In the first four—reading from right to left—are Pte. Slade, resting with both hands on his rifle ; Lce.-Cpl. Wilson, Pte. Guy, and Pte. McCafferty, who is turning to look at the other men falling in behind. . . . On the extreme left is Pte. H. Bristol. . . . Directly behind Pte. Guy are two men in waterproof sheets : Pte. Kennington [the artist] in a blue trench helmet and Pte. W. Harvey. . . . On the ground is Pte. A. Todd. . . . He has fallen exhausted by continual sickness, hard work, lack of sleep, long hours of " standing-to," and observing.

This picture shows quite another aspect of realism. It is a stately presentation of human endurance, of the quiet heroism of the rank and file. The deadliest enemy here is the piercing cold, which seems to pervade the whole picture. Apart from its human emotional appeal, this large picture—in which the figures are two-thirds life-size—possesses a peculiar technical interest in that it is painted on glass. The advantage of this method is that the pigment is hermetically sealed, and so long as the thick plate-glass endures unbroken the colour of the surface will remain for centuries as fresh as on the day when it was painted. The technical difficulties, however, will be apparent even to laymen when it is realised that in order to use this method the whole picture has to be painted backward. Not only

690

"THE KENSINGTONS AT LAVENTIE," BY ERIC H. KENNINGTON

This picture presents a typical moment in the life at the Front during the terrible winter of 1914–15. After enduring twenty degrees of frost in the trenches for four days and nights, these Territorials have been relieved and are now forming up in a ruined farmyard outside the communication trench. Each figure in the picture is an actual portrait.

has the subject to be reversed on the other side of the glass, but the process of painting has to be reversed also : the upper touches, which on a canvas would have been the last, must be laid first on the glass, and what would have been the first brush-stroke on a canvas must be put on the glass last. Looking at the apparent ease with which the whole picture has been painted, and remembering the infinite difficulties of the method employed, " The Kensingtons at Laventie " must be pronounced a great technical achievement as well as a noble memorial of British fortitude.

§ 3

" Often," says a character in one of Sudermann's novels, " Art leads us astray because she has deliberately tried to reflect something quite different from the spirit of her time." Many visitors to the Royal Academy and other exhibitions in 1915 and 1916 felt vaguely that the pictures they saw there were leading them astray. Eric Kennington's picture and the paintings of Nevinson acted on them differently, because these seemed truer to the spirit of the time. The outworn conventions of the older artists seemed powerless to convey an adequate expression of the clash of the world conflict, and possibly it was the general failure of well-known and eminent painters to deal with the 1914–18 war that led the British Government to select a black-and-white artist as the first " Official Artist." In addition to the useful propaganda work accomplished by poster-artists and cartoonists, it was felt that the nation should possess permanent records of typical scenes and episodes in the greatest war the world had ever known. The outcome of this feeling was the appointment in August, 1916, of Muirhead Bone as an official artist on the Western Front. The appointment was eminently appropriate, for this artist's known ability to make memorable designs from scaffolding and the demolition of buildings argued that he was the right man to depict the havoc of war.

Born at Glasgow in 1867, Muirhead Bone came to London in 1901, and was a prominent member of the New English Art Club long before the war. His masterly etchings and drawings of architectural subjects have long been highly prized by connoisseurs. In 1915–16 Muirhead Bone had devoted much of his time to the interpretation of British war industries, sketching " The Building of a Liner," " The Yards on the Clyde," and similar subjects. After his new appointment the regular publication in parts, from the Office of *Country Life*, of reproductions of Muirhead Bone's drawings made on the Western Front, opened a new era in the pictorial treatment of the war. Drawings like the " Sketch in Albert " show with what economy and distinction this artist achieved

" A SKETCH IN ALBERT," BY MUIRHEAD BONE

A drawing made on the spot by the first " Official Artist " sent by the British Government to the Western Front in the first World War. Muirhead Bone gives a vivid impression here of the ravaged state of this Belgian town, and invests its ruin with a dignity of his own.

693

"R.N.D., CRYSTAL PALACE," BY JOHN LAVERY,

From the Painting in the Imperial Museum

An impression of the Royal Naval Division lined up on parade in the grounds of the Crystal Palace, by an artist who is equally adept in the deft sketching of a passing pageant or in the portraiture of a society beauty.

his task of presenting with pictorial dignity and actual truth the aspect of ravaged buildings and wasted landscape. Though Muirhead Bone's reputation was made before the war, these portfolios increased his admirers a hundredfold, and the unexpected popularity and wide demand for his books of sketches soon convinced the authorities that there was room and to spare for other official artists.

In April 1917 James McBey, another Scottish artist, born in Aberdeen-shire in 1883, who was akin in style to Bone, and also chiefly known for his etchings and drawings, was appointed the Official Artist for Egypt and Palestine. The same month William Orpen, R.A., was sent to France as an official artist. A large collection of the paintings he made there was freely presented by the artist to the nation and they are now in the possession of the Imperial War Museum.

§ 4

Some two months after these last appointments, a small collection of water-colours of " The Ypres Salient " was exhibited at the Goupil Gallery. They were the work of a young soldier, Paul Nash, who then was practically unknown, though he and his brother John Nash had already exhibited at the New English Art Club water-colours which had attracted attention among connoisseurs by reason of their unsophisticated simplicity and naïve charm. Though enthusiastically welcomed by some of the leading art-critics, Nash's first exhibition passed almost unnoticed by the public, but a second exhibition of his war-drawings, held later at the Leicester Galleries, aroused widespread interest, and the publication by Country Life of a book of his water-colours established his reputation as an original artist who had and could express poignantly his own vision of the war. In the introduction to this volume of reproductions, C. E. Montague wrote :

In drawing strange places so strangely, Mr. Nash contrives to bring back to the mind the strange things felt by men who were there at moments of stress. One does not see with the eyes alone, but with brain and nerves too, and if these are worked upon in unusual ways, then the messages brought in by the little waves of light that break on delicate shores in the eye are changed—some may say disturbed or blurred ; others may say refined into an uncommon rightness, not to be had at other times. If an artist succeeds in expressing effects of such changes, his work may well delight some of those who have felt the changes go on in themselves.

A picture like " Sunrise : Inverness Copse " may not be " true " as the camera sees truth ; but it is true to the memory of a nerve-racked fighting-man. Granted that it contain exaggerations, they are exaggerations of significant elements in the scene. The lumps and holes in the foreground are a pointed commentary on the deeply pit-marked earth exposed to constant shelling. Paul Nash painted his subjects as seen by the mind's eye, and the mind of man ever enlarges that which it has cause to fear. A sensitive and emotional artist, Nash painted in these water-colours not only what he had seen, but what he had *felt*. As a landscape painter, what he felt most deeply was the abomination of desolation caused by war. Whereas Nevinson showed us soldiers as cogs in the war-machine, Nash presented the Earth as a tortured and violated entity. These two painters, the first realist, the second imaginative, each formed and inspired by the 1914–18 war, were the complement of each other. Nevinson showed the complicated, man-driven machinery of war ; Nash its devastating effects. Many other artists of great skill and talent painted pictures of the war which were perhaps more pleasant to look upon ; but none exhibited its inner ghastliness with more power, originality, and intensity of feeling. By midsummer 1917 the best judges of modern painting were convinced that the two men who had most to say about the war in paint were C. R. W. Nevinson and Paul Nash. Representations were made to the proper authorities, with the result that during the next few months a new batch of " Official Artists " included C. R. W. Nevinson, Paul Nash, Eric Kennington, and John Lavery. As became his age and position, John Lavery—who was born at Belfast in 1857—was enlisted, so to speak, for " home service." " The Royal Naval Division, Crystal Palace, 1916 " is an excellent example of the war-pictures—charming in their delicate colour and atmosphere—which Lavery was able to paint without crossing the seas. Happy in its Whistlerian Impressionism, in which this artist was an adept, this picture is entirely worthy of the reputation of one of our leading portrait painters, but it is no new revelation either of the spirit of the times or of the significance of war.

The artistic activity of Great Britain was at its height in 1917. In March the Imperial War Museum was instituted, and during the summer the Canadian War Memorials Fund was founded by Lord Beaverbrook and Lord Rothermere, who, acting under competent expert advice, accumulated a notable collection of pictures. When the collection was exhibited at Burlington House, prior to its dispatch to Canada, the work of the younger artists revealed to a significant degree the new spirit that was abroad in art. Nevinson and Nash were no longer alone ; other artists of their own generation exhibited war-pictures in which similar tendencies could be discerned. Conspicuous among those who stressed the Cubist point of view, presenting soldiers as automata and emphasising the mechanism of war, were P. Wyndham Lewis and William Roberts ; still

"SUNRISE: INVERNESS COPSE," BY PAUL NASH

From the painting in the Imperial War Museum

"In drawing strange places so strangely Nash contrives to bring back to the mind the strange things felt by men who were there at moments of stress." In this picture of a wood after being exposed to constant shelling, a landscape painter imaginatively expresses his horror at the way in which war distorts and devastates a peaceful scene.

" ADVANCED DRESSING STATION ON THE STRUMA, 1916,"
BY HENRY LAMB,

City Art Gallery, Manchester

The artist, who served in Macedonia with the Red Cross, shows another aspect of war in this picture of a dressing station behind the firing-line. Clear in every detail, natural yet delicately balanced in design, the work as a whole is wonderfully eloquent of the weariness and boredom felt in this quiet moment when the men are waiting for the wounded to arrive.

" TO THE UNKNOWN BRITISH SOLDIER IN FRANCE," BY WILLIAM ORPEN

This painting, the " picture of the year " in the Royal Academy of 1923, was the artist's tribute to the Unknown Soldier. The gilded pomp of the Palace of Versailles, where the Peace Treaty was signed, is imaginatively contrasted with the ragged misery of the ghostly boy-soldiers who watch over the coffin of their comrade. Festooned Cupids and the Cross shining in the distance are symbols of the " Greater Love " of those who have laid down their lives. Scrupulous fidelity to reality and high powers of imagination are shown in this much-discussed picture.

"THE UNDERWORLD," BY WALTER BAYES

From the painting in the Imperial War Museum

This remarkable painting of a London "tube" station during an air-raid was a conspicuous exhibit in the Royal Academy of 1918.   It is at once a true human document of a typical episode and a grandly planned decorative painting in which the alien figures are stated with monumental simplicity and grandeur.

more numerous were those who adopted a post-Impressionist simplification of statement, among the most prominent members of this school being the brothers Stanley and Gilbert Spencer, Paul and John Nash, and Henry Lamb. Pictures by all these artists and many others were also acquired for the Imperial War Museum.

Henry Lamb, another member of the New English Art Club who had attracted attention before the 1914–18 war by his powers of drawing and the emotional force in his pictures, was a comparative late-comer; for having been formerly a medical student he was fully occupied with Red Cross work up to and following the Armistice. When he resumed the brush, however, it was seen that he had taken notes during his service in Macedonia, and his picture " Advanced Dressing Station on the Struma, 1916," now in the Manchester Art Gallery, is a notable contribution to the pictorial exposition of the psychology of war. It is not the excitement or frenzy of fighting that Lamb shows us, but the boredom and dreariness of the men who are waiting for unutterable things to happen. Precisely drawn, wonderfully clear and simple in its design, this painting depicts a quiet moment in the campaigners' life, a moment when the weariness of all concerned finds abundant expression.

To deal with all the artists who painted war-pictures between 1914 and 1918 is obviously beyond the scope of this chapter; and therefore the work of many eminent painters—several of whom will be referred to subsequently—must be passed over in silence for the moment. Turning to a new subject does not necessarily change an artist's style, and it is the evolution of a new style rather than the discovery of a new subject which vitally affects the history of art. The number of Official Artists appointed was evidence of the curious way in which the 1914–18 war persuaded a " Business Government " to treat art with more seriousness and consideration than it had yet received in Great Britain. While many artists, like John Lavery and Muirhead Bone, continued their former style and practice when engaged on these new subjects, other artists, as we have seen, were fired by their experiences in the trenches to the invention of new styles for the expression of new emotions. This direct or indirect influence of the war on art was not limited only to the artists who had served abroad; occasionally it made itself felt in the work of the men who stayed at home.

The most remarkable war-picture in the Royal Academy of 1918 had for its subject a London " Tube " station during an air raid. Walter Bayes's great canvas " The Underworld " is a vigorous and haunting painting which in its style approaches the new manner of post-Impressionism. Designed as a mural decoration, the picture shows an appropriate monumental treatment of the alien figures who sprawl about the platform.

The faces are not English faces, but on occasions such as the artist depicts London's underworld was full of these types. Bayes ably commemorated in their characteristic attitudes and dishevelled condition the dreary languor of these semi-orientals waiting in safety for the " All Clear " signal which will tell them it is safe to return to the surface of the Metropolis. Walter Bayes, who was the Head of the Westminster School of Art from 1918 to 1934 and is a member of a well-known family of artists, has long been known as a decorative painter of great talent, but he had never previously produced a painting so precious as a human document.

The public, as well as the technical expert, can appreciate good drawing, attractive colour, and well-balanced design ; but these things alone will not serve to capture its imagination. It demands rightly that a picture should contain an idea or an emotion that can be clearly grasped. To some artists—mostly of the younger generation—the war afforded the most astounding experience they had ever undergone, and, overwhelmed by it, they burst through the barriers of school-taught orthodox painting to express with a primitive ferocity the intensity of their own sensations. By placing on permanent record, not only the scenes caused but the emotions evoked by the first Great War, they have rendered services to both History and Art which posterity will know how to value.

XXXVI

BRITISH ART AFTER THE FIRST WORLD WAR

FROM JOHN S. SARGENT TO AUGUSTUS JOHN

§ 1

SINCE the First World War art has become a cosmopolitan business. Rapidity of communications and the interchange of international ideas have broken down the old frontiers of thought, so that while painters of various styles can now be found in all civilised countries, the styles throughout the world are very much alike, and it is difficult to make out a case for any distinctive national art. If it be hazardous, however, to assert that there exists a " British School," distinct from the schools of painting in France, Spain, Italy, and other countries, it may nevertheless be said with sufficient confidence that since 1919, in the words of Sir Robert Witt, " British art has stood second to none in the world."

Writing over thirty years ago, the late Sir Walter Armstrong said : " The Pre-Raphaelite revolt is the last great movement which really belongs to the history of British Art. Those developments which have taken place since are more cosmopolitan than British. They have been moved towards assimilating our insular ideas to those of the Continent, which, in painting, means the ideas of France and Holland. Being all moves in one direction, they have had considerable similarity one with another, and it is scarcely worth while to dwell much on the differences which separate the neo-Scots school from that of Newlyn, or both from those franker disciples of Paris who have been so greatly encouraged by the genius of two Americans, Whistler and Sargent."

John Singer Sargent, R.A., who has been perhaps the greatest influence in portrait-painting in our time, was himself Paris-trained. Born at Florence in 1856, the son of American parents—his father being a physician at Boston, U.S.A.—Sargent was educated in Italy and Germany, studied painting under Carolus Duran at Paris, and finally settled in England during the 'eighties. In his own person, therefore, Sargent represented in the most marked manner the cosmopolitan experiences which go to the making of a modern painter. A word may be said here as to his master, Carolus Duran, who was born at Lille in 1837, for though this painter won the coveted Prix de Rome and spent four years in Italy, he became the leading French portrait painter of his time by reason of his later study of Velazquez in Madrid. Carolus Duran, then, was one of the pioneers who turned away the thought of his contemporaries and pupils from the Italian and Flemish to the Spanish schools of painting, and his art, like that of his still more famous pupil Sargent, is largely derived from Velazquez. The English portraiture of the eighteenth century, as has already been shown, was modelled firstly on the practice of Van Dyck and secondly on that of the Venetians; the new note introduced into portrait-painting towards the middle of the nineteenth century, and still dominant at the present day, is based on the work of Velazquez and Goya.

While many have drawn inspiration from this common source, the results obtained from following, in the main, the Spanish tradition, have varied considerably according to the individual temperaments of the artists. In Sargent's painting we see the irrepressible energy which we associate with Transatlantic business enterprise; he was a " hustler " in paint who swept us off our feet by the amazing vivacity of his brush-work and by the almost uncanny actuality with which he set a living being before us. A vigorous draughtsman, using sweeps of paint with economic mastery, Sargent developed powers of psychological penetration which made him supreme in the rendering of character. Some of his male portraits have been so merciless in their unmasking of the real minds of his sitters that they have justified the amusing but apt comment of " Mr. Dooley " :

" Stand there," he sez, " while I tear the ugly black heart out av ye."

At the same time his " Lord Ribblesdale " proves how noble a rendering of human dignity the artist can achieve when he is in complete sympathy with his sitter. The wonderful series of Wertheimer portraits, now in the National Gallery, is at once a revelation of the artist's power in the expression of different characters and a souvenir of his long association with the astute and esteemed art-dealer who, from his earliest days, stoutly affirmed his belief in the genius of Sargent.

From the time he first exhibited at the Paris Salon in 1879, Sargent's career was one of a steady upward progress. It was not till 1894 that he was elected an A.R.A., but before this he had exhibited with distinction both at the Academy and at the New English Art Club. His early portraits show traces of the influence of the Impressionists, but Sargent's connection with this school is less obvious in his portraits than in his landscapes and water-colours.

In water-colour Sargent created a new and distinct style which had a great effect on his contemporaries. How skilfully he used it as a brilliant

"LORD RIBBLESDALE," BY JOHN S. SARGENT
National Gallery, London

Painted in 1902, this noble full-length portrait presents Lord Ribblesdale, then Master of the Buck-hounds, in hunting costume. It was given to the National Gallery by the sitter as a memorial of his wife and of his two sons who were killed respectively in Somaliland and in Gallipoli.

"THE PIAZETTA, VENICE," BY JOHN S. SARGENT

Tate Gallery, London

The intense realism of this water-colour is best seen when it is observed from some little distance. It is a brilliant study of sunshine playing on gondolas, the blue-green water of the canal, and on the arcades of a marble palace. In its breadth, vigour, and wonderful realisation of light and air, this characteristic water-colour is a masterpiece of impressionist illusionism.

sketching medium may be seen in " The Piazzetta, Venice." Here, like Manet, he saw " no lines in Nature," but built up a vivid impression of the scene before him by brilliant touches of colour and strong contrasts of light and shade. It is a broad, vigorous style which, despite its summariness, gives a marvellous sense of actuality in the hands of a master. Though pre-eminent as a portrait painter and as a sketcher in water-colour, Sargent executed notable works in a variety of styles and media. He painted important decorative works for public buildings in the United States, and he also did some sculpture, notably his " Crucifixion " for the Boston Library, U.S.A., a bronze study of which may be seen in the Tate Gallery.

Sargent died, at the age of sixty-nine, in 1925.

§ 2

Glancing briefly at the number of British artists who have attained eminence during this period by the character and individuality of their work—a number so great that it excludes any possibility of doing justice to them all within the space of this chapter—it is not without significance to note how few of them have received their training in the Royal Academy schools. Since the first World War the most fruitful forcing-grounds for British Art have been the Scottish schools and the Slade School in London ; other painters of distinction have come from the Royal College of Art in South Kensington or have received their training abroad.

It has often been said that the rank of a living artist can most fairly be gauged by the esteem in which he is held by foreign countries. By this reckoning a high place must be assigned to Frank Brangwyn, R.A., for few British artists have been more fêted than he on the Continent and in America. Paris, Munich, Vienna, Brussels, Madrid, Holland, and Italy, all have showered honours and distinctions on this artist. Born at Bruges in 1867, of Welsh extraction, Brangwyn was from boyhood familiar with the splendours of Flemish tapestry, and though he first obtained notice by his power of drawing as an illustrator, his real bent has always been towards decorative art. In his early boyhood he worked with William Morris, executing designs for tapestries, etc. ; but when he was only sixteen he left Morris and went to sea, and the knowledge of shipping and seafaring life which he thus gained stood him in good stead when he again returned to London and the practice of art. All his most important early pictures were of subjects he had seen at sea ; among them may be mentioned " Ashore " (1890), " Burial at Sea " and " Salvage " (1891), and " The Convict Ship " (1892). The sturdy drawing, glowing colour, and spacious

"THE POULTERER'S SHOP," BY FRANK BRANGWYN

Tate Gallery, London

Frank Brangwyn has a world-wide reputation as a decorative artist. This picture, originally exhibited in the Academy of 1916, is a splendid example of his original powers of colour and design, and reveals the romantic imagination which enables him to turn common-place things like fruit, vegetables, dead poultry, and shop utensils into a glowing pageant full of splendour and opulence.

design in these works marked out the decorative painter of the future, though at this time the artist was earning his living principally by seafaring drawings, executed for the *Graphic* and other illustrated papers. In addition to his drawings and paintings Brangwyn also devoted himself to etching, and his plates of the working maritime life on the lower reaches of the Thames were among the earliest of his works to attain a wide popularity.

Influenced to some extent perhaps by the Belgian painter and sculptor Constantin Meunier (1831–1905), whose vigorous art illustrated the industrial and mining life of the "Black Country" of Belgium, Brangwyn soon made his reputation as a painter by his unique gift of basing heroic decorative designs on typical scenes and episodes of modern industrialism. In 1895 his "Trade on the Beach" was bought for the Luxembourg, Paris, and a few years later his panel "Commerce," in the Royal Exchange, London, made his decorative gifts widely known to his own compatriots. His decorations for the Skinners' Hall and the series of panels illustrating typical modern industries, originally designed for the British Pavilion in the Venice International Exhibition and now in the Leeds Art Gallery, may be cited as brilliant examples of the decorative mural painting which this artist did so much to revive. Another fascinating series is that which the artist painted for the House of Lords, but which ultimately found its home at Cardiff.

Though a number of projects of decorative painting in the United States have taken up much of Frank Brangwyn's time, so that he is now a comparatively rare exhibitor in London, he has been a prolific producer of pictures, water-colours, and etchings in addition to his mural painting. He is limited neither in method nor in subject, but whether the latter be a scene in Italy, an impression of Pittsburg, or a table laden with the rich fruits of a sumptuous dessert, the presentation of the theme is invariably decorative and grandiose. "The Poulterer's Shop," which was bought for the nation by the Chantrey Trustees from the Academy of 1916 is a glowing example of the sense of opulent splendour which Frank Brangwyn's imagination and executive skill can extract from dead poultry, a heap of vegetables, and commonplace utensils.

§ 3

Since Pettie and Orchardson, Scotland has always been strongly represented in the Royal Academy. The younger Scottish School originated in Glasgow, whither about seventy years ago a very large number of fine pictures by the French romanticists found their way into public and private

"BEN LEDI," BY DAVID YOUNG CAMERON

Tate Gallery, London

Equally distinguished as a landscape-painter and as an etcher, D. Y. Cameron is one of the most personal artists of the day. This painting of a Highland landscape illustrates the delicate drawing and fine simplicity of design which characterise all the artist's works.

collections. In the appreciation of Corot and his contemporaries, Scotland was far ahead of England, and since Whistler also found favour more quickly in the north than in the south, the Scottish painters were, generally speaking, more advanced than their English confrères during the latter part of the nineteenth century. Of the group of painters known as the Glasgow School, it may be broadly said that the figure painters were chiefly influenced by Whistler, the landscapists by Corot and the French romanticists. Among the most distinguished of the figure painters were the late James Guthrie (1859–1930), who was elected President of the Royal Scottish Academy in 1902, and who added much of the robustness of Raeburn to a Whistlerian elegance and colour harmony ; John Lavery (1857–1941), who developed very successfully in his own way the graceful style and dainty colouring of Whistler, whether in portraying manly dignity, feminine loveliness, or in painting landscapes ; the late E. A. Walton (1860–1922), who was equally at home in portrait and in landscape ; Harrington Mann, George Henry, and the late Edward Hornel (1865–1933), who, with thick, enamel-like paint, invented a new style in which children are usually seen decoratively disposed amid flowery gardens of a semi-tropical luxuriance. In this school a place apart was held by the late Joseph Crawhall, whose animal paintings, and particularly his water-colours on brown holland, had an inevitability of line and simple grandeur of design which related his work to that of the greatest oriental artists.

Among the Glasgow landscape painters, most of whom, like the late W. Y. Macgregor, who died in 1923, and David Gauld, followed either the Barbizon or Modern Dutch Schools, the premier place has now been won by D. Y. Cameron, R.A. Born at Glasgow in 1865, David Young Cameron has made a foremost place for himself as an etcher, rivalling Muirhead Bone in his masterly interpretation of architectural and landscape subjects, while he has also developed a most personal style as a painter, depicting the hills and lakes of Scotland and the picturesque houses in her cities with a fine simplicity of design and clear, translucent colour. While in his use of delicate hues, harmonised with subtlety, D. Y. Cameron shows more than a passing acquaintance with Impressionism, in his emphasis of line and tendency towards simplification he exhibits in a mild and restrained form that reaction from Impressionism which ran to excess in Paris.

While there has never been a definite Edinburgh School, several modern painters of distinction have been associated with the Scottish capital, among them being James Pryde, one of the most original and gifted artists of recent years. Born in 1869, Pryde was the son of the late Dr. David Pryde of St. Andrews and subsequently of Edinburgh. Though nominally

"THE VESTIBULE," BY JAMES PRYDE

Property of the Earl of Crawford

Dramatic design is the supreme quality in the work of this most original artist. We do not know who are the figures in the foreground nor exactly what they are doing, but the stage is so beautifully set that we feel intensely that something is about to happen, and spellbound by the dignity of the scene we also wait in " The Vestibule " content with a spectacle of life that is mysterious but suggestive.

he received his training, like so many others, at the Atelier Julien in Paris, very little French influence appears in his work. He learnt the decorative value of the silhouette from Whistler, something about the effective disposal of masses, perhaps, from the brilliant French poster-designer Toulouse-Lautrec (1864–1901), and a good deal about dramatic composition from Hogarth. In other words, Pryde made his own choice among the masters and built up his own art by affinities and observation. It was by poster work that Pryde first roused the attention of the public. He had a sister, Mabel Pryde, who married another artist, William Nicholson, and the brothers-in-law, working under the pseudonym of " Beggarstaff Brothers," produced a series of posters in the 'nineties which electrified London by their outstanding artistic qualities.

After he gave up poster-designing, Pryde never made any attempt to obtain popularity. A fastidious and self-exacting painter, his output was comparatively small, and the pictures which he showed at the old Grosvenor Gallery, at the New Gallery, and at the exhibitions of the International Society, of which he was a distinguished member, appealed more to the collector and connoisseur than to the general public. As a painter he is difficult to place, for he was neither a realist nor an out-and-out romanticist. His subjects are a little mysterious, and though his pictures often have an eighteenth-century look, we hesitate to assign them to any definite period. What is happening in the picture is rarely clear, yet the artist contrives to hold our interest by a suggestion that something is about to happen. There is a strong feeling of latent drama in his work, because he excelled in Dramatic Design.

" The Vestibule," in the Earl of Crawford's Collection, is a characteristic example of the peculiar qualities in Pryde's work. Here, as in all his pictures, we find a stage beautifully set, a scene which so bewitches us by the nobility of its design, by the monumental splendour of its masses, by rich glows of colour from a whole of harmonious sombreness, that we catch our breath with delight at the spectacle, just as we might do in a theatre as the curtain goes up and before we have any knowledge of what action will take place on the scene. Pryde died in 1941.

William Nicholson, who was born at Newark-on-Trent in 1872, served a lengthy apprenticeship before he developed into the popular painter of portraits and still-life that he is to-day. After the success of the posters which he designed jointly with his brother-in-law, he laid the foundations of his individual reputation by a remarkable series of woodcuts in colour. Three of his books, an *Alphabet*, an *Almanac of Twelve Sports*, and *London Types*—all published in 1898—widened the base of his popularity and made the name of William Nicholson known to thousands who rarely visit picture exhibitions.

z*   713

"PORTRAIT OF MISS JEKYLL," BY WILLIAM NICHOLSON

Tate Gallery, London

Equally distinguished as a designer of posters and woodcuts and as a painter of realistic portraits and still-life subjects, William Nicholson in this portrait presents his sitter with the uncompromising realism of a seventeenth-century Dutchman and with the decorative dignity of a Whistler.

More definitely realistic, less imaginative, and less mysterious than Pryde, William Nicholson has this much in common with him, that he, too, is pre-eminently a designer. This much we may see in a work so remarkable for its fidelity to nature as his " Portrait of Miss Jekyll." In its suave rendering of character and atmosphere this portrait is descended from Velazquez through Whistler, but in its arresting simplicity, the effective placing of the chair-back, head, and hands as the accented notes of a diagonal composition, the picture is also related to the posters of the Beggarstaff Brothers and to the masterly designs of the Far East.

Another group of Scottish artists, of whom the best known are the late S. J. Peploe, J. D. Fergusson, and the late Joseph Simpson, were connected with Edinburgh, not Glasgow, and formed another distinct group. All of them were at first influenced by Whistler and subsequently by Manet and later French artists ; strong drawing, bright clean colour, and emphatic design are characteristic to the work of all three. J. D. Fergusson is the only one of the trio alive to-day, and his work has amply fulfilled its early promise.

The once much-talked-of Newlyn School was never a local development, like that of Glasgow, but consisted of a group of artists drawn from various places who found this Cornish fishing village, near Penzance, a pleasant place in which to settle and practise open-air painting. Stanhope Forbes, Napier Henry, the sea-painter, and Frank Bramley have been considered the leaders and founders of this school. Other artists have founded colonies at St. Ives and elsewhere along the Cornish coast, some of the best known being the marine painter Julius Olsson, R.A., the landscape painter Lamorna Birch, R.A., and that particularly brilliant pair, alike in portraiture, landscape, and figure subjects, Harold and Laura Knight, both of whom are now Academicians and who have now gone to Malvern.

§ 4

No two institutions in the United Kingdom have produced a more remarkable sequence of illustrious artists than the New English Art Club and the Slade School of Art, and since, though separate in their origin, the two have come to be closely related to each other, it is convenient to consider them together. The New English Art Club was founded in the 'eighties by a number of young artists whose bond of union was a Paris training. Among the founders were the painters P. Wilson Steer and Frederick Brown (died 1940), and the sculptors J. Havard Thomas and T. Stirling Lee ; while other early members included John S. Sargent, H. H. La Thangue, Mark Fisher, and George Clausen. For nearly forty years the New English Art Club has supplied the Royal Academy with nearly all its most distinguished members. During this period many Academicians and Associates are or have been exhibitors at the New English Art Club, while almost all the most important official art positions in London were gradually captured by members of this Club. Charles J. Holmes, who died in 1938 and who was Director of the National Gallery ; D. S. MacColl, who was for some time Keeper of the Wallace Collection ; William Rothenstein, who was Principal of the Royal College of Art at South Kensington from 1920 to 1935, were all former members of the New English Art Club.

Since its foundation the New English Art Club has largely recruited its strength from students of the Slade School, and the close alliance between the School and the Club is easily understood when we remember that the bond of union between the original clubmen was a Paris training, and when we discover that French influence has been paramount at the Slade School. This school of drawing and painting, situated in Gower Street and connected with University College, was named after Felix Slade (1790–1868), a famous art collector, who left money for the endowment of (Slade) professorships of fine art in Oxford, Cambridge, and University College, London.

The first Slade Professor at University College was E. J. Poynter (1871–75), under whose direction the teaching was much the same as that given in the Royal Academy Schools, but in 1876 he was succeeded by a distinguished French artist, Alphonse Legros, who, more than any other one man perhaps, may be said to have changed the character of British painting. Born at Dijon in 1837 and afterwards studying in Paris under the famous teacher of drawing, Lecoq de Boisbaudran, Alphonse Legros came to England in 1863. He was befriended by Whistler, Rossetti, Watts, and other English artists, and made his living principally by etching and by teaching. For a time he taught at the South Kensington School of Art, but in 1876 he was appointed Slade Professor at University College, a position he held till 1892. His picture of French peasant women at prayer, painted at University College in 1888, is a characteristic example of the seriousness and earnestness of his art, and by its fine precision of drawing shows that Legros was a lineal descendant of Ingres. To a generation absorbed in problems of colour, lighting, and atmosphere, this broad-minded exponent of the French classical school came as a prophet in his insistence on impeccable drawing as the sure foundation of all good painting.

At the Slade, Legros worked wonders in two ways. His great reputation as a teacher attracted the most promising art students of the time ; and his influence on these students had far-reaching effects. Legros, it has been well said, " brought English art again into closer touch with the

W. F. Mansell.

"FEMMES EN PRIÈRE," BY ALPHONSE LEGROS (1837–1911)

Tate Gallery, London

A characteristic picture of French peasant-women at prayer in a church by the great teacher of the Slade School, who, coming from Paris to London in 1863, " contributed largely to the noticeable revival of draughtsmanship in England at the close of the nineteenth century." Legros was naturalised as an Englishman in 1881.

main European tradition, and contributed largely to the noticeable revival of draughtsmanship in England at the close of the nineteenth century." Among the most gifted of his pupils were Charles Wellington Furse, William Strang, and William Rothenstein, all of whom laid the foundations of their reputations as painters by sterling drawing. After Legros left the Slade in 1892, the great tradition he bequeathed to the School was ably maintained by Professor Frederick Brown, among whose pupils were William Orpen and Augustus John, and after Professor Brown's retirement, Henry Tonks, who died in 1937, also of the New English Art Club, successfully conducted the Slade School along the lines laid down by Legros. The present head is Professor Randolph Schwabe.

While Legros was responsible for the renewed attention paid to drawing, other artists gradually made England familiar with the new ideas about colour which had originated in France. Conspicuous among the pioneers in this direction was George Clausen, R.A. Born in London in 1852, he was an art student at South Kensington from 1867 to 1873, and then went to Paris, where he was at first chiefly influenced by J. F. Millet and his follower, Jules Bastien-Lepage (1848–84). His well-known picture at the Tate Gallery, "The Girl at the Gate," a comparatively early work painted in 1889, shows George Clausen still dominated by the art of Bastien-Lepage. Later, the artist was profoundly influenced by the colour of the Impressionists, especially by Monet and Pissarro, and in his second manner, while frequently adhering to pastoral and peasant subjects which recall Millet, Clausen presented them in prismatic colours in which the illumination of real sunshine is rendered with exquisite truth and delicacy. George Clausen has painted both the life and the light of the fields, fusing the humanity of J. F. Millet with the Nature-worship of Claude Monet. Possessing a wide range, he has painted portraits and allegorical subjects as well as landscapes and pastorals. All his work is distinguished by its beauty of colour, radiant illumination, and human tenderness.

P. Wilson Steer, O.M., was born at Birkenhead in 1860. After studying at the École des Beaux Arts, Paris, he returned to England full of enthusiasm for the Impressionists, and among his early works may be found experiments in the style of Manet, Degas, Monet, and Renoir. But while he has always preserved their keen interest in light, Wilson Steer gradually broke away from the close imitation of the Impressionists and developed a style of his own in which the vivacity and broken touch of the French painters were mingled with elements derived from such British painters as Gainsborough, Constable, and Turner. The later art of Steer may be described as a blend of English and French traditions. In the landscapes of his maturity he has used pinks, mauves, and blues very sparingly and concentrated on the varied greens and yellows of Nature,

718

THE GIRL AT THE GATE," BY GEORGE CLAUSEN

Tate Gallery, London

Tender and sympathetic in its feeling for the sweet simplicity of rural life, this picture shows the influence of J. F. Millet and his follower the peasant-painter Bastien-Lepage. Painted in 1889, it is the best-known example of the first manner of an accomplished artist who in more recent pictures added a prismatic beauty of colour to his interpretations of the life of cottagers and agriculturists.

P. Laib.

"PORTRAIT OF MRS. HAMMERSLEY," BY P. WILSON STEER

In this radiant, sunlit portrait we see the confluence of British and French influences—Gainsborough, Constable, Watteau, and the Impressionists—which are happily blended in the distinctive art of Wilson Steer, who, as this picture proves, excels equally in portraiture and landscape painting. Steer is one of the founders of the New English Art Club, and as one of the teaching staff of the Slade School he has had a widespread influence on English art.

excelling in the rendering of wooded country with trees glittering in the sunshine after rain, and also in depicting the light and atmosphere in great vistas of spacious countrysides.   Equally distinguished as a figure painter, Steer is represented by a self-portrait in the Pitti Gallery, Florence, by " The Music Room " in the Tate Gallery, and by figure subjects as well as landscapes in many other public galleries.   Apparently averse to Academical honours, Steer remained the most loyal member of the New English Art Club.   The grace and refinement of his portraiture are beautifully exemplified in his " Portrait of Mrs. Hammersley," in which the background also reveals his powers as a landscape painter.   Steer was awarded the Order of Merit in 1931, and died in 1942.

Two other members of the New English Art Club who have helped to introduce Impressionism into England are Lucien Pissarro and Walter Sickert.   The former is the eldest son of Camille Pissarro.   He was born at Paris in 1863, and grew up among the Impressionists and neo-Impressionists, so that he may be said to have been impregnated with the science of colour from his early boyhood.   In 1893 he settled in London, where he came into touch with William Morris, and setting up a private press he made a European reputation as a wood-engraver and printer of beautiful books.   As a painter he made his way more slowly, but his landscapes have always aroused the enthusiasm of his brother artists by their just observation and masterly statement of the actual hues in Nature.

Walter Richard Sickert, born in 1860, was in his youth a pupil of Whistler, but the influence of this master was later superseded by that of the Impressionists, especially that of Degas, after the artist took up his residence in Paris, where he remained for several years.   Making a speciality of painting low-life scenes, portraying humble interiors, the galleries of theatres and music-halls, costers and flower-girls, Sickert but rarely explored, even in his landscapes, scenes at Dieppe, Venice or Bath, the realm of full sunshine which was the happy hunting-ground of the earlier Impressionists.   In his interiors Sickert is known chiefly as an exquisite interpreter of the subtle beauties of twilight, in his exteriors he usually preferred grey days or at least moments when direct sunshine was masked ; but within his self-imposed limits he was a true Impressionist, always giving his first attention to the lighting, and making lights even in darkness sparkle and vibrate with the magic of his deft broken touches.

§ 5

Returning to the pupils of Legros, first attention must be given to Charles Wellington Furse (1868–1904), who, but for his early death, would assuredly have attained a position in the art world rivalling that of

"THE RETURN FROM THE RIDE," BY CHARLES WELLINGTON
FURSE, (1868–1904)

Tate Gallery, London

But for his early death at the age of thirty-six, this gifted artist would have been the rival of Sargent. His genius for the grand style both in figure-painting and in landscape culminated in this great equestrian portrait group of his friends Mr. and Mrs. Aubrey Waterfield. This picture was exhibited at the Academy in 1903 and bought for the nation two years later by the Trustees of the Chantrey Bequest.

722

Sargent and Orpen. Born at Staines, Furse was only sixteen when he began to study under Legros at the Slade School. Later he worked in Paris, and returning to London he soon made his mark at the New English Art Club, where his portraits especially attracted attention. He was only twenty-five when he began his heroic equestrian portrait of Lord Roberts —now in the Tate Gallery—a great work which, being interrupted by illness, he was never able to complete, for after his recovery he was too much occupied with other work to return to it at once.

Between 1899 and 1901 much of his time was taken up in painting the decorative spandrels for Liverpool Town Hall, and his remarkable capacity for executing imposing works on a large scale was clearly revealed to the world in 1903, when " The Return from the Ride " was the " picture of the year " at the Academy. In this magnificent portrait group of his friends, Mr. and Mrs. Aubrey Waterfield, the figures are nearly life-size and the whole picture is painted with the assurance and exuberance of a master. In the following year, when he was elected A.R.A., he repeated his success at the Academy with an open-air portrait of his wife, entitled " Diana of the Uplands," another life-sized work full of breeziness and polished brilliance. For many years the artist had suffered from lung trouble ; and this finally caused his death in the very year in which he had won his Associateship. The breadth and dignity of his outlook equalled the felicity of his execution, and while the great performances in which his art culminated may be said to have been based to some extent on the practice of Velazquez, his own personal gifts and his keen observation of Nature gave an individual distinction to his works which makes them essentially original.

William Strang (1859–1921) was born at Dumbarton, came to London in 1875, and developed remarkable powers as a draughtsman under Legros at the Slade School. The first works of his to attract notice were his portrait drawings and his etchings, which attained distinction in two very different fields. His portraits, whether drawn or etched, were intensely realistic, of a Holbeinesque clarity and simplicity, strong in line and character ; but in etchings of other subjects Strang displayed imaginative gifts of the highest order, and his illustrations to the Bible, *Don Quixote*, and to some of Kipling's stories revealed a mind as alert to think and philosophise as his eye to see and his hand to record.

As a painter Strang had two distinct styles : in the first his colour was based on that of the great Venetians, in the second his palette became much brighter and lighter and the influence of Manet was apparent. The union of his incisive drawing with this pure clean colour produced in his second manner pictures of arresting brilliance. " Bank Holiday," painted in 1912 and now in the Tate Gallery, is a fine example of his later style,

"BANK HOLIDAY," BY WILLIAM STRANG (1859–1921)

Tate Gallery, London

Notable alike for its incisive drawing, clear, brilliant colour, effective design, and humorous, but sympathetic, observation of life, this picture of the embarrassment of a holiday-couple unused to the ways of restaurants marks the culmination of the artist's second manner, in which he united the severe classical drawing of Legros to the clean-coloured realism of Manet.

and while displaying the severity of his line and the emphatic realism with which he presented figures and objects, it also reveals his imaginative gifts in the subtle rendering of the embarrassment of a holiday couple unused to the etiquette which prevails in restaurants.

§ 6

While the painters mentioned above are far from exhausting the list of distinguished artists who received their training directly from Legros, his successor, Professor Brown, may be said to have been fortunate in having still more brilliant pupils. Of these first attention must be given to William Orpen (1878–1931) and Augustus John, who, by common consent, were the most richly gifted of the many students of the Slade School who have attained eminence in their profession.

Now and again in the history of art there are happy individuals who seem to escape the student stage altogether and appear as masters from the first. Lawrence was one ; Millais was another ; Orpen was a third. Born on November 27, 1878, William Orpen attracted the attention of London connoisseurs while he was still a student at the Dublin Metropolitan School of Art. The writer can remember the sensation caused at South Kensington over forty years ago by a drawing from the life with which this young Irishman won the gold medal at the National Competition for works by students at schools of art all over the country. Never before or since has there been so much unanimity of opinion about a prize-winner. Everybody was talking then about " young Orpen's " drawing, for while it satisfied the academic mind by its flawless perfection and anatomical correctness, it roused enthusiasm among more independent critics because it was not a dead thing—as so many prize-drawings are—but a real human figure in which every line pulsated with life. It was clear that a great draughtsman had come to town, and when Orpen left Ireland and came to the Slade School his drawings and paintings soon became conspicuous in the exhibitions of the New English Art Club. In the first decade of the twentieth century this youth in his twenties was already ranked, not with other students, but with artists, like Wilson Steer, who were recognised as masters. What distinguished Orpen at once from other able draughts-men of his age was his precocious facility in the manipulation of paint. Most students have to learn slowly how to handle pigment ; the first paintings Orpen exhibited proved that he had a mastery of the brush. A beautiful example of his early fluency is the picture in the Tate Gallery, entitled " The Mirror," painted in 1900. Even at this period Orpen showed a wide range ; he painted portraits, still-life, nudes, and subject pictures, while perhaps the most characteristic of these early works were interiors with figures, pictures which seemed to have the fullness of content of a Van Eyck, though painted with the exuberance of a Hals.

In " The Mirror," traces of the influence of Whistler may still be seen ; in his later works Orpen's style became broader and more vigorous, his colour grew lighter and more brilliant, and in portraits his penetration into character gained in profundity. But the characterisation was keen in several early portraits, notably the " Charles Wertheimer," the first and only picture the artist exhibited at the Royal Academy prior to his election as Associate in 1910.

After his entry into the Royal Academy the art of William Orpen grew steadily in power and public favour, but his phenomenal success never warped his sincerity as an artist. While he contributed a generous measure of portraits to the exhibitions of Burlington House, he remained loyal to the New English Art Club, and there he again and again showed those inimitable pictures which an artist paints for his own delight and pleasure. Among them may be mentioned some notable scenes of vagrant and peasant life in Ireland, and playful allegories, like " Sowing the Seed," in which a true Irish sense of humour had been blended with pictorial and decorative charm. It was characteristic of Orpen's independence as an artist that of all the hundreds of portraits which he painted in Paris during and after the Peace Conference, the very best of them should be, not one of the famous statesmen and soldiers who sat to him, but a man who was a nonentity till his portrait was exhibited. The now famous " Chef de l'Hôtel Chatham " was not only the " picture of the year " at the 1921 Academy, it is a picture for all time which has and will have the wide human appeal of Moroni's " Portrait of a Tailor." In this portrait of the Chef in his immaculate white cap and jacket, standing beside his grill, we have Orpen at his very best, using all his amazing facility and dexterity in the handling of paint for the purpose of putting on canvas the rich, full humanity of a living being.

This artist's two great Peace pictures in the Academy of 1920, " Signing of Peace in the Hall of Mirrors, Versailles," and " A Peace Conference at the Quai d'Orsay," were an expansion of the delightful little interiors which he had sent in earlier days to the New English Art Club, and in a way his allegory, " Sowing the Seed," may be regarded as a prelude to the very different and far more serious painting, " To the Unknown Soldier," which was the centre of interest in the Academy of 1923. For both these paintings show high powers of imagination, and warn us that in marvelling at the quickness of his eye and at the unerring skill of his hand, we must not forget that William Orpen was also an artist with a keenly intelligent brain and with a warm imaginative heart, a man who

W. F. Manseli.

" THE MIRROR," BY WILLIAM ORPEN (1878–1931)

Tate Gallery, London

Painted in 1900—when the artist was only twenty-two—this charming picture is already a master's work, showing nothing of the hesitancy or tentativeness of a novice. In the mirror is seen a diminished reflection of the other end of the room ; with the artist at work before his easel.

727

"CHEF DE L'HÔTEL CHATHAM," BY WILLIAM ORPEN

Diploma Gallery, Royal Academy

In this portrait of a chef in a Paris hotel William Orpen uses his amazing powers as an artist to create a monumental work which makes the subject live for us in all its humanity. It is typical of our times that a great artist should choose such a subject, and should regard the painting so highly that he makes it the diploma work for the Royal Academy Gallery on his election.

could see both the humour and tragedy of life, who could feel deeply and could express his emotions either in genial satire or in a majestic allegory of epic grandeur.

The foundations of Augustus John's reputation were also laid in the drawings which he showed at the New English Art Club during the first decade of the present century. The exuberant flow of his line, his powerful modelling of form by subtleties of light and shade ; the extraordinary vitality of his heads in chalks and sanguine—all seemed to suggest that in Augustus John was reincarnated the princely art of Rubens. One thing alone at that time limited his popularity. It was asked why did he draw such " ugly " people. The truth was that John, having an exceedingly original mind, found beauties in new types. A Welshman by birth and descent, John in his early days was a Borrow in paint, happiest and most at home among the Romanies. The apparent strangeness of his early drawings and paintings was largely due to his preference for gipsy types. While teaching at the Liverpool University School of Art, round about 1904, he would periodically disappear to go roving with the gipsies and then reappear, bringing with him pictures of the raggle-taggled life of the caravan. These pictures, bright and clear in colour, incisive in line, and effective in composition, were a new thing in painting. As a painter John did not possess the precocious facility of Orpen, and his early work often shows a certain heaviness of handling when compared with his present-day pictures, and in acquiring mastery of the brush John gradually evolved two distinct manners. Influenced to some extent by the modern French painters, he has shown a tendency to simplification which is most marked in his decorative work. In mural decorations, like " The Mumpers " at the Tate Gallery, John deliberately sacrifices roundness of form for decorative effect. Like Pierre Puvis de Chavannes (1824–1898), the great painter of the Ste. Geneviève series in the Panthéon, Paris, John found that the qualities he aimed at necessitated a certain flatness of treatment. At the same time his colour in these decorative works has become lighter and brighter. To this extent, in so far as it has tended to simplify rather than to complicate painting, the art of Augustus John may be said to illustrate a reaction from Impressionism. But while his decorative works often have primitive qualities, in his portraits he uses his full power of expressing form, and one of his greatest masterpieces, " Madame Suggia," proves that when this is his aim, John is second to no living man in realistic force and characterisation. His landscapes are closer to his decorative work than to his realistic portraiture. Finding his favourite subjects among the mountains and lakes of his native Wales, John invented a new genre in landscape. Emphatic in their design, simplified in form, and brilliant but still in colour, they struck a new note in British art.

W. F. Mansell.

" MME. SUGGIA," BY AUGUSTUS E. JOHN

A masterpiece of modern portraiture, this brilliant painting of a distinguished 'cellist shows the extra-ordinary power of Augustus John, who here presents his sitter in the " grand style."   Encased in a setting that is simple yet eminently decorative, the figure of the performer is amazingly alive and full of action.

"THE BURNING KILN," BY CHARLES JOHN HOLMES

Tate Gallery, London

An impressive example of the new type of "industrial landscape" invented by C. J. Holmes, who was for many years Director of the National Gallery and formerly Slade Professor of Fine Art at Oxford University.

731

"MR. MINNEY," BY WALTER W. RUSSELL

Tate Gallery, London

This racily observed and dexterously painted portrait of a professional model " in his best clothes "
was the most discussed picture in the Academy of 1920. Russell was a pupil of Professor Frederick
Brown, and for some years was a member of the teaching staff of the Slade School of Art.

732

"THE COUNTESS OF ROCKSAVAGE AND SON," BY CHARLES SIMS

This radiant portrait of the married sister of Sir Philip Sassoon and her son was deservedly the " picture of the year " in the Academy of 1922. While the actuality of the figures and the delicious play of sunlight on the flesh-tints reveal more than a passing acquaintance with the secrets of Impressionism, the clear design of the decorative setting has a formal beauty that reminds us of the work of the Italian Primitives.

Limitations of space prevent all but the briefest mention of another member of the New English Art Club, who created a new type of landscape. Charles John Holmes, a former Director of the National Gallery, was born in 1868 and died in 1938. The son of a Cornish clergyman, he distinguished himself as a classical scholar at Eton and Oxford, and made a reputation as a writer on art before his water-colours and paintings became generally appreciated. Always a stylist in design, simplicity was the outstanding quality in his work, and while he painted many impressive landscapes of the grim, gaunt scenery of the Lake Country, it was his peculiar distinction to invent " industrial landscape," pictures in which the factories and power-stations of modern industrialism are powerfully presented. " The Burning Kiln " is a fine example of the imaginative grandeur with which C. J. Holmes invested these new subjects.

Another pupil of Professor Brown, Walter W. Russell, R.A. (born 1867), added to the laurels of the New English Art Club by his brilliant portrait, " Mr. Minney."

In the period under review the two most distinguished artists who came from the Royal Academy Schools were Frederick Cayley Robinson (1862–1927) whose poetic and decorative work showed a mingling of Pre-Raphaelite ideals with the noble simplicity of Puvis de Chavannes, and Charles Sims, R.A. (1873–1928), who, after first attracting attention by the sheer beauty of his romantic idylls, astonished even his admirers by his exquisitely gracious and accomplished portrait " The Countess of Rocksavage and Son."

The premature death in 1914 of Spencer F. Gore robbed native art of a rarely gifted painter. Gore's work was all done before the 1914–18 war started, but full recognition of this achievement only came in the period following it. He was born in 1878, educated at Harrow and trained at the Slade. Sickert and Lucien Pissarro were early influences and before his short life closed he had created his own beautiful style of Impressionism. He died at Richmond in his thirty-sixth year, and among his last works are some superb paintings of the park.

In this short chapter it has been impossible to cover all the achievements in the field of British art that took place in the years that immediately followed the end of the first World War in 1918, but the record reveals that the academic tradition, modified by the newer tendencies, produced a notable body of good work.

XXXVII

ART ACCEPTS ALL MEN'S VISION

A WORD ON THE NEW MOVEMENTS

THE study of modern art is often profoundly disturbing to those who have been trained in the traditions which prevailed during the latter part of the nineteenth century. It appears anarchic, perverse, unmannerly, ugly. There is no evidence of technical prowess nor of that craftsmanship which for hundreds of years has been accepted as an essential of the artist's equipment. *Naïveté* stands cheek by jowl with over-sophistication. The work of children, of infants even, is looked upon with deep interest, not merely as a promise of eventual development into worthwhile art, but as something standing in its own right and having a claim upon our attention as vision and as ideas of the visual world expressed in form and colour. The work of the most highly valued artists does not appear to differ widely from these lispings of the immature. The foremost critics write highly intelligent books about this seemingly unintelligent stuff—books that are often so highly intelligent, so profoundly philosophical, that the average reader is defeated by the abstract learning in their pages. Lecturers expound the significance of this new art. The expensive art galleries and public museums devote their wall space to exhibitions of this type of work. Newspaper critics treat it with respect and the deepest seriousness in their precious space. Connoisseurs and directors of galleries buy it.

Is all this simply contagious nonsense ? Or a racket between dealers and critics and the artists to put a high price upon specious rubbish ? Or a vast joke in bad taste ? Or a sign of the prevailing madness of our times which, for all their marvellous advancement, are not free from much more universal and dangerous lunacy ? Any of these, or a combination of some of them, suggest themselves as explanations, and might be accepted unless there is, in fact, justification for modern art in some other direction more rational and more honest.

First of all we must accept the fact that the traditional line, which painting and sculpture have followed in Europe almost unswervingly since Giotto led us away from Byzantine symbolism, has been broken. One writes " almost " because it is well to remember that artists as eminent as Botticelli

735

in his final period, El Greco, and William Blake did not truly follow that tradition, but prophetically worked in the modern manner. However, the main line is clear : an endeavour to represent in line and form and colour the appearance of objects in the natural world under the influence of light. All the slowly acquired knowledge of the Renaissance artists, all their accumulated technique, was devoted to this end. The rediscovery of Greek and Roman sculpture, which had pursued this same path to its own perfection, gave fresh emphasis to the European trend. The knowledge of scientific perspective of a Uccello, the understanding of anatomy of Michael Angelo or Leonardo, of light and shade by Rembrandt, the science of colour in the hands of a Delacroix or the Impressionists : everything over hundreds of years contributed to perfect this art of appearances, based on the duplication of their form and colour as the eye received it. Pictures and sculpture represented them as they could be seen from one point of space at one point of time. That was accepted as the end and ideal of art, and the craftsmanship which created that illusion most perfectly was accepted as the ideal workmanship of the artist.

Towards the end of the nineteenth century certain advances in applied science had their inevitable repercussion in this realm of art. The invention of photography, with its marvellous potentiality of depicting objects as the artist was striving to do, was one factor. The speeding up and ease of transport and the consequent opening up of the culture of the whole world, was another. The third was a movement in the mind of mankind which was in essence a reaction against the materialism which had been itself a by-product of scientific progress. The fourth element was the new science of psychology and the emphasis on the subconscious under the leadership of Freud and his disciples.

The first of these shook the faith of the artist in the essential necessity of his task of representation. If the camera were going to do the task as well or better, why so laboriously produce works of art ?

The second revealed the fact that other peoples had produced works of art along quite other lines than this European one of realistic representation. So-called savages created sculptural forms which evoked a response as lively as the sublime works of Michael Angelo ; Chinese or Persian perspective did not depend upon a single point of view at a single moment of time ; Africa, India, South America, the South Sea Islands, the art of Byzantium fossilised in the conservative ikon art of the Russian church : these and a score of other modes of expression were seen to be fulfilling the basic needs of art.

The third asked whether art might not find its real function in presenting ideas about the world rather than representing and depicting the outward appearance of things. It linked up with the former factor, for

"HOMAGE TO MANET," BY WILLIAM ORPEN

Manchester Art Gallery

In this great portrait group Orpen paid homage not only to Manet, the leader of the French Impressionists, but also to a number of his own most illustrious contemporaries. The scene is a studio in Bolton Gardens. On the wall hangs Manet's portrait of "Eva Gonzales." Seated round the table from left to right are George Moore, Philip Wilson Steer, Sir Hugh Lane (resting his head on his hand) and Professor Henry Tonks. Standing behind Lane are D. S. MacColl and Sickert (holding the lapels of his coat).

SEATED LOHAN

British Museum

A giant ceramic sculpture of the Tang Dynasty (A.D. 618–906), made of hard white pottery and glazed in the usual colours of this period. There were sixteen Lohans, the disciples or apostles of Buddha, and a series of these over-life-size statues of them was discovered. Eight were in magnificent condition, this one, now in the British Museum, being the finest of them all.

Seated on a rock, the symbol of stillness and timelessness, with the long ears which betoken holiness, the folded hands and the pose of contemplation, this work is one of the world's masterpieces of sculpture and cermaic art.

" THE RICE GOD "

This ancient Steatite carving from Sierra Leone would once have been dismissed as art because it failed to conform to the standards of European Classic beauty. During our century, however, we have grown to appreciate the power and the sense of rhythm (even though it be a new rhythm) of these works by primitive people working to express their own emotions and ideas.

anthropologists were making us aware of the symbolic power of the non-realistic images of these exotic arts.

The fourth proposed the whole non-rational world of the subconscious as a possible territory where the artist might work, and alongside this emphasised the importance of the expression which children indulged in before their minds were moulded by the imitation of adults or the imposition of teaching.

In spite of these disturbing factors the artists were, as ever, under the compulsion to create, as they had been since Man first scratched figures on the walls of his cave. Art, therefore, switched itself along these new lines of development. If the artist could not compete with the camera he could take refuge in non-representational design which had always been so important an element underlying his work. If Polynesians and Chinese could express themselves in fantastic or ultra-simplified forms, could move away from the three-dimensional perspective, why should that not be done in the studios of Paris and London? If we were going to present the things of the mind which have nothing to do with time or space, why be bound by the representation of temporal and spacial actuality. Finally, if the subconscious were a province of art, why think at all?

In this development of art Impressionism was the last word in direct vision. It was rightly complained that Monet was "only an eye." He saw and put down exactly what he saw under the effect of light at that moment. The three great Post-Impressionists, Cézanne, Gauguin and Van Gogh, were reactions from this too-visual art although all of them owed much to it, particularly in the way of brilliance of colour. Cézanne painted not so much Nature as the geometrical forms which his intellect told him lay beneath Nature. "Every form of Nature can be expressed by the cube, the cone and the cylinder," he asserted. Gauguin turned more and more towards decoration built up in two rather than three dimensions—a repercussion probably from the Japanese art which so affected the Paris of his day. Van Gogh expressed in his very brush-work the inner vitality of the world rather than its mere outward appearance.

From Cézanne derived all that art which is basically Cubistic, and in its extreme manifestation abandoned the appearance of Nature altogether for the fascination of pure solid geometrical forms and their relationship one with another. From Gauguin one branch of art increasingly pursued the primitive; whilst Van Gogh had opened the way to frankly subjective ideas about things rather than their visual form and colour. In these and other directions the barriers were down.

Actually we have to remember that Mankind inhabits two separate worlds. One is the world he shares with the animals, a sensuous world which he sees, hears, feels, tastes, and smells. These five senses are limited

By permission of Berkeley Galleries.

"ELEVEN-HEADED AVALOKITO" FROM TIBET

Beside the art of Primitive people we have grown to appreciate the wonderful forms of the East where religious art, harking back to the fecundity of the Hindu faith, has given us the many-limbed and many-headed figures. This jewelled sculpture from Tibet reveals how wonderfully the formal problems can be overcome once we have released the mind from representation.

By permission of Berkeley Galleries.

"TIKI" ANCESTRAL FIGURE

The Maoris of New Zealand yield yet another type of sculpture with an age-old tradition differing entirely from the European one. The strong, simplified forms, the deep shadows, the formalised arrangement of the limbs, the decorative tattooing on the face : these things combine to make a powerful work of art of this figure from the house of a Maori chief.

by immediate time and a narrow range in space. As soon as Man began to think consciously he created another world in his mind, a world vague at first but becoming fixed and permanent when he created language. Words—definite articulated sounds each linked to a special idea and accepted in that association between one man and another—were more than a means of communication. They were the furniture, the contents of this new world of human consciousness. It was free from the limitations of space and time. In that world things which were not present could be evoked as easily as things which were. It was the world of ideas. The great change-over which took place in art towards the end of the nineteenth century and has continued throughout our own time was the granting of the freedom of that world of the mind to the artist instead of confining him to the limitations of the world of the visual sense in which European art at least had walked steadily for several hundred years.

The artist still had the limitation that he had to use visual symbols, but he was free to use any kind of symbol which expressed any idea, and not only the reiteration of the appearance of the thing. His task was to invent visual symbols which should be as universal and entirely satisfying in his realm as words had proved in this vast world of the mind. (Actually any symbol has to be translated into a word or words before it can have its place in the world of the mind. If an artist draws a cat we mentally say " cat " in order to make the picture part of the furniture of our mind.) It has to be granted that so far the artists have often failed to invent satisfying symbols, and some thinkers assert that by the nature of things he never can. But at least we owe it to the progressive contemporary artist to believe that he is trying to reach this goal, that he is honest and sincere. This belief, and not a cynical accusation of dishonesty, facile humour, or aggravating lunacy has to be our approach to modernist art.

Thus if a Simultanist or Futurist puts on his canvas many aspects and segments of a subject which in real life can only be seen from different viewpoints (since only one material thing can occupy one space at any given point of time) we can realise that such things can be in the world of the mind which he is depicting. If a sculptor so analyses the forms of a figure that he is dealing only with abstract masses and stresses ; if he expresses himself in the art mannerism of Byzantium or India ; if a Surrealist puts down on paper the irrational associations which come and are unquestionably accepted by the mind in the dream state ; if a Fauvist abandons everything but a single vital line to express the idea he wishes to emphasise ; if some other artist draws a boat looking rather like a toy boat than a real one, being concerned only with its decorative value and simplifying accordingly ; or yet another expresses the essential nature of sunflowers by a riot of brilliant yellow paint around a central vortex of purple brown,

741

"PADMA PANI AND SCENES FROM LIFE OF BUDDHA"

The East has inspired European artists not only through its sculpture, but in painting also. Buddhist art in China, Tibet, and Japan has given us some exquisite paintings on silk of scenes from the life of the Buddha and similar sacred themes. These, freed from our conceptions of perspective and representation, have an inspiring beauty.

742

sacrificing for that emphasis on colour the exquisite lines of the sunflower form in nature ; if, in the last resource, the artist wishes to draw literally nothing on earth but only an abstract pattern of form and colour from the recesses of his own mind : if any or all of these things become an artist's intention, the door is open. This is freedom finding new laws, not merely licence abandoning the old ones.

For these principles of art, this freedom from our European tradition based on the Greeks as it was passed down to us at the time of the Renaissance, we have turned to the strangest sources, and everywhere have found fresh vision and methods. The first reaction to such newness has inevitably been one of mistaken comparison with our own European standards, but then it has been realised that these works are things of power and often of grace. Who can deny the lovely Bodhisattvas of Buddhist art their tenuous beauty ? The great Exhibitions of Chinese and of Persian Art held at the Royal Academy in the years before the war were revelations of new things created according to standards other than our own. We came to see that a figure might have a hundred arms and a dozen heads and yet not be monstrous, that a painting might be planned on a two-dimensional scheme and have arresting beauty. But we were forced to go further than this. Long before, Paris and then London had grasped the power of much absolutely primitive work, the magic sculpture of African tribesmen, of Maories, of South Sea Islanders. At one time Negro sculpture became a rage in Paris. Vlaminck and Derain were chief among its " discoverers." In truth, the time was ripe, as we have seen, for this extension of men's æsthetic vision.

Some recent exhibitions, particularly of sculpture, at the small Berkeley Galleries in London, have revealed anew to us the wealth which can come from such sources. One of Primitive Art from Africa, and the islands of the Southern Atlantic and Pacific, including New Zealand, was a wonderful demonstration of the evocative strength of the forms which these " savages " could create. The direct carving of wood and stone, and the decoration of handicraft had a beauty based on their own age-long traditions. At the same Galleries there was a further exhibition of Tibetan work, sculpture, paintings, and craftwork. Again it proclaimed new beauty, linking, as it did, the ancient culture of China with that of India. The excavations in Northern India, those in Mesopotamia, and all this opening up of the East and of the primitive peoples of the far islands has opened new doors to the artist who can now be sure that his audience will grasp new intentions and methods.

It has to be remembered in all this traffic with exotic forms and even more exotic ideas that these works were created as the expression of deep religious, community and social ideas. To the native of Africa or Polynesia they are linked with fertility ritual or devil worship in evocative magic or

743

taboo as the Hindu or Far Eastern work is linked with ancient Asian religious systems. To the European artist and lover of art such meanings do not exist, however interested anthropologists and ethnographers may be in them. The images come to us, therefore, as pure art forms : shapes, masses, patterns, lines, colours. Many of them are frankly hideous from the viewpoint of our conceptions based on Classic and Christian art, but others have a formal beauty and invariably there is the charm of fine craftsmanship. This distinction between outward form and inner meaning should be remembered if our acceptance of the new thing is to be sincere and not a mere cult.

Let it be granted that it also opens the door to charlatanism and deliberate eccentricity. That is always the price of freedom. It is for common sense to make its own bargains, to accept, reject, approve, or disregard. This has been the way of art throughout the ages.

XXXVIII

ART IN THE 'THIRTIES

THE ROYAL ACADEMY, SOME INDEPENDENTS AND FRENCH PAINTERS

§ I

IN the short interval between our wars, there has been much activity in art at home and abroad. One of the forms this expenditure of energy took in England was a movement within the Royal Academy to make the Annual Exhibitions more truly representative of the living art of the day. To this end a number of new Associates and Academicians were recruited from among the more famous members of the New English Art Club, and the work of others of lesser repute was accepted regularly for exhibition. Walter Richard Sickert, Augustus John, and the late William Orpen were the most famous new exhibitors in the early 'twenties. The art of these masters has already been described and it is only necessary here to record that national and private collections have been greatly enriched by their many masterpieces of the period. Among other well-known members of the Club who became associated with the Royal Academy, either officially or as exhibitors, were Ambrose McEvoy, Philip Connard, Stanley Spencer, Charles Cundall, and Henry Lamb.

Ambrose McEvoy was born in Wiltshire, at Crudwell, in 1878, and he died at the age of forty-eight in January, 1927. He entered the Slade School at the early age of fifteen, and his promise was immediately recognised by his teachers. In the beginning he steeped himself in the study of the Old Masters, and his first exhibits were small genre-paintings and sparkling little interiors rather in the manner of seventeenth-century Dutch art. Although he had considerable gifts as a landscape painter, it was as a portraitist that he became widely known. He has often been called the " twentieth-century Gainsborough," perhaps because of the air of delicate distinction and spirituality he imparted to his sitters. The title could not but please him, for he is quoted by R. H. Wilenski, the distinguished critic, as saying : " There are days when I think Gainsborough the greatest painter that ever lived." McEvoy's draughtsmanship is firm and decided, and this is apparent in even the most elusively iridescent of his paintings. He aimed at a very high degree of finish and worked many times over the

2A*

745

whole canvas. Yet there was nothing fixed or rigid about his work. The tale of the last brush-strokes McEvoy ever made illustrates vividly how flexible it was. " Only a few days before he died he saw how to give greater life and movement to the nearly finished portrait of Lady Wimborne, and with incredible swiftness and sureness, swept the broad lines of a new rhythm across the picture, so that the figure seems to move lightly across the field of vision ; and so the canvas remains, unfinished but alive, for he never touched a brush again." [1]

McEvoy's work is well-known outside England. Examples are in the Musée du Luxembourg in Paris and in the Johannesburg Gallery, and he visited America to execute several portrait commissions. His striking portrait of Ramsay Macdonald is now in the Scottish National Portrait Gallery, and one of his finest male portraits, that of Dr. James Ward, D.Sc., is in the Fitzwilliam Museum, Cambridge. But although he did several successful paintings of men, it is as a painter of women that he made his name, for the grace and charm of his style is peculiarly suited to femininity. There are ten of his works in the Tate Gallery, among them his last Academy exhibits, a portrait of Mrs. Claude Johnson, and a painting, presented by the Department of Overseas Trade, of the Searchlight Tattoo at Wembley. He was made an A.R.A. in 1924.

Another New English artist who became an Academician in the period is Philip Connard. His first reputation was made by his airy landscapes and sunny interiors, and then his luminous portrait groups earned him wider recognition. Of recent years he has produced much purely decorative work, and the name " Connard " now calls to mind at once one of those charming panels on which, in pale sweet colours, birds and flowers display their fragile grace. A happy use of his decorative gifts is seen in the set of paintings of royal castles he executed for the adornment of the room at Windsor which contains the Queen's Doll's House.

Soon after the Armistice Stanley Spencer began to exhibit at the New English his strange new art, and in the intervening period he has been in, and out again, of the Academy. He studied at the Slade School, and went through the first World War, and he has contributed officially to the War Records.

Stanley Spencer's æsthetic forbears are the Pre-Raphaelite Brotherhood, and the chief source of his inspiration when he began to paint was the New Testament. He illustrated the Gospel stories in an unorthodox manner, however, for he used the village of Cookham in Surrey, where he lived, for their setting, and present-day villagers in clumsy modern clothes as participants in the sacred scenes. Thus, in " The Visitation," an early work, the Virgin was shown as a servant-girl in cotton frock and

[1] " Painters of England," by S. G. Kaines Smith.

"MRS. CLAUDE JOHNSON," BY AMBROSE McEVOY

Tate Gallery

Presented to the nation by the sitter in memory of her husband, this luminous painting is a character-istic example of the artist's skill in feminine portraiture. McEvoy is chiefly known for his fine series of oils of beautiful and distinguished women, but he also experimented with much success in portrait sketches in water-colour. He was a pupil of Professor Brown at the Slade School, and after his student days was associated with John and Sickert. He died, at a comparatively early age, in 1927.

" THE RESURRECTION," BY STANLEY SPENCER
Burghclere Memorial Chapel

This large altar-piece is one of the most striking mural paintings of the era. In his treatment of the subject the artist has used to the full his remarkable talent for investing a mystical event with something of the appearance of a familiar phenomenon. It is as though yet one more *Reveille* has just sounded in ears that have heard so many. and once again the camp begins to stir, for a new day has come.

apron, calling at a typical Surrey cottage ; and in " Christ Carrying the Cross," the Via Dolorosa runs between iron railings by red brick villas. In this last painting symbolism is mixed with realism, as befits the subject.

About seventeen or more years ago, Stanley Spencer showed a collection of drawings and designs for a War Memorial Chapel, which existed only in his imagination ; but there it had a very real existence, for the whole project was most elaborately worked out. The drawings were both decorative and dramatic, and the immediate result of their exhibition was such as few present-day artists would dare to hope for. Mr. J. L. Behrend decided to build a Memorial Chapel to the specified requirements and to commission the artist to decorate it. The chapel was built at Burghclere in Hampshire. Its mural decoration was finished in 1933. There can be no doubt that this is one of the major events in the history of native art during the last two decades.

The artist served in Macedonia from 1914 to 1918, and for most of the time as hospital orderly. He has drawn on his memory of those years for subject-matter. The paintings cover three walls ; their subjects include war scenes and life in hospital. Behind the altar on the central wall is a large painting, " The Resurrection." The paintings are full of detail, but there is nothing sensational or morbid about the scenes chosen. They are vivid records of remembered scenes and they are also very decorative works of art. It is only in the large central picture that the artist has allowed his imagination full rein. Macedonia is the scene of the Resurrection. The soldiers are shown waking slowly from their long sleep. In the foreground are the heaped crosses ; in the far distance the unknown goal.

It took several years to complete the work and while it was in progress Spencer also executed a number of other important paintings. About 1926 he painted the eighteen-foot " Resurrection of the Dead," now in the Tate Gallery, which was the cause of much comment when first seen. The Burghclere version of the same subject is entirely different in design. Another beautiful work (some think it the most beautiful of all the artist's paintings) was also done while the chapel decoration was going forward. This is the long narrow landscape, " Cottages at Burghclere," now in the Fitzwilliam Museum, Cambridge. The exquisitely rendered detail, enamelled brilliance of colouring, and enhanced realism of the whole composition make this painting one of the most memorable achievements of our time.

Stanley Spencer was made an Associate of the Royal Academy, but he resigned several years ago following a difference of opinion with the Selection Committee concerning a painting he sent for exhibition.

Charles Cundall's career was also interrupted by war service, and he was hampered for a long time by the results of a wound in his right arm. Nevertheless he managed to paint so effectively that he was elected to the New English Art Club and some years later made an A.R.A. He is Lancashire born and Slade trained. His successes have been obtained in fresh, brightly coloured pictures of contemporary life. Football and tennis matches, the Coronation and Barnet Fair, London parks and squares have all provided him with subjects well-suited to his mood. One of his major works, " The Demolition of Waterloo Bridge," was exhibited in the Academy in 1936, and it is now of historic interest as the beautiful bridge has gone. " Chelsea *versus* Arsenal at Stamford Bridge," painted in 1937, is a " documentary " which achieves æsthetic beauty.

The achievements of Henry Lamb as a painter in the Great War have already been considered. His work was first seen at Burlington House in the 'twenties. At one time his paintings showed a lively medley of very bright clean colours, but later their colour-schemes grew more orthodox and restrained. He is chiefly known for his portraits and portrait groups ; the latter are true " conversation pieces," and full of psychological interest. Two of his early works each had a sensational success : the poignant " Death of a Peasant," a most moving portrayal of grief, and the famous portrait of the late Lytton Strachey, author of *Eminent Victorians*, which was on loan for many years to the Tate Gallery. He was elected A.R.A. in 1940.

Among those artists whose careers have been closely identified with Academy successes, and whose reputations have greatly increased during the past twenty years, are the Royal Academicians, A. J. Munnings, now President of the R.A., Gerald Brockhurst, and the late Glyn Philpot.

The art of A. J. Munnings, R.A., has a secure place in public esteem. His large painting, " The Prince of Wales on Forest Witch," which was the Academy sensation in 1921, ushered in the most successful phase of his career. Since that date his work has attained a world-wide reputation, and to its popularity to some extent is due the newly revived interest in English sporting pictures. Alfred J. Munnings was born in 1878 at Mendham, in Suffolk, where his father, like Constable's, was a miller. After schooldays at Framlingham College he was apprenticed to a printer in Norwich, but soon he was attending the local School of Art, where he studied poster-designing as well as painting. Some thirty years later a loan exhibition was held in Norwich Castle of the works of the one-time printer's apprentice, and every phase of his work was represented there, from his first childish drawings to " The Drummer," a sketch in oils which was sold in the same year for £1300. He has shown at the Academy

"KILKENNY HORSE FAIR," BY ALFRED J. MUNNINGS

This brilliant work shows Sir Alfred Munnings in his threefold power as a supreme painter of horses, as a landscape artist, and as an impressionist able to catch the poses of the figures in a crowd under the light of a given moment. Every slightest touch of the brush leaves an impression of a person or animal caught in significant movement, and the crowded scene is yet realised as one single unity.

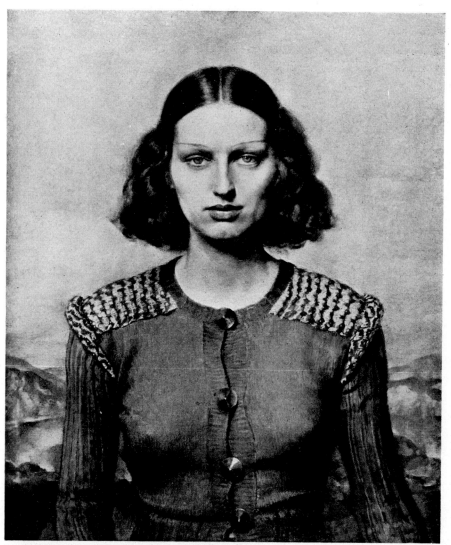

"JEUNESSE DORÉE," BY GERALD BROCKHURST

In this fine portrait of a beautiful, grave young girl may be seen the æsthetic qualities and the masterly technique which have made the artist one of the most admired and fashionable portraitists of the day. The decorative values of modern dress have seldom been more happily emphasised than in Brockhurst's compositions. Among his successes are his portraits of the Duchess of Windsor and the Countess Haugwitz-Reventlow. He has also won distinction as an etcher of figure subjects, and had produced some exquisite pencil portrait drawings.

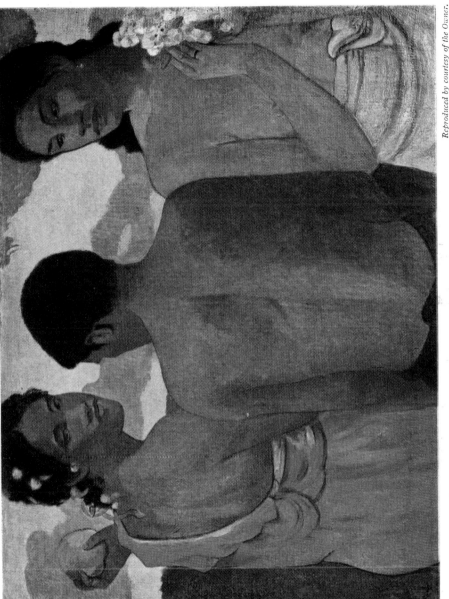

"THE THREE TAHITIANS," BY GAUGUIN

Alex. Maitland Collection, Edinburgh

This calmly beautiful work was painted when Gauguin had returned to Tahiti, ill, poor and in a mood of utter revolt and despair at the death of his daughter Aline. Yet he could create this rich simplicity of form and colour, for there among the primitive people he discovered a fundamental beauty and some sort of meaning to life.

"ENNUI," BY WALTER RICHARD SICKERT

Tate Gallery, London

Few artists of recent times have shown the enormous versatility in subject and in medium of Sickert, but perhaps he is best represented by that line of democratic painting which made him so great an influence with the Camden Town Group. In this picture he expresses in a daringly built-up design the utter boredom of Sunday afternoon in a working-class home. This was a new kind of realism, touched with pity and humour

every year since he was twenty, and in 1920 he was made an R.A. During the 1914–18 war he executed forty-five war pictures for the Canadian Government. He is a keen huntsman and race-goer, and it is not surprising, therefore, that he has been moved to depict the grace and beauty of race-horses and thoroughbreds. He has also an appreciative eye for the natural loveliness of the English scene, and to this we owe a very pleasant series of landscapes in fresh and lively colour.

Gerald Brockhurst is another artist who has consolidated his position as a gifted portrait painter and etcher during these last years. The longevity and vitality of the Pre-Raphaelite tradition is borne witness to in his early work. He received his first training at the Birmingham School of Art, where he came under the influence of Southall and Gaskin ; afterwards he entered the Royal Academy Schools. He was made an A.R.A. in 1928, and an Academician ten years later.

It has been said that his portraits evoke Renaissance Italy, and certainly his impeccable draughtsmanship and the deep-toned clarity of his colour recall the Italian mode. Also, in some of his admirable half-length portraits he has used the fascinating Renaissance convention of giving emphasis to the subject and depth to the canvas by painting in miniature landscapes as the far-away background. And then, again, he invests his sitters with a dignity and aloofness which recall the life and mood of a more spacious age than ours. His portrait of Henry Rushbury, R.A., painted in 1929, which is now in Philadelphia, remains one of his most striking successes. Brockhurst has chosen to paint his fellow-artist at his most characteristic, while he is at work, and it is the portrait of an artist intent upon his " subject " that he shows us, and not merely the features of his friend. " Young Womanhood," of 1931, " Jeunesse Dorée," of 1934, and " Armida," of 1936, are typical of his best work. He has also made another reputation for his masterly pencil portraits and portrait etchings.

Although he was an Academician for many years, Glyn Philpot went through several phases in the course of his career. In none of them did he depart markedly from academic tradition, except perhaps in the last (he died in 1938), when he was drawn to experiment in the Impressionist manner. He studied at the Lambeth School of Art, and then in Rouen and Paris, but contemporary French art hardly interested him. At any rate, it left no mark on his style of painting for almost the whole of his career. At first he painted symbolical subjects ; such was his " Pilgrimage of the Soul." After a phase of realism, he returned to religion for inspiration, and produced, among many in this genre, his well-known " Threefold Epiphany " and " Annunciation." In portraiture he also had much success. His later style aroused some comment among his

753

admirers, but to the non-academic mind there is nothing very revolutionary about it.

R. O. Dunlop was made an A.R.A. as late as 1939, but his reputation as a talented artist who was extraordinarily adept with the palette knife, has been steadily growing during the last decade. At one time he produced still-lives and over-life-size heads, rather sombre in colour, and the surfaces of these, covered with an extremely thick crust of paint, were very rough and uneven ; but the colour has cleared and the surface grown smoother as technical difficulties were overcome. The artist was born in 1894, in Dublin, of Scottish parents. He went to the Manchester and the Wimbledon Schools of Art. His work is in the Tate Gallery and in some of the provincial galleries, and an example has been acquired by a public gallery in New South Wales. Dunlop's reputation as a fine portraitist has been recently growing.

Two painters who look out on the twentieth-century scene with the eyes of disciples of Crome and Cotman, or Richard Wilson, have gained an appreciative public within the recent past. Of the two, widest recognition has come to Algernon Newton, who was made an A.R.A. in 1935. It was about ten years or more earlier that this accomplished artist began to show at Burlington House his serenely beautiful pictures of London canals, which to many were a revelation of the neglected beauty of the capital. These glazed, meticulously finished, clear-tinted paintings were something quite new in contemporary art—to find anything like them one had to go back at least a hundred years—and their success was immediate. Later, in the same mood and manner, the artist produced a number of remarkably fine river scenes and a series of dignified paintings of country houses seen in their right setting of spacious parks.

Bertram Nicholls also draws his chief inspiration from the British landscape painters of the late eighteenth and early nineteenth centuries. He works usually on a small canvas, and he has re-discovered with signal success the charm of carefully applied varnish as the final surface of his pictures. His colour is dark-toned and liquid, his compositions quiet and mellow in mood, his subject-matter at one time Provence and the Roman Campagna, but more often of late years the peaceful face of Southern England. Nicholls studied at the Slade School and in Madrid and France. Two of his works are in the Tate, one has gone to the National Gallery of Canada, and others are in the principal provincial galleries.

Of the thousand and more exhibits which are seen at Burlington House every summer, portraits by the Royal Academicians, W. G. de Glehn, Francis Dodd, and Gerald Kelly, and landscapes by Arnesby Brown, A. K. Lawrence, and George Henry will always be singled out for admiration, for each of these distinguished artists has his well-established place in the art of our time.

A notable feature of Academy policy during the past twenty years is the recognition extended to women painters. Mrs. A. L. Swynnerton (who was born only seven years after Victoria came to the throne), was admitted as Associate in 1922, and thus became the first woman since the eighteenth century to be so favoured. The next feminine recipient of official honours was Laura Knight, who became A.R.A. in 1927. Since that date she has been made a Dame of the British Empire, and a Royal Academician. Mrs. Knight is chiefly known for her large-scale vigorous paintings of circus and ballet-life. " Charivari," into which she has managed to crowd very amusingly all the characters of the circus ; " Ballet Girl and Dressmaker," acquired by Mr. Earl Hoover of Chicago ; " London Palladium," a strikingly composed theatre interior ; and " Circus Matinée " are the titles of some well-known and characteristic works.

A third woman Associate is Dod Procter, who attained that status in 1934. From her home in the artists' colony at Newlyn in Cornwall, Mrs. Procter sent regularly to the Academy without attracting marked attention until 1925, when her emphatic painting, " The Model," created a stir ; then, in 1927, the public at large was made to realise her existence when her *tour de force*, a full-length of a sleeping girl, entitled " Morning," had a sensational success and was bought by the proprietors of the *Daily Mail* for presentation to the nation. Before being lodged in the Tate the picture was sent on tour in the provinces. The figures in all this artist's work are highly modelled, solid, three-dimensional. A characteristic feature is the pallor of her flesh tints. In " Morning," the broad passages of blue-white in which the linen is rendered combine with the pale flesh tones to make a novel harmony. Of late, Mrs. Procter's work has grown softer and gentler in outline and atmosphere.

One of our most distinguished woman painters was not similarly honoured until April 1940, when she was elected A.R.A. Ethel Walker, elected a member of the New English Art Club as long ago as 1900, and exhibitor at Burlington House for many years, has produced a long series of very beautiful sea pieces, flower studies, and portraits in her own luminous version of Impressionism. Professor Frederick Brown, Slade Professor at University College, has placed her " among the few really great colourists of the day." The artist has also made several large-scale decorations, drawing on Homeric subjects for inspiration. " Nausicaa," now in the Tate Gallery, is one of the best known of these. Miss Walker was made a C.B.E. within the last few years.

755

Reproduced by permission of the Artist.   *A. G. Cooper.*

"BALLET GIRL AND DRESSMAKER," BY LAURA KNIGHT

In the possession of Mr. Earl Hoover of Chicago

Laura Knight has been exhibiting at Burlington House since 1903, and her pictures enjoy immense popularity. "Ballet Girl and Dressmaker," which was shown at the Royal Academy in 1930, is indeed a masterpiece of modern realism. Laura Knight is equally expert with water-colours as with oils.

§ 2

Meanwhile, outside the Royal Academy, work of the first importance in the history of native art was being shown at the London Group exhibitions. The London Group was formed shortly before the 1914–18 war by a band of artists who were dissatisfied with the policy of the New English Art Club. Among its original members were Sickert, Spencer Gore, Robert Bevan, Epstein, Wyndham Lewis, Charles Ginner, and Harold Gilman. Its first president was Harold Gilman (whose lovely " Leeds Market " and " Canal Bridge " now hang in the Tate Gallery), and he held that office until his untimely death in the influenza epidemic of the black spring of 1919. Gilman's close friend was Ginner, with whom he had held a joint exhibition at the Goupil Gallery soon after the London Group was formed. The catalogue of this far-away venture is of great interest now, for it contains as foreword a reprint of an article written by Ginner for the *New Age*, in which he set forth with admirable lucidity the credo of certain of the founders of the London Group, who were, incidentally, some of the finest non-academic realistic artists of our time. They called themselves Neo-realists—but not very seriously, and rather as a joke aimed at the current fashion for labels. Ginner put their standpoint quite clearly :

It is the common opinion of the day, especially in Paris (even Paris can make mistakes at times) that Decoration is the unique aim of Art. Neo-Realism, based on its tradition of Realism, has another aim of equal importance. . . . It must interpret that which, to us who are of this earth, ought to lie nearest our hearts, *i.e.*, Life in all its effects, moods, and developments. Each age has its landscapes, its atmosphere, its cities, its people. Realism . . . interpret its epoch by extracting from it the very essence of all it contains of great or weak, of beautiful or sordid, according to the individual temperament. . . .

Thus, with intelligence and assurance, a stand was made against what was considered by these artists to be the growing emptiness, incoherence, and incomprehensibility of much of the art of the day.

Charles Ginner has remained faithful to the tenets of his æsthetic creed in the quarter century that has elapsed since he formulated it with his friends, Spencer Gore, Harold Gilman, and Robert Bevan. Ginner was born and educated at Cannes, in the south of France. When he grew up he entered an architect's office in Paris, but he soon left this for the atelier of the Spanish painter, Anglada. His first exhibition was held in Buenos Aires, and it was not until he was over thirty that he settled in England, where his work instantly attracted the sympathetic attention of

A. G. Cooper.

" ST. JOHN'S CHURCH, CHESTER," BY CHARLES GINNER

Intricacy of design combined with great subtlety of colour harmonies are outstanding characteristics of this artist's work. These qualities are superbly illustrated in this beautiful composition. Though he was for many years a member of the Sickert Circle, Ginner, who has been a pupil in Paris of the Spaniard Anglada Camarasa, has never in his painting shown any sign of being influenced by Sickert. His work exhibits rather a curious blend of pre-Raphaelite precision of detail with the colour passion of Van Gogh.

his fellow-artists. Since then he has steadily continued to paint in his own peculiarly individual way. New movements interest him, but he has always been too sure of what he wanted to do and how he wished to do it, to waste time and energy in useless experiment. His subject-matter is often the commonplace : rows of slate-roofed houses, suburban streets with tram-lines, London back gardens, dockyards. And as often it is the infinitely varied face of Nature : fields and woods, the downs and the sea. Traces of his short architectural training may be noted in his orderly method of dealing with design. In all his work there is chromatic richness, satisfying composition, and superb handling of detail. Paintings by him have been acquired by many of the provincial galleries, as well as by the Tate Gallery, and examples of his remarkable water-colour drawings are in the British Museum and in the Victoria and Albert Museum. His painting of St. John's Church, Chester, is an excellent example of his style.

An early member of the London Group, and one of the youngest, was John Nash, who has become so widely known for his lovely interpretations of English rural beauty. John Nash began by producing amusing water-colours, which were very unsophisticated in manner and naïvely drawn. This gaucherie was to be expected, for the artist never attended any art school. At first, the lack of an orthodox training hampered the full development of his gifts, but his isolation from the schools and coteries has also served to preserve unimpaired the freshness and individuality of his vision. During the last decade he has come to be recognised as one of our very finest landscape painters in oil and water-colour. He has also made two other reputations, one as a book-illustrator of great comic gifts, and another for his superb engravings and water-colours of flowers and plants. John Nash is well represented in the national collection and was one of the two official war artists appointed by the Air Ministry early in 1940.

Ethelbert White, member of the N.E.A.C. and one-time member of the London group, has drawn his inspiration largely from his native land. In his early work he showed affinities with John Nash, but these soon disappeared as he found himself. He has developed an attractive personal style which is very well suited to the rendering of English landscape, and particularly of wood scenes. " Over the Hills," in the Tate Gallery, is a good example of his painting.

The London Group was greatly expanded during the early 'twenties, mainly through the enthusiasm and initiative of Roger Fry, the well-known critic and painter. As a result of this influx of new life, small groups, chiefly under the pronounced influence of contemporary French artists, were formed within the society. Duncan Grant was the nucleus, and Vanessa Bell, Mark Gertler, Matthew Smith, Keith Baynes, and Frederick

Porter other adherents of the group to which Roger Fry was chiefly attached by æsthetic sympathies.

Duncan Grant was born in Rothiemurchus, Inverness, in 1885, and he studied art at the Westminster School of Art and in Paris. Roger Fry gave him his benediction from the outset of his career. The critic was at that time conducting, in a lovely old Adams house in Fitzroy Square, the Omega Workshop for applied art, and it was natural that Grant, with his marked gifts for decorative design, should join Fry's talented company of artists and craftsmen. So, for a short period, he was employed designing textiles and pottery. Fry included some of his paintings in the Second Post-Impressionist Exhibition held at the Grafton Galleries in 1913. About this time the artist was commissioned, with others, to do murals for the Borough Polytechnic, some of his designs for which are now in the Tate Gallery. It was as a purely decorative artist that Duncan Grant first made his name—arabesques of sweet creamy colour flowed from his brush with charming effect whatever the subject-matter—but, as his work matured, mere decoration ceased to occupy him exclusively and his beautiful paintings gained in atmosphere, solidity, and depth. For many years now Duncan Grant has been generally recognised as our most gifted and accomplished exponent of Post-Impressionism. The influence of Cézanne hovers over his work as a whole, but this does not cause his style to be any the less individual. He is one of the small body of British painters whose work commands respect in Paris at the present time. An interesting example of his early manner is the Tate exhibit, " The Queen of Sheba," painted on wood.

Vanessa Bell was also closely connected with Roger Fry in the Omega Workshop days and later, when he turned his attention to the London Group. She is the daughter of the well-known Victorian man of letters, Sir Leslie Stephen, and sister of the famous woman writer, Virginia Woolf. Her æsthetic sympathies have always been with the French Post-Impressionist school, and although she has experimented, she has never been drawn to follow the extremists. She has collaborated agreeably with Duncan Grant in decorative work. Their " Modern Music Room " caused a stir when it was shown at the Lefevre Gallery. It was the target for much amusing, and some indignant, criticism—but then, that has been the fate of a great deal of modern art. In common with Duncan Grant, Mrs. Bell has been working towards a more realistic and less stylised manner of painting for several years now. Her flower-paintings (one was bought by the Contemporary Art Society for the nation) show her gifts at their most charming.

Mark Gertler's work also has an important place in the art of the epoch. This talented Jewish artist was born in 1892, and he died, aged forty-six,

" PROVENÇAL LANDSCAPE," BY DUNCAN GRANT

There is always something mellow and satisfying about this painter's landscapes, and especially in his paintings of Southern France. In this picture of Cézanne's country, the Midi, with its glowing colour and the finely rounded forms of the rolling fields, one is made to feel the richness and fertility of the sun-drenched earth.

761

in 1938. In his early circumstances there was much struggle and hardship. The winning of the Slade scholarship in 1911, and that of the British Institute a year later, momentarily solved material difficulties and brought him to the notice of a number of artists and art-patrons who greatly encouraged him. The Contemporary Art Society bought his " Fruit Sorters " while he was still practically a student. He had always a taste for very rich, and even garish colour, and a highly developed sense of form. In the main he was a realist who liked his reality flamboyant and exuberant. Street fruit-stalls under flaring lights, and merry-go-rounds were youthful favourites as subjects. Later, his work shed something of its first gaudiness and he produced in a low-toned colour-scale highly finished compositions, in which his handling of the pigment gave a curiously liquid effect to the surface. It was as though one looked at a Gertler painting through a film of clear water which heightened the colours without distorting the forms. There was often something monumental and static in his figure groups and portraits. The well-remembered " Coster Family," and the fine portrait of the artist's mother evince these qualities admirably. The full-length nude of a girl of fourteen or fifteen, " Young Girlhood," is a well-known and representative example of his art at its surest. His later experiments in the *surréaliste* manner were not very successful. The Tate Gallery has acquired one of his paintings, and his portrait of Sir George Darwin is in the National Portrait Gallery.

Akin to Gertler in his love of warm-hued pigment is Matthew Smith, whose first work was shown in the London Group in the 'twenties. Matthew Smith did not begin to paint until he was over forty. He was born in Halifax, Yorkshire, in 1879. The first part of his adult life was spent in business, for like Gauguin, he postponed the beginning of his real career until he had entered early middle life. But, as with Gauguin, there never was a doubt that painting was his true vocation. His preference is for the utmost exuberance of colour, and this led him at one period to produce a remarkable series of nudes, in which the flesh-tints of the well-rounded models had been translated into flaming scarlet and ruby. As his art developed the necessity to express himself in such chromatic extremes lessened, and the crimson flesh grew gradually rosy, and then became beautifully golden. Later, Matthew Smith turned to landscape, to the interpretation of which he brings the same dash and brilliance that characterise his flower studies and nudes.

Other British artists who do not fit very exactly into any particular group or category now, and who have achieved well-established reputations are Edward Wadsworth and William Roberts. Wadsworth and Roberts were allied with Wyndham Lewis and the Vorticists at one time, but each went his own way early in his career.

" GIRLHOOD," BY MARK GERTLER

Mark Gertler succeeded in many fields of art. When he was quite young the perfectly depicted study
of his room in Spitalfields and a portrait of his mother created a sensation by their quality. Later he
turned his powers to such exquisite and firmly modelled studies as this, and to flower painting in
the same vein of stylised naturalism.

By permission of Arthur Tooth & Sons Ltd.

"MARINE SET," BY EDWARD WADSWORTH

Wadsworth's art is evocative. He has chosen to turn to the objects of the sea for his subjects, and to assemble them on his canvasses according to his own desires as a designer. He presents them with strong drawing and clean, brittle colour, so that the mind of the beholder reacts immediately to his sea-mood, though there is no naturalistic seascape.

Edward Wadsworth was born in Yorkshire in 1889, and his art studies were conducted in Edinburgh and Munich and at the Slade School. About 1922 he began to experiment with painting in tempera, and got such satisfactory results that he has used this medium ever since. During the next three years he produced some attractive pictures of ships in harbour, only slightly stylised in drawing ; and then came a series of paintings which were quite unlike anything his English contemporaries were doing. They were still lives, in which against a flatly painted stretch of sky and sea (often there was a minute white-sailed ship on the horizon), were grouped some lovely shells, bits of cork or rope, perhaps an anchor, a lifebelt or a screw, or some other mysterious marine object, and the whole collection was rendered with the utmost precision of detail, and in exquisite light sweet colour. " Regatta " is an excellent example of this style of painting. Then, for a time, Wadsworth's compositions became quite unrepresenta-tional, and on his paintings were shown dynamic shapes, strongly sug-gestive of movement and excitement. Later, the artist returned to a more realistic manner, but his imagination still lingers about the incidents of marine life—perhaps because of his naval experience in the Great War. There are works by him in the Tate Gallery and in some of the chief pro-vincial galleries. He was one of the artists chosen to represent English art at the Biennial International Art Exhibition which, but for the outbreak of war, was to have been held in Venice in 1940.

William Roberts won a scholarship to the Slade when he was sixteen. His work has always shown cubist tendencies, and at one time the figures in his compositions resembled robots, but they have gradually grown more human. Emphasis is on design in his virile semi-realistic paintings, and there is a marked ironic note in all his work. " Sun Bathers " is an excellent example of his matured art. A painting by him is in the national collection.

Cedric Morris is another independent who is a member of the London Group. He is self-taught, which may account for his originality, for he has invented a particular genre of bird and flower painting. His landscapes also have much charm and novelty. Insects and butterflies busy among the flowers, and even small birds sipping the honey from the blossoms are often included in his flower paintings, with vivacious effect. But it is for his studies of wild birds in their natural surroundings that this artist is particularly known. " Night Jars " is a typical example. These are done largely from memory, being worked up from notes. Often the marvellous beauty of the birds is shown against a distant landscape, with grasses and pebbles, or fragments of rock, making a close-patterned foreground. The colour is bright and clean and the workmanship detailed and careful.

Laib.

"LANDSCAPE," BY CHRISTOPHER WOOD

Christopher Wood reduced the objects before his eyes to their utmost simplicity of form and colour for the purpose of his design. All art is a choice of the essential things which will convey truth or beauty, and in this Breton landscape the artist has organised those essentials into a charming composition.

A little reminiscent of Cedric Morris in the bright vividness of its colour is the work of a young artist who died at Salisbury in 1930, aged twenty-nine. Christopher Wood was born at Knowsley, near Liverpool, in 1901. He studied art at Julian's in Paris, and later made friends with Picasso and Jean Cocteau. In 1926 he was commissioned by Diaghlieff to design the costumes and *décor* for a ballet, which project was afterwards abandoned. By 1929 he had had two one-man shows, and had shared the honours with Ben Nicholson of an exhibition entitled, " Deux Peintres Anglais," at the famous Bernheim Galleries in Paris. In the same year C. B. Cochran asked him to do the *décor* and costumes for a ballet. Before the commission could be carried out the artist was dead. After his Memorial Exhibition in 1932, a characteristic painting, " Brittany Landscape," was accepted by the Tate Gallery. Christopher Wood specialised in small brilliantly coloured paintings of harbour scenes, fishing boats, and Breton fisherfolk. " Seascape, Brittany, 1929 " shows his art at its surest. Although his talent had not time to mature, the work he has left entitles him to a place in contemporary British art.

A New Zealand born artist who came to Europe to study art before the last war, and in the years since has brought her gifts to fruition, is Frances Hodgkins. Miss Hodgkins' decorative Post-Impressionism has long been known to the more discriminating amateurs, but she has had to wait until comparatively recently for the admiring appreciation of a wider circle.

In 1937 a war novel, *In Parenthesis*, won the Hawthornden Prize for literature. It was written by an artist who had been wounded at the Battle of the Somme while serving with the Welsh Fusiliers during the Great War. The book was illustrated by the author but the prize was awarded for its literary merit. Thus David Jones added a second reputation to the one he had already gained as an extremely subtle and delicate water-colourist. His 1940 London exhibition was a triumphant success. In spite of the adverse conditions of the times, most of the exhibits were acquired by collectors within the first few days of its opening. Four of the water-colours were secured for the nation by the Tate Gallery, the Victoria and Albert Museum, and the British Museum.

There is not space here to describe the work of several other British artists which has attracted much attention and admiration within the period. It is only possible in this short account to name a few of the better-known painters not already referred to, and from whom, judging by past successes, interesting and distinguished work may be expected in the future ; such are Bernard Meninsky, Gilbert Spencer, Ivon Hitchens, Vivian Pitchforth, Richard Eurich, Evan Kirke, James Fitton, Raymond Coxon, Robin Wallace, John Piper, and Edward Le Bas ; and among the younger generation, William Coldstream and Victor Pasmore, Anthony Devas and Rodrigo Moynihan.

§ 3

During the past quarter-century world-wide fame has been achieved by a brilliant company of French artists, many of whom are, to within a few years, of the same generation.

André Derain, whose name first became widely known in England when crowds flocked to applaud the Russian ballet, " La Boutique Fantasque "—he had designed the *décor* and costumes—has an eminent place in this confraternity. Derain was born in 1880. He intended to be an engineer, but took up painting instead. His first master was Carrière, but the strongest influence of his early days was his friendship with Vlaminck. Together they discovered negro sculpture, which has given such a powerful stimulus to a certain school of modern art. Derain was one of the Fauves, and in touch with all the " advanced " movements, but his natural tendency to direct statement was reinforced by his great admiration for Cézanne. His paintings have solidity and coherence, and they are realistic without being naturalistic.

His lifelong friend and fellow-artist, Maurice de Vlaminck, is credited with having been a professional motor cyclist, a violinist, a popular novelist, and a worker in the Sèvres porcelain factory before becoming a painter. When he did settle down to art, however, he succeeded in inventing and developing a very original style. His landscapes have a stormy and dramatic quality, due largely to his brilliant handling of light and shade in deep-toned greens, scarlet, black, and white. Referring to academic painting he has written : " I flee from the monotony, the severity, the very smell of picture galleries." So it is not surprising that he, too, was at one time a Fauve !

Paintings by Dunoyer de Segonzac began to appear frequently at mixed exhibitions in this country in the 'twenties. He was born in 1884, and his career had just got under way by 1914. His war service consisted in directing camouflage in the French lines. Before the 1914–18 war he had been a pupil of Jacques Emile Blanche and had travelled extensively in Spain, Italy, and Africa. He has always been a vigorous realist. He lays his paint on very thickly and his special preference is for wide flat country in landscape, and for extremely well-rounded forms in nudes. His work is sent regularly to the Salon des Indépendants and the Salon d'Automne, and he has designed theatrical costumes which Poiret, the famous costumier, has carried out. In the latter's memoirs is described how Poiret found in the artist's studio an unstretched canvas thrown away as rubbish, which

"PAYSAGE DE BONLIEUE," BY MAURICE UTRILLO

At one time Utrillo was so fascinated by the prosaic streets of little French towns, villages, and suburbs, with their strings of small shops and grimy whitish houses, that he would paint nothing else. Hence the many well-known canvases of what has come to be called his "white period." The "V" of the signature (often missing) is for his mother's name, Vallodon.

"PORTRAIT," BY MARIE LAURENCIN

No woman artist has ever been so delightfully feminine as Marie Laurencin. Her light-toned colour schemes in which only the eyes often strike a darker note, give to her girls an ethereal quality and charm which almost removes them above flesh and blood humanity.

"PORTRAIT OF THE PAINTER, HUBERT," BY AMEDEO MODIGLIANI

Extreme simplification to emphasise the basic pattern and colour elements marks Modigliani's work.

he bought, to de Segonzac's amazement, for 3000 francs. Ten years later, at the Hotel Drouot sale, the same painting was sold for 90,000 francs.

Maurice Utrillo is the son of the well-known artist, Suzanne Vallodon, who was a professional acrobat as a child. Her son was born when she was sixteen, and soon afterwards she became a model for Renoir and Puvis de Chavannes. When, later, she began to paint, she was encouraged by Degas, Toulouse-Lautrec, and Cézanne. In such an atmosphere Utrillo's gifts were certain of attention. Ill-health has dogged him always, but his output has been considerable nevertheless. He paints largely from memory, in artificial light—and, some say, from post cards. He, too, is a realist, and he has evolved a peculiarly original style of painting to express the melancholy beauty of those long muddy grey-white streets of suburban Paris, with their tattered plane trees and decrepit green shutters. " Paysage de Bonlieue " is a good example of his work.

Raoul Dufy is the decorative artist *par excellence* of the period ; sophisticated, ironic, and irreverent. As well as painting in oils he has specialised in very large water-colours, delightfully gay and frivolous in colour and mood, and amusingly calligraphic in design.

Marie Laurencin has also created a very charming form of decorative art, to which she strictly limits herself. Children and young girls (with a sly suggestion of malice in their enormous dark eyes), doves, flowers, and slender ponies with elegant arched necks provide her with subject-matter, which she renders on canvas in pale pinks and blues and white and grey, with sometimes a touch of black. Her charm and her art are essentially French, as will be realised from a glance at " Portrait."

Examples of the work of all these artists have been acquired by the principal galleries in Europe (including Moscow) and in the United States of America. Other French painters who have made international reputations in the period are Othon Friez, Lurçat, Marchand, Rouault, Léger, L'Hote, Lotiron, Marquet, and Dufresne.

Posthumous fame came in the 'twenties to the Italian, Modigliani, whose art owes its strange distinction to the painter's admiration of negro sculpture. The reputations of the Polish painter, Kisling ; the Spaniards, Picabia and Juan Gris ; the Finnish artist, Survage ; and the Russians, Chagal and Tchelichev, were all made in the " School of Paris " within the last two decades.

XXXIX

THE UNENDING STORY

EUROPEAN ART TO-DAY AND TO-MORROW

§ I

ART does not " stop short in the cultivated court of the good Queen Anne," nor in that of Victoria. Inevitably it goes on as the experiences of humanity continue and demand expression. Two great wars and an interim period of social upheaval which interfered with the life habits of practically every person in Western civilisation ; the wild forward surge of scientific discovery ; the coming of the motor-car age and the approximate change over to urban living : such things have their repercussions on the artist and his patrons, and therefore upon art itself.

From such an age of turbulence we can hardly expect a quietist art. The academic painters, catering still for the remnants of aristocracy and the new plutocracy which imitates aristocracy, are still devoted to hunters and heiresses and the park-like landscapes wherein they disport themselves. They do their task magnificently ; and the prime representative of this type of work, A. J. Munnings, has been elected to the Presidency of the Royal Academy and has been knighted in recognition of his work. Impressionism and Post-Impressionism have had an effect even on the most academic painters, however. Their colour has become brighter and more vibrant, their concern with light more pronounced. Sometimes there is a far echo of Cézanne in the most tidy English landscapes, or a decorative reminder that Gauguin passed across the field of art. Very much of the best English work might be thought of as Impressionism called to heel.

The vortex of art until the beginning of the second World War was Paris, and it was from Paris that the newer ideas came. London, New York, and the capitals of Europe swung round that vortex. With the rise first of Bolshevism in Russia, then of Fascism in Italy, and finally of Nazism in Germany a new element came into art in the form of State interference. The Russian government stigmatised almost all the existing art as bourgeois and decadent. Art for art's sake, the intellectualism of the newer schools, the academic old schools : all were recognized as under the patronage of the aristocracy and the capitalist and were condemned accordingly. Art

773

must be " Proletcult " ; it must subserve the State, idealise the workers and their leaders, reflect the new age of the machine and the new order of society.   At first it was greatly moved towards expression in abstract machine forms as Lenin's ideas of an electrical paradise caught the imagination of the Russians.   Later it swung back to something akin to late-Victorian romanticism and story pictures ; revolutionary leaders addressing meetings, workers going to the fields or in the factories, taking the place of the domestic sentiment in our own story-telling pictures.   Gaponenko painting " Farm Workers going to Work," or Kuznetsov turning his Post-Impressionist art to subjects in the Eastern provinces under the new industrialism, or Alexander Deineka showing the town people of the Soviet : these are the type of artist and subject of the newer Realism and Impressionism now emerging from the early censorship.

Fascism in Italy had an entirely different approach.   Marinetti, the Futurist (that much-abused word used loosely as a synonym for all modernist art methods), had a great deal of influence.   He glorified war and violence and advocated an art which would express these dynamics.   Nothing much came of it ; and ultimately it quietly passed away when the State department of the Syndicate of Fine Art organized all the artists under a scheme of official patronage.   This official art, with its ultimate reward of salaried membership of the Fascist Royal Academy, led to naturalism and realism which was of little importance, a slight harking back to the traditional painting of Italy in her great days in the hands of such men as Funi, or of Umbrian landscape in those of the Siennese, Dario Neri.

In Germany all modernism in art was suppressed as decadent, Bolshevik, Jewish, or any other word with which unofficial ideas could be belaboured. Hitler's own taste for tepid late eighteenth-century German art naturally established the fashion.   An exhibition of the proscribed " Decadent Art " organized by the Nazis in Munich as a kind of Chamber of Horrors to shock good Nazis was enormously patronized (and, one suspects, enjoyed) but not necessarily in a manner which would have been approved by the authorities.   Another exhibition of the work of artists accepted by the Government failed to evoke any popular excitement, although the work exhibited was often soundly academic as well as politically innocuous. Let it be granted that art in Germany after the 1914–18 war, reflecting the neurosis of that most febrile and unhappy country, had rushed down a steep place after every form of the bizarre.   But official interference with German artists and the general sense of the loss of personal freedom resulted in the artists coming out and leaving the Germans in, if we may paraphrase Whistler's *mot*.   As with Russian official art, the insistence on the importance of the subject swung things back to literalism and story-telling realism. Elk Eber picturing Storm Troopers passing grim factory workers under the sacred sign of the Swastika, or Adolf Wissel's Nain-like peasants posing for their portraits, may be good statecraft and are not entirely negligible as painting, but it is not on such painting that great art is founded.

§ 2

From all this totalitarianism either of left or right the freedom-loving artist flees. Perhaps it was the artist's passion for freedom which caused him to gravitate to pre-war Paris, for there to the artist even the economic bondage of comparative poverty mattered little if at all. The life of the studios and of the cafés was one of the freest in the world. Nearly forty thousand students made up that world. The masters of all countries and the men and women who took art with deadly seriousness came there. As rigid authoritarianism clamped down on various states the free artists fled to the French capital where liberty, equality and fraternity still were words with meaning. The Isms followed one another with bewildering rapidity : Cubism, Futurism, Simultanism, Dadaism, Surrealism, the names were legion. It was all a little mad and neurotic, but the world in which it was born was mad and neurotic. Art has to be a little mad anyway.

The French Fauvists, the " wild beasts " of 1905, were settling down into accepted masters. If the wildness of Derain had swung over to a distinctively French style influenced by Cézanne among the moderns and by the French primitives ; if Matisse, one-time leader of the Fauves, had grown comparatively tame in a style of delightful decoration ; if Edouard Vuillard had become something of an old master with his intimate studies of French interiors and of French scenery ; and Vlaminck, who had once stirred the art world with his passion for Negro Sculpture and had once been a leading Cubist, had now swung to the other extreme with loosely drawn and dramatically coloured landscapes wherein the paint overlay the basic form ; if Marie Laurencin was repeating her feminine dainties *ad infinitum* (and perhaps, alas, *ad nauseum*) ; there was still excitement. Braque, the Cubist, was true to his self-created formula of map-like decorations based on still life and abstract form. Georges Rouault remained an Expressionist, telling his vision of tortured humanity with the utmost emotionalism, with the thick outlines and rather chalky colour which he had made his own. Utrillo still evoked magic from the most unpromising dull streets of provincial and suburban France and from the drab bricks and mortar of Montmartre ; and Dunoyer de Segonzac carried on magnificently the pure Impressionist tradition.

Moreover there was the Spaniard Picasso who had long been the accepted leader of movements in Parisian circles. He had been everything in turns but nothing long. The restless mind which had once stood for Cubism tried a score of methods old and new, sane and mad. He is the overwhelming influence towards change. The younger men accept him as their leader though they do not dare to imitate his highly individual vision. Most important of his more recent work was the great cartoon " Guernica," his impassioned protest against the martyrdom of the little Basque town, the dress-rehearsal of modern war methods with which we have now become all too familiar. There is a story that when the German invaders, examining his Paris studio, saw the work, one of them asked Picasso, " Did you do that ? " and the intrepid Spaniard replied : " No, you did." If the story is not true, it should be. The cartoon, appalling in its ugliness, " purges with pity and terror," as Aristotle demanded of the art of tragedy. Clawing hands and gaping mouths and trampling beasts amid the shells of buildings, " Guernica " is a vision of hell. It is terribly ugly, utterly distorted, unreal, yet with its own overpowering realism. Almost everything Picasso does to-day is a challenge, although in such a painting as " The Virgin of Toledo " he can express himself with a winning and tenuous charm.

The exhibition in London of work which Picasso had done during the German occupation of Paris proved to be an art bombshell, causing furious controversy. It was a mixture of the earlier Cubist style and of the highly individual method of depicting the ugly which he had used in the " Guernica. " Its apologists explained that it presented his reactions to the hatefulness of the situation in an occupied country. True it was powerful, but its morbidity evoked much criticism.

Two other Spaniards were with Picasso in Paris. One was Salvator Dali, who has since gone to New York ; the other Joan Miro. Both were linked with the Surrealist movement.

Surrealism, or as some prefer to call it, Super-realism, has been the only new movement of any importance during the last twenty years. Herbert Read writes of the aims, methods, and meaning of the surrealists as follows :

As the word implies, the main doctrine of the school is that there exists a world more real than the normal world and this is the world of the unconscious mind. . . . I doubt if *surréalisme* would ever have existed in its present form but for Professor Freud . . . for just as Freud finds a key to the perplexities of life in the material of dreams, so the *surréaliste* finds his best inspiration in the same region. It is not that he merely makes a pictorial representation of dream-images ; his aim is rather to employ any means which will give him access to the repressed contents of the unconscious, and then to mingle these elements freely with the conscious images. . . .

Here then is the clue to the meaning of the fantastic, incoherent, and often repellent pictures which have been seen in some London galleries during the last few years. They are pictorial expressions, in symbols taken

"LADY IN A ROCKING CHAIR," BY PABLO PICASSO

An example of Picasso's later method. The forms have been so broken and rearranged as non-realistic patterns to express the essence of the subject as the artist conceives it that there is little nature or representation left.

from the dream-world, of whatever the artist could uncover of his " un-conscious " ; and because there is usually some strange beauty and emotion in dreams, many of these paintings have æsthetic value, and some can communicate a disturbing emotion.

Max Ernst, who was exiled from the Third Reich in the Nazi purge of " decadent art," possesses, according to M. Breton, the French poet who launched the movement in 1924 with a manifesto, " the most magnificently haunted brain of to-day "—a very useful possession, one surmises, for a *surréaliste* ! And certainly, his " Couple Zoomorphique en Gestation," a typical example of his art, gives the impression of a very bad dream indeed !

Dali, however, is a strictly conscientious draughtsman of naturalistic appearances. If the association of ideas evokes the image of a lobster when he sees a bald head, and the consequent picture is, in essence, a lobster poised on a bald head, both are very carefully drawn and painted. His famous " Suburbs of the Paranoic-Critical Town " is full of classically depicted things in the weirdest juxtaposition : a temple, an arm-chair, a horse's skull a girl with a bunch of grapes. Miro is a much closer disciple of Picasso ; a Cubist as well as a Surrealist, who makes no attempt to represent realistically " the stuff that dreams are made of."

One other Surrealist who finally gravitated to Paris is the Italian, Georgio di Chirico. He was born in Greece of Italian parents, which probably accounts for the pronounced vein of classicism in his painting. It is cold, hard, remote, and unemotional ; yet it is grand and beautiful. His horses (which are so often the motif of his pictures) are perfect creatures, full of life and movement, but somehow they belong to dreams. Broken fragments of classical temples lie about ; strange, cotton-wool clouds are static in the cold blue of the skies. It is a visionary world of the imagination but it is excellently rendered. Chirico goes to nature for his models, as the dreaming mind does, but his juxtapositions have a strangeness and incongruity only just short of those of Dali.

Surrealism has another exponent in the Belgian, Delvaux. He also paints a classic, timeless and utterly irrational world wherein women can change into trees below the waist. Again his environment is often that of ruined classical architecture stated in coldly objective terms.

§ 3

Two other extremists belonging to the International Brigade of Art are Paul Klee, the German-trained Swiss, and Kandinsky the Russian. Both have become complete abstractionists, pursuing expression to a point of anarchy which makes it almost valueless as communication. That is

"HORSES BY THE SEA," BY GIORGIO DE CHIRICO

Chirico has made in his art a world of fantasy where nobly stylised horses move against a background of ruined classic temples. It is a dream-world, but the artist does not abandon the truth to visual appearances of waking reality, however strongly he insists on the design values of his paintings.

one of the dangers of all this subjective art, for there should be acceptable symbols if art is to fulfil its function of speaking from mind to mind. Klee and Kandinsky both create rather thin and entirely non-representational works. Klee's contribution is a kind of automatic writing. He worked at the celebrated Bauhaus of Weimar with Gropius and Kandinsky, and was a professor of Dusseldorf Academy until he had to leave Nazi Germany. An extract from Klee's own exposition of his method may be illuminating. (The process described has been called " Going for a walk with a line.") " From a dead full-stop the first act of movement sets off (line). After a short time a halt to take breath (interrupted line, or line jointed by repeated halts). A look back, what a long way we have already gone (opposite movement). Then taking thought of the way hither and thither (bundle of lines) . . ." and so on. The result makes cheerful patterns, sometimes reminding one of the untutored drawings of children and peasants. Such is the amusing and disarming " The Trout in the Forest." It may be significant as the reaction against over-sophistication and against the smooth naturalistic finish of late nineteenth-century art.

The exhibition of Klee's work at the Tate Gallery early in 1946 revealed a lyric personality which had expressed itself by many methods. The technical charm of his harmonious colouring and delicate draughtsmanship amply compensated for the loss of the merely representational element which throughout his career he has so firmly avoided. Sometimes, however, the result looks remarkably like childish nonsense.

Kandinsky was born in Moscow, but went to Germany and with Klee and Marc formed a group called *Der Blaue Reiter*. He moved more and more towards abstraction and was one of the Dadaist Group, who in the hectic 'twenties consciously exalted utter nonsense and irrationalism as the right thing in art. He became almost morbidly anxious to avoid natural appearances, trying " to eliminate from his painting any memory of visible objects in nature "—an almost impossible task, be it said, for the visual memory of the spectator tends to see resemblances to natural objects in the most meaningless scribble.

This work of Klee and Kandinsky was the approximate extreme to which the search for new methods of expression and the rejection of old carried modern art. It was suspiciously like emptying out the baby with the bath, and it opened the door to the charlatanism which lacked the draughtsmanship to depict the baby anyway. On the other hand we have to remember that dull academic art, even though it demands a certain power of handicraft and is subject to visual cross reference with the things of Nature which it is depicting in pigment, can be so uninspired that it has no value beyond the merest surface appeal or the sentimental literalism which accompanied that.

"LADY WITH NECKLACE," BY PAUL KLEE

Klee has made a study of masks in Ethnographic museums, and has experimented with their power to startle the imagination. Some of his pictures remind us of the scrawls of children, some of primitive savage art, some of things seen in a mental hospital; but even Klee's most nightmarish products usually show a feeling for craftsmanship in the quality of their paint, and often a calligraphic quality of line. His abstract designs are pure inventions rather than abstractions of things seen.

The German Expressionists who flourished in the years after the 1914–18 war and before the rise of the Nazis were much less abstract. They sought to express in colour and line the emotional life of their unhappy land. The colour was vivid and crude often, the line tortured and undraughtsmanlike; but they got something compelling. It was neurotic, so was the world it expressed. It was ugly, so was the life it depicted. Beckmann and Baumeister and Nolde were its exponents among many others, and that vicious cartoonist, Georg Grosz, who depicted so terribly the night life of decadent Berlin. The brilliant woman artist, Kathe Kollwitz, contributed her telling pictures of the starving mothers and children of Germany under the blockade. Most outstanding of the Expressionists, perhaps because he so developed a style of his own which surpassed Expressionism, was Franz Marc. He took animal forms and made of them the most thrilling rhythmic designs; and although he used colour subjectively and contorted form to suit his own purposes, his paintings became accepted classics and were world famous. He was killed in the last war when he was only thirty-five, and despite the Nazi dislike of non-representational art he has been accepted by them as a great German painter. The Austrian, Egger-Lienz, was another man who won universal approval. He may be said to have anticipated Expressionism with his terrible studies of peasant life long before the 1914–18 war. Although he was too big a man to be neatly labelled, his " Dance of Death," painted in 1925, a year before his death, was a piece of pure Expressionism and a terrible comment on war.

Another interesting German modernist, albeit now his work belongs to the Cubist and Futurist past, is Lyonel Feininger. He was born as far back as 1871 and was actually American by birth, but he lived and painted much in Germany, where he created interesting cubistic studies of buildings, the interpenetrating planes and sharp angles reorganized to make fascinating designs of form and light.

§ 4

The smaller countries of Europe have, as one would suppose, each produced artists working in these newer styles. Usually their works have not been so extreme. France intellectually and Germany emotionally led art down these strange by-paths. The quieter and more balanced Scandinavian peoples were not given to such excesses; nor were the Dutch; and even the Czechs, who might have been expected to be caught up in the Central European storm, kept their feet on the ground. In Czechoslovakia, or rather in old Bohemia, Josef Manes led the way for new art ideas in the middle of last century, and towards the end of that century a society was founded in his name to encourage Impressionism and new ideas. Josef Capek, part author of the Insect Play, and an altogether delightful artist; Kubista; Slavicek, the Impressionist; and Kubin, who has since migrated to France and changed his name to Coubine, are outstanding Czech painters; with such younger men as Jan Zrzavy who simplifies his forms and eliminates all non-essentials.

Holland's most outstanding personality is Toroop, although Jan Sluyters is a more popular artist with a reputation beyond the Netherlands; whilst Willink, the one-time Surrealist, and Hynckes, the Cubist, probably have their appeal rather to the younger generation. The sculptor, Hildo Krop, should be also mentioned, for he has created some monumental work in the new spirit including the great public clock at Rotterdam with its massively sculptured heads emerging from the stone. Another Dutch artist whose work is more familiar to Londoners is Jan Poortenaar, for he worked in England for some years and has exhibited his etchings and his studies of the Dutch East Indies here since he returned to Holland.

Charley Toroop, the daughter of Jan, showed work of conspicuous power in an exhibition in London of work done in Holland during the German occupation, and in this same exhibition the Expressionist work of Hendrik Chabot was remarkable.

One other Exhibition held since the war in London has brought to us almost our first acquaintance with the Belgian, James Ensor, whose work has long been known on the Continent. Ensor, whose technique has in it something of the gaiety and colour of Renoir, but who is too individual to claim for any school or master, delights in strangely macabre subjects. He makes queer genre pictures of skeletons and disembodied masks.

The Scandinavian countries have, as we have seen in an earlier chapter, produced a number of first-rate sculptors, and also certain painters with pronounced individuality, although the inspiration in painting more than in sculpture is cosmopolitan and derives from Paris. Edvard Munck, the Norwegian, was by far the greatest and most outstanding figure. He was a daring Impressionist with a courage in the abstraction and synthesis of form which carried him far beyond any mere visualisation of the scene or figure. He achieved the standing of a master in these Northern countries and his brilliant colour-schemes influenced the painting of his day. Munck has recently died. Alongside him as an influence is Anders Zorn, the brilliant Swedish etcher, who also carried the Impressionist technique into this graphic realm. Denmark made her contribution with Johannes Larsen, a noble painter of animals and of the quiet Danish landscape.

Against this background of the earlier men, all influenced by the French Impressionists, must be set the newer school who found their inspiration in the Post-Impressionists and in some of the Fauvists, Matisse being a particular influence. Einar Jolin, Leander Engstrom, Hilding Linqvist, and

"SKELETONS WARMING THEMSELVES," BY JAMES ENSOR

An exhibition in London during early 1946 of the work of the Belgian artist, Ensor, enabled us to appreciate the power of his fantastic mind and his ability to express it in paint. He owes little to anybody, though one sometimes seems to detect echoes of Renoir's palette and brushwork. His subjects often take the form of bodiless masks or clothed skeletons, and have an element of social satire.

Johan Johansson. Linqvist in particular, with his deliberate simplification of scene and figure, is regarded in his own country, where the folk quality in his work naturally has an immediate appeal.

One other of the smaller nations needs to be considered. Poland has long had a tradition of art, and has of recent years contributed magnificently to the graphic arts, bringing to them her riches of tradition and folklore. Perhaps it is hardly fair to claim Suzanne Eisendieck for Poland, for she was born in Danzig and studied first in Berlin and then in Paris. She has a curious feminine charm, something of a Northern version of Marie Laurencin, although her work is entirely different and is, indeed, highly individual. The theatre, the music-hall, the circus, the café, these are her hunting-grounds for subjects, and her period is that quaint one which in England we call Edwardian. The dressed-up feminine types particularly appeal to her, and she renders them in gay, high-toned paint.

Moise Kisling is another Pole who went to Paris and stayed there, giving us well-built work in a classically simplified draughtsmanship. But for more typically Polish work we must look to the woman painter Zofia Stryjenska, who still depicts the peasant, fairy-tale Poland of our dreams, with delightful brilliantly coloured costumes, painted wooden architecture, and the fir trees of the North. The Pole who has sprung into well-deserved fame of recent years, however, is the brilliant cartoonist Topolski. His has brought to perfection as a means of expression a nervously alive line which brings a kind of Impression into linear art. His sepia drawings shimmer on the paper, and when he has the opportunity to transfer them to walls he keeps this vital quality. The war, and his national fury with his country's enemies, has brought out the bitter satirical power of his mind and given new motives for his brilliant work. Topolski has settled in London.

The emergence of Diego Rivera as a major artist is one of the most interesting events of the period. Diego Rivera was born in 1886 and brought up in Mexico City. In 1907, with the help of the Governor of Vera Cruz, he came to Europe to study art, and after extensive travel in Spain and Italy he settled in Paris and joined Picasso's circle. His paintings of this period show his preoccupation with Cubism, but the Byzantine mosaics seen in Italy had profoundly impressed him and their influence can be traced in the great series of frescoes he did years later in Mexico City, in Detroit at the Ford Works, in New York, and elsewhere. Especially is this evident in the powerful use made of simplification to give dignity and impressiveness to the figures in his famous Mexican murals. Rivera's chance came after his return home in 1921, when Vascencelos, Minister of Education under Obregon, engaged him with other native artists to decorate the three-tiered patio of the new education offices. This was his first great work, and others were to follow. The scheme of the frescoes is simple.

"SOLSTICE OF THE SUNFLOWER," BY PAUL NASH

Nash painted a series of four great canvases on the theme of the Sunflower and the Sun. In three of them the sunflower stands in the sky in place of the sun, but in this the sun shines from its zenith moving the firewheel of the flower on its mystical way through the standing corn. This symbolises the blessing of the midsummer fire, the link between the heavenly body and the fulness of Nature.

On the ground-floor walls the labouring life of the common people provides the theme ; the life of the mind is illustrated on the second-floor galleries by school and laboratory scenes ; the top-floor walls reflect the life of the spirit, by which the artist understands primarily the self-sacrifice and ardour of Mexican revolutionaries, symbolical, full-length portraits of many of whom are included in the paintings. At Chapingo in the agricultural school, Rivera has done one of his most famous frescoes : " The Distribution of Land to the Peasants," and here, too, he has used well-known Mexican personalities as models. His output has been enormous and his work is one of the chief influences in contemporary American art. Of late the artist has turned to landscape and portraiture.

§ 5

And what of England ? Among moderns three men in particular have emerged during immediately recent years : John Piper, Henry Moore, and Graham Sutherland. As we have seen in Chapter XXXVII, there were and are a host of men and women doing good work based on the English tradition of sound craftsmanship modified by the influence of Impressionism. Speaking generally, Britain does not encourage wildness. On the other hand we must not assume that the English lack courage in art, for it has to be remembered that we produced Constable and Turner, both of whom were pronounced influences in founding the French Impressionists and thereby upon the whole development of modern art. Our galleries and critics have, moreover, given welcome to the new ideas, and our connoisseurs have become their patrons. Sir Kenneth Clark as the Director of the National Gallery pursued a policy of patronage and propaganda which if it erred in its catholicity erred on the side of the moderns. During the war years also C.E.M.A., the Committee for the Encouragement of Music and the Arts, organized many exhibitions, and again the policy has been to give encouragement to new men and ideas. A grant from the Pilgrim Trust to commission artists to record England threatened by German bombs has also been interpreted as a means to patronize specific artists approximately of the progressive wing, although for that particular purpose many of us feel that a more catholic selection of art work and a choice nearer representation would have been a sounder policy, the idea being to record Britain and not to record contemporary art or the individualised work of a comparatively few selected artists. Of the older masters, Sickert and Steer have won forward to increasing fame and popularity, fine exhibitions of their work at the National Gallery having revealed more than ever their high standing. The official patronage of many painters as war artists (often on the home front which was itself so much a war front) has kept art vividly alive and concerned with vital subjects. One interesting phenomenon of war-time painting has been the depicting of London under the Blitz, a subject which has caught the imaginations and the brushes of a number of artists actually engaged in the Fire Service. Exhibitions of these paintings took place at Burlington House, and although the tremendous subject tended to overpower the purely aesthetic appeal, much of the work had more than documentary value.

The regular Exhibitions of the work of official war artists, on the whole, yielded nothing startling beyond this same documentary value. The men with established reputations have discovered new and often thrilling subjects. Eric Kennington, long established for his virile masculine portraits, found magnificent material in the men of the Air Force. Muirhead Bone brought his genius to bear on places, and Dame Laura Knight turned hers out of the circus and the caravan to record the munition factory. An interestingly individual contribution was made by the late Eric Ravillious who based his war drawings on a kind of impressionistic pen line and wash which brilliantly expressed the effects of light or other dynamics of Nature.

In England the Surrealist movement has been taken up with enthusiasm by many of the youngest generation of painters, and among the older artists of repute Paul Nash, John Armstrong, Roland Penrose, and Edward Burra. Paul Nash, whose death was a great loss to English art, had long abandoned his very beautiful and original form of stylised realism, which gave us a lovely pale-tinted series of interiors and landscapes. At one time, like his younger brother John Nash, he used simplification brilliantly in his efforts to impose design on nature, but his work became progressively more abstract as he experimented.

John Armstrong began by making decorations for a cabaret, which earned him the title of " the modern Beardsley " from one critic, and later he designed amusing stage settings, in a pseudo-naïve, Early Victorian idiom, a little reminiscent in their bright crude colouring of the old " penny plain, twopence coloured " theatrical prints. Now he has joined the newest movement, which gives considerable scope for his talent for precise decoration in clean flat colour. A panel by him is in the Tate Gallery.

A development of abstract art is the Constructivist School of which Piet Mondrian, Naum Gabo, and Ben Nicholson in painting, and Barbara Hepworth in sculpture are the principal exponents of distinction. The Dutch painter, Mondrian, is the real leader of the group. In many of his paintings straight lines are drawn heavily and evenly across the whole surface of the work so as to make rigid rectangular patterns. Naum Gabo,

"SHELTERERS IN THE TUBE," BY HENRY MOORE

From the painting in the Imperial War Museum

Henry Moore is primarily known for his highly stylised or abstract sculpture and the drawings he makes for it. During the second World War, however, he did a series of powerful and expressively pathetic studies of the people sheltering from air-raids in the Tubes. This study compares interestingly with the picture by Walter Bayes, made in 1918 and reproduced on page 700.

who was born in Central Russia in 1890 and who worked in Germany during the 'twenties, holds that what he calls the " unseen subjects," the reality that lies deeper than surface appearances, are the real matter of the art of the future, of which Constructivism is a foretaste. In a broadcast discussion he stated that the Constructivist's aim is to invent a new harmony and a new scale of emotion, and that to do this there is no need to borrow subjects from the external world.

Ben Nicholson arrived at Constructivism after many experiments. Ten years and more ago he was producing attractive landscapes in charming colour, drawn somewhat in the downright way in which a child draws, with blobs of trees sticking up and great emphasis on contours ; and at the same time he was making amusing still lives, again in high, sweet colour and often on big empty canvases, with a mug or a cup and a plate or two isolated in the centre. Then he " arranged " or " composed " and mainly in chalk white, rectangles and circles in low relief. No one can deny the decorativeness of these austere compositions.

Graham Sutherland's art is peculiarly un-English. It depends chiefly upon the challenge of its colour, which is particularly violent. He sacrifices form and all else to this, although he was attracted by the shapes of giant girders twisted by heat and wrecked by explosives during the bombing of London. With such a subject his anarchic style is more at home than when he presents Nature, for the sense of beauty in Nature is bound up with a certain delight and intimacy, and the crude greens and violent orange-reds of Sutherland's work miss altogether that aspect. His style and colour are explosive and belong to a world of violence so that he found his rightful place as a war artist.

Henry Moore is primarily a sculptor but during the second World War was preoccupied with the forms of people sheltering in the Underground stations, usually expressed in pen and wash. These were curious rhythmic dehumanised studies, terrible in their intensity and pathos. They were the modern English equivalent of Expressionism, and yet they had a classical coldness. In no sense representational, these drab studies of dehumanised humanity were an indictment of the misery of war as telling as Goya's of two centuries ago. Moore's sculpture is an attempt to get sculpture out of pure, abstract form. Arguing that sculpture is primarily an affair of masses and holes, as Rodin asserted, this modernist became preoccupied with the effects obtained by the wearing of rocks and pebbles by water, and has built up a number of works on this sort of rhythm and relationship of masses. In their own way they are interesting but are remote from human interest, except that of a very few profound intellectuals. It is again a matter that art must have accepted symbols if it is to fulfil its function of communication between mind and mind. Moore adapts this same technique

"THE THORN TREE," BY GRAHAM SUTHERLAND

Graham Sutherland's pictures are ideas not representations. Here is the essential thorniness of the thorn tree, its basic character translated into curious semi-abstract shapes.

791

to approximations of the human female figure, seeing that too as an arrangement of rounded masses and the sort of holes which are worn in rocks by the action of water and the grinding of pebbles. In these works the difficulty of acceptance is added to by the half-resemblance to the human form and the feeling of utter distortion which comes from this. His work has, however, found a number of powerful advocates, is frequently exhibited, and is much discussed. Time alone will show whether this excitement is a passing fashion for the bizarre or an early recognition of a new form of art and expression.

John Piper, the third man whose work has recently emerged into the limelight, is a painter of landscapes and architecture which wins through by dramatic colouring and chiaroscuro. The somewhat dull façades of churches or barns become startling things of brilliant orange set against smoky blue-greys. A series of studies of Windsor Castle, bought by the Queen, showed the historic pile like some strange theatre scene. Indeed, this element of theatricality is paramount in Piper's work. There is sound draughtsmanship underneath his surfaces, and a vivid imagination. Even at its most bizarre, it is beautiful and exciting as art should be.

One other English artist of outstanding personality is Edward Burra. He is one of the most exotic painters of our time, a depicter of rococo horror, in a style so tense in design and brilliant in colour that his work cannot be missed. He goes for his subjects to the underworld, the torture chamber, the night club, and to that decadence of religion which we find in the churches of Mexico and Spain. In one mood he follows Georg Gross, the German satirist, of the night haunts of Berlin, but his more personal style is one of thick, rich water-colour of startling solidity.

For the rest, art in England pursues much the path it had taken in the days after the last war. Paul Nash became more than ever a Surrealist seeking his subjects in the recesses of his own mind and creating landscapes of macabre significance in the cold greys and pale blues and browns he had always loved. Wadsworth continues to bring together strange objects of the seashore in a kind of weird assembly which has only its nautical associations as a link. John Armstrong is a classical Surrealist who brings excellent draughtsmanship to portray the strangely assorted objects of his dreams. And a host of less outstanding or less challenging people produce good work nearer the academic tradition. One phenomenon worth recording is the revival in the graphic arts. Wood-cutting and engraving have found a number of first-rate exponents and the art of book production —always at its best in England—has benefited. The work of Robert Gibbings, of Clare Leighton, Agnes Miller Parker, John Farleigh and Eric Underwood stands out from the many who are creating noble illustrations and decorations for books.

" COUNCIL CHAMBER, HOUSE OF COMMONS," BY JOHN PIPER

John Piper has used his characteristic style of dramatically illuminated architecture to show the ruined chamber of the House of Commons after the Blitz.

793

§ 6

So it moves still : this practice of art which nearly twenty thousand years ago began in the caves or on the bones of animals. In this machine age the cinema, the demands of advertisement in poster and magazine, the need for design in a thousand directions has almost superseded the creation of the mural and the easel picture. In this democratic age the art of the mural is having a resurgence on the walls of community centres, restaurants, and great public buildings such as the magnificent Town Hall at Stockholm. Stores and public restaurants employ the artists who once were patronised by the lords spiritual and temporal. Cinemas are decorated instead of churches and palaces. Books costing a few pence each are illustrated instead of the Missals and Books of Hours of the Middle Ages. Posters are purchased for the hoardings where once the merchant princes bought precious landscapes or interiors to adorn their walls. But art goes on in the new ways. It explores new aspects of man's mind, new activities of his body. And always it continues to evoke the magic which for twenty thousand years has been conjured by that strangest of all human creatures, the artist.

XL

ART IN THE COMMONWEALTH

THE PAINTERS AND SCULPTORS OF CANADA, AUSTRALIA,
SOUTH AFRICA, AND NEW ZEALAND

§ 1

THERE may have been a tendency in Britain to think of the great overseas dominions and colonies as fields of giant physical rather than cultural exercise, but recent years have tended to correct the extremes of this view. We became intensely aware, for instance, at the Empire Exhibition at Wembley in 1924–25 of the claim of the contemporary Canadian artists at least to very considerable attention, realising that out of the characteristic grandeur and beauty of their country one group of painters especially had established a style of their own almost independent of European artists. Since then our awareness has broadened. Not the least aspect of it has been the acceptance of the arts of the primitive and the native peoples of the smaller colonies and dependencies chiefly in highly stylised sculpture, folk and ritual in origin but nevertheless possessing fascinating formal qualities. As we have noted in a previous chapter there has been an absolute vogue for this type of work, some of it, such as the Benin sculpture and the Ifi heads from West Africa, having a beauty and classical perfection not in the least exotic or bizarre. We have, however, long realised the sense of rhythm of almost all African peoples and Polynesians, and, if anything, the cult of this art among ultra-sophisticated European aesthetes has been overdone. It is, therefore, with the painting and sculpture of the white settlers rather than with that of the native peoples that we are dealing here.

§ 2

Canadian art history does not really commence until the nineteenth century when Paul Kane (1810–71) came with his family from Ireland and settled in what was then York, and is now Toronto. This was about 1819. Kane from the beginning was attracted by the colourful Indian encampments and the magnificent Canadian Indian types. In the early 'forties he visited Europe, and when he returned to Canada he arranged

795

with the Hudson Bay Company to make an expedition with their fur traders into the wilderness of the West and North-West. His book, *Wanderings of an Artist among the Indians of North America*, became something of a classic and a definite contribution towards anthropology. On this journey, which was pursued right across the Rockies to the Pacific coast, Kane made some of his studies of the Indians and their encampments, and it was this work which he continued.

The next name is that of Cornelius Krieghoff (1815–72), a German-born artist who first studied in Holland and then settled in Canada after joining the American army, deserting, and marrying a French Canadian girl. Somewhat in the manner of the earlier Dutch artists, Krieghoff depicted the life of the early settlers, especially at a famous tavern, Chez Jolifou, which he himself frequented. He also worked for the coloured engravings which were growing in popularity in his time, and in these he records vividly the scenery of the country and the picturesque Indians.

These two were the pioneer painters. After them Canada seems for a long time to have been concerned chiefly with its material development, and it is not until towards the end of the century that we again find anything of outstanding merit. By then, of course, the artists are no longer European born. Four men born in the 1850's were destined to play a large part in creating a definite Canadian art : Homer B. Watson (1855–1930), Horatio Walker (1858–1938), Franklin Brownell (1856–   ), and William Brymner (1855–1925). Watson and Walker both saw the possibilities of rendering the beauty of the Canadian countryside they knew, the farms, and farm life. "To make pictures of attractive moods of Nature," Watson declared his aim, and though often the moods are fierce rather than softly attractive, his robust style was equal to the task. Both men working well into the twentieth century painted in the thick impasto which seemed so right for conveying the bold effects of this sturdy land.

Maurice Cullen (1877–1934) and James Wilson Morrice (1865–1924), the next two Canadian artists, owe their style much more to the French of the late nineteenth century. Cullen was an enthusiastic Impressionist when he returned to Montreal from Paris, and found in the snow scenes and the ice glow of his native land fascinating effects of light. He was an open-air painter and catches marvellously the effect of the air filled with snow. Morrice is probably the most important of all Canadian artists, his reputation extending well beyond the boundaries of the Dominion and his pictures being in a number of public galleries abroad. He divided his time between France and Canada, returning there in the winters to get the effects of the scenery under snow. A friend of Harpignies, of Matisse, and of Condor, Morrice had the international feeling for art, and in his own work a lovely sense of colour, suffusing his cold skies with a delicate

"LAURENTIAN VILLAGE," BY CLARENCE A. GAGNON

A typically Canadian painter, and one of the founders of the style of bold forms and colouring which we associate with the art of Canada, Gagnon found his subjects in the snowbound villages nestling in the fold of the hills. He made a motive of the solid little sleighs and the brilliant touches of colour of the clothes of their drivers.

797

rose-pink. He exploited, too, the solid shapes of the typical sleighs of the farmers, their squat, low-bodied forms set on the ruts in the snow-covered roads. It was all absolutely Canadian, with the whole knowledge of European painting behind it. His pictures of the various places in Europe, Africa, and the West Indies, which he visited, fine as they are, never quite achieve the place personality of the Canadian works.

Linked in spirit with Morrice was Clarence Gagnon (1880–1942). Trained first in Canada under Brymner, who was himself an enthusiastic admirer of Whistler and a great influence on the young men of Montreal as the Head of the Montreal Art School, Gagnon began as a Whistlerian. When he went to Paris to the Académie Julien where so many of the Canadian artists studied, he quickly achieved a reputation as an etcher and as a painter in the simplified style of Whistler, with clean broad patches of colour. Returning to Canada and working in the countryside near Quebec, he strengthened this style into something more three-dimensional and with an echo of Morrice, seeing, as the elder artist had done, the pictorial value of the villages under snow against the surrounding forests and hills, the solid forms of the little sleighs.

One other artist, Tom Thomson (1877–1917) stands before we come to the famous Group of Seven whose work has counted for so much in Canadian art. Thomson was largely a self-taught painter, something of a recluse in his passion for the magnificence of nature which he found in the wild regions of Algonguin Park, a government reserve with innumerable lakes and streams and fine forests. Here and elsewhere in the wilds Thomson loved to travel by canoe, fishing and camping at will, and here at last he settled as guide, painting the scenes he loved. His studies of trees, put in bold simplified masses, are brilliantly coloured and sensitive to the basic forms. His technique is a kind of pointillism often done with square touches which remind one a little of Seurat, but he came to these methods through his own experiments with his pigment and by his contacts with other Canadian painters. In 1917 his upturned canoe was found on one of the lakes, and Canada mourned one of her most interesting artists.

The story of Canadian art in the twentieth century is largely bound up with the Group of Seven, which, although it was not definitely formed until 1920, consisted of the seven men whose work had then been long operative in the art of their country : J. E. H. Macdonald, Lawrens Harris, Frank Carmichael, Arthur Lismer, Alexander Young Jackson, Franz H. Johnson, and Frederick Horsman Varley.

Macdonald must be regarded as the moving spirit, and 1907, when he returned to Toronto from England, the opening date. In Toronto, as the chief designer for a firm called Grip Limited, he met Tom Thomson, and later, Lismer, Carmichael, and Varley. These men began to take long trips, largely by canoe, into the heart of Canada and to work out the brilliant technique which was to bring them fame. In these canoe trips for the purpose of sketching they were following the lead of a slightly older artist, John William Beatty (1868–1941), who had studied in Paris and worked in Europe but then went back to Canada and taught for many years at the Ontario College of Art. In his style of broad Impressionism Beatty was also a pioneer of the characteristic Canadian painting.

Macdonald soon decided to devote himself entirely to painting. By 1912 he was elected to the Royal Canadian Academy, and exhibited his typical early picture " Tracks and Traffic," bold in colour and design and essentially national. After that he created work after work in this vein. His painting was given a mixed reception by critics and public : one picture of 1916, " The Tangled Garden," especially calling forth a great deal of critical abuse. Nevertheless this style was winning recognition as a definitely Canadian expression.

The first World War inevitably cut across the art activity and the association of these men. It was responsible for one contribution to Canadian art in that Lord Beaverbrook launched a scheme for commissioning a number of foremost Canadian painters to make a record of the war, and Jackson, Morrice, Beatty, Lismer, Varley, and others were chosen to make this documentary collection. When these Government War Memorial paintings were subsequently exhibited in London, Varley especially won high praise.

With the end of the war in 1918 all these men returned to the work of depicting the wild beauty of Canada. Hitherto they had worked largely in the region of Algonquin Park, but now Macdonald discovered the more distant Algoma with its magnificent panorama of mountain, forest, and lake, and its even greater challenge. By 1920 they were all meeting regularly, and the idea of joint exhibition came into being, and that Group of Seven which yet could claim " we have no Group formula, and are conscious of widely divergent aims." Thirty pictures from that first " Exhibition by a Group of Seven Painters " were sent to the United States the next year, and at home in Canada their own second exhibition revealed how united they were by an almost common vision of that lovely land. The National Gallery of Canada began to buy their pictures in face of some controversy. But from thenceforward Macdonald, Jackson, Harris and Lismer especially, went almost everywhere in Canada and painted in the idiom they had evolved. When in 1924–25 this work came to the Canadian Pavilion at the British Empire Exhibition at Wembley it was magnificently received, as it was in Paris in 1927.

A word about the other men who formed this group with Macdonald : Alexander Young Jackson was born in Montreal in 1883, studied at the

Académie Julien in Paris, was elected to the Royal Canadian Academy in 1919, but eventually resigned. He tremendously simplifies his forms, emphasises the natural rhythms for the sake of design, and paints in the vivid colours common to all these men.

Arthur Lismer was an Englishman, born in Sheffield in 1885, who went to Canada in 1911 after studying first in his native city and then in Antwerp. He has held many academic and educational posts in Canada, among them that of the Vice-Principal of the Ontario College of Art which has played so large a part in this movement.

Lawrens Harris was born in 1885 and after studying abroad also returned to Canada in 1911. His work, which began in the typical style of the Group, moved to a much greater simplification of the forms and such complete emphasis of the decorative rhythm of cloud, water, mountain, and ice that it verges on the abstract. He painted largely in the lakeside country of Lake Superior.

Frederick Horsman Varley, like Lismer, was a Sheffield man, born in 1881, and, like Lismer, he studied at the Académie Royale des Beaux Arts in Antwerp. He went to Canada in 1912. He is the one of these men who applied the bold style of the Group to portraiture and figure painting ; and, as we have seen, his work for the Canadian War Memorial received the especial praise of the critics.

Franz H. Johnson was born in Toronto in 1888. He exhibited in the 1920 show of the Group of Seven, but then withdrew.

Franklin Carmichael, the youngest member of the Group, was born in 1890 in Orillia, Ontario. He, too, studied at the Ontario College of Art where eventually he became himself a teacher in 1932.

A few other men joined the Group at different times during its career : Alfred Joseph Casson (1898–) a very typical painter in the style, but with the distinction of being also a fine water-colourist ; Lemoine Fitzgerald (1890–) who became Principal of the Winnipeg School of Art ; Edwin Headley Holgate (1892–) who, like Varley, was a strong figure painter as well as a landscape artist. Mention should also be made of Albert Henry Robinson (1881–), who, though not a member of the Group, painted in the typical manner of these others.

All these artists are, as we would expect, represented in the National Gallery of Canada at Toronto, as well as in galleries abroad and in many private collections. The Group of Seven reached its zenith between 1924 and 1927 when, as we have seen, the exhibitions at Wembley and in Paris gave it European fame. In 1933 as a Group it came to an end when it merged with the larger Canadian Group, but by that time the style was established as typical of Canadian painting : the simplification of form, brilliant colour, curving strokes of pure pigment, emphatic rhythm ;

everything applied to the typical Canadian scene of mountain, forest, lake, or simple buildings, and using often the brilliant effects of snow to pictorial advantage.

In October to December of 1938 there was another great Exhibition of Canadian art in London, this time at the Tate Gallery, where " A Century of Canadian Painting " enabled us to review the whole story from Paul Kane to that date. Naturally there are now many painters pursuing highly individual techniques, some of them working in modernist subjective manner inspired by the later School of Paris. But it is too soon to decide which of them will live. Names spring to mind : Fritz Brandtner, a violent Expressionist, who turns his eyes to the docks and factories ; Alexander Bercovitch, the Russian figure painter, with his vivid palette ; the semi-abstract Marion Scott ; Carl Schafer, who continues to paint the rhythmic hills or the farm life in thin oils or in water-colour ; or Lilian Freeman, whose delicate line is something new in Canadian art. Unless it be Emily Carr, however, who has carried forward the bold traditions of the Group of Seven to the verges of Expressionism, it is impossible to see any painter of such outstanding Canadian individuality that we can safely consider as a new addition to that national contribution which the Group of Seven and its followers made to the art of the world.

§ 3

Art in South Africa has followed the line familiar to the great lands which called for physical effort and endurance rather than cultural development, so that only of comparatively recent years has there arisen a body of artists supported by the understanding and appreciation of a sufficient public. Now, in our own century, life has become wealthy, settled ; and a healthy artistic life has established its roots. These, again, as we would expect, draw their nourishment partly from the nature of South Africa itself, and partly from the art-life of Europe, in this case often of Holland since the Dutch influences share with the British.

Among the painters of the early nineteenth century we would name Samuel Daniel (1775–1811), the son of a Royal Academician and himself an exhibitor of the Royal Academy, who went to the Cape and in 1804 produced a series of fine colour plate books called *African Scenery and Animals*. His water-colours of the life of the colonists of that time are of both documentary and artistic interest. The work of a Dutch artist, J. C. Poortemans (1786–1870) is less sophisticated as art, but equally of value as a record of the colonial life. He endeavoured after he came to the Cape in 1833 to establish the art of lithography there. Our own period would probably enjoy the very *naïveté* of the paintings and drawings he made.

About the same time that Poortemans arrived at the Cape two other artists came, one on a visit, the other as a settler who became South Africa's leading artist. Sir Charles D'Oyley was a gifted amateur, an official in the Civil Service in India, who left some fascinating studies of Cape life. Thomas William Bowler (1813–69) was a fine water-colourist, who loved to portray the splendour of the East Indiamen riding at anchor or entering Table Bay. Shortly after came Thomas Baines (1820–75) who was an explorer as well as a daring artist. He depicted much that he saw with tremendous verve : landscape (he was the first to paint the grandeur of the Victoria Falls), hunting scenes, fighting and historical incidents, and the normal life of the colonies. His works in the Africana Museum at Johannesburg are an invaluable record of the period. Two other lesser names belong specifically to the nineteenth century : Wilhelm Langschmidt (1805–66) and F. Timpson I'ons (1802–87). The former was a German artist who settled at the Cape as a farmer and worked there as a portrait painter ; the latter went out to the Eastern provinces and left us delightful impressions of the native tribal life and of the exotic landscape.

All these men, however, were colonial artists ; and it was not until the beginning of this century that art in South Africa with roots in Europe moved into a new dimension. Frans David Oerder (1867–1944) may be considered a transition painter. He was a Dutchman who came to the Transvaal in 1890, worked for the Boers as a war artist during the South African War, left his adopted country when that war resulted in defeat, but eventually returned there towards the end of his life. His pictures of life in Pretoria are delightful records of the old Boer capital.

Most of the earlier men had gravitated to South Africa as colonists, and had, in fact, not been professional painters. Now the position was reversed. The new artists were born in South Africa and came to Europe for training, to Paris, London, Amsterdam. Sometimes they stayed and became absorbed in the body of European art ; sometimes they returned to their native land, but, alas ! too often only as an echo of the " isms " of the contemporary School of Paris.

Outstanding among them is the doyen of South African painting, Jacob Hendrik Pierneef (1886–   ). He is, by far, the most important of the artists of the country : individual, decorative, an exciting colourist, perhaps a shade too eclectic and thereby sacrificing an impressive Pierneefism for echoes of other men's work. He can execute paintings on a large scale, as the murals at South Africa House in London testify, or he can create sensitive small easel pictures of lyric loveliness such as " The First Rain, Lichtenberg " which is in the Johannesburg Municipal Gallery. Pierneef was born in Pretoria and as a young man worked there under Oerder and the sculptor, Anton van Wouw. Thence he went to Holland, and at

Amsterdam and Hilversum contacted the newer movements, being especially influenced by Cubism. Back in South Africa, however, his individual sense of decoration caused him to become an interpreter of the South African scene in a stylised, but not a distorted, manner. The most appreciated of artists in the Dominion, Pierneef is still working in his native city.

An even earlier artist of note is Hugo Naude (1869–1941), who was really the first South African artist to study abroad and to return as a professional painter. It was Olive Schreiner, that brilliant authoress of *The Story of an African Farm*, who took Naude up as a young man, sent him to London to study at the Slade, and then to Munich and to France. He returned to Worcester, his home town in the Cape Province, lived down prejudice against what was at that time a new vision out there, and became an honoured artist.

Pieter Wenning (1874–1921) is the next important figure. He was a poor man when he first came to South Africa in 1906, and for ten years he pursued his painting in the scarce leisure hours available to a man working hard for his living. For him there was no training in Europe, but he studied reproductions of the European Impressionists and he learned much from Japanese colour-prints. By about 1916 he had won a certain recognition and was able to rely entirely upon a growing patronage, so that in the few years left to him he became one of the most sought after and honoured of South African painters.

Two men of the 'nineties migrated to Europe and became part of the European art story : Neville Lewis (1895–   ) and Enslin du Plessis (1894–   ). Lewis often returned to Africa for the subject-matter of his pictures, and, indeed, may have returned there for good ; Enslin, painter of still-life and of landscape, has worked chiefly in London and has only occasionally gone back to his native land.

Merlyn Evans (1910–   ) is another artist who vacillates between South Africa and London. Actually he is a Welshman, having been born in Cardiff ; but after his training he settled in the Dominion though more recently he has returned to London. Evans's most characteristic work is conceived in a vein of sinister horror of the modern world, and his themes are often of trials, executions and such phenomena of the contemporary political scene. These he presents in a highly organised, decorative Cubism, almost, but not quite, abstract.

For its size, wealth and importance, the art life of South Africa is still surprisingly unorganised. The last few years have, happily, shown a sense of this shortcoming, and given us the fine Municipal Art Gallery at Johannesburg, directed by one of the most scholarly of South African artists, Anton Hendricks ; the establishment of The New Group in Cape Town, with something of the spirit of The London Group ; and that of the Pretoria Art Centre whose director is Le Roux Smith le Roux, whose murals are a feature of South Africa House, London, and of the liner *Queen Elizabeth*.

The New Group includes most of the men and women with modern vision. One of the founders was Gregoire Boonzaier (1909–), with Terence McCaw (1913–), and the fine woman painter, Frieda Lock. Another important woman artist is Irma Stern, who has a reputation not only in the Dominion but in the foremost European capitals where she has had one-man shows. Wisely she has seen the aesthetic possibilities of the native types. Another artist who has exploited this material is Alexis Preller (1911–) who was a student of Mark Gertler in London, and who has brought many African influences to bear on his work. This is true also of Walter Battiss (1906–), who turned for his inspiration to the prehistoric cave paintings which have been discovered of recent years in Africa and have added so considerably to our knowledge of early art. Battiss is the author of a number of books on this subject, on which he is a scientific worker, and apart from his own original contribution to art— such as "Quagga Race, 1948" which was exhibited at the Olympiad Exhibition in London that year—he has made many careful copies of the cave paintings.

We are only beginning to understand the importance of the primitive art of Africa and its people, and most of this comes from the people of the coastal regions or of the interior farther north. One interesting portent in a recent exhibition of South African Art at the Tate Gallery, London, was the work of Gerard Sekoto (1913–), a native painter, a self-taught Bantu artist, who was born at a mission station in the Transvaal, and is now an accepted professional painter. His studies of the people in the coloured quarters of the great towns are direct visions of a phase of life full of picturesque and formal qualities.

Along with these painters South Africa can also claim a number of distinguished sculptors, some of them working in the remarkable exotic woods of the region. The earliest was Anton van Wouw (1862–1945), who was working on a statue of President Kruger when the South African war broke out in 1899. He has made some fine bronzes of the Bantu people. Kruger's grandson, Stephanus Eloff (1885–1947), was himself a sculptor of standing with a reputation in Africa and in Paris where he did much of his work. Moses Kottler (1896–) is the most eminent of the living sculptors. His portraits, and his studies of the Bantu people, are noble expressions carried out in wood, stone or bronze in a technique of simplified forms he has made his own.

Since the end of the war the Dominion has become art conscious to an extent never achieved before, and the South African Association of Arts working as a co-ordinating official body will probably further still more the output and appreciation of good work already well begun.

§ 4

The pattern of the art activities of the Antipodes follows that of the other great Commonwealth nations. As in Canada and South Africa, the necessity of colonising, the sheer physical task of settlement and the building of the cities, militated against the establishment of a culture over many decades ; the first manifestation of art was an echo of that of Europe, a kind of nostalgic transplanting of the styles prevalent earlier in the Old Country ; this was followed by a realisation that the characteristic landscape, light and people offered the possibility of something new ; and then, as communication with Europe became easier, artists were increasingly influenced by the newer revolutionary ideas of European art.

In the case of Australia this condition was emphasised by the fact that at first it was so largely a penal colony, and later was invaded by the gold rush of the 1850's : neither event likely to prove a very fertile field for culture. This early history has long since given place to a community with a very high standard of living and a rising culture, and of recent years some of the finest modern paintings and some important Old Masters have gone to Australia to the magnificent art galleries of her big cities, whilst her own artists have, in some cases, earned world-wide reputations especially in the field of black-and-white drawing. Names like Phil May, Will Dyson, Norman Lindsay and David Low are so well known that we tend to forget that they are Australians.

Australian art began in a strange direction, for the first was almost scientific, being the work of men whose draughtsmanship was devoted to recording natural history. Thus Sydney Parkinson was the recording naturalist of Captain Cook's vessel, *Endeavour* ; William Westall in a like capacity on the *Investigator* made drawings of the Australian coast ; and John Webber served on the *Resolution*. The first land artist of any note is Thomas Watling, actually one of the freed convicts who had once used his talent as a forger, been deported, and on the expiry of his sentence had turned to topographical water-colours. All the early work, practically, is in water-colour, for the immense distance of Australia from European sources meant that the actual material of oil-painting was not easily come by. Also, as we would imagine, it is topographical, and the names of John Eyre, M. Taylor, and J. W. Lewin arise. There was a kind of vogue —dictated maybe by the vastness and grandeur of the landscape—for panoramic views, especially of the rising township of Sydney.

Between 1809 and 1821, a stroke of good fortune came to the colony by the appointment of Lachlan Macquarie as Governor. Removed so far from any interference by the authorities in London he ruled his territory like a European prince, commissioning and setting a fashion for portraits, miniatures, and pictures in the eighteenth-century British tradition. From that time forward Australian art had its patrons and its exponents. Frederick Garling was one fascinating painter of marine subjects who boasted that he painted every ship which sailed into Sydney harbour. The next artist of importance was Conrad Martens, a pupil of Copley Fielding, who in 1832 sailed as the official artist in the *Beagle*, famous for its association with the young Charles Darwin. He settled in Sydney in 1835 and stayed there until he died in 1878, painting in oils as well as in water-colour in the manner of the prevailing English water-colour school. He made some fine studies of Sydney harbour.

One interesting untrained painter of the early period was James Wallis, who was attracted by the life of the natives and left us such records as that of a " Corroboree at Newcastle."

The gold rush of 1851–61 affected the fortunes of Australia in every way and not least of it art. It helped considerably to populate the country, it brought Australia into world prominence ; it established the wealth of the lucky few ; and, not least, it provided genre subjects and a form of popular art of illustration in lithography and engraving. Samuel Thomas Gill is the outstanding name. As a young man of twenty-one we hear of him at Adelaide in 1839. In common with so many out there he took part in the gold rush, for he was a " tough " fellow who drank, gambled, rode, quarrelled, and generally lived the rough life of the earlier settlers. But he saw the pictorial possibilities of the gold fields and equally their financial ones for an artist, and he turned his Rowlandson-like talent to the creation of series of engravings and lithographs of such subjects as " Gold Digging at Victoria," and so stood at the beginning of that tradition of illustrative black-and-white work in which Australians have done so well. Almost from the beginning of the Australian Press the newspapers, especially the excellent *Sydney Bulletin*, have taken seriously the service of culture both to art and literature and have published good drawings as well as short stories, poems, and expert criticism.

The settling down of the gold rush left the colony much richer in people and industry, and it is noteworthy that in 1860 at Melbourne was opened the first National Gallery and School of Art.

By the 'eighties, Sydney, Melbourne, and Adelaide were established modern cities, and towards the end of that decade Impressionism, which proved so attractive to the Australian artists, gained its ascendancy. Tom Roberts in particular realised that the strong light, the subtle colouring, and the tree forms of the country demanded a treatment in the new theory of outdoor painting which was stirring France. He had been preceded by an important Swiss-born artist, Abram Louis Buvelot (1814–88), who came to Melbourne in 1865 and gave us such fine work as the " Waterpool at Coleraine," which is in the National Gallery at Melbourne. He was followed by the man who stands at the peak of Australian art of the nineteenth century, Arthur Streeton. Streeton painted in the open air ; he used a heavy, square-headed brush admirably suited to expressing the leaf forms of the prevailing gum trees ; he pitched his work in very high tones, painting the foliage under the blinding sunlight of the country. Apart from his actual contribution of paintings he made his own enthusiasm contagious and trained other artists in the painters' camp which he established at Heidelberg. This " Heidelberg School " remains, even to-day, the main influence in Australian art. Along with Streeton should be mentioned Frank McCubbin, an Australian-born artist, painter of somewhat sentimental subject pictures like " Down on his Luck," a study of a settler for whom Australia had not proved a land of gold. There was a big Impressionist Exhibition in Melbourne in 1889 where this style of painting effectually won out.

By this time the artists were well aware of the pictorial possibilities of the Australian landscape and life. Emanuel Philip Fox, a teacher in Melbourne who had himself studied in Paris, exploited to the full the possibilities of broken colour even for the life-sized nudes which he painted, and which gained him (perhaps with some hyperbole) the title of the Australian Renoir. Hans Heyden, who worked as a landscapist in the arid central lands, exploiting the full pictorial and decorative possibilities of the scenery and the gum trees, was the apotheosis of the Australian approach. Max Meldrum, a Scottish artist who went out to Australia in 1889 and after travel and study abroad returned in 1913, establishing an art school and writing a great deal upon art, was another pronounced influence of the rising men.

Meantime Norman Lindsay had established his reputation with his almost Beardsleyesque black-and-white work for the *Bulletin* and in the books which he illustrated. His daughter, also a fine artist, who worked under the name of Ruby Lind, married Will Dyson, one of the most brilliant of cartoonists of the twentieth century, whose work in London for the *Daily Herald* has only been equalled by that other great Australian cartoonist, David Low.

The new century saw the establishment of the modernists. Roi de Mestre about 1919 became a leader of the movement in Sydney with Roland Wakelin ; whilst in Melbourne, George Bell, although himself something of an Academic artist, fought for the new ideas and encouraged the new generation to work with a new vision. Arnold Shore brought the

Post-Impressionism of Van Gogh, and William Frater that of Cézanne, while Kah Fizelle struck an individual note with a linear technique of sensitive beauty especially in studies of the nude. Along with these came inevitable echoes of all the later " isms " of the School of Paris, and violent controversy as to their right to be called art. Sir Lionel Lindsay, himself a good water-colourist, etcher, and woodcut artist, became one of the most slashing critics of modern art, and his diatribes against it in book-form and in news-paper articles are famous in art circles. Nevertheless a number of names of men practising in the modernist techniques achieved a place as Surrealists, Neo-Realists, and the rest : James Gleeson, Max Ebert, Peter Reeves-Smith, Eric Thake, and others. Not least was that of William Dobell, when the award of one of the Australian art prizes for his " Portrait of Joshua Smith," a Neo-Realist work, veered the whole controversy for a time round his work.

Recently some of the younger Australian artists have achieved a certain *réclame* for their exhibitions in London : Russell Drysdale, Brian Midlane, Mollie Paxton, and a promising young artist, Justin O'Brien, who works in a curious, almost Byzantine, style and is largely inspired by religious feeling. In less controversial manner the airy water-colours of J. S. Loxton have created interest in London, both at the Royal Academy and in a one-man show.

Art in Australia, therefore, has established itself firmly since its difficult beginnings in the early years of last century ; and her fine galleries (some with magnificent bequest funds) and the propaganda work of the Australian Contemporary Art Society, founded by George Bell in 1938, go far to ensure an interesting future.

In some ways art in New Zealand has had advantages : the settlement there of the British in any quantity came later than in Australia, and under the gracious climate and lovely natural surroundings there was almost from the beginning a possibility of establishing a cultured life. Naturally it imitated the life left behind in Britain as far as it could, but the abundance of timber made the fashion for the architecture, and architecture inevitably affects the other visual arts. There was also the wonderful indigenous art of the Maoris, one of the finest and best preserved of the primitive arts of the world. If the later arrivals brought to the cities in the second half of the nineteenth century a much poorer conception of architecture, painting and sculpture, this has been largely corrected by a revival of good taste.

New Zealand, even more remote from Europe than Australia, suffers in that her artists are less known in the old world. Best of them probably is Stewart Maclennan, who has recently been appointed Director of the National Art Gallery and is himself a fine water-colourist and lithographer.

Australian News and Information Bureau, London.

MARGARET OLLEY," BY WILLIAM DOBELL

Dobell is one of the controversial modern artists of Australia. His portrait of Joshua Smith, awarded the Archibald Prize in 1943, created great discussion. In 1948 he won this prize again with this highly stylised portrait. The manner owes something to Renoir, but William Dobell is too individual a painter to label.

He trained in London at the Royal College of Art. Russell Clark, another versatile New Zealand artist, who is now art master at Canterbury College ; Cedric Savage, who paints in a very direct style the beautiful Takaka region ; Vida Steinart, and a number of other lively artists reveal that if New Zealand came fairly late into this field she is now intensely aware of its possibilities.

ART IN AMERICA

THE story of painting in America is one of curious frustration. Material forces have from the beginning worked against the establishment of the pronounced national art which we might expect from this virile people. Indeed, their very virility has worked against it, for it has continually directed energy into other channels ; and, moreover, the culture of Europe has always acted as a lodestar to the most promising men. Benjamin West, John Singleton Copley, and Gilbert Stuart in the eighteenth century all came to England and became virtually British artists ; so did Whistler and Sargent in the nineteenth ; while Mary Cassatt went to France and became one of the established French Impressionists. In our own day we have lured Jacob Epstein so thoroughly from his native New York that we forget he is not British-born.

The need of colonising the vast areas of the country, the rise of the world's greatest industrial life, and the swift accumulation of enormous riches into the hands of men not intrinsically cultured even though they became the most spectacular collectors of pictures and *objets d'art* : all these things also have worked against the creation of the native school. The mere fact that the great millionaire industrialists bought the art treasures of Europe had, in some ways, a bad effect upon the growth of an indigent art. Nevertheless there have been the men who stayed at home, who saw in the American scene and the American way of life subjects worthy and inspiration compelling. They may have accepted the European tradition of manner of painting, echoing eighteenth-century portraiture, the Barbizon school of landscape painters, the Impressionists, and the wilder spirits of the modern School of Paris, but they have applied these mannerisms to the personalities, the landscapes, and the way of life of their own country. Washington Allston, George Inness, Winslow Homer, Thomas Eakins, Albert Pinkham Ryder, John la Farge and others are names to conjure with, as the exhibition of American painting at the Tate Gallery in 1946 proved. Modernist art has to-day some notable exponents in the United States, and certainly has the encouragement of innumerable galleries and widespread patronage, especially by the Museum of Modern Art in New

York which is certainly the greatest collection of modernist painting in the world.

§ 2

In the beginning America suffered somewhat from the Puritan inhibitions of her first settlers, for the Puritan tradition has always been inimical to all arts other than music. Soon, however, the colonies began to echo as far as they could the cultural life of eighteenth-century England and France, and the wealthy merchants and administrators began to collect paintings, especially portraits, in the prevailing European mode, particularly, of course, that of England. The first name which has real importance is that of John Smibert (1688–1751), a Scottish artist who went to the New World and carried there the British tradition. His group portrait of "Bishop Berkeley and His Entourage," painted in 1729, and now at Yale University, is a fine example of group portraiture. The first native-born painter, however, was Robert Feke (c. 1705–50), who became the portraitist of the foremost members of colonial society. The best known of his works is also a group portrait, "Isaac Royall and His Family," at Harvard Law School. With the growth of settled conditions and the establishment of the fine colonial houses, American painting might have established itself firmly on the English model yet with an American note, as the architecture had already done ; but it met its first check in the War of Independence. Copley, anticipating the Revolution, left America in 1774 after he had contributed nobly to the Colonial art. West left in 1760, and at Rome embarked on that triumphant career which never wavered until he died as President of the Royal Academy in 1820, having succumbed to the lure of Europe. Gilbert Stuart left America just at the start of the War of Independence, entered West's by that time flourishing studio in London, became a dandy of the town and then, in 1792, returned to America declaring that he wished to paint Washington's portrait. Elegant, aristocratic, he was one of the fine portrait painters of that period of fine portraiture, and the picture which he eventually did make of the great Washington is one of his best works.

All these men belong largely to the story of European art. Benjamin West (1738–1820) especially was an influence, his studio becoming the centre for all Americans visiting London, and a training ground for American artists. He cultivated the great neo-classical story-painting, but added to it a note of romance. When he painted his famous "Death of General Wolfe," now in the National Gallery of Canada at Ottawa, he broke new ground by putting the characters in correct costume instead of the customary classical one. His vast "Death of Bayard," owned by His Majesty the King, anticipated the sheer romanticism of Walter Scott, and it comes as a surprise that it was painted in 1771. He was by common consent the only man to succeed Sir Joshua Reynolds as the President of the Royal Academy, a position which he occupied until his death in 1820.

John Singleton Copley (1737–1820) was greatest as a portraitist, but when he came to London he worked in the vogue which West had largely created of the large historical picture. His genius lay in incorporating good and authentic portraits into these histories. His " Death of the Earl of Chatham " (Tate Gallery), for instance, contains fifty-five portraits. Successful as he was with such enormous canvases, or in the royal portrait groups which he painted, many will prefer him in the earlier pieces painted before he left America, such as the glorious " Boy with a Squirrel " or the portrait, " Mrs. Thomas Boyleton," at Harvard University.

Meantime in America itself art suffered from that paradoxical success of the other phases of American life. There were portraits of the heroes of the new Republic. Two of these, of Lafayette, introduce to us two of the noteworthy painters, Rembrandt Peale (1778–1860), one of a family of artists largely influenced by Dutch art, and S. F. B. Morse (1791–1872), who is remembered best as the inventor of the Morse Code. Morse was a good artist, broad in his treatment and getting the essential character of his sitters. The City of New York commissioned a series of full-length portraits of the military and other leaders of the Republic, and in 1817 commissioned the murals for the Rotunda of the Capitol. As so often happens with grandiose schemes of art patronage very little of intrinsic worth resulted. John Trumbull (1756–1843) alone succeeded as a " historiographer," his " Battle of Bunker's Hill," now at Yale University, being a fine battle picture. But America had set her face towards the enormous exploitation of her rich possessions of natural wealth, and art was not her *métier*. The rise of the mercantile classes in the North ; the continuous movement into the great regions of the West : these gave no time for the cultivation of art.

§ 3

Despite the magnificence of the American landscape practically nothing had been done in this way. A few fascinating anonymous " primitive " paintings have come to us from the early nineteenth century, perhaps done by gifted amateur artists. " The Runaway Horse," a great black horse set against a beautifully simplified background, is one of the best of these ; and a curious " Meditation by the Sea," where a tiny figure in a bowler hat stands beside a turbulent sea, might have been painted by a modern Surrealist. Around this time, however, there arose a number of artists whom we call the Hudson River School who did turn to the

Catskills and the White Mountains and the definitely American scenery for their subjects, investing it with something of the moral sublimity we would associate with the Lake School of English poets. Thomas Doughty (1793–1856); Thomas Cole (1801–1848), who painted the mountains in the purity of their snow with Wordsworthian sublimity, are the outstanding early landscape men.

Washington Allston (1779–1843), the promisingly beautiful youth who charmed all who met him, who spent his life partly in Europe and partly in his native land, never quite fulfilling his early great possibilities, was the painter of subject pictures and of romantic ideal landscape. These were followed by George Inness (1825–94), a painter of the American scene in the manner of the French painters of Barbizon. He, too, was largely concerned with the moral teaching of the sublimity of Nature, and expressed this by vast views of the river valleys.

In the later part of the nineteenth century we have that cleavage again between the artists who were allured by European culture, and those who remained and gave American art its finest contribution. Of the former were Whistler, Sargent, and Mary Cassatt, with all of whom we have dealt in the preceding pages. Over against these were Winslow Homer (1856–1910), Thomas Eakins (1844–1916), and Albert Pinkham Ryder (1847–1917).

Homer and Eakins are America's best artists. Homer's subjects were of Nature at her most inimical to man. He himself left New York and settled to a hermit's life on the bleak coast of Maine where he painted pictures of the sea in its fury, or of snowy landscape such as his magnificent " Winter "—a study of a fox and great hovering birds on a snow-covered coast—which is in the Pennsylvania Academy of Fine Arts. His pictures of man at grips with the storm-swept sea are his most typical work, though now and again he does a dainty water-colour of this seashore he loved in its summer gentleness.

Eakins, with something akin to an Impressionist technique, turned to the active man, especially the sportsman, for his subjects. His studies of rowing men are his most typical. He was a friend of Walt Whitman, whom he painted, and who declared that he " never knew of but one artist, and that's Tom Eakins, who could resist the temptation to see what they thought ought to be, rather than what is." He has been called " the American Courbet," but this may be misleading for it applies to the realism of his subjects, but by no means to his somewhat lyrical style of painting, influenced as it became by Impressionism.

If Homer and Eakins may be classed as Realists, the third of the trio of foremost nineteenth-century American painters stands as a fine imaginative artist. This is Albert Pinkham Ryder. In actual technical power he was

"MAX SCHMITT IN A SINGLE SCULL," BY THOMAS EAKINS

Eakins, whom Walt Whitman hailed as one of America's greatest artists, was at his happiest in depicting men of action, and not least among them the rowing men. This subject gave him opportunity to put in landscapes in a brilliantly luminous technique which owes something to the French Impressionists.

"LONG BRANCH, NEW JERSEY," BY WINSLOW HOMER

A charming early work by one of the foremost American painters, recalling the *Plage* pictures of such French artists as Boudin. Later Homer thought of the task of American painting as that of showing the struggle between man and Nature, and settled on the wild Maine coast to paint the sea in storm and the hardy fisherfolk of the region.

a lesser man ; in content a greater. He is a symbolist sometimes in a mood which reminds us of the eerie genius of Odilon Redon ; always there is in his pictures a sense of brooding and solitude. We watch " The Flying Dutchman " barely distinguishable from the wild seas over which everlastingly it sails ; or we stand with scarce discernible figures before the vast doorway of " The Temple of the Mind." If we think of the mind of Coleridge we have an analogy with Ryder. Elemental forces, wildness, loneliness, moonlight in wild valleys, everything mysterious is in his work. An interesting painter who belongs spiritually to the Surrealists long before they were operating or had established their theories.

One other nineteenth-century painter of eminence should be mentioned, John la Farge (1835–1910), an eclectic painter, French in racial origin and echoing all through his highly studious work the influences of European art. He took painting as seriously as Whistler or Sargent, wrote ably about his own and other men's work, executed a vast body of work much of it on a most ambitious scale, turning his attention to the designing of stained glass towards the end and achieving fine effects ; but there is a journeyman's air about its very ability which puts it behind the work of a man such as Ryder who could not approach him in technical prowess. One of the influences upon him was that other American artist, William Morris Hunt (1824–79), an impetuous painter who seldom carried his work far enough to achieve lasting greatness, but who was at his best when he painted the nude in a luminous stippled manner which conveyed the sensuous beauty of the flesh.

So we pass to the moderns and almost away from purely American painting, for they are all too often products of or echoes of that School of Paris which is not a school at all. America has taken kindly to modernity. It finds ready admission to the galleries, a ready market, attention in the Press. It is part of America's abounding youthfulness, and a little of her self-assertion against the traditions of the Old World. Nothing is too wildly modern to shock this all-embracing taste.

It has to be remembered that the American collectors bought the French Impressionists before there was any big European interest in them, and since commercial values operate a great deal in this matter in the States there is a tendency to gamble on the anarchic in the belief, or at least hope, that it will win out in the same way as did American support of the great Frenchmen.

Charles Burchfield (1893–   ), Charles Demuth (1893–1935), and Lionel Feininger (1871–   ), stand among the forerunners ; Demuth with such work as " My Egypt " and Feininger with his studies of architecture in the purely Cubist manner paying tribute to that fashion of painting. Feininger worked for many years in Germany, where he obtained a considerable fame, but he returned to the United States in middle age. Max Weber was another ultra-modern man who was connected with the German Expressionist movement.

The first concerted movement towards a modern technique came much earlier when under Robert Henri (1865–1929), an enthusiastic painter of purely American life in a manner derived from Impressionism, established the group " The Eight," itself a successor of a Paris-inspired group " The Ten." The Eight were out for Realism in subject-matter and for directness in manner. They were scornfully called " The Ash-Can School " for their proclivity for finding subjects in the slum quarters and in low life of the great American cities. One of the best of them was George Luke (1867–1933) who searchingly depicted the children. John Sloan (1871–   ) succeeded as well as any in conveying the pity for the underdog which underlay their work.

Since their time the fighting leadership has been taken by Alfred Stieglitz (1864–   ), a man who, characteristically for America, graduated into the arts through his own art of photography which he used as brilliant formal and social comment. He it was who established a pioneer gallery on Fifth Avenue, began a revue " Camera Notes " which crusaded for the new forms in art, and introduced to the American public almost all the new men and the most daring European artists. Later at the New York Armory and at " An American Place " this work continued. Now there are altogether too many contemporary American galleries and artists working in the modern manner to attempt to list them ; and time will tell which of them have the genius capable of outlasting contemporary fashion. In the tragic economic slump of the late 'twenties and early 'thirties an attempt was made by the government to do something for the impoverished artists by means of a great Federal Art Project, but like that early scheme at the establishment of the Republic it did little aesthetically despite its grand ideas for public murals and paintings. Art, even in well-organised America, bloweth whither it listeth, and does not take kindly to State cossetting.

BOOKS FOR FURTHER READING

THE enormous number of books upon art and artists already existing and continually being added to makes any recommendation seem invidious ; but the following list of established authorities will be helpful in pursuing the subject in greater detail. Some which are out of print can nevertheless be consulted at libraries or borrowed from them. The *Encyclopædia Britannica* should also be consulted, and its own bibliographies of each artist or aspect noted. There are also the great dictionaries of artists, chief of which is *Thieme and Becker's Lexicon* ; but this vast 36-volume work is in German, and *Bryant's Dictionary of Artists* will serve most purposes.

GENERAL HISTORY :

> *History of Art,* by J. Piljoan (3 vols.).
> *History of Art,* by E. Fauré (5 vols., Lane).
> *The Story of Art,* by E. H. Gombrich (Phaedon).
> *A History of Art,* by H. B. Cotterill (2 vols., Harrap).
> *The Arts of Mankind,* by Hendrik van Loon (Harrap).
> *A History of Art,* by G. Caroti (2 vols., Duckworth).
> *A Miniature History of European Art,* by R. H. Wilenski (Oxford).
> *European Painting and Sculpture,* by Eric Newton (Pelican).
> *The National Gallery,* by Sir Charles Holmes (3 vols., Bell).
> *History of Painting,* by R. Muther (Putnam).

PREHISTORIC, EGYPTIAN, SUMERIAN, BABYLONIAN, CRETAN :

> *Primitive Art,* by L. Adam (Penguin).
> *Lascaux Cave Paintings,* by Fernald Windels (Faber).
> *Methods and Aims of Archaeology,* by W. M. Flinders Petrie.
> *The Romance of Archaeology,* by W. H. Boulton (Sampson Low).
> *Digging up the Past,* by Sir Leonard Woolley (Penguin).
> *Ur of the Chaldees,* by Sir Leonard Woolley (Penguin).
> *The Palace of Knossus,* by Sir Arthur Evans (Macmillan).
> *Discoveries in Crete,* by R. M. Burrows.

GREECE : ROME, BYZANTIUM :

> *Greek Art and National Life,* by S. C. Kaines-Smith (Nisbet).
> *A Handbook of Greek Sculpture,* by Ernest Gardner (Macmillan).
> *Six Greek Sculptors,* by Ernest Gardner (Duckworth).
> *Roman Sculpture,* by Mrs. Arthur Strong.
> *Roman Portraits* (Phaidon).

CHINESE, INDIAN, ISLAMIC :

Chinese Painting, by W. Cohn (Phaidon).

Chinese Art, by Leigh Ashton and Basil Gray (Faber).

Chinese Art, edited by Leigh Ashton (Kegan Paul).

The Chinese Eye, by Chiang Yee (Methuen).

Introduction to Chinese Art, by Arnold Silcock (Oxford).

Indian Art, edited by Sir Richard Winstedt.

A Handbook of Mohammedan Decorative Arts, by M. S. Dimand (Quaritch).

An Introduction to Persian Art, by Arthur Upham Pope (Peter Davies).

ITALIAN ; GENERAL :

New History of Painting in Italy (Central), by Crowe and Cavalcaselle (Dent).

History of Painting in Northern Italy, by Crowe and Cavalcaselle (Murray).

Venetian Painting of the Renaissance ; Florentine Painting of the Renaissance ; Central Italian Painting of the Renaissance ; Northern Italian Painting of the Renaissance, by Bernard Berenson (Putnam).

Short History of Italian Art, by A. Venturi (Macmillan).

Italian Painting, by Paul Konody and R. H. Wilenski (Jack).

The Italian Masters, by Horace Shipp (Sampson Low).

A History of Italian Painting, by F. Jewett Mather (Stanley Paul).

Civilisation of the Renaissance, by Jacob Burckhardt (Phaidon).

Lives of the Painters, by Gioggio Vasari (Everyman).

Mornings in Florence, by John Ruskin (Allen & Unwin).

INDIVIDUAL ARTISTS :

The Phaidon Press have published monographs with excellent illustrations on Bellini, Botticelli, Donatello, Leonardo, Michael Angelo, Raphael, Tintoretto, Titian, and others.

Michelangelo, by A. Venturi.

Michael Angelo, by Roman Rolland.

Leonardo da Vinci, by Edward MacCurdy (Bell).

Leonardo the Florentine, by Rachael Annand Taylor (Grant Richards).

Leonardo's Notebooks, edited by Edward MacCurdy (Bell).

Botticelli, by Yukio Yashiro (Medici).

Botticelli, by Herbert P. Horne.

Raphael, by Paul Konody (Nelson).

Titian, by Sir Claude Phillips (Seeley Service).

Cellini, Autobiography (Everyman).

FLEMISH :

Flemish Painting, by Sir Paul Lambotte (Studio).
Flemish Painting, by Emile Cammaerts (Avalon).
Great Dutch and Flemish Painters, by Wilhelm Bode.
Flemish Painting in the Seventeenth Century (Hyperion Books).
Van Eycks and Their Followers, by Sir Martin Conway (Murray).
The Holy Lamb, by Leo van Puyvelde (Collins).
Breughel (Hyperion Books).
Rubens, by R. M. Stevenson (Phaidon).
Masters of Past Time, by Eugene Fromentin.

GERMAN :

Dürer, His Life and Work, by T. D. Barlow (Quaritch).
Holbein, by R. Reinhardt (Phaidon).
Modern German Art, by Peter Theone (Pelican).

DUTCH :

Great Masters of Dutch and Flemish Painting, by Wilhelm Bode (Duckworth).
Dutch Painting in the Seventeenth Century, by C. H. Collins Baker (Studio).
Introduction to Dutch Art, by R. H. Wilenski (Faber).
Rembrandt. Introduction by Thomas Bodkin (Collins).
Rembrandt, by Jakob Rosenberg (Oxford).
Paintings of Rembrandt, by A. Bredius (Phaidon).
Works of the Most Eminent Painters of the Seventeenth Century, by C. Hofstede de Groot.
Vermeer, by T. Bodkin (Phaidon).

SPANISH :

Spanish Painting, by Philip Hardy (Avalon).
History of Spanish Art, by C. Rathfon Post (In progress, Oxford).
Velazquez, by R. A. M. Stevenson (Duckworth).
Velazquez, by E. Lafuente (Phaidon).
El Greco, by L. Goldscheider (Phaidon).
El Greco, By Meier Graaf.

FRENCH :

Short History of French Painting, by Eric Underwood (Oxford).
The French Masters, by Horace Shipp (Sampson Low).
French Painting, by R. H. Wilenski (Medici).

French Eighteenth-Century Painters, by Edmund and Jules de Goncourt.
The French Impressionists, by Camille Mauclair (Duckworth).
Art in France, by Louis Hourticq (Heinemann).
French Painting of the Sixteenth Century, by L. Dimier (Duckworth).
Modern French Painters, by Jan Gordon (Lane).
French Painting in the Twentieth Century (Hyperion Books).
Cézanne, by Roger Fry (Hogarth).
Van Gogh. Letters to Theo, edited by Irving Stone (Constable).
Van Gogh, by W. Uhde (Phaidon).
Degas Drawings, by Lilian Browse (Faber).

ENGLISH :

Short History of English Painting, by Eric Underwood (Faber).
English Painting, by Charles Johnson (Bell).
The British Masters, by Horace Shipp (Sampson Low).
British Painting, by William Gaunt (Avalon Press).
Art in Great Britain and Ireland, by Sir William Armstrong (Heinemann).
History of British Water-colour Painting, by H. M. Cundall (Batsford).
English Water-colour Painters, by A. J. Finberg (Duckworth).
English Mediaeval Painting, by E. W. Tristram and Tancred Borenius (Pegasus).
English Painting of the Sixteenth and Seventeenth Centuries, by C. H. Collins Baker and W. G. Constable.
Hogarth, by William Gaunt.
Gainsborough, by W. T. Whitley (Murray).
Reynolds, by C. R. Leslie and T. Taylor (Murray).
Romney, by A. B. Chamberlain (Methuen).
Turner, by Sir William Armstrong.
Turner, Ruskin's " Modern Painters " (Dent).
Constable, by the Hon. Andrew Shirley (Medici). See also *The Rainbow*, by the same author (Michael Joseph).
Blake : The Paintings, by Darrell Figgis ; *The Engraved Designs*, by Laurence Binyon (Benn).
The Pre-Raphaelite Tragedy, by William Gaunt (Cape).
Pre-Raphaelitism and Pre-Raphaelite Brotherhood, by Holman-Hunt (Macmillan).
Nineteenth-century Art, by D. S. MacColl (Maclehose).
Reynold's Discourses (Everyman).

AMERICAN :

History of American Painting, by Samuel Isham (Macmillan).
American Painting, by Denys Sutton (Avalon).
Canadian Painters (Phaidon).

MODERNISM : AND GENERAL WORKS :

Modern Masterpieces, by Frank Rutter (Newnes).
Introduction to Modern Art, by E. H. Ramsden.
Modern Movements in Painting, by Charles Marriott (Chapman & Hall).
Modern Movement in Art, by R. H. Wilenski (Faber).
Art Now, by Herbert Read (Faber).
Contemporary Painting in Europe, by Anthony Bertram (Studio).
The Meaning of Art, by Herbert Read (Faber).
Vision and Design, by Roger Fry (Penguin).
What is Art, by D. S. MacColl (Penguin).
Landscape into Art, by Kenneth Clark (Murray).
Language of Painting, by Charles Johnson (Cambridge).

The " Faber Gallery " is an excellent series of books of reproductions with short, authoritative introductions.

SCULPTURE :

The Tradition of Sculpture, by Alec Millar (Studio).
The Art of Carved Sculpture, by Kineton Parkes (Chapman & Hall).
Some Modern Sculpture, by Stanley Casson (Oxford).
Twentieth-century Sculpture, by E. H. Ramsden (Pleides).

GENERAL INDEX

2D*

INDEX TO ILLUSTRATIONS